TOTAL QUALITY CONTROL

TOTAL QUALITY CONTROL
Engineering and Management

The Technical and Managerial Field for Improving Product Quality, Including Its Reliability, and for Reducing Operating Costs and Losses

A. V. FEIGENBAUM

Manager, Manufacturing Operations and Quality Control, General Electric Company, New York City
President, American Society for Quality Control

McGRAW-HILL BOOK COMPANY, INC. 1961

New York Toronto London

TOTAL QUALITY CONTROL
(Revision of the book originally published under the title "Quality Control.")

 Library of Congress Catalog Card Number: 61-11051

20352

To H. S. F. and to the memory of J. V. and I. V.

PREFACE

Product quality, always of importance, is rapidly becoming the most significant factor in customer decisions. This is true whether the purchaser is a housewife, a large industrial corporation, or a military procurement agency.

The engineering and management field that is concerned with product quality has had, and is continuing to have, an almost phenomenal growth. Once the interest of a few technical men, quality control is today the primary concern of an increasingly large number of managers, engineers, and statisticians.

The problems to which these men and women direct their attention exist in many forms: the assurance of a positive customer reaction to products; the development of appropriate levels of reliability in a company's components and assemblies; the maintenance of the maximum control of process in the factory; the performance of the right kind of job of preproduction testing; the establishment of meaningful relations between vendor and purchaser; the improvement of expenditures on quality costs and the corresponding improvement in business results.

Inevitably the field of quality control has rapidly matured technically and deepened organizationally in response to the wealth of industrial operating experience over the past few years. There has now emerged a systematic body of principles, practices, and technologies today identified as *total* quality control to distinguish it from some of the more limited, more fragmentary work of the early beginnings of the field.

It is the purpose of this book to review the total field of quality control in depth. Quality control is presented as a body of technical, analytical, and managerial knowledge. It is discussed from the business point of view, with regard to the economics of cost and profit as well as to organization and management. It is considered in terms of a thorough review of the kinds of engineering activities that must be carried on.

I

The materials presented in this book have been developed in many companies for use in meeting a wide variety of practical industrial applications. They have been used in a number of plants both as the "plan of attack" for organizing new quality-control programs and as text material for in-company training courses.

"Total Quality Control" is directed to those men and women in industry who are responsible for the successful operation of a business or some part of it. These persons may be termed *manager, superintendent, engineer, quality manager, quality-control engineer, process-control engineer, reliability engineer*, or *development and design engineer.*

The book is designed to help them meet the challenging problems that they face daily in improving product quality and in reducing the costs of its control. The book may be used in the following ways:

1. As a guide for men and women who are establishing a quality-control program for the first time.
2. As survey material for industrial managers in appraising the potentialities of this activity.
3. As a text for use in quality-control educational courses.
4. As a methodological refresher for currently operating quality-control personnel.
5. As a reference for men and women interested in certain types of preproduction engineering methods, purchasing procedures, inspection and testing methods, and administrative systems.

II

The book contains nineteen chapters, which are consolidated in six parts. Each part is written so that it can be used as a unit in itself. This is intended to facilitate use of the book by those whose operations comprise only a portion of a complete quality-control program.

At the beginning of the book several fundamental principles are presented together with the plan for their development in the succeeding chapters.

The contents of "Total Quality Control" stated by its six parts are as follows:

Part One—Business Quality Management. This section presents a brief review of quality-control activity and its scope throughout the entire business system of a company. Executives may quickly gain here a perspective toward quality control.

Part Two—Quality-control Management. The administrative problems are presented here together with the elements of managerial work involving planning, organizing, integrating, and measuring the quality-control function.

Among the topics discussed are the elements of quality-control work, the organization required to get the work accomplished, methods for measuring the effectiveness of the function, and integration of the various quality-related activities of the organization into a quality system.

Part Three—Engineering Technology of Quality Control. The body of knowledge required for quality-control work is identified and classified into three distinct engineering technologies. Some of the techniques used in each are described.

Part Four—Statistical Technology of Quality Control. Industrial statistics is a field of knowledge that continues to provide quality control with many useful techniques. It has often been presented in a fashion requiring advanced mathematical training for its interpretation. The purpose of this section is to present, in basic algebra and arithmetic, the point of view that is represented by these methods.

Formulas, charts, and tables are furnished to the extent that they seem required. Reference material is suggested for those readers whose interests and background make further detail about statistics and reliability desirable.

Part Five—Applying Total Quality Control in the Company. The purpose of this section is the discussion of applications of quality-control methods to company problems. These methods are woven into a general pattern that may be found useful in organizing quality control for a particular company.

The four jobs carried on in an over-all program are treated in some detail. Examples are discussed, and representative tabular forms and plans are outlined.

Part Six—Quality-control Education and Training. The successful installation of a quality-control program is dependent upon people's willingness to follow certain courses of action. This section considers motivation within the company organization.

Persons must not only be willing; they must also be able. Training programs are thus discussed with respect to audience and content.

The importance of communicating product-quality information both to vendors and to customers is considered. The growing professional nature of quality-control work is discussed.

III

For the author to include his individual debt to those who have influenced this book, he would have to list scores of quality-control associates in his own company and many colleagues in other companies, in universities, and in the American Society for Quality Control. A particular debt is owed to the author's close professional colleagues: Leon Bress, William Masser, Winthrop Spencer, and Stanton Yingling. With respect to some of the concepts discussed, the author is acting much as a recorder of the work of these men. Appreciation must also be expressed to Fred Berkenkamp, Harold Freeman, Frank McLaughlin, and Theodore Schultz for the basis of some of the conceptual work.

Special appreciation must be given to Halbert Miller and Arthur Vinson, who stimulated the original operating work, some of the results of which are reviewed in this book. And without Mr. Miller's encouragement, this book would not have been possible.

Particular personal appreciation must be given to Wyatt Lewis, who worked intimately with the author in various aspects of this book and who contributed much independent creative thinking. Mr. Lewis was extremely helpful in the development of the book.

Appreciation must also be given to William Vinson, who carefully gave his attention to certain aspects of the statistical chapters and made a number of improvements, as well as several independent and primary contributions to the text.

The author is particularly indebted to Donald S. Feigenbaum for assistance rendered during the book's development.

Help to the book's progress has also been provided by the competent secretarial assistance of Miss Albina Fellini and Mrs. Betty Lawler.

It should also be recalled that this book draws heavily on a previous volume by the author, "Quality Control: Principles, Practice, and Administration." The many persons who contributed to that earlier volume thus have played a significant part in this book.

A. V. Feigenbaum

CONTENTS

Preface vii

The Principles of Quality Control and Plan of the Book 1

Part One: BUSINESS QUALITY MANAGEMENT

1. Product Quality and Total Quality Control 11
2. What Are the Factors in Controlling Quality? 24

Part Two: QUALITY-CONTROL MANAGEMENT

3. What Are the Jobs of Quality Control? 33
4. What Is the Organization for Quality Control? 43
5. Quality Costs 83
6. The Quality System 107

Part Three: ENGINEERING TECHNOLOGY OF QUALITY CONTROL

7. Quality-control Engineering Technology 123
8. Process-control Engineering Technology 150
9. Quality Information Equipment Engineering Technology 166

Part Four: STATISTICAL TECHNOLOGY OF QUALITY CONTROL

10. Frequency Distributions 203
11. Control Charts 248
12. Sampling Tables 307
13. Special Methods 374
14. Product Reliability 403

Part Five: APPLYING TOTAL QUALITY CONTROL IN THE COMPANY

15. New-design Control 437
16. Incoming-material Control 481
17. Product Control 521
18. Special Process Studies 579

Part Six: QUALITY-CONTROL EDUCATION AND TRAINING

19. Communicating Total Quality Control 597

Index 621

THE PRINCIPLES OF QUALITY CONTROL AND PLAN OF THE BOOK

A series of "principles" has begun to simmer out of industry's experience with total quality control.

An interpretation of these principles is presented below. It is offered as a summary of the management point of view toward quality control. It may also be used as a list of operating rules for organizing quality-control programs.

1. Total quality control may be defined as

An effective system for integrating the quality-development, quality-maintenance, and quality-improvement efforts of the various groups in an organization so as to enable production and service at the most economical levels which allow for full customer satisfaction.

2. In the phrase "quality control" the word *quality* does not have the popular meaning of "best" in any absolute sense. It means "best for certain customer conditions." These conditions are (*a*) the actual use and (*b*) the selling price of the product. Product quality cannot be thought of apart from product cost.

3. In the phrase "quality control" the word *control* represents a management tool with four steps:

   a. Setting quality standards.
   b. Appraising conformance to these standards.
   c. Acting when the standards are exceeded.
   d. Planning for improvements in the standards.

4. Several quality-control methods have been carried on in industry for many years. What is new in the modern approach to quality control is (*a*) the integration of these often uncoordinated activities into an

over-all administrative program for a plant and (*b*) the addition to the time-tested methods used of the new quality-control technologies which have been found useful in dealing with and thinking about the increased emphasis upon reliability in product design and upon precision in parts manufacture.

5. Total quality control is an aid to, not a substitute for, the good engineering designs, good manufacturing methods, and conscientious inspection activity that have always been required for the production of high-quality articles.

6. The fundamentals of quality control are basic to any manufacturing process, and the tools have been and can be used in industries ranging from radios, electric motors, and turbines to bakery, drug, and brewery products. Although the approach is somewhat different if the production is job shop rather than large quantity, or small components rather than large apparatus, the same fundamentals still obtain. This difference in approach can be readily summarized: in mass-production manufacturing, quality-control activities center on the *product,* whereas in job-lot manufacturing, they are a matter of controlling the *process.*

7. The details for each quality-control program must be tailored to fit the needs of individual plants.

8. The core of the quality-control approach is "station control" of product quality during the process of design and manufacture so as to prevent poor quality rather than to correct poor quality after an article has been produced.

9. Benefits often resulting from total-quality-control programs are improvements in product quality and design, reductions in operating costs and losses, improvement in employee morale, and reduction of production-line bottlenecks. By-product benefits are improved inspection methods, sounder setting of time standards for labor, definite schedules for preventative maintenance, the availability of powerful data for use in company advertising, and the furnishing of a factual basis for cost-accounting standards for scrap, rework, and inspection.

10. Certain kinds of costs, associated with the improvement and control of product quality, provide a means for measuring and optimizing total-quality-control activities. Costs for attaining and maintaining a certain level of product quality are brought together and consolidated with costs resulting from failure to obtain that particular level of quality. Such consolidated costs are known as *operating quality costs.*

11. Operating quality costs can be distributed among four different classifications for convenience of analysis and control. These are

a. Prevention costs, which include quality planning and other costs associated with preventing defects. These involve such costs as quality-control engineering expense.

b. *Appraisal costs,* or the costs incurred in evaluating product quality to maintain established quality levels. These include inspection and testing costs.
c. *Internal failure costs,* caused by defective materials and products that do not meet company quality specifications. These include scrap, rework, and spoilage.
d. *External failure costs,* caused by defective products reaching the customer. They include complaints and in-warranty product service costs.

12. Cost reductions—particularly reductions in operating quality costs—are possible results of quality control for two reasons:

a. Industry has often lacked quality standards. It has, therefore, unrealistically tilted the scales in the balance between the cost of quality in a product and the service that the product is to render.
b. In almost every instance an expenditure in the area of prevention has a severalfold advantage in reducing costs in the areas of appraisal, internal failure, and external failure. A saving of many dollars for each dollar spent in *prevention* is often experienced.

13. Present-day factors affecting industrial product quality have developed as a result of three pressures:

a. Increasingly high quality requirements on the part of customers.
b. The necessity to upgrade in-plant quality control practices and techniques to meet these demands.
c. Rising quality costs which tend to place companies in an unfavorable competitive position.

14. These three upward pressures can be met by total quality control which provides

a. A means for assigning quality responsibilities to *all* key personnel in the company.
b. A support to this broad assignment of quality responsibilities in the form of the organization of a specialized quality-control component whose *only* area of concentration is product quality.
c. A set of specialized technologies for measuring, evaluating, controlling, and improving product quality.

15. The factors affecting product quality may be divided into two major groupings: (*a*) the technological, that is, machines, materials, and processes; (*b*) the human, that is, operators, foremen, and other company personnel. Of these two factors, the human is of greater importance by far.

16. Quality control enters into all phases of the industrial production process, starting with the customer's specification and the sale to him

through design engineering and assembly through shipment of the product to a customer who is satisfied with it and ending with proper installation and field service.

17. Effective control over the factors affecting product quality demands controls at all important stages of the production and service processes. These controls may be termed the *jobs of quality control,* and they fall into four natural classifications:

a. New-design control.
b. Incoming-material control.
c. Product control.
d. Special process studies.

18. New-design control involves the establishment and specification of the desirable cost-quality, performance-quality, and reliability-quality standards for the product, including the elimination or location of possible sources of quality troubles before the start of formal production.

19. Incoming-material control involves the receiving and stocking, at the most economical levels of quality, of only those parts the quality of which conforms to the specification requirements.

20. Product control involves the control of products at the source of production and through field service so that departures from the quality specification can be corrected before defective products are manufactured and so that proper product service can be maintained in the field.

21. Special process studies involve investigations and tests to locate the causes of defective products and to determine the possibility of improving quality characteristics.

22. Product reliability is, in effect, "product function over the product life expectancy (time)." It is a part of the balanced total product-quality requirement—just as are also appearance, maintainability, serviceability, supportability, etc.—and hence cannot be treated separately from total quality control.

23. Statistics are used in an over-all quality-control program whenever and wherever they may be useful, but statistics are only one part of the total-quality-control pattern; they are not the pattern itself. The four statistical tools that have come to be used in quality-control activities are

a. Frequency distributions.
b. Control charts.
c. Sampling tables.
d. Special methods.

The point of view represented by these statistical methods has, however, had a profound effect upon the entire area of total quality control.

24. The statistical point of view in total quality control resolves essentially into this: variation in product quality must be constantly

studied—within batches of product, on processing equipments, between different lots of the same article, on critical quality characteristics and standards. This variation may best be studied by the analysis of samples selected from the lots of product or from units produced by the processing equipments.

25. The demands on total quality control are increased by automation of the manufacturing process. With automatic equipment, higher quality levels for parts usually have been found necessary for trouble-free operation. In fact, until higher quality levels are attained, excessive down time may make operation of the automated process uneconomic. Rapid detection of out-of-control conditions, feedback for process adjustment, and quick response of the process to correction are essential to low defect rates.

26. An important feature of total quality control is that it controls quality at the source. An example is its positive effect in stimulating and building up operator responsibility for, and interest in, product quality through measurements taken by the operator at his station.

27. Necessary to the success of quality control in a plant is the very intangible but extremely important spirit of *quality-mindedness*, extending from top management right to the men and women at the bench.

28. Whatever may be new about the total-quality-control program for a plant must be sold to the entire plant organization so as to obtain its willing acceptance and cooperation. Participation by many members of the company organization in developing details of the quality-control program is very desirable.

29. A quality-control program must have the complete support of top management. With lukewarm management support, no amount of selling to the rest of the organization can be genuinely effective.

30. Management must recognize at the outset of its total-quality-control program that this program is not a temporary cost-reduction project. Only when the inefficiencies represented by the cost reductions are out of the way can the quality-control program take over its long-range role of the management *control* over quality.

31. Organizationwise, quality control is management's tool for delegating authority and responsibility for product quality, thus relieving itself of unnecessary detail while retaining for itself the means of assuring that quality results will be satisfactory. There are two basic concepts important in organizing for quality control.

The first is that *quality is everybody's job*. Every component has quality-related responsibility, e.g., Marketing for determining customer's quality preferences, Engineering for specifying product quality specifications, and Shop Supervision for building quality into the product.

The second concept is that, *because quality is everybody's job, it may become nobody's job.* Management must recognize that the many individual responsibilities for quality will be exercised most effectively when they are buttressed and serviced by a well-organized, full-time, genuinely modern management function whose only area of operation is in the quality-control jobs.

32. This quality-control organizational component has twin objectives: (*a*) to provide quality assurance for the company's product, i.e., simply to be sure that the products shipped are right, and (*b*) to assist in assuring optimum quality costs for those products. It fulfills these objectives through its three subfunctions: *quality-control engineering, process-control engineering,* and *quality information equipment engineering.* These quality-control subfunctions provide basic engineering technologies that are applicable to any product for assuring its right quality at optimum quality cost.

33. *Quality-control engineering* does the quality planning which establishes the basic framework of the entire quality-control system for the company.

34. *Process-control engineering* monitors the application of this quality-control system on the shop floor and thus gradually supplants the older policing inspection activity.

35. *Quality information equipment engineering* designs and develops the inspection and testing equipment for obtaining these process-control measurements. Where justified, this equipment is combined with production to provide automatic feedback of results for control of the process. All pertinent results are then analyzed as a basis for adjustment and corrective action on the process.

36. From the human relations point of view, the quality-control organization is both

a. A *channel of communication* for product-quality information among all concerned employees and groups.

b. A *means of participation* in the over-all quality-control program by these employees and groups.

The quality-control organization is a means of breaking down the attitude sometimes held by factory operators and functional specialists that "our quality responsibility is so small a part of the whole that we're really not a part of the plant quality-control program nor are we important to it."

37. Total-quality-control programs should be allowed to develop gradually within a given company. It is often found wise to select one or two troublesome quality problems, to achieve successful results in attacking them, and to allow the quality-control program to grow step by step in this fashion.

The foregoing principles will provide a focus through which the reader may wish to approach the field of quality control as it is developed and reviewed in the body of this book.

This review will consider the five key elements of total quality control:

1. Its *scope:* the extent of its activity throughout the entire business system of a company (covered in Part One, Chap. 1 and 2).

2. Its *management:* the planning, organizing, integrating, and measuring of quality-control activity (covered in Part Two, Chap. 3 through 6).

3. Its *technology,* both *engineering* and *statistical:* the bodies of knowledge required to accomplish quality-control work (covered in Part Three, Chaps. 7 through 9, and Part Four, Chaps. 10 through 14).

4. Its *applications:* the "tools," techniques, and procedures to get the quality-control job done (covered in Part Five, Chaps. 15 through 18).

5. Its *training:* the preparation of men and women to accomplish the work of total quality control (covered in Part Six, Chap. 19).

PART ONE

BUSINESS QUALITY MANAGEMENT

CHAPTER 1

PRODUCT QUALITY AND TOTAL QUALITY CONTROL

The outstanding quality accomplishments of industry during the past decade are familiar history. The major challenge that has resulted from more complex consumer products, such as automatic home laundry equipment with increased functions and performance requirements, is being met with increasing effectiveness. The high degree of reliability required for complex military weapons systems, such as missiles, rockets, and space vehicles, is well on the way to being attained. This results side of the quality picture makes impressive reading.

Not so pretty a picture is presented when the behind-the-scenes effort to assure these high-quality standards is examined. It may be summarized by noting that many industries are now in a position where, for every dollar spent in planned production, many additional cents are lost owing to the poor quality of their products while in process of manufacture or while being serviced in the field.

These data show that, although we have generally found our quality failures in the factory instead of after shipment, our techniques for so doing are often excessively costly and wasteful. They also show that in some cases products which may fail soon after being placed in service have not always been detected in the factory. These conditions cannot be tolerated by any industry striving to maintain and improve its competitive position.

This is a situation with which industry is vitally concerned. It is one calling for the new techniques that have come to be popularly classified under the label of quality control.

1.1 What Is Total Quality Control and What Is Its Purpose?

The goal of competitive American industry, as far as product quality is concerned, can be clearly stated. It is to manufacture a product into which quality is designed, built and maintained at the most economical costs which allow for full customer satisfaction.

It is to the over-all, company-wide program for attaining that goal that this book refers when it uses the phrase "total quality control." Or, as a definition:

Total quality control is an effective system for integrating the quality-development, quality-maintenance, and quality-improvement efforts of the various groups in an organization so as to enable production and service at the most economical levels which allow for full customer satisfaction.

Since this activity is one of the major responsibilities of management, quality control[1] must be classified as a "management tool," along with similar "tools" such as production control and budget control. As a management tool, quality control has produced for many American industries outstanding improvements in product quality and design, and reductions in operating costs and losses.

Effective human relations is basic to quality control. A major feature of this activity is its positive effect in building up operator responsibility for, and interest in, product quality. In the final analysis it is a pair of human hands which performs the important operations affecting product quality. It is of utmost importance to successful quality-control work that these hands be guided in a skilled, conscientious, and quality-minded fashion.

Sound technological methods are also basic. A wide variety of these methods is now being used. Included are systems for specifying engineering tolerances, accelerated test methods for evaluation of component and systems reliability, classification of quality characteristics, vendor rating methods, sampling inspection techniques, process-control techniques, design of quality-control measuring equipment, gaging systems, product quality evaluation and rating schemes, application of statistical techniques from $\overline{X}$ and R charts to designed experiments, and many others.

It is of interest to note that these individual methods have themselves been used as definitions for quality control over the years. The written and spoken word often finds quality control defined as some form of sampling inspection, as a portion of industrial statistics, as reliability

[1] "Quality control" and "total quality control" will be used interchangeably throughout the balance of the book.

work, or as the inspection act itself. These several definitions have described only individual parts of, or methods in, an over-all quality-control program. They may have contributed to the confusion with which the term is sometimes associated in industry.

1.2 The Meaning of "Quality" in Industry

In the phrase "quality control," the word *quality* does not have the popular meaning of "best" in any absolute sense. To industry, it means "best for certain customer conditions."

Important among these customer conditions are (1) the actual end use and (2) the selling price of the product. In turn, these two conditions are reflected in five additional conditions: (1) the specification of dimensions and of operating characteristics, (2) the life and reliability objectives, (3) the manufacturing and engineering costs, (4) the production conditions under which the article is manufactured, and (5) the field installation and maintenance objectives.

It is neither practical nor economical for these conditions to have perfection as their aim: "that's why we have tolerances." This aim is rather the level of quality that establishes the proper balance between the cost of the product and the service it renders.

For example, a punch-press manufacturer in upstate New York was recently faced with two alternatives in the manufacture of a 4-inch washer type. On the one hand, he might use a stock die and scrap materials to produce a washer that would sell for ¼ cent and whose quality he could not guarantee for any conditions of excessive load or temperature. On the other hand, he might purchase a special die and special materials to produce a washer which would sell for 2 cents and which he could guarantee for high-load and elevated-temperature conditions.

The customer for the washers, who was contacted by the manufacturer's sales department, had an application where load and temperature conditions were of no consequence but where price was very important. The manufacturer's decision was, therefore, in favor of the ¼-cent washer made from scrap materials, which became his "quality" product and the requirements of which were reflected back into his factory.

Product quality can then be defined as

the composite product characteristics of engineering and manufacture that determine the degree to which the product in use will meet the expectations of the customer.

This brings to attention some other terms, such as *reliability, serviceability,* and *maintainability,* that have sometimes been used as definitions for product quality in themselves. These terms are, of course, individual *characteristics* which go to make up the composite of product quality.

It is important to recognize this fact, because the key requirement in establishing what is to be the "quality" of a given product requires the economic balancing off of these various individual quality characteristics. For example, the product must perform its intended function repeatedly as called upon, over its stipulated life span under intended environments and conditions of use—in other words, it must have good *reliability*. The planned amount of service and maintainability must be performed, so the product must have proper *serviceability* and *maintainability*. The product must have appearance suitable to the customer requirements, so it must have *attractability*. When all the other product characteristics are balanced in, the "right" quality becomes that composite which provides the intended function with the greatest over-all economy, considering among other things product obsolescence, and it is the total concept of "quality" that must be controlled.

1.3 The Meaning of "Control" in Industry

In industrial terminology, the process of delegating responsibility and authority for a management activity, thus freeing management of unnecessary detail while retaining for it the means of assuring that results will be satisfactory, is generally labeled a *control*. The procedure for meeting the industrial quality goal is, therefore, termed quality "control," just as the procedures for meeting production and cost goals are termed, respectively, production "control" and cost "control."

There are generally four steps in such a control. For quality control, these steps break down as follows:

1. *Setting standards.* Determining the required cost-quality, performance-quality, and reliability-quality standards for the product.
2. *Appraising conformance.* Comparing the conformance of the manufactured product to these standards.
3. *Acting when necessary.* Taking corrective action when the standards are exceeded.
4. *Planning for improvements.* Developing a continuing effort to improve the cost, performance, and reliability standards.

1.4 The Product-quality Challenge Facing American Industry

There are three distinct product-quality trends that must be taken into account by the company which designs, processes, and sells products in today's competitive market place.

1. *Customers—industrial, consumer, and military—have been increasing their quality requirements very sharply.* This tendency is likely to be amplified by intense competition in the period ahead. Several under-

lying causes are responsible. New technology has made possible product offerings that provide more functions and higher performance. The trend has been made significant by the fact that products continue to grow more complex. This means that there is greater opportunity for failures to occur; hence to maintain product reliability, even at old levels, requires progressive increases in component quality levels. Complexity also has the effect of making it difficult for the customer accurately to judge the quality of a product at the time he buys it. Increasingly, he expects a product that will provide its functions satisfactorily and reliably over its intended life.

2. *As a result of this increased customer demand for higher-quality products, present in-plant quality practices and techniques are now, or will be soon, outmoded.* The rapid development of new product technology and demands for increased product performance have made tolerances more stringent. Thus, the machined part that could once be checked with a pocket scale or a pair of micrometers must now be carefully measured with an air gage; material that could once be visually accepted if it were "reddish brown and shiny" must now be carefully analyzed, both chemically and physically, to assure that it is beryllium copper instead of phosphor bronze. At the same time, automation, in which rapid quality evaluation is a pivotal point, has magnified the need for mechanization of inspection and test equipment, much of which is now in the hand-tool stage. Indeed, the quality-control content of the manufacturing equipment investment dollar, already 10 to 20 per cent in some companies, may well double in the next decade to purchase the benefit of this mechanization.

Likewise, improvements in labor-management relations are reemphasizing the operator's responsibility for controlling quality at its source rather than overemphasizing inspection of the product upon completion.

3. *Quality costs have become very high. For many companies they may be much too high if these companies are to maintain and improve their competitive position over the long run.* In fact, quality costs (inspection, testing, laboratory checks, scrap, rework, customer complaints, and similar expenses) have crept up to become a multimillion-dollar item. For many businesses they are comparable in degree with total direct labor dollars, with distribution dollars, or with purchased-material dollars. Evidence points strongly to the fact that many businesses have quality-cost expenditures representing 7, 8, or 10 per cent, and even more, of their cost of sales.

Taken together, these three problems spell out the twin quality challenge that competitive conditions present to American management: (1) considerable improvement in the quality of many products and many quality practices and, at the same time, (2) substantial reductions in the over-all costs of maintaining quality.

1.5 Total Quality Control

Fortunately, there is a way out of the dilemma imposed on businessmen by increasingly demanding customers and by ever-spiraling costs of quality. This "way out" seems to lie in a new kind of quality control, which might be called *total quality control.*

The underlying principle of this total quality view, and its basic difference from all other concepts, is that, to provide genuine effectiveness, control must start with the design of the product and end only when the product has been placed in the hands of a customer who remains satisfied.

The reason for this breadth of scope is that the quality of any product is affected at many stages of the industrial cycle (Fig. 1.1):

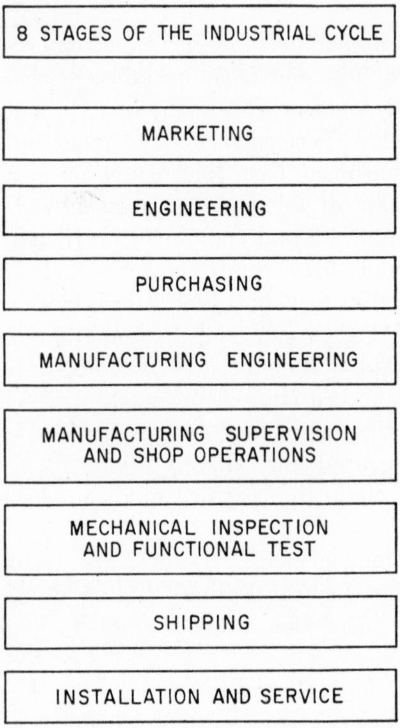

8 STAGES OF THE INDUSTRIAL CYCLE

MARKETING

ENGINEERING

PURCHASING

MANUFACTURING ENGINEERING

MANUFACTURING SUPERVISION AND SHOP OPERATIONS

MECHANICAL INSPECTION AND FUNCTIONAL TEST

SHIPPING

INSTALLATION AND SERVICE

FIG. 1.1.

1. Marketing evaluates the level of quality which customers want and for which they are willing to pay.
2. Engineering reduces this marketing evaluation to exact specifications.
3. Purchasing chooses, contracts with, and retains vendors for parts and materials.
4. Manufacturing Engineering selects the jigs, tools, and processes for production.
5. Manufacturing Supervision and shop operators exert a major quality influence during parts making, subassembly, and final assembly.
6. Mechanical inspection and functional test check conformance to specifications.
7. Shipping influences the caliber of the packaging and transportation.
8. Installation helps ensure proper operation by installing the product according to proper instructions and maintaining it through product service.

In other words, the determination of both quality and quality cost actually takes place throughout the entire industrial cycle. This is the reason why real quality control cannot be accomplished by concentrating on inspection alone, or design alone, or reject trouble shooting alone, or operator education alone, or statistical analysis alone, or reliability studies alone, important as each of these individual elements is.

The breadth of the job makes quality control a new and important industrial management function. Just as the theme of the historical inspection activity was "they (i.e., bad parts) shall not pass," the theme of this new approach is "make them right the first time." Emphasis is on defect prevention so that routine inspection will not be needed to as large an extent. The burden of quality proof rests not with inspection but with the makers of the part: machinist, assembly foreman, vendor, as the case may be.

Like traditional inspection, the quality-control function in this total quality view is still responsible for assurance of the quality of products shipped, but its broader scope places a major addition on this responsibility. Quality control becomes responsible for quality assurance *at optimum quality costs.*

The total quality view sees the prototype quality-control man not as an inspector but as a quality-control *engineer,* with an adequate background of the applicable product technology and with training in statistical methods, in inspection techniques, in reliability studies, and in other useful tools for improving and controlling product quality.

1.6 Total Quality Control Compared with Other Quality-control Programs

It is worth noting that total quality control has resulted from a half century of evolution. There have been five steps in this evolution, and each has generally taken a 20-year period from inception to realization (Fig. 1.2).

The first step, *operator quality control,* was inherent in the manufacturing job up to the end of the nineteenth century. Under that system one worker, or at least a very small number of workers, were responsible for the manufacture of the entire product, and therefore each worker could totally control the quality of his work.

In the early 1900s we progressed to *foreman quality control.* During this period we saw the large-scale advent of our modern factory concept, in which many men performing a similar task were grouped together so that they could be supervised by a foreman, who then assumed responsibility for the quality of their work.

The manufacturing system became more complex during World War I, involving large numbers of workers reporting to each production foreman. As a result, the first full-time inspectors appeared on the scene, initiating the third step, which we can call *inspection quality control.*

This step peaked in the large inspection organizations of the 1920s and 1930s, separately organized from production and big enough to be headed by superintendents.

This remained in vogue until the tremendous mass-production requirements of World War II necessitated the fourth step of quality control, which we now identify as *statistical quality control.* In effect, this phase was an extension of the inspection phase and boiled down to making the big inspection organizations more efficient. Inspectors were provided with a few statistical tools, such as sampling and control charts. The most significant contribution of statistical quality control was that it provided sampling inspection rather than 100 per cent inspection. But the job

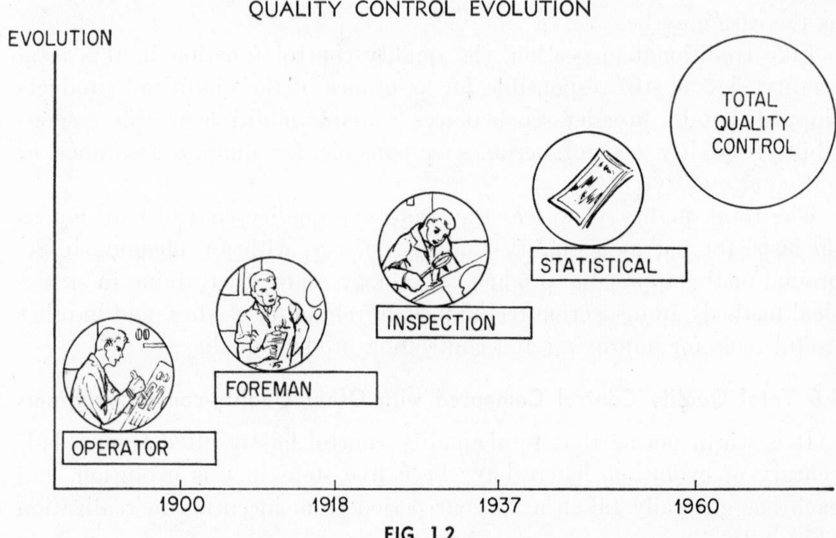

FIG. 1.2.

being done was still basically the shop-floor inspection job, which could never get its arms around the really big quality problems as business management itself saw them. This need brought us to the fifth step, which has come into being recently: *total quality control,* as discussed above.

1.7 The Place of Total Quality Control in the Modern American General-management Concept

Business managers are aware of the axiom that salability plus producibility plus productivity equals profitability. It takes but a moment's reflection to realize that total quality control contributes substantially to each element in this business formula.

Salability is enhanced through total quality control in that the balancing of various quality levels and the cost of maintaining them is planned in an organized manner. The result is that the manufactured product really can meet the customer's wants *both* in the satisfactory function of the product and in the price that he has to pay for it.

Producibility is improved because quality control offers guidance, based on quality experience, to the designing engineer while new products are being developed. Such guidance takes many forms; for example, consulting on the relationship between new design standards and the quality capabilities of the manufacturing plant.

Productivity is increased by emphasizing the positive control of quality rather than after-the-fact detection and rework of failures. The amount of salable production that comes off the assembly line becomes much higher than it would otherwise be, without increasing a penny in the cost of production or increasing a single unit in the rate of production. Furthermore, positive action taken in the incoming-materials area frequently increases the production rate of the manufacturing equipment itself. This is because defective purchased material is prevented from reaching the assembly line where it will waste the efforts of skilled workers and expensive machines.

It should thus be noted that total quality control has a vigorous impact on each of the three factors which influence profitability. Through careful analysis of customer wants and needs, the product can be provided with those qualities which motivate purchase by the consumer and thus increase *salability*. When the quality of the product design is established with *producibility* in mind, manufacturing costs can be substantially reduced. With necessary manufacturing capability for quality production in place, *productivity* rises as costs per unit decrease. Thus, the industrial manager finds in total quality control a powerful new tool to increase the *profitability* of his business.

1.8 The Place of Total Quality Control in the Modern American General-management Concept—Some Examples

To make these points more specific, let's look at the performance of three companies whose general managers failed to include in their business-management plans the contribution of total quality control to salability, producibility, productivity, and profitability. Refer to these companies as A, B, and C (Fig. 1.3).

In Company A, the basic business strategy was to increase product volume in an effort to climb above the break-even point. Company B's strategy was to market a new product, seeking much wider customer coverage. Company C's business technique was to obtain substantial cost reduction by moving from its old company location to a new plant. Let's look at the results in each case.

Company A never made its planned production volume. Product

rejects in process saw to that. One measure of the resulting lack of effective utilization of capacity is Company A's quality costs of 24 per cent of net sales billed.

Company B, with a new product, was unable to develop any real element of customer acceptance in the market place. One reason is shown in its quality costs of 18.7 per cent of net sales billed.

Company C has not obtained the cost reduction sought from its new location. In this company, quality costs of 6.4 per cent of net sales billed are most significantly compared with its direct labor base and come to 140 per cent of direct labor.

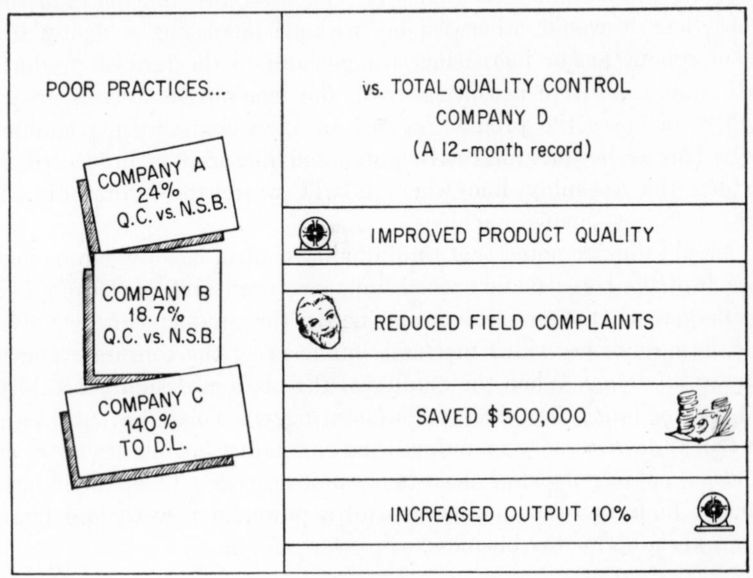

FIG. 1.3.

As you might suspect, Companies A, B, and C are not very profitable. In each case, total quality control would have substantially helped each company to meet its particular objectives.

In contrast, let's examine Company D, whose general management did include total quality control in its business-management plans. Company D is a moderate-sized manufacturer of electrical devices with a business volume of approximately $10 million a year. Its total quality activity in 12 months improved product quality substantially, reduced field complaints severalfold, and reduced the going level of quality costs from an annual rate of about $1 million a year to a new annual rate of less than $500,000, a total savings of more than $500,000. This resulted in a more than one-third increase in the profitability of Company D. In the process, Company D's output increased 10 per cent.

Many similar examples can be cited extending throughout American industry. These only serve further to emphasize the tremendous potential profit that lies hidden and untapped in terms of greater salability, producibility, and productivity. Total quality control provides managers with a significantly important means to acquire such profit.

1.9 Where Is Quality Control Used?

Since the fundamentals of quality control are basic to any manufacturing process, the program has been and can be used in industries ranging from radios, electric motors, and turbines to bakery, drug, and brewery products. Although the approach is somewhat different if the production is job shop rather than high quantity or small components rather than large apparatus, the same basic fundamentals still obtain.

A major source of confusion in the question "Where is quality control used?" lies in the fact that quality control is often defined in the questioner's mind as one of the individual quality-control methods rather than as a broad integrated program. An analogy is that of thinking only of screw machines when the phrase "manufacturing processes" is used or of considering electrical engineering as the study of only electric motors and generators.

Quality control refers to the broad administrative area of developing, maintaining and improving product quality. It does not mean simply any single technical method for accomplishing these purposes. Such a definition would be too restrictive.

The answer to the question "Where are quality-control *methods* used?" will, of course, depend upon the circumstances. The several methods available are not all satisfactory for every application but must be carefully selected to meet the conditions of each job.

1.10 What Results Are the Objective of Quality Control and When Will They Appear?

Experience has shown that, when an improved quality level is attained by controlling product quality within the factory, operating costs are generally reduced. This reduction in operating costs is made possible because, in its past efforts to make a balance between the cost of a product and the service it renders, industry has tilted the scales considerably in the direction of product costs that are too high. Many of the "costs of quality" are spent either to correct mistakes or to police them. These high costs in quality assurance, internal failure due to rejections, and other similar categories have been substantially reduced by an effective program of quality control in many shops.

Varying with the circumstances of each application, the six benefits that may be expected from an over-all quality-control program are:

1. Improvement in product quality.
2. Improvement in product design.
3. Reduction in operating costs.
4. Reduction in operating losses.
5. Reduction of production-line bottlenecks.
6. Improvement in employee morale.

The benefits to be derived from a quality-control program are by no means confined to industry and its profit-and-loss ledgers. A number of contributions to the social and public welfare result from such an activity.

The activity of establishing proper balances between the cost of an industrial product and the service it renders is important in the effort to produce more goods at less cost and at lower prices. There are several outstanding examples of just such a result.

Again, no quality-control activity can continue very long without pointing up the great importance of cooperation and participation in the program by the workmen. This type of thinking and the resulting action can be a positive factor in effective industrial relations. The possibilities in this direction have scarcely been explored in quality-control activities.

The greater protection to the consumer in the development of new and better checks on quality characteristics is well known. Recent emphasis on the part of customers has pointed up the importance of adequate environmental tests and simulation of end-use conditions employing a specified operational period.

1.11 What Will Be the Effects of Automation on Quality Control?

A look into the future shows what the long-range future of total quality control will be as automation becomes more and more effective. Studies show that with automation there will be *more* quality problems instead of fewer; there will be even *more intense* upward pressures on quality costs than exist today; there will be *much greater,* rather than less, need for high-level quality-control work.

These points can be illustrated by an example from the plant of a New England manufacturer making precision instruments.

For most hand-assembly lines, a 1 per cent reject quality level for hardware is a very respectable goal and is achieved only with consistently good work. Examination shows what this 1 per cent level means for one of the factory's automated subassembly operations: the magnetic bearing support.

This operation requires the use of two thin washers per subassembly, to be used as magnet spacers. The machine produces 720 subassemblies per hour, thus using 1,440 washers. If 1 per cent of the 1,440 washers have a small burr or a slightly rounded edge, there will on the average be 14 machine stoppages per hour—one every 4 minutes—due to washers jamming the track feeding the machine. Thus, with a respectable 1 per cent level for hardware, the automated equipment will be out of operation more than it is in operation. Obviously, such a 1 per cent reject level doesn't begin to be good enough for instrument automation.

If one multiplies this example manyfold and adds a liberal sprinkling of other examples which reflect much greater quality complexities, one will find the true nature of the quality problem under automation emerging: it is that, unless the "make-it-right-the-first-time" total-quality-control principle is *really* made to work, there will *be* no automatic production: down time will see to that.

Compared with today's *hand* operations, automation will require far *better* procedures for determining the quality ability of new designs prior to the start of production; it will require far *tighter* controls over incoming-material quality and over in-process quality; it will require the development of far more *effective* inspection and test, measuring, and feedback control devices; it will also require the creation and use of far *higher* levels of total-quality-control engineering technology.

1.12 How Is Quality Control Set Up?

All the benefits to be gained from quality control remain only verbal promises, however, unless some action is taken in a company to bring them into being. The most important factor in setting up quality control is the establishment of the organization to do the job.

For this organization to be properly constructed, it is first necessary to determine what problems it is being established to solve and to set up the plan of "ground rules" for solving them, after which it is possible to conceive the type of organization required. These matters are discussed in Chap. 2, Part One, and Chap. 3, Part Two.

CHAPTER 2

WHAT ARE THE FACTORS IN CONTROLLING QUALITY?

During the past two decades, industry has seen an extremely pronounced growth of competition in product quality. This competition has been most apparent in appliance lines, such as toasters and washing machines, but the same situation has prevailed in the heavy industries and has been reflected in their cost pictures. On large steam turbines, for example, costs due to ever-improved quality have substantially increased elements of the manufacturing costs of this type of apparatus.

A natural result of these circumstances has been for many factories to place a premium upon the establishment and maintenance of a good quality reputation. Such a reputation can be exploited among customers by the sales department, and it can be the keynote of advertising policies. A poor quality reputation, on the other hand, presents one of the most difficult points of sales resistance that the sales department of a company has to overcome.

A dip in consumer-goods sales during an interval in our national economy was attributed in significant measure to a "consumer quality strike." Concerted buying resistance was in evidence as a result of such things as loose connections occurring in appliances, nuts working off automobiles, and seams coming apart in clothing. Major factors in restoring purchases in certain products were significant quality improvements by manufacturers.

A reputation for quality, whether good or bad, is not a thing of chance. It is the direct result of the internal policies of a company. It depends on an aggressive product-planning function to determine the true wants and needs of the customer. It depends on innovation in product-design work, coupled with a manufacturing capability to create the product; it depends on careful planning of the quality system so each step in the process will assure the desired quality result. The product must have reliability to perform its intended function over the expected life of the product and under the conditions it will encounter in service. All this must be backed by an organization that is quality-minded from top to bottom—a company that is willing to back its product with adequate guarantees and product service to ensure complete customer satisfaction.

Unfortunately, some companies have not recognized the rapidly changing quality demands of the consumer. Consequently, their internal policies have not been continuously geared up to produce the required product-quality result. Their quality-control methods and technologies have not been kept current to meet new product-quality demands.

2.1 What Fundamental Factors Affect Quality?

The effects that these changing demands have on a company can be reviewed by considering their effects on the "seven Ms." These so-called Ms are the fundamental factors which affect product quality. They are

1. Markets
2. Men
3. Money
4. Management
5. Materials
6. Machines and Methods
7. Miscellaneous

2.2 How Have Current Conditions Affected Quality?

Industry today is subject to a great number of conditions which bear upon production in a manner never experienced in any previous period. These conditions have affected each of the seven factors in product quality.

1. Markets. The number of new and improved products offered in the market place is growing at an explosive rate. Many of these products are an outgrowth of new technologies involving not only the product itself but also the materials and methods by which it is manufactured. Consumer wants and needs are carefully identified by today's businesses as a basis for developing new products. The consumer has been led to believe that there is a product to fill almost every need. Customers are demanding and getting more and better products today to fill these needs. Markets are becoming broader in scope and yet more functionally specialized in the goods and services offered. This has required that businesses be highly flexible and able to change direction rapidly.

2. Men. The rapid growth in technical knowledge and the origination of whole new fields, such as industrial electronics, have created a great demand for men with specialized knowledge. Specialization has become necessary as the fields of knowledge have increased not only in number but also in breadth. Although specialization has its advantages, it has the disadvantage of breaking the responsibility for product quality into a number of pieces. At the same time, this situation has created a demand for the systems engineer who can bring all these fields of specialization together to plan, create, and operate various systems that will assure a desired result. The numerous aspects of the business system which includes industrial, manufacturing, and quality-control systems are just beginning to be appreciated.

3. Money. The increase of competition in many fields has shaved profit margins. At the same time, the need for automation and mechanization has forced large outlays for new equipments and processes. The resulting increase in plant investment, which must be paid for through increased productivity, has made losses in production, due to scrap and rework, extremely serious. Quality costs associated with the maintenance and improvement of quality have reached unprecedented heights, until they are equaling or surpassing total direct labor dollars in many businesses. This fact has focused the attention of managers on the quality-cost area as one of the "soft spots" in which its operating costs and losses can be decreased to improve profits.

4. Management. Responsibility for quality has been distributed among several specialized groups. Once the foreman had sole responsibility for product quality. Now Marketing, through its product-planning function, must establish the product requirements. Engineering has responsibility for designing a product that will fulfill these requirements. Manufacturing must develop and refine the process to provide a capability adequate to make the product to the engineering specification. Quality Control must plan the quality measurements throughout the process flow that will assure that the end result will meet quality requirements. Even quality of service, after the product has reached the customer, has become an important part of the total "product package." This has increased the load upon top management, particularly in view of the increased difficulty of allocating proper responsibility for correcting departure from quality standards.

5. Materials. Owing to production costs and quality requirements, engineers are working materials to closer limits than ever before and using many new, so-called exotic metals and alloys for special applications. As a result, material specifications have become tighter and diversity of materials greater. The visual inspection and thickness check of a few years ago no longer serves for acceptance. Instead, rapid, precise, chemical and physical measurements must be made, using highly specialized laboratory machines, such as the spectrophotometer and machinability test equipment.

6. Machines and Methods. The demand on the part of companies to get cost reductions and production volume to satisfy the customer in intensely competitive markets has forced the use of manufacturing equipment which is steadily becoming more complex and much more dependent upon the quality of material fed into it. Good quality is becoming a critical factor in maintaining machine up time for full utilization of facilities. This is true for the entire span of manufacturing equipment, from deep-draw dies to automatic subassembly machines. The more companies mechanize and automate to get cost reductions, the more critical good quality will become, both to make these reductions real and to raise man and machine utilization to satisfactory values.

7. Miscellaneous. Great advances in the intricacy of engineering designs, demanding much closer control over manufacturing processes, have made the formerly ignored "little things" of great potential importance. Dust in an electronic tube assembly area, floor vibration transmitted to a precision machine tool, or room temperature variation during adjustments to inertial guidance systems are hazards to modern production.

Increased complexity and higher performance requirements for products have served to emphasize the importance of product reliability. Constant attention must be given to make certain that no factors, known or unknown, enter the process to decrease the reliability of components or systems. Inherently reliable designs can deliver such reliability only as a result of such vigilance. Thus we see that many of these seven factors affecting quality are continually undergoing change. These, in turn, must be met with corresponding changes in quality-control programs.

2.3 How Complicated Are Modern Quality Problems?

Entwined within many company problems of product quality are several combinations of these seven technological and human factors.

As far as the technological factors are concerned, it is often difficult to trace a quality problem back to a single cause. The failure of an instrument assembly to pass a final preshipment inspection may be due to earlier acceptance of faulty purchased materials, to improper machining or processing of certain component parts, to faulty assembly jigs, or to any of a dozen other possibilities.

When these technological conditions have been traced, it is equally difficult to pin down the human factors. The faulty machining of a part may be due to carelessness of the machine operator, to incorrect instruction by the foreman, to defective methods set up by the job planner, or to a poor design by the engineer. Curtly blaming a foreman, operator, or engineer on a superficial basis may have little bearing on the true problem.

The situation was vividly illustrated in the recent experience of an Eastern factory which manufactures permanent magnets. One of the factory's small magnets was subject to very high rejects because of poor magnetic quality at the final electrical test, where each magnet was checked individually. This magnet type was produced in a process that had five major steps:

1. *Material mixing,* involving the bringing together of the necessary raw materials—aluminum, nickel, cobalt, and others—in the correct proportions.

2. *Pressing,* involving the pressing into the desired shapes of the mix, which had been impregnated with certain hydrocarbons.

3. *Sintering,* involving the subjection of the pressed mix to a temperature and an atmosphere in which the mix fused.

4. *Grinding,* involving the machining of the magnet to the desired dimensions.

5. *Inspection and test,* involving the 100 per cent mechanical check of the magnets to assure their having the proper physical dimensions and the 100 per cent electrical check to assure their magnetic quality.

A member of the factory's planning and methods group took it upon himself to help the foreman reduce the high rejects on the small magnet line. After an analysis of the nature of the test rejects and at the completion of several process checks, the planner came to the conclusion that the defects were being caused by unsatisfactory furnace conditions during the sintering process.

The planner attempted, therefore, to adjust the furnace conditions so that satisfactory magnets could be produced on a continuous basis without an appreciable number of rejects. After several furnace changes, which seemed to have little success, he came to the conclusion that, although the furnace might be the most important factor affecting magnetic quality, there were undoubtedly other contributing conditions, one or more of which had to be adjusted along with the furnace.

Where to allocate the responsibility for further study and corrective action of these other factors was a question the planner found difficult to answer with the sketchy information at his disposal. There were at least six groups that might have been responsible:

1. *The manufacturing personnel,* from the standpoint of operator care and skill, proper instruction, and adequate care of, and attention to, the furnace and its controls.

2. *The planning and methods group,* in the selection of the furnace process and the design of the jigs and fixtures used in connection with it.

3. *The design engineers,* from the viewpoint of the original design, the

selection of tolerances and operating characteristics, and the selection of materials.

4. *The materials-ordering section,* in the choice of vendors and the quality guarantees it had required from these vendors.

5. *The laboratory engineers,* in the standards they had set for the materials and the furnace atmosphere and annealing conditions they had recommended.

6. *The mechanical-inspection and electrical-test activities,* from the standpoint of their judging the quality of the incoming materials and the results of the processes previous to the annealing operation.

The planner took into account only the persons immediately concerned with the problem. He did not, therefore, include on his list the sales department, whose original contract with the customer had set up the specifications that were causing the magnetic rejects.

No immediate action was taken by any of these groups except the planner's own. In fact, attention was soon drawn completely from the reject problem because, three days after the planner's apparently unsuccessful furnace trials, the rejects mysteriously dropped to a negligible percentage, and it seemed that they would remain low.

The planner uneasily shared credit with the foreman for the elimination of the rejects, doubtful in his own mind that the minor furnace adjustments he had made were actually causing the improvement. As he had feared and almost expected, the rejects suddenly soared a few weeks later and the furor was again on.

The problem was finally solved when the factory management, recognizing this situation and other similar ones, made a complete and effective reorganization of its controls over product quality. It is of interest to note that this new program, after a month of hard work, had suggested not one but three major changes in the small magnet. These suggestions, which were put into effect, called for a tolerance change by Engineering, a closer control over furnace temperature by Manufacturing, and a different means of gaging by Inspection. These changes largely eliminated the high rejects at a savings of several thousand dollars on an annual basis and with a corresponding improvement in the quality of the magnet.

A member of the management group of the magnet company was asked to express his ideas about what he had learned from this experience concerning what an effective quality-control program should do. "Well, that's an easy one," he told his questioner. "It ought to find out what quality troubles there are and then see that the troubles are fixed so that they don't happen again."

He was asked how this situation could be brought about. "Why, by making it so that they pay some attention to quality ahead of time instead of waiting until everybody is all excited because a batch of bad parts is winged at final inspection or in the field. They all start blaming the factory for the whole business, when maybe it was because of a build-up of mistakes by the engineers, the production men, the purchasing people, the planners, and the inspectors."

There have been many glossier and more diplomatic descriptions of the jobs a quality-control program should do than this one. But none has pointed up more clearly the fact that, to have any real control over the conditions affecting product quality, it is necessary to have controls at all important stages of the production process, from the inception of the engineering design through to the final assembly and packaging of the product. Nor has it been better illustrated that preventive rather than corrective thinking must be at the core of the entire quality-control program.

These results are the objective of *total* quality control.

PART TWO

QUALITY-CONTROL MANAGEMENT

CHAPTER 3

WHAT ARE THE JOBS OF QUALITY CONTROL?

It has been shown that the broad concept of total quality control encompasses the complete industrial cycle. It involves many persons and components throughout the organization in a number of specialized functions. The quality-related activities are many, and they range from the planning phases, so the right quality can be made the first time, on through the control of processes and customer service.

Because of the many quality-related activities, there is a need to classify the work of total quality control to identify the assignable packages of work for each position.

3.1 What Are the Jobs of Quality Control?

The *jobs* of quality control gear right in with the production and service processes, and one means of distinguishing among them shows that there are four natural classifications into which they fall.

The first job of quality control may be termed *new-design control.* Included here is the quality-control effort on a new product while its marketable characteristics are being selected; while design parameters are being established and proved by prototype tests; while the manufacturing process is being planned and initially costed; and while the quality standards are being specified. Both product and process designs are reviewed to eliminate possible sources of quality troubles before the start of formal production in order to improve maintainability and to eliminate threats to product reliability. In the case of quantity production, new-design control ends when pilot runs have given proof of satisfactory production performance, and with job-shop production the

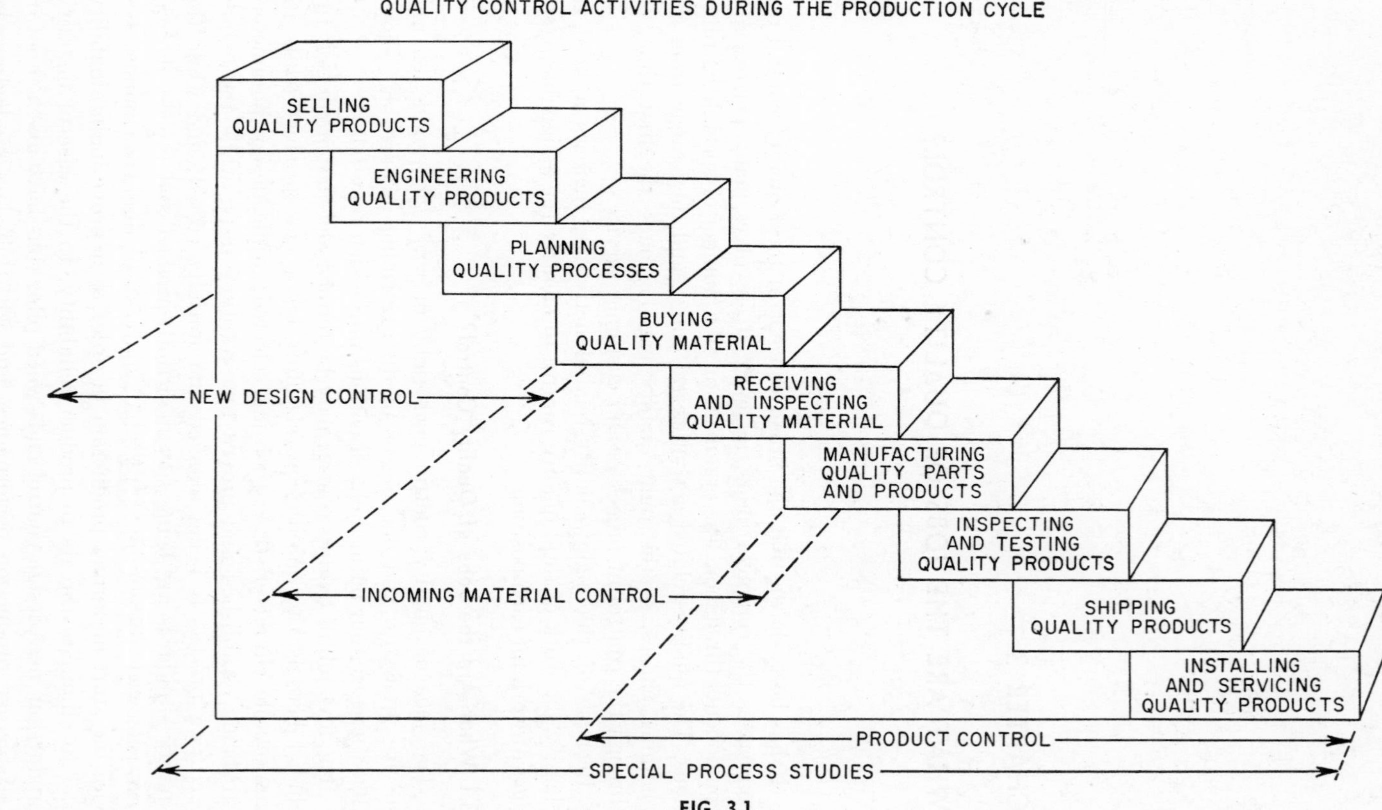
QUALITY CONTROL ACTIVITIES DURING THE PRODUCTION CYCLE
SELLING QUALITY PRODUCTS
ENGINEERING QUALITY PRODUCTS
PLANNING QUALITY PROCESSES
BUYING QUALITY MATERIAL
RECEIVING AND INSPECTING QUALITY MATERIAL
MANUFACTURING QUALITY PARTS AND PRODUCTS
INSPECTING AND TESTING QUALITY PRODUCTS
SHIPPING QUALITY PRODUCTS
INSTALLING AND SERVICING QUALITY PRODUCTS
NEW DESIGN CONTROL
INCOMING MATERIAL CONTROL
PRODUCT CONTROL
SPECIAL PROCESS STUDIES

FIG. 3.1.

routine ends as work is being started on production of the component parts.

The second job of quality control is *incoming-material control.* Involved here are the procedures for actual acceptance of materials, parts, and components purchased from other companies or, perhaps, from other operating units of the same company. Occasionally, incoming-material control applies to parts produced in one area of the same factory for use in another area.

Specifications and standards are established as criteria for acceptance of raw materials, parts, and components. A number of quality-control techniques are applied to provide acceptance at most economical levels. These techniques include vendor quality evaluations; certification of material, parts, and components by the vendor; acceptance sampling techniques; and laboratory tests.

When the design has been released for production, tools have been procured, and materials, parts, and components have been received, *product control,* the third job of quality control, comes into play. Product control involves the control of products at the source of production so that departures from quality specifications can be corrected before defective products are manufactured. It not only involves the materials and parts themselves but also control of the processes that contribute the quality characteristics during the manufacturing operation. It seeks to deliver a reliable product that will perform satisfactorily during its expected life and under the conditions of use. It therefore also involves quality activities after production and in the field and product service which assures the consumer recourse in obtaining the intended product function, should recourse be necessary for any reason.

The fourth job of total quality control is *special process studies.* It is concerned with investigations and tests to locate the causes of defective products. Elimination or control of these causes results in product and process improvement, not only in improving quality characteristics, but also in reducing costs.

Figure 3.1 shows how the quality-control jobs gear in with the production process.

3.2 What Is New-design Control?

As a definition:

New-design control involves the establishment and specification of the desirable cost-quality, performance-quality and reliability-quality standards for the product, including the elimination or location of possible sources of quality troubles before the start of formal production.

Techniques used in new-design control include analysis of product function, environmental and end-use tests, classification of quality characteristics, establishment of quality levels and quality standards, process-capability studies, tolerance analysis, quality-ability analysis, log of prototype inputs, prototype tests, establishment of process parameters, product evaluation, manufacturing process review, establishment of reliability standards, development of maintainability and serviceability standards, and pilot runs. This work is treated in detail in Chap. 15.

3.3 What Is Incoming-material Control?

As a definition:

Incoming-material control involves the receiving and stocking, at the most economical levels of quality, of only those parts the quality of which conforms to the specification requirements.

There are two phases in incoming-material control:

1. Control on materials and parts received from outside sources.
2. Control on materials and parts processed by other plants of the same company or other divisions of the plant.

Techniques used in incoming-material control include vendor capability evaluations; vendor-rating plans; vendor certification of material, parts, and component quality; clear delineation of quality requirements; inspection and test procedures, including use of gages, standards, and specialized quality information equipment; selection of economical sampling plans for use at specified levels of quality; and measurement of inspection performance. This work is treated in detail in Chap. 16.

3.4 What Is Product Control?

As a definition:

Product control involves the control of products at the source of production and through field service so that departures from the quality specification can be corrected before defective products are manufactured and so that proper product service can be maintained in the field.

There are two phases in *product control:*

1. Control of machining or processing of component parts.
2. Control of assemblies and packaging of batches.

Techniques used in product control include implementation of a complete quality plan for in-process quality control and final product acceptance; process capability studies; process sampling; control-chart technique; tool, jig, and fixture control; calibration of quality information equipment; operator instructions and training; analysis of complaints; and analysis of quality costs for their optimization and field service quality techniques. This work is treated in detail in Chap. 17.

3.5 What Are Special Process Studies?

As a definition:

Special process studies involve conducting investigations and tests to locate the causes of defective products and to determine the possibility of improving product-quality characteristics.

Techniques used in special process studies consist largely of special applications of the standard methods used in the other *jobs* of quality control. This work is treated in detail in Chap. 18.

3.6 Does a Quality-control Program Always Include These Four Jobs?

In a particular company, the actual details of the jobs of the quality-control program will depend upon the production circumstances. A company that purchases parts and materials and then machines and processes some of them, after which it assembles the various components, will probably include all four jobs of quality control in its program.

A producer of studs, nuts, and bolts, whose only mechanical facilities are screw machines, will very likely use only *product control* on machines and, possibly, *special process studies* in his quality-control program. The mail-order house may use chiefly *incoming-material control* and the textile manufacturer, both *incoming-material control* and *product control.* The chemical manufacturer, with his "batch" production, may depend upon *new-design control* and *special process studies.*

All four jobs of a total quality-control program came into successive use by a device manufacturer during the design and production of a controller for a jet airliner. The controller was an electromechanical device with two coils that provided electrical force, against which the mechanical force of spring-loaded contacts operated. It was produced in an area in which the following sequence of operations prevailed:

1. *Incoming materials.* Parts and materials from outside vendors were received, checked for conformance to specification, and then stocked.

2. *Processing parts.* These materials and parts were worked by a variety of manufacturing equipments ranging from spot welders and punch presses to varnish dip tanks and wire strippers.

3. *Assembly.* The various components converged on an assembly line and were assembled to form the final product, which was mechanically and electrically checked.

This controller was an improved version of an earlier device which had been subject both to poor quality within the factory and to excessive quality costs. Neither of these conditions could be tolerated on the new design. The objective of the quality-control program on the controller was, therefore, to set up controls at each important stage of the design and manufacturing process so as to provide and maintain a high level of quality at a minimum of cost. The procedures that were used to accomplish this goal were classified as follows:

New-design Control. While the controller was still in the design and planning stage, special reliability tests and pilot runs were used to analyze the design in order to make possible adequate guarantees to the customer, to provide reasonable specifications to the shop, and to make available sufficient advance information to the mechanical-inspection and electrical-test supervisors. Experience with previous designs of similar type; studies on the accuracies of the machines, tools, and processes to be used; and the full utilization of purchasing information were integrated to anticipate and minimize sources of possible quality troubles before production started.

Incoming-material Control. Information gained from the new-design control procedures showed, with respect to the parts and materials purchased from vendors, those parts and those dimensions which were critical. Based on these data, careful checks were made on the first lots of parts shipped in by the vendors to determine their quality and workmanship. Where parts were unsatisfactory, immediate contact was made with the vendor. This contact was followed up until the parts were satisfactory or the vendor in question was replaced.

As soon as there was assurance of the quality of a vendor's workmanship, reliable, cost-saving sampling schedules were set up to serve as controls. These sampling checks formed the basis for vendor ratings and, after production had started, for a continuing review of where and how specifications could be so changed without impairing quality that it would be possible for the vendor to reduce his billed prices.

Product Control. As the controller started into active production, each operator was carefully instructed in his or her part of the job. Similar instruction was given to new and replacement operators. A preventive maintenance program on the manufacturing equipment largely limited factors that had previously been problems, such as use of undersize machine-tool fixtures, taps, drills, and reamers and the gradual working down of the consistency of the varnish in the dip tanks used to impregnate the controller coils.

On the parts and subassemblies being machined and processed, suitable gaging equipments were made available to each operator. Patrol inspection, on a definite time schedule, gave additional assurance that any defective work would be located at its source. At the important points in the assembly cycle for the device, control charts and defect breakdowns were set up so as to "telegraph" to the shop supervisors the magnitude and the location of the quality troubles. Packaging and shipping were closely controlled.

Special Process Studies. When control charts, patrol inspection checks, and reject breakdowns registered the presence of quality troubles that shop supervisors could not clear up, aid was furnished them by those of the functional groups which could be most helpful in analyzing and taking corrective action on the problem. In cases of this sort, the quality-control organization had the responsibility of seeing that there was no duplication of effort in these studies and that the talent of the entire organization was effectively utilized.

Many of these studies involved straightforward problems that were solved by bringing together the proper individuals or groups to agree on specification improvements or fixture and tool redesign. Generally, tests were made to determine the nature of this corrective action. In a few instances, on complicated problems where several variables were involved, some of the statistical special methods were found useful in setting up and interpreting the test runs.

Compared with the previous design, considerable improvements in quality and reduction in losses and costs were noted on this controller. One interesting sidelight is that these improvements were obtained at the same time that inspection and testing expenses were reduced about 40 per cent below similar costs on the previous design.

3.7 What Part Does Statistics Play in the Quality-control Job?

In the light of the considerable publicity accorded the use of statistics in quality-control activity, a natural question is "What is the application of statistical methods in the four jobs of quality control?"

Statistics is used in a total quality-control program whenever and wherever it may be useful. But statistics is only one of the tools to be used as a part of the total quality control pattern; it is not the pattern itself.

The *point of view* represented by these statistical methods has, however, had a profound effect upon the entire area of quality control. This point of view is represented by four statistical tools which may be used separately or in combination in the four quality-control jobs. These tools are

1. The *frequency distribution,* which is a tabulation or tally of the number of times a given quality characteristic occurs within the samples of product being checked. As a picture of the quality of the sample, it may be used to show at a glance (*a*) the average quality, (*b*) the spread of the quality, and (*c*) the comparison of the quality with specification

requirements. This tool is used in the analysis of the quality of a given process or device.

2. The *control chart,* which is a chronological (hour by hour, day by day) graphical comparison of actual product-quality characteristics with limits reflecting the ability to produce, as shown by past experience on the product-quality characteristics. When the curve of the graph approaches or exceeds the limits, some change is suggested in the process that may require investigation. This tool may be used to maintain control over a process after the frequency distribution has shown that the process is "in control."

3. *Sampling tables,* which are a series of schedules for representing the probable quality relationships (usually expressed in percentage terms) of the entire lot to the samples properly selected from that lot. This tool is used when assurance is desired for the quality of material either produced or received.

4. *Special methods,* which include such techniques as the analysis of tolerances, correlation, and the analysis of variance. These methods have been hewn, for industrial quality-control use, out of the general body of statistics. This tool is used for special analyses of engineering designs or process troubles.

For general factory use, the frequency distribution, the control chart, and the sampling tables have been reduced to simple shop mathematics.

A general survey of the point of view represented by statistical methods is contained in the five chapters of Part Four: Chap. 10, Frequency Distributions; Chap. 11, Control Charts; Chap. 12, Sampling Tables; Chap. 13, Special Methods; Chap. 14, Product Reliability.

3.8 What Part Does Other Methodology Play in the Quality-control Job?

Statistics is essentially one of several techniques that may be applied to the solution of problems in total quality control. What are some of the other techniques that can be used in quality control?

There are many of an engineering character that have developed in recent years. The technology of quality information equipment design affords solution for the measurement of quality characteristics and for their rapid analysis. The technique of reliability evaluation and analysis provides a basis for predicting the reliability of a product under end-use conditions. The techniques of simulation also facilitate reliability prediction for various environmental conditions.

A general survey of the engineering technology of quality control is contained in the three chapters of Part Three: Chap. 8, Quality-control Engineering Technology; Chap. 9, Process-control Engineering Technology; Chap. 10, Quality Information Equipment Engineering Technology.

3.9 Do These Jobs Apply to Job-lot as Well as to High-quantity Production?

Much of the original quality-control publicity was accorded the spectacular accomplishments of statistical sampling on articles produced in quantities of millions. An unfortunate carry-over from this early publicity is the attitude still prevalent in some factories that the quality-control jobs are essentially tools for mass production.

Both practical experience and common sense show that this is not the case. The quality-control jobs are as applicable to job-lot production as to high-quantity production.

It is fully as necessary and useful to control the quality of the design of a new generator when only one unit is to be built as it is to carry on similar activity for a relay whose production rate will reach the thousands. It is fully as important to control the materials and parts for this generator as it is to superintend them for the relay. It is fully as basic to oversee the machining of parts and their assembly into a complete generator as it is to control this work for the relay.

The methods used in the quality-control jobs may differ between the two products. Certain types of sampling methods will be better applicable in the quality-control jobs for the relay. Process-capability studies will probably be relatively more useful in the generator program. The type of control chart that is ideal for the relay will require considerable adaptation for use with the generator.

The administration of an over-all, integrated quality-control program will be of equal value for both products in place of a sprawling, disjointed series of activities. It is likely that the administration and organization of this program will not differ very widely between high-quantity and job-lot production.

Another way of describing the basic differences between job-lot and high-quantity quality-control programs is as follows:

In mass-production operations, product quality can be effectively controlled by types of parts, since all parts will be manufactured to the same drawings and specifications. However, in job-lot manufacture, the parts differ from job to job and only the process by which they are produced is common to all types of products.

Therefore in mass-production manufacturing, quality-control activities center on the product, whereas in job-lot manufacturing, it is a matter of controlling the process.

For example, in the mass-production manufacture of coils, the emphasis of quality-control activities is on the coil type itself: its dimensions, fiber wrappings, etc. But where varying types and sizes of coils are produced on a job-lot basis, the quality-control activities center on the common manufacturing process for producing the coils.

3.10 How Are the Jobs of Quality Control Accomplished?

In Sec. 1.3, it was shown that the four steps in the over-all control of quality are

1. Setting standards.
2. Appraising conformance.
3. Taking corrective action.
4. Planning for improvement.

Although, to different degrees, these four steps are combined in each of the jobs of quality control, they appear to tie together effectively with these jobs in one-two-three-four order: a major portion of new-design control is setting standards; incoming-material control is largely a question of appraising conformance; product control is, in part, the procedure for taking corrective action; and special process studies have planning for improvement as one of their major aims.

From this breakdown of an over-all quality-control program into its component parts, it can be readily seen that there are several by-product benefits over and above the major improvements which result from such a program. Successful prosecution of the jobs of quality control makes possible greatly increased knowledge about the accuracies and capabilities of machines and processes. It makes factual material about product quality available for market planning and merchandising activities. It stimulates better engineering designs by promoting reliability studies of new products before they have been placed in active production. It promotes improved inspection methods and relieves inspection monotony by substituting careful checks of samples for mass sorting of the 100 per cent variety. It enables sounder setting of time-studied standards for labor by establishing quality standards for shop operations.

An important by-product of quality control is the provision of a reasonable and definite schedule for preventive maintenance to replace the hit-or-miss type of schedule that often leads to trouble. When product quality is to be emphasized in company advertising, quality control makes available powerful information for trade journals, magazines, and catalogs. It also furnishes a factual basis for cost accounting on such standard costs of quality as prevention, appraisal, and failure costs.

Successfully to secure these major and by-product benefits from the four jobs of quality control requires integrated, organized action by the various individuals and groups involved in the production process. Chapter 4 discusses how this organization can be set up.

CHAPTER 4

WHAT IS THE ORGANIZATION FOR QUALITY CONTROL?

The task of a quality-control organization is administration of the activities of the persons and groups who work within the technological framework represented by the four quality-control jobs.

The spirit motivating this organization must be one which stimulates an aggressive quality-consciousness among all company employees. This spirit depends upon many intangibles, among which management's attitude toward quality is paramount.

It also depends upon some very tangible factors. The most important of these is that the structure of the quality-control organization permit a maximum of results and of integration with a minimum of personal friction, overlap of authority, and dissension among functional groups.

Establishing an adequate quality-control organization for a company is a job of human relations. Guides to the structural patterns that are useful may be found in industry's experience with quality control during the past several years. This experience may be gaged against the backdrop of the organization planning methods which are now being widely used by management.

The patterns emerging as most successful may be readily summarized in terms of their essentials:

Basic quality responsibility rests in the hands of company top management. Over the past several decades top management, as part of the general industrial trend toward specialization, has delegated portions of its quality responsibility to such functional groups as Engineering, Planning, Manufacturing, and Inspection. In addition, the all-important responsibility of each workman for producing quality products has, if anything, increased over this period of years with the increasing complexity both of products and of production machinery.

In present-day industry, the four jobs of total quality control cannot be effectively pursued with quality responsibilities for their various elements thus widely diffused and separated. There must be an associated mechanism to assist in integrating and measuring these responsibilities. In the larger companies where top management cannot of and by itself act as such a mechanism, present-day management establishes an organizational component as the pivotal point of its total-quality-control organization to provide the required integration and control.

Creation of this quality-control component does not relieve other company personnel of their delegated quality responsibilities, for the discharge of which they are best qualified. The component does, however, make the quality-control whole for the company greater than the sum of its individual engineering, manufacturing, inspection, and marketing parts, through the functions of integration and control. It thus provides the core of the organizational pattern for making effective the total-quality-control technological framework, an effectiveness which has not been at all equaled by the more traditional quality-control organizations of the past.

It is the purpose of this chapter to develop and discuss this total-quality-control organizational pattern and to review some of the factors which have contributed to the need for this type of organization.

4.1 What Has Been the Formal Organization for Quality Control in the Past?

In companies which have devoted real attention to quality-control activities, many have given only casual attention to quality-control organization. A majority of their time and effort has been devoted to developing the technological aspects of quality control.

As a result, several company quality-control components have, like Topsy, "just growed." They have become appendages to existing inspection departments, "new" functional groups developed with little preliminary analysis of what their function should really be, or additional assignments for strong personalities in the plants.

The quality-control organizations that are formally recognized on company organization charts are often not adequate to administer the quality-control jobs. Some plants do not recognize that all four jobs are within the province of their quality-control organization. Often a quality-control program is allied with the traditional inspection department. It concerns itself with job 2, incoming-material control, and with certain phases of job 3, product control.

Equally frequently encountered is the practice of creating a quality-control organization simply by adding such methods as statistical sampling to the activities of the plant's existing inspection department.

Again, there are often basic inadequacies in the program of those plants which concentrate upon the development of "new" functional quality-control organizations. Many of these groups have been built around a single quality-control technique or a single quality-control objective. Some of these groups are statistical bureaus; others carry on specialized versions of sampling work or study only "manufacturing losses"; still others are responsible for trouble shooting field complaints or for writing factory inspection and testing instructions.

These groups are limited in scope to job 1, new-design control; to job 3, product control, or to job 4, special process studies. Their members typically are extremely conscientious and often gain local successes in the individual projects they attack. In the final analysis, however, as is almost inevitable, the results of their work in relation to the over-all plant quality objective may be analogous to the results obtained in attempting to restrain a balloon by squeezing one end.

Failure to meet the company quality objective is not the only difficulty that has been experienced from these types of quality-control organizations. They have often been characterized by lack of integration among the several activities and by sprawling, disjointed quality-control planning. The new quality-control techniques, most of which cut across all four quality-control jobs, are frequently overlooked or misapplied because there has been no single channel through which they might be introduced on a company-wide basis.

More recently some companies have organized in such a way that product-reliability responsibilities are set up separate from basic product-quality responsibilities. Large and costly reliability organizations have been established which, in some cases, largely duplicate the product-quality responsibilities that already exist. Naturally, conflicts between the two groups develop, and the interests of neither over-all product quality nor its product-reliability element are served.

Knotty personality problems have sometimes arisen when management has been led to expect from these forms of quality-control organizations the over-all improvements in quality and reductions in cost that have been reported in the literature. Friction with other company groups and employees and high turnover of quality-control personnel have characterized these programs. Employees throughout the company are often not clear as to the scope of the quality-control organization and sometimes level "empire-building" charges against its members.

On the one hand, management becomes dissatisfied with its quality-control program and suspicious of the national claims being made for the activity. On the other hand, members of the quality-control organization become frustrated and privately berate management for its lack of understanding and for its refusal to grant the group more power.

4.2 What Has Been the Status of Quality Responsibilities in These Organizations?

In the final analysis, many of these quality-control organizations of the past have been so informal or so restricted in scope that they have not been quality-control organizations at all in the total-quality-control sense of coordinated administration of an integrated program of the four quality-control jobs. Individual elements of these jobs have been carried on, not as a part of the preconceived plant-wide total-quality-control program, but as uncoordinated portions of the regular responsibilities of several functional groups in the plant. New-design-control activities have usually been the exclusive province of Design Engineering and, possibly, Manufacturing Engineering. Incoming-material control has generally been supervised by Inspection and Laboratory Engineering.

Product control has often been directed by Manufacturing Supervision. Special process studies have frequently resolved into free-for-alls in which all groups would participate at one time or another.

A typical breakdown of some of the major functional groups which have, as a practical matter, key responsibilities for product quality may be developed as follows:

1. *Product Planning, Marketing, and Sales,* for the product description that will best fulfill the customer's wants and needs, for the presentation of product-quality data to the customer, and the determination of quality standards with him.

2. *Product Engineering,* for the original product design, the writing of specifications, the establishment of guarantees, and the selection of materials, tolerances, and operating characteristics.

3. *Manufacturing Engineering,* for the selection of machining and processing equipments, for the design of appropriate jigs and fixtures, for analysis of certain types of manufacturing difficulties which may arise in producing quality of the desired standard, and for the selection of methods, development of work places, and provision of satisfactory working conditions.

4. *Purchasing,* for choosing vendors and for the quality guarantees demanded from the vendors.

5. *Laboratory,* for the quality standards set for materials and processes, for the approval of the quality of critical materials, either purchased or processed, and for recommendations on the use of special processing techniques.

6. *Factory Supervision,* for operator education, for proper attention to, and care for, manufacturing facilities, for proper interpretation of

drawings and specifications, and for actual control over the manufactured parts as they are being produced.

7. *Factory operators,* for skill, care, and workmanship.

8. *Inspection and Testing,* for judging the quality of incoming parts and materials and for appraising the conformance of manufactured parts and assemblies to specifications.

9. *Packaging and Shipping,* for the adequacy of the container into which the product is placed and for the shipment of the product.

10. *Product Service,* for providing the customer with the means for fully realizing the intended function of the product during its expected life: e.g., maintenance and repair instructions and replacement parts.

Other groups like Production Control, Wage Rate, and Personnel share in these quality responsibilities. Some newly created specialized activities—motivational research, for example—have product quality as one of the major reasons for their existence.

Management has thus been paying the price for the quality-control jobs. The issue in quality-control organization is, therefore, *not* "Shall we organize for administration of the quality-control jobs?" It is rather "What type of quality-control organization shall we have?"

4.3 What Issue Has Arisen from This Distribution of Responsibilities?

It may be granted that the hydra-headed responsibility and lack of genuine organization for the four quality-control jobs is a major cause for the high costs of industrial quality and for the occasional low quality of these products. As everybody's job, quality control may often become nobody's job.

It may be granted that coordination among quality-control activities has occurred more according to whim than according to any adequate organizational procedure. Budget factors and personality considerations have tended to Balkanize product-quality responsibilities and to insulate functional groups from each other.

It may be granted that several of the quality-control activities have developed in contradictory directions. Product-quality responsibilities are so widely distributed that it is naive to expect that they will synchronize with each other "spontaneously."

It may be granted that modern quality problems are too complex technically to be adequately solved on this hit-or-miss basis. Industrial quality problems have simply outgrown the organization structure designed in a previous era to cope with them.

But what is to be done about this situation?

The basic issue at stake is that these individual quality responsibilities are integral parts of the day-to-day work of the line, staff, and functional groups which hold them. They cannot be effectively separated out from the other activities of these groups. The few efforts to organize quality control in this direction have proved abortive.

Thus, responsibility for specifying tolerances and other quality requirements and for making suitable tests to determine what this quality should be is intimately connected with the product engineering function. An important part of manufacturing engineering work is development of the assurance that the tools and processes selected will produce parts of the required quality standard.

It is right and appropriate in most companies that key responsibilities for product quality be distributed among various organizational components. How can quality control be organized so that integration and control are provided without relieving the rest of company personnel of their basic responsibility for quality?

4.4 What Is the Process of "Control"?

This problem of diffused responsibility is not so knotty as it may seem at first glance. It has been faced and solved by management on several previous issues.

It was faced in the development of organization for personnel administration. It was inconceivable that all personnel activities be stripped from the hands of the line organization and be placed in the hands of a personnel group.

It was faced in the development of production-control organization. It was clearly seen at the outset of this program that responsibility for many phases of production must remain where it was: in the hands of the factory foreman, the engineer, and other parties to the production process.

It was faced in the development of financial and cost accounting organization. It was obvious that responsibility for expenditures should be placed with the many individuals and groups who knew about the work being done; such responsibility could not be totally placed in the hands of a cost accounting group.

The organizational technique developed by management to meet these conditions can be simply described. It may consist initially in leaving untouched responsibilities and authority in the hands of the groups to which they have been delegated. This procedure is followed whether this delegation had previously been formally made by management or whether the responsibilities had informally gravitated to the groups in question.

A means is then created for assuring management that the results of these groups are satisfactory in relation to preset management standards. In the process of this results check, it may become necessary to coordinate the activities of the several delegants and to redistribute some of their responsibilities.

Management often has not the time to carry on the work that is required. It may therefore "extend its personality" by creating a functional man or functional group to do this work for it.

This process is one of *control*. The term "control" is usually applied to the organization that is correspondingly created as in budget "control," production "control," financial "control" and, of course, quality "control."

This process may be rephrased in relation to product quality. Analyzed from this organizational point of view, quality control becomes merely what the phrase implies: management's control over product quality. It is a device whereby management delegates authority and responsibility for product quality, thus relieving itself of unnecessary detail and permitting the benefits of specialization while retaining for itself the means for assuring that quality results will be satisfactory, in terms of top management's standards and policies.

4.5 Organizing Principles

Fundamental to building the organization structure which puts this process to work, and thereby brings the four quality-control jobs to effective use, are two quality-control organizational principles that sum up the concepts discussed above. The first principle is that *quality is everybody's job* in a business.

In defiance of this principle, many businesses over the years have attempted to centralize their company quality responsibility by organizing a function whose job has been handsomely described as "responsibility for all factors affecting product quality." These experiments have had a life span of as long as 6 to 9 months, that is, when the job incumbent had the advantage of a strong stomach, a rhinoceros hide, and a well-spent, sober boyhood. Others not similarly endowed did not last the 6 months.

The simple fact of the matter is that the *marketing man* can best evaluate customer's quality preferences. The *design engineer* is the only man who can effectively establish specification quality levels. The shop *supervisor* is the individual who can best concentrate upon the building of quality.

Total-quality-control programs thus require, as an initial step, top management's reemphasis of the respective quality responsibilities and accountabilities of all company employees in new-design control, in incoming-material control, in product control, and in special process studies.

The second principle of total-quality-control organization is a corollary to this first one: *because quality is everybody's job in a business, it may become nobody's job*. Thus, the second step required in total quality programs becomes clear. Top management must recognize that the many individual responsibilities for quality will be exercised most effectively when they are buttressed and serviced by a well-organized, genuinely modern management function whose only area of *specialization* is product quality, whose only area of *operation* is in the quality-control jobs, and whose only *responsibilities* are to be sure that the products shipped are right—and *at the right quality cost.*

The two basic responsibilities of this total-quality-control function may be formally stated as *first,* to provide quality assurance for the business's products, and *second,* to assist in assuring optimum quality costs for those products.

The quality-control function fulfills these responsibilities through its

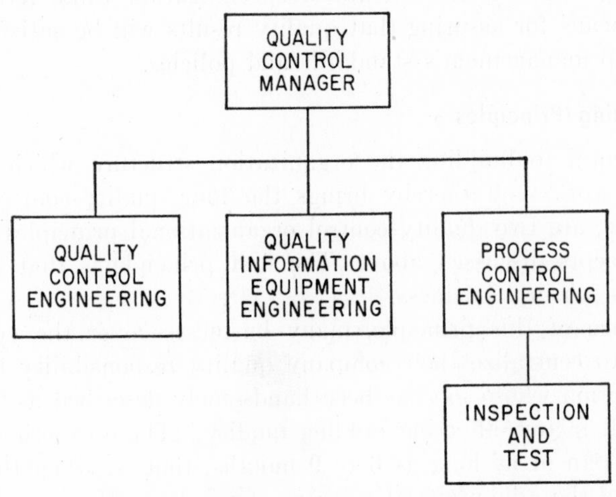

FIG. 4.1.

three subfunctions, which are quality-control engineering, process-control engineering (including also inspection and testing), and quality information equipment engineering.

Quality-control engineering does the quality planning which establishes the basic framework of the entire quality-control system for the company.

Process-control engineering (including also inspection and testing) monitors the application of this quality-control system on the shop floor and thus gradually supplants the older policing inspection activity.

Quality information equipment engineering designs and develops the inspection and testing equipment for obtaining these process control measurements. Where justified, this equipment is combined with production to provide automatic feedback of results for control of the process. All pertinent results are then analyzed as a basis for adjustment and corrective action on the process.

The basic structure for such a quality-control function is shown in Fig. 4.1. Figure 4.2 is a typical position guide for the manager of the

---

XYZ COMPANY

POSITION GUIDE

MANAGER—QUALITY CONTROL

I. *Broad Function*

The Manager–Quality Control has managerial and functional responsibilities for the operation of the quality-control component. He will integrate the quality-connected functions of the various sections into a quality system designed to fulfill the customers' needs at minimum quality cost. To this end he is responsible for assuring that quality requirements have been adequately defined to permit appropriate quality planning; and that these quality requirements have been met.

II. *Principal Responsibilities*

Within the limits of approved policies, programs, budgets, and procedures, the Manager–Quality Control is responsible for, and has the authority to fulfill, the duties listed below. He may delegate portions of his responsibility together with the necessary authority for their fulfillment, but he may not delegate or relinquish his over-all responsibility for results.

A. Managerial Responsibilities

The Manager–Quality Control is responsible for providing leadership to all employees of the quality-control component by performing the work of a manager, in which he will, as to

1. Planning
   a. Keep himself and his supervisors informed of the objectives, policies, plans, and budgets of the business.
   b. Develop the company's quality-control program, including policies, objectives, plans, organizations, procedures, and appraisals, and assure the documentation of the program and its distribution to company personnel to promote the proper concept of the quality-control program.
2. Organizing
   a. Develop a sound organizational structure for the performance of all phases of the quality-control component activities.
   b. Establish appropriate subfunctional components within the quality-control component, man them with qualified personnel, and delegate appropriate responsibilities and authority for conducting their particular phases of the quality-control program.
   c. Instruct, advise, counsel, and review the performance of the unit and subunit supervisors of the quality-control component.
3. Integrating
   a. Provide for the systematic utilization of all resources of the com-

ponent to achieve effectively and economically the desired objectives.

b. Acquaint each person in the component with his responsibilities, authority, and accountability and promote individual development and the necessity for unity of effort.

4. Measuring

a. Establish standards for measuring the performance of the Unit and Subunit heads and other personnel of the quality-control component and inform them of their progress.

b. Analyze and appraise the progress of the component as measured against the objectives set up, and take or suggest action necessary for improvement.

B. Functional Responsibilities

The Manager–Quality Control, by contributing his own knowledge as well as working through those reporting directly to him, will

1. Formulate basic policies, plans, programs, standards, and techniques necessary to carry out the objectives of the Quality Control component, and upon their approval, carry out such policies, plans, and programs.
2. Provide for adequate facilities and equipment necessary for inspecting, testing, and measuring the quality of the company products and for the most economical maintenance of such equipment and facilities.
3. Provide and have distributed to all appropriate personnel of the business programs designed to promote the spirit of quality thinking throughout the component and to encourage participation of Quality Control personnel in any educational courses that may be available to keep themselves informed of the newest developments that involve quality-control procedures.
4. Maintain relationships with Marketing units to understand thoroughly the functions of the product necessary to fulfill customer needs.
5. Maintain relationships with Engineering units to discuss quality considerations, as early as possible in the product-design stage.
6. Maintain proper relationships with vendors to ensure that their products meet company quality standards.
7. Work with cost-accounting supervisors to determine costs of quality so that these costs can be easily analyzed and controlled.

III. *Authority and Reservation of Decision-making Authority*

The Manager–Quality Control has full authority to make decisions and take action necessary to carry out the responsibilities assigned to him so long as such action does not deviate from established business and company policies, practices, and position guides and is consistent with sound business judgment, except for the following specific limitations placed upon his authority.

1. Certain additions to payroll and salary adjustments of certain employees.
2. Changes in the organizational structure at the unit level or above.

3. Major changes affecting the other components.
4. Approval of certain expense accounts.

IV. *Accountability*

The Manager–Quality Control is fully accountable for the fulfillment of his responsibilities and for their proper interpretation. He may not delegate or relinquish any portion of his accountability. Performance of the Manager–Quality Control will be measured by the extent or degree to which he and his quality-control component fulfill the following accountability measures:

1. The quality of his leadership in all areas of the quality-control component.
2. The quality and timeliness of his decisions and actions as to all responsibilities of the position.
3. The quality of his managerial leadership by his own actions and the action of others in the quality-control component reporting directly to him.
4. The attainment of the objectives and fulfillment of the responsibilities of his position as indicated by the level and trend of
   a. The control of the quality of incoming materials and completed parts as compared with engineering specifications.
   b. Action taken to correct cause of complaints due to poor material or workmanship.
   c. Adequacy of equipment and facilities with which to perform quality-control functions.
   d. Adequacy of process measurements to provide necessary information to Shop Operations for process control.
   e. Adequacy and timeliness of quality information feedback to organizational units that can take corrective action.
   f. Accuracy in diagnosing quality difficulties and analyzing underlying causes.
   g. Accuracy of product-quality measurements indices and in reflecting the true quality of the product reaching the customer.
   h. Realization of quality costs as compared with budget and estimates.
   i. Realization of cost-reduction and manufacturing-loss goals.
   j. Safety of component personnel as indicated by the frequency and severity of accidents in the subsection.
   k. Morale of the component employees as indicated by the number of grievances as well as by absenteeism, employee turnover, and productive man-hours lost because of work stoppage.
   l. The effectiveness of promotion of the suggestion plan and other employee benefit plans as measured by comparative employee participation in the benefit plans.
   m. The effective utilization of manpower, facilities, and equipment indicated by the work produced against predetermined standards.

FIG. 4.2

function. Figure 4.3 reviews typical work elements of the quality-control-engineering, process-control-engineering (also including inspection and test), and quality-information-equipment-engineering subfunctions.

WORK ELEMENTS QUALITY CONTROL

The major subfunctions in Quality Control are

- Quality Control Engineering.
- Quality Information Equipment Engineering.
- Process Control Engineering, including Inspection and Testing.

Quality Control Engineering

General Description

This component of the quality-control function has responsibility for the action required to

1. Determine that quality objectives and goals have been defined sufficiently to permit adequate quality planning to satisfy customer expectations.
2. Review proposed products and processes for the purpose of avoiding or eliminating unnecessary quality difficulties.
3. Plan the quality measurements and controls on materials, processes, and product to provide adequate control of quality at minimum quality-related costs.
4. Determine that manufacturing processes have sufficient capability to meet quality requirements.
5. Analyze quality information and feed back analyses and recommendations for adjustment to product design, manufacturing process and equipment, and the quality system.

Work Elements

1.* *Quality Objectives and Goals.* Recommend realistic company product-quality objectives and goals. Work with Marketing and Engineering in establishing specific quality requirements on individual products on the basis of customer need, the function of the product, and its reliability, salability, and value.

2.* *Preproduction Quality Ability.* Review new and revised designs for quality ability. Recommend improvements to Engineering that increase product uniformity and reliability and improve quality characteristics to reduce field failures and complaints. Recommend improvements for simplifying control of manufacturing processes and evaluating quality, thereby reducing costs.

3.* *Review of Engineering Prototype Evaluations.* Review performance, environmental, life, shipping test results, etc., and other information resulting from Engineering development work. Analyze and evaluate prototype performance as a basis for reliability studies and for planning the required controls on quality and associated information feedback.

* Work elements which normally are not delegated to Shop Operations.

4.* *Quality Standards.* Participate with Marketing and Engineering in establishing and defining those quality standards which cover such items as appearance, surface roughness, color, noise, and vibration.

5.* *Shop-practice Standards.* Participate with Manufacturing Engineering and Shop Operations in establishing shop standards that will be followed in the absence of engineering specifications; e.g., radii on bends and squareness of sheared stock.

6.* *Product- and Process-quality Planning.* Determine and establish the required quality procedures for controlling product and process quality, including reliability requirements. Planning should include the relative importance of quality characteristics and required quality levels; points in the flow for quality measurements to be made; methods and procedures for quality measurements by operators, quality checkers, inspectors, testers, auditors, etc.; applicable statistical quality-control techniques; quality information feedback; required quality measurement and control equipment; defective-material disposition procedures; and other pertinent quality procedures. Assure incorporation of applicable quality measurements into the manufacturing process planning. Provide appropriate components with cost estimates and time schedules pertaining to the above controls on quality. Periodically review quality planning to assure continued adequacy and effectiveness.

7.* *Purchased-material Quality Control.* Determine the relative importance of purchased-material quality characteristics and the required quality levels, keeping in mind design, manufacturing process, and reliability requirements. Ensure adequate delineation of quality requirements to vendors through Purchasing. Designate quality characteristics to be measured and methods and procedures for performing quality evaluations, including sampling plans and required inspection and test equipment. Evaluate new vendor facilities and systems for controlling quality. Plan for vendor ratings and materials certification by vendors.

8.* *Controls on Production Devices Directly Affecting Quality.* Assist Manufacturing Engineering in specifying the required quality capability of new production devices directly affecting quality; i.e., equipment, tools, dies, fixtures, etc. Establish methods and procedures for evaluating original adequacy to the required quality capability. Establish procedures for ensuring adequate preventive maintenance controls, qualitywise, on the above.

9.* *Quality Capability Requirements.* Determine that manufacturing processes and equipment have sufficient capability to meet quality requirements by analyzing process-capability studies, control charts, and other statistical data. Determine which product- and process-quality characteristics require process-capability studies. Analyze results of studies and feed back recommendations for selection or improvement of machine or process to meet manufacturing quality requirements.

10.* *Outgoing Product-quality Index.* Establish a current, timely, and continuous index of outgoing product quality by means of customer-oriented quality audits and ratings, including life, reliability, and environmental evaluations.

11.* *Quality Information Feedback.* Ascertain the specific quality information

* Work elements which normally are not delegated to Shop Operations.

feedback needs of all key personnel in Manufacturing and, as applicable, in Engineering and Marketing; ensure timely delivery of action-centered data and reports which make for optimum quality-related decision making.

12.* *Manufacturing Quality Problems.* Diagnose chronic manufacturing quality problems referred by Process Control Engineering to determine basic cause of difficulties. Also provide technical assistance as required to other functions. Present analysis of facts to establish the nature of the problem for solution and action by the appropriate component. Follow and report progress to applicable management.

13.* *Quality-cost Analysis.* Analyze all elements of quality costs, and provide analyses as a basis for initiating positive action in the areas of prevention, appraisal, and failure, for over-all reduction in quality costs.

14.* *Product-quality Certification.* Develop quality-certification plans for products shipped to customers. Assist Marketing in publishing brochures outlining the quality system, showing the advantages to the customer in buying quality-controlled and certified products.

15.* *Customer Complaints and Field Failure Analysis.* Analyze, identify basic causes, and feed back analyses and recommendations, participating with other functional components in instigating corrective action. Follow and report progress to appropriate management.

16.* *Quality-control Training.* Develop and implement quality-control orientation programs for all operational personnel in the company to ensure understanding of quality-control objectives, programs, plans, and techniques. Provide quality training programs for personnel in Shop Operations and other subfunctional components.

17.* *Quality-control Communication.* Develop and initiate efficient methods for regularly reporting to managers and other interested personnel the current status of product quality with respect to quality objectives and goals to stimulate quality improvement and continued quality efforts. Keep management regularly informed on status and progress made on quality-control programs and plans.

18.* *Quality-system Manuals.* Write and furnish quality-system manuals, in cooperation with Engineering and Marketing, in the fulfillment of government and commercial contracts.

General Comments on Quality Control Engineering

In a small business, it is possible that all the above work elements would be assigned to one position.

In larger companies, the above work elements might be divided among several positions. For example, Advanced Quality Control Engineering would be responsible for work elements 1 and 2. The quality-control engineer who does the planning of specific controls on quality would be responsible for work elements 3–10, 14, and 18. Work elements 16 and 17 would normally be assigned to the appropriate engineer or engineers by the Manager–Quality Control. The remainder would be given to a quality-control engineer assigned to a product line. In some cases, a quality-control analyst would be assigned to the numerical

* Work elements which normally are not delegated to Shop Operations.

analysis portion of the quality-control-engineering work elements. All work elements, as denoted by asterisks, are normally retained in Quality Control.

Quality Information Equipment Engineering

General Description

This component of the quality-control function has responsibility for the action required to develop, design, and provide the required quality-measurement equipment for evaluating, measuring, and controlling product and process quality, including reliability requirements.

Work Elements

1. *Test and Inspection Equipment Design.* Design, construct, and prove in required testing equipment, inspection tools, fixtures, and gages or procure this equipment or service. Plan for continued effectiveness of such equipment and tooling, including calibration schedules.
2. *In-process Quality-measuring Devices.* Ensure that in-process quality-measuring devices are provided to indicate, and in some cases record, the quality at the instant it is produced so the operator can provide rapid control of the process and have proof of in-process quality. Plan for continued effectiveness of such devices, including calibration schedules.
3. *Mechanization and Automation.* Work with Manufacturing Engineering to incorporate, where possible, the quality-measurement and control devices with the manufacturing equipment to provide optimum mechanization and automation through integrated analysis and feedback of quality data.
4. *Advanced Quality-measuring Techniques and Equipment.* Devise, develop, and prove feasibility of advanced quality-measurement and control techniques and equipment required to achieve continually improving manufactured product quality, including reliability, at reduced costs.

Process Control Engineering

General Description

This component of the quality-control function has the responsibility and takes the action required for

1. Providing technical assistance for understanding quality standards and solution of Manufacturing quality problems.
2. Evaluating the quality capability of processes and providing quality maintenance throughout Manufacturing.
3. Interpreting the quality plan and assuring its understanding and effective implementation throughout Manufacturing.
4. Assuring the maintenance and calibration of quality information equipment and safe operating practices.
5. Assuring that the quality level of the finished product, purchased materials, and components are commensurate with engineering specification and the quality plan.

6. Performing the actual physical operation required to help provide quality assurance, such as inspecting, testing, and quality auditing.

7. Appraising the quality plan and contributing to its continuing effectiveness.

Technical Work Elements

1.* *Appraise the Quality Plan.* Appraise the continuing effectiveness of the quality plan in terms of quality levels, nature of manufacturing quality problems, customer complaints, and economical operation as the result of implementing and working with the plan.

2.* *Interpretation of Quality Plan.* Furnish to Shop Operation and other Manufacturing organization components all necessary interpretation of the quality plan: its use, operation, and intent.

3.* *Review and Maintain Quality Standards.* Inspect all quality standards, both written and physical, for clarity and furnish interpretation to assure understanding and proper use. Provide for the maintenance of all quality standards. Also provide for or maintain necessary company-wide primary and secondary standards, such as instruments and gage blocks.

4.* *Determine Conformance to Quality Planning.* Provide to Shop Operations and others an evaluation of conformance to quality planning, to aid in making effective use of such planning.

5.* *Temporary Quality Planning.* In urgent situations, when not prescribed in the quality plan, provide Shop Operations temporarily with inspection, test, and process-control criteria, procedures, measurements, etc.

6.* *Quality Trouble Shooting.* Provide advice, counsel, and assistance in the understanding and solution of quality problems in manufacturing.

7.* *Contribute to Reducing Quality Costs and Manufacturing Losses.* Seek out and demonstrate ways and means for reducing quality costs and manufacturing losses. Work closely with Quality Control Engineering, Manufacturing Engineering, and Shop Operations in effecting such improvements.

8.* *Product Special Testing.* Conduct, or arrange for, special tests as an aid to Engineering and other organization components for product development, product specification development, and new processes and equipment development.

9.* *Laboratory Tests, Measurements, and Analyses.* Make, or arrange for, laboratory tests, measurements, and analyses of materials, processes, and products for process- and product-quality control. Provide special tests and measurements as required.

10.* *Material and Product Disposition.* Investigate nonconforming materials, components, and products for causes. Work closely with Engineering, Manufacturing Engineering, Materials, and Shop Operations for prompt and economic use or disposition, and for correction of the cause for nonconformance.

11.* *Customer Contacts.* Work closely with Marketing in maintaining contact with the customer's inspection or quality-control representative as to current quality problems. Interpret standards, specifications, quality requirement, and quality planning for in-plant customer inspection.

* Work elements which normally are not delegated to Shop Operations.

12.* *Analyze Rejected and Returned Product.* Analyze products returned because of customer complaints to determine the cause of complaint. Advise and counsel appropriate organization components for corrective action.

13.* *Service and Repair Shops Contacts.* Consult with, and offer advice to, Service and Repair Shops on evaluating returned product quality. Also assist in evaluating the quality of the repaired product.

14.* *Intercompany Quality Responsibility.* Investigate differences in interpretation of quality criteria between companies in a supplier-customer relationship. Promote quality understanding and acceptance practices that result in increased use of company-built components and products. Work closely with Purchasing, Ordering, or Production Control as required.

15.* *Quality of Manufacturing Equipment.* Assure that all purchased equipment, tools, dies, and fixtures meet quality capability specifications by interpreting results of capability studies and requirements of the quality plan.

16.* *Vendor Contacts.* Work closely with Purchasing in maintaining contact with the vendor's quality-control representative as to the vendor's quality performance and for interpreting the standards, specifications, requirements, and objectives of the quality plan. Serve as direct contact with in-plant vendor inspection. Refer chronic problems to Quality Control Engineering with recommendations for solution.

17.* *Determine Process and Equipment Quality Capability.* Perform quality-capability studies of processes and manufacturing equipments, tools, and dies to assist in the solution of manufacturing quality problems and to provide quality information to be used in improving the quality plan.

18. *Record Quality Data.* Record quality measurements and maintain quality records as required by the quality plan.

19.* *Foster Quality Awareness.* Aid in fostering quality-mindedness throughout Manufacturing and in suppliers of purchased materials.

20.* *Maintenance of Quality-control Equipment.* Provide for standardization, calibration, and maintenance for process instrumentation, process-control and test equipment, laboratory equipment, inspection equipment, meters, and gages.

21.* *Improve Measuring Techniques.* Recommend to Quality Control Engineering and Quality Information Equipment Engineering improvements in measuring techniques.

22.* *Safety.* Provide safety rules and practices for use in the design, operation, and maintenance of quality information test and inspection equipment. Inspect designs and resulting quality information equipment for safety. Establish and maintain safe working conditions, equipment, and procedures for all such equipment used in the component. Advise managers as to safety training needs, and provide for the training of users of quality information equipment in safety.

Inspection and Test Work Elements

1. *Operational Planning and Scheduling.* Plan inspecting and testing work load, in accordance with over-all schedules and available facilities, to meet production requirements.

2.* *Receiving Inspection and Test.* Perform specific inspection and test opera-

* Work elements which normally are not delegated to Shop Operations.

tions to confirm that only materials meeting established specifications are accepted. Make use of vendor contacts, process analysis, other laboratory data, and application of incoming-material certification plans.

3. *In-process Inspection and Test.* Perform specific inspection and test operations to confirm that parts in process meet established specifications.

4.* *Final Inspection and Test.* Perform specific inspection and test operations to confirm that only finished products meeting established specifications are shipped. Assure that all products furnished to customers conform to engineering specifications and the quality plan, making use of information from in-process controls, inspection, performance testing, quality auditing, and customer contacts.

5.* *Quality Auditing.* Perform quality audits as required.

6.* *Quality-records Maintenance.* Maintain accurate up-to-date inspection and test records as prescribed by the quality plan to indicate quality trends and need for corrective action.

7.* *Training Personnel.* Assure that inspection and test personnel are trained in job requirements.

Comments on Process Control Engineering

With today's manufacturing practices an advantage is gained by having a technically competent engineer on the manufacturing floor to handle the day-to-day quality problems as they arise and to implement the quality plan. Process Control Engineering fulfills this responsibility. Such an arrangement relieves the quality-control engineer of short-range quality problems so he can accomplish his function of quality planning. It provides specialized technical assistance on matters of quality in the shop, thus permitting routine in-process inspection and test work to be assigned to Shop Operations. Final inspection and testing and receiving inspection and testing are normally assigned to the process-control engineering component.

General Comments on Work Elements

Elements marked with asterisks are normally retained in the quality-control component. Under certain circumstances, the unmarked elements may be delegated to other components in the business.

FIG. 4.3

It was noted above that total-quality-control programs require the identification of the quality responsibilities of all company employees in the four quality control jobs. Figure 4.4 shows a typical set of relationships among these responsibilities, including those of the quality-control function. This diagram, called a *relationship chart,* is a most useful means for analyzing, identifying, and establishing the primary quality responsibilities of the various organizational components of the company.

* Work elements which normally are not delegated to Shop Operations.

RELATIONSHIP CHART
(Applied to Product Quality)

Code: (R) = Responsible
C = Must contribute
M = May contribute
I = Is informed

Areas of Responsibility	General Manager	Finance	Marketing	Engineering	Manager–Manufacturing	Manufacturing Engineering	Quality Control	Materials	Shop Operations
Determine needs of customer			(R)						
Establish quality level for business	(R)		C	C	C				
Establish product design specs				(R)					
Establish manufacturing process design				C	M	(R)	M	M	C
Produce products to design specs			M	C	C	C	C	C	(R)
Determine process capabilities					I	C	(R)	M	C
Qualify suppliers on quality							C	(R)	
Plan the quality system	(R)		C	C	C	C	(R)*	C	C
Plan inspection and test procedures						C	(R)	C	C
Design test and inspection equipment						C	(R)		M
Feed back quality information			C	C	I	M	(R)	C	C
Gather complaint data			(R)						
Analyze complaint data			M	M			(R)		
Obtain corrective action			M	C	C	C	(R)	C	C
Compile quality costs		(R)	C	C	C				
Analyze quality costs		M					(R)		
In-process quality measurements							(R)		C
In-process quality audit				C		C	(R)		
Final product inspection			C	C	M	C	(R)		

* Responsibility typically delegated to Quality Control, as discussed in detail in Chap. 6.

FIG. 4.4

4.6 Organizing the Quality-control Function in a Company

Companies vary widely in products and history and markets and personalities. So, too, will it be appropriate for them to vary in their particular adaptations of the basic quality-control structure shown in Fig. 4.1.

What is the right way for a particular company to go about organizing the three subfunctions of the quality-control component? Should some quality-control work be decentralized, or should the function be centralized? To whom should Quality Control report? The rest of this chapter is directed toward answering these questions.

Let's turn first to the half-dozen steps for planning any sound quality-control organization structure.

First: Define the company quality problems for whose solution the organization is being created.

Second: Establish the objectives that the organization must achieve if it is regularly to solve these problems.

Third: Determine the basic work elements that must be accomplished in meeting the organization objectives. Classify these work elements into an appropriate number of basic functions.

Fourth: Combine these basic functions into job packages which pass the screen of seven acid-test questions:

a. Does the position comprise a logical, separate field of responsibility?
b. Is the position clear-cut and definite as to scope, purpose, objectives, and results to be achieved?
c. Can a single man be held responsible and know the measuring sticks by which he is being judged?
d. Are the functions of the position closely related and do they "belong together"?
e. Does the position have authority commensurate with its responsibility? In other words, is it tooled up for results?
f. Does the position have easy, workable relationships with other positions in the organization?
g. Can the number of men reporting to the holder of the position be genuinely supervised?

Fifth: Consolidate the job packages into an organization component or components best suited to specific company requirements, recognizing the particular character of the organization component that has been created.

Sixth: With this in mind, locate the component in that segment of the larger company organization where it can do its job and achieve its objectives with maximum effectiveness and economy and a minimum of friction. Establish the relationships with other organization components that are necessary to the organization objectives.

The first four steps have been discussed earlier in this and previous chapters. When steps 5 and 6 are considered, the detailed ways in which Quality Control can be organized begin to take shape.

Sections 4.7, 4.8, and 4.9 discuss the considerations involved in step 5 above, namely, the factors involved in establishing specific organization structure for Quality Control.

Section 4.10 discusses the considerations involved in step 6 above, namely, the factors involved in placing this quality-control structure within the larger structure of the company organization.

4.7 Basic Questions for Organization Structuring

In establishing the specific organizational structure for quality control, a company must answer these basic questions:

1. Are all the work elements (as shown in Fig. 4.3) of the three subfunctions to be placed in a central quality-control component reporting to the Manager–Quality Control? Or should suitable work elements be decentralized and placed in other components in the company? As an example of such decentralization, should some routine inspection and test work be assigned to the superintendent in charge of shop operations?

These questions are discussed in Sec. 4.8 below.

2. When the decisions have been made as to how centralized the quality-control component is to be, another series of questions follows. How is the work assigned to the quality-control component to be structured in detail? For example, should there be one or more quality-engineering components reporting to the Manager–Quality Control? Should there be more than one process-control-engineering group? Is the quality-information-equipment-engineering activity of a sufficient magnitude to warrant a separate component, or should it be combined with quality-control engineering in a single component?

Perhaps the most typical question is whether inspection and testing should be broken out of process-control engineering to form a separate component reporting to the Manager–Quality Control. In turn, should there be more than one inspection component or more than one test component?

These questions are discussed in Sec. 4.9 below.

4.8 Should the Quality-control Function Be Centralized or Decentralized?

Figure 4.5 illustrates those work elements of quality control which, industrial experience indicates, can be considered "fixed" within the quality-control component as well as those elements which are "variable"

FIXED AND VARIABLE WORK ELEMENTS

	Quality Control Engineering	Quality Information Equipment Engineering	Process Control Engineering
FIXED (Always retained within subfunction)	• Quality objectives • Prescribe quality-control plan: where, when, who, how, and how much to inspect and test, for example • Quality-cost analysis • Quality-control training • Quality information feedback • Diagnosis of quality problems	• Design and provide quality information equipment • Mechanization and automation of quality-measuring equipment • Measurement development	• Interpret and implement quality-control plan • Quality audit • Process-capability studies • Maintenance of quality-control equipment • Receiving inspection and test • Final inspection and test
VARIABLE (May decentralize to Shop Operations)			• In-process inspection and test • Data recording • Operational planning

FIG. 4.5

and may be suitable for decentralization to other organizational components in the company. It may be noted from the chart that the work elements appropriate for decentralization are primarily to be found in the process-control-engineering component and include in-process inspection and testing elements.

Inspection and Test Reporting to Shop Operations. In companies with a well-established quality-control organization of proved effectiveness, certain advantages may be obtained by assigning the routine in-process test and inspection elements of process-control engineering to shop-operations components. Certain criteria must be observed to make this decentralization effective. Typical of these criteria are the following:

1. That a suitable written quality plan must be prepared by Quality Control Engineering and that it be vigorously followed by Shop Operations.

2. That a process-control-engineering function must exist within the quality-control component to provide competent technical support to Shop Operations for help in solving day-to-day quality problems.

3. That Process Control Engineering must conduct a continuous audit on product quality being shipped.

4. That Process Control Engineering must conduct a continuous audit on the degree to which the planned quality procedures are being followed.

5. That quality information equipment must be maintained on a planned schedule to assure accuracy and precision of measurements.

6. That inspectors and testers must be trained to have the capability required to perform the work to which they are respectively assigned, and this training must be kept up-to-date.

RELATIONSHIP CHART

(Applied to Product Quality)

Code: (R) = Responsible
C = Must contribute
M = May contribute
I = Is informed

Areas of Responsibility	General Manager	Finance	Marketing	Engineering	Manager–Manufacturing	Manufacturing Engineering	Quality Control	Materials	Shop Operations
Analyze quality costs		M					(R)		
In-process quality measurements							C		(R)
In-process quality audit				C		C	(R)		
Final product inspection			C	C	M	C	(R)		

FIG. 4.6

7. That there must be a clear and continuous understanding of the primary responsibilities for accomplishing each element of quality work on the part of each organizational component in the company.

The use of a relationships chart proves quite useful in establishing this primary responsibility for each organizational component. A segment of a typical chart is shown in Fig. 4.6.

Figure 4.7 shows an organization where all the variable elements of routine inspection and testing have been decentralized from Quality Control and assigned to Shop Operations.

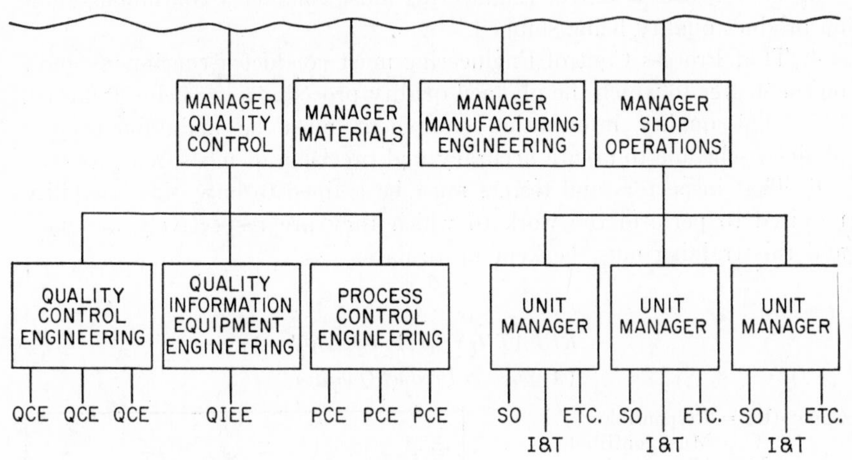

FIG. 4.7.

The Closed Feedback Loop in Quality-control Organization.[1] It may be noted from Fig. 4.5 that the major part of the work elements shown tend to be in the fixed category. This is because the quality-control function itself is primarily a planning and control, or "feedback," function in which "too much division" changes the basic purpose of the function. The continuous feedback cycle of quality control activities are as follows:

First, *quality planning* is done by Quality Control Engineering; this establishes the basic framework of the quality-control system for the company's products. Included also is planning for the quality measure-

[1] Part of Sec. 4.8 according to an unpublished paper by J. S. Macdonald, General Electric Company.

ment equipment, which is performed by Quality Information Equipment Engineering.

Second, *quality appraising* is performed by Process Control Engineering (also including inspection and testing). It evaluates, in accordance with the quality plan, the conformance and performance of the parts and products with engineering specifications.

Third, there is rapid feedback by Process Control Engineering for *quality analysis,* which results in new planning, thus completing the cycle (Fig. 4.8). This analysis also fosters corrective action for product-quality deviations.

THE FEEDBACK CYCLE IN QUALITY CONTROL

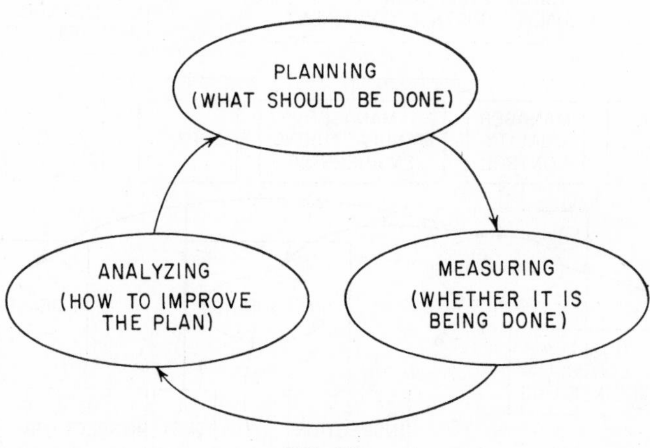

FIG. 4.8.

Within this structure, the fixed elements of quality-control work provide for clear-cut responsibility. Through the structure, the Manager–Quality Control is able to make his direct contribution to product quality in the company by having full accountability for his two basic responsibilities of assuring the right quality at the right quality cost.

Of at least equal importance, as discussed earlier in the chapter, there is clear and full accountability on the part of all other company functions for their basic quality responsibilities. The superintendents in Shop Operations, for example, have the clear responsibility for producing in accordance with the specifications and the quality system plan, and for performing the "variable" work elements of their own in-process measurements.

But now let's see what happens to these direct responsibilities for the feedback cycle if some of the fixed work elements were to be removed from the quality-control function.

Figure 4.9 will serve as an example. Here all the fixed elements of quality-control-engineering work remain with the quality-control function. But a part of the fixed elements of process-control-engineering work is removed from the quality-control function and assigned to the superintendents of Shop Operations. Also assigned to the superintendents is the in-process inspection and test function.

Single, clear-cut responsibility for the feedback cycle no longer resides with the quality-control function. Because of the elimination of the fixed elements of process-control-engineering work, the fundamental character of the quality-control component has been changed. It is no longer a genuine planning-and-control and feedback function.

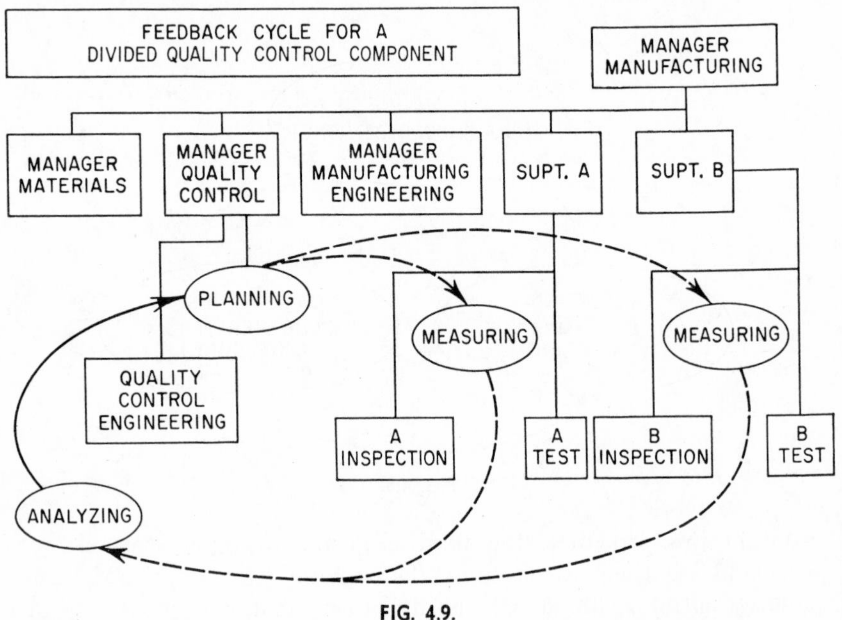

FIG. 4.9.

It instead becomes a loosely knit activity which carries on only certain elements of quality control work; the feedback cycle itself can come together only at organizational levels well above that of the quality-control function. In fact, however, it is unlikely that this feedback cycle will be brought back together at these upper management levels because of the many other responsibilities that exist there.

For such divisionalization of what here have been called fixed work elements in fact distorts the basic purpose of quality-control organization, as discussed in Sec. 4.3. Top management no longer has, in its quality-control function, a device whereby it delegates authority and responsibility for product quality, thus relieving itself of unnecessary detail and permitting the benefits of specialization while retaining for itself the means for assuring that quality results will be satisfactory in terms of top management's standards and policies. In substance, top management has no such device.

Lack of understanding of this basic feedback and planning-and-control nature of the quality-control function has perhaps been the primary reason for the large number of failures in quality-control organization that have taken place throughout industry. There may be full agreement about the work elements, as shown in Fig. 4.3, but a company may nonetheless assume—wrongly—that the contribution of its quality-control function can be adequate so long as all these work elements are assigned "somewhere" rather than on an organized basis of fixed and variable structure discussed here.

This philosophy assumes that quality-control organization is merely the bits-and-pieces sum of its individual quality-control engineering, process-control engineering, and quality information equipment engineering activities. It assumes that, so long as strong individual responsibilities have been established for each of these activities and each is located somewhere in the larger organization, then a strong quality-control contribution will necessarily result, regardless of the assignment of responsibility.

One way to demonstrate the flaw in this reasoning is to compare the diagram of the quality-control feedback cycle of the organization structure shown in Fig. 4.8 with one for the structure shown in Fig. 4.9. Figure 4.10 reflects the properly organized structure. Figure 4.9 reflects the improperly organized structure.

You will note that Fig. 4.10 shows short, direct tie-ins among the three feedback phases. In contrast, Fig. 4.9 shows dashed rather than direct tie-ins and additional loops and lengths that must be traveled to complete the cycle. Readers familiar with technical feedback circuits will no doubt suspect from these diagrams that in Fig. 4.9, as compared with Fig. 4.10, there is a tendency to slower response and to back-and-forth "hunting"—or "buck passing," in organizational language. They will suspect that it is inherently a more difficult loop to organize and probably cannot be made to work entirely effectively. That suspicion is, in fact, confirmed both by organization theory and by organization practice.

Experience throughout industry over the past decade shows that not only is slowness of action a problem with such back-looping structures but also that the resulting "hunting" may lead to dissatisfaction with the quality-control organization pattern on the part of all company personnel and to the gradual disappearance in actual practice of any dashed-line relationship at all. Quality Control, whose very life blood is the fast, automatic response of the feedback loop to assist company personnel to prevent poor quality, will be eliminated as a feedback function, as a result of the improper structuring of fixed work elements from the quality-control function. Only some individual bits of quality-control engineering, process-control engineering, and information equip-

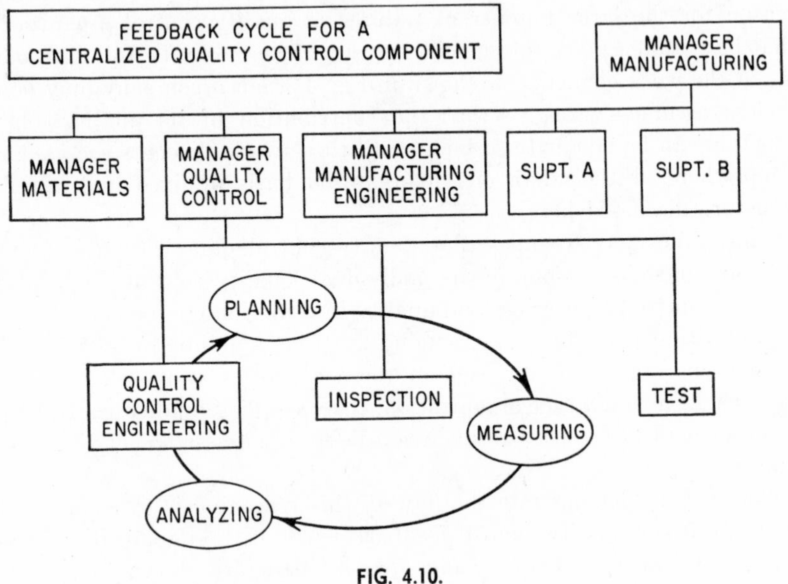

FIG. 4.10.

ment work will remain in the function. Certainly, total-quality-control programs cannot be pursued with so piecemeal an organization.

4.9 How Should the Quality-control Component Be Structured?

After deciding what quality-control work is to be decentralized to other organizational components, the next task is the internal structuring of the quality-control function itself. There are many alternatives for structuring the quality-control component, depending upon the particular situations faced by a company. A few of the alternate ways of structuring the quality-control function are discussed in this section. When such alternatives are being chosen, certain criteria need first to be considered. A few of the more important of these criteria are the following:

1. Keep "layers" of supervision to a minimum so lines of communication can be kept as short as possible.

2. Keep "spans" of supervision as broad as possible. (This follows if "layers" are to be kept to a minimum.) The "span" is the number of persons reporting directly to a supervisor or manager. The lower in the organization one goes, the greater the spans should become. This is be-

cause the work of the reporting positions usually becomes more uniform in nature.

3. Place similar elements of work into a single work package that can be handled by a person in the position considered.

With these criteria in mind, let us look at some examples of particular situations in which companies have structured their quality-control component best to suit certain situations. The following examples will be considered:

1. A multiproduct plant.
2. A plant with one basic product line at a single location.
3. A number of different product lines in a single plant location.
4. A number of different manufacturing sections in the plant, involving specialized technologies.
5. A small company.

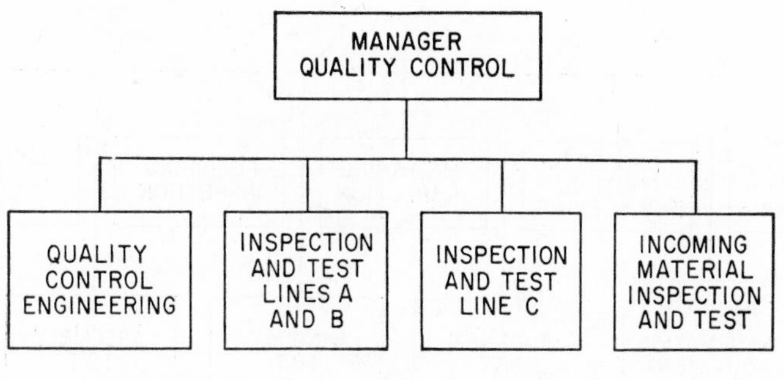

A MULTIPRODUCT PLANT

FIG. 4.11.

6. A large company.
7. A highly automated plant.
8. A multiplant situation.

A Multiproduct Plant. Figure 4.11 shows the organizational structure for the quality-control component where there are three product lines (A, B, and C) at a single plant location of moderate size. The technical content of both product and process is relatively limited; hence all the engineering activity for the quality-control function is centralized in a single quality-control-engineering component. In addition to regularly assigned quality-control-engineering work, process-engineering work is applied to the respective product lines as required. Quality-information-engineering work is also done by this same component as the need arises.

Inspection and testing are decentralized, according to product line. One inspection and test component serves lines A and B, which are assembly operations of similar products. Another inspection and test component serves line C, a fabrication line. The incoming-material inspection and test component checks purchased materials, parts, and product components for all lines.

One Basic Product Line—Single Plant Location. Figure 4.12 shows a situation in which a single product is being manufactured at a single plant location. At first one might think this to be even simpler than the previous example. In this particular case, however, the manufacturing operation consists of a number of closely integrated processes, each involving its specialized technologies. The size of the operation is such that it is difficult to justify assigning a quality-control engineer to each process section. Consequently there is one quality-control-engineering

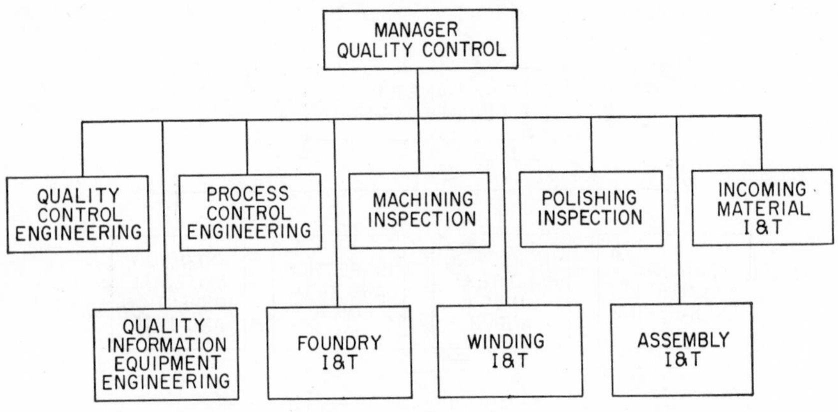

ONE BASIC PRODUCT LINE—SINGLE LOCATION

FIG. 4.12.

component which does the quality planning for all the processes. The total process-control-engineering demand is high; however, the load varies considerably from process to process depending on where current quality problems arise. Hence, a single process-control-engineering component serves all processes as the needs arise. A quality control information equipment component serves the entire plant.

Each process is assigned its separate inspection and test component since the type of inspection and/or test is highly specialized with respect to each of the processes.

A Number of Different Product Lines. The quality-control organization shown in Fig. 4.13 is for a single plant location of moderately large size that has a number of different product lines. The technical content of each product line is comparatively high with respect to the process. As a result, process-control engineering is decentralized by product line. Inspection and test activities are included within the process-control-engineering components in this particular plant. In one case, lines B and C are combined to occupy fully one person's time with respect to process-control work. Line responsibility has also been combined (A with D and B with C) to round out the quality-control-engineering assignments. One quality information equipment component serves all product lines since the work is similar regardless of the type of product line being served. One or more engineers are employed in this component depending on the work load.

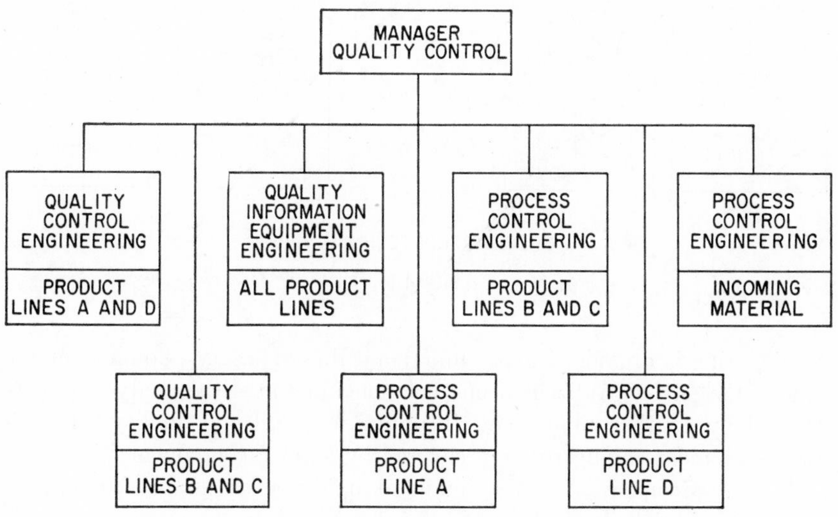

A NUMBER OF DIFFERENT PRODUCT LINES

FIG. 4.13.

Manufacturing Involving Specialized Technologies. Figure 4.14 shows a quality-control organization for a large heavy-apparatus company. Although the plant is in a single location, each of the components is manufactured in its respective building. Some buildings are separated by as much as a mile. The process technologies differ considerably. For example, the insulator section requires a chemical engineer or ceramics engineer to fill the process-control-engineering position. Tanks involve steel plate fabrication, welding, and painting; cores involve coil winding, treating, and baking; and laminations involve metal stamping and enameling. As a consequence, a process-control engineer is located in each of the manufacturing buildings to provide the required specialized technical backup for shop operations. In contrast, Quality Control

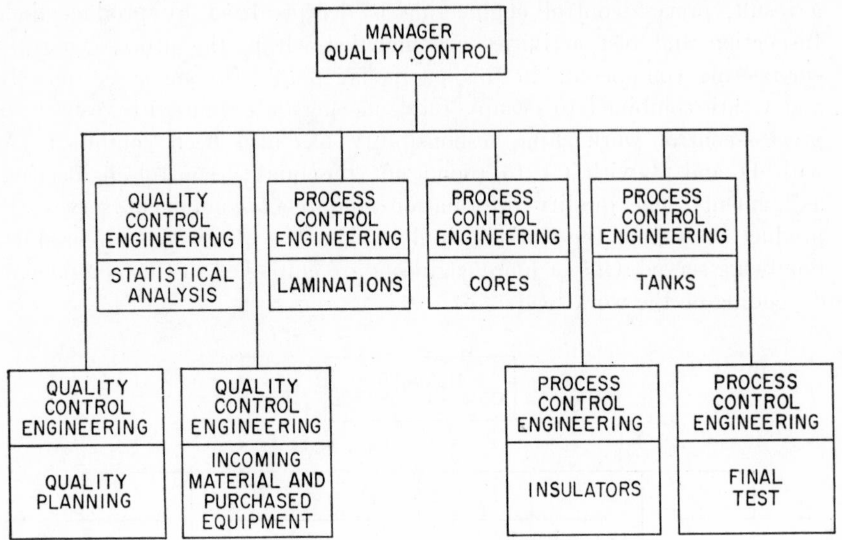

SPECIALIZED TECHNOLOGIES

FIG. 4.14.

Engineering is organized along functional lines. Quality planning for the entire plant is centralized in one component. Statistical analysis is performed by another component. Incoming material and quality information equipment engineering are covered by a third component.

A Small Company. Another dominant influence on quality-control organization is the physical size of the plant in terms of number of products, number of processes, number of operators, and square feet of floor space. Figure 4.15 shows a small quality-control component where three functions, quality-control management, quality-control engineering, and

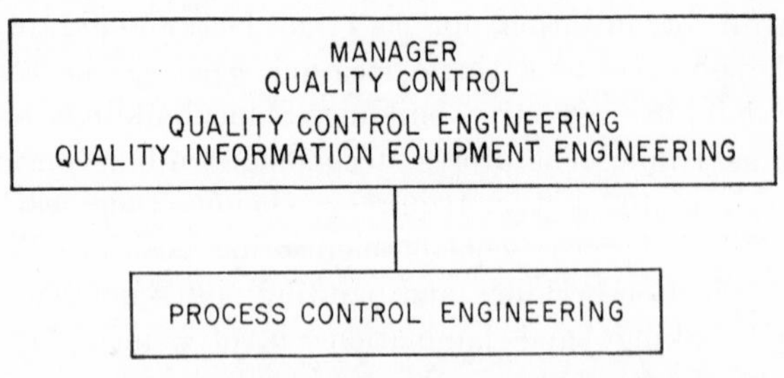

A SMALL ORGANIZATION

FIG. 4.15.

quality information equipment engineering, are combined into one position. Reporting to this position is a process-control engineer for providing hour-to-hour technical support to shop operations.

A Large Company. In contrast to the small company is the inherent complexity of the large company. The number of highly specialized operations increase, there are often a number of product lines, and the degree of automation may tend to increase. The very number of positions that must be filled to handle the quality-control function properly in a large company dictates an organization similar to that shown in Fig. 4.16. In order to keep the span of the Manager–Quality Control within reason, it is necessary to place managers or supervisors over the specialized engineering activities. All the quality-control-engineering work is supervised by one manager. Another manager supervises quality-control information equipment engineering. Still another manager supervises the process-control-engineering activity. A manager is also given responsible charge of the quality-control laboratories, where physical and chemical tests and analyses are made for material acceptance and process control. The quality-control component field responsibility is placed under a separate manager reporting to the Manager–Quality Control.

A Highly Automated Factory. The character of the processing equipment is a major factor to be considered. For example, the organization structure is influenced by the degree to which a factory is mechanized or automated. The quality information equipment activity may be of major proportions, although other subfunctions may be moderately small. In such a case, a quality information equipment engineer may have to be assigned to each product line or each manufacturing section.

The Multiplant Situation. The preceding pages have implicitly assumed that there is only one administrative unit in the plant or company for which the quality-control component must be established. In actual practice, there are often several such administrative units.

The responsibilities of the quality-control component in these situations are the same as have been developed above. But practice in organizing for this situation is somewhat more complex.

The multiplant issue may be resolved by creating a quality-control component for each administrative unit. For the entire company or entire plant, a general quality-control staff position may also be created to report directly to company or plant management.

The individual quality-control organizations will report directly to the management of their administrative units. They will also have a functional relationship to the general company or plant staff position for purposes of standardizing quality-control policies and for control personnel. Figure 4.17 shows the appropriate organization pattern for a large company.

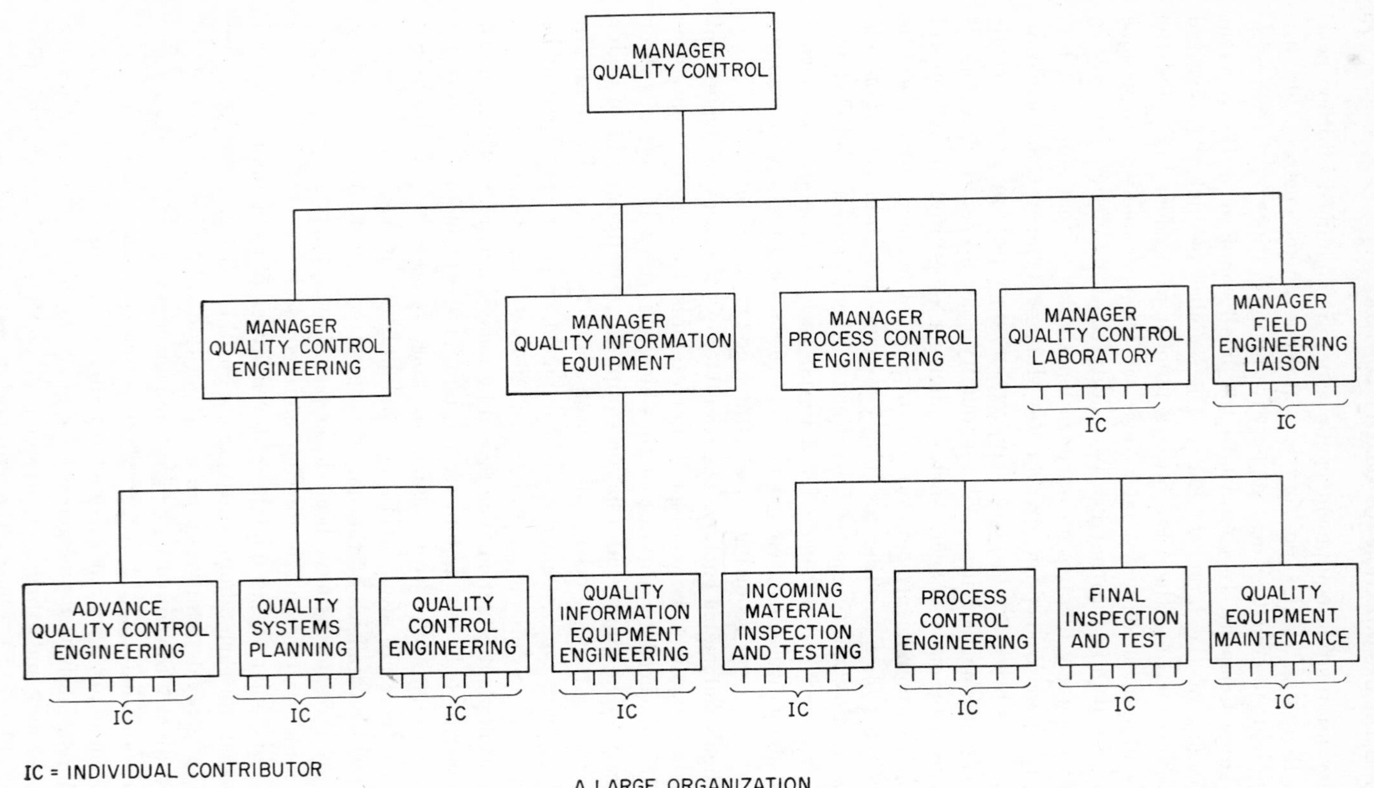

A LARGE ORGANIZATION

FIG. 4.16.

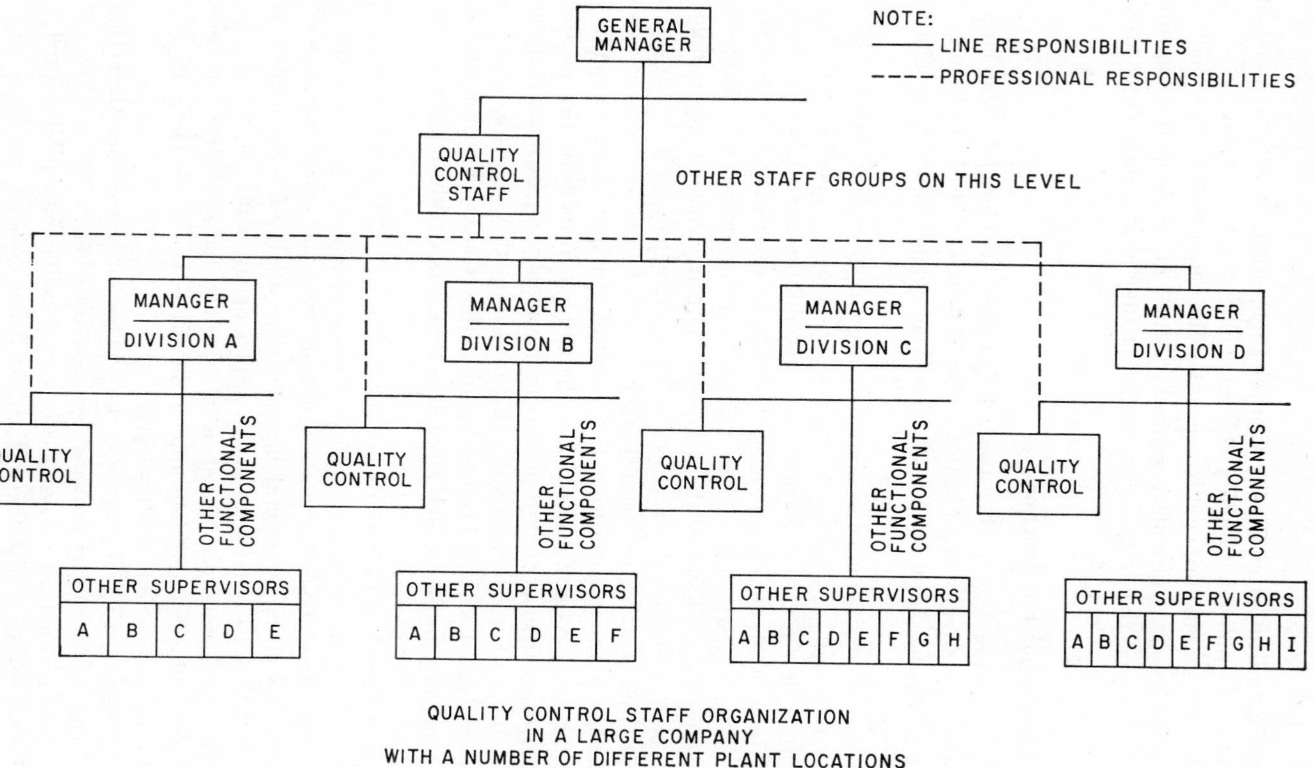

QUALITY CONTROL STAFF ORGANIZATION
IN A LARGE COMPANY
WITH A NUMBER OF DIFFERENT PLANT LOCATIONS

FIG. 4.17.

The Centralization of Quality Control Engineering. It will be noted in the above examples that quality-control engineering has usually been centralized. This occurs principally because of the major need for the quality-control function to provide a central channel of working relationships with the Engineering, Marketing, and other functions in such major areas as New-design Control.

4.10 Location of the Function

Where should the quality-control function be placed in the larger structure of company organization? Should it be a part of Marketing, of Engineering, of Manufacturing? Should it report directly to general management?

These are crucial questions, but they are not susceptible to categorical answers. Certainly, Quality Control in any company should report high enough so that it can implement its responsibilities for quality assurance at optimum costs. Certainly, also, it should be close enough to the firing line so that it will be able to fulfill its technological role. However, companies vary widely in their objectives, their character, their philosophy of organizational structure, and their technology. The answer to the question of where to locate Quality Control will necessarily vary also.

The approach to answering this question for any given company is this: first, to determine what are the quality responsibilities as they exist in the larger structure of the total company organization; second, to establish where in the total structure the quality-control component is to be located always keeping in mind that Quality Control must be organized in a fashion which recognizes that it is a multifunctional, company-wide activity.

It may be worthwhile to report one firm's approach. In this company, there are a number of product departments, each of which operates as a decentralized business, with profit-and-loss accountability reposing with the department general manager. The cycle of basic quality responsibility is as follows for each product department:

· The marketing component is responsible for evaluating customer quality preferences and determining the prices these customers are willing to pay for various quality levels.

· The engineering component is responsible for translating Marketing's requirements into exact drawings and specifications.

· The manufacturing component is responsible for building products to these drawings and for knowing that it has done so.

Within this structure of responsibility, Quality Control clearly emerges as a manufacturing component. Thus, in the product department, the Manager–Quality Control reports to the chief manufacturing executive in that department—the Manufacturing Manager—and operates at the same organizational level as the Manager–Materials, and the Manager–Manufacturing Engineering.

An important concept in this company being used as an example is that each major organizational component should have direct measurements of its own work. Manufacturing not only must know that it has produced products of specified quality but also be responsible for the costs incident to assuring a specified quality level. It must minimize these costs consistent with the specified quality level. It is fundamental, therefore, that quality assurance and assistance in minimizing quality costs are basic in manufacturing and that, as a consequence, the quality-control function should report to Manufacturing.

This example illustrates the type of organization planning incident to determining the exact organization location of Quality Control. An important consideration is that Quality Control is a multifunctional, business-wide activity, and, in this case, the greatest opportunity to contribute to the business resided in the Manufacturing component. It is not an uncommon practice to take any multifunctional, business-wide activity and place it in the component where it can make the greatest contribution. Product Planning, for example, is often assigned to the marketing component for this reason.

The particular decision, however, must be made by each company, based upon its own circumstances. This decision may take several forms. The above example is one such form. Quality Control, reporting directly to general management, may be another form under particular circumstances.

4.11 Organizing for Reliability and Other Product-quality Parameters

As was noted in Chap. 1, certain product "qualities" are singled out and incorrectly used as the description of the *composite* total quality of the product. One of the more significant of these has been "reliability." New terms that have more recently come over the horizon are "maintainability" and "serviceability." It is vitally important to recognize that these, while important, are nonetheless individual "qualities" of the product and must be considered together with all the other quality characteristics that make up product quality. To do otherwise creates the danger of excluding important characteristics. Frequently, under the stress of specific quality problems, the temptation arises to organize separately for these individual problems. This makes achieving over-all product quality more difficult.

It has been argued that reliability is a very special product quality of overriding importance and, hence, deserves special consideration and emphasis. Some have sought to gain this emphasis by means of special reliability organizations. These organizations have sometimes tended to become large and costly "empires," often duplicating, or in conflict with, other product-quality organizations in the company. When a separate reliability organization is established, experience has shown that its integral relationship with the many other "qualities" of the product often conflicts with the established functional organization. Certainly, Product Engineering plays a major role in determining product reliability, but so also do Manufacturing and Quality Control in maintaining, or enhancing, that reliability.

Total quality control provides the most workable organizational solution to these problems. The quality system, which will be discussed in Chap. 6, establishes the quality responsibilities, and hence the reliability responsibilities, for the respective functions and their corresponding organizational components. It also identifies the "interfaces" among these components and establishes procedures for smooth handling of all quality matters. Total quality control also provides a truly "open-ended" organizational solution, meeting other quality requirements that inevitably will receive emphasis in the future, such as maintainability, serviceability, system effectiveness, and the like. The point is to organize once for the purpose of quality on a full "strength-of-the-company" flexible basis.

4.12 What Are Some Problems in Organizing for Quality Control?

It is only to be expected that the critical problems in organizing for total quality control will be matters of human relations. The major difficulty usually faced is the natural resistance by members of the organization to change of any sort.

One example of this resistance is the automatically negative reaction with which some company employees may greet a program like quality control. Such grumbled statements may be made as "We're doing exactly what we did before, except that they call it quality control now, and that man they have as head of the quality-control organization gets all the credit for our work."

A major cause for attitudes of this sort is that delegation of product-quality responsibilities preceded by many years the creation of the quality-control organizational component. Unless they are convinced otherwise, holders of these responsibilities may fear that the quality-control component will somehow usurp their prerogatives.

A different type of human problem is represented by the initial administrative difficulties that the new quality-control component may face. One functional group may try to pass responsibility to another group. The engineering and marketing groups may rail against lack of interest in quality by the manufacturing group and refuse to cooperate because "It won't do any good unless those manufacturing fellows become more quality-minded."

Manufacturing may, in its turn, criticize Engineering for lack of realistic quality standards and criticize Inspection for unnecessarily harsh product rejections. Manufacturing Supervision may see reasons for going slow with the introduction of statistical methods. Overzealous proponents of these methods may wish to place a control chart on every factory operation and be sharply critical if this is not done.

After an initial fanfare in introducing the quality-control component, top management may forget that the component is only an extension of itself and give it the lukewarm support that may be the kiss of death to the quality-control program. Marketing and Sales may be extremely polite to the advisory efforts of the component but feel that the quality-control program is really only an internal plant matter.

Some quality-control programs have been well organized on paper but have failed to meet their objectives because they were improperly introduced to the company. The statement is sometimes made by quality-control personnel in this type of program that their company organization is "not quality-conscious" and that it "isn't going along with the quality-control program." This may be largely an admission by the quality-control men that, in introducing their program, they took into proper account only technical and not human factors.

Experience seems to indicate that a program should be allowed to develop gradually within a company, both to aid in "selling" it and to permit tailoring of the general routines to meet the particular needs of the various shops. It is often found wise to select one or two troublesome quality-control problems, to obtain successful results in attacking them, and to allow the quality-control program to grow step by step in this fashion until it is in a position to encompass all four quality-control jobs.

A detailed discussion of some of the human problems of introducing quality control is reserved for Part Six of this book.

4.13 What Is a Broad Human Relations View of Quality-control Organization?

In the human relations language of the psychologist and the sociologist, quality-control organization is both (1) *channel of communication* for product-quality information among all concerned employees and groups; in effect, an information system; and (2) *means of participation* in the over-all company quality-control program by these employees and groups.

The problems of communication that have been generated by the high degree of specialization in the modern industrial organization are well known by management. Inspection may not know what product characteristics Engineering considers really important until production has started and articles are actually in the hands of customers.

Operators may not understand that the close tolerances to which they are working are critical for proper product performance. A complete meeting of minds may never take place between the foreman and the inspector on what is important on certain machined parts.

Equally well known to management is the need by employees to feel "part of it." Some factory operators and functional specialists feel that "our quality responsibility is so small a portion of the whole that we're not a part of the company quality-control program or important to it."

With proper quality-control organization, the foreman will more readily get the chance to suggest to Engineering certain design changes that would make manufacture easier and more economical. These suggestions will be forthcoming *before* production has started instead of becoming criticisms afterward. Quality Control will have the opportunity to participate with Manufacturing Engineering in the development of key inspection stations while a manufacturing layout is still on the drafting board.

4.14 What Is the Size of the Quality-control Component?

Under the total-quality-control approach, the Manager–Quality Control can focus his attention on meeting the company's quality objectives at the lowest quality cost, and the dollars for quality control can be budgeted on the basis of producing such a result rather than on the basis of a historical inspection and test ratio. The size of the quality-control component then is balanced by considering what can be accomplished at most economical levels. The collection, analysis, and use of quality costs, discussed in the following chapter, provides a means for determining this economic balance.

As a matter of fact, it may be noted from industrial experience that sound total-quality-control organization requires no long-term increase in quality-control expense. Quite the contrary, quality-control expense, as a proportion of total company expense, will be reduced in the long run. Improvements of one-third or more in over-all quality costs are not unusual. When the organization of the quality-control component includes, as has been shown in this chapter, technically competent manpower whose efforts can be devoted to preventive quality efforts, inevitably the number of persons in the quality-control organization will be fewer than in earlier, less technical forms of organization.

CHAPTER 5

QUALITY COSTS

It was noted in Chap. 1 that the twin quality challenge that competitive conditions present to American business management is (1) *considerable improvement in the quality of many products and many practices* and, at the same time, (2) *substantial reductions in the over-all costs of quality.*

Total-quality-control programs in actual practice have been successful in meeting this twin challenge of better quality at lower quality cost. The reason for the satisfactory better-quality result is fairly clear from the very nature of the prevention-centered, step-by-step, technically thorough program. But the explanation may not be nearly so obvious for the accompanying by-product of lower over-all quality cost. This needs to be spelled out, especially since it includes, in the long run, lower expenses for the quality-control activities themselves as compared with the costs of traditional inspection and testing.

5.1 Costs of Quality

The reason for the favorable cost result of total quality control is that it cuts the two major cost segments of a company's quality costs (segments which might be called *failure* and *appraisal* costs) by means of much smaller increases in the third and smallest segment (which might be called *prevention* costs). Why this is possible can be seen as soon as the character of these three categories is considered

- *Prevention costs* are for the purpose of keeping defects from occurring in the first place. Included here are such elements as quality-control engineering and employee quality training.

· *Appraisal costs* include the expenses for maintaining company quality levels by means of formal evaluations of product quality. This involves such cost elements as inspection, test, outside endorsements, and quality audits.

· *Failure costs*[1] are caused by defective materials and products that do not meet company quality specifications. They include such loss elements as rework, scrap, field complaints, and spoilage.

In the absence of formal nationwide studies of these operating quality costs in various businesses, it is impossible to generalize about the relative magnitude of these three elements throughout American industry. However, it would probably not be far wrong to assume that failure costs may represent about 70 cents out of every quality-cost dollar and that appraisal costs probably range in the neighborhood of 25 cents. In many businesses, however, prevention costs probably do not exceed 5 cents out of the total quality-cost dollar.

In a nutshell, this cost analysis suggests that we have been spending our quality dollars the wrong way: a fortune down the drain because of product failures; another large sum to support a sort-the-bad-from-the-good appraisal screen to try to keep too many bad products from going to customers; comparatively nothing for the true defect-prevention technology that can do something about reversing the vicious upward cycle of higher quality costs and less reliable product quality.

The fact is that historically, under the sorting-inspection type of quality-control function, failure and appraisal expenses have trended together, and it has been extremely difficult to pull them down once they have started to rise. The reason is clear.

An unprofitable cycle is at work that operates something like this: the more defects produced, the higher the failure costs. The traditional answer to higher failure costs has been more inspection. This, of course, means a higher appraisal cost.

Now this tighter inspection screen does not really have much effect in eliminating the defects. Some of the defective products are *going* to leave the plant and wind up in the hands of complaining customers. Appraisal costs thus stay up as long as failure costs remain high. And the higher these failure and appraisal costs go, the higher they are likely to go without successful preventive activity. So the total-quality-control approach is to turn this cost cycle downward by establishing the right

[1] Later in this chapter, failure costs are broken down, in Fig. 5.1, into internal failure costs and external failure costs as an aid to control.

amount of prevention, supporting the right, though modest, amount of quality-control engineering, process-control engineering, and quality information equipment engineering.

This plainly means an increased expenditure for prevention to bring about reduced failure costs *and* reduced appraisal costs, with the balance of quality-cost dollars going to profit. The 5 cents out of every dollar that is now being spent for prevention may well need to be doubled and tripled, with much of the increase going toward test-equipment automation and improved efforts in the engineering activities of quality control. These increases in prevention are financed by a portion of the savings in failure and appraisal cost; they do not represent net, long-term additions to total company quality cost.

Let's examine what actually does happen, costwise, in total quality control:

First, when prevention costs are increased, to pay for the right kind of engineering work in quality control, a reduction in the number of product defects occurs. This defect reduction means a substantial reduction in failure costs.

Second, the same chain of events takes place with appraisal costs. An increase in prevention costs results in defect reductions, which, in turn, have a positive effect on appraisal costs, since defect reduction means a reduced need for routine inspection and test activities.

Finally, when there is an upgrading of quality-control equipment, personnel, and practices, an additional reduction in appraisal cost results. Better inspection and test equipment, a general modernization of quality-control practices, and the replacement of many routine operators by less numerous but more effective process-control inspectors and tests have a positive downward pull on the cost of the appraisal function.

The end result is a substantial reduction in the cost of quality and an increase in the *level* of quality. Improvements of one-third or more in quality costs are not unusual. The major element of this improvement goes into profit improvement for the company.

5.2 Quality-cost Items—What They Are

An essential element in operating a total-quality-control program is the identification, analysis, and control of quality costs for the business. Let us consider specifically typical items that make up these *operating quality costs.*

Figure 5.1 lists the items in each of the four areas of operating quality costs and contains the definitions of these items. Each company must determine the significant items in this figure it will include in its quality costs. Some companies may, indeed, find it desirable to include additional items in this list and develop the quality cost structure best suited to their particular needs.

Definitions of Operating Quality-cost Items

I. *Cost of Prevention*

A. *Quality planning (quality-control-engineering work)*

Quality planning represents costs associated with the time that personnel in the quality-control function spend in planning the quality system and in translating product design and customer quality requirements into specific manufacturing controls on quality of materials, processes, and products through formal methods, procedures, and instructions.

B. *Process control (process-control-engineering work)*

Process control represents costs associated with the time that personnel in the quality-control function spend studying and analyzing manufacturing processes, for the purpose of establishing a means of control as well as improving existing process capability, and in providing technical support to shop personnel for the purposes of effectively applying or implementing quality plans and initiating and maintaining control over manufacturing operating processes.

NOTE: Quality planning and process control may be performed in some businesses by the same quality-control engineers. The first activity may be thought of as preproduction planning and the second as providing technical support during production. Process control is aimed at controlling process-quality problems. This should be distinguished from test and inspection, defined under II, *Cost of Appraisal.*

C. *Quality planning by functions other than Quality Control*

Quality planning by functions other than Quality Control represents costs associated with the time spent in quality-planning work such as: reliability studies; preproduction quality analysis; writing instructions or operating procedures for test, inspection, and process control by personnel who do not work for the Manager–Quality Control. In some operations, for example, work of this nature is performed by Product Engineering.

D. *Design and development of quality information equipment*

Design and development of quality information equipment represents costs associated with the time that personnel spend in *designing* quality-assurance measurement and control devices. This item should include the personnel in the business performing this activity regardless of whom they report to. It does not include the cost of equipment or depreciation.

E. *Quality training*

Quality training represents the cost of developing and operating formal quality training programs throughout the company operations designed to train personnel in the understanding and use of quality-control techniques. It does not include training costs of instructing operators to achieve normal quantity proficiency.

F. *Other prevention expenses*

Other prevention expenses represent all other expenses for which the Manager–Quality Control has control responsibility and which are not specifically included elsewhere, such as secretaries, telephone and telegraph, rent, and traveling.

II. *Cost of Appraisal*

A. *Test and inspection of purchased materials*

Test and inspection of purchased materials represent the costs associated with the time that inspection and testing personnel spend on evaluating the quality of purchased materials and any applicable costs of supervisory and clerical personnel. Also this may include the cost of inspectors traveling to vendors' plants to evaluate purchased materials.

B. *Laboratory acceptance testing*

Laboratory acceptance testing represents the cost of all tests provided by a laboratory or testing unit to evaluate the quality of purchased materials.

C. *Laboratory or other measurement services*

Laboratory or other measurement services represent the cost of laboratory measurement services, such as instrument calibration and repair and process monitoring.

D. *Inspection*

Inspection represents the costs associated with the time that inspection personnel spend evaluating the quality of the product in the shop, and applicable costs of supervisory and clerical personnel. It does not include the cost of inspection of purchased materials included in II-*A*, inspection equipment, utilities, tools, or materials.

E. *Testing*

Testing represents the costs associated with the time that testing personnel spend evaluating the technical performance of the product in the shop and applicable costs of supervisory and clerical personnel. It does not include the cost of testing purchased materials included in II-*A*, test equipment, utilities, tools, or materials.

F. *Checking labor*

Checking labor represents the costs associated with the time that shop operators spend on checking quality of own work as required by the quality plan, checking product or process for quality conformance at planned points in manufacturing, sorting lots which are rejected for not meeting quality requirements, and other in-process evaluations of product quality.

G. *Setup for test or inspection*

Setup for test or inspection represents the costs associated with the time that personnel spend in setting up product and associated equipment to permit functional testing.

H. *Test and inspection material*

Test and inspection material represents the cost of power for testing major apparatus, such as steam or oil, and materials consumed in destructive tests, such as life test or tear-down inspections.

I. Quality audits

Quality audits represent the costs associated with the time that personnel spend performing routine quality audits on the in-process or finished product.

J. Outside endorsements

Outside endorsements represent Underwriters' Laboratories fees, insurance inspection costs, etc.

K. Maintenance and calibration of test and inspection equipment

Maintenance and calibration of test and inspection equipment represent the costs associated with the time spent by maintenance personnel in calibrating and maintaining test and inspection equipment.

L. Product-engineering review and shipping release

Product-engineering review and shipping release represent the costs associated with the time of product engineers who review test and inspection data prior to release of the product for shipment.

M. Field testing

Field testing represents the costs incurred by the department in field testing the product at the customer's site prior to final release. These costs might include traveling costs, living expenses, etc.

III. *Cost of Internal Failure*

A. Scrap

For the purpose of obtaining operating quality costs, scrap represents the losses incurred in the course of obtaining the required level of quality. It should not include materials scrapped for other reasons, such as obsolescence, overruns, and product design changes resulting from further evaluation of customer needs. Scrap might be further subdivided, e.g., between fault of own manufacture and fault of vendor.

B. Rework

For the purpose of obtaining operating quality costs, rework represents the extra payments made to operators in the course of obtaining the required level of quality. It should not include extra payments to operators for any other reasons, such as rework caused by product design changes resulting from further evaluation of customer needs. Rework might be further subdivided, e.g., between fault of own manufacture and fault of vendor.

C. Material-procurement costs

Material-procurement costs represent those additional costs incurred by the material-procurement personnel in handling both rejects and complaints on purchased materials. Such costs may include getting disposition from vendors for rejected materials, making certain that vendors understand quality requirements for either rejects or complaints, etc.

D. Factory contact engineering

Factory contact engineering represents the costs associated with the time spent by product or production engineers who are engaged in production problems involving quality; e.g., if a product, component, or material does not conform to quality specifications, a product or production engineer may be requested to review the feasibility of product specification changes. It does not include engineering development work which may be performed on the factory floor.

IV. *Cost of External Failure*

A. *Complaints*

Complaints represent all expenditures for the adjustment of customer complaints.

B. *Product service*

Product service represents any product-service expense directly attributable to correcting imperfections or special testing, not included in complaints. It does not include installation service or maintenance contracts.

FIG. 5.1

5.3 Quality Costs—How to Get Them

The cost data necessary to provide an operating quality-cost report are generally available from the existing accounting system. Often it is only a matter of pulling the data together to provide the different elements of quality cost and to place these in the categories previously discussed. When data are not available for a certain element, e.g., time spent by design engineers in interpreting quality requirements, it is often possible to make accurate estimates to arrive at a value for the element. However, the accounting component should make such estimates on a sound financial basis.

At first it may be necessary for the Manager–Quality Control to put together a few consolidated quality-cost reports to demonstrate what it is and how it can be used. When the value of the report has been demonstrated, the quality-cost reporting function should be taken over by Accounting, since it is the appropriate component to issue financial data.

5.4 Analysis of Quality Costs

After quality costs have been identified and obtained, it is necessary to analyze them before they can be used as a basis for action. The analysis process consists in examining each cost element in relation to other cost elements and the total. It also includes a time-to-time comparison, i.e., comparing one month's operation with the previous several months' operation, or one quarter with the previous several quarters. Such a comparison is more meaningful when the absolute dollars of quality costs for a period are related to the degree of total manufacturing activity for that period. For example, this quantity can be stated as a ratio of quality-cost dollars to the dollars of manufacturing output or to other suitable bases, as discussed below.

Comparison Bases. It is suggested that operating quality costs be related to at least three different volume bases. The bases selected will vary depending upon the product and type of manufacture for a particular business. Examples of volume bases that should be considered are (1) direct labor, (2) productive direct labor, (3) shop-cost input, (4) shop-cost output, (5) manufacturing-cost output, (6) contributed value, (7) equivalent units of productive output, and (8) net sales billed. In addition, the interrelationship of the four quality-cost segments should be of interest, particularly the relationship of costs of external failure to total operating quality costs.

Breakdown by Product Line or Process. To pinpoint the areas which merit the highest priority of quality-control effort, a breakdown of overall operating quality costs by major product lines or areas of the process flow is often needed. For example, with cost information readily available, it is possible to report certain items of quality costs in terms of a particular machining or assembly area or for a specific model.

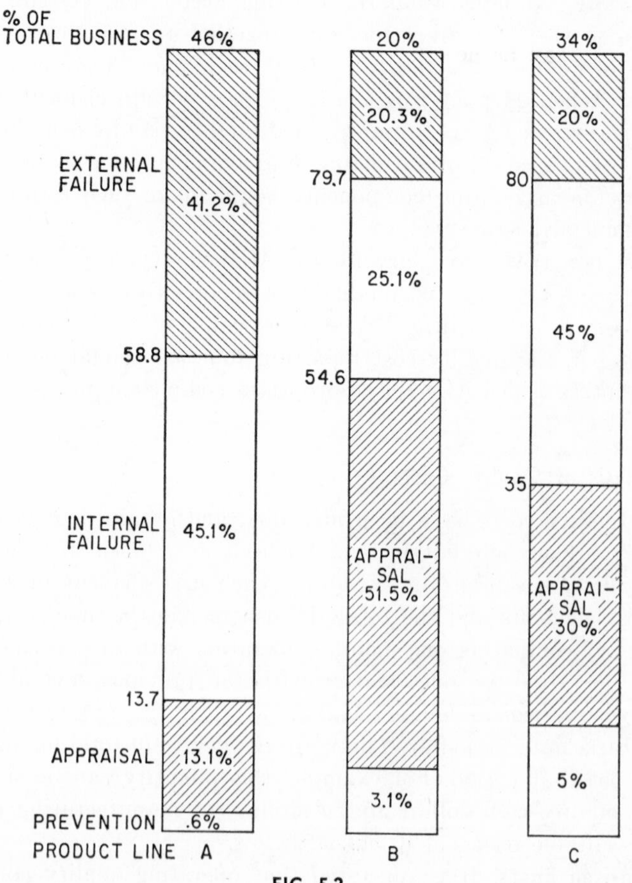

FIG. 5.2.

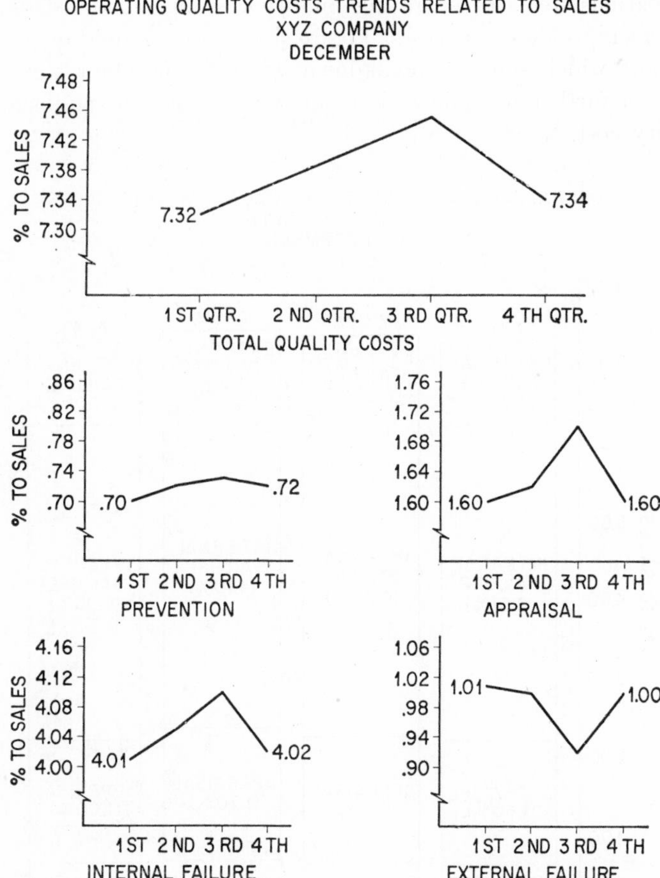

FIG. 5.3. In considering operating quality costs, it should be kept in mind that they may be related to other bases than sales.

Figure 5.2 shows the quality costs for three separate product lines: A, B, and C. Line A shows a disproportionately high failure rate with very little prevention and appraisal effort. Appraisal appears high for line B. Although a high percentage of prevention effort is going into line C, internal failure remains high. This indicates that a greater proportion of existing preventive effort should be expended in reducing internal failure.

Reports. Regular operating quality-cost reports should be issued periodically on a weekly, monthly, or quarterly basis as required. These reports include the expenditures for the items selected from Fig. 5.1, as well as the comparison bases. The reports include quality-cost data applicable to previous periods for the purpose of indicating trends. Figures 5.3 and 5.4 demonstrate two methods of showing cost trends.

The various items of operating quality cost are classified under the four segments of quality costs. Figure 5.5 is an example of a quality-cost report which shows a breakdown by the four major segments. In addition, a further breakdown is made with respect to significant items of quality cost.

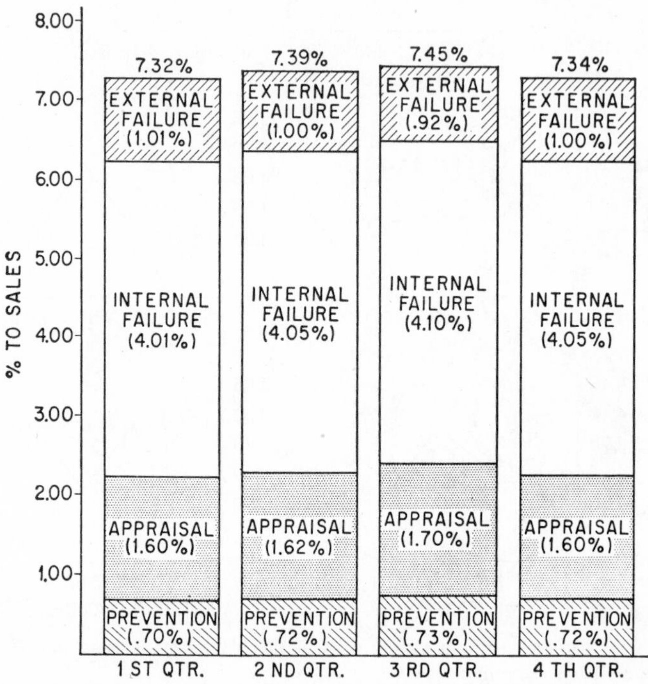

FIG. 5.4. In considering operating quality costs, it should be kept in mind that they may be related to other bases than sales.

5.5 Selection of Measurement Bases for Operating Quality Costs

Measurement bases are an important part of the operating quality costs and should be selected with care. Because of diversified businesses, bases selected for one may not satisfy the requirements of another; therefore, it is best to consider the advantages and disadvantages of several measurement bases before making selections.

Some Questions to Consider for the Selection of Measurement Bases.

1. Are they sensitive to increases and decreases in production schedules?

2. Will they be affected by mechanization and the resulting lower direct-labor costs?

3. Are they affected by seasonal product sales?

4. Are they oversensitive to material price fluctuations?

If the business is affected by such influences as the above, bases should

OPERATING QUALITY COSTS
XYZ Company
December

	1st quarter	2d quarter	3d quarter	4th quarter
Expenditures (in thousands of dollars):				
Prevention	$ 14.2	$ 14.6	$ 15.1	$ 14.3
Appraisal	32.1	33.5	37.2	33.2
Internal failure	84.1	86.2	92.2	83.1
External failure	20.4	21.1	21.4	20.1
Total	$150.8	$155.4	$165.9	$150.7
*Per Cent to Sales:**				
Prevention	.70	.72	.73	.72
Appraisal	1.60	1.62	1.70	1.60
Internal failure	4.01	4.05	4.10	4.02
External failure	1.01	1.00	.92	1.00
Total	7.32	7.39	7.45	7.34
*Per Cent to Sales—Significant Categories:**				
Quality planning	.32	.35	.36	.37
Inspection	.70	.71	.83	.82
Scrap and rework	3.90	3.92	3.98	3.72
Complaints	.80	.82	.81	.81

* Other bases such as shop cost of output, total direct labor, or contributed value may be used.

FIG. 5.5

be selected to reflect current relationships. Because of the possibility of the above influences occurring at a future date and making past data obsolete, it is advisable to select more than one measurement base. Such selections should, in the majority of cases, include three from each of these four bases: labor; manufacturing cost; sales; and units of product.

Descriptions of the suggested bases will be broken down into two parts:

I. Advantages and Disadvantages
II. Definitions and Calculations

I. Advantages and Disadvantages

A. Labor bases

1. Total direct labor
2. Operation or standard labor

Operation or standard labor, when available, is always superior to total direct labor because it represents planned performance rather than planned plus variances.

Both labor bases are sensitive to the ups and downs of the business. They are not appreciably affected by material price changes, by many end products, by sales lagging production, or by long manufacturing schedules.

Both are affected by mechanization that results in a reduction of operators.

B. Manufacturing cost bases

1. Shop cost of output (SCO)
2. Manufacturing cost of output (MCO)
3. Shop cost of input (SCI)

Manufacturing cost of output is superior to shop cost of output where the product has a high technical content, since MCO reflects the design-engineering cost. Conversely, if the design-engineering cost is less of a factor, SCO is a better base.

If the manufacturing cycle is extremely long, both the output bases would have little relationship with current quality costs. For these conditions SCI would be a better base.

C. Sales bases

1. Net sales billed
2. Contributed value (net sales billed minus direct material)

Both the above bases are considered good if the manufacturing cycle is relatively short and the product is sold soon after completion.

Contributed value is used in preference to net sales billed whenever material is a large part of the sales dollar and where price fluctuations in material would distort a NSB base.

D. Unit bases

1. Production related to contributed value
2. Production related to quality costs
3. Quality-cost dollars per equivalent unit of production output

These three bases are useful because they relate unit output or actual production to a dollar base. The first two are not recommended where there are several end products of different values. A change in the production mix would distort the base but would not be reflected in the total production. Of course, this is not an influential factor where quality costs are kept by product lines.

By selecting and using several of the bases recommended above, it is possible to measure more accurately the trends in quality costs. If all bases do not show the same improvement, the cause of discrepancy in any base should be determined.

II. Definitions and Calculations

A. Total direct labor (self-evident)

B. Operational labor (planned direct labor)

C. Direct labor
Direct material } Shop cost
Indirect cost
plus

D. Production engineering costs and expenses
Provision for complaints
Box, pack, and ship

(*C* and *D* together: Manufacturing cost)

E. Contract-engineering costs and expenses
Product installation construction and misc. direct charges
Other accounts (plant, etc.)

(*C*, *D*, and *E* together: Cost of sales)

F. Net sales billed
Minus cost of sales equals gross margin
Minus commercial and administrative expense equals income before taxes
Minus taxes equals income after taxes

G. Contributed value is equal to net sales billed minus direct materials

H. Production related to contributed value: multiply the contributed value per unit times the production for the period

I. Production related to quality cost: divide the total quality cost by the number of pieces produced and express as dollars per unit or per thousand units.

J. Quality-cost dollars per equivalent unit of production output: when more than one end product is involved and the manufacturing cost of each is unequal, it is desirable to equate the production to equivalent units before relating to quality costs. To do this, follow these steps:

1. Select the end product that makes up the largest dollar volume and call product 1.

2. Get the manufacturing cost or contributed value (whichever is more applicable) of product 1.
3. Assign this cost the factor 1.
4. Get the manufacturing cost or contributed value of product 2.
5. Find the related value factor for product 2 (divide step 4 by step 2).
6. Multiply the production of product 1 times the factor 1.
7. Multiply the production of product 2 times the factor from step 5.
8. The total of steps 6 and 7 is the equivalent units of production output.
9. Total quality costs divided by equivalent units of production output in step 8 gives the quality-cost dollars per equivalent unit of production output.

Example:

Product	Unit mfg. cost of contrib. value	Factor ×	Production output for period	Equiv. prod. output for period
A	$250	1 ×	10,000	10,000
B	$400	1.6 ×	3,000	4,800
C	$50	.2 ×	10,000	2,000
	Total equivalent units of production output =			16,800

Assuming total quality-cost dollars for this period amounted to $59,576, the relation is

$$\frac{\$59{,}976}{16{,}800} = \$3.57 \quad \text{quality-cost dollars per equivalent unit of production output}$$

As the product mix in the output changes, the equivalent units produced will also change. This provides an extremely sensitive and easily understood comparison base which closely follows production.

Complaint Comparisons. In some businesses, the reporting of complaint expenditures lags actual production from 6 to 24 months. In these cases, the inclusion of complaint charges with current quality costs may give a somewhat distorted picture. Under these circumstances, it may be well to make two comparisons: total quality costs to the applicable comparison bases, and total quality costs *less complaints* to the applicable comparison bases. To facilitate making such comparisons, the failure area is divided into internal and external failures. All external failure deals with complaints.

5.6 Establishment of Quality-cost Goals

When an analysis of quality costs has been completed, it has to be interpreted in terms of actions that will be taken. Certain goals must be set in bringing about the desired relationships. For example, a balance is sought between dollars invested in preventive effort versus dollars saved as a result of reducing failure costs. When a quality-cost program is first initiated, it may be found that a dollar spent in prevention will save many dollars in failure costs. As the program progresses and the most costly cases of failure are brought under control, further prevention effort may not pay off at as high a ratio. In time, the "curve" will flatten out, so further preventive effort cannot be justified on the basis of available reduction in failure costs. A minimum exists for total operating quality costs when the quality-cost elements are in optimum balance. Complete reporting and analysis of quality costs assist in determining this optimum point.

If dollars are spent in "debugging" a product or process to prevent defects, there will be less need for inspecting or testing the product and less cost for failures in the plant or complaints in the field. Because of this interrelationship, expenditures in any one of the four quality-cost segments must be evaluated in terms of the resultant savings in the others.

This does not mean, however, that a straight dollar-for-dollar relationship exists between the various items of quality costs. For example, the quality costs included in the segment of costs of external failure should be given considerably greater significance than the items falling within costs of internal failure. A dollar of complaints is normally of much more market impact than a dollar of scrap.

The usual situation is covered by the foregoing discussion, but there are other situations that require special consideration with respect to operating quality costs. One must always bear in mind the objective of the business. For example, some companies may be doing research and development work, in which case the only manufacturing would involve a few prototypes. This should mean a heavy investment of preventive effort toward obtaining designs of product and process that result in high product reliability. Such expenditure would have to be analyzed and then agreed to in order to assure meeting the long-range objectives of the business even though external failure costs are, and would be, extremely low because of limited current production.

5.7 Applications of Quality Costs

The Manager–Quality Control is constantly making decisions which affect the costs in the various segments in order to obtain the minimum total operating quality cost at the desired outgoing quality level. Quality costs provide some basically sound "tools" for arriving at such decisions. They may be used as follows.

Quality Costs Serve as a Measurement Tool. Since quality costs are broken down into segments, the Manager–Quality Control easily can obtain a dollar measurement on each quality activity. For example, the dollars invested in quality planning can be measured in terms of the quality-control-engineering costs devoted to that activity. Justification for this investment can be measured in terms of reduced failure costs as a result of quality planning and in terms of reduced quality-appraisal costs as a result of more efficient inspection methods.

Quality costs provide comparative measurements for evaluating quality programs versus the value of the results achieved.

Quality Costs Serve as Process-quality Analysis Tool. To use only the measurement tool is not enough. The Manager–Quality Control needs to analyze particular quality costs. Quality costs, when properly broken down by product lines or segments of the process flow, will pinpoint major problem areas and serve effectively as an analysis tool.

Quality Costs Serve as a Programming Tool. An analysis provides a basis for specific courses of action. Planning for carrying out these courses of action involves establishing a program. One of the important functions filled by a program is the assignment of available manpower, and other resources, for carrying out the action. Since resources are usually limited, quality costs provide a means for identifying those actions which provide the highest potential pay-off, hence those actions which should have priority with reference to time sequence.

Figure 5.6 is an example of such a program. It will be noted that it specifically describes the action and states when it is to start, the individual responsible for the action, the time required in each period, and the results expected. This type of programming provides a means for obtaining maximum contribution from company personnel toward product-quality improvement and quality-cost reduction.

Quality Costs Serve as a Budgeting Tool. Quality costs guide the Manager–Quality Control in budgeting the necessary expenditures for accomplishing the desired quality-control programs. Such programs, of course, take into account the objectives and goals of the business. As shown by a previous example, the long-range objective may be to attain high product reliability. In such a case, the program would be directed toward staffing a strong quality-control-engineering effort to do pre-production evaluation and quality planning.

All programs may not be immediately feasible in view of available resources. Programs may have to be brought along successively, building toward goals that take 2 to 3 years to realize. Such a procedure helps assure realistic budgets and attainment of specific reliability goals.

An Example of Operating Quality Costs. Let us look at an example of what can be achieved when the Manager–Quality Control uses quality costs as a tool for programming and arriving at supporting budgets to reach specific goals. A small company is used as an example. This company had many trying problems in the quality area and was fighting desperately to pull out of a loss position.

An analysis of quality cost showed the high rate of 9.3 per cent to shop cost of output. Furthermore little was being spent for preventive effort. The 9.3 per cent was divided as follows: prevention, 0.2 per cent; appraisal, 2.8 per cent; and failure, 6.3 per cent to shop cost of output. The company decided to start a total-quality-control program, "investing" in two quality-control engineers doing the kind of technical work discussed in Chap. 4. In a little less than 2 years and after an investment of $26,900 for preventive effort, total quality costs dropped from 9.3 per cent to 6.8 per cent. Prevention went from 0.2 per cent to 0.4 per cent, appraisal dropped from 2.8 per cent to 2.4 per cent, and failure from 6.3 per cent to 4.0 per cent to shop cost of output. This improvement was brought about by reductions in a number of quality-cost items as follows:

- Appraisal costs were reduced $43,000.
- Scrap and rework were reduced $206,800.
- Complaints were reduced $53,600.

In total, this company made a net quality-cost improvement of more than $276,000 in a little less than 2 years; and its product quality is now looked upon as one of the best in its field.

This kind of quality and cost improvement clearly helped this company to progress successfully to a profit position within the first year's operation of the program. A solid profit position was attained in the second year. In small businesses or large businesses, this same approach can be taken, and experience has shown that comparable results can be achieved.

5.8 Other Quality-cost Categories

Although *operating quality costs* are the most important category of quality costs, from the standpoint of both dollars and control, there are other categories of quality costs that should not be ignored. Two are mentioned here as being of importance. One major category is *indirect quality costs,* and the other is *equipment quality costs.*

Indirect quality costs include those quality costs which are hidden in other business costs. They need to be reported separately so attention will be given to reducing these items of cost. For example, the purchase price

PROPOSED PROGRAM

Date: ____________

XYZ COMPANY

PURCHASED MATERIAL PLANNING, EVALUATION, AND CONTROL

Elements of Quality-control Work	Area, Line, or Product	Input Coverage: Basis of Input Measurement	Input Coverage: Current	Goals: 3/31	Goals: 6/30	Goals: 12/31	Proposed Start. Date	Responsibilities: Function Basically Responsible	Responsibilities: Indiv. Responsible	Responsibilities: Key Assoc. in Other Components	Est. Total Input Req. (Man-hr by Indiv. Respons. and Dollars Other Than Compens.): Man-hrs	Est. Total Input Req.: $	Estimated Effort Application by Individual Responsible (in Man-Hr): Jan-Feb	Mar-Apr	May-Jun	Jul-Aug	Sep-Oct	Nov-Dec
Formally classify quality characteristics on purchased material as to relative importance, and establish acceptable quality levels and standards considering manufacturing process requirements as well as end-product requirements.	Product A	% of all parts, and materials fully covered	20	25	45	70	Feb. 4	Q.C. Engr.*	J. Dunn	George–Engr. Green–Purch. Arp-Mfg. Eng.	180	. . .	15	50	40	30	25	20
	Product B		15	20	40	65	Feb. 18	Q.C. Engr.*	C. Brill	Jones–Engr. Black–Purch. Smith–Mfg. Eng.	180	. . .	10	40	50	30	30	20
Develop specific methods, procedures, and operations for each acceptance test, inspect or check on each part or material, and reduce to formal written planning.	Product A	% of all parts, materials, and quality characteristics fully covered by written planning	30	40	60	85	Jan. 6	Q.C. Engr.	R. True	George–Engr. Dunn–Q.C.E. Silk-Insp. & Test Equip. Design	240	1,300	35	60	60	20	40	25
	Product B		15	25	50	80	Feb. 4	Q.C. Engr.	R. True	Jones–Engr. Brill–Q.C.E. Silk-Insp. & Test Equip. Design	280	600	30	80	70	25	50	25

Improvement Results Expected in Quality-cost Flow

	Performance Measurement	12/60 (Current)	Goals, 6/61–12/61		% Rel. Improv. Per Year
Productivity	1. Dollars of direct material processed per dollar of incoming-material acceptance costs	198	210	240	20
Effectiveness	2. % incoming-material acceptance costs divided by manufacturing losses attributable to vendors	44%	47%	60%	36
	3. % manufacturing losses (O.V.) recovered divided by total manufacturing losses attributable to vendors	15%	25%	40%	165
Timeliness	4. % of lots found not fully meeting all quality requirements as received	8%	12%	5%	38
	5. Average number of lots per week not processing through in less than a day	120	70	30	75

Reduction in acceptance costs and net losses 1961 over 1960 = $55,000

Reduction in annual rate of acceptance cost and net losses (end 1961 vs. end 1960) = $109,000

Formally delineate quality requirements including relative (importance and acceptance levels on individual quality characteristics) to vendors through purchasing of direct materials and parts. Includes checks to be made by vendor and data to be supplied.	Product A	% of all parts, materials, and quality characteristics fully delineated to vendors, understood, and accepted	0	20	40	70	Jan. 6	Q.C. Engr.† through Purchasing	J. Dunn	Green–Purch. White–Prod. Contr.	220	150	50	40	40	30	40	20
	Product B		0	15	35	60	Jan. 20		C. Brill	Black–Purch. Rogers–Prod. Contr.	220	150	30	50	50	30	40	20
Perform vendor quality servicing to assure scheduled quality output.	Product A	Av. no. of vendors *not* consistently supplying material meeting all quality requirements.	27	24	18	3	Mar. 1	Qual. Control (Process Control Spec.)*	A. Mack	Brill, Dunn QCE; White, Rogers Prod. Cont.	190	650	...	60	45	30	35	20
	Product B		18	15	12	2	Mar. 1		A. Mack	Green, Black Purch. Blue–Insp. Fore.	210	400	...	70	70	25	25	20
Establish systems of measuring the productivity, effectiveness, and timeliness of incoming-material control. Develop feedback to ensure that corrective action is taken as required.	Product A	% of functional performance measurements in place and reported monthly.	0	100	100	100	Jan. 6	Mgr. Qual. Control	D. Adams	King–Mgr. Mater.	20	...	15	5				
	Product B		0	100	100	100	Jan. 6		D. Adams	Borne–Acctg.	20	...	15	5				
Remaining elements of work in *incoming-material control*, major area of the total quality system.	Products A and B	...	...	...	...	...	Jan. 6	Qual. Control generally	C. Brill J. Dunn R. True A. Mack F. Blue D. Adams	As indicated or required	290	500	10	20	40	60	80	80
TOTAL..........	...	...	...	...	...	...	...	...	...	...	2,050	3,750	210	480	465	280	365	250

* Previously divided responsibility.
† Responsibility not previously specifically assigned.

FIG. 5.6

of materials include, in effect, the supplier's (operating) quality costs. If the supplier can reduce such quality costs by a substantial amount, this might be reflected in a lower sales price to his customer. Other indirect quality-cost reductions as savings unequivocally attributable to total-quality-control activities include design improvement requiring less labor or material; process improvement requiring less labor, material, or equipment; reduction in inventory of materials held for inspection and test, rejected materials awaiting disposition, overstocking of purchased material as a hedge against rejections; reduction in down time; savings to customers through elimination of their incoming inspection afforded by the producer certifying product quality.

Equipment quality costs represent the capital investment in equipment specifically obtained to measure product quality for purposes of acceptance and control. This investment is made for some of the same reasons that operating quality costs are incurred, namely, for prevention of quality failures and for economies in appraisal. In the case of operating quality costs, these costs are expended mostly for personnel services; in the case of equipment quality costs, they represent expenditures for measuring equipment (inspection and test machines). When properly identified, amortized, and consolidated with operating quality costs, a more complete and realistic basis for measuring the effectiveness of the total-quality-control program is provided by equipment quality costs.

5.9 Other Measures for Decision Making in Quality Control [2]

A number of other numerical quality-cost measurements are needed by the Manager–Quality Control and will have to be developed as required by his particular situation. The approach to developing such measurements may be illustrated, by examples in relation to job 2 of total quality control: incoming-material control.

Productivity Measurement. The first of these examples concerns a productivity measurement which reflects the relative quantity of work performed. The performance measurement is

Direct Material Dollars
divided by
Incoming Appraisal Costs

Productivity is normally measured in terms of *output* over *input*. In incoming-material control, direct material represents *output*. Incoming appraisal costs, which include all incoming testing, inspection, and laboratory-acceptance testing, are the quality-related input. This ratio

[2] This section is according to a paper by F. J. Berkenkamp, General Electric Co.

provides a direct measure of productivity—output over input—reflecting the relative *quantity* of work performed. As *more* work is appraised for quality at *less* cost, productivity rises.

Effectiveness Measurements. The next measurement is one of *effectiveness,* which reflects the relative quality of work performed. Here we need two measures.

The first measure is

Incoming-material Appraisal Costs
divided by
Manufacturing Losses Attributable to Outside Vendors

Incoming-material appraisal costs reflect the effort applied. Manufacturing losses attributable to outside vendors reflect the effectiveness of the applied effort in keeping poor-quality incoming material from reaching the factory floor.

As the *quality* of the applied effort in appraising incoming material rises, associated manufacturing losses should *decrease* and effectiveness should *go up.*

This effectiveness index shows no bona fide improvement by merely increasing incoming appraisal costs. These increasing appraisal costs will also make the *productivity index* go down, thus indicating no legitimate over-all improvement.

The second measure of effectiveness is

Outside Vendor Losses Recovered from Vendors
divided by
Total Losses Attributable to Vendors

The quality of work performed in incoming-material control applies not only to effectiveness in screening out poor quality but *also* to effectiveness in being able to recover increasingly higher percentages of vendor-associated losses. This recovery percentage is as low as 15 per cent in some businesses and the total outside vendor-attributable losses as high as several hundred thousand dollars a year. This is another important measure of potential for increasing profits through improvement of the effectiveness of work performed. The better the job done by Quality Control in the defect-prevention and after-the-fact phases of incoming-material control, the greater is the probability that Purchasing will be able to recover higher percentages of vendor losses.

Timeliness Measurement. *Timeliness of action* provides another measurement reflecting the timeliness of work performed. Here again we need two measures to present potential contribution to profits fairly.

The first is

Per Cent of Lots Failing to Meet Fully All Requirements as Received

This is a measure of *timeliness of defect-prevention work* in the incoming-material control area. It is one thing to become increasingly effective in sorting good from bad. It is equally or more important to take preventive action which ensures the proper quality as received. Better defect-prevention work done not only with vendors but also with Engineering and Purchasing should reduce the per cent of lots failing to meet all requirements. A reduction in this percentage is reflected as an improvement in timeliness of action.

The second measure for timeliness of action reflects efficiency in processing incoming material:

Average Number of Lots per Week *Not* Processing through from Receipt at Receiving Dock to Release for Stock or Use in Less than 1 Day (24 Hours)

Timeliness of action here is reflected in terms of material *not* processing through rapidly, of material awaiting disposition or corrective action before release for stock or use. A high number of lots reflects poor timeliness of action. Very positive contributions to profits are available from reduced purchasing lead times, lower inventories, fewer production hold-ups for needed material, and fewer "use-as-is" disposition of marginal-quality material to keep production lines running. As materials flow through faster and disposition procedures are improved, timeliness of action through incoming-material control improves.

Managerial Decision Making. How are these performance measurements used as managerial decision-making tools?

The measures that have been discussed are ratios in the three basic performance areas of *productivity, effectiveness,* and *timeliness of action* in incoming-material control. To be of value, these ratios must be converted into decision-making tools. This is accomplished by plotting *performance* versus *time* and noting the relative improvement achieved and progress made in meeting goals.

As an example, consider the first of these measurements as a graph, namely, productivity for incoming-material control in a business. The actual numbers on the graph are typical of some businesses. Figure 5.7 shows productivity reflecting the *quantity* of work performed.

In terms of direct material dollars divided by incoming-material appraisal costs, productivity has become static at $200 of direct material for every dollar of incoming appraisal costs. This level is considerably below the $240 goal set by the Manager–Quality Control for productivity improvement by year's end. If this goal is to be achieved, the Manager–

Quality Control must make decisions to *ensure* that action is taken. It may be a decision to make a work-sampling study to determine what percentage of total incoming appraisal time is *nonproductively* spent in materials handling, in obtaining blueprints and measuring devices, and in keeping records. It may be a decision to look into the substantial amount of dollars being expended in routine laboratory-acceptance testing. A substantial portion of this routine laboratory testing might well be *reduced* to skip-lot sampling with *no loss* in protection.

These are just two of many possible avenues to explore to bring productivity up to the goal in terms of more work performed at less cost. The important point is that the Manager *knows* productivity has become static and recognizes the need for a *decision* to motivate positive action. He has a direct measure of how sound this action was in achieving the

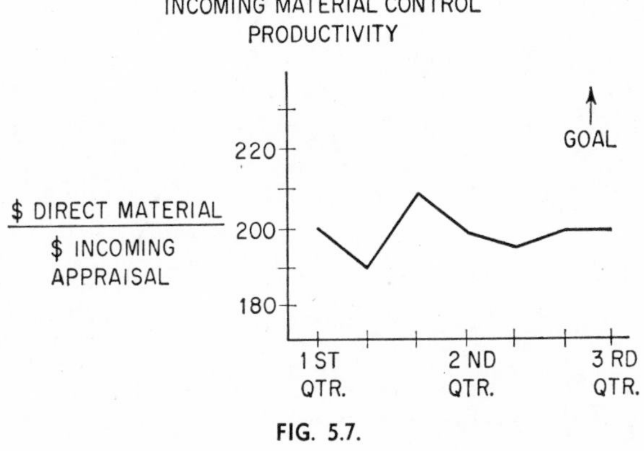

FIG. 5.7.

results he desired in the productivity area. Similarly, graphs can be constructed for the remaining four performance indices that have been discussed in the incoming-material control area.

Combined Measurements. The basic performance indices, noted above, each tell a separate story. Any one alone would provide an erroneous measure of the contribution being made. In combination, however, these performance indices provide a powerful decision-making tool for increased profits through positive and effective incoming-material control.

The Manager–Quality Control also has a sound, numerical basis for *establishing* specific *programs, goals,* and *budgets* and for a close, cooperative relationship with the Manager–Materials. Equally important, these performance indices make an excellent report for top management. The control of quality and its contributions to profits are translated in terms that are readily understood and, in graphical form, readily measured.

In this discussion, only one area, incoming-material control, has been considered. Performance indices covering productivity, effectiveness, and timeliness of action can likewise be developed for each of the major jobs of total quality control. Periodic reports on all indices provide a composite, continuing measure of performance for the quality system in a business.

If a quality-control manager can regularly report positive improvements in a high percentage of these performance indices, the indications are good that his component is operating satisfactorily in making its contributions to the effectiveness of the business.

Managing through these indices, and within the framework of operating quality cost data, is one of the major keys to sound total quality control for a company.

CHAPTER 6

THE QUALITY SYSTEM

In order to accomplish any task efficiently, it is necessary to plan the required courses of action. For example, when building a house, the numerous parts of the job must be done in a certain sequence. After architectural drawings are complete, the foundation must be staked out and excavation started. The framework cannot go up until foundation and first floor are completed. Electric wiring and plumbing must be scheduled when partitions are completed but before the walls are constructed, and so on to completion.

Just as the construction of a house requires sequencing and timing of the work of many individual artisans in proper relationship one to the other, so it is with the total-quality-control jobs. Chapter 3 discussed how the four jobs of total quality control extend across the entire product cycle; hence sequencing and timing are involved. Chapter 4 reviewed how every function in the industrial organization has a part to play in the ultimate delivery of a finished product of the desired quality. This means that many different positions, under these several functions, are carrying out tasks that influence product quality. These tasks must bear the proper relationship and timing to one another if the company is geared up to produce the desired end result. Hence, the need for *planned* courses of action becomes apparent.

6.1 The Systems-engineering Job

There are many functions that must be brought together in proper relationship to provide the single major function of getting a quality product to market. In this respect, planning the structure that will permit execution of the total-quality-control job takes on the aspects of systems engineering.

In any system, there are numerous individual components, each with a specific function that is contributed toward the single, major function of the system. For example, a missile is a system whose major function is to deliver a pay load from one location to another location. It is made up of several subsystems, such as those for guidance, pay load, propellant, and fire control. Besides these purely physical systems, there are also *business* systems, such as postal systems, educational systems, and railway systems.

All these systems are characterized by numerous individual components providing specific functions that contribute to the function of the system. In every case, there must be some one individual or small group of individuals who understands the system as a whole, how the components must fit together, and how they must relate one to another. This is the individual or group to do the necessary systems engineering.

6.2 The Quality System

Specifically, then, what is the definition of the quality system?

The quality system is the network of administrative and technical procedures required to produce and deliver a product of specified quality standards.

These procedures establish the elements of work that must be done, the sequence and timing that are necessary to produce the desired result, and the positions responsible for carrying out the individual elements of work.

6.3 Why the Quality System Is Necessary

The only case in which the quality system would be *unnecessary* is that of the Yankee pot maker, who did the entire job, from defining his market, designing his product, procuring materials, making pots, to peddling them. If he received any customer complaints, these were factored in next time he designed or made a pot.

As soon as the pot business became big enough to justify the Yankee pot maker in hiring a "hand" or a "peddler," the need for a quality system came into being. The activities of the various "hands" as they related to product quality had to be related to each other with respect to timing and responsibilities.

When an industry grows to such an extent that the labor must be divided among either several or many persons, there is a need for formal planning. Quite obviously, the share of the work that each individual is responsible for must be defined. Since the work is most generally part of an over-all "team" effort, it must be related to that of the other members of the team. Hence, not only does the *division* of labor become a consideration, but also the *integration* of labor becomes an equally important consideration. The whole purpose of organization is to get division of labor but with integrated effort leading to singleness of purpose. If the individuals are working at cross-purposes or are interfering with each other's efforts, either the people or the system are not working as they should be.

The quality system provides the network of procedures that the different positions in a company must follow in working closely together to get the four jobs of total quality control done.

6.4 Who Plans the Quality System?

Since the quality system cuts across all functional lines, who should plan the quality system? Theoretically, the position to which all functions of the business report should have this responsibility. Since such a position may be that of president or the general manager of a business, with broad responsibilities, it may be necessary for the detailed task of planning the quality system to be delegated to one of the functional organizations. Quite logically, this typically falls to the quality-control organizational component. Since it has been shown to be a systems-engineering type of job, this work requires a high-level quality-control engineer who has a knowledge of the complete quality system and can plan its broad structure, including the "interfaces" between functions.

Regardless, however, of who may have primary responsibility for planning the quality system, much of the work must be accomplished on a teamwork basis, employing representatives from all functional components of the business. Detailed quality procedures within each function may be established by an assigned person within each respective function. Then the person responsible for planning the total quality system can work with these assigned persons to relate the individual procedures, making necessary adjustments with the concurrence of the involved parties.

6.5 The Quality-system Plan

There are hundreds of individual actions taken by many different persons throughout the organization, all directed toward getting a product of satisfactory quality to the customer at a reasonable cost. These numerous individual tasks must bear the correct relationship to each other. There must not be tasks left undone, and there should not be duplication of effort. The tasks must have the right time sequence. In other words, there must be a quality-system plan. To a considerable degree, the quality-system plan for a business or a product line exists as written documents that appear in many forms: as reliability procedures, as laboratory instructions, as inspection and test plans, and as manpower development programs.

These detailed documentations of individual segments of the plan will be considered in later chapters. What is significant to establish in this chapter are some broader principles about the quality-system plan. These principles are as follows:

1. Implementation of the four jobs of total quality control requires, as an early step by a company, recognition that a systematic approach is needed to knit together the elements of the four jobs.

2. This approach is based upon what is really a point of view, namely, thinking of the business quality system as a network of interrelated plans and procedures which tie together and do not fight each other.

3. It is unlikely that it will be practical or economical to reduce to writing each and every element of this quality system plan: some of it must be based upon common, well-understood practices. But the *critical* elements in the plan must exist in documented form.

4. To provide the foundation for a company quality-system point of view, it is necessary to identify the segments of this quality system, covering both the elements that are documented and those that are understood.

Each company will want to develop the over-all quality system, and its subsystems, which meets its own particular requirements. However, 10 of these subsystems, which are typical of the quality system in many companies, will be considered in this chapter. They are:

1. Preproduction Quality Evaluation, discussed in Sec. 6.6
2. Product- and Process-quality Planning, discussed in Sec. 6.7
3. Purchased-material Quality Planning, Evaluation, and Control, discussed in Sec. 6.8
4. Product- and Process-quality Evaluation and Control, discussed in Sec. 6.9
5. Quality Information Feedback, discussed in Sec. 6.10
6. Quality Information Equipment, discussed in Sec. 6.11
7. Quality Training, Orientation, and Manpower Development, discussed in Sec. 6.12
8. Postproduction Quality Service, discussed in Sec. 6.13
9. Management of the Quality-control Function, discussed in Sec. 6.14
10. Special Quality Studies, discussed in Sec. 6.15

Figure 6.1 illustrates the contribution made by each of these subsystems to implementation of the four basic jobs of total quality control.

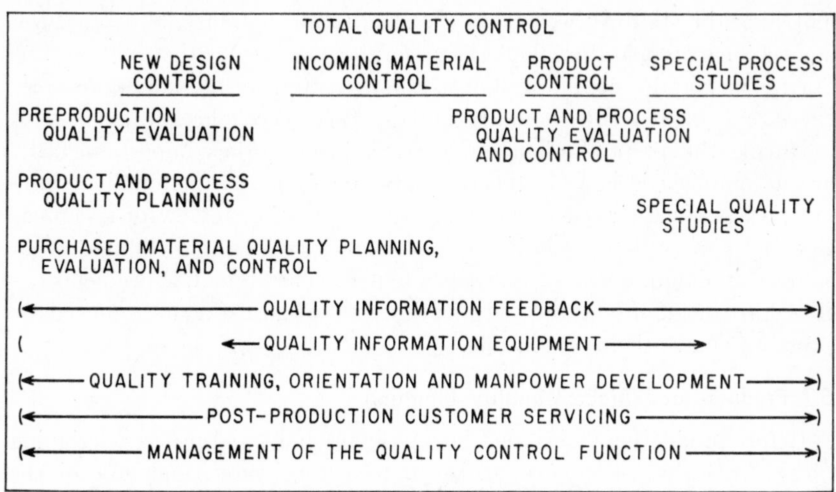

FIG. 6.1.

A Check-list Summary of Key Elements

Companies which have studied and designed these 10 subsystems have learned that at least 300 separate activities are involved within their quality system—further emphasizing that so many elements are not likely to synchronize "automatically" unless some formal planning is done. Since in quality-control it is the single activity that is missed which frequently creates the problems, quality systems planning cannot be adequately dependable for a company unless it has reviewed *all* major activities.

To take account of this detail, Secs. 6.6 through 6.15 below will depart from the descriptive format used elsewhere in this book. They will, instead, provide a detailed summary of key system activities from which the reader can extract a "check list" of some of the significant elements that must be identified in the quality system for his company.

6.6 Preproduction Quality Evaluation

Procedures are established to analyze formally both the product design and the process design to ascertain that the resultant product will fulfill the customer's requirements. Product Engineering should review its own designs with appropriate assistance from analyses made by other functions. A fresh point of view often contributes valuable suggestions. The same review of process is required by Manufacturing Engineering.

Product evaluation should be done, where feasible, under actual end-use conditions. Environments should be duplicated, even to the extent of matching the skill of the persons expected to understand and operate the device. Such an operator should be given the instructions that will be supplied. During the course of the evaluation, any unsatisfactory experiences that might result should be noted and corrective action taken.

During the preproduction quality evaluation, other important tasks are accomplished, such as the identification of important quality characteristics and their classification as to importance; review of specifications for clarity, compatibility, and economy; location and elimination of sources of manufacturing troubles and out-of-control quality problems before start of manufacture; and identification of adjustments to design or process to make them compatible.

6.7 Product- and Process-quality Planning

Before production starts and during the product- and process-designing phases, plans must be formalized to measure, attain, and control the desired product quality. This requires an analysis of product-quality requirements to determine what quality characteristics should be measured, how they should be measured, to what extent (sample or 100 per cent), where in the process flow, who should take the measurement, and the limits of the measurement beyond which corrective action should be taken. Procedures should also be established for planning the devices required for taking the required quality measurements.

Quality planning also includes determination of numbers, qualifications, and training of quality-assurance personnel; methods and formats for recording quality data; preventive maintenance procedures for tools and processes; standardization, calibration, and maintenance for quality-measuring equipment; material flow, routing, and disposition procedures; in-process and outgoing quality audits; and issuance of detailed instructions covering quality-assurance activities.

6.8 Purchased-material Quality Planning, Evaluation, and Control

This subsystem of the system provides the procedures necessary to the control of a very important quality input: purchased material. Such procedures ensure the means for clear delineation of quality requirements to vendors and for communicating to them the classification of quality characteristics by their relative importance. Procedures also provide for appraising the vendor's quality capability, facilities, and quality system prior to placement of the order. Establishment of procedures is made whereby vendors certify the quality of the lots they ship by means of objective quality measurements accompanying each lot. Other procedures include quality evaluation of purchased materials and feedback of quality information to vendors; correlation of vendor quality-measurement methods and equipment with purchased-material inspection; servicing of vendors to assure scheduled quality output; conducting incoming test, inspection, and laboratory examinations.

All these procedures, when established and followed, permit accomplishment of incoming-material control. This calls for close integration with the purchasing unit. Usually buyers have the responsibility for making all agreements and arrangements with vendors. Hence, quality information flow should take place through the buyer, or at least he should be kept advised of any information flowing back and forth.

The important point is that the vendor fully understands what is important to the purchaser from a quality standpoint. The purchaser gets a measure of input quality and feeds back any information needed to correct or adjust the vendor's processes.

6.9 Product- and Process-quality Evaluation and Control

The procedures established under this quality system component provide for *implementing* the product- and process-quality planning. Those procedures having to do with service to the shop operator include the following:

1. Formally delineate relative importance of quality characteristics to shop personnel.
2. Formally establish quality checks by shop personnel and monitor performance.
3. Assure adequate measuring means to operators.
4. Calibrate and maintain measuring devices used by operators.

A number of procedures identify necessary measurement activities to be carried out by members of the quality-control organization:

1. Perform in-process quality evaluation to ensure parts conformance to specification.
2. Perform in-process tests on components and subassemblies to assure function in final assembly and under end-use conditions.
3. Perform audits; audit adherence to in-process quality procedures.
4. Perform end-of-line quality evaluations and inspections.
5. Perform end-of-line quality performance evaluations and tests.
6. Make customer-centered, outgoing quality audits and life-testing, environmental, and reliability evaluations.
7. Establish index of outgoing quality based on audit results.
8. Provide quality-measurement service.
9. Evaluate material not fully acceptable and determine disposition.
10. Measure over-all productivity, effectiveness, and timeliness of product and process control, obtaining needed corrective action.

Still other procedures are concerned with the work done in maintaining measuring equipment and quality ability of tools:

1. Operate and monitor system for preventive maintenance on tools, jigs, and fixtures.
2. Calibrate and maintain quality-assurance measuring devices.

A number of analytical procedures are identified in this quality-system component such as those which:

1. Establish manufacturing-analysis and cost-reduction programs.
2. Analyze quality-generated production delays.
3. Make analyses of productivity, effectiveness, and timeliness of action of quality-assurance personnel.
4. Correlate factory and field performance data to permit prediction of field failure and service-call rates.
5. Establish complaint-analysis and reduction programs.

Provision must be made for temporary and short-range planning to be carried on, such as to:

1. Perform quality-assurance operational planning.
2. Maintain physical quality standards for use of shop.

The establishment and maintenance of various types of quality standards is a concern in product control, such as:

1. Establish process-control limits.
2. Maintain physical quality standards for use of shop.
3. Periodically review specifications, drawings, etc., for currency and accuracy.

Other procedures required have to do with carrying out certain work assignments, as follows:

1. Perform disposition and routing of defective or nonconforming material.
2. Obtain corrective action by appropriate position; follow up and determine effectiveness of action taken.
3. Develop and establish customer quality-certification programs.
4. Operate safety programs.
5. Maintain quality records.

As can be seen from the nature of these "elements of work," this group forms the part of the quality system that is used in the shop or on the factory floor for the day-to-day control of quality. It will be noted that some of the work is done by production operators, some is done by inspectors, and some would be the responsibility of the process-control engineer, as will be shown in Chap. 8.

6.10 Quality Information Feedback

This, in effect, is the information system which forms a part of the quality system. It supplies the quality information needs of key personnel in the various functional areas. Procedures are established to analyze the quality information needs of all positions, i.e., vendors, purchasers, production control men, shop supervisors, shop personnel, manufacturing planners and engineers, quality-control engineers and equipment designers, quality-assurance supervisors, quality-assurance personnel, product-design engineers, product planners, salesmen, product-service supervisors and personnel, customers, and general and functional managers. In analyzing needs, criteria are established for content, frequency, and permissible time delay. This is done for each position to provide timely decisions for effective action in quality areas.

Specific procedures are established which implement data collection, tabulation, analysis, and distribution. Included here are formats that will be concise with respect to responsibility for corrective action and sound with respect to measurements and their comparison bases. Formats for the following kinds of reports should be developed: incoming-material quality evaluations, in-process quality evaluations, end-of-line quality evaluations, product-reliability and life evaluations, manufacturing losses, in-process quality audits, outgoing product-quality audits, field failure and service-call rates, complaint expenditures, special studies reports, various quality costs, and quality-system measurements reports.

Periodic review of the quality information system is necessary to keep it current in meeting the changing needs of the company. Besides identifying new positions that require certain quality information, attention should be given to eliminating distributions whereby no useful purpose is currently being served.

The development and use of automatic quality-level-indicating devices is also considered an element in the quality information system. The past few years have seen a rapid growth of instrumentation which provides the means for communicating quality information to a control center. The chemical industry has some especially noteworthy installations for petroleum refining and other continuous-process operations.

6.11 Quality Information Equipment

Quality measurements that are necessary for the control of quality are identified during product- and process-quality planning. Planning also includes identification of measurement methods and the type of measuring and control equipment that is to be used. The quality information equipment subsystem provides the procedures for procuring this measuring and control equipment. Such activity has advanced development aspects which include study of the long-range needs of the company's business with respect to measuring equipment on the basis of new products, new processes, and improvements in product quality, flow, and costs. Special studies are made to develop new basic measuring techniques, their adaptation and integration into mechanized and automated manufacturing equipments. Procedures for programming advanced information equipment development are included in the system.

Procedures for equipment design and application include development of design requirements, analysis of the quality system to determine most effective and economic measurements, required precision and accuracy, and determining best method for measuring each quality characteristic; development of specifications for quality information equipment and cost estimates covering design, development, construction, and initial application costs; execution of such work, keeping the quality information equipment updated to meet new needs arising as a result of design changes, process revision, and application experience in the field; provision for proper maintenance and calibration; origination and maintenance of schematics, blueprints, layouts, replacement parts lists, and operating and maintenance instructions, including safety precautions; and means for measuring over-all effectiveness of the quality information equipment area.

As manufacturing operations become more mechanized and automated, the quality information equipment activity gains increasing importance. As a matter of fact, a proper degree of development in automated measurements is often a prerequisite to automated manufacture. This is discussed further in Chap. 9.

6.12 Quality Training, Orientation, and Manpower Development

The procedures under this component of the quality system provide the means for developing the "people capability" required to properly operate the quality system. It includes not only those persons directly engaged in control-of-quality work but also those others in the company in other functions whose training affects product quality. Programs for training personnel not directly engaged in quality control are directed at the following: product know-how; quality-control function indoctrination; shop-operations indoctrination in quality-control methods, procedures, and techniques; management quality-control-program orientation, specialized education in quality-control techniques for product-design engineers, manufacturing engineers, and buyers, and other specific areas of activity; shop personnel proficiency evaluations; quality-mindedness programs, trainee education, vendors, and industrial customers.

Programs for those directly connected with control-of-quality work include the following: basic quality-control principles, rotational programs, trainee assignments, personnel performance measurement, guidance, and counseling; company-sponsored course participation, professional society participation, university extension courses, manpower inventory, and promotion programs; continuous quality training through letters, bulletins, periodicals, and personal association.

The effectiveness of quality training, orientation, and manpower development is measured by personnel capability that has come about as a result of this part of the quality system. Availability of capable persons to fill open positions is also a measure of its timeliness as well as of its effectiveness.

6.13 Postproduction Quality Service

When the customer or consumer purchases a product, he is, in effect, purchasing the *function* he expects the product to perform for him. Furthermore, he expects that the product will continue to provide that function over some period of time. If, for some reason, the product fails to perform its intended function over its life expectancy, most companies feel an obligation to see that the customer receives the product function he expected as a result of his purchase. Many companies have an organizational component known as *product service* which fulfills this function. Although such an organization has many of the primary responsibilities in this area, Quality Control has a number of contributing responsibilities. A close working relationship between the components is essential to success (see relationship charts, Sec. 4.5, Fig. 4.4).

The total activity in this area is covered by that component of the quality system known as *postproduction quality service*. Here procedures are established for answering complaints and making adjustments that will result in a satisfied customer. More specifically, this component of the quality system includes procedures covering the following activities: review of product guarantees and warranties to establish relationship with respect to product reliability, to place limitations on the company's liability, and to make adjustments or concessions beyond the warranty period; comparative tests and quality evaluations with competitive products; information to Marketing on quality costs, timing, and adverse effects of schedules on quality, anticipated difficulties, and corrective action being taken; quality-certification plans as advantage to the customer in buying the particular company's products; quality audits on warehouse stocks for deterioration and damage, on purchased material shipped directly to the customer, and on repair items; renewal parts, including technical data, quality control, and required availability period; review for adequacy and recommendation for improvements on instruction books covering installation, maintenance, and use; review of serviceability of the product, tools, and techniques for repairs; review of quality, cost, and timeliness of service work; field failure rates and costs and the reporting system for these, including the data-processing and analyzing systems; correlation of field failures with the factory quality index; information from Marketing to Manufacturing and Engineering on unanticipated difficulties and adverse trends.

6.14 Management of the Quality-control Function

This component of the quality system includes the procedures the manager uses in getting his job of managing done, namely, procedures for planning, organizing, integrating, and measuring. These procedures include the following: accumulation, compilation, and reporting of quality costs; establishment of quality-cost-reduction goals and programs; development of systems for measuring the true outgoing quality level of the product; establishment of product-quality improvement goals and programs by product line; establishment of objectives, goals, and programs for the quality-control organizational component and the publication of these for use of appropriate personnel; classification of quality-control work as to generic kinds of work; organization to get the work done and staffing of the organization; issuance of position guides or job descriptions; issuance of procedures for getting the work done; acceptance of the work assignments by individuals; integration of all individuals in the quality-control organizational component; development of measures of effectiveness to determine the contribution of the quality-control function to the profitability and progress of the company.

6.15 Special Quality Studies

This component of the quality system provides procedures and techniques for identifying specific quality problems and finding specific solutions for such problems. Included in these procedures and techniques are machine- and process-capability analysis; quality-measuring equipment capability and repeatability analyses; studies on economic partitioning of tolerances; formal analyses of specific areas of manufacturing variability contributing to high manufacturing losses, high cost of evaluating and controlling quality, and high complaint expenditures; evaluation of proposed new methods, new processes, and new materials and their effects on ease of manufacture, quality, and quality costs; optimum adjustment of processes based on correlation of product-quality characteristics with process conditions; diagnosis of quality problems, taking corrective action, and following up to measure effectiveness of action.

Using the Quality System for Design and Evaluation

6.16 Using the Quality-system Concept for Self-evaluation

There are many values that are brought to a company's quality-control program by the concept of a quality-system plan that welds together all activities. One of them is the identification, by the quality-control component, of the elements, both documented and undocumented, that are significant to sound quality-control performance in the business.

This listing provides a foundation on which to base systems engineering

MAJOR SUBSYSTEM: PURCHASED MATERIAL QUALITY PLANNING, EVALUATION & CONTROL DATE: ____

	ELEMENTS OF TOTAL QUALITY SYSTEM WORK	Degree of Positive and Effective Coverage	Relative Need	Function(s) Specifically Responsible for Element of Work
	COLUMN	A	B	C
1.	Formally classify quality characteristics of vendor-supplied parts and materials as to relative importance, and establish acceptable quality levels considering *manufacturing process requirements* as well as *end product* requirements			
2.	Develop specific methods and procedures for each quality check or evaluation on each part or material, and reduce to *formal, written* planning			
3.	Ensure adequate formal delineation of specific quality requirements per (1) above to vendors (through Purchasing) on purchased parts and materials. Includes quality checks and tests to be performed by vendor and substantiating data to be supplied with each shipment			
4.	Survey and evaluate vendor quality capability, facilities, and quality control systems prior to order placement, and make specific recommendations to Purchasing			
5.	Develop and establish formal material flow, routing, and disposition procedures to ensure rapid flow			
6.	Develop and establish Incoming Material quality record systems, rating plans, and systems of regular rapid feedback of pertinent quality information to Purchasing and to vendor			
7.	Perform first sample acceptance on new material and new vendors, and closely follow first *production* qualities supplied			
8.	Correlate vendor quality measurement methods and equipment with own measurement methods and equipment, and ensure maintenance of furnished gaging and tooling			
9.	Perform operational planning and work-load scheduling for Incoming Test and Inspection			

FIG. 6.2.

to extend and modify the system to meet changing quality requirements for the company. It also provides a company with a specific check list against which it may evaluate the adequacy of each element within the system, as a basis for determining where improvements are needed.

One company, for example, has identified about three hundred elements of work encompassed by its quality system. These are subdivided into the 10 subsystems discussed in Secs. 6.6 through 6.15. The company has then developed a check list of rating sheets to evaluate the adequacy of each subsystem. Figure 6.2 shows a section of a rating sheet for the subsystem "purchased-material quality planning, evaluation, and control." The degree of coverage is noted in the status column. The company makes a rating at 6- or 12-month intervals. Any item which shows lack of coverage is programmed as an item needing development during the ensuing period. Such a program sheet is shown as Fig. 5.6.

6.17 The Quality System—A Part of the Total Business System

The quality system provides the channels through which the stream of product-quality-related activities flow. This, together with other systems, makes up the main line flow of the total business system. Quality requirements and product-quality parameters change, but the quality system remains fundamentally the same, always providing the proper channels through which essential product-quality-related activities must proceed.

PART THREE

ENGINEERING TECHNOLOGY OF QUALITY CONTROL

CHAPTER 7

QUALITY-CONTROL ENGINEERING TECHNOLOGY

Previous chapters have considered the scope and management of total quality control. Part Three reviews the specialized technological knowledge required to make total quality control effective and shows how this specialized knowledge is fitted into separate work packages.

7.1 The Technological Triangle

Figure 7.1 shows the technological triangle, which provides a useful structure for relating the technologies of quality control to each other.

The apex of the triangle provides the caption for the *field:* in this case, total quality control. The first tier divides the field into the *technical work areas,* or jobs of quality control, which have previously been described as new-design control, incoming-material control, product and process control, and special process studies.

The jobs of quality control are accomplished by the *technologies* in the field. There are three in the field of quality control:

1. Quality-control engineering.
2. Process-control engineering.
3. Quality information equipment engineering.

These are shown on the second tier of the technological triangle and are overlaid by training in many associated technologies and disciplines.

The third tier shows the *techniques* employed by the technologies. It is important to point out that any single technique or combination of techniques may be selected by any one of the three technologies for use in any of the technical work areas. This area of techniques can be looked upon as a storehouse of tools from which all the technologies are free to draw in accomplishing work in the technical work areas.

The fourth, and bottom, tier shows the *applications* for the various techniques in accomplishing certain parts of the work. For example, the technique of quality-cost optimization may be applied to cost reduction and product-design selection and many other listed applications.

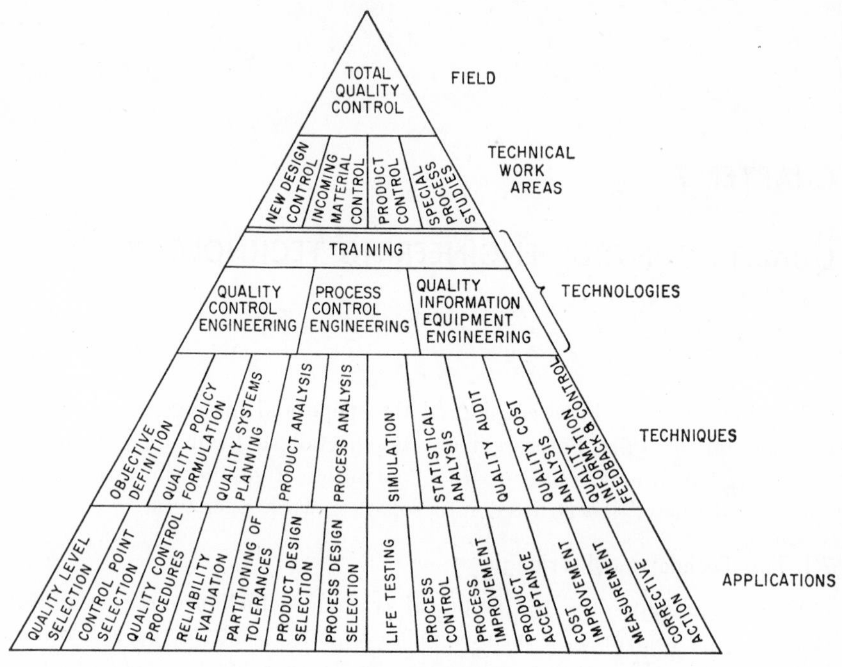

THE TECHNOLOGY TRIANGLE

FIG. 7.1.

This chapter and the two following chapters will discuss the three technologies of total quality control and typical techniques they employ. A few examples of specific applications are given. In Part Five detailed examples will be given, showing how these techniques are used in the four jobs of quality control throughout industry.

7.2 Quality-control Engineering Technology[1]

Quality-control engineering technology may be defined as

The body of technical knowledge for formulating policy and for analyzing and planning product quality in order to establish that

[1] Several of the quality control engineering techniques discussed here have been developed by the following individuals: W. J. Masser, L. N. Bress, F. J. Berkenkamp, H. L. Freeman, D. S. Holmes, W. H. Lewis, F. C. McLaughlin, W. D. Vinson, W. G. Warwick, and S. T. White, General Electric Company.

quality system which will yield full customer satisfaction at minimum cost.

There are many techniques that relate to this technology. One example is that for *analysis of new designs for product function and for the identification of those quality characteristics that are essential to the product function.* Use of this technique makes it possible to plan controls on important quality characteristics with respect to their quality levels at various points throughout the manufacturing process.

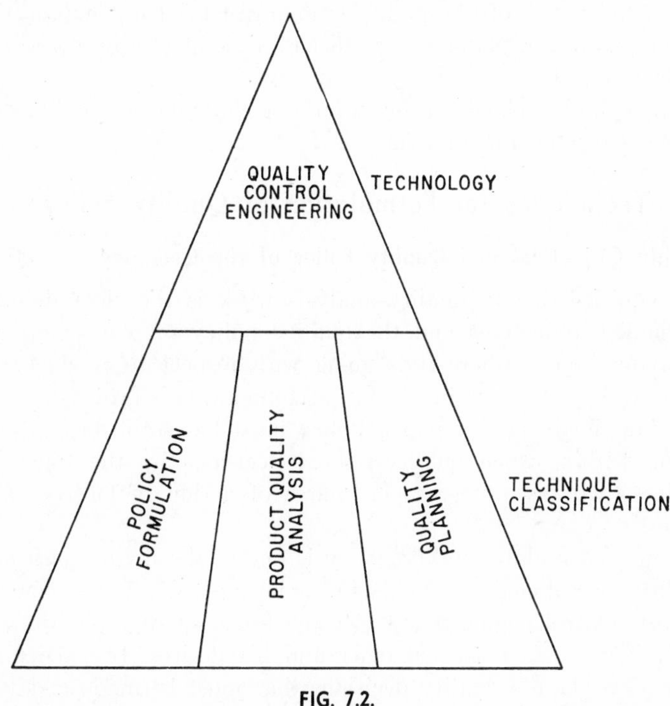

FIG. 7.2.

The entire range of techniques used in quality-control engineering technology may be grouped under three major headings:

I. Formulation of Quality Policy

Included here are techniques for identifying quality objectives of a particular company. Also included are techniques for developing guidelines that are related to the realization of these objectives and which serve as a foundation for quality analysis and planning. (Techniques used for quality policy formulation are discussed in Sec. 7.3.)

II. Product-quality Analysis

Techniques for analyzing include those for isolating and identifying all the factors that related to the quality of the product in its served market. These factors are then studied for their effects toward producing the desired quality result. (Techniques used for analyzing are discussed sequentially in Secs. 7.4 through 7.12.)

III. Quality Planning

Techniques for planning emphasize the development in advance of a proposed course of action and of methods for accomplishing the desired quality result. These are the techniques used for planning the procedures which, when taken together, comprise the documented elements of the quality system discussed in Chap. 6. (Techniques used for planning are discussed sequentially in Secs. 7.13 through 7.28.)

The three major classifications of the techniques of quality-control engineering are shown in Fig. 7.2.

Techniques for Formulation of Quality Policy

7.3 Quality Objectives and Quality Policy of the Company

A prerequisite to any quality-analysis work is the clear delineation of the quality objectives and the quality policy of a company. Until the company knows where it is going with respect to product-quality standards and product-quality levels, no foundation is provided on which to build functional quality plans. Policy must be established to provide the limits within which quality-related decisions by the functions of the business will assure a proper course of action in meeting quality objectives.

Helping to formulate quality policy is one of the major contributions the quality-control engineer makes to the business. To do this effectively, the quality-control engineer must see the broad quality picture, particularly as it relates to the customer and his desires. In particular, he must identify (1) the quality decisions that must be made and (2) the quality problems that must be solved. He can then (3) help in the specific documentation of the quality policy for the company.

Decision Identification. First, the integrated product plan for the business is charted step by step from inception of a product idea on through all the actions required to deliver the product to the customer and to service that product. All the quality-related decisions are identified at each step.

Then the limitations that have to be placed on each decision, in order to assure meeting the quality objectives of the business, are identified. These limitations provide the guidelines within which managers are free to make alternative decisions and take courses of action toward reaching quality objectives.

For example, when a particular product-design concept has been completed for a company by one of its design engineers, a decision must be made by the company whether or not to accept the concept as developed or to subject it to review. Individual cases, taken of and by themselves, may cause internal frictions incident to such a decision. If it has been established by policy that design reviews always are necessary to assure desired product quality, then the issue instead becomes just how the design review will be conducted.

Guidelines, in the form of supporting procedures, will delineate the components or individuals from the various functional organizations who will participate in the review. These procedures also will identify the criteria to be used in accepting the design concept.

This area of decision identification is one of the approaches required in formulating the elements of company quality policy. Another is through identification of quality problems.

Problem Identification. All the quality problems that have been encountered with the product under any circumstance, during development, in customer service, etc., are listed. The question is put in each case as to how the problem came to *be* a problem. Then the further question is posed: "What decision could have been made that would have prevented this from becoming a problem?" The required element of policy is then identified by putting the question "What policy is required to assure getting these 'right kinds' of decisions?"

For example, in a Western company, a consumer-product model was rushed to market to gain the advantage of an innovation in design. Insufficient time was scheduled to determine the reliability of the model. As a result, many quality complaints were received from the field. A policy element was subsequently established which required a 95 per cent reliability at an 80 per cent confidence level before future models in the product line could be released for market.

When the elements of policy have been established through use of the techniques in decision identification and problem identification, the third area of policy formulation—documentation—becomes active.

Policy Documentation. There are many different forms of presentation that can be used to document policy, depending upon the individual requirements of particular companies. Many of these forms in their fundamentals are equally effective in communicating written policy to the company managers. However, the majority include a basic format that covers the following points:

Policy title

Need for policy

Policy statement (this defines the basic quality interests that must be preserved for the company)

XYZ ELECTRONICS COMPANY

PRODUCT QUALITY POLICY

Need for Policy

To enhance the Company reputation, competitive position, and profitability, it is necessary to produce products of good quality. Meeting this objective requires a properly directed approach by all functions to the elements which concern product quality.

Statement of Policy

It is the policy of the XYZ Electronics Company to market only products of a quality that will merit and earn customer satisfaction by performing expected functions reliably and effectively in accordance with customer expectations, and which are discernibly better than competitive offerings. In support of this objective, the XYZ Electronics Company continuously strives to lead its product field in research and development, design, manufacture, and marketing of work related to its area of business responsibility.

Courses of Action

1. Selection of Business Opportunities

   This Company will not accept business which will compromise its product quality reputation. In this regard the customer's specifications will be reviewed to determine that they serve the common interests of the customer and the Company and to ensure that minimum quality standards can be met. When these conditions are not met, the Company will not submit a proposal. A comprehensive contract review will be carried out by all functional areas before a contract is signed in accordance with Company instructions.

2. Product Development and Design

   1) Only approved components and processes shall be used. In cases where new components and processes are needed to meet product requirements, adequate qualification tests or process capability measurements will be carried out prior to their use. Department instructions shall specify procedures for obtaining component and process approval.

FIG. 7.3.

Courses of action (these are the procedures that are followed for implementing the policy)

Responsibility and authority (this area defines the position assignments in the organization that have responsibility for enforcing the policy and for interpreting it)

Definition of terms (if needed)

To assure adherence to the quality policy and to provide for its proper implementation, the required step is a formal communication to the managers responsible for administering the functional work within the company. This is best accomplished by equipping each manager with a loose-leaf binder containing all elements of the quality policy. As issues become superseded, they can be replaced in the binder with new issues.

Figure 7.3 shows a representative section of a quality policy formulated by an Eastern electronics manufacturer.

Techniques for Product-quality Analysis

7.4 Approaches to Analysis

Before planning of the quality system is undertaken, not only should the objective and quality policy of the business be developed, but also the quality aspects of the product itself and those of the served market should be analyzed.

Analysis of all the quality factors bearing on the product defines the areas in which courses of action must be established to meet business objectives. After those needed have been identified, planning can then be undertaken to establish the methods and procedures for carrying out the courses of action.

A subsequent section, 7.13, will consider some of the general approaches to planning. This section will consider some of the general approaches to analyzing.

The act of analyzing involves breaking down a situation into all its elements and then synthesizing these elements back to the whole. In quality-control work there are many separate elements to any product-quality situation. Some examples are

1. Function to be performed by the product.
2. Environments encountered by the product.
3. Life or durability requirements.
4. Product design.
5. Manufacturing process.
6. Shipping conditions.
7. Installation.
8. Maintenance.
9. Characteristics of served market.

10. Competitive offerings.

Each of these items can be further analyzed. For example, item 4, product design, can be described in terms of each individual quality characteristic of the product, and even further analysis can be made by considering various aspects of these quality characteristics. They can be analyzed on the basis of their importance in supporting the principal functions of the product. They also can be analyzed by considering each quality characteristic with respect to its producibility, i.e., its ability to be manufactured easily and economically.

Sections 7.6 through 7.12 consider some representative examples of the specific analyzing techniques used in quality-control-engineering work. Section 7.5 presents these representative techniques in tabular form related to the purpose of the analysis.

7.5 Quality-control-engineering Analytical Techniques

Purpose of Analysis	*Technique*
To identify the needed quality	Delineation of Quality Requirements (Sec. 7.6)
To examine the proposed design	Designed Experiments (Sec. 7.7) Economic Partitioning of Tolerances (Sec. 7.7) Analysis of Prototype Tests (Sec. 7.7) Analysis of Environmental and End-use Effects (Sec. 7.8) Review of Designs Using Earlier Experience on Quality Aspects (Sec. 7.8)
To examine the effect of process and methods	Evaluation of Effects of New Methods, New Processes, and New Materials (Sec. 7.9) Adjustment of Product and Process for Compatibility (Sec. 7.10)
To study vendors	Vendor-facilities Evaluation (Sec. 7.11)
To evaluate the quality-cost balance	Quality-cost Optimization (Sec. 7.12) Simulation Technique (Sec. 7.12)

7.6 Delineation of Quality Requirements

A detailed delineation of quality requirements for each product, its parts, components, and subassemblies, is a necessary technique in the attainment of the desired quality in the finished product. This means that each quality characteristic of any significance must be specified with allowable tolerance limits.

For this to be done intelligently requires a thorough knowledge of the product and how each quality characteristic affects its function. The setting of the product specification is usually accomplished by the product-design engineer, who should be most knowledgeable with respect to the product parameters. The functions the customer expects from the product, the environments and conditions under which he uses it, the expected life and product reliability—all have a determining influence on the design parameters.

Quality requirements are applied in determining the precision and accuracy of manufacturing equipment employed for making the product. They are also used in determining required quality information equipment and quality-control procedures.

7.7 Designed Experiments

These provide the technique for selecting the best of several design approaches or the best of alternate manufacturing methods. The effects of significant factors at different quality levels or values are studied. Such analysis permits selecting the most favorable combination of quality levels for the significant factors. This type of analysis provides a sound basis for planning the design for the product and process. Designed experiments will be discussed more fully in Sec. 13.10.

Economic Partitioning of Tolerances. Where two or more dimensions are involved in a fit, it may be possible to take more tolerance on one member, provided the tolerance is tightened up on the other member or members. Economies may be possible by applying the technique of economic partitioning.

If certain conditions can be met, tolerances of individual parts can be increased without exceeding the total tolerance of the build-up. The certain conditions that must be met are discussed in Sec. 13.8. This section also shows how the tolerance on certain dimensions may be increased without causing an excessive build-up in the total tolerance.

Analysis of Prototype Tests. The building and testing of prototypes is a significant technique for analyzing product quality. During prototype testing, it is necessary carefully to log the history of the prototype as to the characteristics of materials along with any special operations or processes required to produce it. Such a log is applied for the analysis of differences in performance between handmade prototypes and tool-made products.

Prototype test results aid the subsequent quality planning. They indicate the characteristics that may offer difficulty from a quality-control standpoint. They also help to establish cause-and-effect relationships between process and product. Materials and components that represent extremes of tolerance can be represented in prototypes so their effects on function can be studied.

7.8 Analysis of Environmental and End-use Effects

A properly planned prototype-testing program should include tests which thoroughly represent the actual environments and end-use conditions which the product will "see." The same can be said of tests conducted on the first tool-made samples resulting from the pilot run. Chapter 14 discusses techniques of product reliability that are applicable here.

Such tests are operated over an extended period of time to simulate usage the product would experience during the early stages of its life. They show up "weak links in the chain"; i.e., they establish modes of failure.

When the weaknesses of the product are identified, they are corrected by changing the design or the method of manufacture so the customer will not experience premature product failure or breakdown.

Review of Designs Using Earlier Experience on Quality Aspects. Review of product designs is the technique of examination of product drawings and specifications in the light of past experience with similar products. The reviewers look for situations that can be recognized as having a potential for creating quality problems. Such an examination serves to eliminate situations that carry quality risks. Correction of the situation prevents the problem from arising when production starts.

A careful analysis is made by relating each quality characteristic to all other pertinent characteristics and applicable process to see if experience would indicate creation of quality problems. Later, pilot runs and tests of the product under end-use conditions may reveal problems where experience has been incomplete. Identified problems are assigned to the appropriate organizational component for corrective action.

7.9 Evaluation of Effects of New Methods, New Processes, and New Materials

Planned experiments involve techniques to evaluate the effects of new factors entering a process. Effects on ease of manufacture, product quality, and quality costs can be evaluated if it is possible to place numerical values on the causal factors and their effects. Some of the special statistical techniques discussed in Chap. 13 (such as Latin squares, factorial designs, regression analysis, and analysis of variance) can be used for this application. Involved experimental designs can be programmed on computers for savings in time and money.

This technique has its application in analyzing the effects of technical changes so that quality plans can be revised to accommodate such changes properly.

7.10 Adjustment of Product and Process for Compatibility

This technique provides the basis on which the design and the process can be brought into compatible relationship with each other without curtailing design function or requiring process capabilities beyond the limits of feasibility and cost.

When a design engineer starts the product design, there are certain functional objectives he is trying to meet with the product. He not only has to consider what is possible from a design standpoint within the limitations of delivery time and prices but also what is possible from a manufacturing point of view. Consequently, he collaborates with the manufacturing engineer early in the design cycle. In this manner, the design engineer hopes to design a product that will perform the functions the customer expects and, at the same time, design a product that can be built within the imposed limitations of time and cost.

Unfortunately, unforeseen difficulties may arise whereby the related manufacturing processes do not meet expectations with respect to precision or accuracy. Problems may arise with the product design itself in that it does not come up to the required performance. In either case, adjustments have to be made to bring about a compatible relationship among (1) product requirements, (2) the design, and (3) the manufacturing process.

In some cases, adjustments may have to be made in all three factors to obtain a feasible product. The technique of adjusting product and process to a compatible relationship has its application in what has come to be called *negotiating product feasibility*.

7.11 Vendor-facilities Evaluation

Before important orders are allocated to vendors, it is valuable to use the technique of vendor-facilities evaluation. This will determine probability of the vendor being able to deliver the required quality on schedule at the quoted price.

Such an evaluation takes into account the vendor's quality system, whether his past experience has included products similar to those being ordered, and the research and engineering skills and also manufacturing facilities available in the vendor's organization.

This technique has its application in the selection of vendors on the basis of their respective quality capabilities.

7.12 Quality-cost Optimization

Evaluation of the various segments of quality costs discussed in Chap. 5 permits balancing of preventive and appraisal costs against failure costs. The technique of quality-cost optimization involves the selection of a course of action that will result in a minimum total quality cost.

Use of such an analyzing technique helps to establish inspection points in the process that are strategic from an over-all quality-cost standpoint. For example, a circuit test to check accuracy of wiring may prove to be economical, particularly if a subsequent operation makes the wiring inaccessible, requiring an expensive dismantling operation. Such analysis influences the quality planning for the product.

Simulation Techniques. The technique of simulating a system or an organism involves operation of a model or simulator which is a representation of the system or organism. The model is amenable to manipulations which would be impossible, too expensive, or impracticable to perform on the entity it portrays. The operation of the model can be studied, and from it properties of the behavior of the actual system or organism are inferred.

Today, such simulation can be accomplished in quality control. For example, a mathematical model may be built to represent the inspection system for the product. Manipulation of the model, possibly through use of a computer, with various per cent defectives, originating at different processes, and use of various inspection stations can predetermine the location of inspection stations that give the greatest over-all economy.

For a further example, the entire area of physical model building of the product is significant. Environmental tests are used to simulate the end-use conditions under which the product is required to operate. Rather than, for example, use costly test flights to check out aircraft instruments, they are subjected to vibration, temperatures, and pressures equivalent to those encountered in flight.

Techniques Used in Planning

7.13 Approaches to Planning

The act of planning is thinking out in advance the sequence of actions to accomplish a proposed course of action in doing work to accomplish certain objectives. In order that the planner may communicate his plan to the person or persons expected to execute it, the plan is written out with necessary diagrams, formulas, tables, etc.

Planning in the field of quality control must, of course, fundamentally be geared for delivering satisfactory product quality to the customer at minimum quality cost. These objectives are realized only by carefully planning many individual procedures which relate properly to each other and make up the documented elements of the quality system, as discussed in Chap. 6.

Many different pieces of work must be performed, by many people, and in a certain time-phased sequence. Different techniques are used in accomplishing the work. Therefore, the development of a quality-control plan is based on using the results of the techniques of analysis progressively to answer the following questions:

1. What specific elements of quality work need to be done?
2. When, during the product development cycle, does each element of work need to be done?
3. How is it to be done: by what method, procedure, or device?
4. Who does it: what position in what organizational component?
5. Where is it to be done: at what location in the plant, on the assembly line, in the laboratory, by the vendor, or in the field?
6. What tools or equipment are to be used?
7. What are the inputs to the work? What is needed in the way of information and material inputs to get the work accomplished?
8. What are the outputs? Do any decisions have to be made? What are they and what criteria should be used for making them? Does any material have to be identified and routed?
9. Is any record of the action to be made? If so, what is the form of the data? What kind of analysis is required? To whom is it sent? What form of feedback is to be used?
10. Are there alternative courses of action to be taken, depending on certain differences in the product quality encountered?
11. What are the criteria for these courses of action?
12. Is any time limit imposed on the work? If so, what is it?

Many more questions are developed as the planning assumes a finer degree of detail.

The final output of the planning process is the set of detailed procedures necessary to carry out the prescribed courses of action in meeting the quality objectives of the business and in carrying out the established quality policy. Fundamental elements of a portion of such a quality-system plan, which require documentation applying to the incoming-material control job of quality control, are shown in Fig. 7.4. Figure 7.5 shows a page of an instruction covering one of these elements within this particular system plan, giving the detailed procedure for sampling and testing one type of purchased material, namely, fuel oil.

Sections 7.15 through 7.28 consider some representative examples of planning techniques used to establish the quality-system plan for a company.

Section 7.14 presents the techniques of planning in tabular form related to the purpose of the plan.

Materials

1. Incoming-material-control Procedures
   a. Sampling plans
   b. Instructions
   c. Data recording
   d. Reporting
2. Vendor Relationships
   a. Delineation of quality requirements to vendors, including classification of quality characteristics and acceptable quality levels
   b. Correlation of measurement methods
   c. Vendor quality capability, facilities, and quality systems surveys and evaluations
   d. Incoming-material rating
   e. Feedback of quality information to vendors
   f. Corrective action and follow-up
   g. Servicing to assure scheduled quality output
   h. Certification of incoming material
   i. Interpretations
3. Incoming-material-control Measuring Devices
   a. Specification (method, accuracy, precision, capacity, service connections, floor space, etc.)
   b. Maintenance
   c. Calibration
   d. Periodic correlation with vendor's devices
4. Laboratory Acceptance Testing
   a. Test specifications
   b. Samples for laboratory
   c. Request for tests
   d. Laboratory results reporting
5. Material Disposition
   a. Identification
   b. Requests for deviation
   c. Routing (scrap, rework, salvage, return to vendor, detail inspection, etc.)
6. Incoming-material Audit
7. Incoming-material Quality-control Personnel Requirements
   a. Number
   b. Qualifications
   c. Special training

FIG. 7.4. Quality-system plan outline, incoming material.

QUALITY INSTRUCTION

COMPANY R

Subject: Fuels, and Oils, including Process Chemicals

IV. SAMPLING JET FUELS AND LUBRICANTS

A. Fuels and lubricants are subject to 120-day sampling by ABC Laboratory.

B. Receiving Inspection will maintain a complete file of records and will be responsible for the schedule of sampling and the preparation and delivery of the samples to the Plant Laboratory.

C. Samples will be processed in accordance with requirements of military fuel specifications.

1. All samples will be analyzed by the Plant Laboratory and the composite report of both ABC and Plant Laboratory findings will be reported to the Receiving section submitting the samples.

V. SAMPLING ON 90-DAY BASIS

A. It is the option of the Quality Supervisor of each section in the Company to require 90-day sampling for the purpose of maintaining a control check on incoming quality of materials.

B. It is the responsibility of the Receiving section to set up the necessary record control for such sampling program.

C. The Plant Laboratory will perform the analysis and furnish a report to the Receiving section submitting materials under a 90-day quality control program.

VI. PROCESS CHEMICALS

A. Process chemicals shall be ordered and received in the same manner as fuels described in paragraph II.

B. It shall be the responsibility of each Operating Section to issue and to conform to detailed instructions providing the necessary control of these materials.

C. Sampling shall be performed at the option of the Quality Supervisor of each Operating Department, analysis to be performed by the Plant Laboratory on request.

APPROVED: John Smith
Manager—Quality Control
Company R

DATE: March 10, 1961

March 12, 1961

Date Issued	Superseded Issue	Dated	Page	No.

FIG. 7.5.

7.14 Quality-control-engineering Planning Techniques

Purpose of Planning	*Technique*
To establish acceptance criteria	Classification of Characteristics (Sec. 7.15) Acceptance Sampling (Sec. 7.16)
To provide acceptance procedure and an acceptance facility	Determination of Quality Measurements to Be Made (Sec. 7.17) Determination of Quality-measuring Equipment Requirements (Sec. 7.18) Quality Personnel Requirements (Sec. 7.18)
To document the plan	Documentation of Quality Planning (Sec. 7.19) Review of Technical Instructions, Procedures, and Manuals (Sec. 7.19)
To communicate and work with vendors	Making Quality Requirements Understood by Vendors (Sec. 7.20) Servicing of Vendors (Sec. 7.21) Material Certification Plans (Sec. 7.22)
To establish quality information	Quality Information Feedback (Sec. 7.23) Data Processing and Use of Computers (Sec. 7.24) Communicating with Other Functions (Sec. 7.25) Feedback of Information from the Field (Sec. 7.26)
To assure continuing customer satisfaction	Quality Control in the Field (Sec. 7.27) Renewal-parts Quality Control (Sec. 7.27)
To promote quality to the customer	Promotion of Quality to the Customer (Sec. 7.28)

7.15 Classification of Characteristics

This technique involves the classification of the numerous quality characteristics of a product, such as dimensions, speed, hardness, and weight, according to their relative importance in contributing to the quality of the product. Such classification affords a valuable tool for weighing the relative importance of these characteristics.

For example, a fourfold classification frequently used is that of critical, major, minor, and incidental:

• A *critical* characteristic is one which threatens loss of life or property or makes the product nonfunctional if it was outside prescribed limits.

- A *major* characteristic is one which makes the product fail to accomplish its intended function if outside prescribed limits.
- A *minor* characteristic is one which makes the product fall short of its intended function if outside prescribed limits.
- An *incidental* characteristic is one such as a small scratch on a painted surface.

Such classification of characteristics enables the quality effort to be directed to the matters of greatest importance, thereby assuring required quality and continuous production at minimum quality cost.

Classification of characteristics also permits selection of sampling plans with producer and consumer risks limited according to the critical nature of the characteristic. For a quality characteristic classified as critical, for example, it is likely that any risk involving acceptance of nonconforming products is undesirable. In such a case, no sampling could be permitted; i.e., 100 per cent inspection would have to be used to assure that every item in a lot conformed to specification.

If, on the other hand, a certain quality characteristic were classified as minor, a sampling plan might be chosen that would permit acceptance of several per cent of the items slightly outside of specified acceptance limits.

The technique of classifying characteristics has application in quality planning. The degree of inspection commensurate with the importance of the quality characteristic is applied.

7.16 Acceptance Sampling

If the vendor is producing to the required quality level, it should be unnecessary to inspect or test the purchased product 100 per cent. Selection of a statistically determined sample from the lot provides a valuable technique for accepting or rejecting the lot on the basis of a maximum permissible number of defects found in the sample.

The purchaser can thereby protect himself against very poor lots with considerable economy of inspection. Unacceptable lots are generally returned to the vendor for sorting. Chapter 12 reviews the tables available to give various acceptance quality levels (AQLs) at given producer and consumer risks.

There is a wide selection of sampling plans to cover almost any situation that might arise in practice. Basic to the selection of a sampling plan is a decision with respect to the quality level that the inspected material must adhere to, *on the average*, if it is to be accepted. Following this decision is the subsequent choice of single, double, or multiple sampling plans. Then the decision must be made as to the type of measurement taken, i.e., attribute (go and not-go) or variable (continuous scale). Sample size and acceptance number are given by the plan chosen.

This type of sampling finds application over a wide range: acceptance of materials or parts or components or assemblies.

7.17 Determination of Quality Measurements to Be Made

The technique of reviewing product function, design, and manufacturing process leads to the determination of which quality characteristics should be measured.

DRAWING No.	PT or GR.	Oper	Rev.	Issued By	METHOD SPECIFICATIONS — REMARKS
101R233	9/10 / 1	X 6	3	J. SISKA	
MAT'L DATA				Date 3/14/60	
				Sheet 6	
				of 9	
				Work Station ZA35	

#	SEQUENCE DESCRIPTION	Surf. #	MEASURING EQUIPMENT	TOOLS FIXTURES	# Cuts	HD. Pass	MAX. DEPTH	FEED	SPEED	LG. of CUT	Handling	Machining	% TOOL MAINT.
52	CHMF HOOKS	11	"	"	2	R	–	.008	6.7	1/16"			
53	CHMF HOOKS	12	"	"	2	R	–	.008	6.7	1/16"			
54	CHMF HOOKS	13	"	"	2	R	–	.008	6.7	1/16"			
55	CHMF HOOKS	14	"	"	2	R	–	.008	6.7	1/16"			
56	CHMF HOOKS	15	"	"	2	R	–	.008	6.7	1/16"			
57	FORM RAD. VIEM "M"	16	TEMP 101R233-11A	165-108-1	1	R	–	.010	9.6	3/8"			
58	TURN PC. OVER, JAWS, STRAPS, IND. TO ALIGN												
59	FIN. FC. (29.718/29.708 PLUS .26/.24)	1	STRAIGHT EDGE INSIDE MIKE	H.S.S.	1	R	.060	.015	8.2	3/4"			
60	FIN. FC.-RECORD DIM. AT (3) PLACES 120° APART (1)____ (2)____ (3)____ OPER.____	2	"	"	1	R	.060	.010	9.6	4 1/4"			
61	FIN. BO. RECORD DIA.____ F.I.R. RUNOUT____ OPER.____	3	VERNIER CALIPER	"	2	R	–	.008	9.6	5/16"			

FIG. 7.6. Process sheet.

• This technique includes considering and deciding upon the methods used for taking the measurement.

• It also includes determining the point in the process flow where the measurement should be taken.

• It further includes the decision as to the extent of measurement; i.e., every article or a sample from the product flow.

• It also establishes the mechanism for taking the measurement.

• In some cases, the operator may be the only person who should make the measurement. In other cases, the product might pass through an inspection or test station, where inspectors or testers would make further measurements. Or such measurements might be made by automatic quality-control equipment and the data automatically processed and used for adjustment of the process.

The purpose served by use of this planning technique is to establish the economic balance between the cost of taking quality measurements and the value of quality control and product acceptance.

Process sheets or flow charts, which show each step in the process, are used as basic working documents. The significant quality characteristics generated at each step are identified, and strategic inspection points are selected on the basis of the process sequence.

Figure 7.6 shows a process sheet with inspection points noted at certain specific operations by means of circling.

7.18 Determination of Quality-measuring Equipment Requirements

Specifications usually attempt to identify the product in terms of measurable characteristics of the end product. When the end-result specifications cannot be written, the technique of specifying measurable characteristics of the process is used as test-methods specifications. In order that the product function can be assured, these require that certain tests be run regularly to evaluate process characteristics. With the aid of these test specifications, together with an analysis of the product function, the product design, and the manufacturing process, detailed test procedures can be planned. They describe test methods, test equipment, test sequence, and test frequency.

After the methods used for taking the measurements are decided, the equipment to implement the measurement must be developed, designed, built, or procured. Its specification must take into consideration: floor space and power requirements, capacity, accuracy, precision, and safety. Chapter 9 discusses application of this technique.

Quality Personnel Requirements. Upon completion of the inspection plan, including inspection-equipment requirements, the number of persons required to implement the plan is determined. Not only must the total number of persons required be determined, but the number in each classification must be established, according to training and experience.

7.19 Documentation of Quality Planning

Detailed quality procedures and instructions must be documented so that all quality-assurance activities are clearly identified. This is essential to communicate the quality plan to the many positions in a plant that have responsibility for implementing various parts of the plan. The necessary types of communication include use of reports, the procedures

MACHINE ROOM INSPECTION

PUNCHED PARTS – DIES

In addition to the usual procedure of inspection certain additional measurements and recording of dimensions will be made. This added procedure will require the assistance of the Machine Room foreman and operator. The procedure will be as follows:

1) The usual setup and in-process spot checking by the inspector will continue.
2) In addition, 4 times during the production run, or once each hour, whichever yields the most samples, the operator will select three parts, tag them, respectively, sample lot 1,2,3, etc.
3) These samples will be turned over to the Machine Room inspector, who will measure them immediately if possible, or at the earliest convenient time within the shift period. Measurements will be recorded on the appropriate card currently used. The job will run regardless of whether these samples can be measured immediately. If such measurements can be made with simple measuring tools, such as scale, calipers, or micrometers, it is expected that the operators will make them merely as a control to determine that parts are within tolerance, so that defective parts will not continue to be made.
4) If the inspector finds that dimensions are in error either before or after the job is completed, the tool will be tagged defective until such time as an investigation can be made to determine whether die, operator, or procedure error is the cause. The tool must not be returned to the tool crib until measurements of samples are completed and disposition is given by the inspector. If the die is rejected, it will be properly tagged and forwarded to the tool room. Appropriate remarks will be made on the inspection record card.
5) After each run is completed, assuming the die is still acceptable, an average of the dimensions measured ($\bar{X}$) will be plotted on the Quality Control Chart Data sheet. Control limits for the dimensions measured serve as the upper and lower control limits. This plot will serve two purposes:
   A) A record of inspection of $\bar{X}$ plots.
   B) An indication as to: (1) when die is approaching need for repair; (2) normal variation of die; (3) accuracy of setup; and (4) effectiveness of control by operator.

W. E. John
SUPERVISOR – QUALITY CONTROL

FIG. 7.7.

for the calibration of measuring equipment, the routing and disposition of material, the form of quality audits, and the necessary inspections and tests.

It is often advantageous to establish a loose-leaf binder in which this information can be kept. A separate page should be used to cover the inspection or test instruction for a particular inspection and test device. These can be coded and indexed for quick reference. Should any change in procedure be necessary, only one instruction sheet need be replaced in the binder.

An example of an instruction is shown in Fig. 7.7.

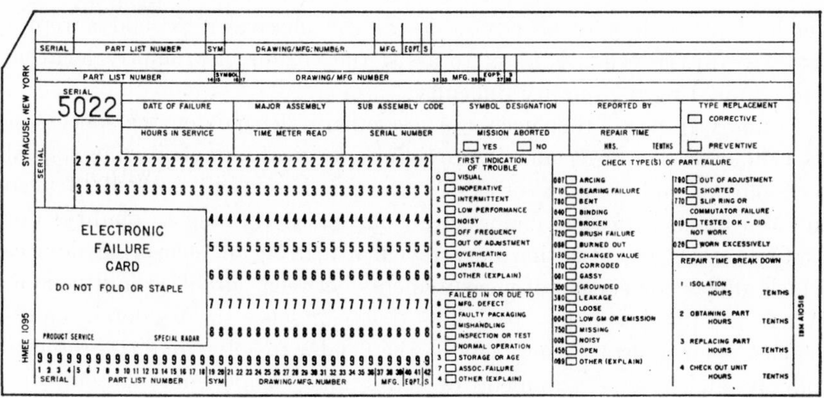

SYRACUSE, NEW YORK
SERIAL | PART LIST NUMBER | SYM | DRAWING/MFG. NUMBER | MFG. | EQPT. | S
PART LIST NUMBER | SYMBOL | DRAWING/MFG NUMBER | MFG. | EQPT. | S
SERIAL 5022
DATE OF FAILURE | MAJOR ASSEMBLY | SUB ASSEMBLY CODE | SYMBOL DESIGNATION | REPORTED BY | TYPE REPLACEMENT ☐ CORRECTIVE ☐ PREVENTIVE
HOURS IN SERVICE | TIME METER READ | SERIAL NUMBER | MISSION ABORTED ☐ YES ☐ NO | REPAIR TIME HRS. TENTHS
ELECTRONIC FAILURE CARD
DO NOT FOLD OR STAPLE
PRODUCT SERVICE SPECIAL RADAR
HMEE 1095

FIRST INDICATION OF TROUBLE
0 ☐ VISUAL
1 ☐ INOPERATIVE
2 ☐ INTERMITTENT
3 ☐ LOW PERFORMANCE
4 ☐ NOISY
5 ☐ OFF FREQUENCY
6 ☐ OUT OF ADJUSTMENT
7 ☐ OVERHEATING
8 ☐ UNSTABLE
9 ☐ OTHER (EXPLAIN)

FAILED IN OR DUE TO
8 ☐ MFG. DEFECT
2 ☐ FAULTY PACKAGING
5 ☐ MISHANDLING
6 ☐ INSPECTION OR TEST
1 ☐ NORMAL OPERATION
3 ☐ STORAGE OR AGE
7 ☐ ASSOC. FAILURE
4 ☐ OTHER (EXPLAIN)

CHECK TYPE(S) OF PART FAILURE
007 ☐ ARCING
710 ☐ BEARING FAILURE
780 ☐ BENT
040 ☐ BINDING
070 ☐ BROKEN
720 ☐ BRUSH FAILURE
080 ☐ BURNED OUT
130 ☐ CHANGED VALUE
170 ☐ CORRODED
001 ☐ GASSY
300 ☐ GROUNDED
380 ☐ LEAKAGE
730 ☐ LOOSE
004 ☐ LOW GM OR EMISSION
750 ☐ MISSING
008 ☐ NOISY
450 ☐ OPEN
099 ☐ OTHER (EXPLAIN)
790 ☐ OUT OF ADJUSTMENT
006 ☐ SHORTED
770 ☐ SLIP RING OR COMMUTATOR FAILURE
018 ☐ TESTED OK - DID NOT WORK
020 ☐ WORN EXCESSIVELY

REPAIR TIME BREAK DOWN
1 ISOLATION HOURS TENTHS
2 OBTAINING PART HOURS TENTHS
3 REPLACING PART HOURS TENTHS
4 CHECK OUT UNIT HOURS TENTHS
IBM A10518

FIG. 7.8. Field failure report card.

Review of Technical Instructions, Procedures, and Manuals. In this area, manuals are reviewed and issued to cover installation, adjustment, testing, repair, maintenance, and user application of the product. Suggestions are also made on the basis of product and process knowledge that will assure customer satisfaction with minimum complaint and service cost.

7.20 Making Quality Requirements Understood by Vendors

At the time a vendor is asked to prepare a quotation for material, parts, or components, the technique of clearly delineating quality requirements to him should be exercised. He should be provided with a formal package which includes a classification of the quality characteristics so that he knows what is of critical, major, minor, and incidental importance. The package should include the criteria by which his product will be accepted or rejected, i.e., the inspection plan that will be used and the maximum percentage of defects, if any, that is permissible.

Such communication to the vendor is essential in directing his resources so that critical quality characteristics will be given the needed attention. In this way, the highest degree of conformance can be obtained without adding excessive costs to materials, parts, and components.

7.21 Servicing of Vendors

The technique of providing technical service to vendors upon request safeguards the scheduled flow of purchased material.

Initially, vendors should be advised of any unsatisfactory trends in the products they ship the company, so that they will be able to adjust their processes before they get into trouble. If scheduled delivery of acceptable material is threatened because of quality problems in the vendor's plant, it may be advisable for the purchaser to send a representative to the vendor's plant to assist the vendor in promptly locating and eliminating the quality difficulty.

In many respects, the success of a company depends on the success of its vendors. Where a vendor is providing a critical part, requiring special technologies and complex processes, the purchaser will do well to keep in close touch with the vendor on all matters pertaining to quality. For example, joint investigation may reveal a drifting of measuring devices which affects correlation of measurements between purchaser and vendor. Where the purchaser has specialists that can serve the vendor in emergencies, their assistance may enable the vendor to solve quality problems quickly and resume shipment of parts and components without disrupting schedules.

7.22 Material-certification Plans

Material certification is a technique for establishing a set of procedures whereby the vendor furnishes the purchaser inspection data and test results as objective evidence that a particular lot of material or parts meets its quality requirements.

Today, certification plans are being used to stop the uneconomic procedure of double inspection; i.e., inspection by the vendor before shipment and inspection by the purchaser upon receipt of the purchased material. Often the purchaser waives inspection if the vendor provides objective data showing that quality requirements have been met.

Such data are included along with the shipping papers accompanying the material or are mailed in advance of shipping. Agreement is reached between purchaser and vendor as to the quality characteristics to be measured and the amount of data required. Since much of the required data are already available from the vendor's quality-control system, usually no increase in price results from including certification as a service. In fact, better planning, brought about by certification, often reduces quality costs, thereby enabling negotiation of cost improvement with the vendor.

An audit of quality is made periodically on received lots to maintain correlation between vendor's and purchaser's measurements.

7.23 Quality Information Feedback

One of the important planning techniques of quality-control engineering is *quality information feedback*. As described in Chap. 6, the quality system is the network of quality-related administrative and technical procedures in a business. The *quality information system* is the communications network that links together the various components of this quality system. Quality information contained in inspection and test reports, customer complaint reports, and accounting reports is the "intelligence" of the quality system.

This quality information system can be looked upon as similar to a telephone system whereby communication is established between a position generating information and another receiving and using information. It provides the actual, physical information feedback loop which was discussed in concept in Sec. 4.5. Through this loop, the specific quality results are measured, analyzed, and then fed back for use in replanning. Quality information provides the factual basis on which quality decisions can be made and action taken.

In planning this information system, the following kinds of questions must be answered:

- What kinds of information are essential?
- How much information is needed?
- To what positions should information be sent? Flow charts are used as a tool in obtaining answers to this question.
- How frequently should the information be sent?
- How fast must it be received to be effective?
- In what form should it be presented to be immediately usable to serve as a basis for decision and action?

The effectiveness of the quality information system that is planned in terms of the answers to these questions should, in turn, be measured periodically to assure that it remains efficient. Such measurements must determine that

- Paper work is kept to a minimum.
- Only usable data are being transmitted.
- Data are going to positions whose responsibilities call for its use.
- Data are adequate and are being properly applied.
- The information system is being adequately maintained.
- The information is producing effective and timely decisions for corrective action.

7.24 Data Processing and Use of Computers

Use of modern data-processing equipment and computers is a technique that greatly speeds up flow in the quality information system. Procedures for quality data collection, tabulation, analysis, and distribution are the important work required to make this equipment usable. Careful planning is also necessary to prevent excessive data-processing costs and yet prevent losses due to lack of quality information.

Besides the economies afforded by trimming down to essentials, modern data-processing equipment offers many other advantages, particularly in large systems. Complaint reporting by field engineers can be reduced to mailing in special cards marked as to type of complaint along with other pertinent data. These "mark-sensed cards" are easily converted for automatic sorting and tabulation. Such a system can also be used as a means for maintaining spare-parts inventories where the original punched cards automatically make out the requisition for replacements.

Similar systems can be used for controlling the quality of incoming materials by reporting on discrepant lots. The system produces all the necessary information to measure quality, rate vendors, analyze costs, and measure the work load and flow of material through incoming inspection.

For in-process control, inspection and test data can be reduced to punched cards for recording quality information such as type of defect, area of occurrence, responsibility for defects, number inspected, number defective, and disposition.

Savings in clerical help is but one of the benefits of automatic data processing. Effectiveness of quality information is increased by the promptness of the report. Time lags that discourage prompt corrective action are eliminated. Trouble spots are immediately brought to the attention of those who can do something about it. Good reporting formats indicate responsibility for action, type of action, and follow-up with a measure of the effectiveness of the action.

7.25 Communication with Other Functions

Establishing a systematic exchange of information among Quality Control, Marketing, and Product Engineering is an effective technique for establishing up-to-the-minute, customer-oriented quality goals.

Specifically, the flow of information includes data on the effect that marketing schedules will have on product quality and quality cost. It includes news on any special tools and techniques that prove valuable in service work.

Progress reports on corrective action being taken to eliminate quality problems can also help sales people to hold customer confidence. Finally, short training programs on the key benefits of a department's quality-control program prove helpful to sales personnel and distributors, especially in a very competitive product line.

7.26 Feedback of Information from the Field

The field organization has an important responsibility in feeding back information to the factory. Such flow provides a further information technique for obtaining action in improving product quality.

Any design features that cause difficulty in servicing need to be made known. Actual product performance data are necessary, along with supplementary data concerning conditions under which the performance data were taken.

Field failure data and customer complaints should be sufficiently detailed to provide a means for analyzing the causes, so that proper corrective action can be applied. Report formats can be designed to make it easy for repairmen to note the cause of the malfunction of a product. Figure 7.8 on page 143 shows such a form.

7.27 Quality Control in the Field

The technique of establishing quality standards in the field and controlling service work to these standards results in maintenance of satisfactory service in the field. The product-service component of the company can establish controls on the quality it generates in the field as a result of servicing the product. Such quality is as important as that of the original product, since the customer expects equivalent quality when he finds it necessary to call for service.

To make this result possible quality standards are established on service work. Means for auditing the work are provided to assure that the standards are being met. Training programs are established for service personnel to provide the skills necessary in meeting these quality standards.

A further technique of quality control in the field is the periodic audit of finished-goods inventory in the warehouse. Stock is reviewed for improper identification and for damage, deterioration, and obsolescence.

Renewal-parts Quality Control. Renewal parts should have a quality level at least as high as, or higher than, that found in the original equipment. The customer may forgive the manufacturer once if the original part fails, but he is slow to forgive a second failure. The planning of quality-control work related to renewal parts is, therefore, an important technique.

One of the major needs for this technique is when material is shipped directly from the vendor to the customer, since difficulty of control is

The Metallurgical Test Laboratory

Deviations in particle size and distribution affect such characteristics as wear resistance and hardness of carbides. So the Metallurgical Test Laboratory checks more than 250 samples a day to insure constant quality.

Special equipment magnifies particles 3000 times; then enough particles are *counted* to plot a distribution curve. Other equipment measures particle diameter on an empirical basis.

The Laboratory also maintains comprehensive files, having access to data on materials made as long as ten years ago.

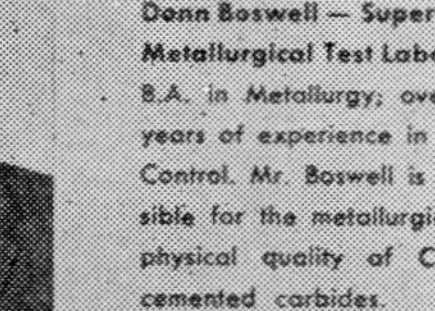

Donn Boswell — Supervisor of Metallurgical Test Laboratory. B.A. in Metallurgy; over eight years of experience in Quality Control. Mr. Boswell is responsible for the metallurgical and physical quality of Carboloy cemented carbides.

Metallograph. Basic research instrument for making microscopic examinations of a carbide's structure and porosity. Used at magnifications up to 1500 X. Camera attachment provides permanent record of each sample's microstructure.

Transverse Rupture Tester. Gives a measure of the basic strength of the material, which is one of the indications of its purity and homogeneity. This machine has a capacity of 20,000 pounds, and is also used to check braze strength of tools.

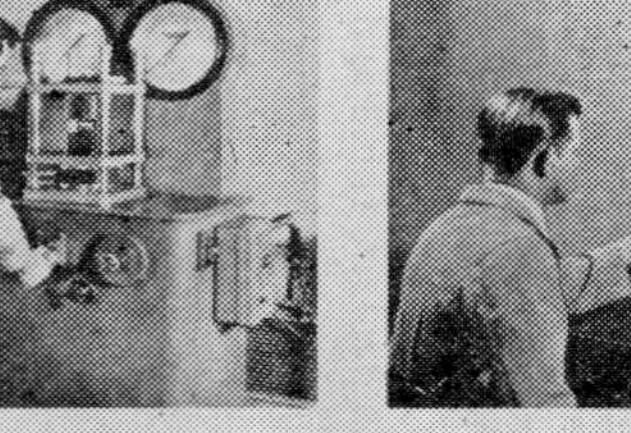

Fisher Sub-Sieve Sizer. Measures average particle size of powders below sieve range (44 microns). Has a range from .2 microns to 50 microns, an accuracy of ±2%. Supplements microscopic and photo-electric particle measurement equipment.

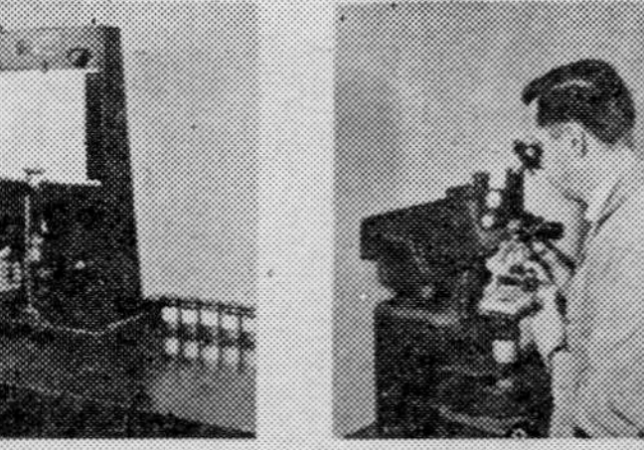

Knoop Hardness Tester. This micro-hardness tester can actually measure the hardness of individual crystals as small as 20 microns. In the background is the Rockwell Hardness Tester used for normal production work.

FIG. 7.9. Sample page from sales brochure using the quality system as a sales mover.

greatly increased; however, procedures must be established that assure compatibility with the original product supplied and the quality of the part. These may include procedures for purging part stocks to eliminate undesirable or obsolete items.

Application of this technique provides a continuing product function to the customer.

7.28 Promotion of Quality to the Customer

The technique of communicating product-quality values to the customer is important in sales work. The system by which a business maintains quality has special significance and may be of great interest to the customer. It assures him that every precaution has been taken to provide him with a product that measures up in every way to its advertised features. Even more to the point on industrial products, quality levels can be certified. This enables the customer to relax his incoming inspection system with confidence.

This type of information is an effective sales mover. It may appear in many forms, such as institutional advertising, brochures, packages, and instructions. Figure 7.9 shows a page from a brochure used to communicate the quality story to the customer.

CHAPTER 8

PROCESS-CONTROL ENGINEERING TECHNOLOGY

We are all rightfully impressed by the flood of worthwhile new devices that modern product technology has provided us. The ingenuity of their design and the intricacy of their function is striking.

An equally striking story, however, is represented in the technological developments behind the manufacturing processes which make these products possible. There has been an almost phenomenal growth in new methods for compounding, molding, cutting, and shaping parts. Many new alloys and materials are being handled in the manufacturing plants of today that were not known a relatively few months ago. These processes not only operate at faster rates of speed, but the greater demands placed on them have tended to make them more complex.

These developments have not been confined to new processes alone. Much greater precision has been developed in the more traditional production equipments. Thus, high-speed, complex, precision processes in drilling, milling, and boring have required closer control; in many cases, automatic control. Older methods, which employed an operator making manual adjustments, are no longer fast enough or precise enough to be applied to modern processing.

The *control* of processes today assumes significantly new importance, not only because it helps these modern processes work more efficiently, but also because many of them are simply not economically practical without satisfactory process control. If a high-speed, complex process goes out of control, major losses in terms of worthless product can mount up with terrifying speed. Even if the product has deviated only slightly from its specification, its later use in complex end assemblies may represent a high risk due to ultimate expensive tear-down operations to replace it.

After the quality-system plan is established through use of quality-control engineering techniques, therefore, implementation within the framework of the plan requires an intensive program of process measurement and analysis applied directly to incoming material, on the shop floor, and in the field. Further, rapid feedback of the resulting analysis is required to maintain control of quality throughout all the production processes. The technology of process-control engineering provides the quality-control tools for accomplishing this work.

8.1 Process-control Engineering Technology[1]

Process-control engineering technology may be defined as

the body of technical knowledge for analysis and control of process quality, including direct control of the quality of materials, parts, components, and assemblies as they are processed throughout the entire industrial cycle.

There are many techniques employed by this technology. They may be grouped under four major headings:

I. Process-quality Analysis

Included here are techniques for analyzing the measurements that have been planned by quality-control engineering technique. These measurements describe the behavior of the process while it is operating, so that there will be sensitive and rapid means for predicting process trends. (Techniques used in process analysis are discussed in Secs. 8.2 through 8.11.)

II. In-process Control

Included here are techniques for applying results of the process analysis actually to adjust process parameters and environments in order to keep the process in a state of control. (Techniques used for in-process control are discussed in Secs. 8.12 through 8.16.)

III. Implementation of the Quality Plan

Involved here are techniques for adjusting and revising elements of the quality-system plan to take into account the dynamic changes of the day-by-day production situation. (Techniques for implementing the quality plan are discussed in Secs. 8.17 through 8.22.)

IV. Quality-effectiveness Audit

[1] Several of the process control engineering techniques discussed here have been developed by the following individuals: W. W. Spencer, L. N. Bress, T. P. Howley, E. F. LaChance, A. W. Meyers, T. E. Schultz, W. P. Sime, and D. D. Ward.

Included here are techniques for performing the constant monitoring that has been planned by quality-control engineering technique. The monitoring covers product and process as well as the attendant costs to assure that the planned quality results are achieved. (Techniques for quality-effectiveness audit are discussed in Secs. 8.23 through 8.26.)

In the final analysis, these process-control engineering techniques are directed toward providing immediate quality information to the operator so he *can* make parts right the first time and knows that he has. To do this, however, requires that the necessary quality information equipment be provided for the operator. As this is done and as this method of operation becomes effective in the shop, the inspectors can then back away from routine sorting in favor of more positive activity. Instead of operating as policemen of manufacturing processes, Inspection and Test can become true parts of the process-control subfunction of Quality Control, as discussed in Chap. 4. These types of process control men can provide positive assistance in the *production* of the right quality

- By becoming auditors of the good quality practices that have been pre-planned.
- By providing as much as possible on-the-spot, shop-floor analysis of defects.
- By feeding back facts about these defects for corrective action.
- By beginning truly to understand process behavior as the basis for process analysis and control.

Techniques Used in Process Analysis

8.2 Process-control-engineering Analytical Techniques

Among the significant techniques associated with process analysis, 12 will be reviewed as representative. They are covered as follows:

Purpose of Analysis	*Technique*
To determine capability	Machine- and Process-capability Analysis (Sec. 8.3)
	Quality-measuring Equipment Capability and Repeatability Analysis (Sec. 8.4)
To determine degree of conformity to planned values	Analysis of Pilot-run Results (Sec. 8.5)
	Incoming-material Testing, Inspection, and Laboratory Analysis (Sec. 8.6)
	Quality-assurance Inspection (Sec. 8.7)
	Production Testing (Sec. 8.8)
	Sorting Inspection (Sec. 8.8)

Purpose of Analysis	*Technique*
To determine source of variation	Process Variation Analysis (Sec. 8.9) Analysis of Variable Quality-cost Performance (Sec. 8.9)
To identify causes of nonconformance	Test-data Analysis (Sec. 8.10) Scrap and Rework Analysis (Sec. 8.10) Field Complaint Analysis (Sec. 8.11)

8.3 Machine- and Process-capability Analysis

Use of this technique permits the prediction of the limits of variation within which a machine or process will operate. Hence it provides a means for measuring the machine and process capability and comparing this against the tolerance required by the specification.

Every machine and every process has inherent variability. For example, if a lathe is set up to turn shafts to an outer diameter of 1.000 inch, it is known that all the shafts produced will not be exactly 1.000 inch. The majority will be near this value, but there may be a few per cent that are as low as 0.998 or as high as 1.002 inches (Fig. 8.1). As will be discussed in more detail in Chap. 10, each machine has a natural pattern of variability; machine- and process-capability analyses establish this pattern on the basis of actual measurements taken under controlled conditions.

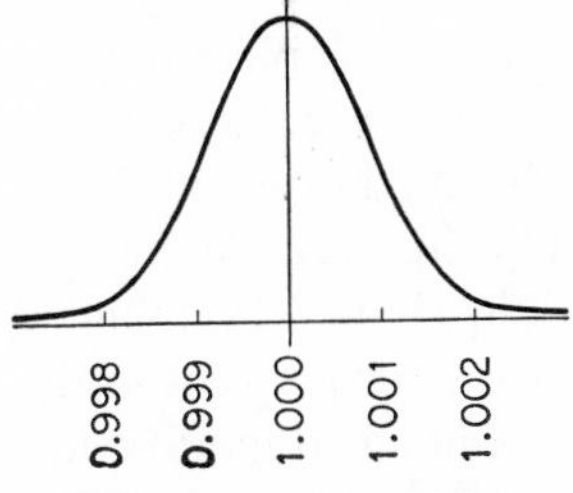

FIG. 8.1. Machine variability as shown by a frequency-distribution graph.

On the basis of this "behavior pattern," it is possible to predict what the machine or the process is capable of producing. If the spread of the pattern is less than that of the tolerance, the machine is capable of producing parts to tolerance. If it is broader than the tolerance, the machine will have to be replaced with one of greater precision or the process will have to be changed.

A detailed procedure for conducting process-capability studies is presented in Sec. 17.16. Examples of process capabilities are also given in that section.

An application of a process-capability study is shown by one conducted by a Philadelphia manufacturer. The study was conducted to determine the capabilities of a Burgmaster, six-spindle, automatic, turret-drill press with General Electric numerical-tape control. Accuracy of hole location was determined under each of the operating conditions ordinarily encountered in practice. Two different methods were employed: one using the master plate to indicate positioning without actually cutting metal, and the other putting a random series of holes in a number of sample pieces.

The sample pieces were measured and analyzed, using the methods discussed in Sec. 17.16. The study proved to be very comprehensive and provided the following information:

1. Accuracy of each of the six spindles when (*a*) drilling, (*b*) reaming, and (*c*) boring.
2. Accuracy of hole locations without center drilling.
3. Repeatability of the machine in coming back to "zero position" after performing a series of operations.
4. Accuracy of the machine in different areas of the work table.
5. Comparison of accuracy with dial- versus tape-controlled operation.

This information was used for programming the machine so it would meet drawing tolerances. This permitted acceptance of the work from the machine with a minimum amount of inspection and a maximum assurance that the pieces were accurate.

8.4 Quality-measuring Equipment Capability and Repeatability Analysis

Just as a piece of manufacturing equipment has a pattern of variability, so does a piece of measuring equipment have its own pattern of variability. For example, if a gage block measures to 1.0000 inch and then repeated measurements are taken on it with an ordinary pair of micrometers, it will be found that most of the readings fall around 1.0000 inch but a few per cent of the readings may be at 0.9998 and 1.0002 inches. The technique of quality-measurement equipment capability and repeatability analysis relates to identifying and controlling this pattern of variability.

Obviously, micrometers without a vernier scale would be unsuitable for measuring a dimension that had a total tolerance of 0.005 inch, since the variability of the measuring instrument, including human variability, is almost as great as that of the process. A rule of thumb is that the precision of the measuring equipment should be such that its total variability does not exceed $\frac{1}{10}$ of the tolerance being measured.

For example, if the shaft has a tolerance of ± 0.001 inch—total tolerance, 0.002 inch—the variability of the measuring equipment desirably should not exceed 0.0002 inch. This equipment should be capable of being read to 0.0002-inch calibration marks, dividing the total tolerance into 10 increments. If such a rule is followed, the observed measurement should be within 1 per cent of the actual measurement.

8.5 Analysis of Pilot-run Results

This analytical technique compares actual versus planned quality performance by means of a pilot run. Any departures from planned performance with respect to either the product or the process calls for investigation and possible adjustment of both.

A pilot run is a trial production run using regular production tooling.

The first manufactured units are subjected to end-use tests and field test to see if the product meets performance requirements.

Besides analysis of data resulting from tests of the pilot-run product, a careful analysis of the pilot run itself should be made to determine which, if any, manufacturing processes depart from planned results and are contributing to the deterioration of product quality.

It is important to point up quality trouble spots so correction to the process or the product design can be made prior to the start of production. An evaluation of the effectiveness of the corrective action should also be made.

The pilot run may also show up inadequacies or "overdesign" in the quality control plan, i.e., points in the process flow where more quality information should be obtained or, conversely, where less quality information would suffice.

As the result of a thorough pilot-run analysis, for example, it was discovered that a special wrench for installing valve orifices in a device was slipping and cutting slivers of metal from the valve body. These slivers would later lodge in the orifice and cause failure of the device. As a result, a new locking wrench was designed that prevented slippage and the attendant quality problem.

8.6 Incoming-material Testing, Inspection, and Laboratory Analysis

Analytical techniques applied to the physical and chemical properties of materials permit measuring the degree to which the materials conform to the quality plan.

The services of a laboratory are often necessary for making these chemical and physical analyses. This can serve for both incoming-material control and process control.

The technique of incoming-material testing and inspection and laboratory analysis has its application in the acceptance of materials, parts, components, and subassemblies that qualify as meeting quality standards. By having the laboratory equipment located in the receiving inspection area much "trotting" of samples to the laboratory and mailing back of laboratory reports can be eliminated, thereby speeding up the whole acceptance procedure.

Examples of such equipment include tensile test machines, Mullens testers (for checking strength of packing materials), hardness testers, magnaflux, moisture testers, etc.

8.7 Quality-assurance Inspection

The technique of quality-assurance inspection is the measuring of the various quality characteristics generated in a production process or inherent in the material. This type of inspection can be a check made on each piece produced (100 per cent inspection) or a check made on a statistical sample of the lot. The inspection may be a mechanical or electrical measurement or a visual inspection, the results of which are compared with standards.

The inspection can be performed by the operator or workman making the part or component, or it can be performed by a second person who is responsible for measuring only.

The purpose of this inspection is to assure that the products being produced meet the standards of quality and the quality levels which have been previously established.

8.8 Production Testing

Production testing is the technique of operating the product under actual or simulated load conditions to determine that the unit will function properly. The actual operating conditions are usually varied to simulate the field conditions, including tests for overload. Tests may be made on each unit of product or on a representative sample. The test method used may make use of automatic equipment or use conventional manual methods and equipment.

Tests of this type not only assure that the product will function, but they aid in reducing customer annoyance due to the product not being properly adjusted. Factory adjustment, where feasible, is less expensive and more accurate than field adjustment. Tests also assist in-process control by making the information available for feedback to contributing processes.

Sorting Inspection. This inspection technique serves to sort those parts which conform to the applicable drawings and specifications from those which do not conform. It is used where the process that produces the part does not have the capability to produce parts to the quality levels required or where a process goes out of control and the lot quality is below the acceptable level. Where the capability of the process is below that required to meet the design requirements of assembly, selective assembly may be used. Under these conditions, the sorting inspection consists of separating the parts into categories or classes according to the dimensions actually generated.

8.9 Process Variation Analysis

Through the techniques used for studying process variations, it is possible either to eliminate or to reduce the cause, thereby decreasing the variation and bringing it under control. In some cases, it may not be possible to identify assignable causes for variation; i.e., the variation may be constant and under control. This situation shows that a fundamental change in the manufacturing process is required to bring about the desired results.

If such basic changes in process are not possible within knowledge, time, and cost limitations, the product design must come under consideration. It may be possible for the product-design engineer to "design around" the difficulty and to accomplish the same product function by means of a different arrangement, e.g., using a mechanical approach rather than electrical. To assist the design engineer here, it is necessary to analyze the design by studying the effects of significant design parameters at varying levels by means of designed experiments.

Analysis of Variable Quality-cost Performance. Where a high degree of manufacturing variability is contributing to losses and production delays, and especially to high quality costs, a formal analysis of the trend is made. The various factors that cause the variability of the process can be brought under study, and those factors which contribute most to variability can be sorted out and identified by various statistical techniques, as discussed in Part Four. Application of these techniques permits elimination or closer control of the factors causing variability; hence it is possible to reduce process variability.

8.10 Test-data Analysis

Fundamental to the maximum usefulness of the technique of test-data analysis is good data on which to base the analysis, such as measurement of the significant parameters at the correct levels and in the proper sequence. These data provide means for detecting symptoms that tell much about the quality of the device being tested.

Proper analysis of data is directed at getting as much quality information as possible from the available measurements. Normal variation in operating parameters such as output voltages and currents, horsepower, noise level and vibration can be distinguished from abnormal behavior by use of statistical techniques.

The resulting analysis often serves to diagnose the basic cause for abnormal operation so that corrective action can be taken on the particular unit under test. It also provides a means for going back into the design or process to make changes that will get away from borderline quality. The analysis of component failure, assembly errors, and finish defects can be used to point out areas where corrective action should be taken or where further study should be made.

Scrap and Rework Analysis. Basic to this technique is the analysis of causes for scrapped parts and necessary rework operations. The collection of data in sufficient detail permits pinpointing of trouble sources. Such data are often available as a by-product of a good quality-cost-accounting system. In such a system, the organizational component responsible for causing the scrap or rework is charged for the loss or repair.

8.11 Field Complaint Analysis

The technique of field complaint analysis uses the data that flow through the quality information network, the planning of which has been discussed in Sec. 7.25. It makes use of servicemen's, dealers' and salesmen's reports concerning customer acceptance and customer returns. Often return of product is requested by the company to determine the quality problems associated with the product in actual use by the customer. Analysis of this kind of information and data points out those things which are failing in the field and those characteristics which are objectionable to the customers. Through this analysis, failure rates can be determined as well as areas where major attention and corrective action is required.

This analysis and subsequent corrective action will result in reduction in the service-call rate and complaint-service expense and enhance the reputation of the manufacturer for quality products. The analysis requires the handling of large amounts of data written in many ways. By accumulating the information into various categories, such as part number, geographical location of the customer, and application, patterns will develop which can be further analyzed. As a result, improved controls can be instituted.

Techniques Used for In-process Control

8.12 Process-control Engineering Techniques Used for In-process Control

Representative techniques for applying results of the process analysis for control purposes are presented by five typical cases as follows:

To control quality during processing	Vendor Rating (Sec. 8.13) Incoming-material Rating Plans (Sec. 8.13) "Structure Table" Control (Sec. 8.14) Control Charts (Sec. 8.15) Work Sampling (Sec. 8.16)

8.13 Vendor Rating

Vendor rating is the technique used in evaluating the performances of each of the suppliers of a business on a comparative basis. This technique is discussed in detail in Chap. 16.

Incoming-material Rating Plans. Various vendors may be rated on their quality performance on a given material or part. This may be on the basis of percentage of acceptable lots to total lots received or on some other suitable basis. The average ratings of vendors may be determined on a monthly or quarterly basis. This quality rating is combined with ratings on price and service, resulting in an over-all performance rating. The final index provides a rational basis for selection of vendors or for dividing the total business among two or more vendors. One such incoming-material rating plan is described in Sec. 16.9.

When a vendor is compared against his competitors, he may insist that the only fair basis is comparison on a given part or component and not on an over-all average performance. This is because some vendors may have more difficult requirements to meet for a particular kind of part not being made by their competitors.

This information can be used to strengthen vendor performance, since, when apprised of a poor quality situation, most reputable suppliers will make every effort to improve their standing or reputation.

8.14 "Structure Table" Control

A "structure table" provides a technique for the tabulation of knowledge in a logical sequence. In quality-control work, such a table is established for a part or a process. The knowledge required for control of the quality attributes is contained in the structure table. Planning for similar parts or operation can be quickly extracted from such tables with a minimum of effort.

Quality information in the body of the table includes process-capability values and percentage yields. Analysis of this information provides a basis for machine routing and expected yield.

For example, if production of a given part involves several different turning operations, the process-capability data will show which lathes should be used to generate a given dimension to a required tolerance. By progressing a step further, the tables will show the expected quality levels which will be produced by following the recommended routing.

Figure 8.2 gives an example of a structure table.

8.15 Control Charts

The control-chart technique is used for in-process control to give an hour-by-hour or day-by-day picture of the process to the shop personnel and the process-control engineer. By use of these charts, the control limits of the process are established, and control of the process is maintained by periodic sampling and plotting the results. By observing the charts, any out-of-control condition of either the central tendency or the spread of the distribution can be detected. Through study of the data plotted on a control chart, advance indications can often detect a process that is tending toward an out-of-control condition. Further investigation and analysis has to be made to determine the cause. Then corrective action has to be taken, preferably before a nonconforming product is made.

Control charts can be used to control such processes as machining,

MACHINE #273
(LATHE–O.D.)

TABLE 0331

A. Q. L. – %	← .1 →				
CAPABILITY – (%) OF TOLERANCE)	≤10	≤25	≤50	≤75	≤75
CHECK–(# PIECES)	1	1	6	10	REJECT
ACCEPTANCE BAND– (% AROUND NOMINAL)	85	64	40	13	REJECT
NEXT TABLE	0332 →				NONE

A. Q. L. – %	← 1.0 →					
CAPABILITY – (%) OF TOLERANCE)	≤10	≤25	≤50	≤75	≤90	<90
CHECK–(# PIECES)	1	1	4	10	10	REJECT
ACCEPTANCE BAND– (% AROUND NOMINAL)	88	70	51	32	18	REJECT
NEXT TABLE	← 0332 →					NONE

A. Q. L. – %	← 2.5 →					
CAPABILITY – (%) OF TOLERANCE)	≤10	≤25	≤50	≤75	≤90	≤90
CHECK–(# PIECES)	1	1	1	6	10	REJECT
ACCEPTANCE BAND– (% AROUND NOMINAL)	90	73	46	38	29	REJECT
NEXT TABLE	← 0332 →					NONE

A. Q. L. – %	← 5.0 →					
CAPABILITY – (%) OF TOLERANCE)	≤10	≤25	≤50	≤75	≤90	<90
CHECK–(# PIECES)	1	1	1	4	6	REJECT
ACCEPTANCE BAND– (% AROUND NOMINAL)	90	76	51	43	35	REJECT
NEXT TABLE	← 0332 →					NONE

A. Q. L. – %	← 10 →					
CAPABILITY – (%) OF TOLERANCE)	≤10	≤25	≤50	≤75	≤90	<90
CHECK–(# PIECES)	1	1	1	2	4	REJECT
ACCEPTANCE BAND– (% AROUND NOMINAL)	92	79	57	45	42	REJECT
NEXT TABLE	← 0332 →					NONE

FIG. 8.2. Structure table.

finishing, assembly, chemical processing, and any other process where the quality characteristics are measurable. The theory and practice of control charts is the subject of Chap. 11.

8.16 Work Sampling

Work sampling is a statistical technique for making a large number of instantaneous or flash observations of a job or worker at random times and for recording the quality activity or state observed. The ratio of each quality activity or state observed to the total observation is a measure of the proportion of time which is spent on various activities. This ratio further determines such information as delay time, the amount of time spent on clerical work, the magnitude of interruptions, and the time spent on different products of a product mix.

It is an analysis tool to obtain facts for programming improvements and assist in measuring the productivity of an activity. It is an excellent technique to determine where further study is necessary to improve productivity. Studies made before and after improvements are made can be used as a measure of an improvement.

Work sampling is an especially useful technique in quality-control work. The variety of different operations that make up most quality control jobs may be effectively analyzed by this method. Excessive time being spent on make-ready work can be identified, such as making electrical connections for testing, collecting samples, or getting report blanks. More efficient, productive quality-control work patterns are often possible as a result of studies making use of this technique.

Techniques Used for Implementing the Quality Plan

8.17 Process Engineering Techniques for Implementing the Quality Plan

Typical of the techniques for implementing and adapting the quality plan to the production situation are the five presented here:

To implement the quality plan	Use of Manuals and Standing Instructions (Sec. 8.18)
	Interpretation of Drawings, Specifications, and Quality Planning (Sec. 8.19)
	Temporary Quality Planning (Sec. 8.20)
	First-piece Inspection (Sec. 8.21)
	Disposition of Discrepant Material (Sec. 8.22)

8.18 Use of Manuals and Standing Instructions

Preparation of process-quality manuals and standing instructions, within the framework of the quality-system plan, represents an important process-control technique. These manuals codify and communicate various procedural details, such as operative procedures and standards of workmanship, which ordinarily are not spelled out on drawings. Specific process references and tolerances should appear on a drawing or in a specification, but generally it is cumbersome to include the detail required for operative procedures and standards of workmanship. Too often, these instructions are not written anywhere. They are transmitted verbally, and like all verbal communications, the information will change each time it is communicated.

Typical manuals are

· *Process-quality procedures manuals,* which include such instructions as material disposition procedures, instructions for completion of forms, maintenance of files, gage-inspection procedures, and procedures for making process-capability studies.

· *Standard shop-practice manuals,* which include such information as the definition of flatness, finish, squareness, undercut for threading, spot-weld depressions, and the like. Instructions of this type are difficult to write, so pictures, sketches, and visual or physical samples may be required to convey fully the meaning of the instructions. Manuals of this type become the reference material for judging quality of workmanship and are useful in training new personnel and for reviews by experienced personnel.

8.19 Interpretation of Drawings, Specifications, and Quality Planning

Interpretation of drawings, specifications, and quality planning is often a necessary technique for their proper implementation in the shop. Even though these instructions are written as clearly as possible, there is always the chance that they may be misunderstood by shop personnel. These men do not always have the same background information that is available to the product engineer who develops the design or the quality-control engineer who develops the plan. This activity helps to give an image of a good part and emphasizes its important characteristics. Information given in this manner is more acceptable than criticism of mistakes and errors by an operator or assembler that result from lack of understanding.

The need for interpretation should never be used as a crutch for poor drawings or instructions or quality plans. When additional information is required, the instruction or drawing or plan should be changed to include it.

Drawings, specifications, and quality planning can be interpreted to the operator, using different methods of communication. This can be accomplished in orientation sessions with either groups or individuals. Another method is to communicate the information to supervisors or lead men so they can instruct their operators. Samples, pictures, and drawings may be used as visual aids. Proper instruction of operators is essential to the "make-it-right-the-first-time" principle.

8.20 Temporary Quality Planning

Temporary quality planning is the technique for instituting a temporary set of quality-control instructions where the established quality plan does not apply. These instructions are generally necessary when the normal or planned production method or planned quality information equipment cannot be used. These situations arise when machines break down and equipment or tooling is removed for maintenance. In other instances, material substitutions are made because of slow delivery or unacceptable purchased material. It is necessary that temporary planning be instituted immediately and on the spot where the problem exists in order that the over-all product quality will be maintained and remain under control, even under adverse conditions.

Temporary planning is generally instituted on the shop floor, using such equipment and gaging as is readily available. In those instances where a permanent change is made in the production process, temporary planning should be used only until quality-control engineering techniques are used to modify the regular quality plan. It is important that a follow-up be made on all temporary quality plans so that inspections, operator checks, laboratory analyses, or tests that were used to control a temporary condition do not continue beyond their need.

8.21 First-piece Inspection

First-piece-from-a-new-tool checking technique is a detailed inspection of a part made using a new tool, fixture, or die under actual operating conditions. The purpose of this inspection is accurately to measure every specified characteristic generated by the new tool and to compare it with the part drawing. Each measurement is recorded and any deviations of the generated characteristic from the drawing are noted. Particular attention is given to such characteristics as squareness, wrinkling, radii, and tool marks. Any deviations recorded must be resolved by either reworking the tool or changing the part drawing to agree with the product.

First-piece inspection becomes the first step in proving in the production tooling and obtaining correlation between manufactured parts and the part drawing. This technique helps resolve major discrepancies between tooling and the product specification. Part-to-part variation can then be determined by a process-capability study.

8.22 Disposition of Discrepant Material

Disposition of discrepant material is the technique used for removing nonconforming material from the operating quality system. Occasionally, material or parts are produced which do not meet specifications. This may be due to vendor problems, material substitution, production errors, equipment failures, or material variation. Whatever the reason, a decision must be made to use as is, to rework the part to drawing, to rework it to a planned deviation from drawing, or, finally, to scrap the part.

Disposition procedures provide an orderly way for the discrepancy to be analyzed for its effect on product. A recommendation is then made for disposition on the basis of the analysis and the necessary approvals requested. A secondary purpose is served by the follow-up for corrective action. The general procedure consists of these steps:

1. The discrepancy is reported on a form with all pertinent inspection data.
2. The discrepancy is analyzed for the effect the defect will have on outgoing product quality.
3. Disposition is recommended.
4. Where design is affected, the design engineer who developed the product specification should approve the disposition.
5. The signed report becomes the authority for disposition, and copies are distributed.
6. Copies are directed to the shop for corrective action.

Techniques Used for Auditing Quality Effectiveness

8.23 Process Engineering Techniques—Quality Effectiveness

Three techniques for monitoring the effectiveness of the quality system are presented as follows:

To measure effectiveness of the quality system	Quality Rating of Organizational Components and Production Personnel (Sec. 8.24) Procedures Audits (Sec. 8.25) Product Audits (Sec. 8.26)

8.24 Quality Rating of Organizational Components and Production Personnel

A product-quality rating for production units or production personnel provides a technique for observing product-quality trends. A product-quality rating is measured by an index number or ratio, which is obtained by taking into account such factors as scrap and rework, level of outgoing quality, the number of rejected lots, and the excess cost in other units due to workmanship errors. Generally changes in the quality of work produced are small. Any noticeable change is the cumulative effect of a gradual degradation of product quality over time. An index number, plotted on a chart chronologically with time, will indicate a trend, either up or down, when one exists. Action can be taken or an investigation can be made when an unfavorable trend is taking place and before serious problems develop.

8.25 Procedures Audits

A procedures audit is a technique for a formal examination and verification that the detailed procedures in the quality plan are being followed. An index can be computed that will indicate the degree to which procedures are being adhered to.

The audit is a detailed examination made on a representative sample of procedures. A record is made of each deviation. Demerits are then assessed for each deviation in relation to the importance of the procedure and the degree of departure from the specified procedure.

The result of the procedures audit can then be stated as an index number. A chart on which these index numbers are plotted will indicate trends as periodic audits are taken. The make-up of the sample should be varied at random from audit to audit.

The procedures audit is a measure of managerial control, since the effectiveness of the quality plan depends on its prescribed procedures being followed. The procedures audit indicates areas requiring better instruction and closer supervision.

8.26 Product Audits

A product audit is a technique for customer-centered evaluations of a relatively small sample of product. It may use environmental, life, and other reliability tests as a means for evaluating product quality. The purpose is not to control quality but to determine the effectiveness of the quality-control system. The audit may be made at the end of the line, it may be made on the completed product, or it may include in-process audits of parts and components. The choice depends on where the different quality characteristics can best be evaluated.

In making an audit, every feature of the product is evaluated with demerits assessed for each discrepancy noted. These demerits are then weighted according to the importance of the quality characteristic. An index is computed by totaling the demerits and relating them to a comparison base, e.g., so many units of product. The index is plotted graphically with time to determine trends of product quality. The audit report is further analyzed to identify specific areas which call for further investigation of design, processing, control methods, or procedures. Corrective action is applied where the results of the analysis dictate.

CHAPTER 9

QUALITY INFORMATION EQUIPMENT ENGINEERING TECHNOLOGY

Modern process control demands equipment which can make quality measurements of precision. The thousandths-of-an-inch pocket micrometer, which once epitomized exactness, is rapidly being replaced by optical flats which measure 10 millionths of an inch.

Dimensional characteristics are, as a matter of fact, but one of a long list of quality characteristics needed for the evaluations of today's products. A whole array of electronic parameters must be measured: voltage, current, power, resistance, capacitance, and frequency, in a wide range of values. Chemical measurements are becoming increasingly common, even in the mechanical goods and electrical industries. Physical strength, thrust, flow, pressures, temperatures, and times (in microseconds) are more and more widely used measurements. Recently an array of radiation measurements has been placed on the list.

Add to this the additional requirements that these measurements must be made rapidly and accurately during the manufacturing cycle, must be compatible with it, and often must be made automatically. Furthermore, consider that these measurements may be used to adjust the process itself automatically. This may involve feeding the measurements into a computer, comparing the results with standards, and then feeding back the needed information for correction of the process, all automatically.

Equipment in the field of quality control is thus assuming a new and much more significant role than was played by the traditional inspection and testing devices.

Historically, inspection equipment was essentially a small incident in the work of the factory methods planner, and the primitive equipment and low productivity of such equipment certainly demonstrates this. Even test equipment, although somewhat more extensively covered, was still largely a matter of selecting manually operated flip-switch circuits that could be mounted in a suitable metal box.

These older equipments had the principal job of accepting or rejecting parts. Their being made automatic usually meant only that they would mechanically sort the bad product from the good, which made no other contribution to the plant's quality objective than that bad parts might be identified more quickly than had ever before been possible. These devices were often set up with almost no preplanned relationship to other segments of the plant quality-control work.

9.1 The Job of Modern Equipment

In contrast, today it is becoming increasingly clear that the basic job of modern quality-control equipment is not merely to inspect or test; it is also to provide usable information about product and process quality. This information may still be used, in part, as the basis for acceptance or rejection. But its other major use is for rapid manual, mechanized, or fully automatic feedback for process control and for true *control* of product quality—often for the first time in some operations.

In fact, these modern quality *information* equipment devices are the representation, in physical equipment, of elements of the quality system of the plant. As such, they are an essential segment of this system and must be fully compatible with its other segments.

Testing and inspection equipments that are designed in terms of the quality *information* concept are often much lower in total cost and less complex in design and operation than are the older testing and inspection devices. This is because it has been all too frequent to mechanize bad quality-control habits in the form of a piece of testing and inspection equipment which turns out to be much more complex and more costly than the planned quality requirements demand.

An example is the Midwestern motor plant that purchased a motor tester for final, 100 per cent, go and not-go checking of 17 quality characteristics. This $90,000 piece of checking equipment did nothing to improve the basic quality level of the motors; its principal asset was that it provided much more rapid separation of the bad motors from the good.

Study, employing the techniques of quality-control engineering, established a quality-system plan for the plant which specified two pieces of in-process equipment to measure and process quality information. These two equipments, whose total cost was $12,000, helped to control the motor process. They soon made the costly, elaborate final motor tester unnecessary.

The principle is this: what is significant is not better quality-control devices as such, but instead those information equipments which integrate with low-cost, high-efficiency quality-control systems. The increasing importance of such equipment is demonstrated by the trends in its use. Only a few years ago, this type of equipment commanded just a few cents out of every dollar spent by plants on their equipment investment. Current forecasts suggest that this may go to 25 or 35 per cent and more of the industrial plant investment dollar in the next few years.

The technology of quality information equipment engineering provides the quality-control tools that must be considered here.

9.2 Quality Information Equipment Engineering[1]

Quality information equipment engineering may be defined as

The body of technical knowledge relating to equipment which measures quality characteristics and which processes the resulting information for use in analysis and control.

There are many techniques used in this technology, any one of which may have several applications. One example is the design of dimensional measuring equipment to send back a signal of the measured characteristics for adjusting the quality of the process. The X-ray gage used to measure the thickness of steel sheets during rolling operations typifies such equipment (Fig. 9.1).

The full complement of techniques of quality information equipment technology may be grouped under four major headings:

I. Advanced Equipment Development
Included here are techniques for creating measurement practices and instrumentation procedures for application to those quality information requirements that are established by quality-control engineering and process-control engineering techniques. (Techniques used for advanced equipment development are discussed in Secs. 9.4 to 9.14.)

II. Equipment-specification Planning
Included here are techniques for establishing the actual specification of the quality information equipment, which is required within the framework of the quality-system plan. (Techniques for equipment-specification planning are discussed in Sec. 9.15.)

III. Design, Procurement, and Construction
Included here are the techniques for the design and procurement of the individual components for the specified equipment. Also included are techniques for constructing the equipment. Further included are

[1] Several of the concepts and developments considered here have been created by S. A. Yingling, E. S. Acton, C. L. Beattie, A. J. Morford, W. J. Seale, and M. E. Stanford.

techniques for procuring the equipment in total, when this is the indicated step for a company. (Techniques for design, procurement, and construction are discussed in Sec. 9.16.)

IV. Installation, Check-out, and Follow-up
Included here are techniques for the installation and application of the quality information equipment following its construction. (Techniques for this phase are discussed in Sec. 9.17.)

FIG. 9.1. X-ray gage used to check thickness of sheet steel during rolling operation (Courtesy of General Electric Company, X-ray Department, Milwaukee, Wisconsin.)

Some companies, which are large enough, will organize their technical efforts so that the entire range of techniques are covered from development through installation. As a practical matter, this means that these companies will design and make their own quality information equipment.

Other companies will organize to concentrate most heavily upon the techniques relating to specification and procurement. This means that they will buy their quality information equipment from one or more of the vendor firms which themselves cover some of the techniques of development, design, construction, and installation.

But the same fundamental need for applying the technology of quality information equipment exists for both types of company; both must specify the type of equipment required by their quality-system plan and must have considered the other information equipment techniques sufficiently to assure the feasibility and proper operation of this equipment. The determination of how this equipment will be obtained then becomes a matter of economics: a practical make-or-buy decision.

9.3 Some Forms of Quality Information Equipment

The modern inspection and testing devices which result from use of quality information equipment technology take many forms from the very simple, very low-cost to the very complex.

For example, a Southeastern manufacturer of electric blankets and heating pads uses equipment that automatically adjusts tiny heating-pad thermostats, tests them for accuracy, and automatically accepts them or rejects them. Totalizers for each category provide information for optimization of the adjusting process.

An example of a job-shop type operation is found in the plant of a manufacturer of complex airborne electronic radar gear. Here punched tapes program tests, which are performed automatically. This equipment today performs in minutes tests that formerly required hours. Printout on each of the quality characteristics tested presents data for setting of process parameters.

In a Southern transformer plant punched cards control the testing of transformers of varying ratings. Formerly 16 hourly rated test employees were required to evaluate the output quality. These have been replaced by one nontechnical employee who performs two operations that have not been automated: connecting and disconnecting the transformers, and placing the card in the reader. Printed-out information for each transformer goes on a tag which accompanies its respective transformer.

Another manufacturer in the Midwest evaluates transformers used on neon signs by means of a fully automated test cycle. The transformers are automatically conveyed into the equipment, the tests are cycled, and the good-quality transformers are transferred to the packing line. Rejects are shunted off with the cause for the rejection identified by means of a piece of paper tape whose length signifies the rejection category. Counters for each category show an instantaneous distribution of defects. This information is used for corrective action on the process.

In addition to these equipments that incorporate already-known technical principles, there are those that continue to emerge from quality information equipment laboratories involving development work on new technical applications. A recent example is a noncontact gage[2] made by

[2] The noncontact gage reports a development by E. S. Acton.

teaming up a new light-sensitive cell with an optical system which can perform highly accurate, mechanical inspection measurements without touching the parts. The information from these measurements is fed back to the "make" equipment for automatic control. This technique has proved an excellent solution to the problem of measuring and controlling, during processing, the thickness of insulation on material while traveling at high rates of speed.

Although these examples are representative of outstanding progress in the field of quality information equipment, they also illustrate the opportunities for further progress that are immediately ahead. With the exception of the last example, for instance, none has the closed-loop feedback feature for control of the manufacturing process.

Advanced Equipment Development

9.4 Advanced Development Areas[3]

Advanced equipment development relates to establishing the fundamental principles of measurement and instrumentation that will provide the foundation for the later work of the detailed design of quality information equipment. This section reviews some general concepts underpinning advanced development, after which Sec. 9.5 discusses the equipment system viewpoint that threads through the work. Then Secs. 9.6 through 9.13 consider some of the more specific techniques for actual points-of-process application of quality information equipment. Section 9.14 then presents evaluation techniques relating, not to new equipment, but rather toward planning to improve existing equipment.

Advanced equipment development basically divides into two general areas which are

1. *Generalized* development.
2. *Specific* advanced developments.

General Development. General advanced development consists of continuous research and investigation of quality information equipment *in toto*. Programs in this area of advanced development are not normally directed at any particular product but rather at a group of them. These programs consist of a systematic approach to the process-control requirements inherent in the quality-system plans.

The basis for these programs lies both in the long-range quality-system plans of the business and in current or new products of the company which have the greatest growth potential.

Specific Developments. The second type of advanced development is that pertaining to the *specific* current or new products to which the busi-

[3] Section 9.4 and material related to it in this chapter are according to unpublished material developed by Donald D. Ward and Walter P. Sime.

OUT OUT OUT

DWG. OR CAT. NO. 2157704-1 — PT. 1 & 4

VENDOR #	VENDOR NAME	DWG. CHG. NO.	DEVICE
	UTC		Transformer Dot 7 & 23

INCOMING PURCHASED MATERIALS

TEST PLANNING

TEST STA.	6	PROG.	
DATE	1-28-60	TEST STD.	
A.Q.L.	1%		

PLANNER: E. D. Fox

TESTMAN:

EQUIPMENT	ACC.	RECORD DATA OF
1. Gertsch "Ratio Trans"		
2. HP 400C or D VTVM		
3. Hewlett packard audio sig. gen.		
4.		
5.		
6.		
7.		
8.		
9.		
10.		

CRITICAL MAJOR MINOR	PROCEDURE
MA	A. Set up circuit as shown for Dot -7.
MA	B. Set up circuit as shown for Dot 23.
MA	C. Check impedance ratio of transformers
	1. Procedure for both Dot 7 and Dot 23
	2. Set DB attenuator as shown
	3. Increase output until meter on HP signal Gen. reads half scale (this places about 0.2V on the transformer)
MA	4. Null voltage on HP400 by turning ratio trans controls.
MA	5. At null the ratio trans should read approx.
	Dot 7 - .07
	Dot 23- .20
	(Dot-7 is 200K to 1K and Dot-23 is 30K CT to 1.2K CT)
	D. Hipot and megger as shown. Minimum insulation resistance 10,000 megohms.

	Dot 7	Dot 23
Hipot at 100VAC RMS - 1 Min.	Green to Red	Red to Black
Megger at 50v d-c	Green to Red	Red to Black

TEST CIRCUIT DIAGRAM

DATA MUST BE RECORDED ON P.O. 2420A & 2420B

CHANGES	REVISION NO.	1.	2.	3.	4.	5.	6.
	DATE						
	SIGNED						

SHEET ____ OF ____

"VISIrecord" PL 20596

PO2420 (7-59) 11X8.75 TRANSLUCENT 060

FIG. 9.2. Preliminary specification for quality information equipment, incoming-material test for transformers.

Check List of Factors to Consider in Establishing Equipment Cost

- I. Equipment Cost
  - Initial cost
    - Development
    - Design
    - Construction
    - Basic equipment
      - Individual components
      - Purchased complete
    - Fixturing or tooling
    - Masters for calibration
    - Equipment for work handling
    - Accessory equipment
      - Recorders, etc.
    - Safety features
    - Installation
      - Footings
      - Enclosures
      - Services
      - Rearrangement of existing facilities
    - Debugging
    - Operator training
    - Replacement parts and spares
- II. Equipment Operating Cost
  - Facilities and services
    - Power
    - Storage
    - Water
    - Air
  - Maintenance
  - Calibration
  - Operator labor
  - Setup
  - Floor space
  - Amortization period
- III. Operating Costs Affected by Equipment Design
  - Cost of bringing work to equipment
  - Cost of bringing equipment to work
  - Information value toward prevention of defects
  - Increased production capacity
  - Increased machine utilization
  - Improved process capability
  - Improved product assurance
  - Improved safety
  - Equipment utilization

FIG. 9.3

ness is committed and to those future products currently undergoing development. The application of quality measurement and control, integrated to the fullest extent with the manufacturing processes, must start at this stage to assure practical success. It is at this time also that the guide rules for development of the quality information equipment are originated. These include the following:

a. The preliminary specifications of that quality information equipment which the quality-system plan indicates should be applied to process or product performance measurements. Figure 9.2 illustrates such a specification for incoming-material testing of transformers.

b. The preliminary quality information equipment cost estimates with breakdowns and cost follow-up procedures. Figure 9.3 shows a check list of cost considerations for quality information equipment.

c. The estimated schedules for design, procurement, construction, checkout, and release of each quality-control equipment component. Figure 9.4 is such a schedule, showing percentage of time and cost represented by each step, together with the position responsible.

d. The productivity and operational cost figures to be associated with each equipment.

e. The organization and personnel required for the quality information equipment design program. Figure 9.5 shows the work of the quality-control engineer, quality information equipment engineer, and process-control engineer with relation to the development steps.

f. The organization and personnel required for operation and performance maintenance of the equipment, along with the associated times and labor costs to be attained.

Equipment development efforts in this stage are of a conceptual nature.

Whether applicable to existing or to new products, the advanced development programs are dependent upon, and to a large extent guided by, the advanced planning being carried on in the quality control engineering area. When new-product designs are involved, however, the quality information equipment design cycle must also integrate with the work of the product-planning group which is materializing new-product specifications; it must also continue into the detailed design of the product by engineering.

Throughout this advanced quality information equipment development activity, recommendations will develop for product-engineering design changes to permit more effective product and process measurement and control. Similarly, recommendations will be developed for Manufacturing Engineering relative to the application of measurement equipment to tie in with the processing equipment itself, for corrective process control or adjustment of the product.

QUALITY INFORMATION EQUIPMENT DEVELOPMENT SCHEDULE

% Time	Step	Description	Responsibility	Cost %
10	1	Development of program concept and problem requirements; analysis of approaches	Qual. Info. Equip. Eng. & Q. C. Eng.	5 10
20	2	Development of tentative (conceptual) design approach, review against requirements, evaluation of economics of program, establishment of schedule	Qual. Info. Equip.	25
40	3	Development experimentation, breadboarding special mechanisms and circuitry, obtaining of test data and analysis, establishing of materials and components decisions	Qual. Info. Equip.	40
	4	Design of circuitry, subassemblies and components, including layout	Qual. Info. Equip.	
55 60	5	Preliminary drafting, parts list and purchasing of prototype materials, review of schedule and economics	Qual. Info. Equip.	
	6	Prototype construction, debugging modifications and improvements	Qual. Info. Equip. Eng.	65
80	7	Pilot run-capabilities evaluation	Qual. Info. Equip. Eng. & P. C. Eng.	
85 90	8	Final drafting, calibration and maintenance plans, theory of operation write-up, operating instruction, time studies, program report	Qual. Info. Equip. Eng. & P. C. Eng.	85 90
100	9	Program application, final economics analysis and program evaluation (6 months to 1 year) after program completion or installations)	Qual. Info. Equip. Eng. & Q. C. Eng.	95 100

FIG. 9.4.

QUALITY INFORMATION EQUIPMENT – RESPONSIBILITY VS. TIME

	Product Development Steps		*Quality Control Engineering*		*Quality Information Equipment Engineering*		*Process Control Engineering*
1	Product planning	1	New design evaluation: Review product specifications Product tolerance; analysis based on capability studies Provision for automatic inspection and test Provide broad equipment requirements	1	Develop program concept, problem requirements; analyze approaches	1	Preprocurement assistance counsel on operating problems and limitations of processes and personnel
				2	Develop tentative design approaches Review and evaluate Establish schedule		
2	Engineering study and design			3	Breadboarding mechanisms and circuitry; obtain data for analysis Decisions on materials and components	2	Equipment design evaluation: Counsel on operation, operator controls, data displays Calibration and maintenance problems
		2	Quality system planning: Classify quality characteristics Determine locations for measurements Develop measurement planning	4	Design and layout of circuitry, components, and subassemblies		
				5	Drafting, parts lists, purchase materials, review schedule		
3	Procurement			6	Construct prototype, de-bug, modify, and improve	3	Operational acceptance: Cooperate on checking out by measuring product under operating conditions Review operating instructions Obtain capability study
4	Preproduction run			7	Pilot-run-capabilities evaluation		
5	Product manufacturing			8	Final drafting, plans, and instructions		
		3	Measurement and Feedback: Plan audit and other techniques to measure and feedback for control	9	Equipment application, cost analysis, and program evaluation		

FIG. 9.5.

9.5 Quality Information System Concept

In order to recognize both the scope and similarity of quality-measurement problems, it is well to consider the quality information equipment from a functional, *systems-design* viewpoint before considering individual components of such a system. Quality information systems can be conceived as consisting in the following seven basic functions.

1. Programming. This function consists in instructing the actual performance of measurements. This includes defining the sequence in which measurements are to be performed, the equipment to be used for measuring the individual quality characteristics, the procedure through which the measurements are accomplished, and the results that are required.

2. Selecting. Here the function is that of selecting the material, part, or product that is to be tested or inspected, the connections to it, the input signals to be applied, the output terminations required, and the measuring devices applicable. This may also include disposition of the material, part, or product at the conclusion of its evaluation.

3. Measuring. Involved is determining the range of measurements to be used and then performing the measurement of product or process quality characteristics.

4. Data Recording and Processing. This function consists in recording pertinent measurements of product or process quality and then tabulating this information in usable form for analysis purposes.

5. Information Analysis and Decision. Here the function is to perform computations on the measurement information, compare these computations with the required results, and determine their acceptability on an individual and trend basis. This function also includes establishing the corrective or controlling action desired.

6. Feedback. Involved is communication of the corrective or controlling action required to the proper controlling areas and of thereupon providing an indication that proper corrective action has been performed.

7. Controlling. Here the function is performance of the required corrective or controlling action on the product design, the manufacturing process, or the individual material, part, or product itself.

The basic block diagram for a quality-measurement system, involving these seven functions, is illustrated in Fig. 9.6, with the functions indicated by number for ease of reference. All seven of these functions may be performed by equipment, or only part of them. All must, however, be considered and accounted for while doing the preliminary planning for the equipment that will fit into the quality system plan. The equipment finally chosen may be nothing more than a simple, inexpensive gage to perform function 3, with the other six functions performed manually or through paper work; or the choice may be for a fully automatic equipment, which performs all seven functions without human intervention.

The selection of the balance of the quality information system among the functions performed by people, procedures, and equipment is a practical matter. It is dependent upon the particular company situation: economics, the labor-to-equipment ratios, and the nature of the manufacturing processes. As noted in Sec. 9.1, the decisions for this selection are based upon the principle that what is significant is not better quality devices of and by themselves but the choice of those equipments which

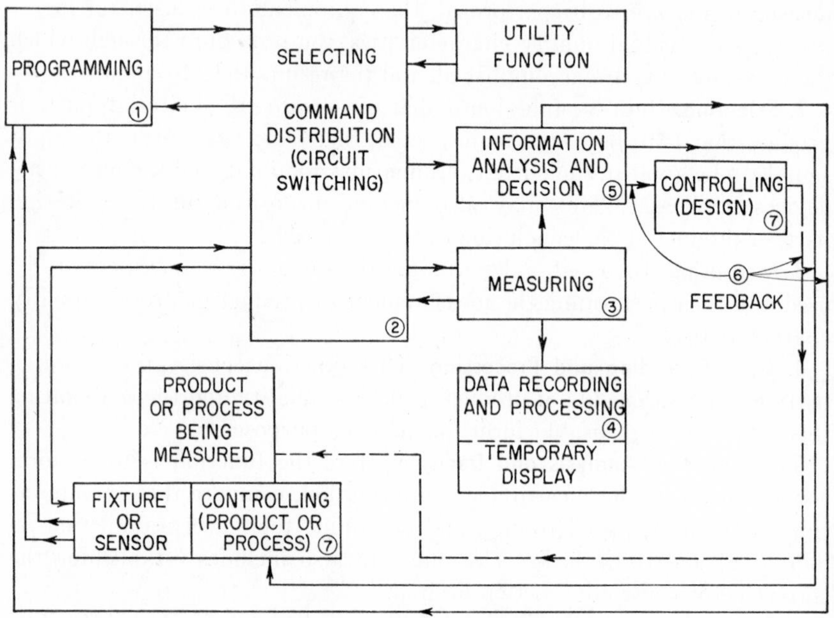

QUALITY INFORMATION SYSTEM BLOCK DIAGRAM

FIG. 9.6.

permit the greatest *over-all* efficiency and operation for the total quality-control system.

9.6 Degree of Mechanization for the Control of Processes

The degree to which this selection leans toward equipment for the control of processes, rather than toward people and procedures, may be determined on the basis of several considerations. These considerations guide what will be the degree of "mechanization" of the quality information system.

The first consideration, and one of the more important, is that of economics: to establish the balance between the cost of accomplishing specific functions automatically as compared with performing them manually. Studied in this establishment of economic balance are processing costs under the two alternatives. Further studied is the value of improved product quality as such.

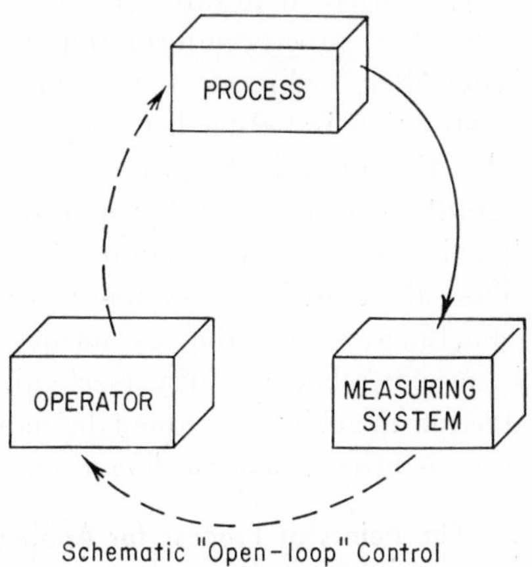

Schematic "Open-loop" Control

FIG. 9.7.

Although the economic consideration is important, other criteria must go beyond that point. For example, product-quality requirements may be very exacting with relation to the capability of available manufacturing processes. When such a situation exists, the process must either have a high degree of inherent stability or be rapidly adjusted when disturbances occur as a result of changing conditions.

In many such high-speed processes, the human being cannot observe, decide, and adjust rapidly and accurately enough to prevent the manufacture of large amounts of nonconforming product. When this is the case, operator adjustment must be replaced by fully automatic equipment control.

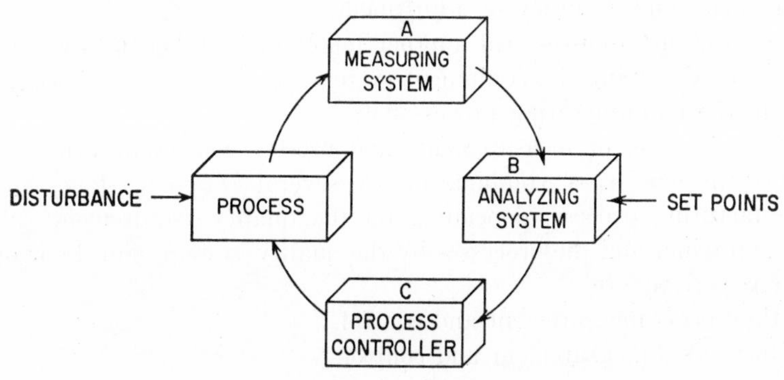

SCHEMATIC PROCESS CONTROL LOOP

FIG. 9.8.

Another consideration on which a decision for fully automatic equipment control should be based is the matter of safety to operating personnel. Greater safety might be assured not only through closer control of hazardous processes but also by removing the operator from hazardous locations, e.g., those subject to radiation, high heat, or explosions.

The two opposing "poles" of process control can be described as *open-loop control,* oriented toward manual adjustment, and *closed-loop control,* oriented toward automatic adjustment. In the open-loop system (Fig. 9.7), process information feedback is to the operator who is the "controller," whereas in the closed-loop system (Fig. 9.8), the process information is fed back to an automatic control system which is physically tied in with the process.

Both types of control system may use quality information equipment, but the closed-loop system uses by far the greater amount. In its strictest sense, the closed-loop system ties all seven of the basic quality information functions together by means of information equipment. When this is accomplished by fully mechanized means, continuous automatic production is achieved without human intervention; this is the objective of what is often termed *automation.*

9.7 The Points of Process for Application of Quality Information Equipment

In Sec. 9.5, the various functions performed in the equipment system were discussed. It was pointed out that many of these functions can be performed by human beings with the remaining functions being performed automatically by machines.

In Sec. 9.6, a set of criteria was presented on which decisions could be based concerning the degree to which the quality system should be automated. These included economics, human safety, required speed of adjustment, and accuracy of adjustment.

This section discusses still another factor to be taken into consideration when designing the equipment system; that is the *point of application* in the manufacturing process flow.

Mechanization of measurements and process control may be accomplished in one or a combination of several different stages of the manufacturing process, depending on the quality requirements placed on the product and the processes by the quality-system plan. Four of the most important are

- Preprocess measurement and control.
- In-process measurement and control.
- Postprocess measurement and control.
- Combinations of process measurement and control.

9.8 Preprocess Measurement and Control

Preprocess measurement and control may be required for the purpose of monitoring or controlling the materials or parts entering the process or for the purpose of controlling the product or the process based on input measurements (Fig. 9.9).

The measurement control of material entering the process is quite necessary in those process industries which require close control of the mix of the constituents of the product by weight or by volume. It also provides a safeguard against expensive, nonpredictable down time in mechanical and electrical goods industries which use long, continuous lines of automatic equipment.

An example of such equipment is a simple gage that automatically checks cast-iron castings for flatiron soleplates prior to a completely automatic milling and machining line. If a casting is undersize so the ogive will not clean up, or if it is oversize so it will not fit down in the

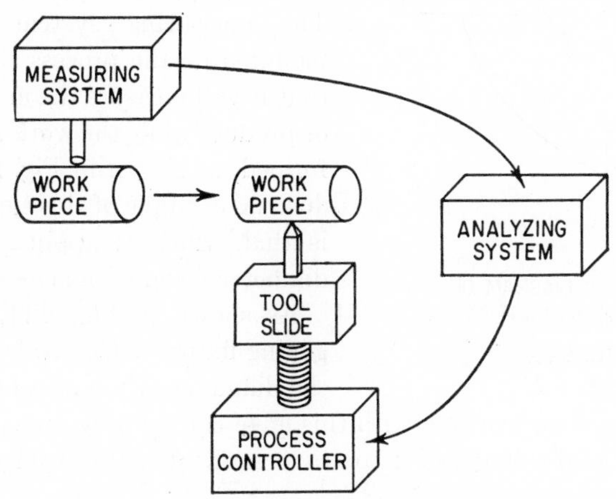

SCHEMATIC DIAGRAM OF PREPROCESS CONTROL

FIG. 9.9.

pockets of the milling machine turntable, the casting is eliminated. In the latter case, cutter breakage with attendant delays is prevented.

9.9 In-process Measurement and Control

Control applied from in-process measurement is based on a measure of the controlled quality characteristic as the product is generated. This in-process measurement and control can initiate signals to regulate or stop the process to prevent substandard production. For instance, in the case of machining processes, signals from the in-process control system may be used to

1. *Regulate the speed or degree of generation.* This may be a signal which changes the tooling from a roughing to a finishing cut as final size is approached for control of accuracy, finish, and eccentricity.

2. *Stop the generation when the predetermined value of the controlled variable is reached.* This is the signal that causes the tool to retract when

finish size is reached, or the one that shuts off the furnace when the house is at the required temperature.

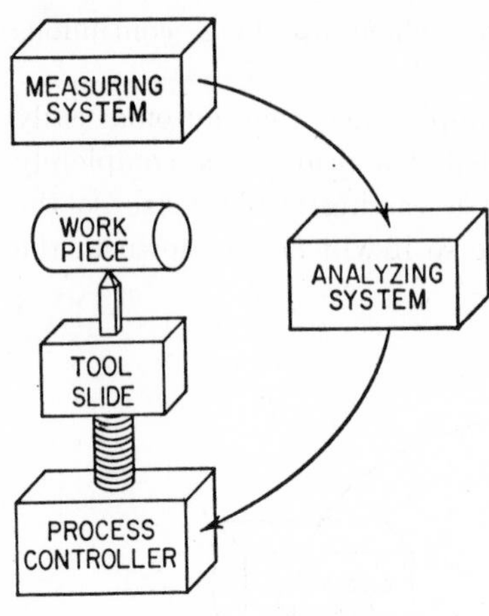

FIG. 9.10.

3. *Stop the generation or the process when it is out of control.* This is the signal that stops the machine when tools become worn or broken and when parts can no longer be held within limits.

In-process measurement is the basis for the in-process control of a process. The measuring system is usually mounted on the process equipment so that it will measure the material, part, or product while the work is being performed, as shown in Fig. 9.10. An industrial example of this type of control is that which is applied to outside-diameter grinding machines.

As shown in Fig. 9.11, a C-frame gaging fixture is clamped directly onto the diameter of the part being ground. The control system working with this gage can be programmed so that it will direct the grinding wheel to traverse in at a fast feed until it gets

FIG. 9.11. Automatic gage controlling grinding process (Federal Products Corporation).

within .001 to .003 inch of finish size and then traverse at slow feed to about 0.0001 inch from nominal size, where the in-feed stops and allows the wheel to start to "spark out." When the analyzing system has determined from the information transmitted from the gage that the piece is ground to nominal size, it tells the controller to retract the grinding wheel.

9.10 Postprocess Control Techniques

Control applied from postprocess, or output measurement, is based on a measurement of the quality characteristics of the completed product. In parts-making processes, the workpiece may be moved out of the chuck or fixtures and into a gaging station, or the gage may be brought

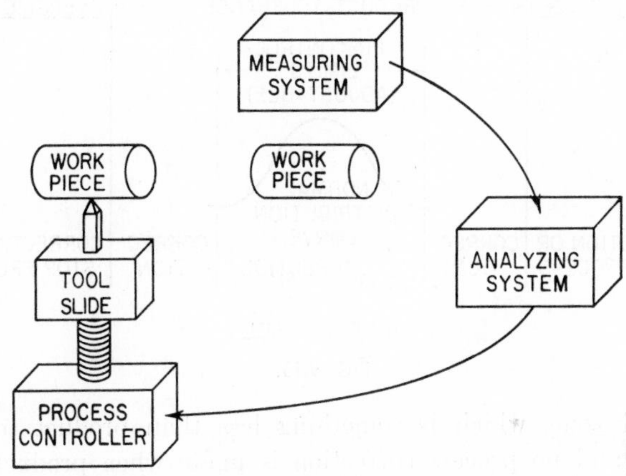

SCHEMATIC DIAGRAM OF POST-PROCESS CONTROL

FIG. 9.12.

to the part before it is moved (Fig. 9.12). In some cases, the gaging station is adjacent to the processing operation; in others, it may be some distance away and the parts from several machines directed to it in sequence.

Postprocess measurement and control may be desirable or necessary for a variety of reasons:

• It may not be possible to find space for in-process measurement equipment.

• Process environment—chips, coolant, temperature, etc.—may be of a nature which makes in-process measurement undesirable.

• It may be desirable to gage the part when it is not under the influence of the processing chuck or fixture.

• The accuracy specified may be beyond the capability of the process, and so the parts may have to be measured and classified for selective assembly.

Signals from the postprocess controller may be used to

1. *Stop the process when it is out of control.* As in in-process control, this is the signal that stops the machine or process when the tools become worn or damaged.

2. *Adjust the process when the product is approaching specified limits.*

3. *Actuate a classifying or segregating mechanism* to identify parts as good, oversize, or undersize, or by size groups for selective assembly or processing.

Postprocess measurements may also be used automatically to control the process by using the technique of zone control. As shown in Fig. 9.13,

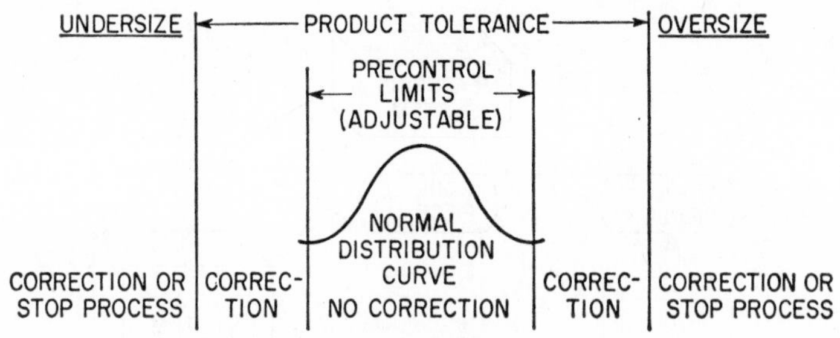

ZONE CONTROL

FIG. 9.13.

a precontrol zone, which is something less than product tolerance, is established, and no process correction is made when products are produced within these control limits. This concept is fully discussed in Sec. 11.22 under "Control Gaging."

This precontrol zone is one answer to the back-and-forth, or hunting,[4] effect of controls which attempt to correct for the normal, inherent dispersion of the process. The precontrol system recognizes the difference between "scatter" and "drift" and corrects only for the drift. The recommended process capability for this type of control is approximately one-half the product tolerance.

The operation of such a precontrol system is as follows: each part is measured after it is produced, and if the dimension in question falls within the precontrol limits, no correction is made and the process receives a go-ahead signal for the next piece. If two successive parts (or, in some cases, three or four parts) fall outside the precontrol limits but are within the product tolerance, a tool correction is made with a signal to the process-controlling element. When a measurement indicates that

[4] The hunting effect is an oscillation of the controller caused by overcorrecting the process, with subsequent swings correcting the overcorrections.

the dimension in question is outside product tolerance, either undersize or oversize, a correction is made (may be indexing a new cutting edge); if the next piece is also outside product tolerance, the machine is automatically shut down.

9.11 Combined Process Measurement and Control Techniques

Combined gaging is a type of process control which utilizes both in-process and postprocess measurement, as shown schematically in Fig. 9.14.

Under this arrangement, the postprocess system monitors the performance of its companion system on the machine and, when corrective action is necessary because of machine drift, causes the system on the

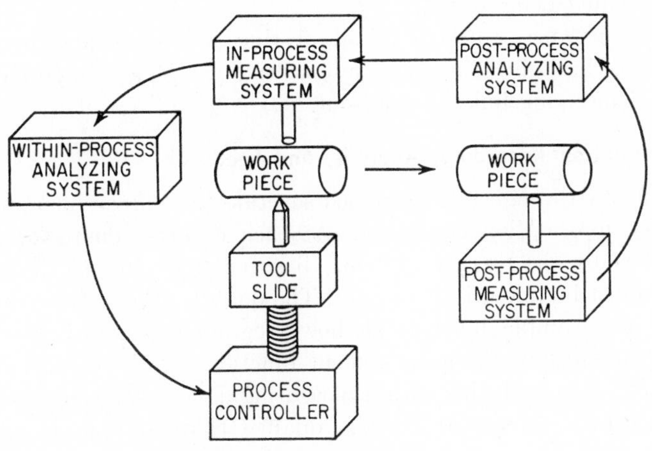

COMBINED PROCESS CONTROL

FIG. 9.14.

machine to reset or zero itself, either in increments or by an amount equal to the variation.

In this way, the in-process system, whose characteristic function is to control random deviation, also compensates for machine drift at the command of the postprocess system. This combined action can permit close control over quality level of machine or process output for extended periods of time.

9.12 Reliability Test Equipment for Laboratory Evaluation

Some of the most exacting quality information equipment engineering is required in the postprocess measurement and control stage for product-reliability evaluation. Although postprocess reliability-testing equipment may not be as totally mechanized over all seven functions as some in-process systems, a high degree of programming and precision on measurement is usually required. Considerable ingenuity is required in accurately simulating end-use conditions. All the conditions that the product may see in use must be duplicated in the combination sequences and time durations that the product will encounter in order to provide accurate reliability evaluation. This means that a number of environments may be in combination, such as temperature, pressure, vibration, and shock. The levels for these environments are dynamically varying with time. Simultaneously, the loading on the product may be varying.

This calls for some very elaborate programming of test conditions with a variety of inputs to the product under test and read-out of product performance at different stages of the test. Duration of the test may be a few minutes up to many days, or even months, depending upon the type of product being tested.

In some instances, such as missile testing, it is necessary to read out performance in flight. This calls for sensitive yet rugged instrumentation with a telemetering link for read-out.

9.13 Information Recording, Analysis, and Feedback

Sections 9.7 through 9.12 discussed several of the areas for application of quality information equipment. At each of these points of process, as specified by the quality system, all seven functions, as discussed in Sec. 9.5, must be taken into account. The quality information equipment engineer, for example, must decide how programming is to be performed. He must decide how the measurement function is to be carried on.

He may accomplish this with a measuring device which senses what is happening to a particular process quality characteristic (speed, size, temperature, volume, etc.) and a transducing device which communicates the value of the controlled variable to an analysis element in terms of pressure, force, position, electrical potential, etc. There are many instances where measuring and transducing are accomplished with the same device.

For another example, he must determine how the information that has been recorded and processed is to be analyzed. He may accomplish this with devices which display, record and store information, analyze, compute and make comparisons, and feed back a signal to the process controlling element. This analyzing element is a device that is programmed to know what *should be happening* and *what should be done* if the event is not occurring.

There are many equipment alternatives open to the quality information equipment engineer as he makes his decisions with respect to how the several functions are to be performed. The very rapid development in these equipment areas make discussion of their details beyond the scope of this chapter

The quality information equipment engineer will keep himself abreast of these developments by studying the literature of industrial electronics and industrial instrumentation technologies; by attending equipment exhibits and shows; by exchanging visits with engineers of companies providing such equipment elements; by continually studying the latest

FIG. 9.15. Automatic relay tester (General Electric Company, Specialty Control Department).

trends in control systems design, information processing, and feedback systems.

This may lead the information equipment engineer to many new devices for accomplishing his objective. For example, he may specify a piece of test equipment which, within itself, performs most of the seven functions of the quality information equipment system.

An instance of such an equipment is an automated tester for relays. The automatic relay tester[5] (Fig. 9.15) employs a unique method for obtaining quality information to monitor and aid control of a process.

[5] The automatic relay tester was developed by C. L. Beattie and M. E. Stanford. The following discussion in Sec. 9.13 and Fig. 9.15 has been provided through the courtesy of the General Electric Company, Specialty Control Department, Waynesboro, Va. where this and similar equipment is manufactured for sale.

A new method of classifying information by converting absolute measurements into cellular form is used. Results, including the decision to accept or reject each tested circuit, are presented both by visual read-out device and by recording on a standard printer.

The relays are set up in two banks of five each. One bank is tested at a time, and a visual display indicates which bank is under test, which test is being performed, and which relay is being tested in the bank. While one bank is being tested, the other can be set up with new units.

All measurement results, such as bounce time, volts, amperes, and ohms are transduced to a common denominator in the data-classifier section and presented in cellular form. Ten cells in the "accept" range (or ± 3 sigma) are used for classifying all parameters, and the visual display as well as the print-out shows a single cell number (0 thru 9). There are also 10 cells above and 10 below the "accept" range so that data can be kept on the degree of failure. For instance, if a measured parameter falls above the "accept" range in cell 7, the digital read-out and print-out will show + 7.

Catastrophic failures beyond the 30-cell range are indicated by red lights on the panel and appropriate print-out.

A second mode of operation can be used utilizing the complete 30-cell range for "accept" and only a reject indication for everything else.

The following measurements are made on each relay:

Parameter measured	*No. of times measured*	*Data classified*
Coil resistance	Once	One value
Contact resistance	10 times each contact	Single highest value
Pickup volts or amperes	Once	One value
Dropout volts or amperes	Once	One value
Pickup time	10 times	Single longest time
Dropout time	10 times	Single longest time
Pickup bounce time	10 times each contact	Single longest time
Dropout bounce time	10 times each contact	Single longest time

The timeliness of the information plus the uniform method of cellular classification for all parameters allows quick detection and analysis of process deviation from normal. The early detection of such deviations as provided by this quality information test system reduces scrap and rework losses in the product. Experience has proved that the dollars saved in this area are equal to or greater than those saved by the automatic and uniform measurement capabilities of the tester.

The output is also suitable for punched tape if further computer analysis is desired.

Modularization and the cellular classification concept make this system adaptable to a wide range of components and parameters.

9.14 Evaluating and Analyzing the Measurement Operation

The foregoing discussion has outlined some basic principles used in planning equipment systems. Use of these principles is essential, not only in providing efficient, effective measurement facilities for new installations, but also in the equally important task of improving quality information equipment that is in service and has been operating for some period of time.

This section discusses a method for evaluating the current status of

TEST AUTOMATION PLANNING SHEET

TEST ____________________ DATE ____________________

INSTRUCTIONS

1. Classify all test operations into basic elements, such as shown on tag chart.
2. Analyze each element; mark automation level on the tag chart. Connect points.
3. Obtain element time (either manual or total) and write in as per cent of total.
4. Obtain test cost for each element (or group) and record (use labor or total test cost).
5. For each element, analyze possible mechanization methods. Consider all improvement potentials and savings. Estimate equipment costs.
6. Determine the highest justified automation level for each test operation element. Mark levels on chart; connect points.
7. Use the work planning section to plan sequence and work schedule for mechanization or automation of test elements.
8. Indicate operation element, initiation date, work detail schedules with completion dates, and show equipment cost (design material, labor etc.), and actual net savings expected. (Use appropriate base-yearly or per unit.)
9. Indicate at bottom completion date and total costs and savings.

TAG · · · TEST AUTOMATION GROWTH · · · TAG

TEST OPERATION ELEMENTS TEST ______ DATE ______			TEST SET UP	POSITION	CONNECT	SELECT TESTS	OPERATE	MEASURE	ADJUST	RECORD	DATA ANALYSIS	FEED BACK	DISCONNECT	REJECT	REMOVE	TEST TEAR DOWN	TOTAL TIME AND COST
Present	% Time																
	Cost																
Proposed	% Time																
	Cost																
Actual	% Time																
	Cost																
AUTOMATION LEVELS — AUTOMATIC	Anticipation, Decision and Correction	100															
	Decision and Correction	90															
	Fault Indicating	80															
	Self Checking	70															
	Simple Decision	60															
	Programmed	50															
MECHANIZED	Operator Initiated	40															
	Operator Cycled	30															
	Hand + Power Aid	20															
MANUAL	Hand + Mechanical Aid	10															
	Hand	0															
	NONE	—															

Tag Chart Benefits
Aids in:

1. Picturing present and proposed test operations.
2. Making a systematic analysis of a test operation.
3. Planning improved test methods.
4. Integrating test operations with manufacturing operations for continuous flow.
5. Analyzing test cost and savings.
6. Spotlighting pay-off areas.
7. Developing realistic improvement schedules.
8. Preparing estimates for equipment appropriations.
9. Selling equipment improvement programs.
10. Maintaining good Employee Relations through adequate and timely information.

FIG. 9.16. Test automation planning sheet.

TAG - - TEST AUTOMATION GROWTH SCHEDULE - - TAG

DATES			Element	Brief Description of Change	Equipment	Cost	Net Savings
Initiate	Target	Complete					
Completion Date					TOTALS		
Special Benefits							

TEST OPERATION ELEMENTS

1. Set up - Prepare test equipment for test.
2. Position - Prepare for test; move into place.
3. Connect - Connect product with motivating sources, measurement devices, etc.
4. Select test - Select for each test: voltages, currents, measuring equip., gages, etc.
5. Operate - Apply power; actuate; bring up to operating condition; etc.
6. Measurement - Perform function of measuring or comparing, including necessary setting of instruments; balance; adjust, etc.
7. Adjust - Adjustments, corrections, settings, etc. on unit to obtain specified operation of unit under test.
8. Record - Record measurement data or results, identification, etc.
9. Data Analysis - Classification of data; computations; preparation for feedback.
10. Information Feedback - Transmit test results or analyses to shop operations. Q.C. Engineering, or Design Engineering.
11. Disconnect - Disconnect motivating sources, etc.
12. Reject - Removal of defective unit.
13. Remove - Remove from test position or location.
14. Test Tear Down - Dismantle set up of test facilities and equipment.

TEST AUTOMATION LEVELS

1. Hand - Use of human faculties alone.
2. Hand + Mechanical Aid - Use of hand operated switches, screw drivers, etc.
3. Hand + Powered Aid - Use of powered clamps, hoists, screw drivers, etc.
4. Operator Cycled - A powered piece of equipment controlled by an operator.
5. Operator Initiated - Completely automatic with the exception of starting.
6. Automatic Program - An operation directed by a fixed cycle programming device.
7. Simple Decision - An operation controlled by a decision from a sensing device.
8. Self Checking - Test equipment compared to standard to insure desired performance.
9. Fault Indicating - Indicates source of faults in test equipment, product or process.
10. Decision and Correction - Sensing device initiates feedback for automatic correction.
11. Anticipation, Decision and Correction - Corrective action before fault occurs.

FIG. 9.16. (Reverse side) Test automation planning sheet.

such equipment with respect to the functions it performs and the degree of mechanization that is indicated. The discussion will use, as its example, the evaluation of a testing position through use of an analytical procedure called *TAG* (*test automation growth*) *charting.*[6] The same analytical procedure is equally applicable to inspection positions, quality-audit position, etc.

Its current mechanization level can be plotted for each element of a test operation on the TAG chart (Fig. 9.16), and after analysis and study of each of these elements, a second, or theoretically desirable, level of mechanization or automation can be established. With the test costs, savings, and other benefits listed for each element and for the test

[6] The TAG chart was developed by E. S. Acton, E. T. Angell, and D. D. Ward after principles originally published by James R. Bright, General Electric Company.

operation as a whole, the chart can readily be used as an aid to the quality information equipment engineer in planning and scheduling for increased mechanization of measurement operations. To measure and gage the mechanization level of a series of operations effectively it is necessary to

1. Classify the operations into discrete and definable elements.
2. Establish a method of evaluating the various levels of mechanization that presently exist and those that may be developed.
3. Conceive and study methods of mechanizing tests.
4. Evaluate proposed changes from an economic and improved quality point of view.

Each of these four steps will be discussed below:

Classifying the Elements of the Test Position.

1. Classify all operations for this test into basic elements, such as those shown on the chart (Fig. 9.16, reverse side).
2. Analyze each element and mark its standing in the proper "automation level." Connect the points thus plotted.

Evaluating the Levels of Mechanization.

1. Add the numerical values assigned to each of the individual elements and divide by the total number of elements to determine the average "automation level." (This numerical rating is an arbitrarily assigned value from 0 to 100 for general rating purposes.)
2. Determine the manual or elapsed time (whichever is under study) for each of the test operation elements and show the percentage of the total time in the space provided.
3. Obtain the test cost for each element (or group of elements) and record in the space provided. All costs relating to the test should be analyzed for inclusion here, since for some operations, power or fuel consumed may be more significant than labor costs, or vice versa.

Figure 9.17 is an example of how the test position for an electrical relay comes out diagrammatically when plotted. Note that, although some of the elements are in the automatic area, several are in the hand stages. Note also the division of the testing time. For instance, in this example, almost half the time of test is consumed in selecting power sources, meters, etc.

Studying for Improvement.

1. For each test element, analyze the possible mechanization methods.
2. Consider all the improvement potentials and savings which would be realized. Estimate the equipment costs for upgrading the various elements.

Evaluating the Necessary Changes.

1. Determine the highest automation level which is justified for each test operation element, in the light of the costs and savings involved.

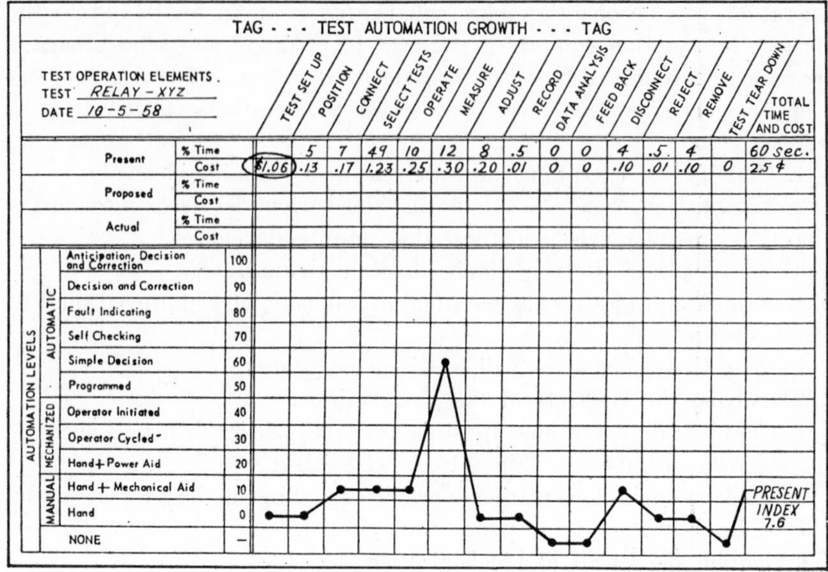

FIG. 9.17. TAG chart for electric relay.

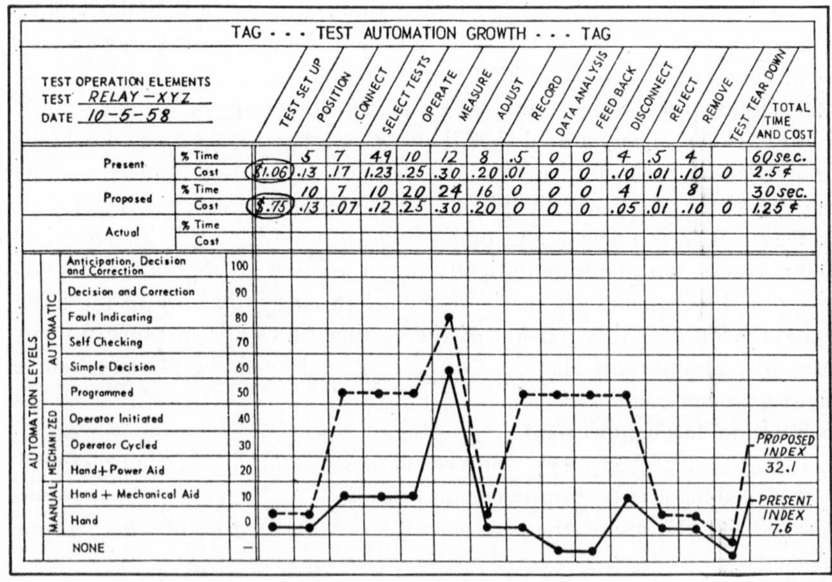

FIG. 9.18. Completed TAG chart for electric relay.

2. Mark these new levels for each element in the appropriate box on the same chart. Connect the new points, using dashed lines or a different colored pencil.

3. This new growth line shows where the advance planning work of the quality information engineer should be directed. The completed TAG chart for the relay test example is shown in Fig. 9.18.

Equipment Specification Planning

9.15 Specifying the Equipment

When a new product design is approximately halfway through its time cycle, the transition of the quality-control equipment-design job begins from advanced conceptual development, as discussed above, to detailed design planning. The design-planning phase consists of finalizing the measurement and control methods, techniques, and equipment in a form that can be used as a specification either for detailed design within the company or for deciding on procurement of the equipment from an outside vendor. Detailed cost estimates for the design and development of equipment are prepared. The specifications for the over-all quality information system are firmly determined, and the detailed specifications for each individual equipment are established, including accuracy, capacity, size, operational requirements, safety, productivity, and operational costs. Figure 9.19 shows a check list for specifying or designing

---

Quality Information Equipment Specification

Check list for specifying or designing equipment

1. Applicable Standards, Codes, and Drawings

NEMA	Sketches
AIEE	Drawings
EIA	Engineering specifications
Safety codes	Operational plannings

2. General Information and Alternate Plans
    - Function of equipment
    - Environmental conditions
        - General
        - Specific

Shock	Lubricants
Temperature	Dirt
Moisture	Chips

    - Delivery requirements
    - Alternate systems of equipment that may fulfill requirements
3. Design and operational requirements
    - Characteristics to be checked

Voltage
Current
Frequency
Power
Dimension
Chemical property
Physical property

Where will characteristics be checked?
Process
Assembly
Final

Input and output requirements
Power
Frequency
Voltage
Connections
Shielding
Pressure

Speed of operation
Number of measurements per unit time
Time available per measurement
Dwell time of paced components
Delay time for information feedback
Time for memory storage of data
Time required for computations
Time required for work classification

Safety requirements
Grounding
Interlocks
Barriers
Safety control circuits

Type of equipment this unit must operate with

Special maintenance features
Plug-in components
Rack-mounted units
Adjustment elements in accessible locations
Test points available
Failure indicating system

Provision for expansion or additions
Physical size
Speed of operation
Quantity of work handled

4. Accuracy and Calibration
State accuracy required
System
Components
Meters
Transducers
Reliability
Calibration
Frequency of calibration
Time required
Self-calibrating

- Separate calibration
  - At location where used
  - At location other than where used
- Master piece required
- Standard required

5. Information output requirements
   - Classification of work checked
   - Visual read-out
   - Records required
     - Statistical chart
     - Digital data
     - Analog data
   - Work identification
   - If used for feedback control
     - What is to be controlled?
     - Control input requirements
     - Connections
6. Materials and Construction
   - Material in
     - Cabinet
     - Chassis
     - Knobs
     - Meters
     - Panels
     - Cabling
     - Control handles
     - Transducers
     - Sensors
   - Construction Features
     - Limitations of
       - Size
       - Space
       - Weight
     - Conformance to
       - Other equipment—give requisition number if available
       - Materials-handling equipment
     - Physical appearance
       - Sloping front
       - Layout of components
       - Layout of controls
       - Paint requirements
       - Type of lettering
       - Name-plate data
     - Method of mounting
       - Fixed
       - Soft tires
       - Portable
       - Locking wheels
     - Special precautions
       - Exclude dust and dirt
       - Explosion proof

Safety precautions
    Ground straps
    Polarized connectors
7. Provision for Instructions
    Operating instructions
    Calibrating instructions
    Maintenance instructions
    Installation instructions
    Parts list
    Spare-parts list
    Schematic drawings
    Wiring diagrams
    Assistance of manufacturer to set up
    Where to get operation assistance
8. Acceptance Checks
    Availability of equipment at manufacturer's plant to ascertain quality of materials and workmanship
    Surveillance of tests to ascertain compliance
    Provision for specified evaluation period after installation
    Process-capability parameters
    Work pieces required for evaluation
        Quantity
        Rate needed

FIG. 9.19. Quality information specification check list.

quality information equipment. The schedule of equipment design, procurement, construction, check-out, and release for operation is timetabled and coordinated with the other segments of the quality system plan.

It is at this time that the details of prototype, sample, and preproduction testing are established and coordinated among quality information equipment engineering, quality-control engineering, and process-control engineering to provide for a team operation of product or process performance analysis and/or determination of rapid corrective action to assure smooth continuity of manufacturing operations.

Design, Procurement, and Construction

9.16 Getting the Equipment Built

The transition from the design-planning stage into the design-procurement and construction phase of the equipment job is essentially one from the planning and organization portion of the program to that of performance and measurement of results. It is in this phase of the equipment job that the detailed design and development of the individual pieces of equipment is either performed within the company or externally subcontracted. Sketches, layouts, circuit diagrams, itemized material lists, and detailed equipment specification sheets are originated. The associated test and inspection operation instructions, which have been developed by quality-control engineering technology, are finalized, and the required equipment operating instructions and calibration and maintenance procedures are drafted. Material is ordered and received and the necessary construction of equipment and facilities performed.

It is normally during this phase of the quality information equipment job, when new-product designs are involved, that the prototype new design is completed and subjected to detailed design evaluation tests to confirm its performance to product requirements and specifications. It is often essential that these tests be followed closely and in detail by the quality information equipment engineers, since performance failures and accompanying design corrections may directly affect the quality-system plan and its associated equipment.

Installation, Check-out, and Follow-up

9.17 Getting the Equipment into Operation

The fourth and last set of techniques of quality information equipment engineering involves equipment installation, check-out, and follow-up.

This phase usually commences just prior to the preproduction run and continues through the build-up to full-rated manufacturing operation. It consists of "debugging" the various equipment components of the quality system, verifying equipment applications and operating, calibration, and maintenance instructions, and instructing and training the operating personnel in equipment usage.

In addition, a capability study is made on the quality information equipment system as a whole, as well as a detailed analysis of the performance of all quality information equipment against its individual specifications.

The concern at this point is in two areas: with the capabilities of the equipment and equipment system to perform satisfactorily to the system specifications; and with the capability of the equipment as it works in conjunction with all the process variables as required by the quality system plan. The process-control engineer is responsible to check the equipment for speed, accuracy, repeatability, and safety under operating conditions. He may find a large margin of safety on accuracy but, for example, poor performance on repeatability in the assigned application.

The quality information equipment engineer may institute a card-record system, which may serve as notification to the process-control engineer that equipment is being built or is on order from a vendor. The process-control engineer may then be alerted to assure that proper incoming checks are made on the equipment. If the equipment has been designed and constructed internally, the equipment engineer will evaluate it against the design specifications; if it is a purchased equipment, satisfactory evaluation may have been performed on a representative unit prior to purchasing the equipment.

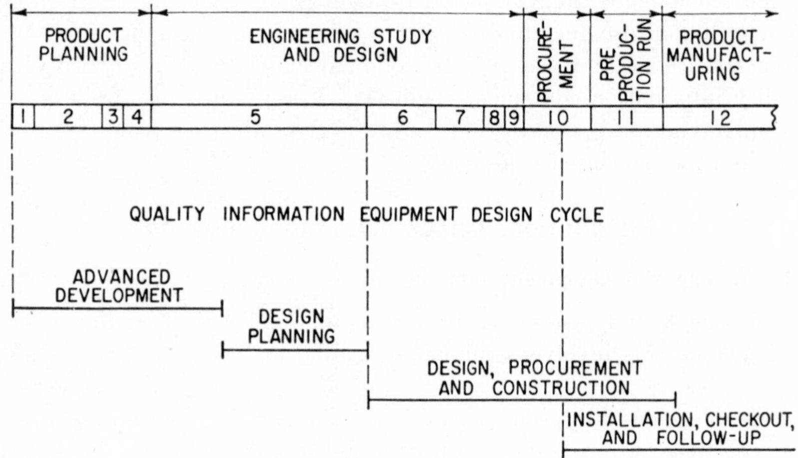

1. Request for product development.
2. Review by product planning.
3. Tentative management approval.
4. Development authorization approval.
5. Preliminary design.
6. Prototype manufacture.
7. Review and final recommendations by Product Planning.
8. Management approval.
9. Final drawings.
10. Conditional manufacturing release.
11. Preproduction manufacture.
12. Full manufacturing release.

FIG. 9.20. Product development cycle.

When the process-control engineer has evaluated the equipment for use under operating conditions, he may retain the notification card from the equipment designer. If the equipment does not perform satisfactorily when installed, or if modification would improve its usefulness, the process-control engineer then sends the card to the equipment designer with a request for the needed changes. For example, he may find that a locating pin on a checking fixture is to drawing but insertion of the product into the fixture scratches one face of the product; or he may find that shop supply voltages fluctuate radically, thus requiring voltage regulation to be added to a piece of testing equipment.

The quality information equipment is jointly released for production use when the quality information equipment engineer and the process-control engineer have assured that the equipment itself functions properly and that it can be used properly in this application.

In order to relate these four phases of the quality information equipment design cycle to the steps in the normal cycle of product development, the chart in Fig. 9.20 is shown.

PART FOUR

STATISTICAL TECHNOLOGY OF QUALITY CONTROL

CHAPTER 10

FREQUENCY DISTRIBUTIONS

The greatly increased precision demanded of manufactured parts has been accompanied by the need for better methods to measure and specify and record it. That statistics, the so-called science of measurements, would become one of the most valuable techniques used in the four quality-control jobs was almost inevitable.

Statistical methods have had a long and rocky road to the general acceptance that they now enjoy in industry. Opposition to them was due, in part, to the natural resistance met during the introduction of any new method.

In part, it was due to the shopmen's fear of the mathematical symbols which seemed to cloak industrial statistics with an air of mystery. In part, it was due to the overabundance of technical statistics and the underabundance of practical administrative applications that characterized the literature which reached industrial management. In part, it was due to the simple fact that the formal education of many graduate engineers overlooked concentration on this subject. Today there is a growing wealth of material on the practical aspects and theoretical details of industrial statistics. The statistical terminology and mathematics have been reduced to simple arithmetic and algebra for general use. A surprisingly large number of industrial employees have been trained in these methods.

The victory of statistical methods in industry really represented a compromise between "pure" statistics and the practical realities of industrial situations. Statistical methods, as actually practiced in total quality control, do not represent an exact science. Their character is strongly influenced by human relations factors, technological conditions, and considerations of cost.

A plant quality-control program may, for example, be faced with the problem of choosing between two sampling tables. One table may be quite precise statistically but may be difficult for shop people to comprehend. The other table may not be so precise statistically but may be much easier to administer. It would be quite typical for the plant to select the latter table.

Probably more important than these methods themselves has been the impact upon industrial thinking of the philosophy they represent. The "statistical point of view" resolves essentially into this: *variation* in product quality must be constantly studied

Within batches of product.

On processing equipments.

Between different lots of the same article.

On critical quality characteristics and standards.

In regard to pilot runs of a newly designed article.

This variation can best be studied by the analysis of samples selected from the lots of products or from units produced by the processing equipments.

This point of view, which emphasizes the study of variation, has had a significant effect upon quality-control activities wherein the actual statistical methods themselves are not used. The study of variation that is recommended has begun to go beyond the bounds of quality control itself into other administrative areas like time study, safety engineering, and personnel administration.

Five statistical tools have come to be used in the quality-control jobs. They are

1. Frequency distributions.
2. Control charts.
3. Sampling tables.
4. Special methods.
5. Reliability prediction.

Some understanding of these tools is useful for full technological comprehension of total quality control. For this reason and because of the relative newness of some of these methods, Part Four discusses them in some detail in its five chapters.

The discussion follows a pattern whereby the general approach to each of the five tools is first presented in the appropriate chapter. Later sections of the chapter present some of the qualifications and limitations that may be required by particular industrial applications of the tool. Industrial experience with presenting the point of view of statistics, as used in quality control, indicates the desirability of this pattern of presentation.

The Concept of the Frequency Distribution

10.1 The Universal Nature of Manufacturing Variations

One of the characteristics of modern manufacturing is that no two pieces are ever made exactly alike. The variations may be small—as in the case of gage blocks, which have been guaranteed to two-millionths of an inch. Whether large or small, variations exist in parts manufactured in all production processes whether they be hand lathes, blanking presses, annealing furnaces, or painting machines.

Some variations are so great that they are immediately shown by modern measuring equipments. Other variations are so minute that successive readings on measuring equipment will reflect primarily the variation of the measuring equipments themselves rather than that of the parts.

Among the types of parts variations, three classifications useful for analytical purposes are

1. *Variations within the part itself,* as illustrated by a small shaft which is out of round at one end and within tolerance at the other end.
2. *Variations among parts produced during the same period of time,* as illustrated by the variation in the length of studs produced by a screw machine during a 5-minute period.
3. *Variations among parts produced at different periods of time,* as illustrated by the variation in length between studs produced at the beginning of the first shift as compared with those produced at the end of the shift.

There are many factors that contribute to any or all of these variations. Among them are tool wear, bearings that loosen, machine vibrations, faulty jigs and fixtures, poor raw materials, careless or untrained operators, and weather changes.

Industry has long recognized the inevitability of these variations. It includes, on drawings and specifications, tolerances which designate the permissible deviation from the standard shape, thickness, color, and size.

10.2 Recording Parts Variations

As closer and closer tolerance limits have been specified, it has been increasingly necessary for shopmen to keep a close check on dimensions. *Go* and *not-go* inspection has been the most widely used procedure for this purpose. Out-of-limits parts are sorted from those which are within limits. Figure 10.1 shows a record of such an inspection.

These data may tell a shop foreman that he must take corrective action to reduce rejects. But it will give him few guides to what that action should be. Were the rejects caused by improper machine setups? By tool wobble? By operator carelessness? By poor materials?

Another type of record was developed by the inspection foreman of an Eastern plant to tabulate the outer diameter dimensions of shafts.

DAILY REPORT AUTOMATIC SECTION		
PART	NO. INSPECTED	NO. REJECTED
STUD DWG. 53415	863	67
BRACKET DWG. 6753	1892	103
STUD DWG. 52318	657	112

FIG. 10.1.

The nominal value for this shaft diameter is 0.730 inch, with a tolerance of ± 0.002 inch.

The form used is called a *tally card.* Shaft dimensions from 0.725 to 0.735 inch are listed across the bottom of the card. While examining completed shafts, inspectors record the outer diameter measurements by placing an x in the appropriate spot on the tally card. Figure 10.2 shows such a card.

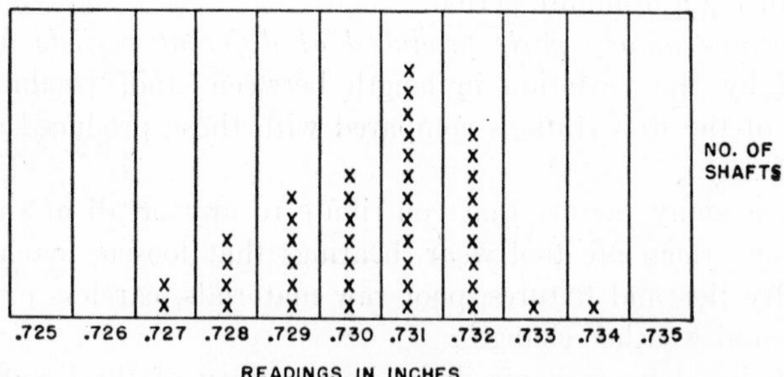

FIG. 10.2.

As compared with Fig. 10.1, this type of record gives a much more effective guide for corrective action. It furnishes at a glance a *picture* of just what and where are parts variations rather than indicating whether the shafts are simply "good" or "bad."

The *where* of parts variations may be learned in many cases because there are certain pictures which are characteristic of causes of variation. If the picture shows a widely spread distribution, it may, as in the case cited above, indicate tool wobble. A picture which shows parts bunched below the nominal 0.730-inch dimension may indicate that the machine-tool setup requires a change.

Figure 10.2 is a form of *frequency distribution.* The common sense of the inspection foreman had led him to the use of the graphic tally, which is the heart of the frequency distribution.

10.3 Defining the Frequency Distribution

The frequency distribution may be defined as a

Tabulation, or tally, of the number of times a given quality-characteristic measurement occurs within the sample of product being checked.

The tabulation may be plotted with frequency of occurrence on the vertical axis and some quality characteristic (inches, volts, magnetic strength, pounds, hardness) plotted on the horizontal scale. It then is properly called a *frequency curve.*

Industrial usage, however, has come to term this type of tabulation a *frequency-distribution curve* or, most popularly, simply a frequency distribution. It is the latter term that will be used here.

10.4 A Frequency-distribution Example

The length characteristic of a certain type of brass stud furnishes an interesting example of the frequency distribution. These studs are produced on a screw machine. Their length is determined by a cutoff operation. The drawing specification for this length calls for 0.500 ± 0.005 inch.

LENGTH OF STUD – .500 ± .005

1.	.498	11.	.500	21.	.505	31.	.503	41.	.502
2.	.501	12.	.499	22.	.502	32.	.501	42.	.501
3.	.504	13.	.501	23.	.504	33.	.504	43.	.504
4.	.502	14.	.502	24.	.504	34.	.501	44.	.502
5.	.503	15.	.504	25.	.501	35.	.500	45.	.500
6.	.504	16.	.499	26.	.503	36.	.502	46.	.502
7.	.502	17.	.503	27.	.502	37.	.499	47.	.504
8.	.505	18.	.502	28.	.500	38.	.502	48.	.501
9.	.503	19.	.503	29.	.501	39.	.503	49.	.503
10.	.500	20.	.502	30.	.501	40.	.503	50.	.503

FIG. 10.3.

Fifty pieces may be arbitrarily chosen as the size of the sample to be checked. The studs are selected as they are successively completed by the machine.

The resulting micrometer readings may be recorded as shown in Fig. 10.3.

This mass of numbers may be scanned for some time without gaining any useful concept of the over-all conformance of the sample of 50 studs to the drawing specification. To clarify this picture, the data can be grouped by like dimension; that is, all 0.500-inch readings will be grouped together, all 0.501-inch readings will be so grouped, and so forth. A card can be prepared which lists the suitable divisions. As in Fig. 10.4, the number of times a reading occurs can be recorded opposite the appropriate division. This represents its *frequency* of occurrence. These divisions are usually termed *cells.*

Figure 10.4 can be converted into a graph by substituting individual *x*s for the numbers listed in the frequency column. Figure 10.5 is the result.

FREQUENCY DISTRIBUTION ON LENGTH OF STUD – .500 ± .005

LENGTH		FREQ.		FREQ. IN %
.495				
.496				
.497				
.498		1		2%
.499		3		6%
.500		5		10%
.501		9		18%
.502		12		24%
.503		10		20%
.504		8		16%
.505		2		4%
TOTAL		50		100%

FREQUENCY DIAGRAM

FIG. 10.4.

LENGTH	FREQUENCY
.495	
.496	
.497	
.498	X
.499	XXX
.500	XXXXX
.501	XXXXXXXXX
.502	XXXXXXXXXXXX
.503	XXXXXXXXXX
.504	XXXXXXXX
.505	XX

FREQUENCY DISTRIBUTION

FIG. 10.5.

It is possible to go still further and to join the tops of the columns of *x*s. This results in the frequency-distribution curve of Fig. 10.6.

The steps illustrated by Figs. 10.3 and 10.4 are often eliminated in practical factory use. Measurements are directly recorded as in Fig. 10.5.

Figures 10.5 and 10.6 present a picture of the length characteristic of the sample of brass studs. Such features about the group quality of stud lengths are shown as

1. *The approximate central value.* This will usually reflect the dimension at which the screw machine was set up.

2. *The spread of the values.* This will reflect the variability of raw materials or possibly that of the screw-machine cutoff operation itself.

3. *The relation of the values to the drawing tolerance.* This will be important as a guide to corrective action if any is necessary.

10.5 The Analytical Use of This Frequency-distribution Picture

Suppose that the 50 studs shown in Fig. 10.6 are being checked for the purpose of approving the setup of the screw machine preliminary to a long production run. Is the setup satisfactory?

Since all the studs are within the drawing tolerance, approval on a go and not-go basis would undoubtedly result in an "O.K." for the setup.

The frequency-distribution picture of Fig. 10.6 furnishes a far more useful basis for approval than this go and not-go approach. It provides a wealth of information that would be unavailable from a go and not-go check. The inspector, operator, or foreman who glances at Fig. 10.6 may see the following:

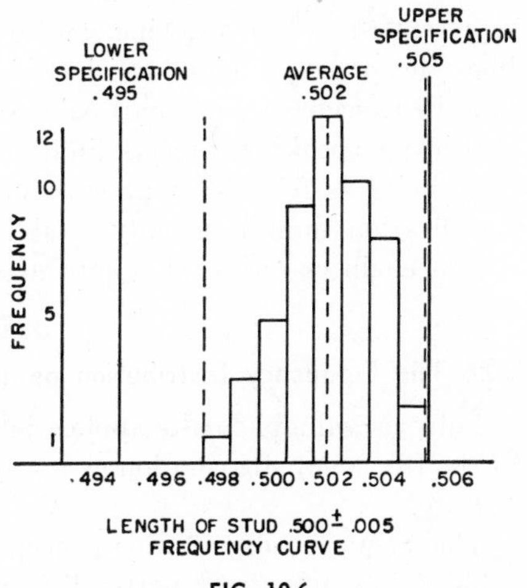

FIG. 10.6.

1. From the way that parts are bunched around 0.504 and 0.505 inch, common sense dictates that some parts may be produced during a long production run that will measure 0.506 or 0.507 inch and so be unacceptable. This condition is all the more critical because, in this particular operation, tool wear tends to produce longer studs. There may be a tendency for parts to measure well over 0.506 or 0.507 inch during the latter part of the run.

2. The total variation of the parts checked is 0.007 inch. This compares favorably with the 0.010-inch total tolerance allowed by the drawing.

3. The machine is set up about 0.002 inch above the nominal dimension; 0.502 inch seems to be the central value on Fig. 10.6.

This information might suggest the appropriate corrective action to the shopmen: a longer, more economical production run may be obtained by taking advantage of the acceptable 0.007-inch spread. The screw machine may be reset so that 0.500, rather than 0.502 inch, will be approached as the nominal reading; or considering the tool wear, 0.499 inch may be used as nominal.

In the actual situation represented by this example, the screw machine was reset in this way. A successful production run was obtained from this action.

This type of application, treating the frequency distribution as a simple picture with no algebraic analysis, is one of its most popular industrial uses. There are many adaptations of this application: different sample sizes are used; different forms are made up for plotting the distribution.

Shop people sometimes like to plot in dashed limit lines at the upper and lower ends of the distribution, as shown in Fig. 10.6. These dashed lines are often called *process limits.*

The shop people usually also plot in somewhat heavier lines, which represent the actual drawing specification. Compared with these heavier lines the process limits furnish a simple prediction of the quality that may be expected from a particular setup on a given machine or process.

Broadly speaking, process limits can be distinguished from specification limits as follows: a process limit is set by the operation itself; a specification limit is usually established by a human being—often the design engineer—who takes into account factors external to the operation.

10.6 The Frequency Distribution as a Way of Thought

Fully as valuable as its application as an analytical method is the use of the frequency distribution as a way of viewing modern product manufacture.

The frequency-distribution concept emphasizes that variation is inevitable in manufactured parts. This variation generally takes a definite frequency pattern, which cannot be learned by examination of only two or three pieces.

Men and women in industry are often prone to think of manufactured parts as individual items, each uniquely representative of the process by which and the design to which they were produced. To learn about these processes and designs, shop people may feel that only a few pieces need be examined. This point of view is probably a carry-over from the days when manufacturing was on an individual job-lot basis.

The frequency distribution states that these individual pieces tell relatively little when they are studied by themselves. The lot of which these pieces are a part yields the significant information. Individual pieces are best thought of as units of a larger lot. Truly to represent the quality characteristics of these pieces requires the study of a sample of adequate size drawn from the lot to which the pieces belong.

Costly errors occur when this concept is not appreciated. An engineer may spend a great deal of time in the design and development of a new product. He may be certain that the article can be produced satisfactorily on the factory floor.

When active production begins, however, manufacturing difficulties may be reported by the shop organization. A large number of articles may be rejected by Inspection. Days may occur when the various parts will not fit together into the assembly of the article.

The engineer may bitterly feel that the shop has not organized itself adequately to produce the article. In its turn, the shop may feel that the engineer has turned out an incomplete design.

What may actually have happened is that the engineer did devote a great deal of attention to tests on two or three sample assemblies and to checks on five or six parts. But he did not test a sufficient number of articles to give a representative picture of the total variation to be expected when all possible variables have come into play.

Figure 10.7 represents this situation. The two xs represent the units actually tested by the engineer. The dashed frequency curve represents the total distribution of which these two units are a part. It is the effect of this distribution curve which may be mirrored in the difficulties the shop is having with this article.

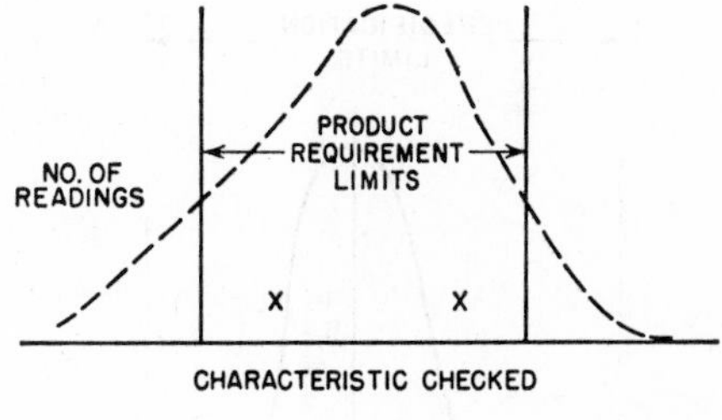

FIG. 10.7.

A similar error may occur when a machine-tool setup is being approved preliminary to a long production run. Only two or three pieces may be checked. In some instances, such as when the variability of the machine is known, this sample size might be satisfactory. In many cases, however, it will not be at all representative of the total variation that may be expected during the production run.

The frequency distribution, therefore, makes such important contributions to the concept of product manufacture as the following:

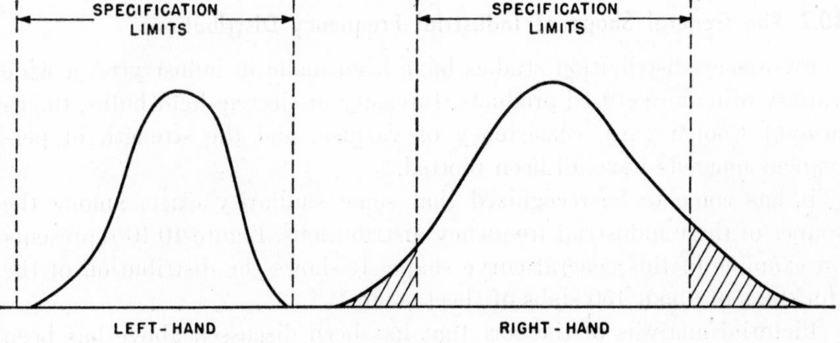

FIG. 10.8.

1. It helps to establish the *principle* that some amount of variation must always be expected among manufactured parts.

2. It helps to establish the *general nature* (see Sec. 10.7) of the graphical shape that this variation will take.

3. It helps to establish an *important approach* to the study and control of this variation.

Thus, it will help answer such questions as

1. Is the variation in a process such that parts can be produced within specification limits as far as a particular quality characteristic is concerned?

In the left-hand chart of Fig. 10.8, the answer to this question is "Yes"; in the right-hand chart, "No." The shaded area represents out-of-tolerance parts.

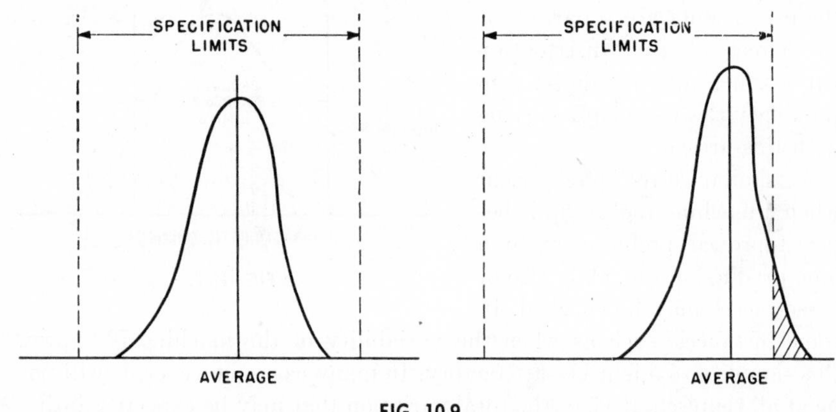

FIG. 10.9.

2. How does the average value for the quality characteristic compare with specification limits?

Figure 10.9 illustrates graphical answers to questions of this sort.

10.7 The General Shape of Industrial Frequency Distributions

Frequency-distribution studies have been made in industry on a wide variety of manufactured products. Intensity of electric-light bulbs, thickness of woolen yarn, consistency of varnish, and the strength of permanent magnets have all been plotted.

It has come to be recognized that some similarity exists among the shapes of these industrial frequency distributions. Figure 10.10 represents an example of this general curve shape. It shows the distribution of the thickness of about 150 slabs of sheet steel.

Pictorial analysis of the sort that has been discussed above has been very useful in many of these studies. But in other applications, there has been need for a more precise sort of analysis. The demand is for consolidation into a set of numbers of the essential information shown by the graphs of Figs. 10.6 and 10.10.

The algebra necessary for this job is to be found in the so-called probability mathematics.

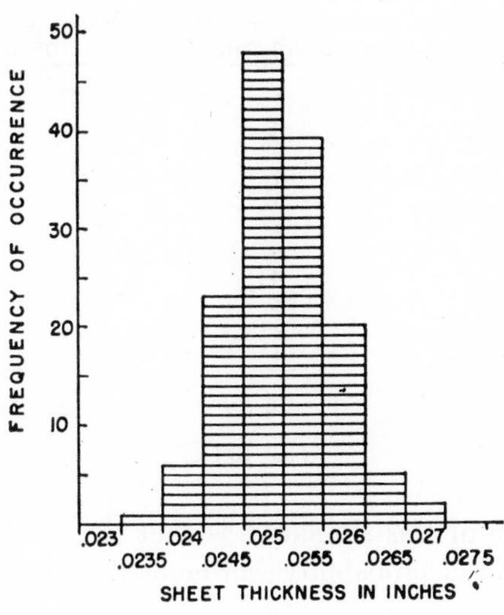

FIG. 10.10.

Mathematics of the Frequency Distribution

10.8 Probability

Everyone who is familiar with games of chance has heard or asked the question "What are the odds?" This question represents the popular recognition that there are *probabilities,* rather than certainties, associated with games of chance—whether tossing coins or waiting for a full house in poker.

The throwing of dice furnishes a useful example of the application of the laws of probability to games of chance.

In throwing one six-sided die, each of the six sides has an equal chance of coming up. In several throws, a 4 should occur as often as a 3.

Two dice may be thrown at once, and their top numbers added. This sum might range from 2 to 12. When two dice are thrown, however, fewer sides are available to turn up totals like 2 or 12 than to turn up a 7. A definite probability, or "set of odds," is associated with this situation and is shown in Fig. 10.11. In the long run, actual throws of two dice would conform to this pattern.

A frequency-distribution curve of the data in Fig. 10.11 can be plotted as shown in Fig. 10.12. The similarity of this curve shape to the industrial distributions already discussed is readily apparent. Presumably, the many variables in an industrial production process have roughly the same effect on parts variations as the so-called chance factors have upon a game like dice.

SUM OF FACES OF DICE	NUMBER OF WAYS OF GETTING THE SUM	"PROBABILITY" OR CHANCE OF OCCURRING
2	1	1/36
3	2	2/36
4	3	3/36
5	4	4/36
6	5	5/36
7	6	6/36
8	5	5/36
9	4	4/36
10	3	3/36
11	2	2/36
12	1	1/36
TOTALS	36	36/36

FIG. 10.11.

The significance of this similarity is that the algebraic measures developed in the field of probability can be used to analyze industrial frequency distributions.

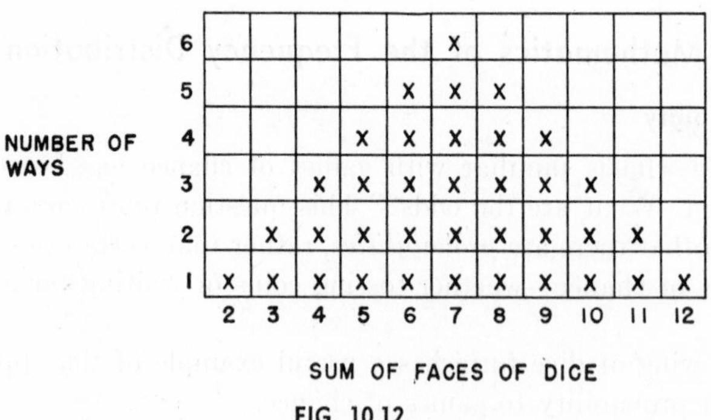

FIG. 10.12.

10.9 Algebraic Measures of the Frequency Distribution

Consider the two characteristics of the frequency distribution that have been mentioned:

1. Its *central tendency*, that is, what is the most representative value?
2. Its *spread*, or *dispersion*, that is, how much variation is there?

For industrial use, the two most valuable measures of central tendency are the *average* and the *median*.

The two most useful measures of spread are the *standard deviation* and the *range*.

10.10 Measures of Central Tendency

Average. The *average* is the most useful measure of central tendency. It is obtained by dividing the sum of the values in a series of readings by the number of readings, or symbolically:

$$\overline{X} = \frac{X_1 + X_2 + X_3 + \cdots + X_n}{n} \tag{1}$$

where $\overline{X}$ = average value (called "X bar") of the series
$X_1, X_2, \cdots, X_n$ = value of each reading
n = number of readings

In order to avoid the awkward numerator in formula (1), it has become customary to speak of the "sum of the Xs" and to use the Greek capital letter sigma (Σ) to denote this sum as (ΣX). Thus, formula (1) becomes

$$\overline{X} = \frac{\Sigma X}{n} \tag{2}$$

If there is a set of five readings—11, 12, 13, 15, 16—the average is obtained as shown:

$$\overline{X} = \frac{11 + 12 + 13 + 15 + 16}{5} = 13.4$$

In a series where there is a large number of readings, the calculation of the average is greatly simplified by first grouping together readings in suitable cells and then summing up these cells. For this condition, formula (2) may become

$$\overline{X} = \frac{\Sigma fX}{n} \tag{3}$$

where f = frequency of readings within a given valued cell (X)
ΣfX = sum of the number of readings in the cells times the value for each cell

When the values of the average for each series of readings in a number of series are calculated, it may be desirable to compute the average of these several averages. This measure is termed the *grand average*.

Symbolically, it is shown as $\overline{\overline{X}}$ (X double bar) and is calculated as in the above formulas. The grand average has its chief value in control-chart work.

Median. The *median* is sometimes used for industrial work. It is that value which divides a series of readings arranged in order of the magnitude of their values so that an equal number of values is on either side of the center or "median" value.

Thus, in a set of readings—11, 12, 14, 16, 17—the value of the median is 14. In another set of readings—8, 9, 9, 10, 11, 11, 12, 12, 13, 13, 13, 15—the value of the median is 11.5.

The median is likely to be somewhat erratic as compared with the average but is often much easier to obtain.[1] For that reason it is preferred in several types of work, particularly with control charts in machine shops.

10.11 The Standard Deviation

The *standard deviation* is used as the measure of spread for almost all industrial frequency distributions. It is the root-mean-square deviation of the readings in a series from their average. The sample standard deviation[2] is obtained by extracting the square root of the sums of the squares of the deviations of each reading in a series from the average, divided by the number of readings, or symbolically:

$$\sigma = \sqrt{\frac{(X_1 - \overline{X})^2 + (X_2 - \overline{X})^2 + (X_3 - \overline{X})^2 + \cdots + (X_n - \overline{X})^2}{n}} \qquad (4)$$

where

σ = standard deviation (called "sigma" from the Greek small letter)

$X_1, X_2, \cdots, X_n$ = value of each reading

$\overline{X}$ = average value of the series

n = number of readings

Thus, in the series 4, 5, 6, 7, 8, where the average is 6, the standard deviation can be calculated as follows:

$$\sigma = \sqrt{\frac{(4-6)^2 + (5-6)^2 + (6-6)^2 + (7-6)^2 + (8-6)^2}{5}}$$

$$= \sqrt{\frac{4+1+0+1+4}{5}} = \sqrt{\frac{10}{5}}$$

$$= 1.414$$

Where there is a large number of readings in a series, it is usually convenient to group together readings of the same value into individual cells

[1] The statistically minded reader will note that the median as compared with the average will tend to be erratic. With large samples, the median is likely to have about 25 per cent more error than the sample average in representing the value for the "true" average (see Sec. 10.18).

[2] This is not to be confused with the estimated "true" population standard deviation (see Sec. 10.18), which can be obtained by multiplying the sample standard deviation by $\sqrt{\frac{n}{n-1}}$. However, for most applications, the sample is of sufficient size to reduce the correction factor to a negligible effect.

before undertaking the calculation of the standard deviation. When the readings have been so grouped, a useful formula is

$$\sigma = \sqrt{\frac{\Sigma f X^2}{n} - \overline{X}^2} \tag{5}$$

where $\Sigma f X^2$ = sum of the number of readings in the cells times the square of the value for each cell

When there is a large number of readings, several techniques may be found useful in simplifying the calculation of the standard deviation. Four of these are listed below:

"Coding" the Readings in a Series. Some series have readings whose values are extremely cumbersome. A case in point is a series whose values are 839.38, 839.42, 839.63. In instances like this it is often useful to "code" the readings by subtracting a constant value from each one.

In the case cited, 839.00 might be subtracted from each reading. This would leave values such as 0.38, 0.42, and 0.63, which are much easier to handle and are symbolized as d.

A general rule is this: any constant value can be added or subtracted from the values in a series without changing the value of the standard deviation. It must be noted, however, that, if the values in a series are multiplied or divided by the same factor, the value for the standard deviation will be multiplied or divided by that factor. To convert back to the original readings it is necessary to multiply or divide the value for the standard deviation by the same constant with which the readings were coded.

"Grouping" the Readings in a Series. One form of grouping the readings in a series has already been mentioned, namely, to gather together readings of the same value into several individual cells. This practice makes for difficulties when it creates too many of these cells.

Thus there may be 200 readings in series ranging from a low of 52.01 through 53.73 to 59.33 on to a high reading of 62.00. All are recorded to the nearest hundredth.

Grouping together all readings which are 52.01, 53.73, etc., may result in 50 to 75 cells. This would probably be a cumbersome total with which to work.

It is possible to group these data in a relatively small number of cells by selecting cells arbitrarily. Thus group 1 may include readings from 52.01 to 53.00 inclusive, group 2 may include readings from 53.01 to 54.00 inclusive, and group 10 may include readings from 61.01 to 62.00. Two hundred widely varied readings can thus be reduced to 10 cells, a far more manageable number than 50 or 75 cells. From 8 to 20 cells are found in industrial frequency distributions, about 12 cells being the most popular number.

The resulting value for the standard deviation for the example cited will be given in terms of the cell interval taken as a unit. This figure can be converted back to the original values for the readings simply by multiplying by the cell interval selected, which in the case cited is 1.00.

"Zeroing." When the readings have been coded or grouped, there are two major alternatives for carrying through the standard deviation calculation:

1. Carry through the calculation with the data as it stands in coded or grouped form. This type of calculation is illustrated in Sec. 10.16.
2. Carry the grouping a step further by selecting one cell arbitrarily as zero, considering the cells in the lower part of the table below the zero cell as positive and those in the upper part of the table as negative. With such grouping, the numbers with which it is necessary to work are often smaller. This is advantageous in certain types of calculations. This procedure is briefly used in Sec. 10.17.

Mechanical and Electronic Calculators. In recent years, there has been an effort to devise mechanical and electronic means for calculating the standard deviation along with other statistics. Although adding machines have always been used for these types of calculations, these newer devices carry on the mechanical portion of the computation much faster than it is possible to do with the adding machine. Large-scale digital electronic computers have been used successfully for solving complex problems using programmed statistical techniques similar to those outlined in Chap. 13. Smaller and more specialized electronic calculators are commercially available for the calculation of specific statistics.

There are also available other calculators such as the process-capability slide rule, discussed in Sec. 17.15, for computing the standard deviation.

There can be little question but that technical devices will eventually eliminate much of the time now required by the standard deviation and other statistical calculations.

10.12 The Range

The *range* is the difference between the lowest and the highest readings in a series, or symbolically:

$$R = X_{\text{high}} - X_{\text{low}} \tag{6}$$

where R = range value
X_{high} = highest reading in the series
X_{low} = lowest reading in the series

In the series 11, 12, 13, 15, 16, X_{high} is 16 and X_{low} is 11. The range is therefore

$$R = 16 - 11$$
$$= 5$$

When the values of the range for each series of readings in a number of series are calculated, it may be desirable to compute the average of these ranges. This measure is termed the *average range*. Symbolically it is shown by $\overline{R}$ (R bar).

10.13 Comparing the Standard Deviation and the Range

While the standard deviation usually provides more reliable information about the spread of a sample than does the range, the range is far simpler to calculate. In a series with 10 readings, the range can be obtained at a glance. The standard deviation would involve a computation.

Because of its relative simplicity, the range has enjoyed wide industrial usage, particularly in control-chart work. Statistically, however, its accuracy decreases as the number of readings increases.

Common sense immediately gives two of the reasons for this decrease in accuracy of the range as sample size increases. In large samples there is more chance of including a "wide-of-the-mark" reading. These "maverick" readings are inevitably reflected to a high degree by the range, which simply measures the spread from the lowest to the highest reading. Also, the range only considers the two extreme readings and disregards the other observations. So all the available information is not used in calculating the spread.

The standard deviation does not have these failings to so great a degree. It is a much more effective reflection of *all* the readings in a series, and any maverick will have far less effect upon its value.

A simple generalization, therefore, is that the standard deviation can be used with samples of almost any number of readings. The range should be used only with samples of small size. Fifteen readings is a practical, rule-of-thumb maximum.

10.14 The Normal Curve

Historically, much of the analytical use of the algebraic measures described above revolved around a type of frequency distribution termed a *normal curve.* This normal curve is the frequency-distribution curve approached in many situations where chance is given full play, as in the case of a large number of throws of dice.

Figure 10.13 illustrates this curve. It has a unique bell shape, which has been likened to a London bobby's hat.

An extremely important relationship exists between the standard deviation and the normal curve. When the standard deviation is computed for a normal frequency distribution, 68.27 per cent of all the readings in the distribution will occur between plus and minus one standard deviation of the average ($\bar{X} \pm 1\sigma$), 95.45 per cent of all readings in the distribution will occur between plus and minus two standard deviations of the average

$(\overline{X} \pm 2\sigma)$, 99.73 per cent of all the readings in the distribution will occur between plus and minus three standard deviations of the average $(\overline{X} \pm 3\sigma)$.

Figure 10.14 shows this relationship between the standard deviation and the normal frequency distribution.

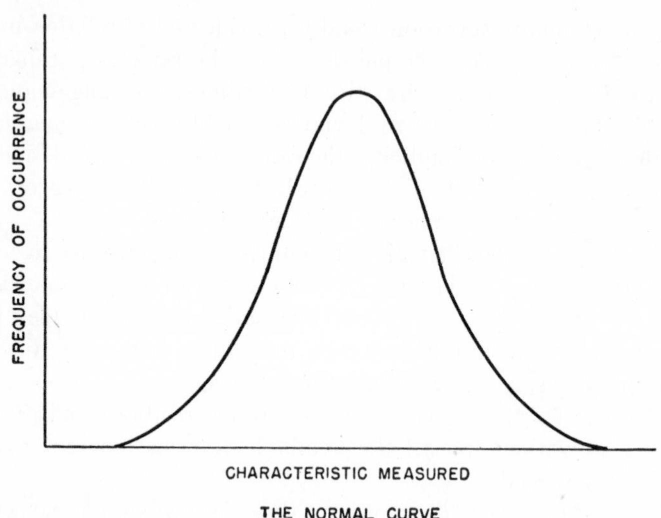

THE NORMAL CURVE
FIG. 10.13.

The importance of this relationship may be readily appreciated. With the average and the standard deviation calculated for a normal distribution, it is possible to compute two additional features of that distribution:

1. The percentage of values that will fall between any two readings of different values. In actual practice, this will be any two dimensions.

2. The total amount of variation that may for all practical purposes be expected from that distribution $(X \pm 3\sigma)$. This so-called 3-sigma value is the algebraic parallel for the process limits that were obtained in Sec. 10.5 by simply drawing dashed lines at the extremes of the distribution.

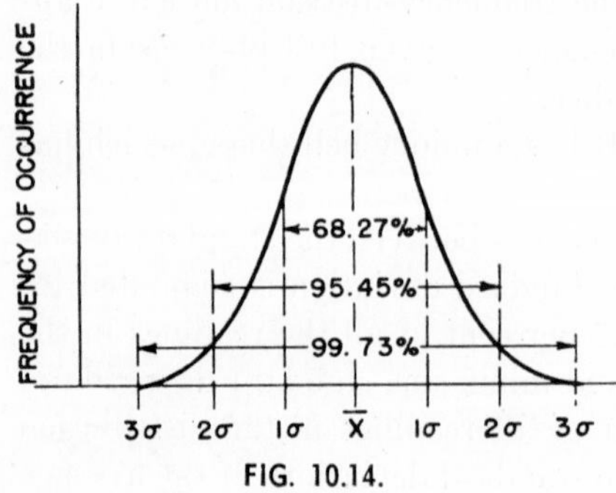

FIG. 10.14.

The task of determining the percentage of readings which fall between any two given dimensions is considerably simplified by the use of the table that is shown in Fig. 10.15. This table relates the decimal fractions of normal curve area to varying distances

DISTANCE FROM AVERAGE DIVIDED BY STANDARD DEVIATION x/σ	AREA	DISTANCE FROM AVERAGE DIVIDED BY STANDARD DEVIATION x/σ	AREA
0.0	0.00000	2.0	0.47725
0.1	0.03983	2.1	0.48214
0.2	0.07926	2.2	0.48610
0.3	0.11791	2.3	0.48928
0.4	0.15542	2.4	0.49180
0.5	0.19146	2.5	0.49379
0.6	0.22575	2.5758	0.49500
0.7	0.25804	2.6	0.49534
0.8	0.28814	2.7	0.49653
0.9	0.31594	2.8	0.49744
1.0	0.34134	2.9	0.49813
1.1	0.36433	3.0	0.49865
1.2	0.38493	3.1	0.49903
1.3	0.40320	3.2	0.49931
1.4	0.41924	3.3	0.49952
1.5	0.43319	3.4	0.49966
1.6	0.44520	3.5	0.49977
1.7	0.45543	3.6	0.49984
1.8	0.46407	3.7	0.49989
1.9	0.47128	3.8	0.49993
1.96	0.47500	3.9	0.49995
		4.0	0.49997

FIG. 10.15.

from the average, $\bar{X}$. x/σ shown in the table equals $(X - \bar{X})/\sigma$, where X is the individual reading. Since the normal curve is symmetrical, most tables calculate areas for only one side of the curve.

10.15 An Example of the Algebraic Analysis of the Frequency Distribution

The philosophy of algebraic analysis of the frequency distribution is similar to that for pictorial analysis, as discussed in Sec. 10.5. The chief difference is the mechanical one of calculating the average and the standard deviation.

An example of such an analysis may be found in a study made by a New York State punch-press factory. This shop wished to examine the amount of variation existing in the sheet steel it was purchasing for its stamping presses.

One hundred forty-four thickness measurements were made on a sample of steel sheets. An indicator gage, reading to an accuracy of 0.0005 inch, was used. Figure 10.16 pictures the tally card which resulted from this series of measurements.

With 144 readings, many of which were the same value, grouping into cells was a simple matter. The first two columns of Fig. 10.17 show this grouping. With data grouped in this fashion, the appropriate formula for the average in Sec. 10.10 is formula (3). Formula (5) is most appropriate for the standard deviation, as presented in Sec. 10.11.

DIMENSION	TALLY	TOTALS
.023		
.0235	X	1
.024	XXXXXX	6
.0245	XXXXXXXXXXXXXXXXXXXXXXX	23
.025	XXXXXXXXXXXXXXXXXXXXXXXXXXXXXXXXXXXXXXXXXXXXXXXX	48
.0255	XXXXXXXXXXXXXXXXXXXXXXXXXXXXXXXXXXXXXXX	39
.026	XXXXXXXXXXXXXXXXXXXX	20
.0265	XXXXX	5
.027	XX	2
	TOTAL VALUES	144

TALLY SHEET FOR STEEL SHEET THICKNESS MEASUREMENTS

FIG. 10.16.

The last two columns in Fig. 10.17 show how grouped data can be further tabulated in a form most useful for substitution into these formulas.

The calculations for the average and the standard deviation are shown at the foot of Fig. 10.17. The importance of carrying enough decimal places in the standard-deviation calculation should be noted.

Some of the information that this analysis made available to management of the punch-press factory was the following:

THICKNESS (IN MILS) (X)	FREQUENCY f	FREQUENCY TIMES THICKNESS fX	FREQUENCY TIMES THICKNESS² fX²
23.5	1	23.5	552.25
24.0	6	144.0	3456.00
24.5	23	563.5	13805.75
25.0	48	1200.0	30000.00
25.5	39	994.5	25359.75
26.0	20	520.0	13520.00
26.5	5	132.5	3511.25
27.0	2	54.0	1458.00
TOTALS( )	144	3632.0	91663.00

AVERAGE :- $\bar{X} = \frac{\Sigma fX}{n} = \frac{3632}{144} = 25.222$ MILS = 0.025222 INCHES

STANDARD DEVIATION:

$$\sigma = \sqrt{\frac{\Sigma fX^2}{n} - \bar{X}^2}$$

$$\sigma = \sqrt{\frac{91663}{144} - (25.222)^2}$$

$$\sigma = \sqrt{636.55 - 636.15}$$

$$\sigma = \sqrt{0.40} = 0.6 \text{ MILS OR } 0.0006 \text{ INCHES}$$

FIG. 10.17.

1. The nominal, or average, thickness for the steel sheets being received was 25.222 mils (thousandths of an inch). ($\bar{X} = 25.222$ mils.)

2. The total variation in the sheet steel was ± 1.8 mils ($\pm 3\sigma = \pm$ 1.8 mils), or a total variation of 3.6 mils.[3]

The standard-deviation figures are rounded off. Three-decimal-place accuracy is meaningless in a situation where the accuracy of the measuring instrument is only 0.5 mil.

An interesting practical circumstance is illustrated by these data. A glance at the tally of Fig. 10.16 would have provided almost the same information as was obtained through these calculations. This glance would have indicated that the spread of the values was from about 23.5 to 27.0 mils.

This condition frequently arises in actual application of the frequency distribution. It is for this reason that much of the use of this distribution is as a simple picture. As will be more fully discussed below, however, there is an important need for calculating the standard deviation in certain types of industrial analyses.

10.16 Algebraic Frequency-distribution Analysis

Management of the punch-press plant may now wish to study another question. How much of this sheet steel would be out of limits were a specification to be established of 25 ± 1 mil, or from 24 to 26 mils?

The answer to this question could be simply obtained by use of the table of areas in Fig. 10.15. Before this table can be used, two values must be calculated:

1. The deviation from the average of the two dimensions in question (24 and 26 mils).

2. The value of this deviation from the average, divided by the standard deviation (x/σ).

Calculation of these numbers is shown in Fig. 10.18.

From Fig. 10.15 it may be seen that an x/σ of 2 corresponds to an area of 0.47725, or 47.725 per cent of the normal-curve area. It may also be seen that an x/σ of 1.3 corresponds to an area of 0.40320, or 40.320 per cent of the normal-curve area. Therefore, the spread between an x/σ of 2 (representative of a reading of 24.0 mils) and an x/σ of 1.3 (representative of a reading of 26.0 mils) equals the sum of these two percentages:

$$47.7 \text{ per cent} + 40.3 \text{ per cent} = 88.0 \text{ per cent}$$

Consequently 88.0 per cent of the area of the distribution falls between

[3] The statistically minded reader will notice the unstated assumption of "normality" of the sheet-steel distribution made throughout this analysis. It is not until Sec. 10.20 and following that nonnormal distributions are formally introduced.

24.0 and 26.0 mils. As a corollary, 12.0 per cent of the area falls beyond 24.0 to 26.0 mils. Were this distribution representative of the thickness of steel sheets henceforth to be received by the punch-press plant, it would indicate that about 12 per cent of the sheets would be unsatisfactory and would be rejected.

COMPUTATION	LOWEST VALUE (24 MILS)	HIGHEST VALUE (26 MILS)
x	$x_L = X_1 - \bar{X}$ $x_L = 24.0 - 25.2$ $x_L = -1.2$	$x_H = X_2 - \bar{X}$ $x_H = 26.0 - 25.2$ $x_H = +.8$
$\frac{x}{\sigma}$	$\frac{x_L}{\sigma} = \frac{-1.2}{.6}$ $\frac{x_L}{\sigma} = -2$ THE ALGEBRAIC MINUS SIGN SIMPLY MEANS THAT THIS DEVIATION REPRESENTS A VALUE BELOW THE AVERAGE OF THE SERIES.	$\frac{x_H}{\sigma} = \frac{+.8}{.6}$ $\frac{x_H}{\sigma} = +1.3$ THE ALGEBRAIC PLUS SIGN SIMPLY MEANS THAT THIS DEVIATION REPRESENTS A VALUE ABOVE THE AVERAGE OF THE SERIES.

WHERE:

x_L = DEVIATION FROM THE AVERAGE OF THE LOWEST VALUE
x_H = DEVIATION FROM THE AVERAGE OF THE HIGHEST VALUE
X_1 = LOWEST VALUE (24 MILS)
X_2 = HIGHEST VALUE (26 MILS)
σ = STANDARD DEVIATION (.6 MILS)

FIG. 10.18.

10.17 Another Method for Calculating the Sheet-steel Distribution

Another method for preparing the data of Fig. 10.17 would have been arbitrarily to select the cell with the highest frequency,[4] 25.0, as the middle, or "zero," cell. The next cell with a value higher than 25.0, namely 25.5, would have been considered as +1; 26.0 would have been considered +2; etc. Similarly, the next cell with a value lower than 25.0, namely 24.5, would have been considered as −1; 24.0 would have been considered −2; etc.

This procedure would result in much smaller numbers in the calculations. In those cases where such a circumstance is desirable, this zeroing technique is very useful in calculating the average and standard deviation.

[4] This is referred to as the *mode* of the distribution.

After the data have been coded and zeroed according to the procedure discussed in Sec. 10.11, the calculations for the average and the standard deviation are exactly the same as shown in Fig. 10.17. When these calculations have been made, however, they must be converted back into original values for the readings. Formulas for this conversion are shown below:[5]

(X)	(f)	(fX)	fX^2
−3	1	− 3	9
−2	6	− 12	24
−1	23	−23	23
0	48	0	0
+1	39	+39	39
+2	20	+40	80
+3	5	+15	45
+4	2	+ 8	32
TOTALS	144	+64	252

AVERAGE $\overline{X} = \frac{\Sigma fX}{n} = \frac{64}{144} = .4444$

STANDARD DEVIATION $\sigma = \sqrt{\frac{\Sigma fX^2}{n} - \overline{X}^2} = \sqrt{\frac{252}{144} - .4444} = \sqrt{1.7500 - .1975}$

$\sigma = \sqrt{1.5525}$

$\sigma = 1.246$

CONVERSION:

TRUE AVERAGE = VALUE OF "ZERO FREQUENCY" + ($\overline{X}$ TIMES CELL INTERVAL)

= 25.0 + (.4444)(.5)

= 25.0 + .2220 = 25.222 MILS

TRUE STANDARD DEVIATION = VALUE OF SIGMA TIMES CELL INTERVAL

= (1.246)(.5)

= 0.6 MILS OR 0.0006 INCHES

FIG. 10.19.

Conversion for average:

Average in original value = value of "zero" frequency + ($\overline{X}$ times cell interval) (7)

Conversion for standard deviation:

Standard deviation in original value = value of sigma times cell interval (8)

Figure 10.19 shows the use of this procedure with the steel-sheet data of Sec. 10.15. It may be compared with the similar calculation in Fig. 10.17.

[5] These formulas are stated rather than shown in symbols in order to simplify them.

10.18 Sample Size and the Frequency Distribution

Several groups of shop supervisors in quality-control training classes had the following question posed to them: "Suppose that a lot of several thousand electrical relays, produced at the same source and under the same manufacturing conditions, is placed on a final test bench preparatory to shipment. The tester at this bench wishes to get a picture of the group quality of the voltage characteristic of these relays. He decides to select a sample of five relays for this purpose.

"Suppose, now, that the tester selects these five relays at random, checks the voltage characteristic of each relay, and plots his results in the form that would be used for a frequency-distribution plot. He calculates the average and the standard deviation for the plot. . . . Do you feel that this five-reading plot will give the tester a good picture of the central tendency and spread of the voltage characteristic of the lot of several thousand relays?"

The answer of the class members was almost unanimously that they did not feel that the plot would give a satisfactory picture.

A second question was then asked of the groups: "Suppose that the tester returns the five relays to the lot and selects five more relays at random. He checks their voltage characteristics and analyzes the resulting plot. . . . Do you feel that the values for the average and standard deviation for the second set of relays will represent about the same picture as that for the first set?"

Again the answer was "No."

The class members were then queried as to why they had answered as they had. Their almost unanimous retort was that the sample size of five was "too small to be representative."

These class members had intuitively placed their fingers on the core of the problem of the sample sizes that should be used to represent the plot or frequency distribution. The class members had pointed out that a sample which is too small may not accurately portray the average and standard deviation of the lot from which it is drawn. They had noted that two or more samples that are too small may vary quite widely in their respective averages and standard deviations even though they have been drawn from the same lot.

The general principles that hold in these cases can be simply stated: the larger the sample size, the less will be the spread among averages and standard deviations for samples drawn from the same lot and hence the more closely will these measures correspond to the comparable measures that would result if the entire lot were analyzed.

The smaller the sample size, the greater will be the spread among averages and standard deviations for samples drawn from the same lot and hence the less closely will averages and standard deviations correspond to the value for the average and standard deviation that would result if sampling were discarded in favor of analyses of the entire lot.

The average and standard deviation values which result from this computation based upon 100 per cent examination of the lot are often termed the *true average* and the *true standard deviation* for that lot.

It follows from the above statements of principle that, for samples drawn from the same lot, values of averages and standard deviations have standard deviations of their own. This standard deviation for the average is symbolized by $\sigma_{\bar{X}}$ (sigma sub X bar). The standard deviation for the standard deviation is symbolized by σ_σ (sigma sub sigma).

These particular measures of spread are represented in the following formulas:

$$\sigma_{\bar{X}} = \frac{\sigma'}{\sqrt{n}} \tag{9}$$

where $\sigma_{\bar{X}}$ = standard deviation of the sample average
σ' = "true" standard deviation of the lot from which the sample was drawn (in actual practice, an estimate from samples is generally used, since the "true" value is seldom known)
n = sample size

and

$$\sigma_\sigma = \frac{\sigma'}{\sqrt{2n}} \tag{10}$$

where σ_σ = standard deviation of the sample standard deviation
σ' = "true" standard deviation of the lot from which the sample was drawn (in actual practice, an estimate from samples is generally used, since the "true" value is seldom known)
n = sample size

It will be noted in the definition of the terms used in formulas (9) and (10) that σ' is said to represent the "true" standard deviation of the "lot" from which the sample was drawn. In the electrical-relay example noted in Sec. 10.18 the "lot" was a physically segregated, already produced group of units.

This sort of lot is only one of many types covered by the term. Broadly, the term may refer to an entire stream of units either already produced or to be produced in the future by the same source and under the same manufacturing conditions. Thus, a "lot" of studs from an automatic screw machine might be the entire output of the machine over a long period under the same setup and operating conditions fully as much as the "lot" might be a single hour's or day's production. Under practical industrial conditions, the decision as to what is or is not a "lot" is often a fairly arbitrary one.

When the frequency distribution for individual readings is normally distributed, then the frequency distribution for the spread of averages, as in formula (9), follows the normal distribution pattern. That for the spread of standard deviations, as in formula (10), is not a perfectly normal curve, but it approaches normality as the sample size increases.

The determination of that sample size of electrical relays wherein the total spread of averages from samples drawn from the same lot will be no greater than 0.90 volt may serve to illustrate the use of one of these formulas. For the sake of simplicity, it may be assumed that, from other data, the true standard deviation of the lot is known to be 1 volt. Also, each calculation will assume a sample average of 14 volts. The relays in question are the same lot that has been discussed in Sec. 10.18.

Using, first, a sample size of five relays, substituting in formula (9) shows

$$\sigma_{\bar{X}} = \frac{\sigma'}{\sqrt{n}} = \frac{1}{\sqrt{5}} = \frac{1}{2.25}$$
$$= 0.44 \text{ volt}$$

Since the distribution of averages is normal, the total spread of averages of samples of five relays will be

$$\bar{X} \pm 3\sigma_{\bar{X}} = 14 \pm 3(0.44)$$
$$= 14 \pm 1.32 \text{ volts}$$

The value for averages computed from a sample of five relays may be expected to range from 12.68 to 15.32 volts when the average value is 14 volts. This represents a spread of 2.64 volts and is greatly in excess of the target of a spread of 0.90 volt.

Additional trial of other sample sizes would show that a sample size of 50 relays would be most appropriate. Substituting in formula (9) shows

$$\sigma_{\bar{X}} = \frac{\sigma'}{\sqrt{n}} = \frac{1}{\sqrt{50}} = \frac{1}{7} = 0.14 \text{ volt}$$

and

$$\bar{X} \pm 3\sigma_{\bar{X}} = 14 \pm 3(0.14)$$
$$= 14 \pm 0.42 \text{ volt}$$

In this case, the value for averages in a sample of 50 relays may range from 13.58 to 14.42 volts. This represents a spread of 0.84 volt and, as such, meets the target that the spread be no greater than 0.90 volt.

10.19 What Sample Size Should Be Used in Connection with Frequency-distribution Calculations?

Use of formulas (9) and (10) in deciding upon the size of a particular sample requires knowing the value of the true standard deviation of the lot from which the sample is to be drawn. In actual industrial practice, this value is often unknown. As a result, formulas (9) and (10) are useful chiefly as theoretical guides rather than as mathematical determinants of industrial sample sizes.

The practical industrial decision as to the appropriate size for a particular sample usually takes two factors into account:

1. *The economics of the situation;* that is, how much does it cost to take each reading?

2. *The statistical accuracy required;* that is, how much error is permissible in the values obtained for spread and for central tendency?

These two factors usually operate in different directions. The economics of the situation calls for the smallest sample size that can possibly be allowed. The statistics call for a generally larger sample size to yield a maximum of protection.

As a result, the sample size that is appropriate for a given frequency-distribution analysis is often not decided in industry on the basis of a fixed statistical formulation. It is developed from a balance between the statistics and the economics of the situation. Past experience with the process in question and judgment of the individuals concerned play a very large part in this decision.

Since the cost of readings and the required statistical accuracy will naturally vary from industry to industry, any generalization about sample size will, of course, be subject to individual adjustment. For practical purposes, however, a sample size of 50 readings is usually sufficiently reliable for most industrial frequency-distribution analyses for shop application. It will be this sample size of 50 which will be widely used in this book.[6]

When the cost of taking individual measurements is low, or when accurate analyses are required, sample sizes of 100 readings or more may be used. In situations where the distribution analysis is relatively new, the individual without formal statistical training may be well advised to use a sample size below 50 readings only in the special cases of competent statistical advice, extensive past experience with the process variation, or where there are desired only extremely rough approximations.

It may be noted that no mention has been made of the size of the lot from which the samples have been drawn. No effort has been made to relate sample size to lot size. The reason is that, in general, the reliability of a sample depends largely upon the size of that sample rather than

[6] The reader interested in further detail on this subject will find in the statistical literature methods for deciding upon a particular sample size with a great deal of precision. See, for example, Leslie E. Simon, "Engineers Manual of Statistical Methods," John Wiley & Sons, Inc., New York, 1941.

upon the ratio of the size of the sample to the size of the lot from which it was drawn.

This principle is of great importance in the development and use of sampling tables. It will be discussed more fully in Chap. 12.

Practical Aspects of the Frequency Distribution

10.20 Shapes of Industrial Frequency Distributions

Many industrial frequency distributions do not follow the bell shape of the normal curve. Sometimes these nonbell shapes represent the standard, accepted condition for the process in question. They may be a reflection of the engineering and manufacturing fundamentals of this process.

Sometimes these shapes represent a purely temporary process condition. They may serve as a guide to detecting the presence of some unusual factor like defective materials or tool chatter.

There is no magic about the normal curve in the sense that those distributions which closely approximate its shape represent "good-quality" processes and those which are not so smooth represent "bad-quality" processes. How "good" is the shape of an industrial frequency distribution is almost entirely a matter of economics.

The jagged, spread-out distribution, which is well within specification limits, may be a good distribution for that particular purpose. The smooth, normal-curve-shaped distribution, which is outside specification limits, may be a bad distribution. Simply because a distribution is "flat-topped," "jagged," or "skewed" is no infallible indication that the process it represents is inferior to that represented by a smooth, normal-curve-shaped distribution.

Five of the typical shapes taken by these distributions are

1. Skewed curves.
2. J-shaped curves.
3. Bimodal curves.
4. Curves of articles that have been 100 per cent inspected.
5. Curves of articles that have been 100 per cent inspected but are subject to variation after the inspection has been completed.

10.21 Skewness

Figure 10.20 represents the distribution shape that is typical for a powdered-metal process in an Eastern factory. This type of distribution is termed a *skewed* curve. The number of readings decreases to zero more rapidly on one side of the "hump" of the curve than on the other side.

A distribution may be skewed to the right, as in Fig. 10.20. It may also be skewed to the left, as in Fig. 10.21, which represents a quality characteristic of a screw-machine part.

Skewness is often the result of the operation of some strong factor or factors. These factors are felt to be fundamental to the powdered-metal process and would be very difficult to identify. For this reason and because the distribution is well within specification limits, its shape is accepted by the factory as standard for this process.

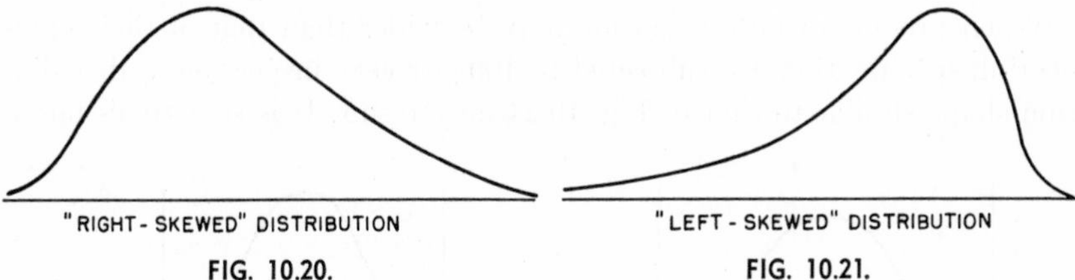

FIG. 10.20. FIG. 10.21.

A skewed curve is not, however, accepted as standard for the screw-machine part of Fig. 10.21. Skewness here is often characteristic of tool chatter. If such action is required to meet the part specifications, the screw-machine process can be investigated for tool chatter and the chatter eliminated.

10.22 J Shapes and Bimodality

When readings are taken of "run-out" or the "out-of-round" of shafts, a distribution shape similar to that of Fig. 10.22 results.

This J-shaped curve is an extremely nonsymmetrical distribution, where one limit is zero and the number of readings approaching the other limit is high.

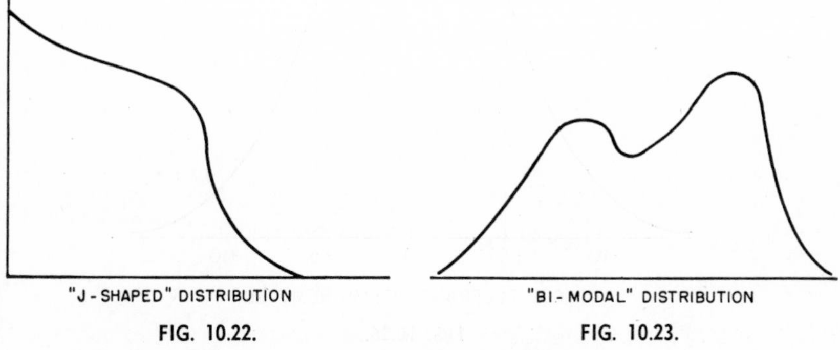

FIG. 10.22. FIG. 10.23.

Batches of similar product from two different sources—different machines, different vendors—may sometimes be mixed together. A distribution shape such as that of Fig. 10.23 may result in these cases.

This *bimodal* curve is a distribution with two peaks, where data of two or more different origins are included.

Bimodality may also result from a shift in conditions when data are being taken on a single machine or process. The machine tool in question may be located on a gallery, and its tool setting may be jarred whenever the crane rumbles by.

10.23 100 Per Cent Inspection Curves

When products whose variation may be wider than that of their engineering specification are subjected to 100 per cent inspection, a distribution shape similar to that of Fig. 10.24 may result. It is sometimes possible for a customer to determine from just such a frequency-distribution analysis the amount of inspection his vendor is placing on a product.

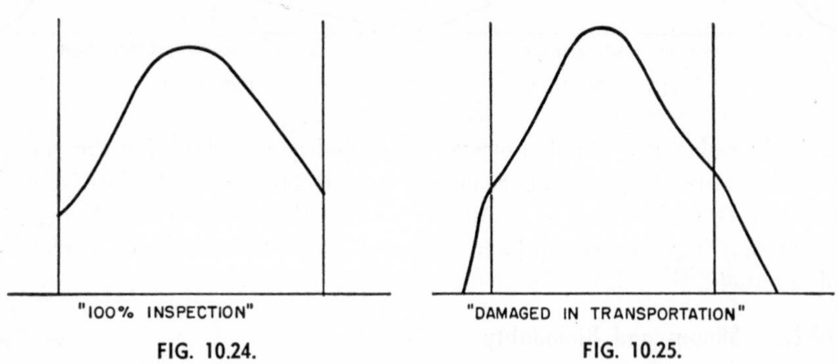

FIG. 10.24. FIG. 10.25.

A product of the sort shown in Fig. 10.24 may be subject to slight changes in its quality characteristics during transportation from vendor to customer. Or there may be some degree of variation between the vendor's measurements equipment and that of the customer. In these cases a distribution shape similar to that of Fig. 10.25 may result.

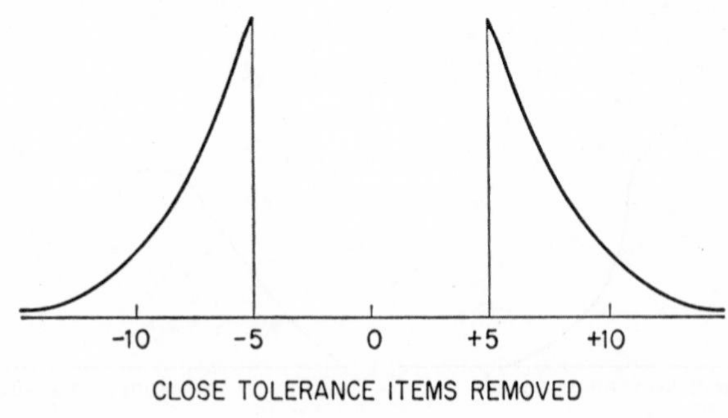

FIG. 10.26.

This distribution is typical of those which obtain on some products, the caliber of whose inspection is in question. The vendor may insist that he has subjected the lot to rigorous inspection before shipment has gone. The customer may insist that the product as received by him contains many defectives—which is also the case.

Some products, such as resistors, are 100 per cent sorted by the vendor and segregated into groupings dependent upon the degree of variation from nominal. For example, Fig. 10.26 shows the distribution of parts shipped to a customer whose tolerance requirements are very broad; the factory has already removed the ±5 per cent tolerance parts for shipment to tight tolerance customers.

10.24 "Normality" and the Frequency Distribution

If curves of the sort discussed above depart so widely from the shape of the normal curve, how meaningful has been the discussion in Secs. 10.8 to 10.19 of the mathematics of the frequency distribution? The discussion there was predicated upon the fact that the industrial distributions would quite closely approximate the shape of the normal curve.

This issue is not so serious as it might seem at first glance. It may be shown that most of the concern with this particular issue is quite academic.

Some of the reasons for the propriety of using normal-curve analysis and algebra as a guide to the study of industrial frequency distributions are the following:

1. Algebraic measures like averages and standard deviations apply to all frequency-distribution shapes. It is only in their interpretation that the degree of similarity of a given industrial distribution to the normal curve may be of importance.

2. Much of the industrial use of the frequency distribution involves no algebraic analysis. The distribution is used as a simple picture.

3. When algebraic analysis is required, experience has shown that a very large number of industrial frequency distributions *do* sufficiently closely approximate the shape of the normal curve.

4. When a distribution is badly skewed or otherwise distorted, the distribution is often used simply as a guide to corrective action. Algebraic analysis may not be made until after this corrective action has been taken. If it is made both before and after, values for the average and the standard deviation furnish excellent indices to the effect of the corrective action.

5. Distribution analyses of many industrial conditions do not require a great deal of precision. In these cases the normality of a distribution may not be of major significance.

6. Normal-curve analysis need not be used where it is inappropriate. There is no magic about these instances. An experienced individual may determine them by a simple glance at curve shape and then apply the

corrections that are discussed in Sec. 10.25. There are also several analytical and graphical methods for determining normality. One of these is the *probability paper,* which is discussed in Secs. 13.3 to 13.6.

Industrial users of these statistical methods know that they are not working with an exact science. No matter how precise their algebraic methods, it is the data used in these formulas that are important. These data are highly perishable in their value. The conditions that the data represent may change overnight.

As a result, algebraic analysis of the frequency distribution is used more as a cautious industrial guide than as a precise and final calculation. If an analysis is improperly made, the rapid industrial production conditions will make that fact soon known.

As these methods come to be used in individual applications, over a period of time, they will probably become flavored with the circumstances of that application. Formulas used will become adaptations to the particular distribution shapes that are involved if these shapes are not normal. In these cases, normal-curve analysis simply furnishes the initial guide for the development of the algebra of the application.

In the final analysis, the measurements-taking philosophy of the frequency distribution is its greatest practical contribution. Once this philosophy has been established, the methods to support the measurements taking will gradually adapt themselves to the particular industrial application.

Frequency-distribution analysis is, of course, subject to the same misuse that characterizes any analytic method. But its user remains safe when he understands its philosophy and limitations, appreciates that it is an inexact science, and uses common sense in its application. Once this background has been developed, abstract discussions of "normality and the frequency distribution" become matters of no great practical concern.

10.25 Frequency-distribution Analysis of Nonnormal Distributions

Section 10.14 described the relationship between the normal curve and the standard deviation, whereby 99.73 per cent of all readings fall with $\pm 3\sigma$ of the normal-curve average. Section 10.16 showed how this relationship could usefully be applied in resolving such questions as expected reject percentages.

This particular relationship between the frequency distribution and the standard deviation does not, of course, hold true when a frequency distribution is appreciably nonnormal in its shape. Yet other useful relationships do still exist between nonnormal frequency distributions and the standard deviation. These relationships can be used to analyze a distribution with just the same approach as was described in Sec. 10.16, except that the formulas presented below now obtain.

For a distribution that is skewed, either to right or left as in Figs. 10.20 and 10.21, but has only one hump and whose average value approximately coincides with the most frequent value, the percentage of values between $\pm(t)\,\sigma$ is shown as[7]

$$\text{Percentage of readings} \geq 1 - \frac{1}{2.25t^2} \tag{11}$$

For a very badly skewed or jagged distribution, Fig. 10.23, for example, the relationship is shown as[8]

$$\text{Percentage of readings} \geq 1 - \frac{1}{t^2} \tag{12}$$

Thus, formula (11) shows that about 95 per cent or more of all values are between $\pm 3\sigma$ of a perceptibly skewed frequency distribution, while about 89 per cent or more of values are, in formula (12), between $\pm 3\sigma$ of the most badly distorted curve shapes that will be found.

PER CENT OF AREA UNDER DIFFERENT FREQUENCY DISTRIBUTION SHAPES

WITHIN →	$\bar{X} \pm 1\sigma$	$\bar{X} \pm 2\sigma$	$\bar{X} \pm 3\sigma$
"NORMAL CURVE" DISTRIBUTION	68.27 %	95.45 %	99.73 %
"SKEWED" DISTRIBUTION	≥55 %	≥89 %	≥95 %
BADLY DISTORTED DISTRIBUTION	—	≥75 %	≥89 %

FIG. 10.27.

Figure 10.27 shows a comparison among areas under frequency distributions which conform both to the conditions of formulas (11) and (12) as well as to that of the normal curve.

[7] This formula is an adaptation, for practical use, of the formula known in the statistical literature as the *Camp-Meidel inequality,* which shows that

$$P_{t\sigma} \geq 1 - \frac{1}{2.25t^2}$$

where $P_{t\sigma}$ is the probability within the interval $\pm(t)\sigma$. The designation $\geq$ in the formula signifies "equal to or greater than."

[8] This formula is an adaptation, for practical use, of the formula known in the statistical literature as the *Tchebycheff inequality,* which shows that

$$P_{t\sigma} \geq 1 - \frac{1}{t^2}$$

where $P_{t\sigma}$ *is the probability within the interval* $\pm(t)\sigma$.

There are also ways to "normalize" some of these nonnormal distributions by such techniques as transformations and computing independently the variation for each half of the distribution.[9]

10.26 The Predictive Value of the Frequency Distribution

It has been implied above that two uses for the algebraic analysis of the frequency distribution are

1. To predict the characteristics of an entire lot of completed units from the characteristics of a frequency-distribution sample drawn from that lot.

2. To predict the characteristics to be expected in the *future* on a process or product design from the characteristics of a frequency-distribution sample drawn from that process or units of that product design.

Certain limitations must be recognized in connection with both of these important applications of the frequency distribution.

Lot Characteristics. The prediction of the average and standard deviation of a lot can be performed accurately and reliably if the following conditions are observed:

1. The sample size must be sufficiently large to permit accuracy.
2. The sample must be properly selected.
3. Practical matters must be dealt with, such as adequate measuring equipment and proper recording of readings.

These sampling details are discussed in some detail in Chap. 12.

Future Performance. The accuracy of a machine tool in performing a given operation may be sought. Appraisal of the performance of a new product may be checked by means of a pilot run whose characteristics must be analyzed. Approval of the setup of a processing equipment, preliminary to a long production run, may be required.

It is not sufficient in these applications merely to be certain that the sample is of adequate size and has been properly selected and measured. A problem of equal importance is "How representative of future conditions is this sample?"

This question can never be answered with complete certainty. But a sample can be made more representative of these conditions in several ways. Past experience with the process in question can be used to gage the seeming reasonableness of sample results. Samples can be examined at separate intervals of time, and the uniformity of their results compared. Analysis can be made of the major variables that may be expected to have an effect at *some* time in the future, and these variables can be introduced into the articles in the sample.

[9] For these and other such procedures, the reader will find much in the statistical literature. See, for example, Dudley J. Cowden, *Statistical Methods in Quality Control,* Prentice-Hall, Inc., Englewood Cliffs, N.J., 1957.

In judging the process capability of a new machine tool, experience has taught personnel in one factory that they must make three or four distribution sample checks at intervals of several days. They then compare the results of these checks, consolidate them if it seems appropriate, or make more checks if such a step seems indicated. Chapter 17 details a method for making a study of this type.

This factory uses only one distribution sample to approve the setup on processing equipments that are already installed. They have had previous experience with this equipment, and sometimes there are available the results of process-capability study on it, such as has been discussed above.

There is no substitute for technical judgment in predictions of this sort. If proper conditions and variables have not been taken into account, mere statistical accuracy in dealing with the data at hand means very little. If the resulting prediction does not conform to common sense, then it is likely to be wrong and should be carefully rechecked. Until he has gained some experience, the new user of industrial statistics in particular should make haste slowly in this predictive use of the frequency distribution.

10.27 Some Guides to the Use of the Frequency Distribution

The frequency distribution usually enjoys a better initial reception in the shop when it is simply called a *tally*. Its record forms may be termed *tally cards*. A wide variety of forms are used for these tallies. Figure 10.28 shows one of them.

Nothing is more disheartening than to analyze a set of readings only to find that they are worthless. The data recorded on these tally cards must be accurate. This requires proper record keeping on the part of the individual assigned that task. The importance of adequate gaging equipment to make the required measurements cannot be overemphasized.

Carelessness or ineffectiveness on the part of the recorder may be a critical problem. Occasionally the readings that are so carefully analyzed in the front office have generated in the head of this record taker. He may have wished to save himself the effort of making the checks, or he may have forgotten to make them.

The record taker may be untrained in the proper use of gages and instruments. He may make a series of reading errors that are not discovered for some time.

When the frequency distribution shown on the tally card seems to take a unique or puzzling form, very careful attention should be paid to its readings. Figure 10.29 illustrates an interesting example of this sort.

The characteristic measured is voltage. The frequency distribution of these voltage readings shows peaks and valleys far more numerous than would be expected due to sampling variation. But it will be noted that the peaks occur at some multiple of 5 and the valleys occur in between.

In this set of readings, the recorder simply "liked" to read numbers that were some multiple of 5 because the instrument was calibrated with markings at 5, 10, 15, 20, etc. The unusual curve of Fig. 10.29 is the result of this simple fact, and not of any more profound mystery that an unsophisticated observer might have attributed to it.

This matter of recorders' "liking" some values better than others becomes a serious problem when very close readings are required. The recorder may unconsciously read the numbers he likes even though he may have the desire and the instruction to do otherwise.

An extremely desirable feature of the tally-type frequency distribution is that sometimes it is almost secured "for nothing." The readings that make it up are often taken in the shop anyway. It takes only slightly more effort to record them on the tally form.

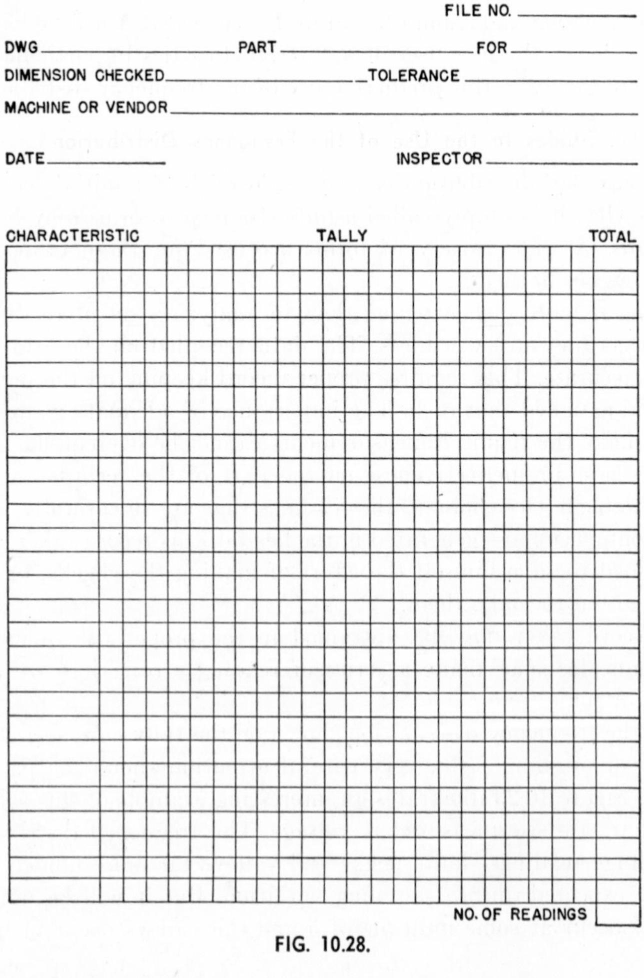

FILE NO. ____________

DWG ____________ PART ____________ FOR ____________

DIMENSION CHECKED ____________ TOLERANCE ____________

MACHINE OR VENDOR ____________

DATE ____________ INSPECTOR ____________

CHARACTERISTIC | TALLY | TOTAL

NO. OF READINGS

FIG. 10.28.

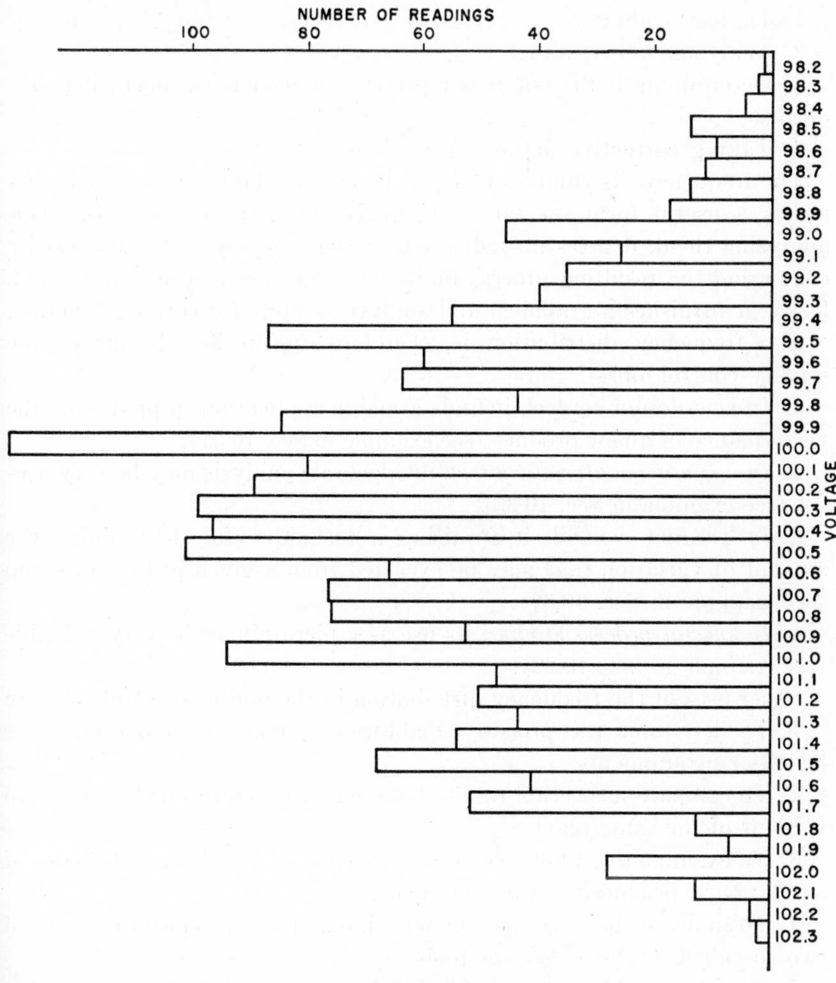

FIG. 10.29.

It is usually desirable to leave all formulas and calculation aids off the tally form that is used in the shop. This carries further the evidence of its simplicity. When practical, it is most desirable to analyze the readings away from the shop in the relatively more quiet, less hurried atmosphere of the office.

The Frequency Distribution in Action—Some Examples

10.28 The Frequency Distribution and the Quality-control Jobs

There are usually four steps in the analysis of a manufacturing process or an engineering design. They are

1. Taking readings.
2. Analyzing the readings.
3. Determining if the readings represent an economical operating condition.
4. Taking corrective action where necessary.

The frequency distribution is useful in each of these four steps: it furnishes a useful form for taking readings and a practical method for analyzing them, it gives an indication of the economy of the process by comparing the resulting process limits with the specification limits, and, lastly, it furnishes a graphical and analytical guide for corrective action.

The frequency distribution is, therefore, useful in all four of the quality-control jobs.

1. *In new-design control,* it finds a major application in predicting the performance of a new product (see example in Sec. 10.31).
2. *In incoming-material control,* its algebraic analysis may be very useful (see example in Sec. 10.30).
3. *In product control,* it furnishes a technique for determining the amount of variation that may be expected from a given process or setup (see example in Sec. 10.32).
4. *In special process studies,* its use as a picture may be very valuable (see example in Sec. 10.29).

Other uses of the frequency distribution in the quality-control jobs are

1. To determine the process capabilities of machine tools and other processing equipments.
2. To compare inspection results between two factories or between two sections of the same plant.
3. To examine the difference between the dimensional characteristics of similar parts produced in different molds.
4. To indicate the variations among similar parts produced by each of two so-called duplicate sets of tools.
5. To examine the accuracy of fit between mating parts.
6. To analyze the effect of tool wear during a long production run on a machine tool.

10.29 A Study of Regulating Equipments That Failed at the Customer's Plant[10]

Plant A produced regulating equipments in quantity for shipment to its customer, plant B. The two plants were about 150 miles apart. Plant B tested each of these equipments carefully after they were received, even though plant A had also tested them.

For the first 6 months of production, plant B found all the equipments

[10] Investigation made by Mr. R. B. Thomasgard and associates, Schenectady, N.Y.

it received to be satisfactory. Without warning, however, a large percentage of the regulators received by plant B in the seventh month were found defective in test.

Lot after lot shipped from plant A were found similarly defective. Plant B demanded that plant A take immediate corrective action.

Staff employees in plant A began to analyze the entire production process for the regulating equipments. They were primarily interested in

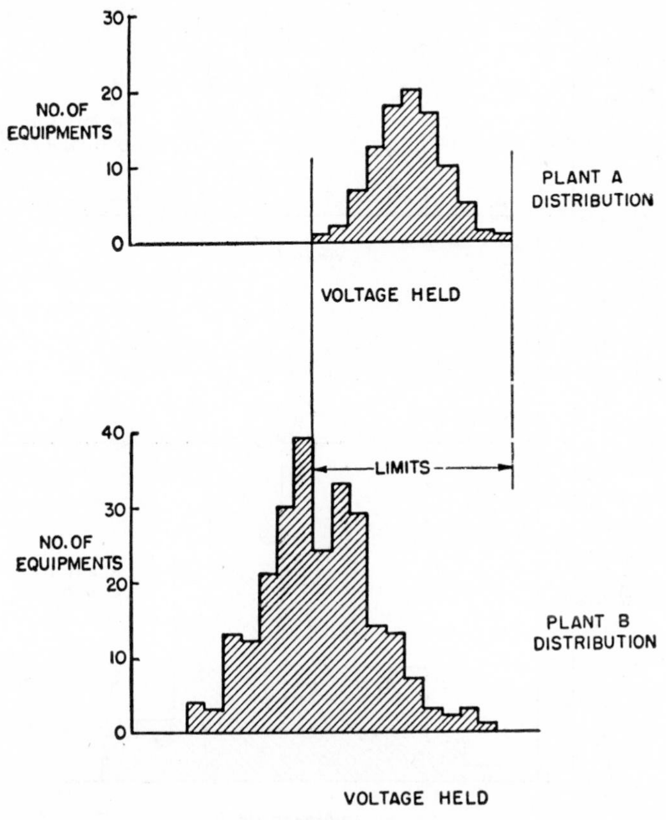

FIG. 10.30.

the factors which affected the "voltage held" characteristic, since this was most critical.

The frequency distribution was one of the analytical tools used. Figure 10.30 shows the frequency distributions plotted for the voltage held characteristic. These distributions compare a sample of equipments tested in plant A after their manufacture with the same sample after its receipt and test in plant B.

These curves led the engineering staff of plant A to conclude that there were two major differences between the distribution as plotted in plant A and that plotted in plant B:

1. The plant B distribution had shifted lower on the voltage held scale. This might have been due to difference in testing methods in the two plants, reasoned the engineers.

2. The plant B distribution had a much wider spread than did the

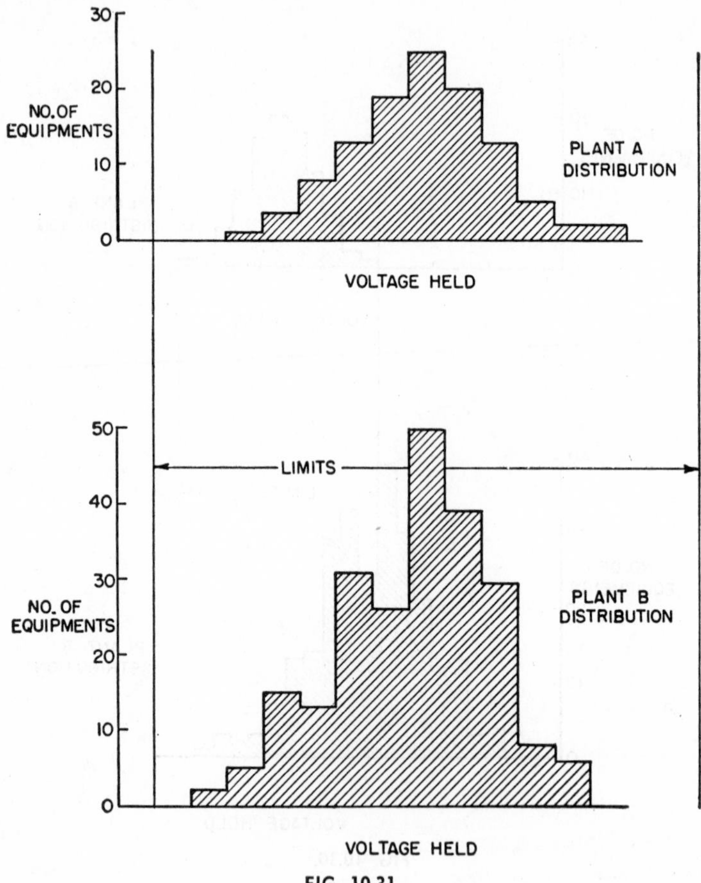

FIG. 10.31.

plant A distribution. The engineers reasoned that this might have been due to some mechanical shift in the regulating equipments while in transportation between the two points.

These two speculations were pursued. After a great deal of investigation, they were borne out in test results. Production testing methods in plant A and plant B were geared together. A mechanical redesign was put into effect on those parts in the regulator that were shifting.

Another set of frequency distributions was plotted on samples manufactured and tested under these new conditions. This is shown in Fig. 10.31, from which the end of the rejections could be predicted.

Subsequent production experience bore out the accuracy of this prediction.

10.30 Predicting the Quality of an Incoming Lot of Bronze Journal Bearings[11]

A shipment was received by an Eastern factory containing a large quantity of bronze journal bearings. These bearings had been purchased for use in the production of an important device. Not completely certain

INSIDE DIAMETERS	TALLY	TOTAL
1.370	X	1
1.371	X	1
1.372	XX	2
1.373	XXXX	4
1.374	XXX	3
1.375	XXXXXX	6
1.376	XXXXXXXXXXXXXXXX	16
1.377	XXXXXXXXXXXXXX	14
1.378	XXXXXXXXXXXXXXXXXXXXXXXX	24
1.379	XXXXXXXXXXXXXX	14
1.380	XXXXXXXXX	9
1.381	XXXX	4
1.382	X	1
1.383	X	1
	TOTAL READINGS	100

FIG. 10.32.

of the workmanship of the vendor from whom the bearings were secured, the factory wanted assurance of the quality of the lot.

The critical characteristic of these bearings was their inside diameter, whose specification was 1.376 ± 0.010 inch. It was decided to make a frequency-distribution analysis of this particular quality characteristic.

One hundred bearings were drawn from the lot, and their inside diameters were measured carefully. The frequency distribution of these measurements is shown in Fig. 10.32.

[11] From a study discussed by Dr. C. F. Green, R. W. Hallock, and associates, Schenectady, N.Y.

An algebraic analysis was then performed. The two values to be calculated were the average and the standard deviation. These computations are shown:

Average:

$$\bar{X} = \frac{\Sigma X}{n} = \frac{137.730}{100} = 1.3773 \text{ inches}$$

Standard deviation:

$$\sigma = \sqrt{\frac{\Sigma(X - \bar{X})^2}{n}}$$

$$= \sqrt{\frac{\begin{array}{l}(1.370 - 1.3773)^2 + (1.371 - 1.3773)^2 + 2(1.372 - 1.3773)^2 + \\ 4(1.373 - 1.3773)^2 + 3(1.374 - 1.3773)^2 + 6(1.375 - 1.3773)^2 + \\ 16(1.376 - 1.3773)^2 + 14(1.377 - 1.3773)^2 + 24(1.378 - 1.3773)^2 + \\ 14(1.379 - 1.3773)^2 + 9(1.380 - 1.3773)^2 + 4(1.381 - 1.3773)^2 + \\ (1.382 - 1.3773)^2 + (1.383 - 1.3773)^2 + \end{array}}{100}}$$

$$= \sqrt{\frac{0.00054300}{100}} = 0.0023 \text{ inch}$$

For a normal curve, 99.73 per cent of the readings lie between $\bar{X} \pm 3\sigma$. Substituting the above values in this expression:

$$\begin{aligned}\bar{X} \pm 3\sigma &= 1.3773 \pm 3(0.0023 \text{ inch}) \\ &= 1.3704 \text{ to } 1.3842 \text{ inches}\end{aligned}$$

On this basis, the bearing quality is shown to be satisfactorily within the drawing range of 1.366 to 1.386 inches. This distribution is somewhat distorted and skewed to the left, however, so that the 3-sigma limits are not strictly accurate. But the distribution is well within drawing limits, nor is the amount of skew excessive, so the factory decided that it could accept the lot of bearings on this analysis.

This conclusion was found to be satisfactory when the bearings were actually used on the production lines.

10.31 Performance of a New Product

The engineering designers of a new product were agreed that its most critical characteristic was "pickup volts." They decided that it would be extremely valuable to learn what might be expected from this characteristic when active production of the article was begun.

A number of samples of the device were made up on a pilot-run basis. The pickup volts of each of these articles were tested, and a frequency distribution was made of the data. The resulting curve is shown in Fig. 10.33.

A brief glance at this distribution showed the design engineers that unsatisfactory performance might be expected. An algebraic analysis of this distribution was made, using a table of areas similar to that of Fig. 10.15. It indicated that about 20 per cent of the devices could be expected to fall outside the specification limit of 15.5 volts that had been established for maximum pickup.

The designers set about to analyze the various factors affecting pickup voltage. They discovered that a spring constant they had specified led to excessive variation. This spring supplied the mechanical force against which the electric force of the product's coil operated.

The problem resolved itself into making some simple change to compensate for the spring constant. It was found most economical to accomplish this by a minor mechanical design change on another part.

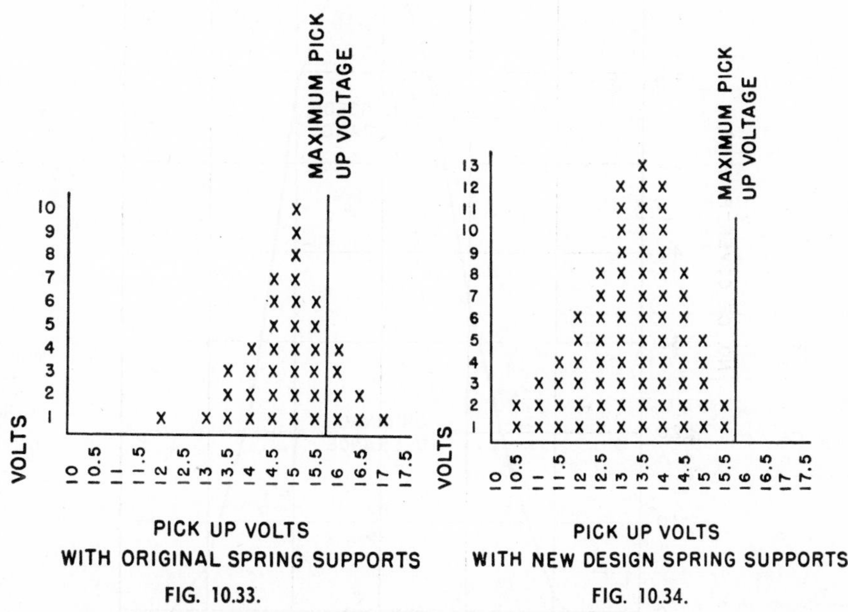

PICK UP VOLTS WITH ORIGINAL SPRING SUPPORTS

FIG. 10.33.

PICK UP VOLTS WITH NEW DESIGN SPRING SUPPORTS

FIG. 10.34.

This change was made, and it was found to have eliminated the trouble that had been caused by the spring. The design engineers were pleased to have eliminated a potential source of manufacturing trouble before actual production had started.

When this article went into active manufacture, a frequency-distribution analysis was made of the pickup volts characteristic of the first production models. This distribution, given in Fig. 10.34, showed that no trouble was being experienced.

10.32 Establishing the Shop Tolerance for a Drilling Operation

The drawing specification for a small, flat cover plate allowed a tolerance of ± 0.001 inch between the centers of two drilled holes. Considerable production difficulty was being experienced in meeting this tolerance, in addition to which a large number of cover plates were being rejected at final inspection.

The shop foreman claimed that a ±0.001-inch tolerance could not be met with existing drilling equipment. The experienced draftsman who had placed that tolerance on the drawing was equally certain that it could be met.

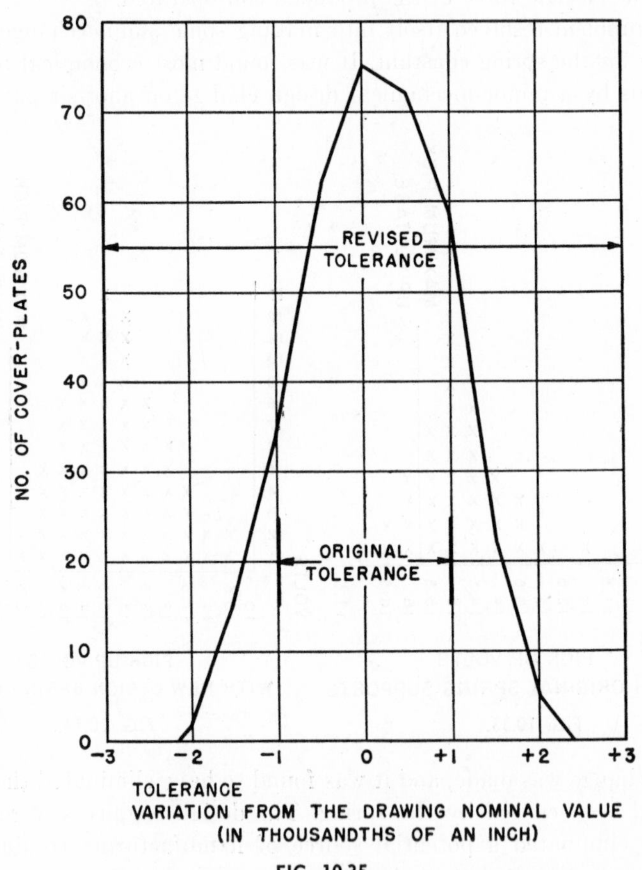

FIG. 10.35.

To resolve the question on a factual basis, a frequency-distribution analysis was made on a typical production lot. Both foreman and draftsman assured themselves that the drill press was properly set up, that its drills were well ground, and that the drill jigs were in good condition.

The resulting frequency distribution of Fig. 10.35 showed a variation of ±0.0025 inch in the center distances of the cover plates in the sample under examination. Since all had agreed that the sample was fully representative, it was decided that the ±0.001-inch tolerance could not be met with existing equipment.

Three alternatives were open:

1. To continue to produce cover plates to this tolerance with existing equipment and make the resulting rejects a part of job cost.
2. To secure new equipment.
3. To widen the tolerance.

As is often the case in instances of this sort, investigation of the device on which the cover plate was assembled showed that a between-centers tolerance of ±0.003 inch would be fully as satisfactory as one of ±0.001 inch.

This change was made on the drawing, and no subsequent trouble was experienced on the part.

CHAPTER 11

CONTROL CHARTS

Controlling the quality of materials, batches, parts, and assemblies during the course of their actual manufacture is probably the most popularly recognized quality-control activity. Much of the present-day literature on statistical methods in quality control is devoted to this subject. The statistical tool most generally recommended for this work is the control chart or some modification of it.

The control chart has been used in industry for many years. Its most prominent pioneer has been Dr. Walter A. Shewhart, of the Bell Telephone Laboratories.

Only a few fundamentals are required for practical understanding of this tool. Although there are many adaptations of the basic control-chart types, these are largely matters of changes in detail to meet particular situations.

Concept of the Control Chart

11.1 The Control-chart Approach

There are several alternative techniques for establishing drawing tolerances and specification limits. Sometimes these limits are carefully determined by test. Sometimes they are arbitrarily "picked out of the air." Often they are based upon past experience with materials and manufacturing processes.

This experience has frequently been consolidated in writing in the form of "shop-practice" tolerance sheets. In other instances it exists as know-how in the heads of veteran shopmen.

It is common for a designing engineer to translate this know-how into engineering data. The engineer may ask the machine-shop foreman if he can maintain a tolerance of ±0.003 inch between drilled hole centers on bearing brackets. The foreman's experience may lead him to answer, "Sure, we can do that." This answer may be the engineer's basis for placing a ±0.003-inch tolerance on the bearing-bracket drawing.

The shop-practice experience may also be very important on the factory floor after drawings have been released to it by the design engineer. The machine shop may, for example, produce a lot of these bearing brackets whose between-centers variation is ±0.005 inch instead of the ±0.003 inch indicated. The shop foreman's immediate reaction will be that something "unusual" has occurred. Perhaps the drill is running off center, perhaps it is improperly ground, perhaps the drill jig is worn.

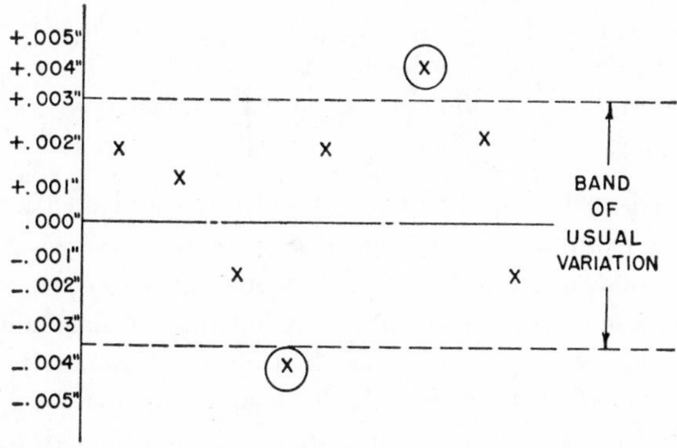

FIG. 11.1.

He goes to the drill press with possible corrective steps well formulated in his mind.

Experienced factory men thus intuitively separate manufactured parts variations into two types:

1. *Usual* variation, which is the amount of deviation that the shopman has learned to expect. In the case of the bearing brackets, this is ±0.003 inch.[1]

2. *Unusual* variation, which is the amount of deviation greater than the shopman has learned to expect. In the case of the bearing brackets, this is the variation beyond ±0.003 inch.[2]

Shopmen therefore conceive of "limits" of usual variation with respect

[1] The statistical control-chart literature might refer to the causes of this type of variation as *unassignable*.

[2] The statistical control-chart literature might refer to the causes of this type of variation as *assignable*.

to those parts and processes with which they are familiar. When these limits have been exceeded by the manufactured parts, the shopmen recognize that something unusual has occurred which requires correction.

Figure 11.1 illustrates this concept. The circled points are those requiring corrective action.

It is analysis of just this sort that is the basis for the control chart. The philosophy of usual variation limits is carried into the control chart in the form of control limits. Because of the nature of control-chart technique, however, the actual numerical value for control limits will ordinarily differ from the value for the corresponding usual variation limits.

11.2 Defining the Control Chart

The control chart may be defined as

A chronological (hour-by-hour, day-by-day) graphical comparison of actual product-quality characteristics with limits reflecting the ability to produce as shown by past experience on the product characteristics.

This comparison is usually made by selecting and measuring samples rather than by examination of each piece produced.

The control-chart method is a device for carrying out, on a factual basis, the shopman's separation of variation into "usual" and "unusual" components. It compares actual production variation of manufactured parts with the control limits that have been set up for those parts.

When these limits have been computed and then judged acceptable for use in production, the control chart takes up its major role—aiding in the control of the quality of materials, batches, parts, and assemblies during their actual manufacture.

11.3 How Much Variation Is Acceptable?

The decision as to whether or not a set of control limits is acceptable is almost purely a question of economics. Is the usual variation they represent less than that required by the specification limits? If so, the control limits will generally be satisfactory.

Is the usual variation represented by the control limits greater than that required by specification limits? Will it cost too much to try to obtain greater accuracy? If so, the control limits may be satisfactory. Will it be cheaper to improve the process than to accept the scrap and rework that seems inevitable? In this case, the limits will not be satisfactory and should not be accepted.

The distinction between usual and unusual variation is, of course, purely relative. What is usual for one machine and operation may be far different from usual variation for another machine and operation on the same material.

Plants and manufacturing areas within plants may vary in all the factors which go to make up usual variation. They may vary in the nature of their equipment, in the state of repair of machines, in the quality of materials used, in their skill in tooling jobs, and in the training and spirit of their employees. Thus, efforts to compare control limits among plants may often result in contradictory conclusions.

With skilled personnel to handle a certain job and with money to spend on it, the variation represented by control limits may almost certainly be reduced. In the example of drilling between centers cited in Sec. 11.1 the usual variation of ±0.003 inch might well have been reduced to ±0.0015 inch by new equipment and better materials.

Once accepted, however, the control limits can be used as an economic guide to corrective action on the job in question. It will cost too much to obtain greater uniformity. But if production results indicate more variation than is permissible by the limits, then it may be economical to spend money to trace down and eliminate the causes of this excessive variation.

11.4 Uses of the Control Chart

Depending for information about variation in product-quality characteristics upon what shopmen carry around in their heads is sometimes a risky business. Benefits in accuracy and record keeping result when this type of know-how is supplemented by the use of control charts.

The time period for learning about the usual variation represented by the control-chart limits may also be greatly reduced. A period of hours or days may suffice in place of the much longer period necessary for the development of certain types of process know-how. This feature is of particular importance where there is a large proportion of green employees and newly appointed supervisors.

With control limits established for materials and parts manufacturing, a number of control-chart applications are readily suggested. Some of them are the following:

Predict Rejects before Defective Parts Are Produced. Quality troubles often gradually "drift" into a process. An improperly ground tool may cause a trend toward unusual variation which will finally result in the production of defective parts. A chart which compares these actual production variations with control limits may "red-flag" the entrance into the process of this sort of quality trouble before scrap or rework is actually caused.

This application may be illustrated by a popular comparison of control-chart limits with highway boundaries. As the quality characteristics of manufactured parts approach the control-limit "shoulders," process correction may be called for to prevent the process running in a "ditch" by producing defective parts.

Judge Job Performance. The perennial question "Are we doing as good a quality job as we can expect with existing equipment?" may be answered factually by comparing actual manufacturing variations with the usual variation represented by control limits.

Establish Tolerances. Specification limits bear a relationship to usual variation only by coincidence. This is true because specification limits relate to the product requirements, whereas the expected variation relates to the process and its capability. However, it is advantageous for the design engineer to be familiar with the capabilities of the existing processes so that he can "optimize" the utilization of these processes in his design selection.

Guide Management. The control chart furnishes management with a brief summary of the success or failure of plant efforts to control product quality.

Forecast Costs. Usual variation may be representative of a plant's methods of manufacture. To reduce this variation may be extremely expensive and may require new machinery, new methods, and better machine maintenance. Unusual variation, on the other hand, may represent temporary difficulties that can be eliminated without excessive expense.

Usual variation may for many processes be associated with the most economical way of manufacturing. Its determination is consequently useful for cost purposes.

In the special case wherein usual variation is wider than specification limits but, for some reason, the factory cannot improve the process, then it must be recognized that some scrap will be produced. The amount of this scrap can be forecast, minimized,[3] and made a part of job cost.

Develop a Bogey for Defective Material. Cost accountants have always had a problem in dealing with the content of "manufacturing-loss" reports and in adding to standard cost systems a realistic factor to account for rejected parts and assemblies. They have long recognized that 0 per cent rejects may be both an impractical and uneconomic target.

A percentage bogey is therefore often arbitrarily chosen at some figure which seems the most economic. This figure is frequently far too high or low—as the accountants themselves would be first to admit—simply because there may be no adequate data upon which to base an accurate estimate. Setting up control-chart limits on various types of operations may furnish a more realistic basis for establishing these bogeys.

[3] See Sec. 17.17 for a discussion of how the scrap can be minimized when such a condition is present.

11.5 Types of Control Charts

Corresponding to the two types of inspection data that are taken in industry, there are two fundamental types of control charts:

1. Measurements or "variables" charts (of which the most popular are the so-called $\overline{X}$, R charts) for use when actual readings are taken.
2. Charts for use with go and not-go or "attributes" data, of which fraction or per cent-defective charts (sometimes called p charts) are most popular.

While the details for computing the control limits for these two types of charts differ, the basic approach is the same in both cases. It is based on the laws of probability that were discussed in Chap. 10.

The steps followed in this approach are as follows:

1. Select the appropriate quality characteristic to be studied.
2. Record data taken on a required number of samples, each composed of an adequate number of units.
3. Determine the control limits from these sample data.
4. Determine if these control limits are economically satisfactory for the job. Are they too wide? Too narrow?
5. Plot the limits on suitable graph paper. Start to record the results of production samples of proper size, which are selected at periodic intervals.
6. Take corrective action if the characteristics of the production samples exceed the control limits.

When a process yields samples whose characteristics remain consistently within the control limits, it may be termed a *controlled process.*

In many instances, when control limits are first being computed for parts or assemblies, the processes are found to be "out of control"; characteristics of several samples exceed the control limits. On these processes, causes for the excessive sample variations can be traced down and eliminated. Steps 2 and 3 are repeated until the process becomes controlled.

Much of the data taken in industry are of the go and not-go variety. Actual measurements are becoming more and more popular, however, as their advantages in the prevention of defective work become recognized.

Go and not-go data merely indicate that parts are "good" or "bad." But an important question for corrective action is "How good or bad?" So in measurements data this question is more adequately answered.

Measurements control charts will be discussed below in Secs. 11.6 to 11.15, after which Secs. 11.16 to 11.25 will treat charts for use with go and not-go data.

Measurements Control Charts

11.6 Form of the Chart

It has been shown above that the computation of control limits really simmers down to a numerical calculation of what shopmen come to consider as usual variation limits. But how can this numerical calculation be made?

Chapter 10 discussed in some detail the universal nature of variation among manufactured parts. It described the frequency distribution as one medium for presenting and analyzing this variation. Sections 10.5 and 10.14 discussed frequency-distribution process limits, between which will fall practically all individual readings on production parts for the quality characteristic in question.

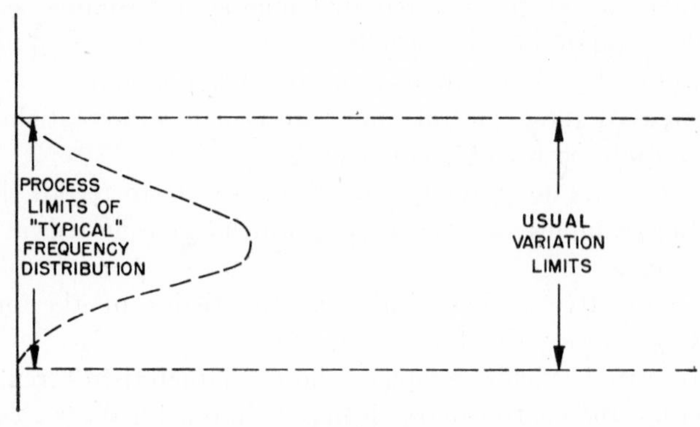

FIG. 11.2.

There is great similarity between these process limits and the usual variation limits that were described above in connection with the control chart. Usual variation limits are, for most practical purposes, the process limits for the frequency distribution that would be "typical" for the product-quality characteristic in question. Figure 11.2 illustrates this.

Because of this similarity, one approach to the form for a measurements control chart might be simply an application of the type of frequency distribution discussed. Steps that might be followed are

1. Make several frequency-distribution analyses to arrive at the "typical" values for process limits.
2. Periodically obtain the readings on production parts required for a frequency-distribution sample.
3. Compare the picture of each of these frequency distributions with the process limits.
4. Take any indicated action.

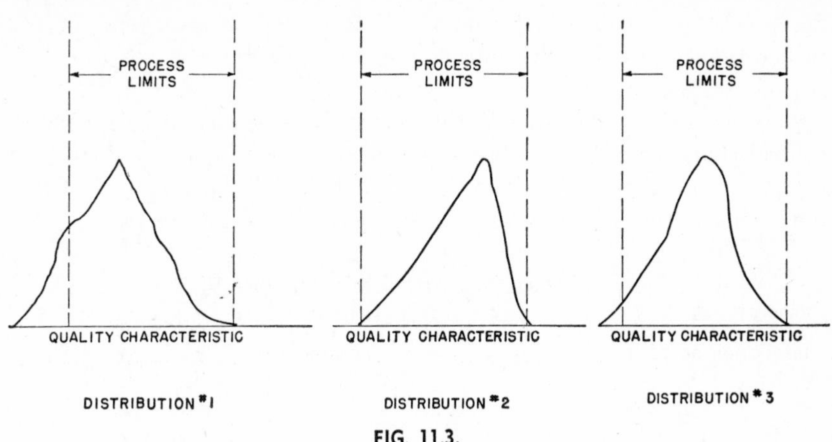

FIG. 11.3.

Figure 11.3 shows the resulting picture of such an analysis.

Many practical problems are involved in this procedure. With a probable sample size of at least 50 readings required, it is possible that cost considerations would permit the measurement of only a few samples during each production period. Yet experience shows that the measurement of many samples selected at more frequent intervals during the production period is the more effective procedure for the control of product quality.

It would, in addition, be clumsy to compare the resulting frequency-distribution pictures with the process limits. It would also be relatively expensive to secure enough samples to calculate any acceptable "typical" values for these process limits.

One way to meet the objection of clumsiness would be to turn the frequency distributions on their side. As shown in Fig. 11.4, this would improve matters very little. And even if it improved them a great deal,

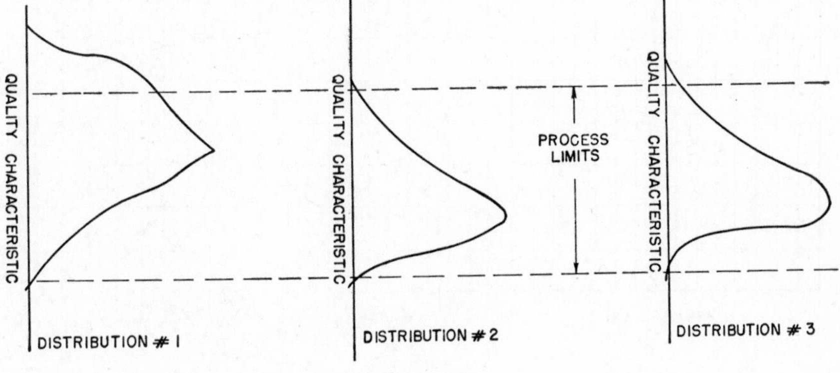

FIG. 11.4.

the procedure of Fig. 11.4 would still force the measurement of few rather than many samples during the production period for the same reasons.

It is because of difficulties of this sort that the modern measurements-control-chart approach has been developed. Instead of selecting the few samples comprising a relatively large number of units, this method permits the selection of many samples of relatively small size.

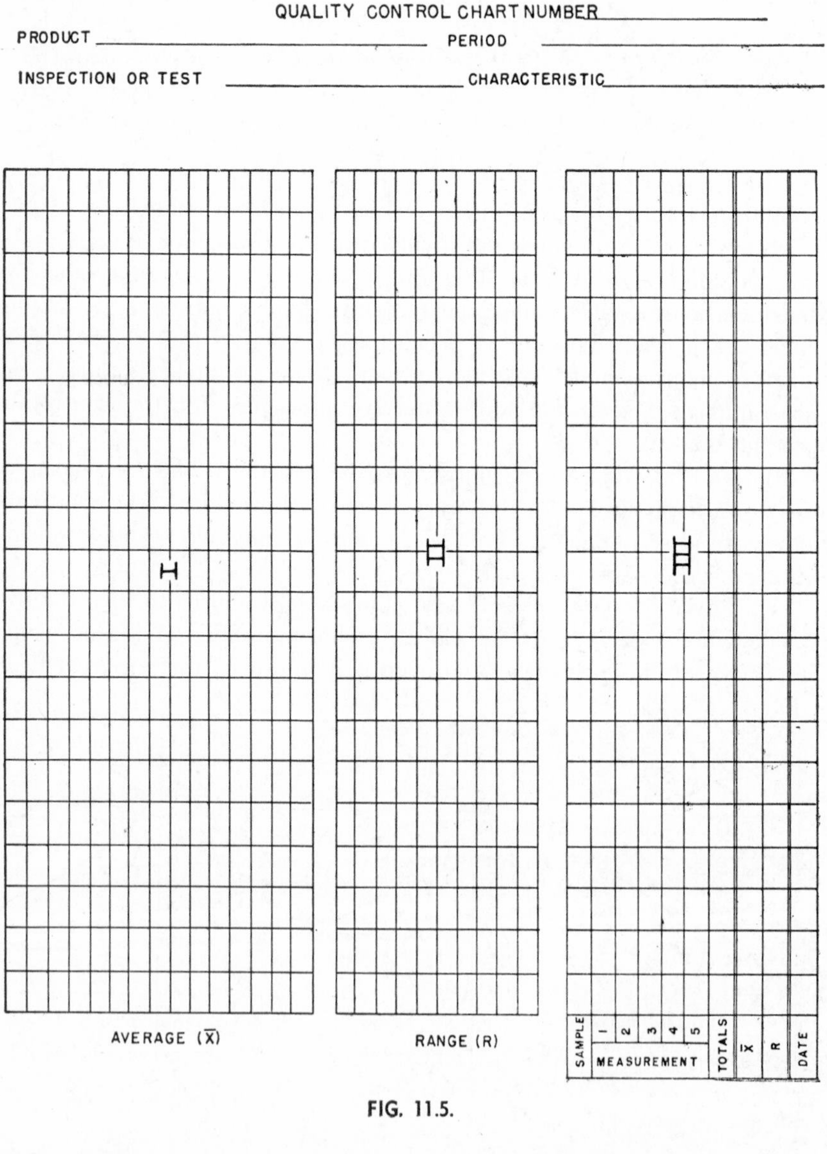

QUALITY CONTROL CHART NUMBER ____________

PRODUCT ____________ PERIOD ____________

INSPECTION OR TEST ____________ CHARACTERISTIC ____________

I

II

III

AVERAGE ($\bar{X}$)

RANGE (R)

SAMPLE | MEASUREMENT 1 2 3 4 5 | TOTALS | ΣX | R | DATE

FIG. 11.5.

Rather than plotting the values for each individual reading in these small samples, measures of central tendency and spread are computed for each of these samples. These measures are then plotted on separate charts—one chart for central tendency and the other for spread. Control limits are established for each of these two charts, and the values of central tendency and spread for each individual sample of production parts are compared against the limits.[4] Corrective action may be indicated when one or both of these values fall outside the limits.

Figure 11.5 illustrates a chart form used with this measurements charting method. Some of its relative advantages may be briefly summarized:

1. The chart simmers out the two important characteristics of the frequency distribution into the simple form of two individual graphs which are easily used on the shop floor. These are

a. A graph for measures of *central tendency*. The average $\bar{X}$ has been found the most useful measure here (see I in Fig. 11.5). However, any measure of central tendency will suffice.

b. A graph for measures of *spread*. The range R has been found the most useful measure here (see II in Fig. 11.5). However, any of the various measures of spread may be used.

Measurements-control-chart limits are relatively easily computed for each of these two graphs and can be simply plotted on the appropriate portions of the graph.

2. The chart makes economical the selection of several samples, each with a few readings, in place of a few samples with as many as 50 readings (see III in Fig. 11.5).

11.7 Measurements-control-chart Limits

The basic principle for computing measurements-control-chart limits is similar to that for computing the frequency-distribution process, or 3-sigma limits, that have been discussed earlier. The difference between the two lies in the fact that the measurements control limits are being established for *measures of central tendency and spread* from samples of relatively smaller size.

It will be recalled from Sec. 10.18 that values of central tendency and spread for samples drawn from the same lot have 3-sigma limits of their own. Limits for the two graphs in measurements control charts—the graph for central tendency and that for spread—are merely these same 3-sigma limits of Sec. 10.18. For the variation being compared in measurements control charts is that reflected in a series of samples drawn from what is presumed to be the same production stream or "lot"; values for central tendency and spread of these samples are simply

[4] It is assumed that the general shape of the frequency distribution does not vary significantly.

gaged against their own 3-sigma limits, a technique that is in conformance with the principles of Sec. 10.18.

3 sigma has been chosen in place of 2 or 4 sigma, for example, because experience has proved the 3-sigma value to be most useful and economical for control-chart applications, since so many frequency distributions encountered in industry tend toward "normality." [5]

Formulas for computing these measurements-control-chart limits can be readily listed:

When Range Is Used as Measure of Spread

Average: Lower control limit $= \bar{\bar{X}} - 3\sigma_{\bar{X}}$
Center line $= \bar{\bar{X}}$
Upper control limit $= \bar{\bar{X}} + 3\sigma_{\bar{X}}$

Range: Lower control limit $= \bar{R} - 3\sigma_R$
Center line $= \bar{R}$
Upper control limit $= \bar{R} + 3\sigma_R$

When Standard Deviation Is Used as Measure of Spread

Average: Lower control limit $= \bar{\bar{X}} - 3\sigma_{\bar{X}}$
Center line $= \bar{\bar{X}}$
Upper control limit $= \bar{\bar{X}} + 3\sigma_{\bar{X}}$

Standard deviation: Lower control limit $= \bar{\sigma} - 3\sigma_\sigma$
Center line $= \bar{\sigma}$
Upper control limit $= \bar{\sigma} + 3\sigma_\sigma$

where $\bar{\bar{X}}$ = grand average (see Sec. 10.10)
$\sigma_{\bar{X}}$ = standard deviation of the sample average (see Sec. 10.18)
$\bar{R}$ = average range (see Sec. 10.12)
σ_R = standard deviation of the sample range
$\bar{\sigma}$ = average standard deviation (see Sec. 10.11)
σ_σ = standard deviation of the sample standard deviation (see Sec. 10.18)

It would obviously be tedious to gather a series of samples of small size, determine the values for central tendency and spread for each of these samples, and then go through the laborious calculations that are involved in the use of the above formulas. As a result, a table of constants—A_1, A_2, B_3, B_4, D_3, D_4—has been prepared to simplify this computation. With the use of these constants, which are listed in Fig. 11.9, the formulas become

[5] Note the possible deviations in the areas contained within $\pm 3\sigma$ shown in Fig. 10.27.

When Range Is Used as Measure of Spread

Average:	Lower limit	$= \overline{\overline{X}} - A_2\overline{R}$	(13)
	Center line	$= \overline{\overline{X}}$	
	Upper limit	$= \overline{\overline{X}} + A_2\overline{R}$	(14)
Range:	Lower limit	$= D_3\overline{R}$	(15)
	Center line	$= \overline{R}$	
	Upper limit	$= D_4\overline{R}$	(16)

When Standard Deviation Is Used as a Measure of Spread

Average:	Lower limit	$= \overline{\overline{X}} - A_1\bar{\sigma}$	(17)
	Center line	$= \overline{\overline{X}}$	
	Upper limit	$= \overline{\overline{X}} + A_1\bar{\sigma}$	(18)
Standard deviation:	Lower limit	$= B_3\bar{\sigma}$	(19)
	Center line	$= \bar{\sigma}$	
	Upper control limit	$= B_4\bar{\sigma}$	(20)

It is these formulas—(13) through (20)—which are used to compute measurements-control-chart limits. The interpretation of these control limits is the same as that for process and normal variation limits. However, the physical location of the limits is different, since one is considering the distribution of averages rather than the distribution of individual observations.

Drawing and specification limits establish the acceptable amount of variation for the individual pieces that are produced. As such, they can be compared with frequency-distribution process limits. These process limits can be directly measured against drawing and specification limits to determine whether or not an economically satisfactory state of control of product quality exists. Section 10.16 illustrated one way in which these limits could be so used.

Measurements-control-chart limits, being based on a distribution of averages, cannot usually be directly compared with drawing or specification limits. When a decision must be made as to whether or not these control limits indicate an economically satisfactory process condition, it is necessary to compare the drawing or specification limits in question with the process limits.

Figure 11.6 illustrates a typical relationship among these limits.

Figure 11.7 illustrates some practical problems that may arise when this type of limits analysis is used to make a decision about the economics of a process condition. The process conditions are unsatisfactory in both charts of Fig. 11.7, even though the reasons for their being unsatisfactory are almost completely opposed.

In the left-hand chart, the process has too much variation for the

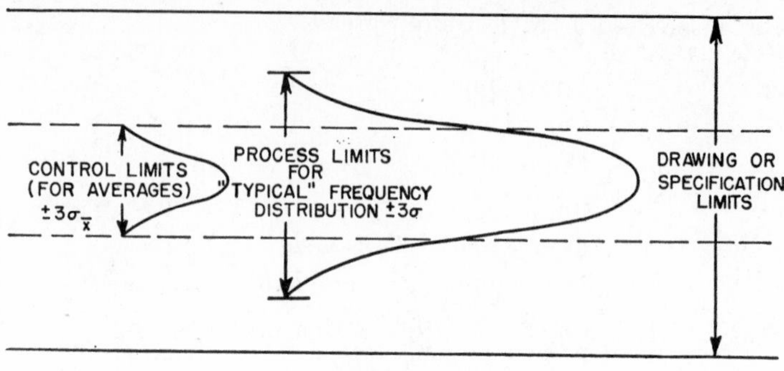

FIG. 11.6.

specification limits. If the control limits were accepted as computed, defective work would be produced. There are three possible alternatives here:

1. The process conditions can be improved.
2. The specification limits can be widened.
3. It can be recognized as part of job cost that, if no change is made, some scrap will be inevitable.

On the right-hand chart, the process condition is "too good." To reset a tool or change a process condition every time sample results showed out of control here would certainly be uneconomical. In this case, there are two alternatives: (1) the specification limits can be narrowed if

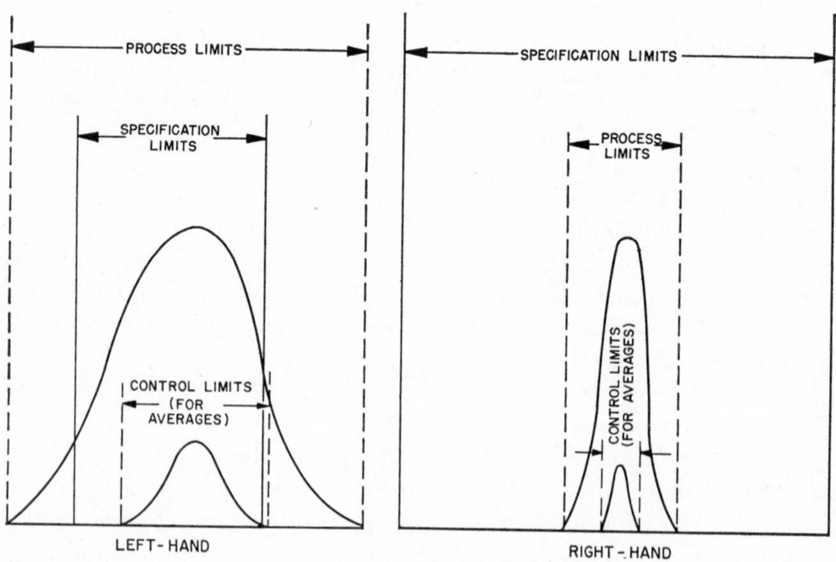

FIG. 11.7.

this will tend to produce a better product or (2) the control limits can be widened by some factor beyond the process limits which has proved satisfactory by experience with the chart in question. This matter will be reviewed more broadly in later sections of this chapter.

11.8 Computing Control Limits in Relation to Process Averages

There are two broad approaches for establishing measurements-control-chart limits:

1. Compute the control limits in relation to the average value for the process, or the so-called process average.
2. Modify the control limits to consider the allowable variation in the drawing or specification limits.

Method 1 will be discussed below, and Secs. 11.13 and 11.14 will discuss method 2.

There are eight steps to be followed in establishing a measurements control chart based upon setting the control limits in relation to the process average:

1. Select the quality characteristic to be controlled: length, width, hardness, etc.
2. Gather data by selecting an adequate number of samples of the part in question and measuring the chosen quality characteristic. Adequacy will vary according to the specific process under examination, but for purposes of illustration, a sample of 25 has been selected.

   Each sample should contain an appropriate number of individual units. A sample size of five units has been found effective for many industrial applications, so the sample size of five will be used in the following example.

   The samples should be taken at successive intervals (every hour, every day), and the data from each one must be recorded in the order that it has been selected and measured.
3. Compute values of the average and range for each of the 25 samples.
4. Compute the grand average $\overline{\overline{X}}$ of the averages of the 25 samples. Compute the average of the ranges $\overline{R}$ of the 25 samples.
5. Compute control limits based on these sample averages and ranges.
6. Analyze the average and range values for each sample with relation to these control limits. Determine if any factors requiring corrective action are present before the control limits are reviewed for approval.
7. Determine if the control limits are economically satisfactory for the process.
8. Use the control chart during active production as a basis for control of the quality characteristic in question so as to be assured that the process average and spread have not changed significantly.

11.9 The Calculation of Control Limits

A screw-machine setup had just been completed for the production of studs whose cutoff-length drawing tolerance was 0.500 inch ± 0.008 inch. A frequency-distribution analysis had been carried on while the setup was being made. This analysis showed the setup to be satisfactory for the start of a long production run.

To establish a measurements control chart to control the quality of these studs during the subsequent production run, the eight steps outlined above would be followed in some detail:

Step 1: Select the Quality Characteristic. The cutoff length of the stud is most critical, and this is the characteristic for the control of which the chart is to be established.

Step 2: Gather Data for a Reasonable Time. About 150 studs are produced each hour. With a sample size of five units—one reading per stud on five studs—it can be arbitrarily assumed that one sample every hour may be selected for the purpose of setting the control limits. This decision is a practical matter of balancing such factors as cost, probable machine drift, availability of inspectors, and accessibility of gaging equipment.

Measurements of the required 25 samples will be taken by an inspector and will be recorded on a form similar to that shown in Fig. 11.5. Figure 11.8 shows the actual form used in this case. The data taken are recorded on Fig. 11.8 as they are gathered.

Step 3: Compute the Average and Ranges for Samples. Referring to sample 1 of Fig. 11.8, the five readings are

$$\begin{array}{r} 0.498 \\ 0.501 \\ 0.504 \\ 0.502 \\ \underline{0.503} \\ 2.508 \end{array}$$

Using formula (1):

$$\overline{X} = \frac{2.508}{5} = 0.5016 \text{ inch}$$

(The fourth decimal is shown in this example simply for illustrative purposes.)

Using formula (6):

$$R = 0.504 - 0.498 = 0.006 \text{ inch}$$

Similar calculations may be made for the other samples in Fig. 11.8. The average and range readings for each of the samples are plotted in the appropriate spot on the control chart.

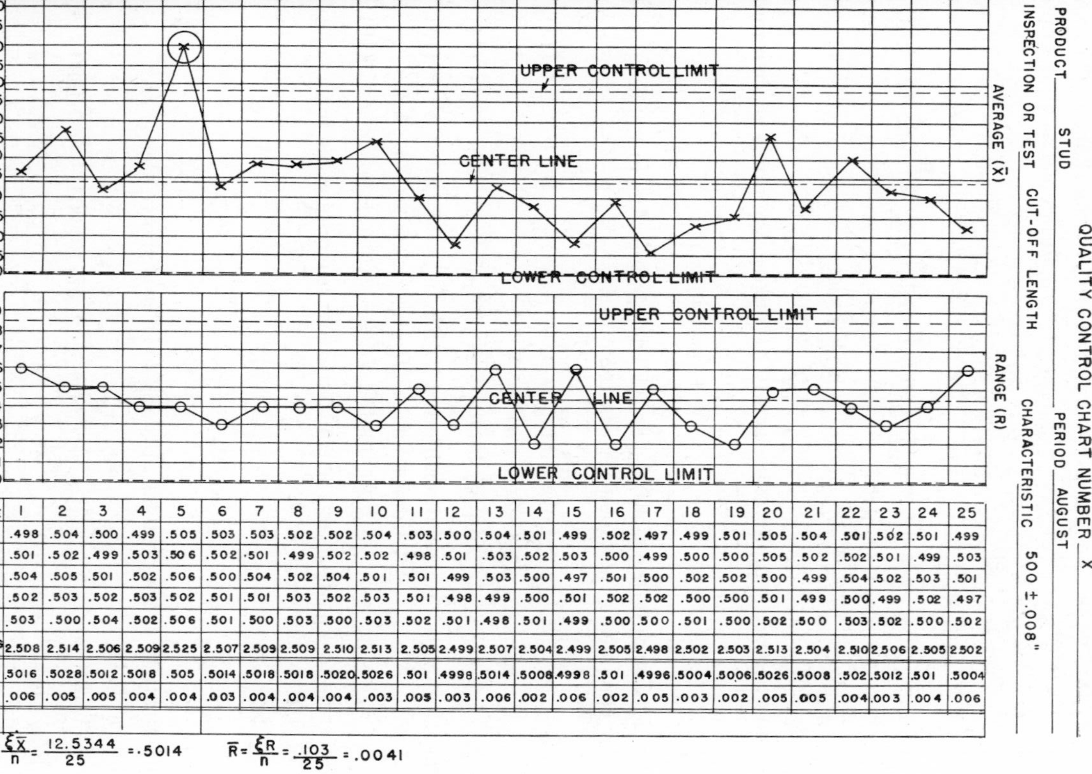

QUALITY CONTROL CHART NUMBER X

PRODUCT STUD PERIOD AUGUST

INSPECTION OR TEST CUT-OFF LENGTH CHARACTERISTIC 500 ±.008"

SAMPLE	1	2	3	4	5	6	7	8	9	10	11	12	13
MEASUREMENT 1	.498	.504	.500	.499	.505	.503	.503	.502	.502	.504	.503	.500	.504
2	.501	.502	.499	.503	.506	.502	.501	.499	.502	.502	.498	.501	.503
3	.504	.505	.501	.502	.506	.500	.504	.502	.504	.501	.501	.499	.503
4	.502	.503	.502	.503	.502	.501	.501	.503	.502	.503	.501	.498	.499
5	.503	.500	.504	.502	.506	.501	.500	.503	.500	.503	.502	.501	.498
TOTALS	2.508	2.514	2.506	2.509	2.525	2.507	2.509	2.509	2.510	2.513	2.505	2.499	2.507
$\bar{X}$	.5016	.5028	.5012	.5018	.505	.5014	.5018	.5018	.5020	.5026	.501	.4998	.5014
R	.006	.005	.005	.004	.004	.003	.004	.004	.004	.003	.005	.003	.006
DATE													

SAMPLE	14	15	16	17	18	19	20	21	22	23	24	25
MEASUREMENT 1	.501	.499	.502	.497	.499	.501	.505	.504	.501	.502	.501	.499
2	.502	.503	.500	.499	.500	.500	.505	.502	.502	.501	.499	.503
3	.500	.497	.501	.500	.502	.502	.500	.499	.504	.502	.503	.501
4	.500	.501	.502	.502	.500	.500	.501	.499	.500	.499	.502	.497
5	.501	.499	.500	.500	.501	.500	.502	.500	.503	.502	.500	.502
TOTALS	2.504	2.499	2.505	2.498	2.502	2.503	2.513	2.504	2.510	2.506	2.505	2.502
$\bar{X}$	.5008	.4998	.501	.4996	.5004	.5006	.5026	.5008	.502	.5012	.501	.5004
R	.002	.006	.002	.005	.003	.002	.005	.005	.004	.003	.004	.006
DATE												

$$\bar{\bar{X}} = \frac{\Sigma \bar{X}}{n} = \frac{12.5344}{25} = .5014 \qquad \bar{R} = \frac{\Sigma R}{n} = \frac{.103}{25} = .0041$$

FIG. 11.8.

Step 4: Determine the Grand Average and the Average Range. The sun of the 25 sample averages is 12.5344. Using formula (2), the gran average is

$$\bar{\bar{X}} = \frac{12.5344}{25} = 0.5014 \text{ inch}$$

The average range may be similarly calculated, using formula (2) in th form that

$$\bar{R} = \frac{\text{sum of sample ranges}}{\text{number of samples}}$$

The sum of the 25 sample ranges is 0.103. The average range is, therefore

$$\bar{R} = \frac{0.103}{25} = 0.0041 \text{ inch}$$

Step 5: Compute the Control Limits. The appropriate formulas in Sec 11.7 for computing these control-chart limits are

Averages:

$$\text{Lower limit} = \bar{\bar{X}} - A_2\bar{R} \tag{13}$$
$$\text{Center line} = \bar{\bar{X}}$$
$$\text{Upper limit} = \bar{\bar{X}} + A_2\bar{R} \tag{14}$$

Ranges:

$$\text{Lower limit} = D_3\bar{R} \tag{15}$$
$$\text{Center line} = \bar{R}$$
$$\text{Upper limit} = D_4\bar{R} \tag{16}$$

Referring to Fig. 11.9 for the constants that are applicable for a sampl size of 5, it is shown that

$$A_2 = 0.577$$
$$D_3 = 0$$
$$D_4 = 2.114$$

Substituting A_2 in formulas (13) and (14), it is shown that
Formula (13):

$$\text{Lower limit} = \bar{\bar{X}} - A_2\bar{R} = 0.5014 - (0.577)(0.0041) = 0.4990$$

Formula (14):

$$\text{Upper limit} = \bar{\bar{X}} + A_2\bar{R} = 0.5014 + (0.577)(0.0041) = 0.5038$$

Substituting D_3 and D_4 in formulas (15) and (16), it is shown that
Formula (15):

$$\text{Lower limit} = D_3\bar{R} = (0)(0.0041) = 0$$

Formula (16):

$$\text{Upper limit} = D_4\bar{R} = 2.114(0.0041) = 0.0087$$

These control limits may be plotted on the appropriate portions o 'ig. 11.8 by means of dashed lines. The center lines are also plotted on his figure, although some forms of control chart eliminate them.

Step 6: Use Limits to Analyze Sample Results. The control chart for he cutoff length of the screw-machined studs is fully constructed at the onclusion of step 5. It may be noted from examination of Fig. 11.8 that ll sample ranges are within limits but that the average value for sample is out of control.

It is possible that, since only one sample reading is out of control, the eason may be pure chance. It will be recalled that all these calculations re based upon the laws of probability. There is the chance (about 3 out f 1,000) that an occasional good sample will show as out of control.

FACTORS FOR COMPUTING CONTROL LIMITS

UMBER OF OBSER-VATIONS IN SAMPLE	CHART FOR AVERAGES		CHART FOR STANDARD DEVIATIONS		CHART FOR RANGES		NUMBER OF OBSER-VATIONS IN SAMPLE
	FACTORS FOR CONTROL LIMITS		FACTORS FOR CONTROL LIMITS		FACTORS FOR CONTROL LIMITS		
n	A_1	A_2	B_3	B_4	D_3	D_4	n
2	3.759	1.880	0	3.658	0	3.268	2
3	2.394	1.023	0	2.692	0	2.574	3
4	1.880	.729	0	2.330	0	2.282	4
5	1.596	.577	0	2.128	0	2.114	5
6	1.410	.483	.003	1.997	0	2.004	6
7	1.277	.419	.097	1.903	.076	1.924	7
8	1.175	.373	.169	1.831	.136	1.864	8
9	1.094	.337	.227	1.774	.184	1.816	9
10	1.028	308	.273	1.727	.223	1.777	10
11	.973	.285	.312	1.688	.256	1.744	11
12	.925	.266	.346	1.654	.284	1.717	12
13	.884	.249	.375	1.625	.308	1.692	13
14	.848	.235	.400	1.599	329	1.671	14
15	.817	.223	.423	1.577	348	1.652	15

FIG. 11.9.

In this case, however, other reasons caused further analysis of sample . Investigation showed that the regular inspector had not taken the eadings but had asked another employee to take them. The employee vho was requested to take these readings was not qualified to handle recision measuring equipment. Other factors led to the suspicion either hat sample 5 had not been measured at all or that the readings had been "faked."

For strict accuracy, therefore, the sampling procedure in steps 2 hrough 5 should have been repeated by gathering more samples. With omewhat less strict accuracy, the computation of steps 3 through 5 ould have been reworked, eliminating sample 5.

In this case, however, the control limits were allowed to stand as they had been originally calculated. It was felt, after examination of the stud data, that a recalculation would not yield sufficiently different results to justify the additional time that would be consumed by it.[6]

The circumstance illustrated by the results with sample 5 is typical of occurrences while control limits are being initially established for a process or an operation. The sample results on which the first computations have been made are usually examined with a judicious eye.

Often, several sample averages or ranges are found out of control during these initial computations. In these cases, efforts are made to trace down, identify, and eliminate the causes. The procedure of steps 2 through 5 is repeated until the process or operation is found to be "in control." This procedure is called *screening* control-chart data.

Step 7: Determine if the Control Limits Are Economically Satisfactory. The decision regarding the economics of control limits can effectively be made by carrying through a frequency-distribution analysis before the control chart is established and by coupling this analysis with a brief glance at the limits themselves after they have been computed.

In Chap. 10 it was pointed out that a process condition was considered economically satisfactory if its frequency distribution was within tolerance limits and was well centered. It was noted in Sec. 11.9 that such a frequency-distribution analysis had been carried on while the screw machine was being set up for the production of studs. This analysis had indicated that the 3-sigma or process limits for the cutoff length compared satisfactorily with the 0.492- to 0.508-inch tolerance limits.

The purpose of glancing at the control limits in addition to the process-limits analysis is merely to substantiate the frequency-distribution conclusions. Thus it is possible that the distribution sample might not have been representative (see Sec. 10.26) or that the process might have been subject to factors causing variation which were not taken into account by the frequency-distribution analysis.

With the studs, however, a glance at the control limits plotted on Fig. 11.8 merely tends to corroborate the frequency-distribution conclusions.

The center line of the $\overline{X}$ chart is on the "high side" of the tolerance rather than at the nominal, but this is a situation often encountered in the shop. It resulted here, as is typical, from the desire of the machine operator to be "on the safe side of the tolerance."

What he had apparently done was to reset his tool so as to produce studs whose average value was somewhat above the nominal length of 0.500 inch. He had done this because studs that were on this "high side"

[6] Decisions of this sort must, of course, be based upon the circumstances peculiar to individual cases. Is the greater accuracy that would be gained by repeating the sampling procedure and "screening out" unrepresentative samples worth the additional time and effort that would be required?

could have excess material removed if a part happened to fall outside drawing limits, whereas studs on the "low side" would have to be scrapped, were parts to fall outside drawing limits.

Yet the control limits are still satisfactory in spite of the high-side center line, although from a purist's point of view they might be improved by centering the process at the nominal value.

Step 8: Use Control Limits for Controlling Quality during Actual Production. With control limits computed and approved, a measurements control chart can be placed right at the screw machine producing the studs. This chart will have control limits plotted on it, and the values for average and range of the periodically selected samples will be marked in the appropriate chart spaces. This will be done by some designated individual, usually a floor inspector or the machine operator. Corrective action will be taken when the chart shows it to be necessary.

In theory, the frequency of making the sample checks may be calculated mathematically. In practice, this decision is an economic judgment based upon such factors as the numbers of inspectors available, the quality history of the job, the quantity of hourly production, and how much it might cost to allow an out-of-control condition to exist undetected.

During the above procedure for computing control limits for the studs, samples were chosen every hour. This same policy is continued when the chart comes to be used for controlling quality of the cutoff length during actual production. For the studs, this hourly period is sufficient normally to highlight such factors as "drift," tool wear, or gradual loosening of setup bolts in sufficient time so that production of defective parts can be prevented.

Since the process conditions upon which the original computations are based may be subject to change, it is desirable that the control limits be reevaluated and possibly completely recalculated periodically. The need for such a computation depends, of course, upon the tendency of process and operation conditions to change. The frequency with which the calculation must be made may be 6 hours, 6 days, or 6 months, depending upon individual circumstances.

For the stud job, a 3-month period is adequate for recalculating limits. Should any methods change be made in the process during that period, however, recalculation of the limits would be required at once.

11.10 Economically Satisfactory Control Limits: Relation of Range and Standard Deviation

When the average range $\overline{R}$ has been computed for a series of samples, as in Sec. 11.9, the value of the standard deviation for the "production stream" (Sec. 10.18) from which these samples were drawn bears a direct relationship to $\overline{R}$, if the distribution considered approximates the normal curve. This relationship is shown as[7]

$$\sigma' = \frac{\overline{R}}{d_2} \tag{21}$$

Figure 11.10 includes a tabulation of the d_2 conversion factor for sample sizes ranging from 2 to 15 units. The reasons for not exceeding 15 units in the sample were discussed in Sec. 10.13.

Use of Fig. 11.10 may be illustrated by the calculation of the standard deviation for the pull of springs. These springs were received by means

Number of readings in sample n	*Conversion factor* d_2
2	1.128
3	1.693
4	2.059
5	2.326
6	2.534
7	2.704
8	2.847
9	2.970
10	3.078
11	3.173
12	3.258
13	3.336
14	3.407
15	3.472

FIG. 11.10

of periodic large shipments to an assembly plant. From these shipments a series of samples was drawn and measured. Five springs were included in each sample.

From the ranges of each of these samples, $\overline{R}$ was calculated as 14.0 grams. To compute the corresponding standard deviation the d_2 factor was secured from Fig. 11.10. For a sample of five readings, d_2 equals 2.326.

Substituting the values for $\overline{R}$ and d_2 in formula (21), the resulting expression was obtained:

$$\sigma' = \frac{\overline{R}}{d_2} = \frac{14.0}{2.326}$$

$$= 6.0 \text{ grams}$$

A very useful application of formula (21) is to be found in those cases

[7] As was noted in Sec. 10.18, σ' represents an estimate of the "true" standard deviation.

where control-chart limits have been computed without first making a frequency-distribution analysis of the process. As was noted in Sec. 11.7, the control limits themselves cannot be directly compared with tolerance limits; 3-sigma, or process, limits for individual pieces must be calculated.

These 3-sigma limits for individual pieces can be computed easily by using the value of $\overline{R}$ that has already been calculated for use in the control limits. The 3-sigma limit can be developed as follows:

$$\sigma' = \frac{\overline{R}}{d_2} \qquad (21)$$

and

$$3\sigma = \frac{3\overline{R}}{d_2}$$

and

$$3\sigma = \frac{3}{d_2}\overline{R}$$

Now the 3-sigma limits for readings on individual pieces equal

$$\overline{\overline{X}} \pm 3\sigma$$

or

$$\overline{\overline{X}} \pm \left(\frac{3}{d_2}\right)\overline{R}$$

The factor $3/d_2$ varies with different sample sizes. This factor will hereafter be termed L in this book. Figure 11.11 lists a tabulation of the factor L for different sample sizes.

Process, or 3-sigma, limits can be computed with this factor by use of the following formulas:

$$\text{Lower limit} = \overline{\overline{X}} - L\overline{R} \qquad (22)$$

$$\text{Center line} = \overline{\overline{X}}$$

$$\text{Upper limit} = \overline{\overline{X}} + L\overline{R} \qquad (23)$$

Use of these formulas can be illustrated by reference to the control-chart data of Sec. 11.9. If, with these data, a frequency-distribution analysis had not been made prior to computation of control limits, the process-limit calculation could have been made as follows:

It will be recalled that, for the studs,

$$\overline{\overline{X}} = 0.5014 \text{ inch}$$

and

$$\overline{R} = 0.0041 \text{ inch}$$

From Fig. 11.11 the value of L for a sample size of five units is 1.290. Substituting these values in formulas (22) and (23):

Formula (22):

$$\text{Lower limit} = \bar{\bar{X}} - L\bar{R} = 0.5014 - (1.290)(0.0041) = 0.4962 \text{ inch}$$

Formula (23):

$$\text{Upper limit} = \bar{\bar{X}} + L\bar{R} = 0.5014 + (1.290)(0.0041) = 0.5066 \text{ inch}$$

These limits compare satisfactorily with the tolerance limits of 0.492 to 0.508 inch, although they are again on the high side for reasons that were discussed in the previous section.

FACTORS FOR L AND M

SAMPLE SIZE (N)	L	M
2	2.659	5.319
3	1.772	4.143
4	1.457	3.759
5	1.290	3.568
6	1.184	3.452
7	1.109	3.378
8	1.054	3.304
9	1.010	3.282
10	.975	3.250
11	.946	3.225
12	.921	3.204
13	.899	3.189
14	.881	3.174
15	.864	3.162

FIG. 11.11.

The computation carried out through formulas (22) and (23) is sometimes not completely accurate when data used in the control-chart computation are skewed. In the case of the studs, for example, close examination of the data would show that there is an appreciable skew to the left. Yet process limits are sufficiently far within the drawing limits so that the above calculation is acceptable as a guide to the conclusion that the control limits in question are economically satisfactory.

This type of calculation, as a matter of fact, is encountered chiefly in the early stages of factory control-chart installations. When experience has been gained with the control chart, the conclusion as to whether or not limits are economically satisfactory often becomes a rule-of-thumb decision which is made by simply glancing at the control-chart data.

1.11 The Standard-deviation Control Chart

Some shops prefer the standard deviation as the measure of spread in he control charts they use, particularly where sample size is more than 0 units. This type of measurements control chart is usually termed an $\overline{X},\sigma)$ chart.

The procedure for calculating control limits is the same as when ranges re used. The chart forms used are similar to those shown in Figs. 11.5 nd 11.8, except, of course, that a standard-deviation chart is used in lace of the range chart. The major difference between this computation nd that discussed in Sec. 11.9 is that different constants are used. These onstants are, as was shown in Sec. 11.7, respectively, A_1 instead of A_2 nd B_3 and B_4 instead of D_3 and D_4. These constants are tabulated on ig. 11.9 in relation to different sample sizes.

The appropriate formulas from Sec. 11.7 for use in these computations re

verage:	Lower limit	$= \overline{\overline{X}} - A_1\bar{\sigma}$	(17)
	Center line	$= \overline{\overline{X}}$	
	Upper limit	$= \overline{\overline{X}} + A_1\bar{\sigma}$	(18)
tandard deviation:	Lower limit	$= B_3\bar{\sigma}$	(19)
	Center line	$= \bar{\sigma}$	
	Upper control limit	$= B_4\bar{\sigma}$	(20)

To convert to process, or 3-sigma, limits for individual readings, the pplicable formulas are

Lower limit	$= \overline{\overline{X}} - M\bar{\sigma}$	(24)
Center line	$= \overline{\overline{X}}$	
Upper limit	$= \overline{\overline{X}} + M\bar{\sigma}$	(25)

Figure 11.11 shows factors for M in relation to different sample sizes. The same caution in the use of these formulas must be observed as that discussed in connection with the use of the factor L in Sec. 11.10.

11.12 Measurements Control Charts: Differences in Detail

Control-chart installations of various plants contain many differences in detail from the types of charts that have been developed above. These differences are the result of efforts to meet individual plant conditions. They relate to such matters as

1. Number of units in each sample.
2. Measures of central tendency.
3. Chart form.
4. Methods of computing control limits.

1. Number of Units in Each Sample. The measurements-control-char sample sizes used in industry range from 2 to 20 units. Because of lov accuracy, 2 and 3 units are infrequently used. Samples of 4 to 6 unit are only slightly less popular than the 5-unit sample. Sample sizes of a many as 20 units are used in occasional cases. Multispindle machines ar an example here; it may be desired to take one or more readings on unit from each of several spindles, a procedure requiring a relatively larg sample size.

The decision as to which of these sample sizes is appropriate in a give situation is one which must be made by striking a balance among suc factors as the number of times samples may be selected in a particula period, the number of units that may economically be included in each o these samples, and the statistical accuracy that may be required fo telegraphing unimportant "outs of control."

2. Measures of Central Tendency. The median is sometimes used as th measure of central tendency in place of the average $\bar{\bar{X}}$. Under productio conditions, the median is simpler to compute than the average, since i can usually be determined simply by circling the reading of middl value in the sample.

The sample median is generally subject to greater statistical variatio than the sample average (about 25 per cent, generally for normal dis tributions), but for practical purposes it is sometimes more useful be cause of this ease of computation. The use of the median is influenced therefore, by such factors as the availability of mathematically com petent personnel, the degree of need for statistical accuracy, and th form of the distribution being observed.

3. Chart Form. Wide variation exists in the form taken by measure ments charts developed for individual installations. On some jobs, it i not necessary to keep both an average and a range chart. For example tool wear and other forms of process change have varying effects o different operations. There are instances where either the range or aver age remains almost constant or is unimportant, while there are wid changes in the other measure. Thus, a chart for either averages *or* range may be all that is required in these instances for control purposes.

Some control charts, as finally developed, lose their graphical forn entirely. Figure 11.12 illustrates such a chart that has been successfull used in a chemical factory for several years. This chart is not a graph uses the median instead of the average, uses no range readings, and call for action when the sample medians exceed a certain specified value Out-of-limits readings are shown by a circle surrounded by bristles.

There are measurements control charts where no numbers at all ar recorded. Individual Xs for every piece in each sample are plotted o an appropriate card form. If no more than a certain proportion of Xs

STATISTICAL CONTROL SHEET

DRWG. NO. 4Y444-3
SPEC. LIMIT 100 MM
CONTROL LIMIT 112 "
TEST METHOD
DATE 6-1-60
OPERATOR A.
SAMPLE 10 PER BOAT
MAGNETS PER BOAT
FURNACE 1

TAP	AMMETER READS	CAL. I	M-10	GALV. DELF.	Ø	COIL NO.	N	RES. SERIES	RES. SHUNT

STANDARD SHOULD READ				STANDARD DOES READ			
NO.	Ø	MM DELF. MAGNETOMETER	CURRENT TO ZERO	NO.	Ø	MM DELF. MAGNETOMETER	CURRENT TO ZERO
2		111		2		111	
4		110		4		112	
5		115		5		116	

DATE THRU FURNACE	5-31-60			6-1-60														6-1-60					
SHIFT THRU FURNACE	3rd.			1st.														2nd.					
BATCH NO.	13107			13107														13107					
BOAT NO.	3			5		8		9		10		11		12		13		1		2		3	
SHOP ORDER	1740-9A			1740-9A														1740-9A					
DISPOSITION	OC			OC		LM		OC		OC		OK		OK		LM		OK		LM		OK	
	117	111		104	110	101	105	117	119	115	109	103	117	119	114	117	115	113	116	118	121	121	112
	112	111		110	103	107	104	110	102	108	116	113	110	116	118	115	120	111	112	113	115	114	117
	116	106		109	110	109	97	114	110	116	117	110	121	118	112	116	122	115	113	118	116	111	118
	114	113		112	112	109	93	112	108	111	102	118	118	117	120	118	115	109	115	108	110	112	118
	111	105		105	110	115	86	110	120	118	111	113	116	121	118	116	91	112	113	114	81	112	116
DATE THRU FURNACE																			6-1-60				
SHIFT THRU FURNACE																			3rd.				
BATCH NO.																			13107				
BOAT NO.	4		5		6		7		8		9		10		11		13		1		2		
SHOP ORDER																			1740-9A				
DISPOSITION	OK		OK		OK		OK		OK		OK		OK		OK		OK		OK		OK		
	119	105	120	114	117	117	118	111	118	117	112	122	114	117	120	116	102	109	119	117	116	111	
	116	115	115	115	115	110	114	112	118	118	113	117	114	120	117	114	116	116	116	119	120	120	
	118	118	119	110	116	116	106	112	114	118	117	118	118	120	117	120	119	114	115	110	118	115	
	120	120	112	114	114	120	120	115	117	117	117	114	114	110	116	114	115	118	120	115	115	112	
	105	117	117	100	117	115	119	114	117	119	102	117	120	110	116	120	119	115	117	119	115	120	

FIG. 11.12.

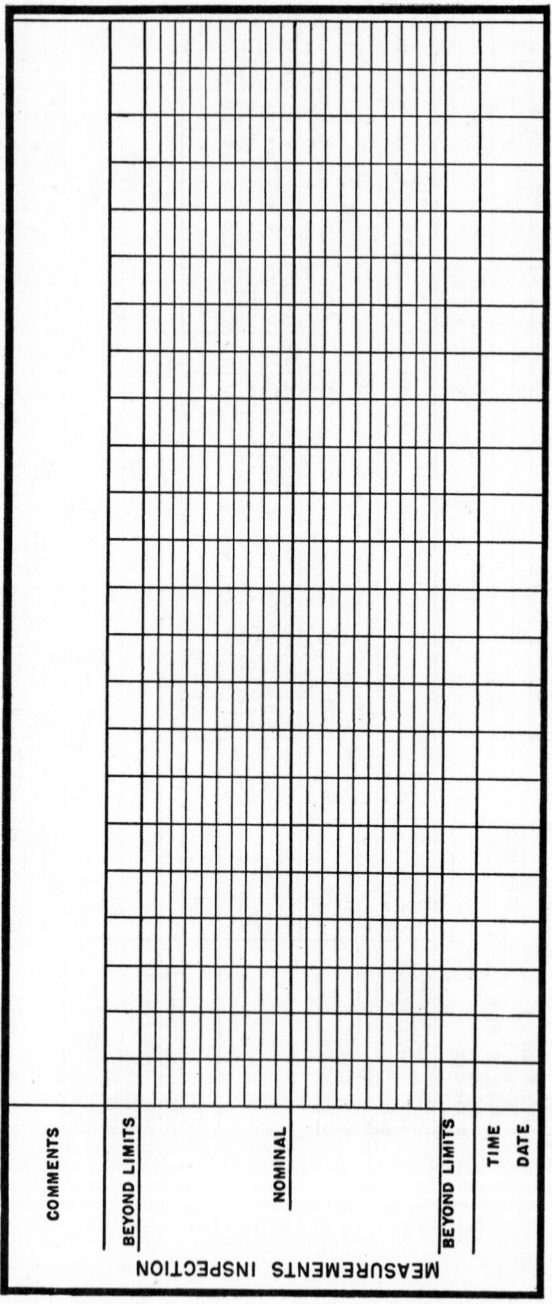
COMMENTS
BEYOND LIMITS
NOMINAL
BEYOND LIMITS
TIME
DATE
MEASUREMENTS INSPECTION

FIG. 11.13.

ı a sample fall outside the control limits, then the sample is considered o be representative of a satisfactory process condition. Figure 11.13 hows a typical form used here.

4. Computing Control Limits. There are many systems in use for computing measurements control limits. Graphs have been made of the onstants of Fig. 11.9. Some plants have issued data sheets on which mits are computed for a wide variety of conditions. Slide rules are now ı use in some factories.

There is no best form of measurements control chart; there are many arieties available, and the type of chart to suit particular needs can est be developed by the quality-control group of a given plant.

1.13 Control Limits in Relation to Specification Limits

Although the preceding methods for setting limits have been the most opular in industry, a somewhat different approach has much to recomıend it in those cases where the process limits are narrower than the pecification limits. In this method, control limits are established in relaion to drawing or specification limits rather than to process averages.

The primary advantage to this approach is that it may result in more conomical production runs. When control limits are established in relaion to process averages, the average or nominal value often becomes he machine operator's target. Every effort may be made to set up and o keep the job-quality characteristic at this average value.

On some jobs with long production runs, where tool wear is an imortant factor, this procedure may prove uneconomical. About one-half he variation allowed by the drawing or specification is simply discarded efore the production run begins. The left-hand chart of Fig. 11.14 llustrates this condition.

In the many cases where specification limits are wider than process imits, establishing control limits in relation to specifications may permit more economical operating condition. These control limits will provide guide to setting up the job, not at the nominal value, but at that end f the control limits which is opposite the direction of tool wear. Thus n a job wherein the tool wear is in the direction of the upper specification imit, the lower control limit will be the target for the initial setup. The ight-hand chart of Fig. 11.14 illustrates this situation. It may indicate better long-term operating condition than does the left-hand chart of he figure, since it may permit a much lengthier run without the need for ooling changes.

However, this procedure may prove inappropriate as in the case of nachining certain mating parts whose over-all tolerance when assembled ıas been established by the designing engineer on the assumption that the arts quality target would be the drawing nominal value (see Sec. 13.8).

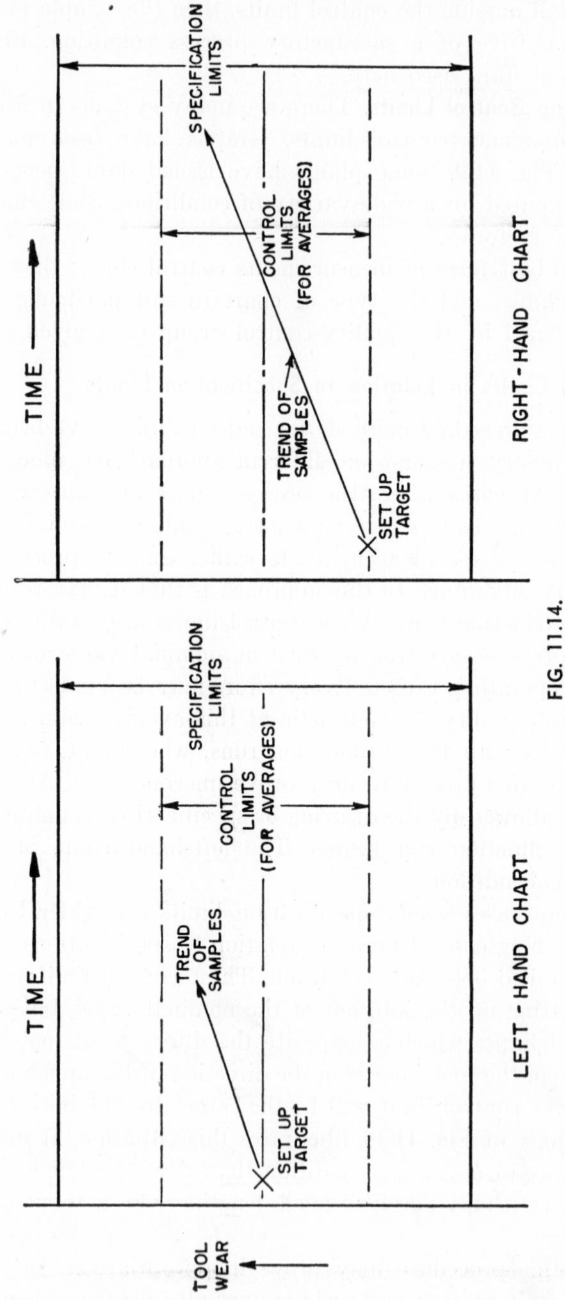
TIME
SPECIFICATION LIMITS
CONTROL LIMITS (FOR AVERAGES)
TREND OF SAMPLES
SET UP TARGET
RIGHT - HAND CHART
TIME
SPECIFICATION LIMITS
CONTROL LIMITS (FOR AVERAGES)
TREND OF SAMPLES
SET UP TARGET
LEFT - HAND CHART
TOOL WEAR

FIG. 11.14.

But for the run-of-the-mill parts that make up the bulk of production in many shops, control limits that relate to specification limits may prove highly satisfactory and extremely economical.

11.14 Computing Control Limits Based on Specification Limits

The general approach to the establishment of these control limits involves the determination of the process conditions that generally apply to manufacturing of the parts in question and the development of a nomograph which is based upon this analysis.

An effective technique for accomplishing this objective has been developed in recent years. It is based upon computing, for each process, its *process capability*. Values for this process capability are equivalent to the process limits for the "typical" frequency distribution for the process in question, that is, the amount of variation that may ordinarily be expected from the process. Section 17.16 discusses one means for determining these so-called process-capability values.

A procedure for computing control limits in relation to specification limits that is based upon process-capability values is as follows:

1. Determine the process-capability values for the process for which control limits are to be established. This value can best be computed by the technique presented in Sec. 17.16, although some shops use know-how values based upon past experience with the process in question.

2. Determine the control limits from these process-capability values by the use of the nomograph (Fig. 17.18) discussed in Sec. 17.16, which has been established in relation to process-capability values. This nomograph may be used no matter what part is to be produced on the machine or process in question. The following formulas are used with the nomograph computation:

$$\text{Lower control limit} = \text{lower specification limit} + Q \tag{26}$$
$$\text{Upper control limit} = \text{upper specification limit} - Q \tag{27}$$

where Q = per cent of the process capability as computed by the nomograph.[8]

3. After they have been judged economically acceptable, plot these control limits on suitable graph paper.

4. Use the chart for controlling production quality of the parts. Select periodic samples, compute their average value, and compare this average value with the control limits to determine if corrective action is required.

[8] The mathematical expression for Q as used in the nomograph is

$$Q = \frac{t_{p_1}\sigma - 1.28\sigma_{\bar{x}}}{6\sigma} = \frac{t_{p_2}\sigma + 1.28\sigma_{\bar{x}}}{6\sigma}$$

where t_p = the normal curve deviate with an associated p per cent in one tail of the distribution.

An example to illustrate the use of this technique for setting control limits may be found in Sec. 17.17.

11.15 Measurements Control Charts: Summary

There are several additional applications of measurements control charts in factory operations over and above their use during actual production. Two typical applications are

1. Informing designing engineers of the manufacturability of the various possible alternative designs.
2. Measuring tool wear as a guide to future tool and gage design.

Detailed applications of this sort are discussed in Part Five of this book, Applying Quality Control in the Company. As far as use of these charts for control of quality during production is concerned, formulas for use in computing the control limits are summarized below:

Limits in Relation to Process Averages

Using the Range as the Measure of Spread

Averages:

$$\text{Lower limit} = \overline{\overline{X}} - A_2\overline{R} \quad (13)$$
$$\text{Center line} = \overline{\overline{X}}$$
$$\text{Upper limit} = \overline{\overline{X}} + A_2\overline{R} \quad (14)$$

Ranges:

$$\text{Lower limit} = D_3\overline{R} \quad (15)$$
$$\text{Center line} = \overline{R}$$
$$\text{Upper limit} = D_4\overline{R} \quad (16)$$

Process limits:

$$\text{Lower limit} = \overline{\overline{X}} - L\overline{R} \quad (22)$$
$$\text{Center line} = \overline{\overline{X}}$$
$$\text{Upper limit} = \overline{\overline{X}} + L\overline{R} \quad (23)$$

Using the Standard Deviation as the Measure of Spread

Averages:

$$\text{Lower limit} = \overline{\overline{X}} - A_1\bar{\sigma} \quad (17)$$
$$\text{Center line} = \overline{\overline{X}}$$
$$\text{Upper limit} = \overline{\overline{X}} + A_1\bar{\sigma} \quad (18)$$

Standard deviations:

$$\text{Lower limit} = B_3\bar{\sigma} \quad (19)$$
$$\text{Center line} = \bar{\sigma}$$
$$\text{Upper limit} = B_4\bar{\sigma} \quad (20)$$

Process limits:

$$\text{Lower limit} = \overline{\overline{X}} - M\bar{\sigma} \quad (24)$$
$$\text{Center line} = \overline{\overline{X}}$$
$$\text{Upper limit} = \overline{\overline{X}} + M\bar{\sigma} \quad (25)$$

LIMITS IN RELATION TO SPECIFICATIONS

$$\text{Lower limit} = \text{lower specification limit} + Q \tag{26}$$
$$\text{Upper limit} = \text{upper specification limit} - Q \tag{27}$$

Control Charts for Go and Not-go Data

11.16 Per Cent-defective Control Limits

In go and not-go (or attributes) inspection a unit is classified as simply meeting the specification limits or not meeting them. Frequently, go and not-go data are represented by the value of their fraction or per cent defective. The fraction defective (often presented as a decimal) is the value obtained by dividing the total number of units inspected into the number of units in which defects have been discovered. The per cent defective is merely the percentage representation of the corresponding decimal value.

Thus, if 3 units are found to be defective out of a lot of 100 units, the fraction defective for that lot is $3/100$, or 0.03. The per cent defective for the lot is, of course, 3.

The variation that is universal among manufactured parts is to be found fully as much in these go and not-go data and their per cent-defective values as it is in actual measurements readings. Per cent- and fraction-defective data can be described by means of values for their central tendency and spread fully as much as measurements readings.[9]

With per cent-defective data, the average is generally used as the measure of central tendency expressed as a percentage. The standard deviation is the measure of spread in that percentage.

The average for per cent-defective data (expressed in integer notation, as in 3 per cent) is symbolized by $\bar{p}$ (p bar). With constant sample size, $\bar{p}$ can be computed by dividing the sample size into the average number of defects for each sample. With sample sizes which vary within the series of samples for which the average value is to be calculated, $\bar{p}$ can be computed by dividing the total number of units in the series into the total number of defects in the series as follows:[10]

[9] This is true since it can be shown that the binomial distribution (describing attribute data) for large samples approximates the normal distribution (describing variables data).

[10] Both the term *defect* and the term *defective* will be used here as follows: "defect" is a failure to meet a requirement imposed on a unit with respect to a single quality characteristic; "defective" refers to a defective unit containing one or more defects with respect to the quality characteristic under consideration.

Go and not-go control charts can be established for either defects or defectives, depending on the inspection system in use.

$$\bar{p} = \frac{\Sigma c}{\Sigma n} \times 100 \tag{28}$$

where c = number of defects

The standard deviation of $\bar{p}$ is symbolized by $\sigma_{\bar{p}}$ (sigma sub p bar). With constant sample size, it can be computed as follows:

$$\sigma_{\bar{p}} = \sqrt{\frac{\bar{p}(100 - \bar{p})}{n}} \tag{29}$$

where n = sample size
$\bar{p}$ = average value for per cent defective

As in the case of measurements data, control-chart limits are merely the 3-sigma values for averages; in this case, average values for per cent defective. These control limits may be represented as follows:

$$\text{Control limits} = \bar{p} \pm 3\sqrt{\frac{\bar{p}(100 - \bar{p})}{n}} \tag{30}$$

Fraction-defective control limits may be computed by a slight adaptation of the formula as follows:

$$\text{Control limits} = \bar{p}_1 \pm 3\sqrt{\frac{\bar{p}_1(1 - \bar{p}_1)}{n}} \tag{31}$$

In formula (31), $\bar{p}_1$ is taken as the decimal value for average fraction defective.

Interpretation of these control limits is similar to the interpretation for the measurements control limits that have been described earlier in this chapter. When per cent-defective values for production samples fall outside the per cent-defective limits, a process change may be indicated which may call for corrective action.

11.17 Two Types of Per Cent-defective Control Charts

Control charts based upon per cent-defective data have proved quite effective in controlling quality during production. Two major variations in the charts used are

Type 1: Constant Sample Size. These are charts which are based upon comparing with control limits the per cent- or fraction-defective values computed from samples of constant size. These samples are selected from the production process periodically—every hour, every 15 minutes, every morning.

Type 2: Varying Sample Size. These are charts established for parts and assemblies which have been 100 per cent inspected as a part of regular factory routine. The sample size for these charts is the total production for the period in question and so may vary from period to period.

Establishing control-chart limits for type 1 charts is a straightforward matter. The approach for setting the limits is the same as has been described in Secs. 10.6 to 10.15, except that control limits are computed throughout with the use of formula (30) and only one chart for per cent defective is maintained rather than individual charts for average and spread. Sample size with these charts is relatively larger than for measurements charts because of the lesser effectiveness of go and not-go data.

A sample size of 25 units is very popular for per cent-defective charts, although various rules have been suggested for determining the minimum sample size. Cowden has suggested that $n\bar{p}$ should be greater than 25.[11] This would mean, for an expected 10 per cent defective, the minimum sample size would be 250 units. Juran, on the other hand, suggests that the sample should be large enough so that the condition of no defects in the sample is a significant improvement over the average per cent defective.[12] This condition requires a sample size that is greater than $(9 - 9\bar{p})/\bar{p}$ units. For an expected average fraction defective ($\bar{p}$) of 10 per cent, the minimum sample size would be $(9 - .9)/.1 = 81$ units.

A major application of type 1 charts is in those cases where measurements data may not exist—as in surface finish or possibly color—or where these measurements are difficult to obtain. Sometimes, also, constant sample size is made necessary by factors not directly connected with the control of quality, such as those cases where, for wage-payment reasons, the number of units in lots presented for 100 per cent inspection is pegged at a certain number of units, like 500, 2,500, or 4,000.

Type 2 charts are probably the more important form of per cent-defective control chart. In addition, because the procedure for computing their control limits is not quite so straightforward as that for type 1 charts, type 2 charts will be discussed below in some detail.

11.18 Form of the Per Cent-defective Chart for 100 Per Cent Inspection

The majority of parts inspection in industry is of the go and not-go variety. Go and not-go examination of units is often 100 per cent inspection, where the checking of each part is assumed to result in sorting all bad units from the good units.

Records of the results of this go and not-go inspection have been maintained in many factories for a number of years. In too many instances, this record keeping has been a relatively fruitless task, since the mass of numbers thus maintained may not furnish a very convenient guide for preventing the future production of defective units.

The effectiveness of this type of inspection in preventing the recurrence of defective work has, however, been considerably increased in recent

[11] Cowden, Dudley J., "Statistical Methods in Quality Control," Prentice-Hall, Inc., Englewood Cliffs, N.J., 1957, p. 357.

[12] Juran, J. M., "Quality Control Handbook," McGraw-Hill Book Company, Inc., New York, 1951, p. 394.

years by presenting go and not-go data in the form of a per cent-defective control chart. Figure 11.15 shows a typical chart form that has been developed for this purpose.

There are four major parts to this chart:

1. A graph for plotting the per cent-defective (see I in Fig. 11.15).

2. A chart for recording the inspection information from which the per cent-defective values can be computed (see II in Fig. 11.15).

3. A chart for periodically summarizing the per cent-defective data (see III in Fig. 11.15).

4. A graph for plotting these summaries (see IV in Fig. 11.15).

The number of units inspected in each period—the sample size—will vary under normal shop conditions. Formula (30) cannot, therefore, be applied to compute a single set of control limits, since the formula is predicated upon the assumption of constant sample size.

In theory, therefore, formula (30) can be used to compute control limits only for the per cent-defective data for each individual inspection period, taking the per cent-defective value for that period as $\bar{p}$. This would, however, result in the unsatisfactory situation wherein there would be different control limits for each inspection period, making the interpretation of these limits quite difficult for practical shop purposes. Control limits for inspection periods where production was relatively low might be wider than control limits for inspection periods where production was somewhat higher.

In practice, if sample size does not vary more than a maximum of 20 per cent, which is a practical criterion for most factory inspection periods, accuracy which is satisfactory for most industrial purposes may be gained by the computation and use of the *average* sample size over the inspection periods in question. This average sample size and other average values can then be substituted in formula (30). The computation can be even further simplified by using charts of constants computed from formula (30) rather than using the formula itself.

The eight steps listed below can be followed to establish a per cent-defective chart of this sort:

1. Determine the quality characteristic to be controlled. This may be a single characteristic like length or weight; frequently it will be the total of all defective units found in those being examined.

2. Select an adequate number of samples. Each sample should contain an appropriate number of individual units. As in computing the control limits for variable data shown in Sec. 11.8, the appropriate number will vary depending upon the process involved. For purposes of illustration, 25 samples are used. The "number of units" in each sample is, in this case, the total number of units examined during a standard inspection period like an hour or a day. The 25 samples must be taken at suc-

QUALITY CONTROL CHART NUMBER ________________

PRODUCT ________________ MONTH ________________

INSPECTION ________________ CHARACTERISTIC ________________

PER CENT DEFECTIVE

DATE	INSP.	DEF.	%
		II	

I

		III	
1 WK			
2 WK			
3 WK			
4 WK			
5 WK			

IV

MO			

FIG. 11.15.

QUALITY CONTROL CHART NUMBER ____________

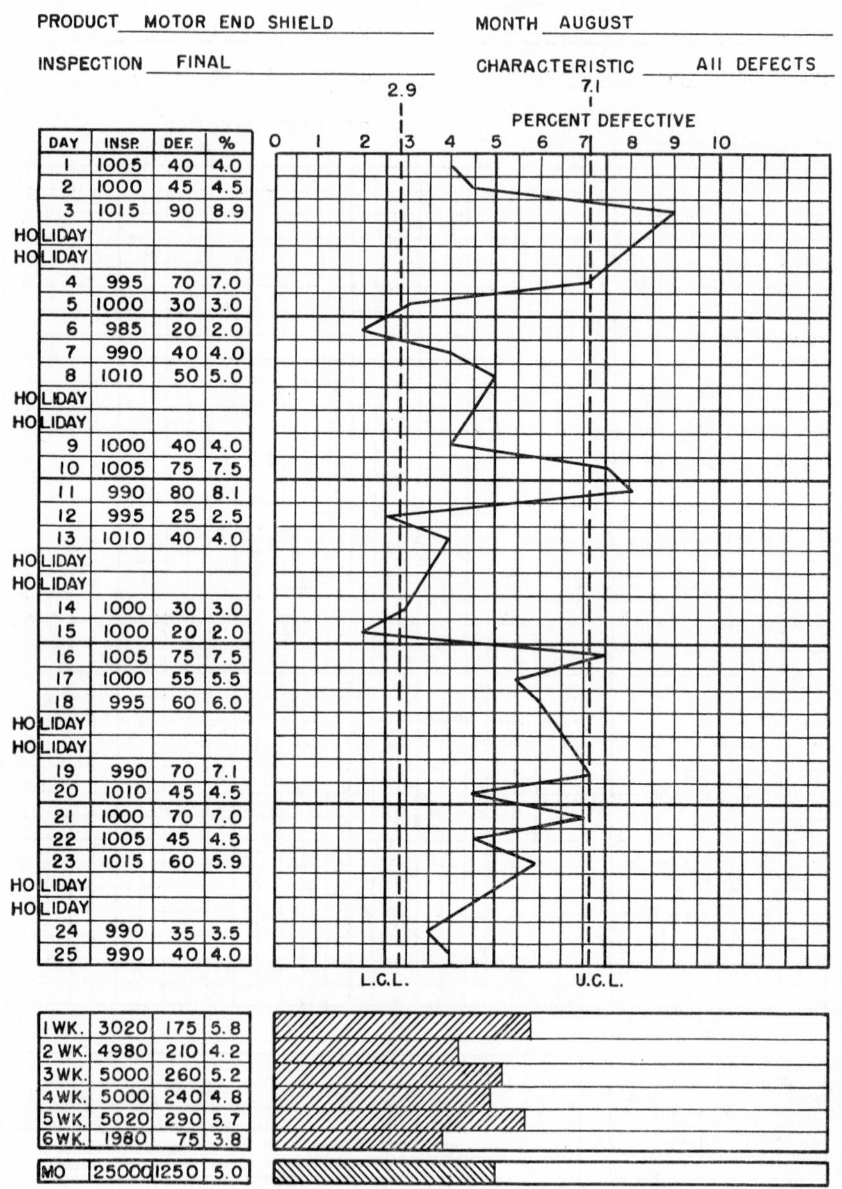

DAY	INSP.	DEF.	%
1	1005	40	4.0
2	1000	45	4.5
3	1015	90	8.9
HOLIDAY			
HOLIDAY			
4	995	70	7.0
5	1000	30	3.0
6	985	20	2.0
7	990	40	4.0
8	1010	50	5.0
HOLIDAY			
HOLIDAY			
9	1000	40	4.0
10	1005	75	7.5
11	990	80	8.1
12	995	25	2.5
13	1010	40	4.0
HOLIDAY			
HOLIDAY			
14	1000	30	3.0
15	1000	20	2.0
16	1005	75	7.5
17	1000	55	5.5
18	995	60	6.0
HOLIDAY			
HOLIDAY			
19	990	70	7.1
20	1010	45	4.5
21	1000	70	7.0
22	1005	45	4.5
23	1015	60	5.9
HOLIDAY			
HOLIDAY			
24	990	35	3.5
25	990	40	4.0

1 WK.	3020	175	5.8
2 WK.	4980	210	4.2
3 WK.	5000	260	5.2
4 WK.	5000	240	4.8
5 WK.	5020	290	5.7
6 WK.	1980	75	3.8
MO	25000	1250	5.0

FIG. 11.16.

cessive intervals (every hour, every day). The data from each one must be recorded in the order that the sample has been selected.

3. Compute the average sample size. In this case where the total number of parts inspected in an hour or day is the sample size, sample size equals average hourly or daily production.

4. Compute the average number of defectives hourly or daily.

5. Compute control limits based upon the calculations of steps 3 and 4 above. Charts are available to simplify the computation that would be required if formula (30) were used directly.

6. Analyze the per cent-defective values for each sample with relation to these control limits. Determine if any factor requires corrective action before the limits are reviewed for approval.

7. Determine if the control limits are economically satisfactory for the process.

8. Use the control chart during active production as a guide toward control of the quality characteristics in question.

11.19 Establishing a 100 Per Cent Inspection Control Chart

In the manufacture of motor end shields, there are several attributes which might cause an end shield to be defective. Some of these attributes are casting fractures, incorrect inner-bore diameters, and poor machined finishes. A typical application of the per cent-defective control chart may be found in the 100 per cent final inspection of these end shields, where any of these several attributes might cause rejection.

Production of end shields varies between 950 and 1,050 units per day. The daily total of shields inspected will be considered sample size. The eight steps to be followed in making up a control chart of this sort will be followed in some detail:

Step 1: Determine the Quality Characteristic to Be Studied. In this case, any attribute which causes rejection of an end shield will be included.

Step 2: Take an Adequate Number of Samples. Data will be recorded on the inspection results for 25 successive days. These data are recorded in the appropriate section of Fig. 11.16.

Step 3: Compute the Average Sample Size. The total production for 25 days is 25,000 units. The average daily production is, therefore, 25,000/25, or 1,000 units.

Step 4: Compute the Average Number of Defectives. The total number of defectives is 1,250 units. The average value for daily defectives is, therefore, 1,250/25, or 50 units.

Step 5: Compute Control Limits. Computation of control limits can be considerably simplified by the use of charts. Figures 11.17 and 11.18 show

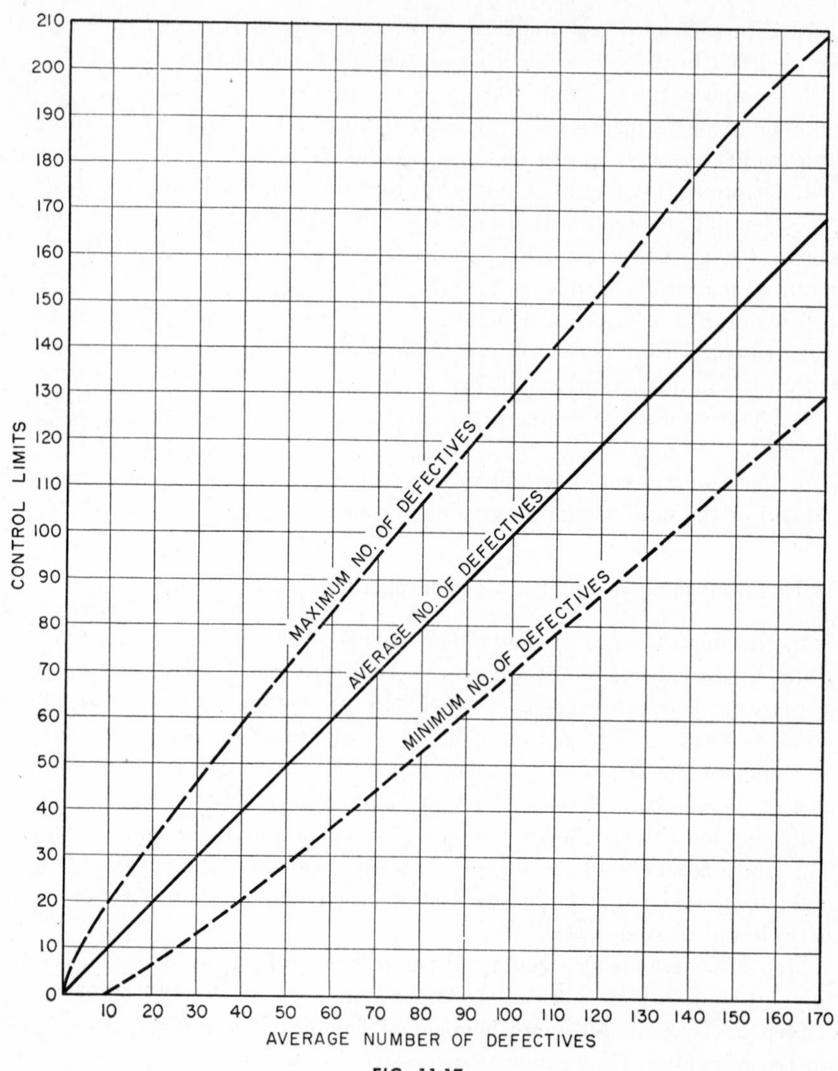

FIG. 11.17.

the charts that are useful for this work. Figure 11.18 differs from Fig. 11.17 in that it has an expanded horizontal scale.

Use of these charts is as follows: the average number of defectives, 50, is located on the horizontal scale of Fig. 11.17. Figure 11.18 is inappropriate, since its horizontal scale does not extend beyond 17 average defectives. The two dashed curves marked "Minimum No. of Defectives" and "Maximum No. of Defectives," respectively, cross the 50 line at 29 and 71 on the vertical scale of Fig. 11.17. These values, 29 and 71, repre-

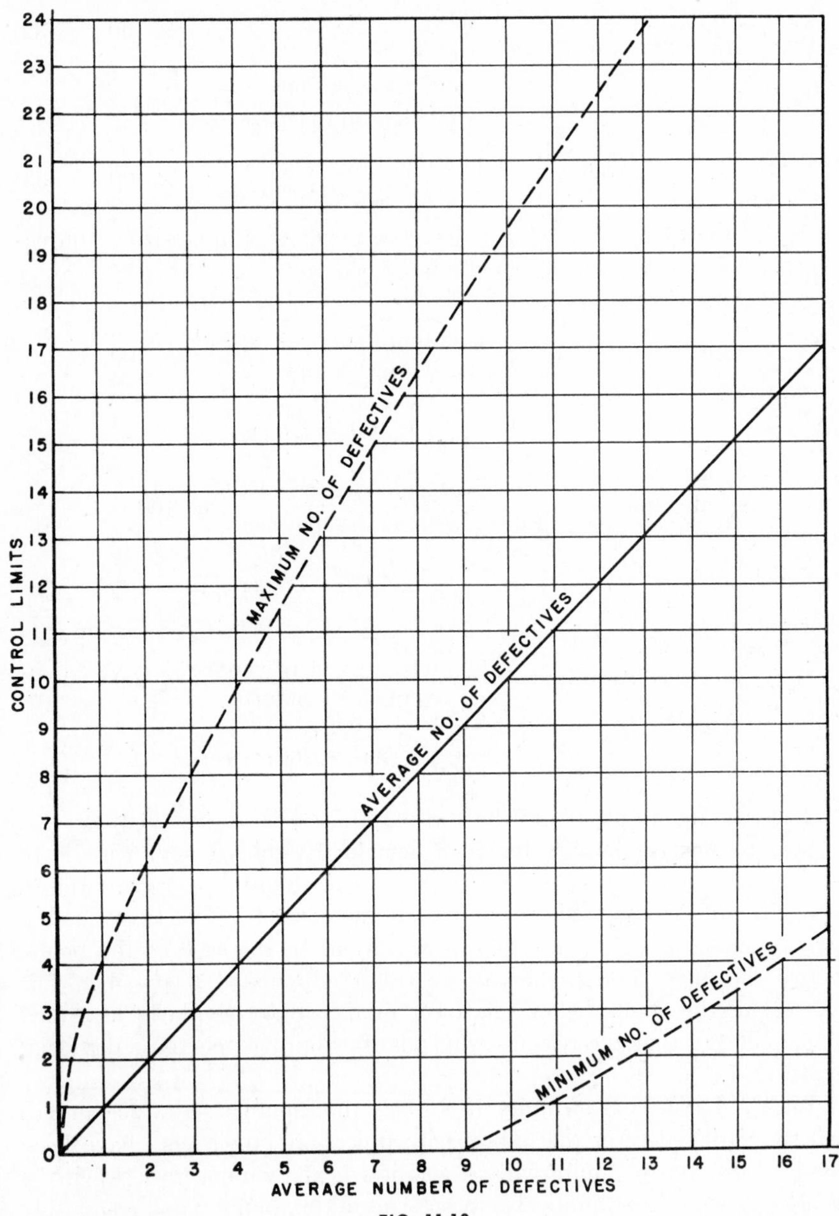

FIG. 11.18.

sent the minimum and maximum numbers of defectives that should be experienced in any day of production.

The upper and lower per cent-defective control limits can now be calculated as shown in the following formulas:

$$\text{Upper control limit} = \frac{\text{maximum no. of defectives}}{\text{average sample size}} \times 100 \qquad (32)$$

$$\text{Center line} = \frac{\text{average no. of defectives}}{\text{average sample size}} \times 100$$

$$\text{Lower control limit} = \frac{\text{minimum no. of defectives}}{\text{average sample size}} \times 100 \qquad (33)$$

It will be recalled from step 3 above that average sample size is equivalent to the average daily production of 1,000 units.

Formula (32):

$$\text{Upper control limit} = \frac{\text{maximum no. of defectives}}{\text{average sample size}} \times 100$$

$$= \frac{71}{1{,}000} \times 100 = 7.1 \text{ per cent}$$

$$\text{Center line} = \frac{\text{average no. of defectives}}{\text{average sample size}} \times 100$$

$$= \frac{50}{1{,}000} \times 100 = 5.0 \text{ per cent}$$

Formula (33):

$$\text{Lower control limit} = \frac{\text{minimum no. of defectives}}{\text{average sample size}} \times 100$$

$$= \frac{29}{1{,}000} \times 100 = 2.9 \text{ per cent}$$

These limits are plotted in the appropriate section of Fig. 11.16.

Step 6: Analyze Results for Each Sample. Examination of Fig. 11.16 shows that sample results on the third, sixth, tenth, eleventh, twelfth, fifteenth, and sixteenth days are outside the control limits. Investigation will be made of the causes of this variation. In the case of the points above the upper limits, the causes will be eliminated if possible. The causes for the points below the lower limits will be similarly identified if possible, so that the reasons why quality improved on these days can be learned.

With 7 samples out of limits, it is likely that another set of 25 samples will be gathered after the appropriate process improvements have been made. New control limits will be computed, and sample results will be compared with these limits. The process of taking samples and computing limits will be repeated until the sample results show that the process is in control.

The new control limits that will be calculated should reflect the improvements that have been made in process conditions as a result of the investigation of out-of-limit samples. This sequence of computing per cent-defective control limits thus serves as an effective guide to improving the process in question.

Step 7: Determine if Limits Are Satisfactory. The decision whether or not per cent-defective control limits are economically satisfactory for use in the control of quality is based on management judgment.

In theory, this decision should be based entirely upon economic factors. If the over-all cost of accepting end-shield rejects, which average 5 per cent and range from 2.9 to 7.1 per cent, is lower than the over-all cost of process improvements that would be required to reduce these rejects, then the control limits might be acceptable. If over-all costs of process improvement are lower than the costs of rejects from 2.9 to 7.1 per cent, then the limits might be unacceptable.

In practice, at least two factors make it difficult to make this decision based upon purely economic factors alone:

1. Particularly in shops which manufacture several products, it is sometimes very difficult to determine accurately the cost of accepting a certain per cent defective for a given process or part.

2. Operator skill and interest may be a much more important factor in process improvement than the much more easily evaluated costs of such factors as better machine tools or jigs and fixtures. A considerable reduction in rejections can be obtained in certain cases simply by posting the current control chart for all operators to see. In some cases, steps to improve morale may have much greater effect in reducing rejections than will investment in new equipment.

As a result, the decision whether or not control limits are satisfactory is based upon a combination of both the economic facts available and the past experience with the process.

In the case of the end shields, the 2.9 to 7.1 per cent control limits represented a process condition unacceptable to management. The thorough investigation of the end-shield manufacturing process that was initiated in step 6 was intensified, and some new equipment was ordered.

Although no "official" control limits were established for the process until this improvement program was completed, the 2.9 to 7.1 per cent limits were used as informal gages to judge just how satisfactory were the results of these improvements. New limits were later calculated periodically as improvements were put into effect, the results of which demonstrated that this recalculation was necessary.

Step 8: Use the Limits for Control. When satisfactory control limits have finally been established for the end shields, these limits will be plotted on a form similar to that shown in Figs. 11.15 and 11.16. These forms will be posted in plain view out in the shop as close as possible to the processing stations. (The per cent-defective results of each day's production lots will be recorded on these charts.) Lots that show out of limits will be the signal for immediate investigation.

These control limits can also be used by the factory accountants as a basis for estimating the amount that should be applied to represent defective work in the standard costs for the end shields. The control limits may also be useful as a factual basis for setting bogeys for manufacturing-loss reports on the end shields.

As with measurements control charts, per cent-defective control limits should be recalculated periodically in line with possible changes in process conditions.

11.20 Control Charts for Number Defective

These are some instances in go and not-go inspection where the number of defective units is preferred for control purposes over charts for per cent or fraction defective. Control limits for these number-defective or (p_1n) charts can be computed for constant sample sizes as follows:

$$\text{Control limits} = \bar{p}_1 n \pm 3\sqrt{n\bar{p}_1(1 - \bar{p}_1)} \tag{34}$$

where $\bar{p}_1$ = average value for fraction defective

$\bar{p}_1 n$ = average value for fraction defective times the sample size

Interpretation, procedures, and forms for computing these control limits are similar to those described above in connection with per cent- and fraction-defective charts. P charts may easily be converted into the (p_1n) form by changing scales and by multiplying the central line and control limits by the sample size n.

11.21 Control Charts for Number of Defects

With certain types of job-shop production wherein go and not-go inspection is carried on, there are at least two reasons why per cent- or fraction-defective control charts may prove of little value:

1. Production quantities may be too low. There may be only a few units produced every day, every week, or every month.

2. With physically large or complex products like bombers, engines, or turbines, some defects are almost always to be found at final assembly. There may be bolts that must be pulled tighter, plates to be painted, etc. Under the conventional per cent-defective system, charts would almost always show 100 per cent rejects, which would make them of little use for control of quality.

For situations of this sort, go and not-go inspection results are most effectively presented in the form of control charts for number of defects per unit, or (c) charts. Thus an engine might be found to have 30 defects during its inspection, or a bomber might have 250 defects. Control limits would be expressed, therefore, in terms of number of defects per unit—perhaps 300 for the upper control limit for the bomber, 45 for the engine, etc.

Control limits for (c) charts can be computed as follows:

$$\text{Control limits} = \bar{c} \pm 3\sqrt{\bar{c}} \tag{35}$$

where $\bar{c}$ = average number of defects per unit

The calculation procedure for (c) charts is similar to that for (p) and (p_1n) charts.

11.22 Variations on Control Charts for Go and Not-go Data

Many variations exist from the types of control charts that have been presented above. Typical of these variations are (1) difference in forms, (2) "control gaging," (3) precontrol. Each of these variations is discussed below.

1. Forms. The forms used to present go and not-go data in control-chart form vary quite widely in industry from the charts shown in Figs. 11.15 and 11.16. Sometimes the forms lose their graphical nature entirely, as in the case of an interesting tabulation developed by Schrock for control purposes.[13]

This tabulation consists of listings of values for average per cent defective and shows the minimum and maximum number of defective units to be expected either with varying or with average lot sizes. Figure 11.19 shows one page of these tables.

It is in this area that distinctions between the control charts, as a method for controlling quality, and the sampling table, as a technique for controlling quality, begin to disappear. This matter will be treated in more detail in Chap. 12.

2. "Control Gaging." For many years a controversial factory issue has been the desirability of having two or more sets of specification limits for parts: one for use in factory processing and a wider set of limits for use in final inspection. This basic philosophy has been adopted as part of certain control-chart installations, which have become compromises between measurements and per cent-defective control charts.

Very often, in establishing inspection stations in factory processing areas, so-called snap gages are employed. These gages have fixed limits which are set at the upper and lower specification limits for the part in question. With "control gaging" these snap gages are made to a set of limits which is somewhat narrower than the actual specification limits.

These control limits are established by the use of generalized formulas, which are usually a compromise between shop experience and statistical methods.

[13] E. M. Schrock, Erie, Pa.

RANGE OF REJECTS IN LOTS FROM A PROCESS HAVING A LEVEL OF 5 PERCENT DEFECTIVE

NUMBER INSPECTED	REJECTS SHOULD NOT EXCEED	FEWEST REJECTS EXPECTED
100	11	--
200	19	1
300	26	4
400	33	7
500	39	11
600	46	14
700	52	18
800	58	22
900	64	26
1000	70	30
1100	76	34
1200	82	38
1300	88	42
1400	94	46
1500	100	50
1600	106	54
1700	111	59
1800	117	63
1900	123	67
2000	129	71
2100	134	76
2200	140	80
2300	146	84
2400	152	88
2500	157	93
2600	163	97
2700	168	102
2800	174	106
2900	180	110
3000	185	115
3100	191	119
3200	196	124
3300	202	128
3400	208	132
3500	213	137
3600	219	141
3700	224	146
3800	230	150
3900	235	155
4000	241	159
4200	252	168
4400	263	177
4600	274	186
4800	285	195
5000	296	204

FROM "QUALITY CONTROL TABLES FOR ATTRIBUTES INSPECTION"; E.M. SCHROCK, ERIE, PA.

FIG. 11.19. Reprinted by permission from "Quality Control and Statistical Methods," by E. M. Schrock, published by Reinhold Publishing Corporation.

The gages must often be manufactured before the parts for which they are intended are started into actual production. As a result, the use of tools like the frequency distribution for deciding upon appropriate limits is necessarily eliminated in favor of standard tables from which the "control-gage limits" can be readily obtained.

A practice frequently followed in control-gaging applications for sampling lots during the course of their processing is to use as the basis for control the *number* of readings in the sample which fall outside the gage limits. Thus two readings out of a sample of five might be allowed to fall out of limits. This type of procedure is extremely convenient under certain mass-production conditions.

It may not be immediately obvious why the signal for corrective action can be based upon the number of readings which fall outside the gage limits. The entire discussion of this chapter thus far has indicated that corrective action may be required when a value for a *single* sample falls out of limits; yet here the control criterion is a specified *number* of individual readings.

It will be recalled that measurements-control-chart limits were established for sample values both for central tendency and for spread. With central tendency, whether the measure was the average or the median, a job was considered as "in control" if the production results showed that the measure plotted at any point within the control limits.

Instead of computing and plotting the average or median values for the sample, however, suppose that the individual readings for each unit in the sample are plotted on the control chart for averages. Suppose that these units are drawn from a sample whose average value is perilously close to the control limit. Obviously, about as many of these individual readings will ordinarily be outside the control limits as will be within these limits.

Since, with control gaging, it is these individual pieces which are being examined, it is quite possible and practical to establish gage limits at the control limits for average values and to allow the number of pieces which do not meet these gage limits to stand as an indication of the state of control of the process.

One interesting variation of this practice is discussed by Dudding and Jennett. A series of generalized techniques for establishing limits for control gages are presented by them in some detail in a pamphlet that was originally published in England.[14]

3. Precontrol. A more recent development called *precontrol*[15] lends itself very nicely to the use of snap gages or other methods for measuring go and not-go data. With "control gaging" and using the precontrol concept, the gages are made to a set of limits that is one-half the actual specification limits. Then these gages are used to measure pieces to

[14] Dudding, B. P., and W. J. Jennett, "Quality Control Chart Technique When Manufacturing to a Specification," Gryphon Press, London, 1944.

[15] "Quality Pre-control: A Simple Effective Process Control Method," Jones and Lamson Machine Co., Comparator Division, Springfield, Vt.

determine the correctness of the setup and the running portion of the operation in the following manner.

A specified number of first pieces are checked on the gage. If each of these pieces falls within the precontrol limits, the setup is approved. Periodic checks are made on a one-piece sample during the manufacture of the parts. If the piece is within the precontrol limits, the operation is continued. However, if the one piece falls outside the precontrol limit, the next piece is checked. If the second piece falls within the precontrol limit, the operation continues. If the second piece also falls outside the limit, the operation is stopped and readjusted.

11.23 Critical, Major, and Minor Defects; Demerits Per Unit; Quality Index

In its most popular form, as noted in Sec. 11.19, the per cent-defective chart records totals of all types of defects which may be the cause for rejected units. The criticism sometimes leveled against this chart is that it considers all causes for rejection as equally bad, whether they be the simple matter of an easily replaced burred screw or basic flaws which will cause the scrapping of the entire assembly.

The effect of bulking together all types of rejects may have results in two separate areas:

1. On factory procedure for the internal control of product quality.
2. On factory procedure for appraising product quality in regard to field performance.

Each of these two matters will be discussed below:

1. Internal-control Procedures. When all types of rejects are bulked together in a per cent-defective chart, an out-of-control point may cause unnecessary concern at the management level when it has been caused merely by a quickly quelled minor epidemic of extremely inexpensive rejections. On the other hand, management may be lulled into false security when it views an in-control point which includes three or four extremely expensive defects.

In spite of this, it remains in many cases sound practice to consider all defects as of equal weight. For one thing, handling time is one of the major product costs. It may be necessary to put fully as much rehandling time on a product with an inexpensive defect as is required for a product with an expensive defect. Again, the repair cost of these expensive and inexpensive defects tends to balance off in the long run, permitting the consideration that all defects comprising the per cent-defective results may be treated as of equal weight.

In those cases where the relative seriousness of different types of defects does vary very widely, however, it may become desirable to weight defects on the basis of their repair cost. In general practice, these weights are based upon three classifications:

a. Critical defects—including those defects with extremely high repair costs.

b. Major defects—including those defects with significant repair costs.

c. Minor defects—including those defects with low repair costs.

The comparative numerical weighting of critical, major, and minor defects will, of course, vary according to the individual product conditions. For example, a major defect may have twice the weight of a minor defect, or it may have five times its weight, depending upon relative costs. These weights may be used in control-chart computations and will enable the chart more accurately to reflect the true economics of the process in question.

If, however, the true repair or replacement costs are known for the individual defective quality characteristics, the dollar repair costs can be used as the defect weights.

2. Field Performance. With relatively complex products, different types of defects may have widely varying effects upon the performance of the product after it has reached the customers' hands. Bulking together all types of rejects in a per cent-defective chart may tend to give management a false picture of the relative effect on performance of the defects shown.

A critical, major, and minor defect classification may be established, therefore, on the basis of the effect of various defects upon the operation of the product. In this case, defects can be classified as follows:

a. Critical defects—including those defects which are certain to cause failure of the product to perform its function during its normal life expectancy.

b. Major defects—including those defects which are likely to have important effects on the operation or life of the product under normal field conditions.

c. Minor defects—including those defects which are likely to have unimportant effects on the operation or life of the product under normal field conditions.

Comparative numerical weightings of these defects will, again, vary according to product conditions. And again, these weights can be used in control-chart computations and will enable the chart more accurately to reflect an appraisal of the quality produced in the process in question.

In some instances, weighting of critical, major, and minor defects will include both internal economic (as in 1, above) and field-performance appraisal factors (as in 2, above).

Sometimes this critical, major, and minor defect classification procedure is carried still further by assigning demerits-per-unit weights to critical, major, and minor defects. Thus, demerit weights of 100, 30, and 10 might be assigned to critical, major, and minor defects, respectively.

Control charts can be established on this demerits-per-unit basis with a procedure and forms similar to those discussed above in connection with per cent-defective charts. Dodge[16] discusses such a control chart in some detail.

With some products, management may require a single index of its product quality. Such a quality index may be obtained from use of demerit-per-unit data, as follows:

$$\text{Quality index} = \frac{\text{observed demerits per unit}}{\text{expected demerits per unit}} \tag{36}$$

This type of index may be extremely valuable in those factories where management wishes a quality index in a form somewhat comparable to indices it receives on such matters as budget realization, weekly output, and cost of living. If quality costs associated with each type of defect can be determined, then the quality index can be expressed in terms of quality-cost dollars and can be used as a gage against which to measure alternative courses of control and appraisal action.

11.24 Some Practical Aspects of Control Charts

A question that may have arisen in the minds of many readers during the foregoing discussions is this: "In view of the effort and expense required to establish and maintain a single control chart for a single quality characteristic, how far can widespread application of control charts proceed in a factory with many parts and many processes?"

This question can be answered simply: "Control charts should be set up only in so far as it is economically desirable and physically practical to do so." Charts should be established only on important quality characteristics. They should be established only in those instances where costs justify close attention to the process. Control charts are simply one of many quality-control tools; any attempt must be condemned which uses them indiscriminately as proof of a "well-functioning" quality-control program.

Again, it may be noted that the foregoing discussions of methods for calculating control limits were a mixture of statistical computation and some fairly arbitrary decisions to adapt the control chart to the needs of particular situations. In factory practice, this adaptation to meet particular needs is widespread and takes many forms. For one instance, it is a policy in some shops never to plot lower control limits on those per cent-defective charts which are posted on the factory floor.

It has been found difficult to explain to the always changing factory employees that these lower limits do *not* place a premium on a certain

[16] Dodge, H. F., "A Method of Rating Manufactured Product," *Bell System Technical Journal,* Vol. 7, pp. 350–358, April, 1928.

percentage of defective work. As a result, lower control limits are recorded only in the office, where they can be reviewed by interested management and the quality-control staff.

Again, as a preliminary to making decisions as to whether or not per cent-defective control limits are economically satisfactory, management aided by the quality-control staff may select arbitrary control-limit targets for the process in question. In the experience of both management and the quality-control staff, these limits can eventually be achieved, and unless strong contrary evidence is presented, only these limits will be approved.

This practice, tempered with good judgment, is often very successful. This success is particularly notable on those many jobs where human relations factors are far more important than technological factors and where the mere selection of control-limit targets may have the psychological result of fostering quality improvements.

Moves such as these are perfectly reasonable parts of developing control-chart installations for a factory, even though they may result in a departure from standard control-chart technique. Experience seems to show that, in the long run, proponents of the control-chart approach in a factory will be most successful if they concentrate upon promoting the fundamental concepts and points of view fostered by the control chart rather than upon endeavoring to push forward any particular control-chart technique or form.

11.25 Summary of Formulas for Computing Control Limits

The formulas for computing control limits for charts using go and not-go data are summarized below:

$$\text{Per cent-defective control limits} = \bar{p} \pm 3\sqrt{\frac{\bar{p}(100 - \bar{p})}{n}} \qquad (30)$$

$$\text{Fraction-defective control limits} = \bar{p}_1 \pm 3\sqrt{\frac{\bar{p}_1(1 - \bar{p}_1)}{n}} \qquad (31)$$

$$\text{Number-defective control limits} = \bar{p}_1 n \pm 3\sqrt{n\bar{p}_1(1 - \bar{p}_1)} \qquad (34)$$

$$\text{Number of defects control limits} = \bar{c} \pm 3\sqrt{\bar{c}} \qquad (35)$$

Other useful formulas for particular applications of go and not-go data are

$$\text{Average, } \bar{p}: \qquad \bar{p} = \frac{\Sigma c}{\Sigma n} \times 100 \qquad (28)$$

$$\text{Standard deviation of } \bar{p}: \quad \sigma_{\bar{p}} = \sqrt{\frac{\bar{p}(100 - \bar{p})}{n}} \qquad (29)$$

$$\text{Quality index:} \qquad \frac{\text{observed demerits per unit}}{\text{expected demerits per unit}} \qquad (36)$$

The Control Chart in Action

11.26 Practical Applications of Control Charts

Uses of control charts were discussed in general terms in Sec. 11.4. It may now be of interest to depart somewhat from the general cases. Listed below are the brief discussions of five fairly specialized control-chart applications to meet specific practical situations:

1. Per cent-defective chart for control of final assemblies (see Sec. 11.27).
2. Measurements control chart for control of parts production (see Sec. 11.28).
3. Measurements control chart for control of incoming material (see Sec. 11.29).
4. Nongraphical control chart for control of screw-machine parts (see Sec. 11.30).
5. Measurements control chart to study tool wear (see Sec. 11.31).

11.27 Per Cent-defective Chart for Measuring Equipments

Very high rejections were being experienced on measuring-equipment assemblies being manufactured by an Eastern factory. The points at which most defects were found were the final inspection stations, at which more than 20 per cent of all equipments submitted for inspection were being rejected. There were several attributes which led to defective assemblies, and any one of them could cause rejection at the inspection station.

To reduce the rejections on these equipments, factory management undertook to develop a quality-control program. One of the features of this program was a series of per cent-defective control charts established to show quality variations on the equipments at the final inspection station.

After an intensive period of effort in improving production conditions, changing machine tolerances, and educating operators, the figure of 20 per cent average defectives was reduced to 7 per cent. Management was presented with the control limits computed for the job at this 7 per cent value for average per cent defective—a lower limit of about 2 per cent and an upper limit of about 12 per cent. Past experience with similar production conditions led management to suggest experimentation with limits which would reflect only one-half of these standard 3-sigma limits.

These new limits ($\bar{p} \pm 1.5\sigma_{\bar{p}}$) would mean that an indication of a process shift would occur more frequently when no actual process shift had taken place; but it also would result in a smaller process shift being detected sooner. This management decision was based on such factors as

QUALITY CONTROL CHART NUMBER RG-

PRODUCT MEASURING EQUIPMENT MONTH NOVEMBER

INSPECTION FINAL CHARACTERISTIC ASSEMBLY

PER CENT DEFECTIVE

DATE	INSP.	DEF.	%
OCT. 30	228	13	5.9
31	145	13	8.9
NOV. 1	186	13	7.0
2	196	13	6.6
3	144	9	6.3
4	144	12	8.3
WK.	1043	73	7.0
NOV. 6	157	14	8.9
7	-	-	-
9	172	11	6.4
10	137	8	5.8
11	132	12	9.1
WK.	598	45	7.5
NOV. 13	146	13	8.9
14	141	14	9.9
15	211	19	9.0
16	167	18	10.8
17	199	18	9.0
18	148	15	10.1
WK.	1012	97	9.5
NOV. 20	152	13	8.6
21	141	11	7.8
22	206	15	7.3
23	193	9	4.7
24	180	10	5.6
25	198	10	5.0
WK.	1070	68	6.4
NOV. 27	190	13	6.8
28	240	19	7.9
29	150	12	8.0
30	179	14	8.0
DEC. 1	180	7	4.0
2	189	12	6.5
WK.	1128	77	6.8

1 WK.	1043	73	7.0
2 WK.	598	45	7.5
3 WK.	1012	97	9.5
4 WK.	1070	68	6.4
5 WK.	1128	77	6.8

MO.	4851	360	7.4

FIG. 11.20.

the relative costs and production delays incurred when a process shift actually took place balanced against the machine adjustments when no process shift had occurred. The values used in the in-this-case successful specialized application were 4.5 and 9.5 per cent.

Figure 11.20 shows the chart for the month following management's approval of these limits for control purposes. This chart was posted right on the assembly lines. A duplicate chart was posted in the management office. Control limits were used as a pictorial basis for judging the day-by-day job being done on the measuring-equipment production line.

Figure 11.20 was substantially duplicated from that month until the satisfactory completion of the job contract about 8 months later. The chart was a guide for several similar control charts developed for other equipment.

11.28 Measurements Chart to Control Jewel-screw Quality[17]

A measurements control chart was established to aid in controlling the quality of a jewel screw, in which the depth of drilling was critical with

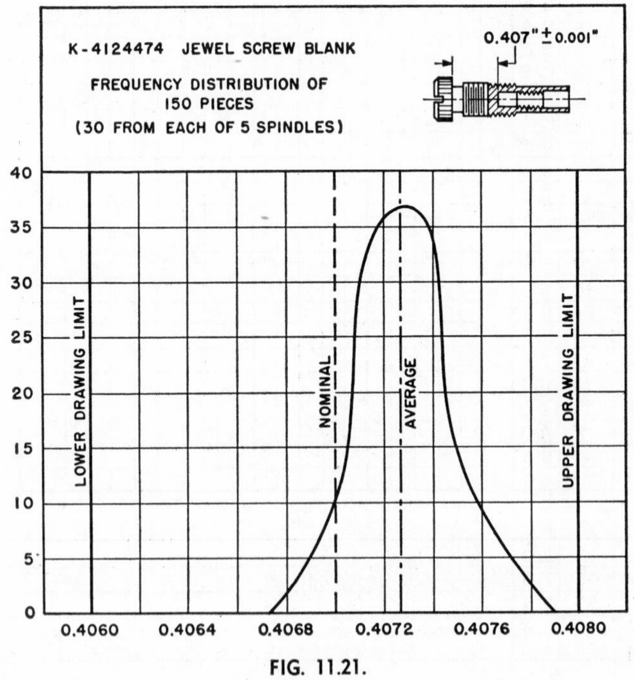

FIG. 11.21.

respect to a turned outside shoulder (see Fig. 11.21). The control limits for this chart were set up in relation to specification limits, using the procedure outlined in Sec. 11.14.

[17] From an unpublished paper by M. D. Benedict, Boston, Mass.

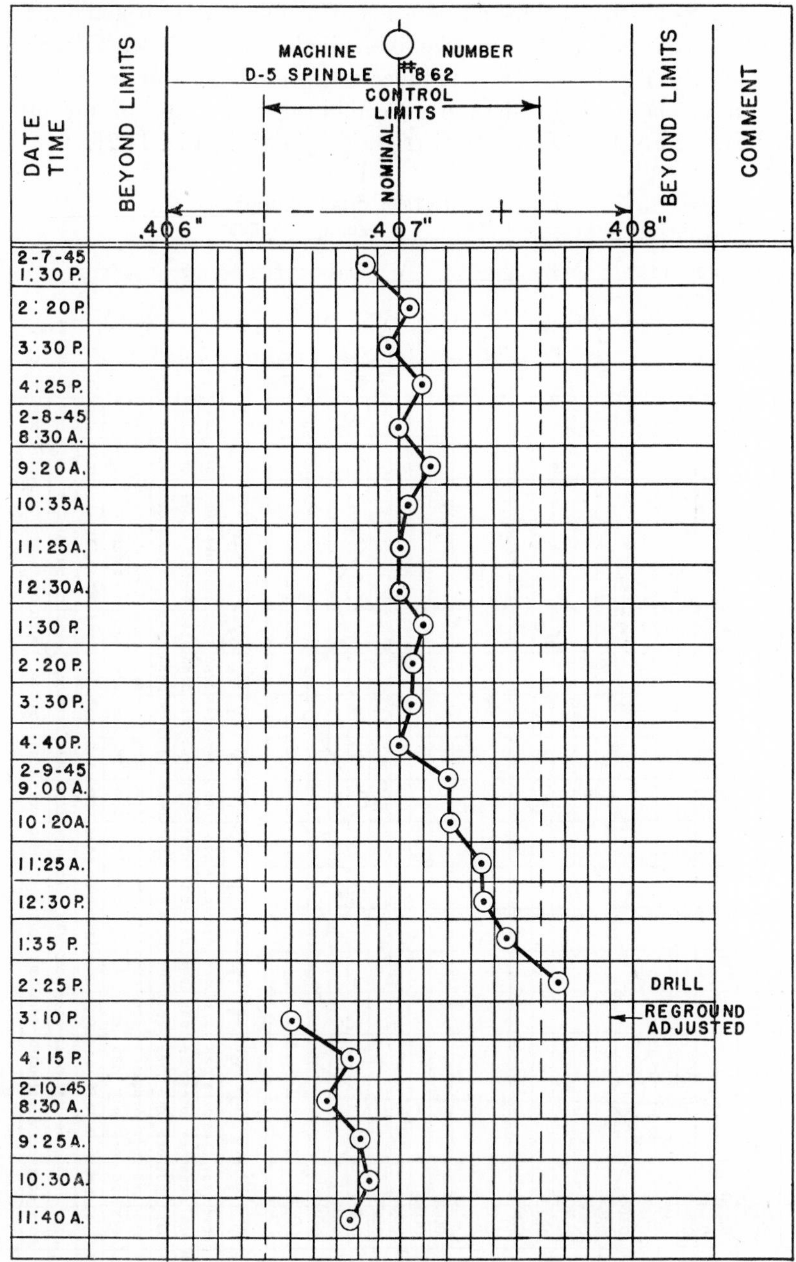
DATE
TIME
BEYOND LIMITS
MACHINE NUMBER
D-5 SPINDLE #862
CONTROL LIMITS
NOMINAL
BEYOND LIMITS
COMMENT
.406"
.407"
.408"
2-7-45
1:30 P.
2:20 P.
3:30 P.
4:25 P.
2-8-45
8:30 A.
9:20 A.
10:35 A.
11:25 A.
12:30 A.
1:30 P.
2:20 P.
3:30 P.
4:40 P.
2-9-45
9:00 A.
10:20 A.
11:25 A.
12:30 P.
1:35 P.
2:25 P.
3:10 P.
4:15 P.
2-10-45
8:30 A.
9:25 A.
10:30 A.
11:40 A.
DRILL
REGROUND
ADJUSTED

FIG. 11.22.

The first step in establishing these control limits was to make a frequency-distribution analysis on the five-spindle, automatic screw machine on which the jewel screw was produced. Each spindle was first studied separately, and then its data were combined with those of the other spindles to form the frequency distribution shown in Fig. 11.21.

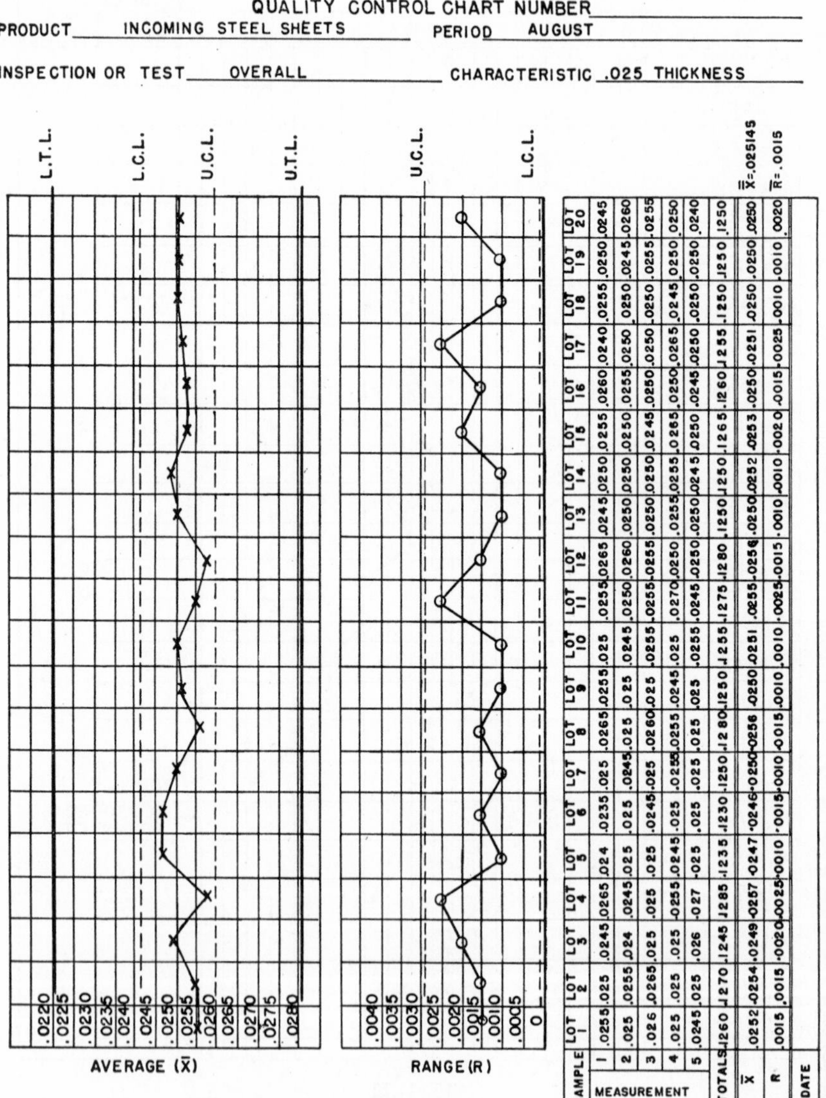

SAMPLE		LOT 1	LOT 2	LOT 3	LOT 4	LOT 5	LOT 6	LOT 7	LOT 8	LOT 9	LOT 10	LOT 11	LOT 12	LOT 13	LOT 14	LOT 15	LOT 16	LOT 17	LOT 18	LOT 19	LOT 20
MEASUREMENT	1	.0255	.025	.0245	.0265	.024	.0235	.025	.0265	.0255	.025	.0255	.0265	.0245	.0250	.0255	.0260	.0240	.0255	.0250	.0245
	2	.025	.0255	.024	.0245	.025	.025	.0245	.025	.025	.0245	.0250	.0260	.0250	.0250	.0250	.0255	.0250	.0250	.0245	.0260
	3	.026	.0265	.025	.025	.025	.0245	.025	.0260	.025	.0255	.0255	.0255	.0250	.0250	.0245	.0250	.0250	.0250	.0255	.0255
	4	.025	.025	.025	.0255	.0245	.025	.0255	.0255	.0245	.025	.0270	.0250	.0255	.0255	.0265	.0250	.0265	.0245	.0250	.0250
	5	.0245	.025	.026	.027	.025	.025	.025	.025	.025	.0255	.0245	.0250	.0250	.0245	.0250	.0245	.0250	.0250	.0250	.0240
TOTALS		.1260	.1270	.1245	.1285	.1235	.1230	.1250	.1280	.1250	.1255	.1275	.1280	.1250	.1250	.1265	.1260	.1255	.1250	.1250	.1250
$\bar{X}$		.0252	.0254	.0249	.0257	.0247	.0246	.0250	.0256	.0250	.0251	.0255	.0256	.0250	.0252	.0253	.0250	.0251	.0250	.0250	.0250
R		.0015	.0015	.0020	.0025	.0010	.0015	.0010	.0015	.0010	.0010	.0025	.0015	.0010	.0010	.0020	.0015	.0025	.0010	.0010	.0020
DATE																					

FIG. 11.23.

The process capability was found to be 1.2 mils, which compared favorably with the specification limits of 2.0 mils. This process capability was then used to determine the Q factor required for the control-limit computation.

Using the nomograph (Fig. 17.24) with $p_1 = 0.3$ per cent, $p_2 = 5$ per cent, $n = 5$ shows the Q factor to be about 0.0004 inch for a process capability of 1.2 mils. Control limits were then directly computed with this value for Q using formulas (26) and (27).

Figure 11.22 shows the resulting measurements control chart, with these limits plotted. The procedure for using this chart for control purposes was established as follows: a sample size of five jewel screws per hour (one per spindle) was selected, with the average reading for each sample recorded on the chart (Fig. 11.22).

11.29 Measurements Chart for Control of Incoming Material [18]

An effective procedure for control of incoming sheet steel by means of measurements control charts was carried on by the punch-press section of a large factory. Control limits were calculated for the average and the range of the sheet steel. Each lot of steel was sampled when it was received from the vendor, and the sample results were compared with the resulting control limits.

Previous difficulties that had been experienced because of the periodic acceptance of unsatisfactory lots of steel were eliminated by the use of this chart. Figure 11.23 shows one of the typical control charts used in this installation.

11.30 A Nongraphical Control Chart for Screw-machine Parts[19]

Figure 11.24 shows a nongraphical type of control chart that was used effectively in a screw-machine factory. This chart was used in connection with patrol inspection. The results of each machine check by the patrol inspector was recorded on the chart, which was posted right at the machine.

During the period of its application, the chart resulted in a considerable reduction in parts rejects. Its extreme simplicity was very useful on the shop floor, since only "High," "O.K.," or "Low" classifications had to be checked by the inspector and machine operator.

The sensitivity of such a chart is limited in detecting small changes in the average. It is primarily effective in detecting operations producing large per cent defectives.

[18] From an analysis made by A. L. Fuller, Schenectady, N.Y.

[19] From a chart developed by N. G. Wickstrom, F. Helms, and J. Boyd, Schenectady, N.Y.

QUALITY CONTROL CHART

DWG. NO. BORE, TURN & C/O DATE 8/23 MACH. NO. 27

5156782	IST. SHIFT OPER. SMITH INSP. JONES																					2ND SHIFT OPER. BROWN INSP. GREEN																				
TIME INSPECTED	8			9-10			10			11-15			12-45			1-30			2-40			4-15			5-30			6-20			7-45			9-00			10-15			11-00		
CHARACTERISTIC	HIGH	O.K.	LOW	HIGH	O.K.	LOW	HIGH	O.K.	LOW	HIGH	O.K.	LOW	HIGH	O.K.	LOW	HIGH	O.K.	LOW	HIGH	O.K.	LOW	HIGH	O.K.	LOW	HIGH	O.K.	LOW	HIGH	O.K.	LOW	HIGH	O.K.	LOW	HIGH	O.K.	LOW	HIGH	O.K.	LOW	HIGH	O.K.	LOW
1.280 + − .001 LENGTH			5		5			5			5			5			5		5				5			5			5				5		5			5			5	
3.75 ± .0002 DIA.			5		5				5		5			5		5			5				5			5			5			5			5			5			5	
.625 ± .0002 DIA.			5		5				5		5			5			5		5				5			5			5				5		5			5			5	
.125 ± .0002 DIA.			5		5				5		5			5		5			5				5			5			5			5			5			5			5	
.875 ± .0002 DIA.			5		5			5			5			5			5		5				5			5			5				5		5			5		5		
.250 ± .0002 BORE			5		5				5		5			5		5			5				5			5			5			5			5			5			5	

IST. SHIFT REMARKS

STOP JOB, DRESS TOOLS AND SET UP FOR 2ND. SHIFT.

2ND. SHIFT REMARKS

O.K. FOR IST. SHIFT. NO SETUP CHANGE NECESSARY

FIG. 11.24.

QUALITY CONTROL CHART NUMBER ________

PRODUCT PRO. & BLANK PERIOD 8/28/

INSPECTION OR TEST ________ CHARACTERISTIC .025 ± .003 HOLE

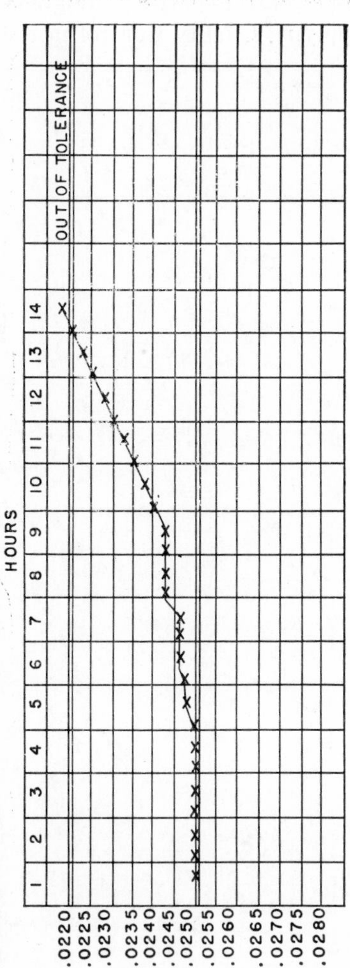

FIG. 11.25.

11.31 Measurements Control Chart to Study Tool Wear[20]

Figure 11.25 illustrates how a measurements control chart may effectively picture tool wear. The chart was used in a machine shop with valuable results.

This control chart for averages was established to study tool wear on

[20] From a study by A. L. Fuller, Schenectady, N.Y.

a pierce and blank punch-press operation. It showed data that not only were useful for patrol inspection purposes but were also of great value to tool and gage men for their future designs of pierce blank and punch equipment.

More detail on practical application of the control chart as a quality-control tool will be given in Part Five, Applying Quality Control in the Company.

CHAPTER 12

SAMPLING TABLES

Every industrial plant purchases some of its raw materials and component parts from outside sources. The vendors may be other companies or other plants of the same company. In the case of some large plants, one division of a plant may consider the output of another division of the plant an outside source.

Assuring that these outside materials are of satisfactory quality has always been a major factory problem. Some of the approaches used to obtain this assurance have been 100 per cent inspection, sampling of lots on a fairly arbitrary basis popularly termed *spot checking,* accepting from vendors certificates of test and inspection in lieu of an examination of the lot, and sometimes no inspection at all until production difficulties with the material call for it.

Another approach to this problem that has developed over the past two decades both in scope and in industrial acceptance has been the use of statistical acceptance sampling tables. These tables have replaced in most instances all other approaches as the core of factory control of the acceptance of incoming materials and parts.

The tables are also enjoying wide factory usage in the final inspections or tests made to assure that shipments to customers are of desired quality. Those government services which maintain inspection forces in industrial plants have also used these tables as their basis for accepting lots of parts and assemblies that have been produced for them.

A somewhat different and equally important need for effective sampling tables relates to the control of parts and assemblies while they are being processed within the factory. Periodic examination of these parts by the so-called patrol, or roving, floor inspectors has too often been guided by hit-or-miss sampling procedures.

Statistical process-control sampling tables have been developed to meet this need. These tables have, indeed, been found very useful in many instances where application of the control chart cannot effectively be made.

A survey of both acceptance sampling and process-control sampling tables is the purpose of this chapter.

The Concept of Acceptance Sampling Tables

12.1 Acceptance Sampling

Webster defines a sample as "a part . . . shown as evidence of the quality of the whole." From the discussion of the previous two chapters, it is clear that samples and sampling methods are a keystone of statistics as used in quality control.

A statistical sampling table is another adaptation of the probability principles that were discussed in Chaps. 10 and 11. It is possible to use "a part as evidence of the quality of the whole" for a simple reason. The variation that is inevitable for manufactured units usually conforms to a certain basic pattern for units that have come from the same manufacturing source. To determine this pattern, it may not be necessary to examine all units that have come from that source; the pattern may be sufficiently well established after examination of only a *certain number* of units—in other words, by sampling. Statistical sampling tables consist of a series of these sampling schedules, each to serve somewhat different inspection objectives.

Sampling may be conducted on a go and not-go (or attributes) basis, that is, determining whether or not the units in the sample conform to specification requirements. Examination of the samples may also be conducted on a measurements (or variables) basis, that is, taking actual readings on the units in the sample.

The first portion of the discussion below will be devoted to go and not-go acceptance. Since the majority of acceptance inspection is carried out on this basis, the usual type of acceptance sampling table is designed for go and not-go data.

The second portion is a treatment of measurements or variables sampling. Section 12.18 is devoted to this topic.

12.2 Why Sample for Acceptance?

When acceptance of incoming materials and parts is based upon inspection at the purchaser's factory, either 100 per cent or sampling inspection can be used. In weighing the comparative benefits of these two methods, 100 per cent inspection will always have this clean-cut advantage over sampling: only through thorough examination of each of the parts in a lot—not through sampling—can complete assurance be obtained that all defective parts or materials have been removed from that lot.

Yet there are several features of 100 per cent inspection which are undesirable as compared with effective sampling carried out on a modern statistical basis. Some of these undesirable aspects of 100 per cent inspection are the following:

1. *It is costly.* Every part must be checked individually.

2. *It may lead to false assurance about the completeness of the inspection job.* The simple statement "100 per cent inspection required" is often considered sufficient information to call for a complete and rigorous inspection job. 100 per cent inspection is seldom, if ever, complete inspection of *all* the characteristics of a part; it is examination of only certain characteristics. The statement "100 per cent inspection required" may leave the selection of the characteristics to be examined in the hands of individuals not at all familiar with those characteristics which are critical and important.

3. *It actually involves sorting.* In essence, 100 per cent inspection means sorting bad parts from good. This is a post-mortem procedure, which may be foreign to the preventive approach of total quality control. Under many types of manufacturing conditions, 100 per cent sorting should be a last resort for use when some control procedure has broken down rather than a standard element of factory routine.

4. *It may result in accepting some defective material.* A number of independent checks on the reliability of 100 per cent inspection in sorting out *all* bad parts from the good have cast considerable doubt upon its complete effectiveness in every instance. Where the per cent defective in lots submitted is low, the monotony of repetitive inspection operations may result in the automatic acceptance of a number of defective parts. Where the per cent defective is high, carelessness or lack of skill in the use of measuring equipments may result in the acceptance of large numbers of defective parts.

5. *It may result in rejecting some satisfactory material.* Some 100 per cent inspection operators feel that they are not doing an acceptable job in the eyes of their supervisors unless they reject some parts. This some-

times results in the hypercritical interpretation of specifications and in the rejection of satisfactory material.

6. *It may be impractical.* In cases where destructive testing is required, 100 per cent checking is, of course, impossible.

In contrast to these liabilities of 100 per cent inspection, reliable sampling procedures may be relatively inexpensive. If conditions permit sampling to be done, cost considerations may make it expedient to allow a certain predetermined percentage of defective parts to remain in a lot until that assembly point is reached where they may be removed by production operators who find that the parts do not fit properly in the assembly.

Sampling may result in a considerable reduction in inspection monotony. The question of whether or not a lot will be accepted, based upon samples drawn from it, may become a matter of considerable interest for inspection operators.

Under many circumstances, sampling may have an effectiveness comparable to or greater than that of well-operating 100 per cent inspection. Also the instruction "sampling required" does not carry with it the impression of automatic accuracy which sometimes accompanies the instruction "100 per cent inspection required." As a result, sampling usually forces the specification of those characteristics which *are* critical and those dimensional tolerances which *must* be maintained.

Obviously, in the case of destructive testing, only sampling is possible. Sampling procedures that have been developed for this destructive testing have achieved great effectiveness and success.

Sampling often lends itself to more efficient administration of the inspection force than does 100 per cent inspection. The reduction in work load that may be permitted by substitution of sampling inspection for 100 per cent examination may allow additional time for wider inspection coverage and for more accurate record keeping. Since sampling inspection may become somewhat of a game to inspection operators, this record keeping may develop into "keeping score" rather than being regarded as monotonous drudgery.

12.3 Early Forms of Acceptance Sampling

Many of these advantages of sampling over 100 per cent inspection have been long recognized. As a result, sampling was carried on in industry long before its features were publicized by the current attention to the statistical sampling tables.

Many of these sampling procedures have been relatively crude and makeshift and have not resulted in the advantages over 100 per cent inspection that were described in Sec. 12.2. "Spot checking" is the phrase usually applied to these hit-or-miss procedures.

In some plants, spot checking has meant a well-regulated and well-defined procedure for examining a certain percentage of the pieces in all incoming lots. In other plants, it has meant the occasional examination of a few pieces from those incoming shipment boxes which were easiest to reach or to pry open. In still other plants, spot checking has resolved, in the final analysis, into a rough examination to determine if the amount of material in the lot corresponds to the amount billed by the vendor.

When, owing to these latter practices, bad material causes quality troubles on the production lines, the amount of inspection may be temporarily increased. This increase in inspection merely constitutes a postmortem step and does not aid in preventing the production of defective work.

The number of parts or the amount of material to be inspected and the size of the lot to be sampled are generally determined in arbitrary fashion under spot-check procedures. Occasionally, too many parts are checked—which is costly. Sometimes too few parts are examined—which may permit defective materials to get into the production line.

In general, little attention is paid to the risk of sampling variation (see Sec. 10.18) associated with the particular spot-check procedure in use. Nor is there any real understanding as to the quality "target" that is being aimed at.

Another feature of the usual spot check is its lack of agreed-upon acceptance or rejection procedure. If a number of defective pieces are found, there is often no definitely specified system as to how to dispose of the lot.

One week, the spot check of a lot of incoming material may show five defective pieces, and the lot may be rejected. A few weeks later, another spot check on similar material may show six defective pieces, and the lot may be passed on to the manufacturing floor. Such inconsistencies in procedure have as their inevitable result friction between vendor and customer, spotty quality of parts and materials released to the manufacturing floor, and strained feelings between the incoming-material inspectors and the manufacturing supervisors.

12.4 A Typical Spot-check Procedure

Spot checking is often carried out with the procedure that a certain percentage of the pieces in a lot are examined. It may be of interest to glance at the effectiveness of such a typical spot-check program. As described in a factory inspection instruction, the plan is presented, as follows: "Ten per cent of the parts in all lots submitted for inspection will be examined on a go and not-go basis. Only those lots represented by samples containing no defectives will be accepted."

At first glance, the acceptance standard of this plan seems to be one which will afford a high degree of protection. Let us see, therefore, just how effective the plan actually is.[1]

Instead of using in our analysis manufactured parts or raw materials as the contents of the lots submitted for inspection, let us instead use a 52-card poker deck from which two deuces are removed. Lot size is therefore 50 cards.

Let us assume that the two one-eyed jacks in the deck are defectives. There will therefore be 2/50, or 4 per cent, defectives in the lot.

A 10 per cent sample from this lot is five cards. The sample from the lot is therefore the equivalent of a five-card poker hand.

To determine the effectiveness of this spot-check plan, suppose that the following procedure is followed: A five-card poker hand is dealt from the deck of cards. The hand is examined to see if it contains a one-eyed jack. The five cards are then returned to the deck, which is shuffled. This procedure is repeated nineteen times to represent a 10 per cent spot check on 20 successive lots of 50 cards.

Students in quality-control training classes made this sort of check many times. Sometimes they found a one-eyed jack appearing in 3 hands out of 20, sometimes in 5 hands out of 20, sometimes in 4 hands out of 20. They found that under this plan from 75 to 85 per cent of the lots submitted for inspection will be accepted containing 4 per cent defectives.

The probability calculation for the 10 per cent spot check under these conditions shows that the most likely situation is that the plan accepts 80 per cent of the lots submitted which are 4 per cent defective. In the most usual case, 16 poker hands out of 20 will contain no one-eyed jacks —a solution that has not surprised poker players in the quality-control training classes.

Figure 12.1 shows a curve plotted from one of the probability calculations analyzing this sampling plan. Sample size (number of cards in the hand dealt) is plotted on the horizontal axis; the probability of accepting a lot with 4 per cent defectives is plotted on the vertical axis.

It may be seen from Fig. 12.1 that a sample size or "hand" of 34 cards would be required if it were desired, for example, to risk passing decks of cards with 4 per cent defectives 10 per cent of the time. This sample size of 34 is in startling contrast to the 5-card sample size called for by the 10 per cent spot check.

There are several other features of this spot-check plan which are undesirable. There is no agreed-upon quality target at which the plan

[1] K. E. Ross has made an analysis of this popular example in an unpublished paper, "Out of the Darkness with Scientific Sampling," Fort Wayne, Ind. Figure 12.1 is after his analysis.

aims. Is it satisfactory to pass lots which are 4 per cent defective? If so, what risk can be taken that an occasional lot with more than 4 per cent defectives will be passed? If not, what quality target should be established? For these questions the sampling plan has no answer.

The plan establishes no organized procedure for the disposition of decks of cards, samples of which contain defectives. It merely specifies that lots of which samples contain *no* defectives will be accepted. It states nothing about the plan of action when one or more defectives are found in a sample. Should the lot from which the samples are drawn be rejected? Should another sample be drawn from the lot? Should the lot be 100 per cent inspected? Again the plan has no answers for important questions.

There is an additional element in this 10 per cent spot check which makes it even more unsatisfactory in actual practice than the limitations described above would indicate. This element is that the protection

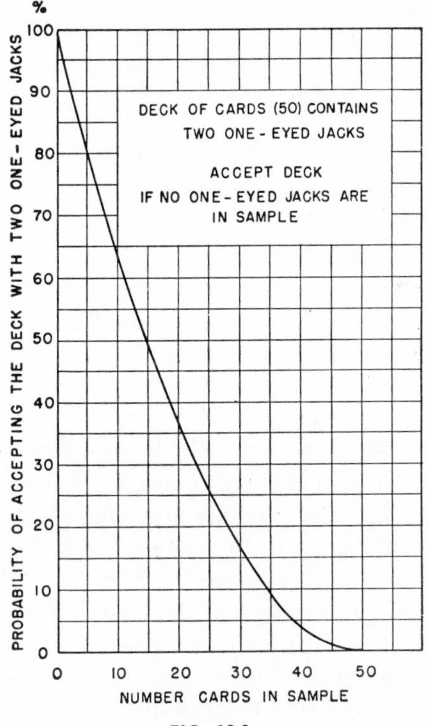

FIG. 12.1.

afforded by the spot check varies with the size of the lots submitted. As a result, the plan may treacherously imply a quality assurance that it cannot fulfill.

Let us assume that the same sampling plan as described above is still in use but that now the lots submitted for inspection contain 1,000 rather than 50 units. Analysis of the protection offered by the sampling plan under these conditions results in a far different picture from that shown by the analysis with a 50-unit sample size. Instead of the plan resulting in the acceptance of 80 per cent of the lots submitted which contain 4 per cent defectives, the 10 per cent spot check now will result in acceptance of only 3 to 4 per cent of the lots submitted.

Under typical factory conditions, it is inevitable that identical parts and materials will be received in lots of varying size. The span of the size of these lots will cover at least the range from 50 to 1,000 units.

The quality target required by the shop floor for this material, however, will obviously be independent of the size of the lots in which material is shipped by the vendor. Yet the protection afforded by the 10 per cent spot check is very dependent upon lot size: the larger the lot size, the greater the protection. The reason for this situation was discussed in Sec. 10.19, namely, that the effectiveness of a sample depends chiefly upon its size rather than upon the ratio of the size of the sample to the size of the lot from which it was drawn.

12.5 Features of Statistical Sampling Tables

It is quite clear that the potential benefits of sampling as compared with 100 per cent inspection are not to be realized from crude spot-check procedures of the sort described above. The need of industry for more effective sampling methods than these has been met by the development of modern statistical acceptance sampling tables. Among the leading American pioneers in the development of these tables have been Harold Dodge and Harry F. Romig while members of the Bell Laboratories.

In contrast to the unreliability and ambiguity of spot checking, modern statistical sampling procedures are reliable and quite specific. They are based upon well-defined probability principles, which have been translated into charts and formulas that are available for use in the construction of individual sampling plans to meet the needs of particular factory conditions.[2]

One of the most important steps in the growth of statistical sampling has been the consolidation of certain of these individual plans into the form of acceptance sampling tables. Figure 12.2 shows such a table.

In contrast to the crude spot-check plans, these tables represent disciplined structures for the performance of sampling in respect to the

[2] See, for example, Freeman, H. A., Milton Friedman, Frederick Mosteller, and W. Allen Wallis, "Sampling Inspection," McGraw-Hill Book Company, Inc., New York, 1948.

Wald, Abraham, "Sequential Analysis," John Wiley & Sons, Inc., New York, 1947.

reliability of the procedures, the handling of the lots, and the costs that are involved. This discipline of acceptance sampling is represented in four definite features of the tables. These tables are as follows:

Specification of Sampling Data
Protection Afforded
Disposal Procedure
Cost Required

Each will be discussed below.

Specification of Sampling Data. That is, the size of samples to be selected, the conditions under which the samples are to be selected, and the conditions under which a lot will be accepted or rejected.

Sample size, as shown in the tables, often is a compromise. The sample must be large enough so that it represents the quality of the lot from which it is drawn. This is a statistical question. The sample size, in some tables, may also take minimum inspection cost into account. This is an economic question, and sample size as well as other data in acceptance tables usually grow out of a balance between economics and "pure" statistics.

Also established as part of the data are the quality "targets" that may be "aimed at" by use of a specific sampling schedule. These targets are usually expressed in terms of values for per cent defective. With some products on which sampling can be done, only a small percentage of defective units may be allowed to pass on to the production line. The quality target in these instances may be 1 per cent defective.

With other articles—nuts and bolts, perhaps—a relatively high percentage of defective articles may be passed. The quality target in these instances may be 5 per cent defective.

A series of sampling schedules, with different per cent-defective values to meet varying conditions, are provided in these tables. Different sampling plans express these quality targets in different forms, among them being average outgoing quality limit (AOQL), acceptable quality level (AQL), and lot tolerance per cent defective (LTPD). Each of these quality targets is designed to serve a somewhat different purpose.

Protection Afforded. That is, the element of risk that the sampling schedules in a given table will reject good lots or accept bad ones.

The very fact that sampling is done brings in such typical risks as (1) passing an unsatisfactory lot as satisfactory and (2) rejecting a satisfactory lot as unsatisfactory.

Condition (1) will be of concern in a case such as that of a factory accepting lots on the basis of a given acceptance sampling table, since unacceptable material may thereby be released to its manufacturing

Table IV-B. Master Table for Normal and Tightened Inspection (*Double Sampling*)

Lot size*	Sample	Sample size	Cumulative sample size	0.015 Ac	0.015 Re	0.035 Ac	0.035 Re	0.065 Ac	0.065 Re	0.10 Ac	0.10 Re	0.15 Ac	0.15 Re	0.25 Ac	0.25 Re	0.40 Ac	0.40 Re	0.65 Ac	0.65 Re	1.0 Ac	1.0 Re	1.5 Ac	1.5 Re
				Acceptable quality levels (normal inspection)																			
2–8 9–15 16–25	No double sampling plans for these sample sizes; use single sampling.																						
26–40	First	5	5																			↓	
	Second	10	15																				
41–65	First	7	7																	↓		†	
	Second	14	21																				
66–110	First	10	10															↓		†		↑	
	Second	20	30																				
111–180	First	15	15													↓		†		↑		↓	
	Second	30	45																				
181–300	First	25	25											↓		†		↑		↓		1	3
	Second	50	75																			2	3
301–500	First	35	35									↓		†		↑		↓		0	3	1	3
	Second	70	105																	2	3	2	3
501–800	First	50	50							↓		†		↑		↓		0	3	1	4	1	6
	Second	100	150															2	3	3	4	5	6
801–1,300	First	75	75					↓		†		↑		↓		0	3	1	3	1	6	2	8
	Second	150	225													2	3	2	3	5	6	7	8
1,301–3,200	First	100	100			↓		†		↑		↓		0	3	1	4	1	6	2	6	3	8
	Second	200	300											2	3	3	4	5	6	5	6	7	8
3,201–8,000	First	150	150	↓		†		↑		↓		0	3	1	3	2	5	2	7	3	8	5	14
	Second	300	450									2	3	2	3	4	5	6	7	7	8	13	14
8,001–22,000	First	200	200	†		↑		↓		0	3	1	3	1	6	2	7	3	8	4	10	6	17
	Second	400	600							2	3	2	3	5	6	6	7	7	8	9	10	16	17
22,001–110,000	First	300	300	↑		↓		0	3	1	3	1	6	2	7	3	9	4	11	6	17	8	26
	Second	600	900					2	3	2	3	5	6	6	7	8	9	10	11	16	17	25	26
110,001–550,000	First	500	500	↓		0	3	1	4	1	6	2	7	3	10	5	13	6	22	9	25	12	37
	Second	1,000	1,500			2	3	3	4	5	6	6	7	9	10	12	13	21	22	24	25	36	37
550,001 and over	First	1,000	1,000	0	3	1	4	1	6	2	9	4	13	5	17	7	26	11	33	15	47	22	65
	Second	2,000	3,000	2	3	3	4	5	6	8	9	12	13	16	17	25	26	32	33	46	47	64	65
				0.035		0.065		0.10		0.15		0.25		0.40		0.65		1.0		1.5		2.5	
				Acceptable quality levels (tightened inspection)																			

↓ = Use first sampling below arrow. When sample size equals or exceeds lot size, do 100 per cent inspection.
↑ = Use first sampling plan above arrow.
* For inspection level II.

† = Use corresponding single sampling plan, table IV-A.
Ac = Acceptance number.
Re = Rejection number.
Tightened sampling plans are not provided for AQL: 0.015.

Lot size*	Sample	Sample size	Cumulative sample size	Acceptable quality levels (normal inspection) 2.5 Ac	2.5 Re	4.0 Ac	4.0 Re	6.5 Ac	6.5 Re	10.0 Ac	10.0 Re
2–8 9–15 16–25	No double sampling plans for these sample sizes; use single sampling.										
26–40	First	5	5	†		†		↓		1	3
	Second	10	15							2	3
41–65	First	7	7	↑		↓		0	3	1	5
	Second	14	21					2	3	4	5
66–110	First	10	10	↓		0	3	1	4	2	6
	Second	20	30			2	3	3	4	5	6
111–180	First	15	15	0	3	1	4	1	5	3	7
	Second	30	45	2	3	3	4	4	5	6	7
181–300	First	25	25	1	4	2	5	3	7	5	11
	Second	50	75	3	4	4	5	6	7	10	11
301–500	First	35	35	1	5	2	7	3	12	6	15
	Second	70	105	4	5	6	7	11	12	14	15
501–800	First	50	50	2	7	3	10	5	15	8	21
	Second	100	150	6	7	9	10	14	15	20	21
801–1,300	First	75	75	4	9	5	12	7	20	12	29
	Second	150	225	8	9	11	12	19	20	28	29
1,301–3,200	First	100	100	5	12	7	17	10	31	14	49
	Second	200	300	11	12	16	17	30	31	48	49
3,201–8,000	First	150	150	7	19	11	29	15	47	21	65
	Second	300	450	18	19	28	29	46	47	64	65
8,001–22,000	First	200	200	9	25	12	36	18	67	27	89
	Second	400	600	24	25	35	36	66	67	88	89
22,001–110,000	First	300	300	12	36	18	55	26	88	38	123
	Second	600	900	35	36	54	55	87	88	122	123
110,001–550,000	First	500	500	18	65	27	89	43	131	62	191
	Second	1,000	1,500	64	65	88	89	130	131	190	191
550,001 and over	First	1,000	1,000	34	113	50	160	79	243	119	348
	Second	2,000	3,000	112	113	159	160	242	243	347	348
			Acceptable quality levels (tightened inspection)	4.0		6.5		10.0			

↓ = Use first sampling below arrow. When sample size equals or exceeds lot size, do 100 per cent inspection.
↑ = Use first sampling plan above arrow.
* For inspection level II.

† = Use corresponding single sampling plan in table IV-A.
Ac = Acceptance number.
Re = Rejection number.
Tightened sampling plans are not provided for AQL: 0.015.

FIG. 12.2. The above table is a modification of Table IV-B of MIL-STD-105A in that inspection level II is used and corresponding lot sizes are incorporated directly in the body of the table.

floor. The term *consumer's risk* is used to describe this characteristic of a sampling table.

The usual technical definition for consumer's risk is similar to the following: consumer's risk is the probability that lots will be accepted which are of a per cent defective equal to the quality target. This quality target is usually the maximum acceptable per cent defective. Consumer's risk is expressed on a percentage basis: thus a given sampling table may have a 10 per cent consumer's risk.

Condition (2) will be of concern to the factory shipping the articles, since the purchaser factory may return as unacceptable satisfactory material which has been rejected under the terms of the sampling table. The term *producer's risk* is used to describe this characteristic of a sampling table.

The usual technical definition for producer's risk is similar to the following: producer's risk is the probability that lots will be rejected which are of a per cent defective equal to the quality target. This quality target is usually the minimum acceptable per cent defective. Producer's risk is expressed on a percentage basis: thus a given sampling table may have a 5 per cent producer's risk.

Disposal Procedure. That is, a set of rules that states what is to be done with the lots after sampling has been completed. Thus, a sampling table may contain the following information: "If the number of defective units does not exceed the number specified in the table, accept the lot. Otherwise, reject or 100 per cent inspect the balance of the lot."

Cost Required. That is, average inspection cost required to accept or reject a lot. Some sampling tables, Dodge-Romig being a particular case in point, are established to permit the use of the minimum amount of inspection necessary to hit a given quality target with a certain consumer's risk or producer's risk. Other sampling tables are established merely to afford a given degree of protection without necessarily providing the minimum inspection cost.

A sampling table will not, of course, specify its inspection cost in dollars and cents. When it is based upon providing the minimum of inspection, it will merely specify the minimum number of units that must be inspected or tested for a given set of conditions. The translation of the sampling schedules into cost figures is, however, an important feature of the use of sampling tables and will be discussed later in the chapter.

12.6 Defining the Statistical Sampling Table

A modern statistical sampling table may, therefore, be defined as

A series of schedules for representing the probable quality relationships (usually expressed in percentage terms) of the entire lot to the samples properly selected from that lot.

The effective sampling table not only must accurately represent the quality of the lot being sampled but also must specify the amount of risk that this representation may be either too high or too low. The number of calculations required to prepare these tables and the necessity for understanding the limitations of these calculations have made the development of sampling tables largely the province of the trained statistician. Yet the fundamentals upon which these calculations are based are quite simple and can be readily understood by all interested in this phase of statistical methods.

Modern sampling tables can be constructed for an almost unlimited variety of situations. The plans may be designed for any degree of accuracy, but they generally represent a balance between this accuracy and inspection cost.

In the final development of a particular table, practical shop circumstances may be of much more importance than theoretical statistical factors. The attitudes of factory personnel and the pressure of everyday factory conditions may make for circumstances not anticipated during the mathematical preparation of the tables. As a result, the trained industrial statistician knows that his objective in preparing a sampling table is not that of constructing a plan which is a mathematician's joy. It is rather that of providing a useful tool to enable a factory effectively to judge its materials and parts—which inevitably involves a table in a form that is easy to administer.

A particular factory may have consolidated in a single card a sampling table that meets all its varying conditions of differing lot size and varying desired quality standards. In developing such a table, certain features of accuracy may have been sacrificed and certain "average values" used—procedures which could be readily criticized on a purely statistical basis. Yet such a table may be far more satisfactory for the use of the factory than would be a number of individual sampling plans which are statistically somewhat more accurate than the table.

12.7 Types of Statistical Sampling Tables

A typical procedure in the construction of a statistical sampling table can be simply expressed: it is first to determine what is the probability of accepting lots containing various per cents defective when acceptance is based upon lot size (N) from which samples (n) are drawn containing (c) or less defectives. Then it is necessary to consolidate into a table those sampling conditions which meet the particular requirements for which the plan is being established.

The relationship between the per cent defective in the lots being submitted for inspection and the probability of acceptance is termed the *operating characteristic,* or OC, of a particular sampling condition. Every combination of lot size, sample size, and allowable number of defectives has a different operating characteristic whose values are usually plotted in the form of a curve. The quality assurance offered by a given table may be judged by the OC curves associated with the table. Figure 12.3 shows such an OC curve for the following conditions:

$$N = 2{,}000$$
$$n = 300$$
$$c = 11$$

While the basic procedures in the construction of several statistical sampling tables may be similar, there are differences both in the details of the construction and in the final form taken by these sampling tables. In line with the two major types of quality protection desired by industrial plants for material being inspected, two major forms of statistical sampling tables have been constructed. They are

1. Those tables which offer protection of the quality of the individual lots submitted for inspection. The types of quality target usually associated with this sort of plan are the acceptable quality level (AQL) target and the lot tolerance per cent-defective (LTPD) target. Several different symbols are used to denote these two points along the horizontal scale. The acceptable quality level is sometimes noted as p_1, and the

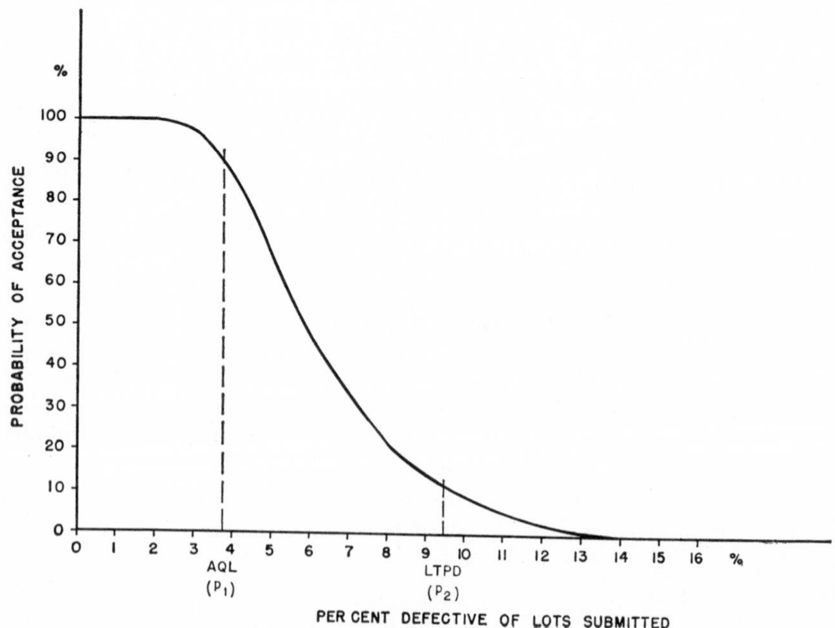

FIG. 12.3.

lot tolerance per cent defective is called the *reject quality level* (RQL), or p_2.

2. Those tables which offer protection of the "in-the-bin" average quality of the material from a large number of lots after inspection. The type of quality target usually associated with this sort of plan is the average outgoing quality limit (AOQL) target.

A sampling plan affording one of these two forms of protection will also afford some degree of protection of the other form. In addition, each of these two forms of sampling table has benefits for particular applications. One type of table cannot be termed "better" than the other.

Where infrequent individual lots of material are received by a plant, lot-quality protection tables may be most appropriate. Where large numbers of lots are being inspected and the average quality of material being released to the factory floor is the important factor, then average outgoing quality protection may be desirable.

Each of these two types of sampling table will be discussed below.

12.8 Lot-quality Protection

When lot-quality protection tables are required, the two most popular tables available are

1. Lot tolerance per cent-defective tables.
2. Acceptable quality level tables.

Lot Tolerance Per Cent-defective Tables.[3] Figure 12.4 shows the OC curves of four acceptance conditions. These four curves are similar in only one respect: they all pass through the point where the probability of acceptance on the vertical axis is 10 per cent and the lot per cent defective on the horizontal axis is 4 per cent. The meaning of this particular sampling-table construction can be simply expressed: under these acceptance conditions, the consumer is sure that 90 per cent of the time lots will be rejected which contain 4 per cent defectives. So for this particular schedule, the lot tolerance per cent defective is 4 per cent at a consumer's risk of 10 per cent.

Acceptable Quality Level Tables. The OC curves for four other acceptance conditions are shown in Fig. 12.5. These curves are similar in only one respect: they all pass through the point where the probability of acceptance on the vertical axis is 90 per cent and the lot per cent defective on the horizontal axis is 4 per cent.

The meaning of this particular sampling-table construction is as follows: under these acceptance conditions lots containing 4 per cent defectives are assured of being accepted 90 per cent of the time. There is a 10 per cent producer's risk that lots conforming to this quality level

[3] The discussion in this section follows an unpublished note by J. W. Gross, Schenectady, N.Y.

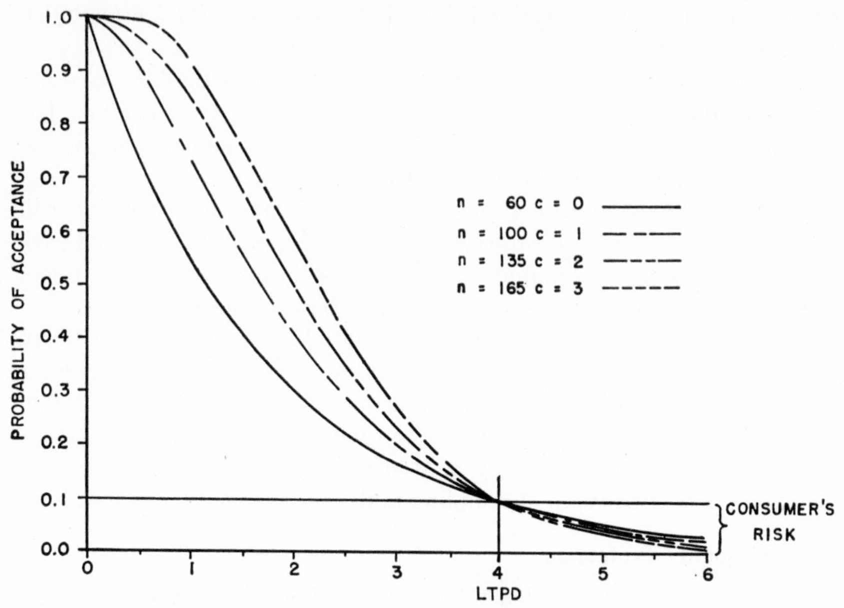

FIG. 12.4.

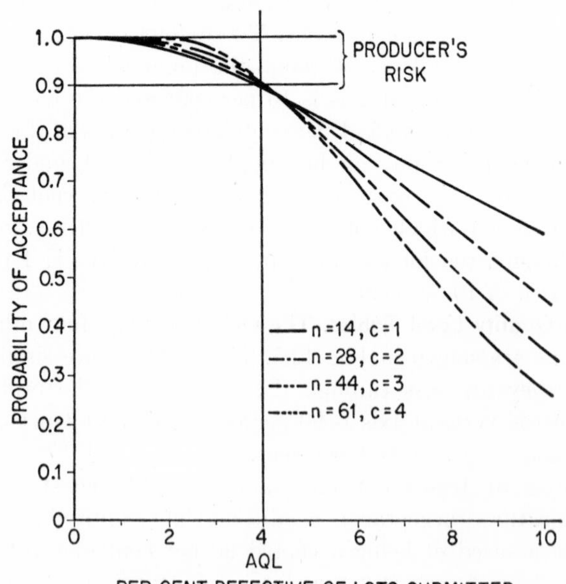

FIG. 12.5.

will be rejected. So for this particular schedule, the acceptable quality level is 4 per cent with a 10 per cent producer's risk.[4]

12.9 Average Outgoing Quality Protection

When average outgoing quality protection is desired, average outgoing quality limit tables are most popular. These tables assure a manufacturer that the per cent defective of his average outgoing quality will be equal to or less than a given level but require that the lots which are rejected under the plan be 100 per cent inspected and that the defective units in these lots be replaced or repaired. The 4 per cent lot tolerance per cent-

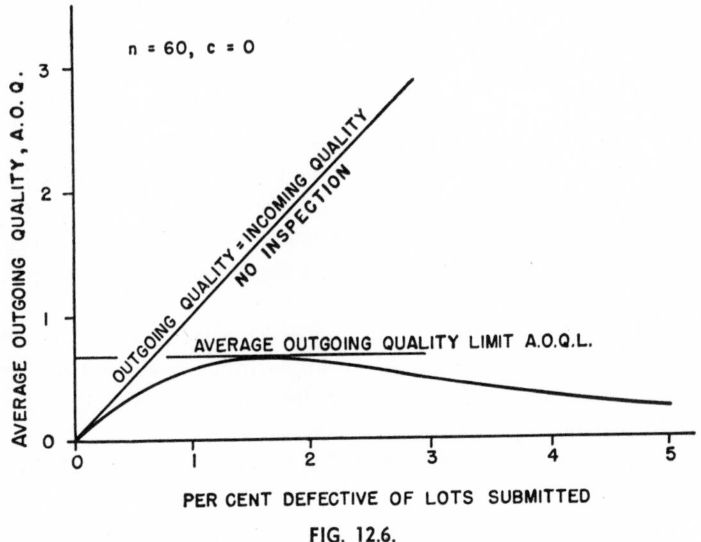

FIG. 12.6.

defective condition, with $n = 60$ and $c = 0$ as shown in Fig. 12.4, will be used to illustrate the AOQL form of sampling plan.

As shown in Fig. 12.4, if lots with a per cent defective of 1 per cent were submitted for inspection, these lots would be accepted 56 per cent of the time. Therefore, 44 per cent of the lots would be 100 per cent inspected, and the defective units in these lots would be replaced or repaired. The average quality after inspection, or average outgoing quality (AOQ), of these lots would be 44 per cent $\times$ 0 per cent + 56 per cent $\times$ 1 per cent = 0.56 per cent.

If lots with a per cent defective of 1.5 were submitted for inspection, Fig. 12.4 shows that 43 per cent of the lots would be accepted and 57

[4] Most acceptable quality level tables are designed for 5 per cent producer's risk, a few for 15 per cent producer's risk, etc.

per cent of the lots would be rejected and 100 per cent inspected. Assuming again that this 100 per cent inspection removes all defectives, the AOQ will be 43 per cent of 1.5 per cent, or 0.645 per cent.

For lots submitted with a per cent defective of 2.0 per cent, the AOQ will be 0.64 per cent. This AOQ value grows progressively smaller for lots with 2.5 per cent defective, 3.0 per cent defective, etc.

These several AOQ values are plotted in Fig. 12.6. This figure shows that the maximum value for average outgoing quality under this plan is to be found with lots submitted for inspection which are 1.7 per cent defective. With lots which are 1.7 per cent defective, the AOQ value on the vertical axis, the average outgoing quality limit (AOQL) is 0.68 per cent defective.

12.10 Single, Double, and Multiple Sampling

With each of these two major types of statistical sampling plans, there may be

1. *Single sampling,* that is, basing acceptance or rejection of a lot upon the units in one sample drawn from that lot.
2. *Double sampling,* that is, selecting one sample of units from a lot and, under certain conditions, selecting a second sample before accepting or rejecting the lot.
3. *Multiple sampling,* that is, basing acceptance or rejection of a lot upon the results of several samples of units drawn from that lot.

Of these three methods, double sampling has probably been the most popular for reasons such as the following:

Double Sampling as Compared with Single Sampling. 1. Psychologically, the idea of giving a lot of material a "second chance" before rejecting it has popular appeal. Double sampling is, therefore, sometimes easier to "sell" in the factory.

2. Double-sampling plans permit a smaller first sample than is called for by the sample size of the corresponding single-sampling plan. When the per cent defective is either low or high in material submitted for inspection, it is possible frequently to accept or reject lots based upon the results of the first sample. In these instances, therefore, double sampling permits lower sampling costs.

Double Sampling as Compared with Multiple Sampling. 1. Double-sampling plans are often easier to administer than are multiple-sampling plans. The need for selecting successive samples in the proper fashion may require greater administrative control and more highly skilled inspection operators.

2. In theory, multiple sampling may often permit lower total inspection than double sampling for a given degree of protection because of the smaller sample sizes required. In practice, however, the greater com-

plexity of multiple sampling may, in some cases, return the over-all cost advantage to double sampling. This is particularly true when the per cent defective in submitted lots is low—say, 0.1 per cent—in these cases, the amount of inspection required by single- and double-sampling plans based upon process averages is much the same as that for multiple sampling.

In spite of the popularity of double sampling, these are certain benefits unique to both single and multiple sampling:

Single Sampling. 1. Single sampling may be the only practical type of sampling plan under conveyorized production conditions when it is physically possible to select only one sample.

2. With lots of material whose per cents defective are close to the acceptable quality level, single sampling may offer more economical inspection protection than double sampling.

Multiple Sampling. 1. When administrative costs can be kept low, multiple sampling may permit lower inspection costs for given degrees of protection than either single or double sampling.

2. New methods currently being developed to simplify multiple sampling, among them automatic "sampling boxes," may result in greatly improved efficiency in administering these sampling plans.

3. Multiple sampling corresponds to the fashion in which an inspector normally selects samples.

The type of product and the way the product is presented for sampling —on a conveyor, in boxes piled on top of each other, etc.—are the factors that must be taken into account.

Again, the choice of single, double, or multiple sampling depends upon the particular conditions for which the sampling plan is to be used. None of the three methods may be termed "best"; they may be merely "best for certain sampling conditions."

12.11 Published Sampling Tables

Of the many statistical sampling tables and plans that have been developed in the past two decades, many have been published in a form which makes them available for general use. The most popular of these published plans are

1. Dodge-Romig tables.[5]
2. Military Standard 105A.[6]
3. Sequential plans.[7]

[5] Dodge, Harold, and Harry F. Romig, "Sampling Inspection Tables," 2d ed., John Wiley & Sons, Inc., New York, 1959.

[6] MIL-STD-105A, "Sampling Procedures and Tables for Inspection by Attributes," United States Government Printing Office, 1950.

[7] Wald, *op. cit.*

SINGLE SAMPLING TABLE FOR AVERAGE OUTGOING QUALITY LIMIT (AOQL) = 2.0%

Lot size	Process average 0 *to* 0.04%			Process average 0.05 *to* 0.40%			Process average 0.41 *to* 0.80%			Process average 0.81 *to* 1.20%			Process average 1.21 *to* 1.60%			Process average 1.61 *to* 2.00%		
	n	c	p_t %	n	c	p_t %	n	c	p_t %	n	c	p_t %	n	c	p_t %	n	c	p_t %
1–15	All	0	...	All	0	...	All	0	...	All	0	...	All	0	...	All	0	...
16–50	14	0	13.6	14	0	13.6	14	0	13.6	14	0	13.6	14	0	13.6	14	0	13.6
51–100	16	0	12.4	16	0	12.4	16	0	12.4	16	0	12.4	16	0	12.4	16	0	12.4
101–200	17	0	12.2	17	0	12.2	17	0	12.2	17	0	12.2	35	1	10.5	35	1	10.5
201–300	17	0	12.3	17	0	12.3	17	0	12.3	37	1	10.2	37	1	10.2	37	1	10.2
301–400	18	0	11.8	18	0	11.8	38	1	10.0	38	1	10.0	38	1	10.0	60	2	8.5
401–500	18	0	11.9	18	0	11.9	39	1	9.8	39	1	9.8	60	2	8.6	60	2	8.6
501–600	18	0	11.9	18	0	11.9	39	1	9.8	39	1	9.8	60	2	8.6	60	2	8.6
601–800	18	0	11.9	40	1	9.6	40	1	9.6	65	2	8.0	65	2	8.0	85	3	7.5
801–1,000	18	0	12.0	40	1	9.6	40	1	9.6	65	2	8.1	65	2	8.1	90	3	7.4
1,001–2,000	18	0	12.0	41	1	9.4	65	2	8.2	65	2	8.2	95	3	7.0	120	4	6.5
2,001–3,000	18	0	12.0	41	1	9.4	65	2	8.2	95	3	7.0	120	4	6.5	180	6	5.8
3,001–4,000	18	0	12.0	42	1	9.3	65	2	8.2	95	3	7.0	155	5	6.0	210	7	5.5
4,001–5,000	18	0	12.0	42	1	9.3	70	2	7.5	125	4	6.4	155	5	6.0	245	8	5.3
5,001–7,000	18	0	12.0	42	1	9.3	95	3	7.0	125	4	6.4	185	6	5.6	280	9	5.1
7,001–10,000	42	1	9.3	70	2	7.5	95	3	7.0	155	5	6.0	220	7	5.4	350	11	4.8
10,001–20,000	42	1	9.3	70	2	7.6	95	3	7.0	190	6	5.6	290	9	4.9	460	14	4.4
20,001–50,000	42	1	9.3	70	2	7.6	125	4	6.4	220	7	5.4	395	12	4.5	720	21	3.9
50,001–100,000	42	1	9.3	95	3	7.0	160	5	5.9	290	9	4.9	505	15	4.2	955	27	3.7

Single Sampling Table for Average Outgoing Quality Limit (AOQL) = 2.5%

Lot size	Process average 0 *to* 0.05%			Process average 0.06 *to* 0.50%			Process average 0.51 *to* 1.00%			Process average 1.01 *to* 1.50%			Process average 1.51 *to* 2.00%			Process average 2.01 *to* 2.50%		
	n	c	p_t %	n	c	p_t %	n	c	p_t %	n	c	p_t %	n	c	p_t %	n	c	p_t %
1–10	All	0	...	All	0	...	All	0	...	All	0	...	All	0	...	All	0	...
11–50	11	0	17.6	11	0	17.6	11	0	17.6	11	0	17.6	11	0	17.6	11	0	17.6
51–100	13	0	15.3	13	0	15.3	13	0	15.3	13	0	15.3	13	0	15.3	13	0	15.3
101–200	14	0	14.7	14	0	14.7	14	0	14.7	29	1	12.9	29	1	12.9	29	1	12.9
201–300	14	0	14.9	14	0	14.9	30	1	12.7	30	1	12.7	30	1	12.7	30	1	12.7
301–400	14	0	15.0	14	0	15.0	31	1	12.3	31	1	12.3	31	1	12.3	48	2	10.7
401–500	14	0	15.0	14	0	15.0	32	1	12.0	32	1	12.0	49	2	10.6	49	2	10.6
501–600	14	0	15.1	32	1	12.0	32	1	12.0	50	2	10.4	50	2	10.4	70	3	9.3
601–800	14	0	15.1	32	1	12.0	32	1	12.0	50	2	10.5	50	2	10.5	70	3	9.4
801–1,000	15	0	14.2	33	1	11.7	33	1	11.7	50	2	10.6	70	3	9.4	90	4	8.5
1,001–2,000	15	0	14.2	33	1	11.7	55	2	9.3	75	3	8.8	95	4	8.0	120	5	7.6
2,001–3,000	15	0	14.2	33	1	11.8	55	2	9.4	75	3	8.8	120	5	7.6	145	6	7.2
3,001–4,000	15	0	14.3	33	1	11.8	55	2	9.5	100	4	7.9	125	5	7.4	195	8	6.6
4,001–5,000	15	0	14.3	33	1	11.8	75	3	8.9	100	4	7.9	150	6	7.0	225	9	6.3
5,001–7,000	33	1	11.8	55	2	9.7	75	3	8.9	125	5	7.4	175	7	6.7	250	10	6.1
7,001–10,000	34	1	11.4	55	2	9.7	75	3	8.9	125	5	7.4	200	8	6.4	310	12	5.8
10,001–20,000	34	1	11.4	55	2	9.7	100	4	8.0	150	6	7.0	260	10	6.0	425	16	5.3
20,001–50,000	34	1	11.4	55	2	9.7	100	4	8.0	180	7	6.7	345	13	5.5	640	23	4.8
50,001–100,000	34	1	11.4	80	3	8.4	125	5	7.4	235	9	6.1	435	16	5.2	800	28	4.5

n = sample size; c = acceptance number.
"All" indicates that each piece in the lot is to be inspected.
p_t = lot tolerance per cent defective with a consumer's risk (P_C) of 0.10.

FIG. 12.7. Reprinted with permission from Dodge, Harold F., and Harry G. Romig, "Sampling Inspection Tables," 2d ed., John Wiley & Sons, Inc., New York, 1959. Two tables: Single Sampling 2.0 per cent AOQL and Single Sampling 2.5 per cent AOQL, in Appendix 6, p. 201.

4. Columbia Sampling Tables.[8]

Rather than designing his own sampling table, many an industrial user of statistical quality-control methods has made successful use of one or another of these published tables. They are, in general, sufficiently flexible to permit their being used in this fashion.

1. Dodge-Romig Tables. These tables include both single- and double-sampling plans. They permit both average outgoing quality limit protection and lot tolerance per cent-defective protection.

To use AOQL tables, for example, it is necessary to know (*a*) the size of the lot submitted for inspection, (*b*) the AOQL protection desired for the material in question, (*c*) the average quality or "process average" of the material presented for inspection.

The AOQL table used will indicate the sample size required and the allowable number of defectives in the sample size. If the sample contains no more defectives than are allowable, the lot is passed. If the sample contains more than the allowable number of defectives, then the lot must be 100 per cent inspected and the defective units repaired or replaced.

The tables specify the consumer's risk involved in each case, as well as other pertinent sampling data. They permit the minimum amount of inspection required for the degree of protection desired for material of a given process average.

Figure 12.7 illustrates a typical page from the Dodge-Romig sampling tables. The figure shows single-sampling lot tolerance per cent-defective tables with a 10 per cent consumer's risk.

2. MIL-STD-105A. These tables include the three types of sampling: single, double, and multiple. The AOQL is not mentioned for any plan.

To use these tables, it is necessary to know (*a*) the size of the lot submitted for inspection and (*b*) the AQL protection desired for the material in question.

The table in question will indicate the sample size required and the allowable number of defectives in the sample size. If the sample contains no more defectives than are allowed, the lot is passed. If the sample contains more than the allowable number of defectives, then the lot may be either rejected or 100 per cent inspected. However, 100 per cent inspection of rejected lots is not required for the maintenance of a given AQL.

There are also contained tables indicating when reduced, normal, or tightened inspection should be used. The criterion for the decision is the magnitude of the estimated process average.

3. Sequential Plans. These plans call for multiple sampling. Seven samples are called for in a popular version of sequential tables. These

[8] Freeman, Friedman, Mosletter, and Wallis, *op. cit.*

tables differ in at least two ways from the types of single- and double-sampling plans discussed above:

a. Since sample sizes are smaller, sample results are analyzed much more frequently than with single- or double-sampling plans for their indication as to whether or not a lot should be rejected.

b. The plans are "double acting." Under standard tables, for example, it is necessary only to specify one quality target: a lot which is X_1 per cent defective will be acceptable, and it is satisfactory to run a Y_1 per cent producer's risk.

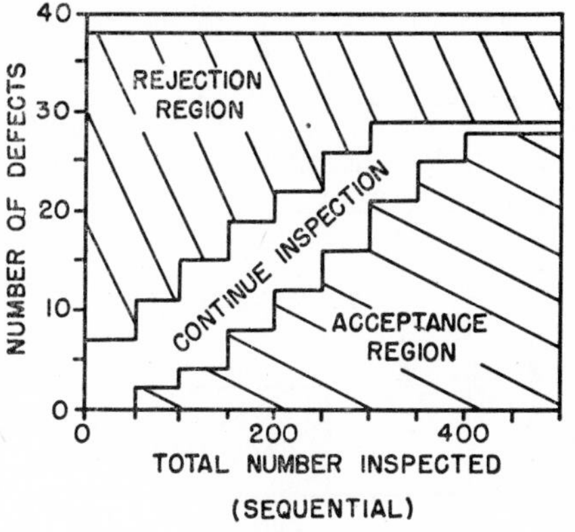

FIG. 12.8.

With sequential plans, the double-acting feature enters in that it is also necessary to establish a second target: it is desirable to reject the lot if it contains more than X_2 per cent defective, and it is satisfactory to run a Y_2 per cent risk of accepting a lot as bad as this.

As a result, sequential plans establish a "band of indecision" between an acceptance and a rejection region, as shown in Fig. 12.8. Sampling is continued until the results from the samples indicate either acceptance or rejection of the lot because the sample results have crossed into either the acceptance or rejection region. This "band of indecision" may be illustrated in a 2 per cent AQL sequential sampling plan calling for a possible five samples and designed for lots ranging from 800 to 1,299 units:

Cumulative sample size	Cumulative acceptance number	Cumulative rejection number
40	0	4
60	1	5
80	2	6
100	2	6
120	3	7
160	7	8

With this sequential plan, if an inspector finds a single defective in a sample size of 40, he can neither accept nor reject the lot but must select another sample. He is operating in the "band of indecision." Examination of 20 more units will bring his sample size to 60, and if he has found one more defective—for a cumulative total of 2—he must select a third sample.

This procedure can be carried on until the maximum sample size—160—is reached. At this point, the band of indecision disappears and acceptance or rejection of the material can be finally decided.

The average amount of inspection required with sequential sampling may be appreciably less than that required for comparable single- or double-sampling plans. Figure 12.9 shows the amount of inspection that would be required with a 4 per cent AQL double-sampling MIL-STD-105A table to gain the same results as from the sequential plan shown in Fig. 12.8. The much greater inspection area in Fig. 12.9 is worthy of note. It illustrates one of the reasons for the greatly increased interest in sequential sampling.

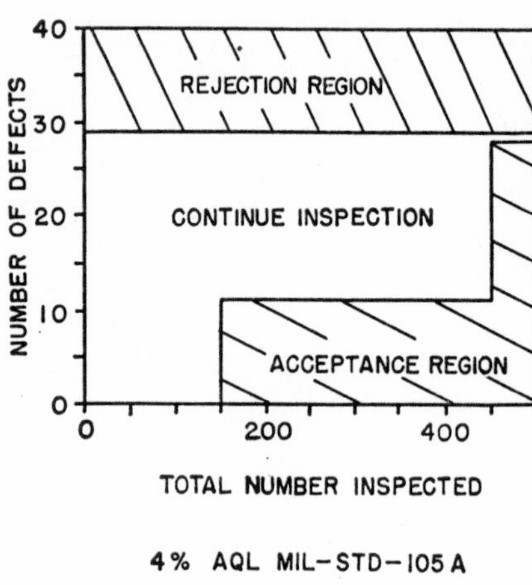

FIG. 12.9.

Figure 12.10 illustrates one form of a sequential sampling table.

4. Columbia Sampling Tables. These extremely flexible tables permit single, double, and multiple sampling as well as AQL and AOQL protection. Their use is similar to that of the tables described above.

12.12 Normal, Reduced, and Tightened Inspection

The standard form of many sampling tables is sometimes termed *normal* sampling tables.

Many well-conceived acceptance sampling procedures, such as MIL-STD-105A, also provide for *reduced*-sampling and, in some cases, *tightened*-sampling plans for use to supplant normal sampling under certain circumstances where it is still desired to hit the quality target specified. While these reduced-sampling plans do not conform to the OC curves for the normal-sampling table in question, their use is justified in that they take advantage of the additional information about the quality of lots submitted that has been obtained from the use of normal-sampling schedules.

When, for example, the quality of lots submitted for inspection is consistently better than the quality target aimed for, which may be demonstrated by the fact that no lots are being rejected, then a reduced-sampling schedule may be used in place of normal sampling under certain acceptance plans. These reduced schedules are usually similar in form to the normal schedules except that the first sample sizes, which correspond to a given lot size, will be smaller. Such tables usually have a first reduced sample one-fifth the size of the first normal sample.

Reduced sampling permits a decrease in inspection cost. This type of sampling can be continued until the quality of the material becomes poorer and calls for a return to normal sampling.

When the quality of lots submitted for inspection is consistently poorer than the quality target aimed for, occasionally a tightened sampling schedule may be called for. This tightened schedule is usually similar to the normal schedule, except that the allowable number of defectives for a given sample size is reduced.

Dodge-Romig tables approach this objective of flexibility and minimum amount of inspection by adjusting sample size to the process average. Instead of normal, reduced, and tightened categories, Dodge-Romig tables have degrees of inspection intensity. Selection from among them is based upon the quality history of the part in question.

A variation of reduced sampling has been proposed by James R. Crawford, which he calls *discovery sampling*.[9] The three major factors forming the basis of discovery sampling are as follows:

1. The entire sampling risk is contained only in the partially defective lots, since any plan will accept the 100 per cent good lots and reject the 100 per cent defective lots.

2. A small fraction defective occurs more frequently than does a large fraction defective.

3. The percentage of partially defective lots delivered to stock is a satisfactory process average measure.

In order to determine the sample size required for discovery sampling,[10] there are three factors to be considered. The first is the AOQL desired. The second is the ratio of lots containing some defectives to the total lots received (less the 100 per cent-defective lots). The third factor is the shape of the distribution of partially defective lots.

[9] Crawford, James R., "Discovery Sampling," Lockheed Aircraft Corp., Burbank, Calif., 1952.

[10] For further information on the mechanics of discovery sampling, see Taylor, Ervin F., "Discovery Sampling," *National Convention Transactions,* American Society for Quality Control, Milwaukee, Wis., 1955, p. 315.

LOT SIZE	SAMPLE SIZE	ACCEPTABLE QUALITY LEVEL (Percent Defective)																													
		0.1		0.25		0.50		0.75		1		1.5		2		3		4		5		6		7		8		9		10		12	
		A	R	A	R	A	R	A	R	A	R	A	R	A	R	A	R	A	R	A	R	A	R	A	R	A	R	A	R	A	R	A	R
499 OR less	40	↓		↓		↓		↓		0	3	0	3	1	4	1	4	1	6	2	6	2	7	3	7	3	8	4	9	4	9	5	10
	50	↓		↓		↓		↓		1	3	1	4	1	4	2	5	2	6	3	7	3	8	4	9	4	9	5	10	5	11	6	12
	60	↓		↓		↓		↓		1	3	1	4	2	5	2	6	3	7	4	8	4	9	5	10	5	11	7	12	7	13	9	14
	70	↓		↓		↓		↓		1	4	2	4	2	5	3	6	4	8	5	9	5	9	6	10	7	11	8	13	8	13	10	16
	80									3	4	3	4	4	5	5	6	7	8	8	9	8	9	9	10	10	11	12	13	12	13	15	16
500 to 799	40	↓		↓		↓		0	2	0	3	0	3	0	4	1	5	1	5	1	6	1	7	2	8	2	8	2	9	4	10	4	11
	60	↓		↓		↓		0	3	0	3	1	4	1	5	2	6	2	7	3	8	3	9	4	10	5	11	5	11	6	12	7	14
	80	↓		↓		↓		1	3	1	4	1	5	1	6	3	7	3	8	5	10	5	11	6	12	7	13	8	14	9	15	10	17
	100	↓		↓		↓		1	4	2	4	2	5	2	6	4	8	5	9	6	11	7	13	8	14	9	16	10	17	12	18	13	21
	120							3	4	3	4	4	5	5	6	7	8	8	9	10	11	12	13	13	14	15	16	16	17	18	19	20	21
800 to 1299	40	↓		↓		•	2	•	2	•	3	0	3	0	4	0	5	0	6	1	6	1	7	1	8	2	8	2	9	2	10	3	11
	60	↓		↓		0	2	0	3	0	3	0	4	1	5	1	6	2	7	2	8	3	9	3	10	4	11	4	12	5	12	6	14
	80	↓		↓		0	3	1	3	1	4	1	5	2	6	2	7	3	8	4	10	5	11	5	12	6	13	8	15	8	15	9	17
	100	↓		↓		0	3	1	3	1	4	1	5	2	6	3	8	5	10	5	11	7	13	7	14	9	15	10	17	10	18	12	21
	120	↓		↓		1	3	2	4	2	5	2	6	3	7	5	9	6	11	7	13	8	14	9	16	11	18	12	19	13	21	15	24
	160					3	4	4	5	4	5	5	6	7	8	9	10	10	11	13	14	15	16	16	17	18	19	19	20	22	23	25	26
1300 to 3199	50	↓		•	2	:	2	•	3	•	3	0	4	0	4	0	5	0	6	1	7	1	8	2	9	2	10	3	10	3	11	3	13
	75	↓		0	2	0	3	0	3	0	4	0	5	1	5	2	7	2	8	3	9	4	10	4	12	5	12	6	14	6	15	7	17
	100	↓		0	2	0	3	1	4	1	4	1	5	2	6	3	8	4	9	5	11	6	12	6	14	8	15	9	17	10	18	11	21
	125	↓		1	3	1	3	1	4	2	5	2	6	3	7	4	9	5	11	7	13	8	15	9	16	11	18	12	20	13	21	15	25
	150	↓		1	3	2	4	2	5	2	5	3	7	4	7	6	10	7	13	9	15	10	17	11	19	14	21	15	23	16	25	19	28
	200			2	3	3	4	4	5	5	6	6	7	6	7	10	11	13	14	17	18	17	18	20	21	22	23	25	26	27	28	31	32
3200 to 7999	50	•	2	•	2	•	2	•	3	•	3	•	4	•	5	0	6	0	7	0	8	1	9	1	10	1	11	2	11	2	12	3	14
	100	•	2	•	2	0	3	0	4	1	4	1	5	1	7	2	8	3	10	4	12	5	13	5	15	6	16	8	17	9	19	10	21
	150	0	2	0	3	1	4	1	5	2	5	2	7	2	8	5	11	5	13	8	15	9	17	10	19	11	21	13	23	15	25	17	29
	200	0	2	1	3	2	4	2	5	3	6	3	8	4	10	7	13	8	16	12	19	13	21	15	24	16	26	19	29	21	31	25	36
	250	1	3	1	4	2	5	2	6	4	8	5	9	6	11	9	15	11	18	15	22	17	25	19	28	22	32	25	35	28	38	32	44
	300	2	3	3	4	4	5	5	6	7	8	8	9	10	11	15	16	17	18	22	23	25	26	29	30	32	33	36	37	39	40	45	46

8000 to 21999	100	•	2	•	3	•	3	•	4	0	5	0	6	0	7	1	9	1	11	3	12	3	14	4	16	5	17	7	18				
	150	•	2	•	3	0	4	0	5	1	6	2	7	2	9	3	11	4	14	6	16	7	17	9	20	10	22	12	24	↑		↑	
	200	0	2	0	3	0	5	1	6	2	7	3	8	3	10	6	13	7	17	10	19	11	22	13	24	16	27	18	30				
	250	0	2	0	4	1	5	2	6	2	8	4	9	5	12	8	16	10	19	13	22	15	25	18	29	19	32	24	35				
	300	0	3	1	4	2	6	2	7	3	8	5	11	6	13	10	18	12	22	16	26	19	29	22	33	24	37	29	41				
	400	1	3	1	4	3	7	4	8	5	10	8	14	10	16	14	22	18	27	23	33	27	37	31	42	34	47	40	52				
	500	2	3	3	4	6	7	7	8	9	10	13	14	16	17	22	23	28	29	34	35	40	41	45	46	50	51	58	59				
22000 to 99999	100	•	2	•	3	•	4	•	5	•	6	•	8	0	8	0	11	1	13	2	16	3	16										
	200	•	3	•	4	0	5	0	6	1	7	1	10	3	11	3	15	6	18	8	20	10	24	↑		↑		↑		↑		↑	
	300	0	3	0	4	1	6	1	8	2	9	3	12	5	14	7	19	11	23	14	26	17	31										
	400	0	3	1	5	2	7	3	9	4	11	5	14	8	17	11	23	16	28	21	33	25	39										
	600	1	4	2	6	3	9	5	11	7	14	10	18	14	23	19	31	27	38	34	46	39	53										
	800	1	4	3	7	5	11	8	14	11	17	14	23	20	28	27	38	37	49	46	58	54	68										
	1000	3	4	6	7	10	11	13	14	17	18	22	23	30	31	40	41	53	54	65	66	76	77										
100,000 and up	200	•	3	•	5	•	7	•	8	0	9	0	13	2	13	2	18	4	20														
	400	•	4	0	6	0	8	0	10	3	12	3	17	7	18	9	25	14	30	↑		↑		↑		↑		↑		↑		↑	
	600	0	4	1	7	2	10	2	12	5	15	7	20	12	22	17	33	24	40														
	800	1	5	2	8	4	11	5	14	8	18	11	24	18	29	24	40	34	50														
	1000	1	5	3	9	5	13	7	17	11	21	15	28	23	35	32	47	44	60														
	1200	2	5	3	9	7	15	9	19	14	24	19	32	28	40	39	55	54	70														
	1600	4	5	8	9	14	15	19	20	24	25	33	34	45	46	61	62	86	87														

A - Acceptance number
R - Rejection number
* Acceptance cannot be made at this sample size

↓ Use first sampling table below arrows
(Form larger lots, if necessary)
↑ Use first sampling table above arrows

FIG. 12.10.

Using Acceptance Sampling Tables

12.13 A Typical Acceptance Plan: Attribute

Figure 12.11 shows a MIL-STD-105A-type acceptance sampling table adopted for use by a multiplant organization to meet the widely varying incoming-material, in-process, and final inspection situations in its various factories.

Fourteen different A.Q.L. schedules are contained in the table.[11] Unlike many sampling plans, there is no fixed probability of acceptance associated with these A.Q.L. schedules. Rather, the probabilities of acceptance range from 0.80 to 0.998 for the fourteen A.Q.L. schedules.

Factory personnel using this table are instructed to select their samples

1. *At random.* It is common sense that a sample may be most representative of a lot of material of unknown quality when the units in that sample have been chosen from all over the lot. As a result, each unit in the sample should be selected in such a way that each unit in the lot has a chance of being chosen.

2. *From a homogeneous lot.* As nearly as possible, the lot from which the sample is selected should consist of articles made under the same manufacturing conditions and drawn from the same manufacturing source.

This is important for practical rather than statistical purposes. For one example, a sample selected from lots shipped into a plant by two vendors may represent as satisfactory the quality of the combined lots. This situation may result only because the quality of one vendor's parts is far better than that required and the quality of the other vendor's parts far poorer than that required. The combined sample may mask over this important difference in vendor shipments.

The table itself consists of six major sections, as shown in Fig. 12.11:

I. Lot size.
II. First sample.
III. Second sample.
IV. Acceptable quality level (normal inspection).
V. Acceptable quality level (tightened inspection).
VI. Procedure.

Each of these sections will be discussed below.

I. Lot Size. This column contains the various ranges of lot size covered by the table. When there is a choice as to what the lot size should be,

[11] The reader will find that no lot tolerance per cent-defective values are listed as such. However, the approximate lot tolerance per cent-defective values can be determined from the operating characteristic (OC) curves for single sampling plans that are included in MIL-STD-105A. This is a departure from former sampling schedules such as the Ordnance tables that preceded MIL-STD-105A.

the decision should be based upon including, within the lot, material from the same source.

If there are two lots each containing 5,000 pieces, the question may arise as to whether lot size should be one lot of 10,000 pieces or two lots of 5,000 pieces. If the two lots are from the same source—perhaps the same vendor—they may be treated as a single lot; if they are from two different sources—perhaps from two vendors—they should be treated as individual lots.

From examination of the table, it will be noted that, in general, the larger the lot size the smaller the percentage of articles that must be checked. Therefore, although it is most economical to use relatively large lot sizes, this policy should not be followed where it becomes necessary to mix materials from different sources. Exceptions to this rule, of course, occur where there is lack of information as to the origin of a lot or where practical experience shows that it is satisfactory to mix lots.

II, III. First Sample, Second Sample. When the particular lot size in question has been chosen, the required sample sizes for that lot size can be read to the right horizontally. The row labeled "First Sample" indicates the number of units to be drawn from the lot and examined. If the acceptance conditions of the table indicate that a second sample must be drawn, its size is shown in the row labeled "Second Sample."

IV. Acceptable Quality Level (Normal Inspection). There are fourteen AQLs listed in the table, ranging from .015 to 10 per cent. Each AQL has associated with it the allowable number of defectives in the first sample (described as Ac) and the rejectable number of defectives in *both* the first and second samples (described as Re).

V. Acceptable Quality Level (Tightened Inspection). The same plans are used but the normal acceptable quality levels have been moved one place

VI. Procedure

1. Choose the desired acceptable quality level.
2. Select first sample indicated in table for lot size involved.
3. Determine in the first sample the number of units D_1 which contain defects.
   a. If D_1 does not exceed acceptance number (Ac) for the desired acceptable quality level, accept the lot.
   b. If D_1 exceeds the rejection number (Re), reject or 100 per cent inspect the lot.
   c. If D_1 exceeds Ac but not Re, select a second sample of size indicated in the table. Determine in second sample the number of units D_2 which contain defects. Then if $D_1 + D_2$ does not exceed Re, accept the lot. Otherwise, reject or 100 per cent inspect the balance of the lot. (The designation c is used for $D_1 + D_2$.)

to the left. This results in a tighter inspection plan being applied to the same AQL.

I TABLE IV-B. MASTER TABLE FOR NORMAL AND TIGHTENED INSPECTION (*Double Sampling*)

Lot size*	Sample	Sample size	Cumulative sample size	IV Acceptable quality levels (normal inspection) 0.015	0.035	0.085	0.10	0.15	0.25	0.40	0.65	1.0	1.5
				Ac Re	Ac Re	Ac Re	Ac Re	Ac Re	Ac Re	Ac Re	Ac Re	Ac Re	Ac Re
2–8 9–15 16–25	No double sampling plans for those sample sizes; use single sampling.												
26–40	First II Second III	5 10	5 15										↓
41–65	First Second	7 14	7 21									↓	†
66–110	First Second	10 20	10 30								↓	†	↑
111–180	First Second	15 30	15 45							↓	†	↑	↓
181–300	First Second	25 50	25 75						↓	†	↑	↓	1 3 2 3
301–500	First Second	35 70	35 105					↓	†	↑	↓	0 3 2 3	1 3 2 3
501–800	First Second	50 100	50 150				↓	†	↑	↓	0 3 2 3	1 4 3 4	1 6 5 6
801–1,300	First Second	75 150	75 225			↓	†	↑	↓	0 3 2 3	1 3 2 3	1 6 5 6	2 8 7 8
1,301–3,200	First Second	100 200	100 300		↓	†	↑	↓	0 3 2 3	1 4 3 4	1 6 5 6	2 6 5 6	3 8 7 8
3,201–8,000	First Second	150 300	150 450	↓	†	↑	↓	0 3 2 3	1 3 2 3	2 5 4 5	2 7 6 7	3 8 7 8	5 14 13 14
8,001–22,000	First Second	200 400	200 600	†	↑	↓	0 3 2 3	1 3 2 3	1 6 5 6	2 7 6 7	3 8 7 8	4 10 9 10	6 17 16 17
22,001–110,000	First Second	300 600	300 900	↑	↓	0 3 2 3	1 3 2 3	1 6 5 6	2 7 6 7	3 9 8 9	4 11 10 11	6 17 16 17	8 26 25 26
11,001–550,000	First Second	500 1,000	500 1,500	↓	0 3 2 3	1 4 3 4	1 6 5 6	2 7 6 7	3 10 9 10	5 13 12 13	6 22 21 22	9 25 24 25	12 37 36 37
550,001 and over	First Second	1,000 2,000	1,000 3,000	0 3 2 3	1 4 3 4	1 6 5 6	2 9 8 9	4 13 12 13	5 17 16 17	7 26 25 26	11 33 32 33	15 47 46 47	22 65 64 65
			V	0.035	0.065	0.10	0.15	0.25	0.40	0.65	1.0	1.5	2.5
				Acceptable quality levels (tightened inspection)									

↓ = Use first sampling below arrow. When sample size equals or exceeds lot size, do 100 per cent inspection.
↑ = Use first sampling plan above arrow.
† = Use corresponding single sampling plan, Table IV-A.
Ac = Acceptance number.
Re = Rejection number.

Lot size*	Sample	Sample size	Cumulative sample size	IV Acceptable quality levels (normal inspection)							
				2.5		4.0		6.5		10.0	
				Ac	Re	Ac	Re	Ac	Re	Ac	Re
2–8 9–15 16–25	No double sampling plans for these sample sizes; use single sampling.										
26–40	First II Second III	5 10	5 15	†		†		↓		1 2	3 3
41–65	First Second	7 14	7 21	↑		↓		0 2	3 3	1 4	5 5
66–110	First Second	10 20	10 30	↓		0 2	3 3	1 3	4 4	2 5	6 6
111–180	First Second	15 30	15 45	0 2	3 3	1 3	4 4	1 4	5 5	3 6	7 7
181–300	First Second	25 50	25 75	1 3	4 4	2 4	5 5	3 6	7 7	5 10	11 11
301–500	First Second	35 70	35 105	1 4	5 5	2 6	7 7	3 11	12 12	6 14	15 15
501–800	First Second	50 100	50 150	2 6	7 7	3 9	10 10	5 14	15 15	8 20	21 21
801–1,300	First Second	75 150	75 225	4 8	9 9	5 11	12 12	7 19	20 20	12 28	29 29
1,301–3,200	First Second	100 200	100 300	5 11	12 12	7 16	17 17	10 30	31 31	14 48	49 49
3,201–8,000	First Second	150 300	150 450	7 18	19 19	11 28	29 29	15 46	47 47	21 64	65 65
8,001–22,000	First Second	200 400	200 600	9 24	25 25	12 35	36 36	18 66	67 67	27 88	89 89
22,001–110,000	First Second	300 600	300 900	12 35	36 36	18 54	55 55	26 87	88 88	38 122	123 123
110,001–550,000	First Second	500 1,000	500 1,500	18 64	65 65	27 88	89 89	43 130	131 131	62 190	191 191
550,001 and over	First Second	1,000 2,000	1,000 3,000	34 112	113 113	50 159	160 160	79 242	243 243	119 347	348 348
			V	4.0		6.5		10.0			
				Acceptable quality levels (tightened inspection)							

↓ = Use first sampling below arrow. When sample size equals or exceeds lot size, do 100 per cent inspection.
↑ = Use first sampling plan above arrow.
* Inspection Level II.

† = Use corresponding single sampling plan in Table IV-A.
Ac = Acceptance number.
Re = Rejection number.
Tightened sampling plans are not provided for AQL: 0.015.

FIG. 12.11. The above table is a modification of Table IV-B of MIL-STD-105A in that inspection level II is used and corresponding lot sizes are incorporated directly in the body of the table.

As an example of the use of the aforementioned table, the case of felt washers may be considered. The inner diameter of these washers is the critical quality characteristic, and these inner diameters are inspected when the material is received from the vendor's plant. An AQL of 2.5 per cent has been established for this quality characteristic.

When a lot of 1,000 washers is received in incoming inspection, the steps that will be followed in the use of the table are as follows:

1. *Select the appropriate lot size.* In Fig. 12.11, it may be seen that the 1,000-unit lot falls in the 801 to 1,300 lot size.
2. *Select the first sample.* First sample for this lot size is 75 pieces.
3. *Measure the first sample.* With the 2.5 per cent AQL, it will be noted that the allowable number of defectives for this lot size is 4. If 4 or fewer defectives are found, the lot can be accepted on the basis of the first sample. If more than 4 but not more than eight defectives are found in the first sample, a second sample must be selected. If more than eight defectives are found in the first sample, the lot either must be rejected or must be 100 per cent sorted.
4. *Select and measure the second sample.* If a second sample has been required, it is shown to be 150 units. If in the combined first and second samples more than eight defectives are found, the lot should be rejected or 100 per cent inspected. If eight or fewer defectives are found, the lot can be passed.

12.14 A Reduced-sampling Plan

As with many acceptance sampling tables, MIL-STD-105A has associated with it a series of reduced-sampling schedules. The reduced-sampling table for single sampling plans is shown in Fig. 12.12. This table is designed for use if three criteria are met.

Condition A: The preceding 10 lots have been under normal inspection and none have been rejected.

Condition B: The estimated process average is less than the applicable lower limit shown in Fig. 12.13.

Condition C: Production is at a steady rate.

Use of the reduced-sampling table is similar to the procedure described in Sec. 12.13. It will be noted that the economy of reduced sampling over normal sampling is obtained in that the size of the sample is far smaller than that for normal sampling.

Reduced sampling is particularly effective with material such as certain types of cast parts, where a lot is generally either uniformly satisfactory or uniformly defective. The small sample size may permit considerable reductions in inspection cost under these conditions.

Lot size*	Sample size	0.015 Ac	0.015 Re	0.035 Ac	0.035 Re	0.065 Ac	0.065 Re	0.10 Ac	0.10 Re	0.15 Ac	0.15 Re	0.25 Ac	0.25 Re	0.40 Ac	0.40 Re	0.65 Ac	0.65 Re	1.0 Ac	1.0 Re	1.5 Ac	1.5 Re	2.5 Ac	2.5 Re	4.0 Ac	4.0 Re
		Acceptable quality levels																							
2–15 } 16–40 }	2	Reduced inspection not available for AQL: 0.015		↓		↓		↓		↓		↓		↓		↓		↓		0	1	↓		↓	
41–65	2			↓		↓		↓		↓		↓		↓		↓		↓		0	1	↓		↓	
66–110	3			↓		↓		↓		↓		↓		↓		↓		0	1	↑		↓		1	2
111–180	5			↓		↓		↓		↓		↓		↓		0	1	↕		↓		1	2	1	2
181–300	7			↓		↓		↓		↓		↓		0	1	↕		↕		1	2	1	2	2	3
301–500	10			↓		↓		↓		↓		0	1	↑		↕		1	2	1	2	2	3	2	3
501–800	15			↓		↓		↓		0	1	↕		↓		1	2	1	2	2	3	2	3	3	4
801–1,300	22			↓		↓		0	1	↕		↕		1	2	1	2	2	3	2	3	3	4	4	5
1,301–3,200	30			↓		0	1	↑		↕		1	2	1	2	2	3	2	3	3	4	4	5	5	6
3,201–8,000	45			0	1	↕		↓		1	2	1	2	2	3	2	3	3	4	4	5	5	6	7	8
8,001–22,000	60			↕		↕		1	2	1	2	2	3	2	3	3	4	4	5	5	6	6	7	9	10
22,001–110,000	90			↕		1	2	1	2	2	3	2	3	3	4	4	5	5	6	6	7	9	10	11	12
110,001–550,000	150			1	2	1	2	2	3	2	3	3	4	4	5	5	6	7	8	9	10	11	12	14	15
550,001 and over	300			1	2	2	3	3	4	4	5	5	6	6	7	8	9	11	12	13	14	16	17	21	22

Lot size*	Sample size	6.5 Ac	6.5 Re	10.0 Ac	10.0 Re	15.0 Ac	15.0 Re	25.0 Ac	25.0 Re	40.0 Ac	40.0 Re	65.0 Ac	65.0 Re	100.0 Ac	100.0 Re	150.0 Ac	150.0 Re	250.0 Ac	250.0 Re	400.0 Ac	400.0 Re	650.0 Ac	650.0 Re	1000.0 Ac	1000.0 Re
		Acceptable quality levels																							
2–15 } 16–40 }	1					1	2	1	2	1	2	2	3	4	5	5	6	8	9	12	13	15	16	19	20
41–65	2	1	2	1	2	2	3	3	4	3	4	4	5	7	8	10	11	13	14	17	18	22	23	29	30
66–110	3	1	2	2	3	2	3	3	4	5	6	7	8	10	11	13	14	17	18	21	22	29	30	37	38
111–180	5	2	3	3	4	3	4	5	6	7	8	10	11	13	14	17	18	22	23	29	30	39	40	↑	
181–300	7	3	4	3	4	5	6	7	8	9	10	13	14	16	17	20	21	27	28	36	37	↑		↑	
301–500	10	3	4	4	5	6	7	9	10	12	13	16	17	19	20	24	25	33	34	↑		↑		↑	
501–800	15	4	5	6	7	8	9	12	13	15	16	19	20	24	25	31	32	↑		↑		↑		↑	
801–1,300	22	5	6	8	9	11	12	14	15	18	19	23	24	31	32	↑		↑		↑		↑		↑	
1,301–3,200	30	7	8	11	12	12	13	16	17	21	22	29	30	↑		↑		↑		↑		↑		↑	
3,201–8,000	45	10	11	13	14	15	16	20	21	27	28	↑		↑		↑		↑		↑		↑		↑	
8,001–22,000	60	12	13	15	16	18	19	24	25	↑		↑		↑		↑		↑		↑		↑		↑	
22,001–110,000	90	14	15	18	19	23	24	↑		↑		↑		↑		↑		↑		↑		↑		↑	
110,001–550,000	150	18	19	23	24	↑		↑		↑		↑		↑		↑		↑		↑		↑		↑	
550,001 and over	300	28	29	37	38	↑		↑		↑		↑		↑		↑		↑		↑		↑		↑	

↓ = Use first sampling plan below arrow. When sample size equals or exceeds lot size, do 100 per cent inspection.
↑ = Use first sampling plan above arrow.
* Inspection level II.
Ac = Acceptance number.
Re = Rejection number.

FIG. 12.12. The above table is a modification of Table V of MIL-STD-105A in that inspection level II is used and corresponding sample sizes are incorporated in the body of the table.

Table II. Limits of the Process Average
(Lower Limits for AQLs from 0.015 to 4.0)

Number of sample units included in estimated process average	Acceptable quality levels											
	0.015	0.035	0.065	0.10	0.15	0.25	0.40	0.65	1.0	1.5	2.5	4.0
25–34	*	*	*	*	*	*	*	*	*	*	*	*
35–49	*	*	*	*	*	*	*	*	*	*	*	*
50–74	*	*	*	*	*	*	*	*	*	*	*	*
75–99	*	*	*	*	*	*	*	*	*	*	*	*
100–124	*	*	*	*	*	*	*	*	*	*	*	*
125–149	*	*	*	*	*	*	*	*	*	*	*	*
150–199	*	*	*	*	*	*	*	*	*	*	*	*
200–249	*	*	*	*	*	*	*	*	*	*	*	*
250–299	*	*	*	*	*	*	*	*	*	*	*	0.38
300–349	*	*	*	*	*	*	*	*	*	*	*	0.67
350–399	*	*	*	*	*	*	*	*	*	*	0.05	0.90
400–449	*	*	*	*	*	*	*	*	*	*	0.20	1.09
450–549	*	*	*	*	*	*	*	*	*	*	0.38	1.32
550–649	*	*	*	*	*	*	*	*	*	*	0.56	1.55
650–749	*	*	*	*	*	*	*	*	*	0.11	0.71	1.73
750–899	*	*	*	*	*	*	*	*	*	0.22	0.85	1.91
900–1,099	*	*	*	*	*	*	*	*	0.05	0.34	1.00	2.10
1,100–1,299	*	*	*	*	*	*	*	*	0.13	0.44	1.13	2.27
1,300–1,499	*	*	*	*	*	*	*	0.004	0.20	0.52	1.23	2.40
1,500–1,699	*	*	*	*	*	*	*	0.045	0.25	0.58	1.31	2.50
1,700–1,899	*	*	*	*	*	*	*	0.080	0.29	0.63	1.41	2.59
1,900–2,249	*	*	*	*	*	*	*	0.119	0.34	0.69	1.46	2.68
2,250–2,749	*	*	*	*	*	*	0.021	0.166	0.40	0.77	1.55	2.80
2,750–3,499	*	*	*	*	*	*	0.061	0.217	0.46	0.84	1.65	2.93
3,500–4,999	*	*	*	*	*	0.020	0.109	0.279	0.54	0.94	1.77	3.08
5,000–6,999	*	*	*	*	*	0.056	0.155	0.388	0.61	1.03	1.89	3.23
7,000–8,999	*	*	*	*	0.020	0.082	0.188	0.380	0.66	1.09	1.97	3.33
9,000–10,999	*	*	*	0.005	0.034	0.100	0.210	0.408	0.70	1.13	2.03	3.40
11,000–13,499	*	*	*	0.015	0.046	0.116	0.230	0.434	0.73	1.17	2.08	3.46
13,500–17,499	*	*	0.003	0.024	0.057	0.129	0.248	0.456	0.76	1.20	2.12	3.52
17,500–22,499	*		0.011	0.033	0.068	0.144	0.266	0.479	0.79	1.24	2.16	3.58
22,500 and up	*	0.003	0.021	0.045	0.083	0.163	0.290	0.510	0.83	1.29	2.23	3.65

* Number of sample units included in estimated process average is insufficient for reduced inspection.

Table II. Limits of the Process Average
(Lower Limits for AQLs from 6.5 to 1000.0) (Continued)

Number of sample units included in estimated process average	Acceptable quality level											
	6.5	10.0	15.0	25.0	40.0	65.0	100.0	150.0	250.0	400.0	650.0	1000.0
25–34	*	*	*	*	5.07	20.47	44.8	82.4	162.7	289.5	509.2	825.3
35–49	*	*	*	1.86	10.72	27.67	53.7	93.3	176.8	307.4	532.0	853.6
50–74	*	*	0.25	5.95	15.90	34.28	61.9	103.3	189.8	323.8	552.9	879.5
75–99	*	*	2.54	8.92	19.66	39.07	67.8	110.6	199.1	335.7	568.0	898.3
100–124	*	1.04	4.02	10.83	22.07	42.14	71.7	115.3	205.2	343.3	577.7	910.4
125–149	*	1.89	5.07	12.18	23.79	44.33	74.4	118.6	209.5	348.7	584.7	918.9
150–199	0.71	2.82	6.20	13.64	25.64	46.69	77.3	122.2	214.1	354.6	592.1	928.2
200–249	1.40	3.67	7.24	14.99	27.34	48.86	80.0	125.5	218.3	360.0	599.0	936.7
250–299	1.88	4.27	7.99	15.95	28.55	50.40	81.9	127.8	221.4	363.8	603.8	942.7
300–349	2.25	4.73	8.55	16.67	29.47	51.57	83.3	129.8	223.7	366.7	607.5	947.3
350–399	2.55	5.10	9.00	17.25	30.17	52.50	84.5	131.0	225.5	369.0	610.5	951.0
400–449	2.79	5.40	9.36	17.72	30.79	53.26	85.4	132.2	227.0	370.9	612.9	954.0
450–549	3.08	5.76	9.80	18.29	31.51	54.18	86.6	133.6	228.8	373.2	615.8	957.6
550–649	3.38	6.13	10.25	18.87	32.25	55.12	87.7	135.0	230.6	375.5	618.8	961.3
650–749	3.61	6.41	10.61	19.33	32.83	55.86	88.7	136.1	232.1	377.3	621.1	964.1
750–899	3.84	6.70	10.95	19.78	33.39	56.58	89.6	137.2	233.5	379.1	623.4	967.0
900–1,099	4.08	7.00	11.32	20.26	34.00	57.35	90.5	138.4	235.0	381.0	625.8	970.0
1,100–1,299	4.29	7.26	11.64	20.67	34.52	58.02	91.3	139.4	236.3	382.7	627.9	972.6
1,300–1,499	4.46	7.46	11.89	20.99	34.93	58.53	92.0	140.2	237.3	384.0	629.6	974.6
1,500–1,699	4.59	7.63	12.09	21.25	35.26	58.95	92.5	140.8	238.1	385.0	630.9	976.3
1,700–1,899	4.70	7.76	12.26	21.46	35.53	59.30	92.9	141.3	238.8	385.9	632.0	†
1,900–2,249	4.82	7.92	12.45	21.71	35.83	59.69	93.4	141.9	239.6	386.8	†	†
2,250–2,749	4.97	8.10	12.68	22.00	36.21	60.16	94.0	142.7	240.5	†	†	†
2,750–3,499	5.13	8.30	12.92	22.32	36.61	60.67	94.6	143.4	†	†	†	†
3,500–4,999	5.33	8.54	13.22	22.70	37.09	61.29	95.4	†	†	†	†	†
5,000–6,999	5.51	8.78	13.50	23.06	37.55	61.88	†	†	†	†	†	†
7,000–8,999	5.64	8.94	13.70	23.32	37.88	†	†	†	†	†	†	†
9,000–10,999	5.73	9.05	13.84	23.50	†	†	†	†	†	†	†	†
11,000–13,499	5.82	9.15	13.96	†	†	†	†	†	†	†	†	†
13,500–17,499	5.89	9.24	†	†	†	†	†	†	†	†	†	†
17,500–22,499	5.96	†	†	†	†	†	†	†	†	†	†	†
22,500 and up	†	†	†	†	†	†	†	†	†	†	†	†

* Number of sample units included in estimated process average is insufficient for reduced inspection.
† Number of sample units included in estimated process average is too great; discard older results.

FIG. 12.13

A major limitation of reduced-sampling tables is, however, this very element of small sample size. In many factories it usually carries with it the danger that the reduced tables may be used indiscriminately in place of normal tables in situations where reduced sampling is not applicable. As a result, the effective introduction of reduced-sampling tables in a factory is usually accompanied by means for careful control over the use of these tables.

12.15 When May Sampling Be Done?

A major problem in the industrial application of statistical sampling plans is unwise use of these plans in situations for which they have no application. The widespread use of sampling plans is no end in itself; there are situations where either 100 per cent inspection or no inspection is to be preferred over any type of sampling plan.

With the exception of those few instances where destructive testing makes sampling imperative or where the possibility of property damage or personal injury makes 100 per cent inspection necessary, the decision as to whether or not sampling should be done may become almost entirely a question of economics.[12]

The question resolves itself into the following parts:

1. In the case of a given part, is it most economical to 100 per cent inspect, to sample, or to carry on no inspection at all?
2. If sampling has been chosen, what sampling plan should be used and what quality targets should be chosen? In the instance of the MIL-STD-105A table discussed above, this question becomes "What AQL should be used?"

Decisions on these questions have most frequently been made in industry in a fashion dictated by practical experience with the individual parts and with individual suppliers. The development of sampling plans has now, however, made it possible to implement this practical experience by means of actual calculations of what is the most economical inspection situation.

An effective approach to determining this most economical inspection situation for the MIL-STD-105A table discussed above involves calculation of the *break-even point*. The break-even point for a given part or quality characteristic may be defined as

> *The percentage ratio between the cost of eliminating defective parts by inspection and the cost for repair when defective parts have been allowed to move onto the manufacturing floor.*

[12] This discussion has been largely influenced by an unpublished paper by J. W. Gross, Schenectady, N.Y.

The calculation of the break-even-point value can be made in regard to a single part or quality characteristic as follows:

1. Determine the cost of removing defective parts by inspection.
2. Determine the average repair cost for units—assemblies, for example—which are made using these defective parts.
3. Calculate the resulting break-even point (BEP) by use of the formula

$$\frac{\text{Cost of inspection (per part)}}{\text{Cost of repair (per defective assembly)}} = \text{break-even point} \qquad (37)$$

4. Determine the actual average per cent defective or process average defective for the part or material in question. This value should be determined from the inspection results of several thousand parts.

These parts should represent as many incoming lots as is practical, in order that variations in the supplier's process can be evaluated. If the average incoming per cent defective is to be determined from the results of sampling inspection, only the results of the first samples should be used.

5. By comparing the BEP (from step 3, above) with the average incoming per cent defective (step 4, above), it can be determined whether 100 per cent inspection, no inspection, or sample inspection is indicated.

Four typical situations may be indicated:

a. If the per cent defective of incoming material is fairly close to the BEP, then sampling inspection may be the economical answer.

b. If the per cent defective of incoming material is somewhat higher than the BEP, 100 per cent inspection will more than pay for itself.

c. If the per cent defective of incoming material is considerably lower than the BEP but is erratic, sampling inspection may be indicated purely for purposes of protection.

d. If the per cent defective of incoming material is considerably lower than the BEP and is stable, then a case might be made for no inspection at all.

If it has been determined that sampling inspection is the most economical procedure in a given case, then some sampling plan and some quality target must be selected. Generalized procedures for relating various break-even points to quality targets are often used in this connection.

For the MIL-STD-105A table of Fig. 12.11, this quality target is, of course, the AQL. Two alternative approaches may be used to select an AQL in Fig. 12.11 which is appropriate to a given BEP:

1. Select the AQL which is closest to or equal to the break-even point. This procedure has the virtue of simplicity and is quite popular for this reason. It is relatively inaccurate, however, and in certain cases it sacrifices some of the economy possible with sampling.

Figure 12.14 shows a typical calculation sheet developed by one factory for determining AQL in this fashion. In the example shown, inspection cost per unit has been determined as \$0.01. Repair cost has been determined as \$1 per unit.

This results in a BEP of 1 per cent which, in the procedure used in

SAMPLING PLAN

PART OR ASSEMBLY STUD

DRAWING NO. 6947328

A. COST PER UNIT FOR COMPLETE INSPECTION OR TEST \$0.01

B. REPAIR COST IF DEFECTIVE UNIT IS FOUND IN ASSEMBLY 1.00

C. ACCEPTABLE QUALITY LEVEL (AQL)-$\frac{A}{B}$ 1% *

* THIS IS THE PROPORTION OF DEFECTIVE UNITS THAT CAN GET INTO ASSEMBLIES WITHOUT HAVING REPAIR COSTS EXCEED 100 PER CENT INSPECTION COSTS.

A. F. Jones
INSPECTOR

3/1/60
DATE

FIG. 12.14.

Fig. 12.14, also becomes the AQL. If the actual incoming per cent defective of these parts is within the range of a 1 per cent AQL, then the 1 per cent value may become the quality target.

2. Relate the break-even point to an AQL by means of the table shown in Fig. 12.15.

This procedure enables somewhat more economical use of sampling tables than is permitted in alternative 1 above. Its use is similar to that of alternative 1 up to the point of calculation of the break-even point; the difference is that the break-even-point value is then used to determine the appropriate AQL value. If the inspection cost per unit is \$0.05 and the associated repair cost is \$1, for example, then the 5 per cent BEP will call for, as shown in Fig. 12.15, an AQL of 4 per cent.

Whether 1 or 2 will be used in a given factory depends almost entirely upon the circumstances in that particular factory—upon the demand for sampling economy, the amount of paper work which will be entailed, etc.

12.16 Uneconomical Use of Sampling Plans

It is well to appreciate the results of indiscriminate use of a sampling plan in those cases where it is uneconomical. One instance is that wherein

RECOMMENDED A.Q.L. VALUES
MIL-STD-105A SAMPLING TABLE SHOWN IN FIG. 12.11
FOR USE WITH VARIOUS BREAK-EVEN POINTS

BREAK-EVEN POINT	A.Q.L.	BREAK-EVEN POINT	A.Q.L.
$\frac{1}{2}$% TO 1%	$\frac{1}{4}$%	6% TO 10$\frac{1}{2}$%	6.5%
1% TO 1$\frac{3}{4}$%	0.65%	10$\frac{1}{2}$% TO 17%	10%
1$\frac{3}{4}$% TO 3%	1%		
3% TO 4%	2.5%		
4% TO 6%	4%		

FIG. 12.15.

the incoming per cent defective consistently exceeds the BEP. If a particular part or quality characteristic were 11 per cent defective in actual practice and the BEP were 7 per cent, then use of Fig. 12.15 would indicate a 6.5 per cent AQL sampling plan.

Should such a sampling plan be used, the great majority of incoming lots would be either rejected or subject to 100 per cent inspection. This makes the plan meaningless at the outset and possibly an added cost burden. In addition, the factor of sampling risk, as discussed in connection with producer's and consumer's risk, would indicate that a certain number of incoming lots would be accepted containing 11 per cent defectives.

In the instance cited, therefore, 100 per cent inspection should be carried on, not sampling, which is both uneconomical and impractical.

In actual practice, accurate details for the break-even-point calculation may not be readily available in a given factory owing to the type of accounting routines used. In addition, AQL selection is often dictated by past experience on a given part or quality characteristic before any detailed cost balance can or has been made.

As a result, the break-even point, in common with other technical methods for answering the question of when sampling may be done, has as its main value the presentation of a point of view rather than the dictation of any hard-and-fast rule for a particular type of formal calculation. Sampling may be desirable under some conditions and undesirable under other conditions; it is imperative that the industrial user of sampling plans know what these conditions are. It is not so imperative, however, as to the form in which he obtains and uses this information—whether to apply it in such an informal fashion as to make the selection of an AQL seem quite arbitrary or to use it as part of a formalized procedure for calculating cost balances.

When Dodge-Romig tables are used, some of this procedure to minimize the cost of sampling consistent with a given degree of protection is "built into" the sampling plan. These tables require that the value for average per cent defective of the material in question be determined before a sampling schedule can be chosen. They automatically afford sampling schedules which minimize inspection in relation to a given quality target.

12.17 Sampling of Multiple Characteristics

The importance of selecting a suitable quality target for a part has been emphasized in the above discussion. But the problem of just what characteristics are covered by this "quality target for a part" has not been fully analyzed. Does a 2.5 per cent AQL for lots of incoming washers apply to all the characteristics of the washer? Does it refer to the thickness and the outer diameter characteristics only? Does it simply apply to the inner-diameter characteristics?

For many parts, to be sure, only one characteristic is critical, so that it is readily obvious what is covered by the quality target for that part. In the case of many industrial applications of springs, it is the "pull" of the spring that will be the only characteristic sampled.

Yet there are many other cases—certain cast parts, for example—where several characteristics are critical. It may be necessary to sample thickness, weight, and length.

As a result, it is desirable that the particular characteristics of a part for which the quality target has been established be specified. When it is necessary to specify more than one such characteristic for parts being sampled, there are two major alternatives for accomplishing this objective:

1. *Establish a quality target for each individual quality characteristic.*

In the case of round-head machine screws, an AQL of 2.5 per cent may be established for the length characteristic, which is fairly critical, while an AQL of 10 per cent may be established for the width of the screwhead, which may be of little importance. The lot may be rejected if either of these quality targets is not hit.

2. *Establish an over-all quality target which applies to several of the part characteristics.* With washers, for example, the thickness, outer diameter, and inner diameter may be combined in a 2.5 per cent AQL. If the sampling plan calls for rejection of the lot if more than five defectives are found, and if two thickness, two outer-diameter, and two inner-diameter defects have been found—a total of six—then the lot may be rejected.

A similar approach to setting these quality targets involves the use of critical, major, and minor defect classifications. These defect classifications are established in a fashion similar to that described in Sec. 11.23. Two alternative means for using this critical-major-minor defect approach are the following:

1. Special sampling tables can be devised which allow a single sample size to be used for several characteristics of a part but which provide separate columns for the allowable number of critical defects, the allowable number of major defects, and the allowable number of minor defects. The allowable number of minor defects is, of course, always larger than that for major defects, which, in turn, is larger than that for critical defects.[13]

2. Standard sampling tables can be used, but the total number of defects in the lot under inspection is determined by weighting critical, major, and minor defects. Thus, with machine screws, minor defects may be weighed as one-quarter the importance of major defects. If the length of the screw is a major characteristic and the width of the screwhead a minor characteristic, and if the allowable number of defects is 5, the lot may be passed if 2 length defectives and 10 width defectives—total 4.5—are found.

Many other reasons can be cited for the importance of clearly specifying those characteristics to which a quality target applies. For one instance, lots of material are often rejected and shipped back to vendors as being "unsatisfactory" without any indication on the reject tag or in the inspection records as to just what is unsatisfactory—whether a single characteristic or a combination of characteristics.

Again, the vague statement that a certain part has a 2.5 per cent AQL may leave the interpretation of the characteristics to which the 2.5 per cent should be applied in the hands of an unskilled inspection operator unfamiliar with the relative importance of the various characteristics. It is quite likely that he will develop his own sampling specification for the

[13] For many operations, no critical defects are allowable.

part, which either may be too severe on unimportant characteristics or may place too little weight on important ones.

12.18 Sampling by Variables

There has been a great preponderance in industry of go and not-go inspection over sampling by actual measurements, or variables sampling. There have been many reasons for this condition, among which have been the relative scarcity of adequate measuring equipments in many factories and, perhaps of greatest importance, the lack of the need for the type of precision that may be furnished by actual measurements.

There are indications on all sides that this situation is rapidly changing. The great growth in the precision demanded of products has been extensively discussed earlier in this book, and there is now both quantity and quality of excellent measuring equipments available to much of industry.

The impact upon sampling procedure of taking actual readings is readily apparent. Much greater accuracy results from these measurements than from a simple statement that a part is "good" or "bad." The several advantages of knowing just where in the tolerance band a part falls as opposed to the mere statement that "it is O.K." may be recalled from previous discussions on frequency distributions and control charts.

Of equal importance but perhaps not so obvious is the fact that variables sampling may be less expensive than go and not-go sampling, since information of equal value may be obtained from a smaller measurements sample than from a go and not-go sample.

Variables sampling takes many forms. One of the most typical is an application of the frequency distribution. A standard frequency-distribution sample size is often established—perhaps 50, perhaps 150 units—and a sample of this size is selected from each incoming lot of the material in question. The measured parts may be plotted on a tally card. Sometimes the sample size is kept flexible, sampling being stopped when an adequate distribution picture for the lot has appeared on the tally card rather than establishing a specific sample size.

Sometimes the resulting frequency-distribution picture is merely visually compared with the tolerance limits as the basis of acceptance or rejection of the lot. Sometimes the 3-sigma limits for the distribution are calculated and compared with the tolerance limits as the basis for acceptance or rejection of the lot. Figure 12.16 shows a lot of condensers that were accepted by visual examination of the frequency-distribution picture.

Measurements-control charts are often used in variables sampling. The procedure involves the establishment of control limits for the part characteristic in question and selection of a sample size. Often this sample size is arrived at arbitrarily after some experience has been obtained with the parts in question.

In place of the methods described above, some factories prefer more precise calculation of the sample size required for a given degree of protection. It can be said in favor of this approach that the individual features of such variables sampling plans are much more closely geared to the needs of particular conditions and that more economical sample sizes and procedures may result. The various formulas required for these calculations are available in the literature.

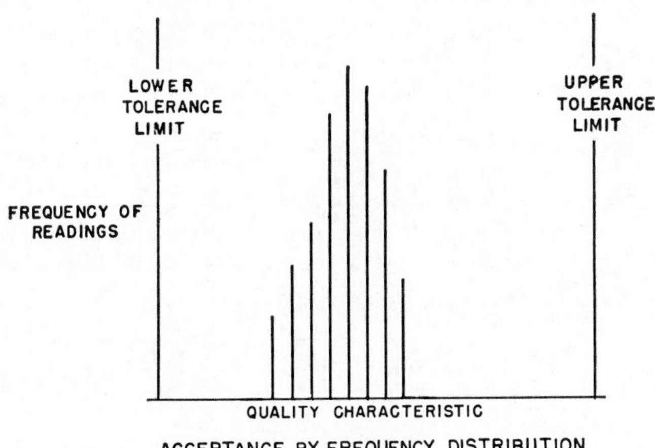

ACCEPTANCE BY FREQUENCY DISTRIBUTION

FIG. 12.16.

Preference in industry is, however, usually in favor of less formal, more rule-of-thumb variables sampling plans of the sort that have been noted above. This is due to the greater simplicity of these plans and the greater ease with which they lend themselves to standardized procedures covering the wide variety of sampling problems that are encountered in any one factory.

12.19 An Acceptance Plan: Variables

Figure 12.17 shows the MIL-STD-414 variables acceptance sampling table for a single specification limit when the variability is known.[14] The table establishes 14 different AQL schedules, each of which is coupled with a specific operating characteristic curve describing the risks involved. Each of these operating characteristic curves is presented in MIL-STD-414.

[14] "Sampling Procedures and Tables for Inspection by Variables for Per Cent Defective," MIL-STD-414, U.S. Government Printing Office, 1957.

The instructions for the selection of the samples are similar to those outlined for MIL-STD-105A in Sec. 12.13, for normal inspection, and in Sec. 12.14, for reduced inspection.

The table itself consists of five major sections, as shown in Fig. 12.18.

I. Lot size.
II. Sample size (n).
III. Acceptable quality level (normal inspection).
IV. Acceptable quality level (tightened inspection).
V. Acceptability constant (k).

With the exception of V, these sections are similar to those discussed in detail in Sec. 12.13. The acceptability constant (k) is the value to which the sample average, the specification limit, and the variability are compared for disposition decision of the lot. How this is accomplished is detailed in the example below:

As an example of the use of this table, consider the instance used

TABLE D-1. MASTER TABLE FOR NORMAL AND TIGHTENED INSPECTION FOR PLANS BASED ON VARIABILITY KNOWN (*Single Specification Limit—Form 1*)

Lot size	Acceptable quality levels (normal inspection)													
	.04		.065		.10		.15		.25		.40		.65	
	n	k	n	k	n	k	n	k	n	k	n	k	n	k
3–40	↓		↓		↓		↓		↓		↓		↓	
41–65	↓		↓		↓		↓		↓		↓		↓	
66–110	↓		↓		↓		↓		↓		↓		2	1.58
111–180	↓		↓		↓		↓		2	1.94	2	1.81	3	1.69
181–300	↓		↓		↓		3	2.19	3	2.07	3	1.91	4	1.80
301–500	3	2.58	3	2.49	4	2.39	4	2.30	4	2.14	5	2.05	5	1.88
501–800	4	2.65	4	2.55	5	2.46	5	2.34	6	2.23	6	2.08	7	1.95
801–1,300	5	2.69	6	2.59	6	2.49	6	2.37	7	2.25	8	2.13	8	1.96
1,301–2,200	6	2.72	6	2.58	7	2.50	7	2.38	8	2.26	9	2.13	10	1.99
2,201–3,800	7	2.77	7	2.63	8	2.54	9	2.45	9	2.29	10	2.16	11	2.01
3,801–8,000	8	2.77	8	2.64	9	2.54	10	2.45	11	2.31	12	2.18	13	2.03
8,001–22,000	10	2.83	11	2.72	11	2.59	12	2.49	13	2.35	14	2.21	16	2.07
22,001–110,000	14	2.88	15	2.77	16	2.65	17	2.54	19	2.41	21	2.27	23	2.12
110,001–550,000	19	2.92	20	2.80	22	2.69	23	2.57	25	2.43	27	2.29	30	2.14
550,001–3,000,000	27	2.96	30	2.84	31	2.72	34	2.62	37	2.47	40	2.33	44	2.17
3,000,000 and over	37	2.97	40	2.85	42	2.73	45	2.62	49	2.48	54	2.34	59	2.18
	.065		.10		.15		.25		.40		.65		1.00	
	Acceptable quality levels (tightened inspection)													

All AQL values are in per cent defective.

↓ Use first sampling plan below arrow, that is, sample size as well as k value. When sample size equals or exceeds lot size, every item in the lot must be inspected.

TABLE D-1. MASTER TABLE FOR NORMAL AND TIGHTENED INSPECTION FOR PLANS BASED ON VARIABILITY KNOWN (*Single Specification Limit—Form 1*) (*Continued*)

Lot size	Acceptable quality levels (normal inspection)													
	1.00		1.50		2.50		4.00		6.50		10.00		15.00	
	n	*k*	*n*	*k*	*n*	*k*	*n*	*k*	*n*	*k*	*n*	*k*	*n*	*k*
3–40	↓		↓		↓		↓		↓		↓		↓	
41–65	2	1.36	2	1.25	2	1.09	2	.936	3	.755	3	.573	4	.344
66–110	2	1.42	2	1.33	3	1.17	3	1.01	3	.825	4	.641	4	.429
111–180	3	1.56	3	1.44	4	1.28	4	1.11	5	.919	5	.728	6	.515
181–300	4	1.69	4	1.53	5	1.39	5	1.20	6	.991	7	.797	8	.584
301–500	6	1.78	6	1.62	7	1.45	8	1.28	9	1.07	11	.877	12	.649
501–800	7	1.80	8	1.68	9	1.49	10	1.31	12	1.11	14	.906	16	.685
801–1,300	9	1.83	10	1.70	11	1.51	13	1.34	15	1.13	17	.924	20	.706
1,301–2,200	11	1.86	12	1.72	13	1.53	15	1.35	18	1.15	21	.942	24	.719
2,201–3,800	12	1.88	14	1.75	15	1.56	18	1.38	20	1.17	24	.964	27	.737
3,801–8,000	14	1.89	15	1.75	18	1.57	20	1.38	23	1.17	27	.965	31	.741
8,001–22,000	17	1.93	19	1.79	22	1.61	25	1.42	29	1.21	33	.995	38	.770
22,001–110,000	25	1.97	28	1.84	32	1.65	36	1.46	42	1.24	49	1.03	56	.803
110,001–550,000	33	2.00	36	1.86	42	1.67	48	1.48	55	1.26	64	1.05	75	.819
550,001–3,000,000	49	2.03	54	1.89	61	1.69	70	1.51	82	1.29	95	1.07	111	.841
3,000,000 and over	65	2.04	71	1.89	81	1.70	93	1.51	109	1.29	127	1.07	147	.845
	1.50		2.50		4.00		6.50		10.00		15.00			
	Acceptable quality levels (tightened inspection)													

All AQL values are in per cent defective.

↓ Use first sampling plan below arrow, that is, sample size as well as *k* value. When sample size equals or exceeds lot size, every item in the lot must be inspected.

FIG. 12.17. The above table is a modification of Table D-1 of MIL-STD-414 in that inspection level III is used and corresponding lot sizes are incorporated directly in the body of the table.

previously, in Sec. 12.13, of felt washers. The inner diameter of these washers is the critical quality characteristic, and these inner diameters are inspected when the material is received from the vendor's plant. These washers are used to alleviate shock, so only a lower specification limit is specified. This lower limit (L) is .500 inch and an AQL of 2.5 per cent has been established for it. The process capability for this quality characteristic is known from past experience to be consistently .006 inch, or $\sigma = .001$ inch.

When a lot of 1,000 washers is received in incoming inspection, the steps that will be followed in the use of the table are as follows:

1. Select the appropriate lot size. In Fig. 12.17 it may be seen that the 1,000 unit lot falls in the 801-to-1,300 lot size.

2. Select the proper sample size (n). The proper sample size of 11 pieces is found at the intersection of the appropriate lot size (801–1,300) and an AQL of 2.5 per cent.

3. Compute the sample mean ($\bar{X}$). The inner diameters of the 11 pieces drawn at random were found to be as follows:

.502 inch	.503 inch
.501 inch	.502 inch
.502 inch	.503 inch
.504 inch	.501 inch
.500 inch	.502 inch
.502 inch	

The sample mean $\bar{X}$ that equals $\Sigma X/n$ was found to be 5.522 inch/11 = .502 inch.

4. Compute the difference between the sample mean ($\bar{X}$) and the lower

TABLE D-1. MASTER TABLE FOR NORMAL AND TIGHTENED INSPECTION FOR PLANS BASED ON VARIABILITY KNOWN (*Single Specification Limit—Form 1*)

I Lot size	Acceptable quality levels (normal inspection)													
	.04		.065 III		.10		.15		.25		.40		.65	
	II n	V k	n	k	n	k	n	k	n	k	n	k	n	k
3–40														
41–65													↓	
66–110									↓		↓		2	1.58
111–180							↓		2	1.94	2	1.81	3	1.69
181–300	↓		↓		↓		3	2.19	3	2.07	3	1.91	4	1.80
301–500	3	2.58	3	2.49	4	2.39	4	2.30	4	2.14	5	2.05	5	1.88
501–800	4	2.65	4	2.55	5	2.46	5	2.34	6	2.23	6	2.08	7	1.95
801–1,300	5	2.69	6	2.59	6	2.49	6	2.37	7	2.25	8	2.13	8	1.96
1,301–2,200	6	2.72	6	2.58	7	2.50	7	2.38	8	2.26	9	2.13	10	1.99
2,201–3,800	7	2.77	7	2.63	8	2.54	9	2.45	9	2.29	10	2.16	11	2.01
3,801–8,000	8	2.77	8	2.64	9	2.54	10	2.45	11	2.31	12	2.18	13	2.03
8,001–22,000	10	2.83	11	2.72	11	2.59	12	2.49	13	2.35	14	2.21	16	2.07
22,001–110,000	14	2.88	15	2.77	16	2.65	17	2.54	19	2.41	21	2.27	23	2.12
110,001–550,000	19	2.92	20	2.80	22	2.69	23	2.57	25	2.43	27	2.29	30	2.14
550,001–3,000,000	27	2.96	30	2.84	31	2.72	34	2.62	37	2.47	40	2.33	44	2.17
3,000,001 and over	37	2.97	40	2.85	42	2.73	45	2.62	49	2.48	54	2.34	59	2.18
	.065		.10		.15		.25		.40		.65		1.00	
	IV Acceptable quality levels (tightened inspection)													

All AQL values are in per cent defective.

↓ Use first sampling plan below arrow, that is, sample size as well as k value. When sample size equals or exceeds lot size, every item in the lot must be inspected.

TABLE D-1. MASTER TABLE FOR NORMAL AND TIGHTENED INSPECTION FOR PLANS BASED ON VARIABILITY KNOWN (*Single Specification Limit—Form 1*) (*Continued*)

I	Acceptable quality levels (normal inspection)													
Lot size	1.00		1.50 III		2.50		4.00		6.50		10.00		15.00	
	II V *n*	*k*	*n*	*k*	*n*	*k*	*n*	*k*	*n*	*k*	*n*	*k*	*n*	*k*
3–40	↓		↓		↓		↓		↓		↓		↓	
41–65	2	1.36	2	1.25	2	1.09	2	.936	3	.755	3	.573	4	.344
66–110	2	1.42	2	1.33	3	1.17	3	1.01	3	.825	4	.641	4	.429
111–180	3	1.56	3	1.44	4	1.28	4	1.11	5	.919	5	.728	6	.515
181–300	4	1.69	4	1.53	5	1.39	5	1.20	6	.991	7	.797	8	.584
301–500	6	1.78	6	1.62	7	1.45	8	1.28	9	1.07	11	.877	12	.649
501–800	7	1.80	8	1.68	9	1.49	10	1.31	12	1.11	14	.906	16	.685
801–1,300	9	1.83	10	1.70	11	1.51	13	1.34	15	1.13	17	.924	20	.706
1,301–2,200	11	1.86	12	1.72	13	1.53	15	1.35	18	1.15	21	.942	24	.719
2,201–3,800	12	1.88	14	1.75	15	1.56	18	1.38	20	1.17	24	.964	27	.737
3,801–8,000	14	1.89	15	1.75	18	1.57	20	1.38	23	1.17	27	.965	31	.741
8,001–22,000	17	1.93	19	1.79	22	1.61	25	1.42	29	1.21	33	.995	38	.770
22,001–110,000	25	1.97	28	1.84	32	1.65	36	1.46	42	1.24	49	1.03	56	.803
110,001–550,000	33	2.00	36	1.86	42	1.67	48	1.48	55	1.26	64	1.05	75	.819
550,001–3,000,000	49	2.03	54	1.89	61	1.69	70	1.51	82	1.29	95	1.07	111	.841
3,000,001 and over	65	2.04	71	1.89	81	1.70	93	1.51	109	1.29	127	1.07	147	.845
	1.50		2.50		4.00		6.50		10.00		15.00			
	IV Acceptable quality levels (tightened inspection)													

All AQL values are in per cent defective.
↓ Use first sampling plan below arrow, that is, sample size as well as k value. When sample size equals or exceeds lot size, every item in the lot must be inspected.

FIG. 12.18. The above table is a modification of Table D-1 of MIL-STD-414 in that inspection level III is used and corresponding lot sizes are incorporated directly in the body of the table.

specification limit (L) in standard deviation units $(\bar{X} - L)/\sigma$. The sample mean $\bar{X}$ is .502 inch, the lower specification limit L is .500 inch, and the standard deviation for this quality characteristic σ is .001 inch. Substituting in the formula, the result is found to be $(\bar{X} - L)/\sigma = (.502 - .500)/.001 = 2$.

5. Select the acceptability constant (k). Using Fig. 12.17, the proper acceptability constant $k = 1.51$ is found at the intersection of the appropriate lot size (801–1,300) and an AQL of 2.5 per cent.

6. Compare the difference found, $(\bar{X} - L)/\sigma$, with the acceptability constant (k). If the value $(\bar{X} - L)/\sigma$ is less than k, the lot is rejected. If $(\bar{X} - L)/\sigma$ is greater than k, the lot is accepted. In this example, $(\bar{X} - L)/\sigma = 2$ inches is greater than $k = 1.51$, so the lot is accepted.

Note that, in this example, the accept decision was made using only 11 pieces, whereas in the case of the double-sampling attribute plan shown in Sec. 12.13, a minimum of 75 pieces was required.

MIL-STD-414 considers other conditions with procedures similar to those in the above example, and, as in MIL-STD-105A, there are tightened sampling plans included in MIL-STD-414.

Process-control Sampling Tables

12.20 The Approach to Sampling for Process Control

Many parts and materials are subject to several successive machining or processing operations before they become finished units. Very often, also, products are assembled on conveyor belts where subassemblies are successively added and various operations are successively performed.

If lots of these finished units are examined for conformance to specification only after they have been completed, large quantities of defectives may very well be found. The preventive approach of total quality control has made it inevitable that "process controls" would be established over the material during the course of actual production, irrespective of any acceptance procedures for examining them after completion.

That process-control sampling is essential has been recognized in industry for some time. The existence in many shops of the so-called patrol or roving floor inspectors is proof that some action has been taken in this direction. In essence, modern process-control sampling techniques represent a better controlled and better planned form of the patrol inspection that has been carried on for many years.

The approach to these modern process-control techniques has taken several forms. When actual readings are made, the measurements-control chart has been found to be by far the most effective process-control technique. When go and not-go inspection has been carried on, per cent-defective control charts have had application and sampling tables for process control have been found particularly useful. It is to a description of these process-control sampling tables that the following discussion is devoted.

12.21 Types of Process-control Sampling Tables

Chapter 11 developed the thesis that parts can be most effectively controlled during production by examining small samples of these parts at frequent, regularly scheduled intervals. The objective of this sort of process check is to provide a continuous picture of the quality of parts being produced.

Plans that attain this objective represent a balance between inspection cost and the statistical accuracy required in indicating part quality. This balance must result in a plan wherein samples chosen are sufficiently representative and the intervals between each check are sufficiently close so that defective parts may be flagged to a stop as soon as they begin to appear in the manufacturing process.

It is this same fundamental approach around which effective process-control sampling tables have been designed. The tables specify

1. A series of sampling schedules which aim at a series of quality targets with a given degree of risk.
2. The frequency with which these samples must be selected.
3. The procedures to be used in implementing the sampling table: steps in accepting or rejecting lots, for example.

Even more than acceptance sampling tables, these process-control tables represent a compromise between practical factory circumstances and "pure" statistics. This situation results from the greater need to recognize in process-control plans such intangibles as the conscientious application of inspectors and operators in the shop and such tangibles as the stability of the process in question.

As a result, some process-control sampling tables represent nothing more than a conscientious effort to place floor inspection on a scheduled basis; others are much closer to ideal statistical sampling procedures.

Perhaps the most important difference among process-control sampling tables relates to the type of production conditions for which the tables are designed. Three major types of process tables to be found are those that apply to

1. Production under those conditions when the output of a given period—a quarter hour, a half day—can be physically segregated in individual lots for process-inspection purposes. Brackets being slotted on a milling machine may, for example, be disposed between process-inspection checks in a tote box by the side of the machine.
2. Production under those conditions when continuous manufacturing flow makes it impractical physically to segregate the output of a given period. Subassemblies being manufactured on a conveyor belt are an example here.
3. Production under those conditions when the lot for process-inspection purposes is automatically segregated during the manufacturing operation. Batch production of chemicals is an example of this type of situation.

The sections below will discuss some of the process-control sampling techniques that have been developed for these production conditions.

12.22 Process-control Table for Use When Output May Be Segregated

A process-control plan originally developed in industry has proved itself highly effective under those circumstances where it is convenient to separate the output of one period from the output of another period. Machining operations such as drilling and tapping have provided a particularly important field for use of this plan.

The plan consolidates the required process-sampling data into two tables, which are shown in Fig. 12.19.

Schedule A provides information on the frequency with which sampling should be carried on.

PROCESS CONTROL SAMPLING PLAN

SCHEDULE A: HOW OFTEN TO SAMPLE - NO. HOURS BETWEEN CHECKS

HOURLY PRODUCTION	PROCESS CONDITION		
	ERRATIC	STABLE	CONTROLLED
UNDER 10	8 HOURS	8 HOURS	8 HOURS
10-19	4 HOURS	8 HOURS	8 HOURS
20-49	2 HOURS	4 HOURS	8 HOURS
50-99	1 HOUR	2 HOURS	4 HOURS
100 AND OVER	$\frac{1}{2}$ HOUR	1 HOUR	2 HOURS

"ERRATIC" - A PROCESS THAT IS INTERMITTENTLY GOOD AND BAD, OR THAT CHANGES FROM GOOD TO BAD WITH LITTLE ADVANCE NOTICE.

"STABLE" - A PROCESS THAT GIVES FAIRLY UNIFORM PERFORMANCE, BUT HAS GRADUAL CHANGE OR DRIFT IN ONE DIRECTION DUE TO TOOL WEAR OR OTHER FACTORS.

"CONTROLLED" - A PROCESS SHOWING PAST AND PRESENT EVIDENCE OF BEING UNDER CONTROL.

SCHEDULE B: SAMPLE SIZES FOR GO-NOT GO INSPECTION

DETERMINE ACCEPTABLE QUALITY LEVEL (A.Q.L.) AS A PERCENT DEFECTIVE; SAMPLE REGULARLY ACCORDING TO SCHEDULE A; USE SAMPLE SIZES BELOW.

ACCEPTABLE QUALITY LEVEL (AQL)	SAMPLE SIZE
UNDER 1.0%	20
1.0 - 1.9%	10
2.0 - 4.9%	5
5.0 OR MORE	2

JOB IS IN CONTROL WHEN NO DEFECTS ARE FOUND IN SAMPLE; WHEN OUT OF CONTROL, CORRECT PROCESS OR START 100% INSPECTION.

FIG. 12.19.

Schedule B provides information on sample sizes appropriate to the desired acceptable quality level for the process or operation in question.

Frequency of sampling in schedule A is determined by two factors:

1. *The production rate.* This rate is simply determined by computing the average number of parts produced each hour.

2. *The condition of the process.* This condition is determined on the basis of past experience. While such descriptions as "erratic," "stable," and "controlled" are necessarily general, the placing of a particular process in one of the three classifications is usually readily accomplished with a sufficient degree of accuracy for the purpose of the plan.

The size of the sample in schedule B is determined by the AQL for the process. This AQL may be either established as described earlier in this chapter or based upon past performance with the process. Selection of AQL based upon past performance is usually the practical alternative; either cost data may not be available or computation of individual break-even points for hundreds of operations may constitute an uneconomic task.

The use of this process-control sampling table usually proceeds with the following steps:

1. An AQL is established for the process or operation in question. Frequently a single AQL is set up to apply to all processes and operations within a manufacturing area. This procedure sacrifices accuracy in individual cases, but it has the benefit of being simple and extremely economical, which tends in many situations to balance out its relative lack of accuracy.
2. Sample size for this AQL is determined from schedule B.
3. The average hourly rate of production is determined for the process or operation.
4. The frequency with which the sample check should be made is obtained from schedule A.
5. The plan is applied to actual production. Output between each process check is segregated. The required sample size is selected from the process at the required intervals. If one or more defects are found, process correction is immediately called for.
6. After the correction has been made, the same sampling procedure may be restored or it may be made somewhat more rigorous for a period of time if conditions seem to call for such action.

Selection of the units in the sample from the production process may be made in three ways:

1. The sample may be selected at random from the segregated lot of parts.
2. The sample may be selected from the parts being produced at the time of the process inspection.
3. There may be a combination of 1 and 2.

Which of these three alternatives should be used will depend upon the conditions of the individual process or operation. Repetitive punch-press operations, where the process is relatively stable for short periods of time but may have "trends" due to tool wear over longer periods, are often best controlled by the use of alternative 2. Drill-press operations carried on by relatively unskilled operators on rather crude fixtures, where the process has little "trend" during the production run but where carelessness over short periods of time may be an issue, are often best controlled by use of alternative 1. Alternative 3 is a compromise plan used in many cases.

12.23 Process-control Table for Use When Output May Be Segregated: Example

The drilling operation on a critical hole in a shoulder plate may illustrate the use of the process-control sampling table of Fig. 12.19.

Past experience has shown that this process varies intermittently from good to bad with little warning and that an AQL of 2.5 per cent should be maintained on the operation. The required sample size may thereupon be determined from schedule B in Fig. 12.19. The appropriate bracket for a 2.5 per cent AQL may be found by reading vertically down the acceptable-quality-level column to the 2.0–4.9 per cent bracket. Reading horizontally across the table to the sample size column, it will be noted that a five-unit sample size is specified.

Average hourly production of these shoulder plates is 85 units. From schedule A of Fig. 12.19, the hourly production column may be followed vertically downward until the suitable bracket is found. Eighty-five units will fall into the 50- to 99-unit bracket. Since the process varies intermittently from good to bad, a process condition of *erratic* applies here. Reading horizontally across the table to the process-condition column for erratic processes, a frequency between checks of 1 hour is specified.

Thus, with the drilling of a critical hole in the shoulder plates, the sampling condition prescribed is the selection of a sample of five units every hour.

12.24 Steps to Take in Application of This Process-control Table[15]

A series of steps are listed below that may appropriately be taken with the practical application of this process-control sampling table when the plan is being used on an over-all basis in a processing area which includes several machine tools and processing equipments:

Step 1: Determine the average number of parts processed per hour by the machines and processing equipments over which control is desired. Determine the total number of machines and equipments that may be operating at the same time in the area.

Step 2: Determine the over-all process condition for the area. Using this and the average production figures from step 1, the frequency of sampling checks can be determined from schedule A in Fig. 12.19.

Step 3: Determine the acceptable quality level for the area.

Step 4: Using the AQL decided upon, determine the sample size from schedule B in Fig. 12.19.

Step 5: Determine the average number of parts that the present inspection force can inspect per hour at the machines in this area.

[15] These steps have been noted by W. T. Short, Schenectady, N.Y., in an unpublished article.

Step 6: Using the information from steps 1 through 5, determine if the present inspection force can apply process control in the area in question. If not, determine how to solve the problem by securing more inspectors, by more effective utilization of the present force, through better gages and equipments, by loosening the process-control plan, etc.

Step 7: Establish some means for recording the results of this process sampling. Usually a card filled in by the inspection department is placed on each machine. The information filled out on the card may be

1. Operator's check number or the machine number.
2. Operation number.
3. Date.
4. Process inspector's identification.

This card is usually divided into time periods, so that the inspector can record in each space the condition of the process at that time.

Figure 12.20 illustrates a typical card used for this purpose. The face of this card carries space for such information as part drawing number, date, and machine number. For each time interval—7:00, 7:30—there are spaces for recording process condition in three categories:

1. "O.K.," that is, whether the parts checked are within tolerance.
2. "High," that is, whether the parts checked are above tolerance.
3. "Low," that is, whether the parts checked are below tolerance.

A column for "Reason" is provided wherein the number code for types of rejects, which is listed on the back of the card, can be used when a process is stopped. The "Stop" column is provided so that it can be punched when the operation is stopped for any cause.

The "S/U" column is included on the card, so that it can be punched when inspection approval has been given to the initial setup parts at the start of the production run. The "Idle" column is printed on the card so that it can be punched if the machine is not operating when the inspector reaches it on his route.

Step 8: Start the process-control sampling plan by filling out appropriate cards similar to the one shown in Fig. 12.20 for each operation or machine for which the plan is being established. Place these tags on an appropriate location on the machines in question.

Step 9: Check the first production units as the operation is being set up. The process inspector should either approve the operation setup or refuse to let it start until the process is corrected to produce satisfactory parts. In the case of the card in Fig. 12.20, he will punch the "S/U" column when he approves the operation.

Step 10: After this approval the operator runs the job, checking his work as he feels necessary or, if the job is on an incentive plan, checking the work as he may be paid in the time-studied price. As parts are completed, the operator disposes them in a tote box provided beside his machine for that purpose. If the operator finds defective parts, the process should obviously be corrected.

Step 11: At the end of the proper interval of time, the inspector checks the required sample size for the job. These parts may be selected either

SPECIAL MFG. DIVISION
INSPECTION

DWG. NO. ____________ DATE ________

MACHINE ____________ OPERATION# ________

STATION# ____________ INSPECTOR ________

OPERATOR CHECK NO. ____________

WITHIN TOLERANCE			TIME	REASON	STOP	S/U	IDLE
HIGH	O.K.	LOW					
			7:00				
			7:30				
			8:00				
			8:30				
			9:00				
			9:30				
			10:00				
			10:30				
			11:00				
			11:30				
			12:00				
			12:30				
			1:00				
			1:30				
			2:00				
			2:30				
			3:00				
			3:30				
			4:00				
			4:30				
			5:00				
			5:30				
			6:00				
			6:30				
			7:00				
			7:30				
			8:00				
			8:30				
			9:00				
			9:30				
			10:00				
			10:30				
			11:00				
			11:30				
			12:00				
			12:30				

FRONT

MACHINE ROOM

1-OVERSIZE	9-DEF. MATERIAL
2-UNDERSIZE	10-BROKEN TAP
3-DEF. FIXTURE	11-BROKEN DRILL
4-ANGLE WRONG	12-BROKEN TOOL
5-DEF. CLS.	13-DEF. CUTTER
6-DEPTH OF HOLE	14-
7-DEF. BURRING	15-
8-DEF. FINISH	16-

PUNCH PRESS

17-ANGLE WRONG	22-UNDERSIZE
18-HOLES OFF. LOC.	23-DEF. MATERIAL
19-BURRS	24-DEF. FIXTURES
20-OVERSIZE	25-
21-UNDERSIZE	26-

SPOT WELD AND BRAZE

27-FLASH	32-DEF. FIXTURE
28-BURNING	33-WELD STRENGTH
29-ALIGNMENT	34-
30-SURFACE COND.	35-
31-DEF. WELD	36-

SHEET METAL

37-OUT OF SQUARE	51-WELD STRENGTH
38-OVERSIZE	52-UNDER CUT
39-UNDERSIZE	53-EXTRA WELDS
40-OMISSIONS	54-POOR GRIND
41-BURRS	55-ROUGH GRIND
42-WARPED	56-DEEP GRIND
43-DEF. MATERIAL	57-DEF. CORNERS
44-DEF. FINISH	58-SHARP EDGES
45-LOCATION	59-DEF. KNOCK OUTS
46-BROKEN WELD	60-
47-DEEP SPOTS	61-
48-FLASH	62-
49-BURNING	63-
50-DEF. FIXTURE	64-

COILS

65-O. DIAMETER	75-TERMINALS
66-I. DIAMETER	76-HARDWARE
67-LENGTH	77-NAMEPLATE
68-INSIDE LENGTH	78-EXPOSED WINDING
69-OUTSIDE LENGTH	79-POOR APPEARANCES
70-INSIDE WIDTH	80-LOOSE COVERING
71-OUTSIDE WIDTH	81-
72-OVER-ALL LENGTH	82-
73-STAMPING	83-
74-LEADS	84-

BACK

A TYPICAL PROCESS CONTROL CARD

FIG. 12.20.

as the pieces that have just been produced by the machine or at random from the tote box. The choice of which of these two means of sample selection should be employed will depend upon the nature of the job and process (see Sec. 12.22).

If no rejects are found, the inspector disposes the parts that have accumulated since his last check into a "completed-work" tote box. With use of the card in Fig. 12.20, he will punch the card "O.K."

Step 12: If a reject is found, the inspector notifies the proper authority —usually the foreman—to get the process corrected immediately. He may place a "defective tag" on the parts that have accumulated since the last check. It may be the responsibility of the operator to sort these parts or, under some systems, for the factory foreman to have them sorted. In the card in Fig. 12.20 the inspector will record the appropriate reject number in the "Reason" space. He will also punch either the "High" space or the "Low" space or possibly both.

Step 13: Whenever the process is stopped to adjust or change the tooling, the procedure of step 9 is followed, as in the case of a new setup.

Step 14: The data on the tags may periodically be analyzed in any of several fashions. There may be daily or weekly breakdowns of reject causes, adjustment of the sampling schedules, examinations of the amount of idle time with the machines and equipments in question. Discussion of analyses of this sort will be deferred for the product-control material of Chap. 17.

It may be worth emphasizing that the process-control sampling table discussed in Secs. 12.22 to 12.24 is a plan that has been developed to meet the needs of the particular factories for which it was designed. There is, for example, no magic in its specification that certain types of processes be checked only every 8 hours; this figure was based upon the fact that the shops worked 8-hour shifts. The fact that the schedules of Fig. 12.19 concentrate chiefly upon production quantities of less than 100 units per hour results from the situation that the shops in question operate at relatively low average hourly production quantities.

The form of process-control sampling tables depends upon the conditions of individual shops rather than chiefly upon any abstract statistical sampling conditions. It is important that this fact be recognized by those factories who are developing applications of such tables for their own shops.

12.25 A "Random-order" Process-control Plan

A somewhat different approach to process control is a random-order plan originally developed by Dodge.[16] This plan is particularly effective when applied to continuous production of parts or subassemblies flowing forward on a conveyor, where it may not be practical physically to segregate lots for process sampling purposes.

[16] Dodge, H. F., "A Sampling Inspection Plan for Continuous Production," *Annals of Mathematical Statistics,* Vol. 14, pp. 264–279, 1943, and *Transactions of the American Society of Mechanical Engineers,* Vol. 66, pp. 127–133, 1944.

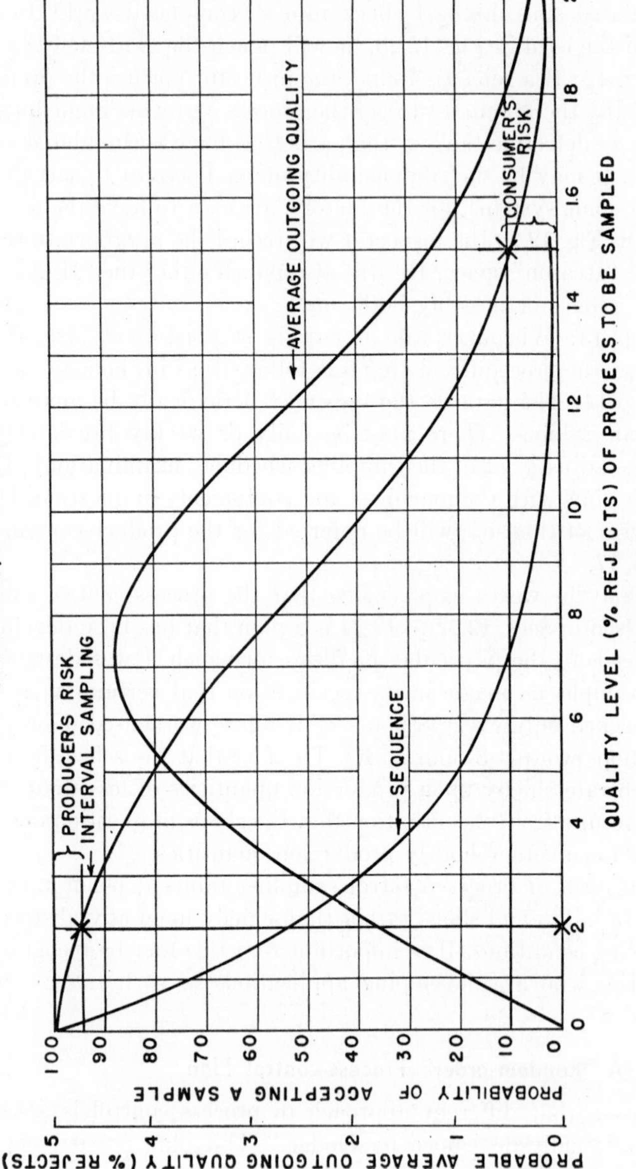

OPERATING CHARACTERISTIC
SEQUENCE = 32 PIECES; INTERVAL = 18
AQL = 2%; LTPD 15%
PRODUCER'S RISK
INTERVAL SAMPLING
AVERAGE OUTGOING QUALITY
CONSUMER'S RISK
SEQUENCE
PROBABILITY OF ACCEPTING A SAMPLE
PROBABLE AVERAGE OUTGOING QUALITY (% REJECTS)
QUALITY LEVEL (% REJECTS) OF PROCESS TO BE SAMPLED
100
90
80
70
60
50
40
30
20
10
0
5
4
3
2
1
0
2
4
6
8
10
12
14
16
18
20

FIG. 12.21.

In its general form, this plan calls for the examination of a consecutive flow of parts, usually as production is starting. If no defects are found, then one out of a certain number of parts coming down the conveyor is examined—one part "every interval," as it is termed in the plan.

If the parts being sampled are found to be satisfactory, this sampling procedure is continued. If a defect is found, then a new sequence of consecutive parts must be examined. If no defects are found in this sequence, interval sampling may be started again.

In Dodge's original plan, all defective units found must be replaced with good units. The plan provides the average outgoing quality limit as the quality target.

Modifications were made on the original plan by Dodge and Torrey.[17] These modifications are designed to reduce the probability of returning to a large 100 per cent inspection because of an occasional defective unit.

Ross[18] has made an interesting adaptation of this type of process-control plan. His plan is designed around the following characteristics:

1. An AQL of 2 per cent at a producer's risk of 5 per cent.

2. A lot tolerance per cent defective of 15 per cent at a consumer's risk of 10 per cent.

Figure 12.21 shows the operating characteristic for this particular plan. It also shows the curve for average outgoing quality that is associated with it.

The sampling schedule developed under this plan requires the inspection of a continuous flow, or "sequence," of 32 parts without a reject. Then 1 part in every 18 is checked until a defect is found.

When a defect is found, a new sequence of 32 pieces without a reject must be found. Because this plan is based upon individual lot protection of the AQL type (see Sec. 12.8) rather than protection of over-all output as in the Dodge AOQL plan, it is not necessary to replace the defective units found in order to maintain the statistical accuracy of the plan.

12.26 Other Process-control Sampling Plans

The process-control plans that have been discussed above are merely a few out of many. Plans have been developed for batch production, for specific foundry applications, for many other situations.

Four other useful approaches to process control will be only briefly noted:

1. The continuous production sampling plans of Wald and Wolfowitz.[19]

[17] Dodge, H. F., and M. N. Torrey, "Additional Continuous Sampling Inspection Plans," *Industrial Quality Control,* Vol. VII, No. 5, March, 1951.

[18] "Out of the Darkness with Scientific Sampling," unpublished paper by K. E. Ross, Fort Wayne, Ind.

[19] The reader may see the original discussion of this plan in A. Wald and J. Wolfowitz, "Sampling Inspection Plans for Continuous Production, Which Insures

2. The "first piece and patrol inspection" plans written of by Manuele.[20]

3. Continuous sampling procedures without control.[21]

4. Multilevel continuous sampling plans of Lieberman and Solomon.[22]

The interested reader may secure information on these plans from the annotated references.

Sampling Tables in Action

12.27 The Relation of Process-control Sampling to Acceptance Sampling

Whenever both process-control sampling and acceptance sampling plans are established in a factory, two questions almost inevitably arise:

1. Why bother with both types of sampling table—why not use only one? Are not the objectives of process-control and acceptance sampling overlapping? Are not acceptance sampling tables fully as economical for process-control purposes as are process-control tables?

2. Is it not uneconomical duplication of effort successively to use both process-control and acceptance sampling procedures on the parts produced within the same factory area by the same manufacturer?

These questions will be discussed in order:

1. In an abstract sense, of course, the objectives of process-control and acceptance sampling techniques are similar. They both aim to aid in the production of satisfactory parts and in the prevention of the production of unsatisfactory ones.

From a practical point of view, however, the purpose served by process-control techniques is very different from that served by acceptance techniques. One is developed to aid in the control of the quality of material during the course of its production; the other to aid in determining the acceptability of lots of finished materials.

Agreeing that the purpose served by the two techniques is different does not tell the complete story; the forms of the techniques themselves are considerably different, and they cannot be used interchangeably in every instance. It is often impractical and certainly frequently uneconomical to use acceptance sampling tables for process-control purposes. Lot sizes

---

a Prescribed Limit on Outgoing Quality," *Annals of Mathematical Statistics*, Vol. 16, pp. 30–49, 1945.

[20] The reader may see one discussion of this plan by Joseph Manuele, "Elementary Principles of Controlling Quality of Product during Manufacture," *The Glass Industry*, Vol. 25, pp. 450–454, October, 1944.

[21] Technical Report No. 39, Applied Mathematics and Statistics Laboratory, Stanford University, 1958.

[22] Lieberman, G. J., and H. Solomon, "Multi-level Continuous Sampling Plans," *Annals of Mathematical Statistics*, Vol. 26, No. 4, December, 1955.

and sample sizes are often too high, and the required acceptance and rejection procedure is often inadequate.

By the same token, process-control sampling tables are equally impractical and uneconomical for use in acceptance sampling. Both sample and lot sizes may be much too small for economy, and acceptance and rejection procedure will probably be inapplicable.

There is a place for both process-control and acceptance sampling tables in a factory program of controlling the quality of its products; the place for one of these techniques cannot be usurped by the other without loss of economy and sampling effectiveness.

2. It is most certainly an uneconomical duplication of effort, in many instances, successively to use both process-control and acceptance sampling plans on parts from the same production area.

There is justification for the use of both techniques when acceptance sampling tables are used as a check upon the effectiveness of newly established process-control plans. It is also justifiable to use acceptance procedures occasionally to audit the quality results in an area in which process-control sampling tables are in use.

These are, however, exceptions; in general, a manufacturer should find no need to follow up process-control techniques with acceptance sampling on the parts from the same factory area.

Acceptance sampling tables often enjoy maximum value in control over parts and materials received from sources external to the factory—over whose production the factory has a minimum of control. Process-control sampling tables enjoy their maximum value in use with the internally manufactured parts and materials over which the factory does have full control.

12.28 Some Practical Aspects of Sampling Tables

Perhaps the most typical practical problem encountered in the use of sampling tables is the tendency toward their misapplication. Acceptance plans are frequently used for process-control purposes; a plan established for a certain AQL and a given process condition is suddenly set up as "the" sampling plan for the entire factory; the existence of reduced sampling schedules may be discovered, and they may be applied to a wide variety of sampling conditions whether or not they are applicable.

In many plants there is a constant struggle to reduce sample sizes and to give "general adaptation" to sampling plans that have been established for certain specific purposes. This objective is both practical and necessary for factory purposes, but it takes a fine sense of judgment on the part of plant personnel to decide how far, if at all, it is possible and feasible to go with such "general adaptations."

It is very interesting to note that this misuse, or perhaps "overuse," of sampling tables is frequently encountered in those plants where the original introduction of scientific sampling encountered its greatest difficulty. It is possible that the problem of misapplication of the plans is, at least in part, due to the basis upon which the plans were originally "sold" to the factory. If, to overwhelm resistance, they were presented as general cure-alls, to be applied under any and all circumstances, the tendency on the part of the shop to apply them in such a fashion is only natural.

The most important cure for this problem of misapplication is, therefore, prevention—proper introduction of the plans and adequate education in their limitations. Sampling tables usually have sufficiently great advantages over existing spot-checking procedures so that their merits can be fairly presented without having to gloss over their limitations. It is of equal importance that the selection and approval of the sampling plans used be placed in the hands of an individual or individuals who are familiar with both the practical and statistical aspects of this tool.

Another problem frequently seen in connection with sampling plans is the attitude that the sampling job is adequately done when a sampling table has been developed or selected. The importance of proper measuring and gaging equipments to successful application of sampling plans seems so obvious as to be scarcely worthy of mention. Yet it is not uncommon to see a great deal of attention devoted in a plant to the development of sampling tables and supporting records, while allowing that sampling be done with worn, outmoded, cumbersome gages or measuring equipments. The proper selection of these equipments and gages is fully as important as the design of the sampling plan with which they will be used.

Also of importance is the proper training of the inspectors and operators in the use and meaning of sampling tables. This training is too often done superficially, resulting in improper use of the sampling plans.

That this situation may exist was brought forcibly home to an inspection supervisor in one factory. He had explained to his inspection force quite briefly—and, he thought, quite fully—the meaning of the double-sampling plan that he had asked them to use in place of 100 per cent inspection. Several days after this explanation, he was stopped by one usually conscientious inspector, who told the supervisor that he liked the sampling plan very well and that he could certainly see that it was aiding in his examining many more lots than he had previously been able to check under 100 per cent inspection procedures. This inspector felt, however, that he had a suggestion whereby the double-sampling plan in use might be even more thoroughly streamlined.

The supervisor eagerly asked for the man's suggestion. He was told that the inspector just could not see the sense in always taking a second sample even though the first sample had shown the lot of material to be satisfactory. Therefore, suggested the inspector, why not make taking of the second sample dependent upon the results of the first sample?

The supervisor had thought that such a double-sampling fundamental as selection of a second sample only upon the basis of evidence from the first sample had been clearly explained to his inspection group. He was astounded by the lack of knowledge of double sampling expressed by his inspector's suggestion. Needless to say, the supervisor scheduled a series of additional meetings for the purpose of instructing his men in the fundamentals of modern sampling plans.

The supervisor should not have been so thoroughly surprised at the lack of insight exhibited by his man; no matter how simplified sampling plans may be made, for their effective application they must still be thoroughly explained to those who will use them. While the supervisor-inspector example cited above is an extreme one, variations on it may be found in many factories whose personnel have not been satisfactorily grounded in the use of statistical sampling procedures.

Another matter the importance of which is frequently overlooked in determining the over-all economy of a given sampling plan is the adequacy of the drawing specification for the characteristic that is being sampled. This is of particular importance in those instances where specifications have been "picked out of the air" and where they may not really be indicative of whether or not the part will be satisfactory for its particular application.

How substantial may be this problem can be illustrated as follows: Results of identical economy can be achieved by inspecting a part characteristic to a tolerance of ± 0.005 inch using a 1 per cent AQL plan, and by inspecting the characteristic to a tolerance of ± 0.004 inch using a 5 per cent AQL plan. The difference in the AQL which is applicable when a change in tolerance of ± 0.001 inch has been made is startling to those who have not previously squarely faced this issue. It leads to this conclusion: determination of the particular sampling plan which is most economical for a given situation is most effectively accomplished when the adequacy of the part specification involved is itself first critically examined before the sampling plan is chosen.

Other practical issues in the application of sampling plans—forms for recording sample results, techniques for the fullest employment of sampling tables—will be discussed in Part Five, Applying Quality Control in the Company.

12.29 Practical Applications of Sampling Tables

The variety of applications possible with sampling tables is almost unlimited. These sampling applications have ranged from standard uses of acceptance tables in the receiving of incoming material to the development of sampling plans for use by factory technical staffs in the product appraisal "life test" of units selected just previous to shipment.

The three examples that will be discussed below cover three of the more usual of sampling plan applications:

1. Reducing the incoming-material inspection force (see Sec. 12.30).
2. Separating the vendors of products of satisfactory quality from those who sell products of spotty quality (see Sec. 12.31).
3. Reducing the number of rejects from factory processing operations (see Sec. 12.32).

12.30 Reducing the Incoming-material Inspection Force[23]

Certain types of complex electronic equipments require for their assembly a wide variety of component parts. When these equipments are produced in large numbers, the problem of assurance that the quality of the many components purchased from outside vendors is of an acceptable standard becomes a major one. Examination of each one of these parts is both an expensive and an extremely lengthy procedure, requiring a very large staff of inspectors.

The problem faced by a factory manufacturing these electronic equipments was, therefore, that of devising an economical system of determining whether or not incoming lots were of a quality level satisfactory for use in assembly operations so that the incoming-material inspection force might be reduced to a reasonable number.

A decision was made to establish a type of sampling procedure which would be sufficiently general in scope to minimize the problem of its administration and yet sufficiently rigorous that only an acceptable per cent defective might be allowed to enter the assembly areas. These defective parts would be detected during the course of test and assembly, so that the problem was one of internal factory economy rather than one of running the danger of customer ill will by shipping equipments with defective component parts.

The factory chief inspector developed for this purpose a Columbia-type double-sampling table. On an experience basis, a $\frac{1}{4}$ per cent acceptable quality level was indicated for a number of the key components. Cost data were unavailable for most of the parts. Even if they had been available, the inspector reasoned, he would be better off to establish one value for AQL which would be generally applicable on an experience basis than to run the risk of administrative confusion by establishing a number of individual AQLs. He therefore established the $\frac{1}{4}$ per cent schedule in his Columbia-type table as the AQL for all incoming parts subject to inspection.

[23] Based upon an application carried on by H. C. Thompson and associates, Schenectady, N.Y.

In connection with use of the plan, the chief inspector also developed a card for recording sampling results, the front and back of which is shown in Fig. 12.22.

The sampling plan was first introduced on a small number of parts and then was gradually expanded until it covered almost all electronic equipment component parts that were subject to inspection. Inspectors were carefully instructed in the use and application of the sampling plan, and their efforts were carefully supervised by the chief inspector during the early stages of the plan.

After 15 months of operation, the factory unanimously agreed that the double-sampling plan had satisfactorily solved its incoming inspection problem on electronic equipment components. Many thousands of dollars in inspection expense had been saved, and the chief inspector concluded that he was actually obtaining better inspection with the ¼ per cent AQL plan than under the old 100 per cent inspection system. He advanced at least two reasons for this conclusion:

1. The rigorous procedure attendant upon a sampling plan, including the maintenance of card records, makes it easier for an inspector to know what characteristics are really of greatest importance to his job of examining the parts in question. For example, the card in Fig. 12.22 listed the critical dimensions to be checked on each part and so did not leave this selection in doubt by use of the sometimes vague "100 per cent inspection required" statement.

2. When an operator is required to inspect only a small number of similar parts, the probability of error due to fatigue is much less than if he is required to inspect a large number of these parts. The caliber of the inspection job is, therefore, likely to be higher.

12.31 Location of Unsatisfactory Vendors of Small Castings[24]

Even though apparatus may be produced on a job-lot basis, it is still perfectly possible that the component parts used on the apparatus may be purchased in sufficient quantity to make a sampling procedure useful. One such example is to be found on a large rotating apparatus, which uses a small casting called a brush holder. Each piece of apparatus uses a large number of brush holders, so the castings are purchased in quantity. While these brush holders are purchased in varying quantities and varying sizes, the characteristics that are important when the holder is assembled to the apparatus are quite similar in all types of the casting.

The factory producing the rotating apparatus had been experiencing large manufacturing losses due to these brush holders being defective after assembly. It was felt that these losses were primarily due to the poor condition in which the brush holders were received from the vendors.

[24] Based upon a study by L. T. Stafford and associates, Schenectady, N.Y.

$\frac{1}{4}$ %

INCOMING MATERIAL INSPECTION RECORD

SAMPLING TABLE		AQL = $\frac{1}{4}$ %	
LOT SIZE	n_1	n_2	c_1 c_2
UNDER 25	7	14	X
25 – 50	10	20	X
50 – 100	13	26	X
100 – 200	20	40	X
200 – 300	25	50	↓
300 – 500	35	70	↓
500 – 800	50	100	↓
800 – 1300	75	150	0 1
1300 – 3200	100	200	0 2
3200 – 8000	150	300	1 2
8000 – 22000	200	400	1 3
22000 – 110000	300	600	1 5
110000 – 550000	500	1000	3 7
550000 & OVER	1000	2000	5 12

(X) USE SINGLE SAMPLING PLAN

(↓) USE FIRST SAMPLING PLAN BELOW ARROW

DRG. NO. X231132

PART COIL

VENDORS

A – JONES COIL CO.

B – BROWN WIRE MFG'S.

C – SMITH PRODUCTS CO.

COMMENTS

FUNCTIONAL DIMENSIONS:

X – $\frac{1}{2}$" ± .005 – I.D. OF HOLE

Y – 2' ± $\frac{1}{32}$" COIL HEIGHT

CHECKING FIXTURE: 24317

FRONT

NO.	VEN-DOR	DATE	LOT SIZE	NO. INSP.	NO. FD DEF.	DISPOSITION PASS	REP.	REJ.	INSPECTOR
1	B	1/10	5000	150	1 - Y 0 - X	✓			A.B.C.
2	A	2/5	825	75	0 - Y 0 - X	✓			A.B.C.
3	C	2/5	1000	225	2 - Y 0 - X			✓	A.B.C.
4	B	2/5	1000	75	0 - Y 0 - X	✓			M.A.D.
5	A	3/6	2000	300	2 - Y 1 - X	✓			A.B.C.
6	C	3/8	1000	75	2 - Y 0 - X			✓	M.A.D.
7	B	3/10	200	25	0 - Y 0 - X	✓			M.A.D.
8									
9									
10									

BACK

FIG. 12.22.

The factory was purchasing its brush holders from three different vendors, and although there was an incoming inspection procedure on these holders, no records were available as to which of the vendors were responsible for the poor quality of the holders.

It was decided to institute an acceptance sampling plan on the holders as they were received from the vendors and to record the results of the sampling on suitable record cards. A 2.5 per cent acceptable quality level was decided upon to cover all characteristics of the brush holders. It was further decided that all brush-holder shipments that did not meet the sampling test would not be sorted but would be shipped back to the vendors, production warranting. The three vendors were so informed and agreed to the procedure.

The results of the sampling plan were soon forthcoming. Sampling record cards indicated that two of the three vendors were consistently meeting the 2.5 per cent AQL sampling plan and that one of the vendors was just as consistently not meeting the plan. The factory purchasing representative discussed this situation quite pointedly with the vendor in question, who improved his processing techniques and came on a par with the quality of the shipments from the other vendors.

As soon as the holders from the unsatisfactory vendor were eliminated from the production stream because of the improvement in his process, the losses of the factory due to this cause dropped off sharply and have remained low. The 2.5 per cent AQL sampling plan has been retained, however, since the factory was certain that it helped assure them of the quality of this important production component.

12.32 Reducing Rejects with Process Control

Recently the machining section of a factory manufacturing electrical devices subjected its production parts to a 100 per cent inspection after they had been completed. It was felt that this rigorous inspection was necessary to prevent any bad parts at all from being received in the assembly area.

Yet bad parts were received by the assembly area in spite of the large amount of inspection that was being applied to them. The decision was made, therefore, that the factory would try an acceptance sampling plan for these parts so that the final inspection force might be reduced, permitting some inspectors to be freed for service as floor inspectors on the machines. It was felt that these floor inspectors would eliminate the rejects at their source.

A MIL-STD-105A acceptance plan was selected, and different values for AQL were applied to various parts. The sampling procedure was established so that those lots which were rejected under the sampling plan would be 100 per cent sorted in the inspection area.

The acceptance plan resulted in some decrease in the final inspection force. But the decrease was not so great as was desired, largely because about 25 to 30 per cent of the lots received failed to pass sampling inspection and so had to be 100 per cent sorted. The parts were small, and there was no means for identifying the machine or operator that had performed the defective operations—each part had an average of 10 different operations, and there simply was not room on the parts for identification marks for the source of each operation. As a result, corrective action in reducing the rejects on the floor was hampered in that there were few positive guides to the actual source of the defective parts.

While some inspectors had been released for duty on the floor, their effectiveness seemed open to question. Little change was noted in the number of rejected lots after these floor inspectors had been in action for several weeks. It was felt that this situation resulted, at least in part, from the hit-or-miss activity of these inspectors.

It was decided, therefore, that the services of these inspectors might better be utilized if a process-control sampling plan were established for the machining area. A sampling plan was devised, very similar in its detail to that shown in Fig. 12.19. The general policy was established for the machine floor that

1. There would be first-piece inspection before a job was allowed to run.

2. The operators would, after this approval, deposit their output into a small tote box.

3. The floor inspector would visit each machine each hour and would examine 10 pieces from the tote box.

4. If no rejects were found, the inspector would dispose the contents of the tote box into a finished work tray. If one or more rejects were found, the foreman would be notified. The foreman would stop the machine if required, have the correction made, and have the parts in the tote box sorted.

5. When the machine was started again, the procedure in 1 above would be repeated.

There were many initial problems in establishing this plan, such as the temptation by all concerned to dispose parts into the finished work tray whether or not they had been inspected. In a period of 6 weeks, however, the number of rejected lots in the final inspection cage had dropped from the 25 to 30 per cent figure to a negligible value. It was later possible to omit entirely the acceptance sampling procedure that had been established earlier and to base assurance of the quality of the parts upon the process-control sampling routine.

The results of this program were a steep decline in the losses caused by rejected parts and also a decrease in the over-all amount of inspection required.

The factory concluded that these results were possible from process-control sampling as opposed to acceptance sampling for the following reason: process sampling could detect and prevent the production of defective work, whereas acceptance sampling could merely reject the parts some time after they had been completed and merely hope for corrective action by reporting these rejections back to the shop floor.

CHAPTER 13

SPECIAL METHODS

Will methods change A make a greater quality improvement in the production process than will methods change B? Do engineers have to assume for their product designs that tolerances of mating parts "build up" arithmetically during production assembly of these parts? Can they take advantage of some more economical form of tolerance buildup?

Are there any graphical methods which simplify the analysis of data taken during investigations of technical quality problems? Do differences in testers' skills account for "significant differences" in the test readings of similar apparatus?

Such problems as these arise almost inevitably in total quality-control programs. It is their solution that is the objective of statistical special methods.

13.1 The Needs Satisfied by Special Methods

A shop may be experiencing quality difficulties on an operation for the heat-treatment of castings. It may be suspected that the critical factor in casting quality at this operation is the temperature maintained in the heat-treat furnace.

The manufacturing engineer may run through the furnace a series of samples, each composed of several castings, to determine the effect of different temperatures on casting quality. One of the temperatures tried may seem to produce somewhat higher quality castings than do other temperatures.

The manufacturing engineer may wonder if this quality improvement is "real"; is the difference between the effect of this temperature and all others "significant" as far as casting quality is concerned? Bitter previous experience may have convinced him of the risks involved in coming to general conclusions from the results of tests using samples of small size. He knows that such risks become particularly dangerous when there is involved, as in this case, the authorization of a sum of money to make a process change which may not actually make for any improvement in the quality of heat-treated castings on a production basis.

The manufacturing engineer may vaguely feel that there "must be" some statistical technique that will be helpful to him in making a decision based upon "significance" of the results obtained from his samples of castings. Yet such standard methods as he may know of do not seem applicable to his problem. The frequency distribution does not appear to him to be useful, or the control chart or sampling tables.

The manufacturing engineer may even wonder if the very basis upon which he conducted his series of sampling tests has been sound. Was his effort to hold all factors constant except furnace temperature wise and reasonable? In effect, was his experiment properly designed?

The statistical technique for which the manufacturing engineer is looking is probably to be found among the variety of special methods that have gradually been hewn out of the mass of mathematical statistics for use in just such quality investigations as that of the castings. These special methods have demonstrated great effectiveness in analyses of a wide range of product quality problems.

Special methods include techniques like "tests of significance" which would be helpful to the manufacturing engineer faced with the heat-treat problem. Special methods are also useful as guides in establishing sampling test programs that will yield the maximum of information with the minimum of time and money, usually termed the *design of experiments;* in determining whether there is an observable relationship between variables—*correlation;* and as an approach to the establishment of tolerances for parts and materials—*tolerance analysis.* Special methods also relate to the use of "probability paper" and other graphical techniques.

The mathematics attached to some of these methods is sometimes more complex than that associated with the statistical tools described in Chaps. 10 to 12. This mathematics may, in many instances, be most effectively used by trained statisticians. But the point of view represented by special methods is probably more important than the technical methods themselves, and this point of view may be readily acquired and applied by those with little or no formal statistical training.

It is the purpose of this chapter to make a survey of the general nature of the more important special methods, with emphasis upon their point of view, and to discuss in detail a few of the more powerful of these techniques.

13.2 The General Nature of Special Methods

Special Methods may be broadly classified in two ways:

Graphical Special Methods. These consist of a variety of techniques which concentrate upon pictorial presentation of quality data in such a form that the picture itself furnishes the basis for decision and action.

Graphical special methods are essentially shorthand techniques. They consist of unique means for tabulating and plotting quality data. As such, their nature and applications are straightforward, and their use requires only an understanding of some relatively simple procedures. Several of these graphical methods have been used for many years in industry. Sections 13.3 to 13.6 will discuss this portion of special methods.

Analytical Special Methods. These consist of a variety of techniques which concentrate upon mathematical analysis of quality data.

Analytical special methods are built around what is basically a philosophy toward the analysis of data. The mathematics and other procedures associated with this portion of special methods may be of secondary importance in the factory to the philosophy that is used and developed by their application.

Unlike the graphical methods, these analytical techniques are new to most of industry. They fill a need in the design and analysis of quality data that had not previously been adequately met in industrial quality-control applications. Sections 13.7 to 13.12 will discuss analytical special methods.

Graphical Special Methods

13.3 Graphical Presentation of Frequency-distribution Data

Frequency-distribution data are usually presented in the standard form that is shown in Fig. 13.1. As was pointed out in Chap. 10, this method of presentation is normally used for pictorial presentation and also during the calculation of the measures of central tendency and spread of a frequency-distribution sample.

In place of this method of presentation, a somewhat different treatment may be used during the determination of these measures. This graphical method often involves a simplification in computation. It consists of presenting the data in cumulative form, such that the percentage of values falling below a given value is plotted against the value.

The plots may be made on either standard rectangular or rectilinear graph paper or on graph paper known as *probability paper,* specially designed for this purpose. Thus, the data of Fig. 13.1 can be plotted on rectangular coordinate paper, as in Fig. 13.2, or on probability paper, as in Fig. 13.3.[1]

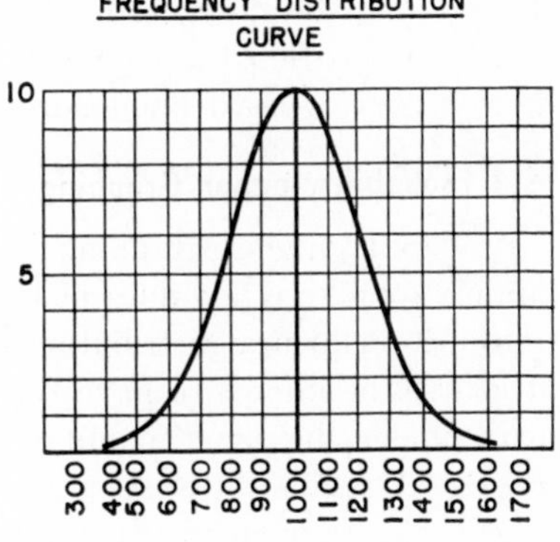

FIG. 13.1.

Both the rectangular coordinate and the probability-paper presentations lend themselves to smoothing out sampling errors and to enabling fair estimates to be made of measures of spread and central tendency. The rectangular coordinate presentation is particularly useful in determining the median and in estimating the average. Probability paper is often of more general utility, however, and it will be discussed in Secs. 13.4 and 13.5 below.

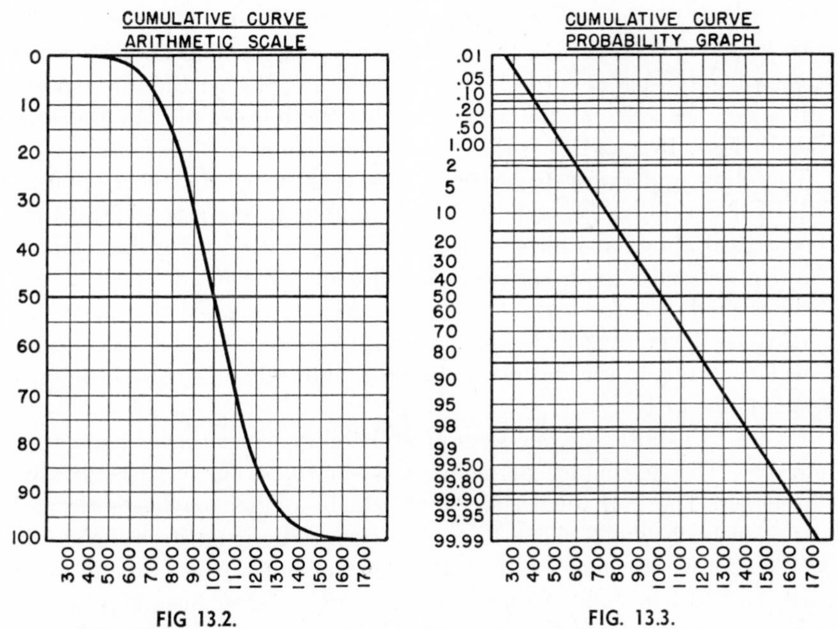

FIG 13.2.

FIG. 13.3.

In analyzing skewed or nonsymmetrical frequency distributions which depart very widely from the shape of the normal curve, this graphical

[1] Much of this probability-paper analysis is after the discussion by W. H. Abbott, Cleveland, Ohio, in an excellent paper "Use of Probability Charts in the Study of Distribution and the Determination of Sigma."

method may be more accurate and more meaningful than undiscriminating application of the more conventional methods applied to these skewed curves based upon normal-curve analysis.

13.4 Probability-paper Graphing

Probability-paper graphing is an extremely useful means for determining approximate values of the average, median, and standard deviation of a frequency-distribution sample. The data in this sample should, of course, be known to have come from a homogeneous source—articles made under the same manufacturing conditions, drawn from the same lot, etc. A probability-paper graph will also show, at a glance, just how closely the frequency distribution in question approaches the shape of the normal curve. It is thus very useful in deciding whether or not a given sample of data can be used in a standardized computation which assumes a fairly close approach to normality in the data used.

Probability paper is a form of graph paper whose scales are so adjusted that a perfectly normal frequency distribution will plot as a straight line. One of the two scales—it may be either the vertical or the horizontal—is laid out in the usual arithmetic fashion found on the standard graph-paper forms. On this scale are plotted the appropriate values for the cells of the frequency-distribution sample. In the case of both Figs. 13.2 and 13.3, this arithmetic scale is the horizontal.[2]

The other probability-paper scale is so constructed that normal-curve data will develop a straight line on the graph. In the case of Fig. 13.2, the vertical scale, on which is plotted the percentage of readings falling below given cell values, has been established in the standard arithmetic fashion, and the resulting curve has taken a reversed-S shape. The vertical scale in Fig. 13.3—the probability graph—has been so established that this curve has been flattened into what is substantially a straight line.

Figure 13.4 illustrates one form of probability paper that is popular in industry. The percentage of readings is shown on the vertical axis on this paper. The individual cell values can be plotted on the horizontal axis. The 1-, 2-, and 3-sigma lines have been so designated on the graph.

Other forms of commercially available probability paper usually differ from Fig. 13.4 in only two major respects: the sigma lines may not be so designated, and the horizontal and vertical scales of Fig. 13.4 may be reversed. Figure 13.5 shows such a form of probability paper. The various sigma lines can be established on this type of form, if so desired, by drawing them in at the required points.

[2] In some instances of probability-paper application, a logarithmic scale may be used here also.

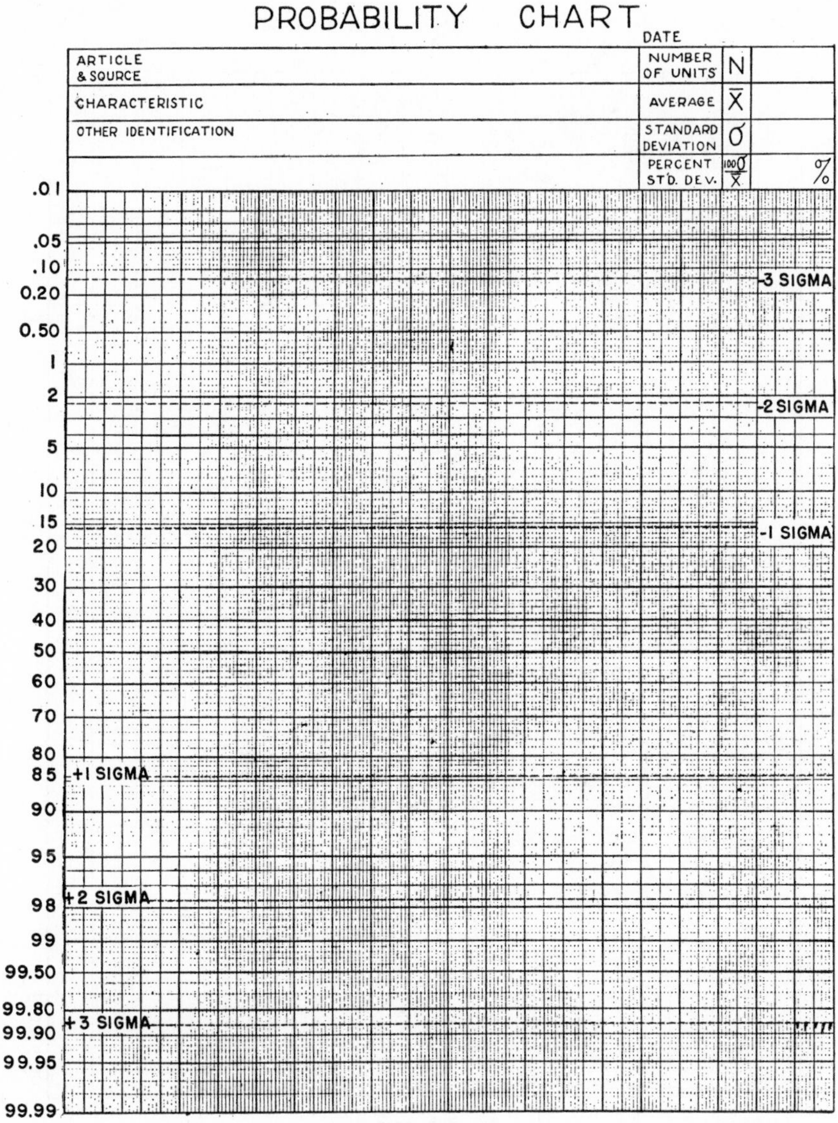

PROBABILITY CHART

DATE

ARTICLE & SOURCE	NUMBER OF UNITS	N	
CHARACTERISTIC	AVERAGE	$\bar{X}$	
OTHER IDENTIFICATION	STANDARD DEVIATION	σ	
	PERCENT STD. DEV.	$\frac{100\sigma}{\bar{X}}$	%

.01
.05
.10 -3 SIGMA
0.20
0.50
1
2 -2 SIGMA
5
10
15 -1 SIGMA
20
30
40
50
60
70
80
85 +1 SIGMA
90
95
98 +2 SIGMA
99
99.50
99.80
99.90 +3 SIGMA
99.95
99.99

FIG. 13.4.

The steps to be taken in probability-paper graphing may be listed, as follows:

1. The particular quality characteristic to be plotted is selected, and sample size is decided. The regular procedure in setting up a frequency-distribution analysis is followed.

PROBABILITY PAPER

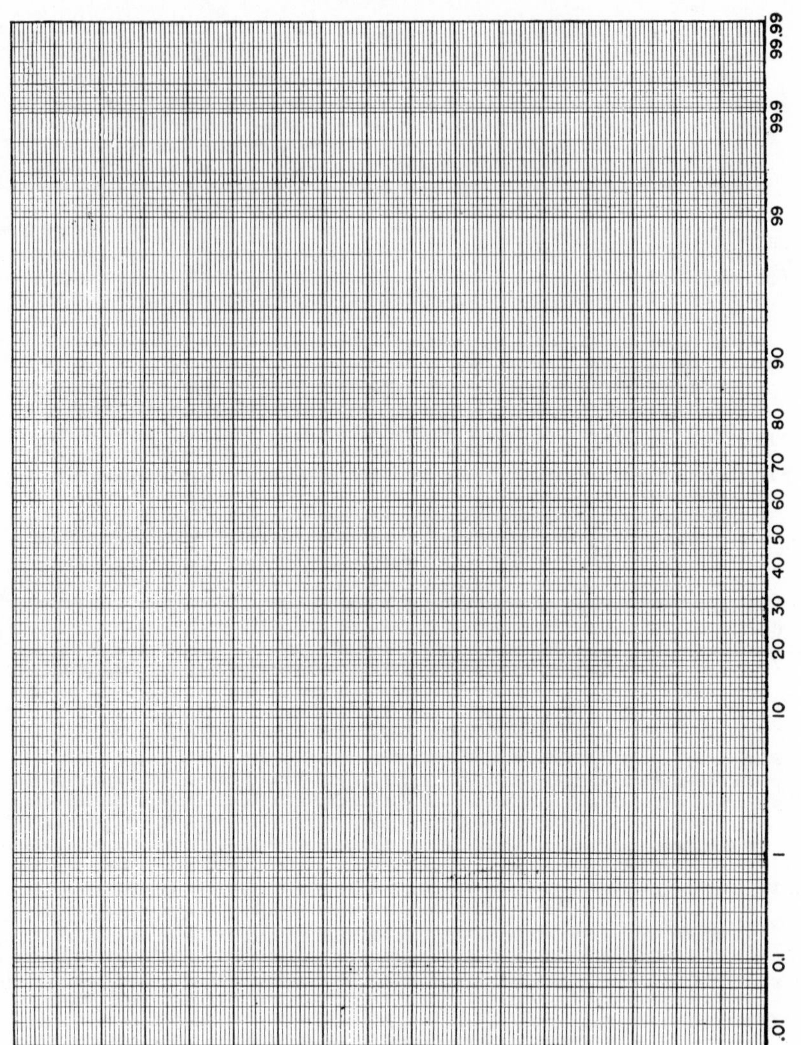

FIG. 13.5.

2. A form is prepared for tabulating the readings, preparatory to the probability plot. Suitable cell values are established. Cells of equal width are usually desirable. For a satisfactory probability graph, 12 to 20 of these cells are generally required. Any logical series of values can be used in establishing these cells.

This tabulation usually includes six columns as follows:

Column no.	(1) Readings to be included in cell	(2) Record as (cell value)	(3) Tally	(4) Tally total	(5) Cumulative total	(6) Cumulative % of total

3. Actual readings are made on the units in the sample. As the readings are taken, a tally is made of those which fall in the appropriate cells.

4. The tabulation of these readings is completed when all sample readings have been taken.

5. The suitable data from this tabulation are plotted on probability paper at the upper limit of each cell.[3]

6. The probability graph is examined in order to determine
   a. The normality of the distribution.
   b. The value of the average, or median.
   c. The value of the standard deviation.

The data may be taken, for example, on the resistance (measured in ohms) of a sample of 100 resistors. It is expected that the total range of the readings will be 145 ohms, or between 25 and 165 ohms. To determine for step 2 above the appropriate number of cells and the steps between cells, it is first necessary to divide 145 ohms by 12 and by 20, since 12 and 20 represent the band of the desired number of cells.

This division operation indicates that the step between cells should be somewhere between the values of 7 and 12 ohms. The most convenient value in this range is 10 ohms, and it is this value which will be used as the step between cells. These cell limits are established at values of 30, 40, . . . , 110, 120, . . . ohms, and a tabular form is prepared as in step 2 above. As readings are made on the resistors, their values are plotted in the tabulation.

Let us assume that the first six readings have the following values: 32, 38, 41, 46, 54, and 67. If, for some reason, resistance readings for the rest of the 100-unit sample were discontinued, the six readings would result in the tabulation on the following page.

The fashion in which the individual readings are placed in their respective cells should again be noted. Column 2, "Record as," represents the upper cell limits and the highest value of readings that will be included in that particular cell. This is unlike the typical practice in standard frequency-distribution plots of recording all readings in a cell against the middle value for the readings that are included in the cell in question.

[3] This discussion is limited to plotting the percentage of values *less than* the curve in question. It is also possible to use probability paper in the fashion of plotting the percentage of values *more than* the curve in question, in which case data are plotted at the lower limit of each cell.

Column no.	(1)		(2)	(3)	(4)	(5)	(6)
	From	To	Record as	Tally	Total	Cumulative	Cumulative % of total
	30 ohms	40 ohms	40 ohms	11	2	2	33.3
	40 ohms	50 ohms	50 ohms	11	2	4	66.7
	50 ohms	60 ohms	60 ohms	1	1	5	83.3
	60 ohms	70 ohms	70 ohms	1	1	6	100.0

13.5 A Typical Probability Graph Example

Suppose that it is desired to determine the value for the average and standard deviation of a 450-unit sample of a certain type of resistor. It is expected that there will be a range of about 1,150 ohms in readings in this sample.

To determine the suitable step between cells, 1,150 ohms may be divided by 12 to 20. The resulting values are shown to be 57 and 95 ohms. The intermediate step of 75 ohms would be less convenient for tabulation purposes than would steps of 50 or 100 ohms. Either 50 or 100 ohms could be selected, but the decision is made in favor of the 50-ohm step because it will enable the tabulation to reflect actual sample readings more accurately than would the 100-ohm step.

The 450 resistance readings are taken and tabulated as shown in Fig.

PROBABILITY PAPER TABULATION
OHMS VALUE OF RESISTORS

(1) FROM	TO	(2) RECORD AS CELL VALUE	(4) TOTAL TALLY	(5) CUMULATIVE TOTAL	(6) CUMULATIVE % OF TOTAL
400	449	450	1	1	0.22
450	499	500	–	1	0.22
500	549	550	1	2	0.44
550	599	600	2	4	0.89
600	649	650	4	8	1.78
650	699	700	7	15	3.33
700	749	750	13	28	6.22
750	799	800	19	47	10.44
800	849	850	27	74	16.44
850	899	900	36	110	24.44
900	949	950	42	152	33.78
950	999	1000	48	200	44.44
1000	1049	1050	50	250	55.56
1050	1099	1100	47	297	66.00
1100	1149	1150	43	340	75.55
1150	1199	1200	35	375	83.33
1200	1249	1250	28	403	89.55
1250	1299	1300	20	423	94.00
1300	1349	1350	13	436	96.89
1350	1399	1400	6	442	98.22
1400	1449	1450	5	447	99.33
1450	1499	1500	2	449	99.78
1500	1549	1550	–	449	99.78
1550	1599	1600	1	450	100.00

FIG. 13.6.

13.6.[4] Thus steps 1 through 4 of Sec. 13.4 are accomplished. It will be noted that this Fig. 13.6 tabulation eliminates column (3) as shown in the tabulations of Sec. 13.4, since inclusion of this column would have made the table too bulky for presentation.

To carry out steps 5 and 6 of Sec. 13.4, the following procedure is followed:

Step 5: *Plot the suitable data from the tabulation on probability paper.* To plot the data of Fig. 13.6 on the probability graph of Fig. 13.7, the steps are as follows:

a. Establish on the horizontal scale the various cell values shown in column (2). On this particular graph there is only sufficient space to record these cells in steps of 100 ohms. It is usually good practice to record cell values both below and above those actually used in the tabulation; thus the values plotted on the horizontal scale run as low as 300 ohms and as high as 1,700 ohms.

b. Plot the cumulative percentages shown in column (6) on the vertical scale of percentage of total against the appropriate values of column (2).

c. Fit a curve to the resulting plotted points. It will be noted that the points between 500 and 1,400 ohms arrange themselves in a straight line. The single point below 500 represents one reading, or 0.2 per cent of the total. The points over 1,400 ohms amount to 2.0 per cent of the total, although the cumulative curve returns to a straight line at 1,600 ohms, leaving only one value, or 0.2 per cent of the total, "out of line."

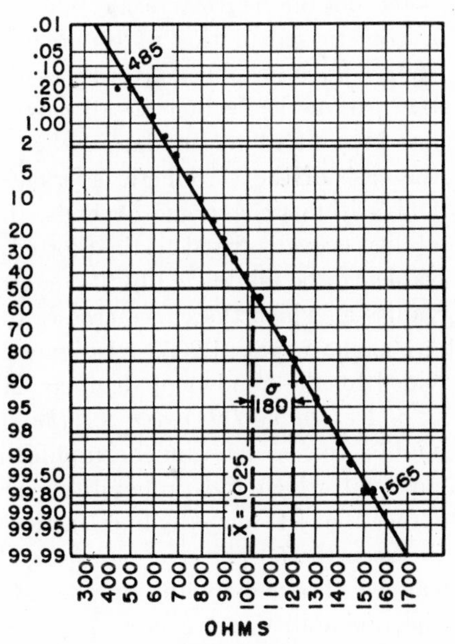

FIG. 13.7.

Step 6: *Determine normality and values for the average and standard deviation.* For these determinations, the steps are as follows:

a. Determine the "normality" of the distribution. In most practical cases, a reasonable conformance to a straight line between 2 and 98 per cent of the cumulative readings is evidence that the distribution in ques-

[4] Data after Abbott, *op. cit.*

tion approaches quite closely the shape of the normal curve. Particularly when the number of readings in the distribution is small, close conformance to a straight line at each end of the plot is quite unusual. In such a case, a straight line between 5 and 95 per cent of the total values is usually sufficient evidence of relatively normal distribution.

Thus the first decision that can be made from the picture of Fig. 13.7 is that the straight-line plot indicates that the data represent a relatively normal frequency distribution.

b. Determine the value for the average. This average value can be obtained from the probability graph by striking it off at the 50 per cent point on the vertical scale. On Fig. 13.7, this is 1,025 ohms. Actual arithmetic calculation of the average will also be found to equal 1,025 ohms.[5] This graphical average will not, however, check so closely with the arithmetic average in all cases; it is determined from a curve that has been fitted to the data rather than from the data themselves as in the case of the arithmetic average. The relation between the graphical and arithmetic average depends, therefore, upon how closely the probability curve is fitted to the plotted data. Error in reading this graphical value can be minimized by its determination as the average of the actual values at which the curve crosses the ± 1-, or 2-, or 3-sigma lines. Thus, $+1$ sigma equals 1,205, -1 sigma equals 845, and their sum, 2,050, divided by the number of readings, 2, equals 1,025 ohms.

c. Determine the value for the standard deviation. The standard deviation can be determined graphically by reading the values between the point at which the probability curve crosses the 50 per cent line and either the $+1\sigma$ or -1σ line. In the case of Fig. 13.7, about 180 ohms is between the 50 per cent point and $+1\sigma$. A more accurate determination can be obtained by taking the difference between the points at which the probability curve crosses the -3σ and the $+3\sigma$ lines and then dividing by 6. In this case, the calculation becomes, $\frac{1{,}565 - 485}{6} = 1{,}080 \div 6 = 180$ ohms.

It is only when the line representing the probability plot is a straight one that the point at which the 50 per cent line is crossed will represent both the median and the average. When the line representing the probability plot is a line curving in one direction, the point at which the 50 per cent line is crossed will represent only the median and not the average. A straight line drawn through the points at which this line crosses -1σ and $+1\sigma$ will cross the 50 per cent line at approximately the average, and the standard deviation will be approximately one-half the difference between the $+1\sigma$ and -1σ points.

[5] This is performed in the usual fashion: $\overline{X} = \frac{\Sigma fx}{n}$.

Even extreme variations from the straight-line form of probability curve do not appreciably affect the rule that the average and standard deviation of a distribution can be determined with a fair degree of accuracy be drawing a straight line through the $+1\sigma$ and -1σ points.

The accuracy of probability-paper graphing in estimating the average and the standard deviation is satisfactory for general purposes. It may not be satisfactory for precision purposes unless there is a large number of readings. For most industrial applications the accuracy is sufficient.

13.6 Graphical Correlation

The objective of correlation is to determine the relationship, if any, existing among variables. These variables are often different quality characteristics of the same part or material.

The correlation technique may be divided into two parts:

1. Simple graphical correlation, which will be discussed in this section.
2. Mathematical correlation, which will be discussed in Sec. 13.11.

For graphical correlation, regular rectangular coordinate paper is generally used. One variable, usually the one assumed to be "independent," is laid out on the horizontal scale. The supposedly related "dependent" variable is laid out on the vertical scale. Readings of the two variables are then made on the parts in question. The values of these readings are plotted on the rectangular coordinate paper.

Effort is thereupon made to fit a curve to the plotted points. The sketched curve should divide the plotted points approximately in two groups; it should pass very close to the median values for the two variables, and the sum of the deviations from the sketched curve should approximately equal zero. This curve may take a very wide variety of forms: a straight line, a curve with one bend, a curve with two bends, a half circle.

When this line has been sketched, the resulting graphical picture may be examined for the amount of deviation from the line shown by the plotted points. If the amount of this deviation is quite small, the band within the points fall may be sketched in and the correlation may be said to represent a well-defined relationship. If the amount of this deviation is quite large, then there may be no reason to attempt to sketch in the band into which it falls and the correlation may be said to represent a poorly defined relationship if, indeed, there be any relationship at all.

Figure 13.8 represents this condition of a well-defined relationship, and Fig. 13.9 represents the condition of a poorly defined relationship.[6]

Thus a factory may be manufacturing small metal inserts for which

[6] The band width should, of course, be compared with the commonly used range of the curve. Thus, if the range of inquiry in Fig. 13.8 is from 5.0 to 6.0 in characteristic A, the curve is no more useful than Fig. 13.9 if the range of inquiry is 5.0 to 15.0.

the elongation under load is a critical characteristic. It may not be practical for the factory to apply load to each insert and to measure the resulting elongation.

It is desired, therefore, to determine if some other quality characteristic of the inserts, which can be determined in a nondestructive fashion, bears a very close relationship to elongation. This other quality characteristic could then be inspected in place of the destructive elongation checks.

Such a related characteristic is thought to exist in the Brinell hardness of the inserts. To check this relationship graphically, factory personnel would pursue the following sequence: suitable cell values for elongation would be established on the horizontal axis of a sheet of rectangular

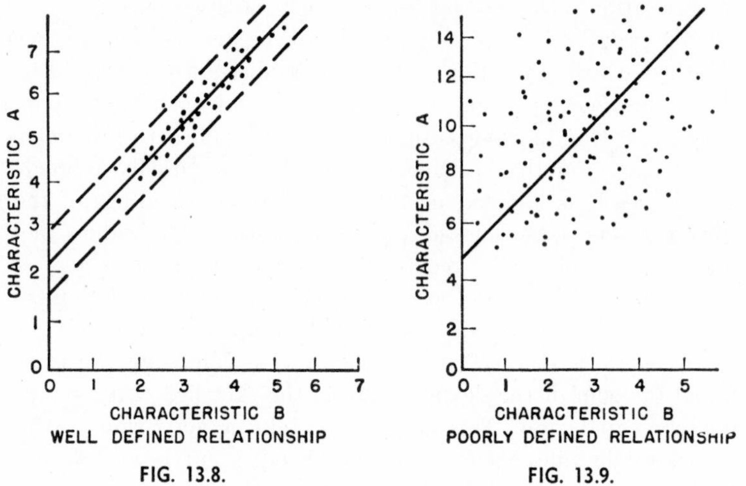

FIG. 13.8.

FIG. 13.9.

coordinate paper, and appropriate cell values for Brinell hardness would be established on the vertical axis.

A series of tests would then be made on sample inserts to determine elongation and hardness under given load. These data would be plotted on the rectangular coordinate paper, just as shown in Fig. 13.8. If the resulting picture were similar to that of Fig. 13.8, the conclusion would be drawn that Brinell hardness may be checked in place of elongation within the band of deviation shown. A corresponding statistical correlation analysis would probably be carried out to determine actual numerical values for the correlation relationship.

If the resulting picture were similar to Fig. 13.9, the conclusion would be drawn that little if any significant relationship can be said to exist between the Brinell hardness and the elongation of these inserts.

Analytical Special Methods

13.7 Analytical Special Methods

Of the several analytical special methods that have been used in industry, probably the following are among the most important:

1. Statistical tolerance analysis.
2. Tests of significance.
3. Design of experiments.
4. Mathematical correlation.
5. Sequential analysis.

Each of these techniques will be briefly discussed in the sections below.

13.8 Statistical Tolerance Analysis

Engineers designing products in which there are subassemblies made up of several mating parts are almost always faced with a common problem: how should the tolerance for the individual parts[7] be balanced off with the tolerance for their subassembly so that

1. The individual parts actually *do* mate when they reach the appropriate point in their manufacturing cycle.
2. These tolerances permit the most economical production costs.

Activity to achieve this balance is usually termed *tolerance analysis.* Historically, it has often resulted in the following situations:

1. The sum of tolerances of the individual parts is allowed to be greater than the tolerance for their subassembly. The engineer "trusts to luck" that he will encounter no production difficulties.
2. The tolerance for the subassembly is made equal to the arithmetic sum of the tolerances of the individual parts. This forces the engineer to
   a. Establish extremely wide subassembly tolerances, with all the attendant problems of such a situation, or
   b. Allow the high manufacturing costs which accompany the narrow individual part tolerances resulting in narrow subassembly tolerances.

Situation 1 is probably the more usual. It has provided relatively so little manufacturing difficulty in many shops that it has become an accepted part of shop custom.

Situation 2, while accepted as not so economical in the short run, has found acceptance in some shops which "want to be sure" that they do not have production difficulties during subassembly and assembly.

[7] In this section it is assumed that the tolerance for each individual part fairly closely approximates its process capability. If this is not true, then process capabilities should be substituted to compute the over-all tolerance for the subassembly.

Even though their approach seems the least logical, those shops which have lived with situation 1 may have chosen the more effective alternative. In trusting to luck, they have had a well-established law of probability working on their side, namely that, *under certain circumstances*, the over-all tolerance of a group of mating parts equals the square root of the sum of the square of the individual part tolerances—a value less than that for the straight arithmetic sum of the individual tolerances. Expressed algebraically:[8]

$$T_t = \sqrt{T_1^2 + T_2^2 + T_3^2 + \cdots + T_n^2} \qquad (38)$$

where T_t = over-all tolerance

T_1, T_2, etc. = tolerances of the individual mating parts

Suppose that an engineer is faced with fixed tolerances for eight mating parts, as follows:

$T_1 = \pm 0.004$ inch $= 0.008$ inch
$T_2 = \pm 0.003$ inch $= 0.006$ inch
$T_3 = \pm 0.003$ inch $= 0.006$ inch
$T_4 = \pm 0.003$ inch $= 0.006$ inch
$T_5 = \pm 0.001$ inch $= 0.002$ inch
$T_6 = \pm 0.002$ inch $= 0.004$ inch
$T_7 = \pm 0.005$ inch $= 0.010$ inch
$T_8 = \pm 0.003$ inch $= 0.006$ inch

The question before him is this: What tolerance should he establish for the over-all assembly of the mating parts? Use of the old custom of arithmetic addition of individual parts tolerances would force him to set a total over-all tolerance of ± 0.024 inch, or 48 mils in this case.

Using formula (38), however, the engineer would develop the following computation (in mils):

$$\begin{aligned} T_t &= \sqrt{8^2 + 6^2 + 6^2 + 6^2 + 2^2 + 4^2 + 10^2 + 6^2} \\ &= \sqrt{64 + 36 + 36 + 36 + 4 + 16 + 100 + 36} \\ &= \sqrt{328} = 18 \text{ mils} \end{aligned}$$

or

$$T_t = 0.018 \text{ inch}$$

This over-all tolerance of ± 0.009 inch, or 18 mils, represents a considerable improvement over the arithmetic total of 48 mils. It provides the engineer with a more realistic and, most likely, a more economical value for the over-all tolerance.

The wide difference between the values of 18 and 48 mils probably represents no real surprise for experienced engineers. They have intuitively recognized this situation in product designs for many years, without the formal analytical apparatus provided by formula (38).

[8] For additional information, see Villars, D. C., "Statistical Design and Analysis of Experiments for Development Research, Wm. C. Brown Co., Dubuque, Iowa, 1951, Chap. 14, pp. 330–334.

Grant, E. L., "Statistical Quality Control," 2d ed., McGraw-Hill Book Company, Inc., New York, Chap. XII, pp. 292–306.

Understanding of formula (38) is of advantage to engineers in the two typical situations that exist when tolerances are being established for a group of mating parts:

1. *When the over-all tolerance is fixed and the individual parts tolerances must be adjusted.* It points the finger at those individual parts to which attention should be directed for reducing the over-all tolerance of the subassembly. Thus in the above example, reducing T_6 from ± 0.002 to ± 0.001 inch might be very expensive and would reduce $\sqrt{328}$ only to $\sqrt{316}$. Reducing T_7 from ± 0.005 to ± 0.004 inch might be less expensive and would have a much greater effect in reducing the over-all tolerance, for it would reduce $\sqrt{328}$ to $\sqrt{292}$.

This problem of the actual reduction of these individual parts tolerances and how far it can proceed is discussed elsewhere in the book. See particularly Chap. 17.

2. *When the individual part tolerances are fixed and the over-all tolerance must be adjusted.* It enables engineers to establish much more economical and realistic over-all tolerance values if the individual parts tolerances are "frozen."

It should be noted that the probability law discussed above stated that it has application *under certain circumstances.* These circumstances simmer down as follows:

Practically all the mating parts in question should pass their individual part tolerances without requiring scrap or rework, or, in other words, the frequency distributions for each of the individual parts should approach fairly closely the shape of the normal curve, with the nominal drawing values corresponding closely to the average value for the part frequency distribution. In addition, each of the mating parts should be drawn from essentially different sources.

In this latter connection, for example, is the case of assemblies consisting of parts made to the same drawing, clamped or welded or riveted together. If the parts are punchings which are stacked together as they are produced so that all those in one assembly come from the same sheet of steel with relatively uniform thickness, the situation is particularly pronounced. For assemblies of this sort—alternating-current solenoids are a case in point—it is not sound practice to depend upon formula (38) for the determination of the over-all tolerance. Here the number of punchings required to meet the drawing dimensions for over-all thickness should be determined by weight or by a similar system.

Another common example is drift due to tool wear when there is little variation between parts at a given instant in time as compared with time-to-time variation.

Another limiting case is that of an assembly of parts made to the same drawing where the frequency distribution for those parts used in each assembly may not approach sufficiently closely the shape of the normal curve. Here also, formula (38) should be bypassed in favor of the procedure of specifying an operation for machining the assembled parts to the required over-all dimension or by controlling this dimension by varying the number of parts used in the assembly.

With these limiting conditions in mind, several factories have made investigations to determine how applicable is formula (38) to their manufacturing conditions. Reports from these companies have indicated that the formula does have wide application in the tolerance analysis of many products and that the conditions for its use are frequently met in actual industrial circumstances.

Experiments conducted by Epstein and Thompson[9] in their respective companies have also tended to confirm the usefulness of this formula.

13.9 Tests of Significance

The purpose of statistical tests of significance is to tell whether the quality of a lot of material, of the output of a given product type, of a batch of parts just received from a vendor differs "significantly" from a standard value or from the quality of a second or more lot or sources. These tests can be used to compare material from two or more sources or to determine which of a number of factors affect the quality of a process.

Collectively, the tests of significance may detect differences in per cents defective, averages, spreads, and other measures. These tests have been evolved to meet the frequently encountered industrial problem that the difference between good- and poor-quality levels is often so slight that it is masked by random variations in small samples.[10] As company quality-control men have learned by long and bitter experience, it is difficult to evaluate such process changes without analytical techniques.

[9] See Epstein, B., "Statistical Control of Assemblies Eliminates Selective Fitting," *American Machinist,* Vol. 89, No. 18, pp. 126–127, Aug. 30, 1945.

P. E. Thompson, West Lynn, Mass., reports similarly positive conclusions in an unpublished note.

[10] When the difference among sample values can be shown so great as to make untenable the assumption of a common source for the lots in question, these differences are said to be statistically significant. An illustration of significance may be made briefly: Part Four has shown that different samples of the same part may well vary in their values of central tendency and spread. Section 10.18 has shown that this will occur with samples drawn from the same lot or same source. When the difference in central tendency and spread is due to this random variation in samples from the same source, the difference among sample values may be said to be statistically not significant. When the difference among the sample values can be shown to be due to their having come from different lots or different sources, these differences may be said to be statistically significant.

a situation pointed up by the example cited in Sec. 13.1. The use of significance tests reduces greatly the chance of coming to incorrect conclusions in such cases.

The two most used significance tests are listed below, along with a description of their most useful application.

1. *The "t" test,* used to determine the significance of differences between measures of central tendency of two samples.[11]

2. *The "F" test,* used to determine the significance of differences among the spread of samples.[12]

Useful presentations of these techniques are available for the interested readers in the references in the footnotes.

13.10 Design of Experiments

Statistical tests of significance are used in the analysis of quality problems under two basically different conditions:

1. *They are brought in at the end of the experiment.* When tests have been run, experiments completed, and all data taken, the analyst is presented with the results and is asked to simmer out accurate information from them. Under these circumstances, the analyst must try to use the appropriate tests of significance under the handicap that all required data may not be available or in proper form.

2. *They are brought in at the start of the experiment.* The analyst is asked to suggest the type of experimental program that will provide the required data before any tests have been started or any data taken. The entire study may then be geared so that the data required for the analysis will be taken at minimum time and expense.

The advantages of condition 2 over condition 1 are obvious. While there will be some circumstances when condition 1 cannot be avoided, both economies in expense and increases in analytical accuracy are to be gained from condition 2 under usual practice.

Tests of significance are also put to use on data taken under two somewhat different philosophies of experimentation.

1. *The philosophy that all factors except the one under study be held constant.* This is the approach that has been used in some factories for many years. While it has resulted in some satisfactory results and must be used under certain conditions, it is subject to such circumstances as the following:

   a. Under the constantly changing conditions in the modern plant—bearing wear, tool use, etc.—it is difficult to be sure that "everything is constant." The experiment may thus be subject to error.

[11] Hoel, Paul G., "Introduction to Mathematical Statistics," John Wiley & Sons, Inc., New York, 1954.

[12] See Hoel, *op. cit.*

b. Fallacious conclusions of cause and effect can be a result of this approach.[13]

c. A very large number of individual tests is required when several variables are being investigated.

2. *The philosophy of randomization, either of all factors, or of all but a few which are deliberately varied.* This is the modern statistical approach, which permits the minimization of experimental error: of the fallacious reasoning to which the "all factors constant" philosophy may be subject, and of the number of tests required to gain a given result.

The approach toward the use of significance tests in experimentation whereby statistics are brought in at the start of the experiment and where randomization and/or deliberate variation is brought into use in the experimental framework is usually termed the *design of experiments.*[14] A test program that has been designed around these techniques almost always yields better results both in reliability and in economy than those conducted under hit-or-miss and "hold constant" circumstances. The economies made possible by the reduction in the number of tests required by designed experiments, as compared with older procedures, is startling in many cases.

Three of the most popular experimental design techniques are listed below, with one of their most useful applications noted. Design technique 1 is the general case of which techniques 2 and 3 are special adaptations:

1. Analysis of Variance Table. This experimental design permits the randomization of all factors. It uses the "F" test in a situation where the quality of a process is affected and where it is desired to study simultaneously the variation among several samples to determine whether a suspected cause of variation in a measured variable is real or is merely attributable to chance.[15]

2. Latin Square. This experimental design permits at least two factors other than the one being studied to be deliberately varied, while all others are randomized. It uses the "F" test in a case such as the following: it is desired to determine which of five springs of different pull characteristics has the best result in increasing the drop-out voltage of a certain relay. It is felt that test machines and test operators are also variables which might affect the drop-out voltage of the relays.

With five spring types to be compared, the Latin-square arrangement

[13] For an able discussion of some of these fallacies, see Leonard A. Seder, "Technique of Experimenting in the Factory," *Mechanical Engineering,* July, 1948.

[14] Cochran, W. G., and G. M. Cox, "Experimental Designs," John Wiley & Sons, Inc., New York, 1957.

[15] See, for example, "Variance, the F test, and the Analysis of Variance Table," *Industrial Quality Control,* March and May, 1948. An excellent, somewhat complex reference on variance analysis is R. A. Fisher, "Statistical Methods for Research Workers," Oliver & Boyd, Ltd., Edinburgh and London, 1948.

requires five test machines and five operators. The machines and operators are allocated to spring A, spring B, etc., in such a way that the separate springs, test machines, and operators are associated in the same trio only once. The tabular arrangement for the analysis is shown in Fig. 13.10, from which the use of the descriptive term Latin square can be readily appreciated.

3. Graeco-Latin Square. This experimental design allows the deliberate variation of variables in order to permit obtaining the maximum of information about the effect of these variables from a minimum of tests. It uses the "F" test in a situation such as the following: it is known that some combination of fixed amounts of five different compounds provides

LATIN SQUARE

		TEST MACHINE				
		1	2	3	4	5
TEST OPERATOR	1	SPRING E	SPRING B	SPRING D	SPRING A	SPRING C
	2	" C	" D	" B	" E	" A
	3	" A	" C	" E	" B	" D
	4	" D	" E	" A	" C	" B
	5	" B	" A	" C	" D	" E

FIG. 13.10.

the best protective coating for mechanical devices being shipped to the tropics. But how should the five compounds be mixed together in fixed amounts in order to achieve best results? If four amounts of each of the five compounds were tried under ordinary experimental procedure, 4^5 tests—1,024 in all—would be required. By arranging each variable in groups that permit one and only one occurrence of each variable with all the others, the Graeco-Latin square design provides the same information from only 16 tests.

Figure 13.11 shows how, in this experimental design, each amount of each compound is given a deliberate association with all the others only once.[16]

[16] See, for example, Kendall, Maurice G., "The Advanced Theory of Statistics," Charles Griffin & Co., Ltd., London, 1948, Vol. II, p. 261.

GRAECO-LATIN SQUARE

	I	II	III	IV
A	1a ①	2b ②	3c ③	4d ④
B	2c ④	1d ③	4a ②	3b ①
C	3d ②	4c ①	1b ④	2a ③
D	4b ③	3a ④	2d ①	1c ②

4 X 4 SQUARE — 4 AMOUNTS OF 5 COMPOUNDS

WHERE

1, 2, 3, 4 — DIFFERENT AMOUNTS OF THE SAME COMPOUND
a, b, c, d — " " " " " "
①,②,③,④ — " " " " " "
I, II, III, IV — " " " " " "
A, B, C, D — " " " " " "

FIG. 13.11.

Useful presentations of these and many other experimental designs are made in the reference in the footnote.

13.11 Mathematical Correlation

Section 13.6 pointed out the instances where, after a graphical correlation plot has been made, it is desired to make a more precise determination as to the strength of the relationship between the variables involved. Three of the basic steps in the technique of mathematical correlation are listed below:

1. The determination of the strength of the relationship in question by computation of the coefficient of correlation r. Ideally, r equals one (1) as in the case of the following two variables x and y:

$$x\text{: } 1, 2, 3, 4, 5 \text{ (independent variable)}$$
$$y\text{: } 2, 4, 6, 8, 10 \text{ (dependent variable)}$$

This type of perfect correlation almost never occurs in industry, however, where r is almost always a value different from 1.

2. The establishment of a mathematical expression that can be used to forecast values of the dependent variable from values of the independent variable. This is merely the mathematical expression of what Sec.

13.6 termed the "sketched line, or curve of best fit." Some important classifications of these lines of best fit, or lines of regression, as they are termed in mathematical correlation, are listed below.

a. A linear relationship between the two variables, for example,

$$y = mx + b$$

This is termed a *linear regression.*

b. Power curves of the form:

$$y = a + bx + cx^2 + dx^3 + \cdots + nx^n$$

Curves of this form are generally termed *curvilinear regressions.*

3. The determination of the significance of the value of r that has been determined and the establishment of limits within which it may be expected that the values obtained from the expression developed in step 2 will fall.[17]

13.12 Sequential Analysis

Section 12.11 discussed the use of sequential analysis as one of the newer techniques for the development of statistical sampling tables.

Sequential analysis is not, however, limited to inspection in its application. It may also be extremely useful in the analysis of complex quality problems.

Sequential analysis may, for example, be used in testing for significant differences in averages or in the uniformity of product manufacture. Section 12.11 pointed out that the sequential approach calls for the establishment of two contingencies: an X_1 and X_2 factor and a Y_1 and Y_2 factor.

In applications cited, X_1 and X_2 become specific values for the differences in averages or uniformity of product manufacture. Y_1 and Y_2 are the associated risks taken in the analysis.[18]

Special Methods in Action

13.13 Practical Applications of Special Methods

Of the four quality-control jobs, special process studies is the one in which special methods find their widest application. Tests of significance,

[17] The reader interested in the details of this method may review such references as Simon, L. E., "An Engineer's Manual of Statistical Methods," John Wiley & Sons, Inc., New York, 1941, pp. 144–155; Croxton, F. E., and D. J. Cowden, "Applied General Statistics," Prentice-Hall, Inc., Englewood Cliffs, N.J., 1955; Shewhart, W. A., "Economic Control of Quality of Manufactured Product," D. Van Nostrand Company, Inc., New York, 1931, pp. 214–229.

[18] The interested reader may obtain detailed information on this subject by referring to the following: Abraham Wald, "Sequential Analysis," John Wiley & Sons, Inc., New York, 1947.

designed experiments, and correlation are among the special methods which have their chief use in special process studies.

Special methods also have varying amounts of practical application in the other quality-control jobs. Statistical tolerance analysis, analysis of variance, and probability paper are extensively used in new-design control, and other special methods have been used in incoming-material control and in product control.

Three practical applications of these special methods are discussed below:

1. Analysis of a lot of questionable quality by graphical correlation (see Sec. 13.14).
2. Study of a proposed methods change by tests of significance and probability-paper analysis (see Sec. 13.15).
3. Examination of a complex assembly temperature-compensation problem by use of a Graeco-Latin square variance analysis (see Sec. 13.16).

13.14 Analysis of a Lot of Questionable Quality: Graphical Correlation

An interesting use of graphical correlation discussed by Armstrong and Clarke[19] involves investigation of a lot of springs whose quality was in question. These small compression springs were being tested for their free length under a given pressure.

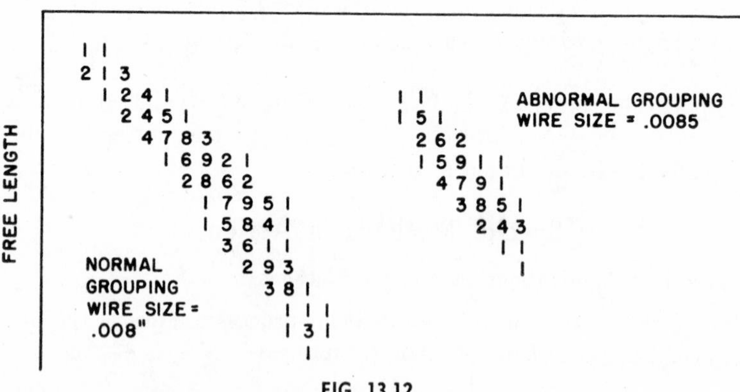

FIG. 13.12.

It was decided to make a correlation study to analyze the quality of the springs. A sample was selected from the lot of springs. Each of the springs in the sample was tested for load, and its free length was measured.

[19] Armstrong, G. R., and P. C. Clarke, "Statistical Methods in Quality Control," published by Hunter Pressed Steel Company.

The results of these tests, as number of occurrences, were plotted on rectangular coordinate paper, with free length on the vertical axis and pressure on the horizontal axis. Figure 13.12 shows this correlation plot and indicates that *two* different patterns were present in one lot.

Further investigation disclosed that there were two different types of spring in the lot, differing in wire diameter. This situation was traced to the fact that some wire of slightly off-standard 0.0085-inch diameter had been inadvertently used on the production line in place of the standard 0.008-inch wire.

Because two different types of springs were mixed in the lot, it was found necessary to sort the entire lot by 100 per cent testing and thus to separate the standard springs from those that were substandard.

13.15 Study of a Proposed Methods Change: Tests of Significance and Probability Paper

On an electronic tube type, one electrical quality characteristic—*grid current*—was the cause for a high percentage of tubes found defective in final test. The specification limits for grid current were 25 to 55 milliamperes, and the rejections were due largely to the excessive spread in production lots of the tubes.[20]

To eliminate this rejection, the engineer in charge of the tube developed a change in the method of one phase of tube assembly. He hoped that this methods change would reduce the excessive spread in grid current.

Before authorizing the expenditure necessary to make the required change in the assembly methods, the engineer wished to investigate the actual effect of the change upon tube quality. He planned his study as follows: 100 standard production tubes would be used. These 100 tubes would be assembled under standard procedure, using the same regular materials, processing equipments, and operators. However, 50 of the tubes would be subjected to the new assembly method. The other 50 tubes, used as a "control" sample, would be assembled in the standard fashion.

The engineer felt that this experiment would permit the full and most effective utilization of tests of significance and gained agreement from the statistical analyst of the plant that this was so under the conditions surrounding the tube type.

As a result, the proposed procedure was followed. The 100 tubes were put through the final test, and the following results were tabulated for the grid-current quality characteristic:

[20] This case reports an analysis made by C. G. Donsbach and associates, Schenectady, N.Y.

	Sample with new method	Control sample
Sample size (n)	50 tubes	50 tubes
Average ($\overline{X}$)	37.4 milliamperes	42.0 milliamperes
Standard deviation (σ)	4.2 milliamperes	7.1 milliamperes

Did the sample assembled by the new method show a reduction in spread that was significant? In other words, were these results statistically significant?

Significance tests, chief among which was the "t" test to determine the significance of the difference between averages, were applied. Their results showed significant differences between the two samples, indicating that the change in methods assembly did make a significant reduction in the spread of the tubes.

The application of significance tests was still relatively new to the plant, however, and the engineer decided to make a further check on the effect of the methods change. He decided to obtain a larger representative sample by running at least one day's production with the new assembly technique. In doing this, the day's production was run with all shifts, all machines, and all other variables completely randomized as encountered in normal production. The results in the final tests of the tubes with the new assembly method, as compared with those manufactured under standard production conditions, are tabulated below:

	Sample with new method	Standard production
n	309	500
$\overline{X}$	36.8	44.1
σ	4.5	8.0
Per cent defective	1.0	14.0

The comparison between the two groups was made graphically by means of probability paper. Figure 13.13 shows the comparison between the groups.

The approval for the new assembly method was given by the engineer after examination of the probability plot. A considerable reduction in rejections, with a corresponding improvement in quality and reduction in cost, was obtained from subsequent production of the tube type while using the new method.

13.16 Examination of Temperature Compensation: Graeco-Latin Square

A plant manufacturing dual tachometer indicators for aircraft was concerned about the temperature compensation of these assemblies. It

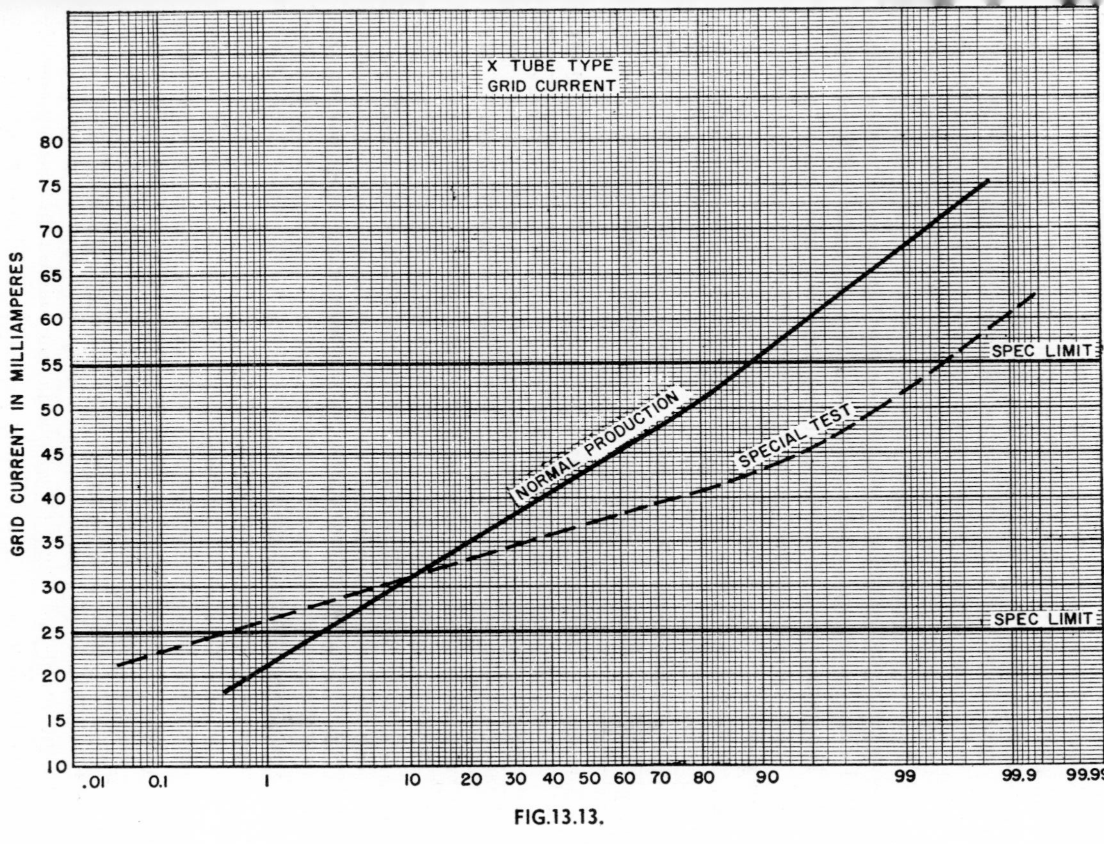
X TUBE TYPE
GRID CURRENT
GRID CURRENT IN MILLIAMPERES
80
75
70
65
60
55
50
45
40
35
30
25
20
15
10
SPEC LIMIT
SPEC LIMIT
NORMAL PRODUCTION
SPECIAL TEST
.01
0.1
1
10
20
30
40
50
60
70
80
90
99
99.9
99.99

FIG.13.13.

was recognized that any analysis of temperature compensation involved the study of a number of combined factors. It was decided, therefore, that the required examination could most effectively be made by designing an experiment through use of the Graeco-Latin square technique.[21]

The plant took four steps in applying this technique:

1. Application of sound engineering principles to select the variables that appeared influential.
2. Design of the experiment from which the data were to be obtained.
3. The actual work of testing and recording the data.

3 X 3 SQUARE

	I	II	III
A	1 α	2 β	3 γ
B	2 γ	3 α	1 β
C	3 β	1 γ	2 α

LOCATION	I .115	II .085	III .055
CONDUCTIVITY	A 1600	B 1800	C 2000
COEFFICIENT	1 .025	2 .040	3 .060
THICKNESS	α .010	β .020	γ .040

TEST SETUP

I .115	II .085	III .055	LOCATION
A 1600	A 1600	A 1600	CONDUCTIVITY
1 .025	2 .040	3 .060	COEFFICIENT
α .010	β .020	γ .040	THICKNESS
I .115	II .085	III .055	LOCATION
B 1800	B 1800	B 1800	CONDUCTIVITY
2 .040	3 .060	1 .025	COEFFICIENT
γ .040	α .010	β .020	THICKNESS
I .115	II .085	III .055	LOCATION
C 2000	C 2000	C 2000	CONDUCTIVITY
3 .060	1 .025	2 .040	COEFFICIENT
β .020	γ .040	α .010	THICKNESS

EXPERIMENTAL DATA

L	+ 1.603	+ .369	− 2.507
MEAN	+ 1.655	− .066	− 2.784
R	+ 1.706	− .502	− 3.062
L	+ 2.312	+ .958	− 1.212
MEAN	+ 1.470	+ 1.290	− .642
R	+ .627	+ 1.622	− .0707
L	+ 2.52	− .378	+ 2.47
MEAN	+ 2.51	− .003	+ 2.32
	+ 2.50	+ .372	+ 2.17

FIG. 13.14.

4. Mathematical treatment of the data to measure the relative importance on temperature compensation of the separate factors.

In making this analysis, it was determined that four factors contributing to the problem being studied on the tachometer indicator assembly were (1) location of the compensator plate, (2) conductivity of the drag disk, (3) coefficient of conductivity of the disk material, (4) thickness of the compensator plate.

Three values of these factors were chosen in the critical region for temperature compensation. They were applied to a 3 by 3 Graeco-Latin square, as shown in Fig. 13.14. Each setup was duplicated for a measure of repeatability. Errors were tabulated at various temperature levels,

[21] This discussion describes an analysis made by P. E. Thompson, West Lynn, Mass.; it directly follows Mr. Thompson's exposition of the project.

VALUES OF STATISTIC F AND CRITICAL VALUES
FOR THE TACHOMETER

FACTORS	SUM OF SQUARES	DEGREES OF FREEDOM	MEAN SQUARE	F	CRITICAL (1%)
LOCATION	15.63	2	7.815	22.10	8.02
CONDUCTIVITY	12.13	2	6.065	17.30	8.02
COEFFICIENT	3.28	2	1.640	4.65	8.02
THICKNESS	14.41	2	7.205	20.60	8.02
RESIDUAL	3.19	9	0.354		

FIG. 13.15.

and the analysis aimed at finding the arrangement that would produce least error.

The data shown were read at $-22°C$; similar work was done at $+49$, -37, and $-56°C$. The final tabulation of results is shown in Fig. 13.15.

From this analysis of temperature compensation, using only nine tachometers, it was found that conductance values were a more critical indicator for locating the compensator plate properly than were thermal coefficients. A considerable saving in labor cost for adjusting the tachometers in the shop was one result from this study.

CHAPTER 14

PRODUCT RELIABILITY

A reliable product is one that can be counted on to perform the function it is designed to perform when called upon. To put it another way, "When you press the button, it works."

The reliability of products is, of course, one of the major areas of quality-control interest. As products have become more complex in function and performance, and as the processes for their production have become more precise, this interest has turned more intensely to quantitative measurements of reliability. Such measurements help to make of reliability a number—a probability—that can be expressed as a standard. They make it possible, rather objectively, to evaluate product reliability, to predict it and to balance it objectively with the other product quality parameters such as maintainability and appearance.

It is the purpose of this chapter to consider the concepts that underpin the statistical and mathematical point of view toward reliability.

14.1 The Increasing Emphasis on Product Reliability

Emphasis on the reliability segment of product quality has been increasing significantly. This has been due to such modern trends as

1. Greater use of automatic or automated products, production processes, and systems.

2. The increased complexity of these products, production processes, and systems.

Each of these two trends will be discussed briefly:

1. When products and systems were manually operated, some person was present to override them and to compensate for maladjustments.

For example, the manually operated carburetor choke on an automobile could be "overridden" by the automobile driver and opened or closed to produce the fuel mixture that would ignite under the conditions encountered.

When such a choke became automatic, however, there no longer was a simple, manual way to override it. If it went out of adjustment, it could not be made to perform by the automobile operator. Hence, the reliability element of automatic choke product quality suddenly became a matter of much greater importance than it had been in manual choke product quality.

When the automatic choke is multiplied by a multitude of the modern, more complex products of today—household automatic washers, automatic machine tools, electronic control equipments, automatic closed-circuit television, automatic electric ranges—the impact of the increased significance of product reliability becomes apparent.

2. In the automatic choke, the importance of reliability was further compounded by the fact that, in order to make a product function automatically, it is sometimes necessary to make it more complex. This increased complexity may tend, in itself, to make the product potentially less reliable because the more parts and functions there are in a device, the greater the probability that one or more will fail.

One of the more dramatic examples of these two trends is in the area of missiles and space vehicles. As compared with its manned-aircraft predecessor, and related to the first trend above, there is no crew aboard a missile to override or adjust its function. Related to the second trend, a missile is a very complex system, consisting of tens of thousands of parts working in electronic, hydraulic, mechanical, and chemical arrangements. Quite naturally, reliability characteristics have been even more heavily emphasized than for earlier manned aircraft. Reliability requirements have been quite rigidly established for missiles, and very specific customer reporting and evaluation of reliability performance has become a contractual requirement.

This emphasis on product reliability is a trend whose significance will continue to increase as products become more automatic and more complex in all product areas: consumer, industrial, and commercial.

Prior to the development of the total-quality-control activity, companies too frequently concentrated on testing their products at the start of product life [time t sub zero (t_0)] rather than also to evaluate product performance at stages during product life (times $t_1, t_2, \ldots, t_n$). In many cases, the related life testing and environmental testing were cursory. This may well explain why, prior to introducing total-quality-control programs, companies in all product areas have experienced extremely difficult reliability problems with their increasingly multifunction products when they were put to use by the customer.

14.2 Reliability and Costs

In the final analysis, the reliability requirements of a product are determined by its customers' requirements. There is a certain product-reliability standard that provides him with the most economical system to meet his needs. If this standard is set too low, actual total cost to the customer may be high, due to excessive repair, maintenance, and out-of-use costs. If an unduly high reliability standard is specified, total costs may still be excessive, due to the greater requirements for components and assemblies.

At some point, there is an optimum reliability value—determined as a balance with other product quality parameters—that provides lowest over-all costs, both to the purchaser and to the manufacturer. This point is probably never fully fixed because of the dynamic efforts of a business toward giving the customer progressively higher reliability without increasing product costs, or even while reducing product costs.

Purchasers have increasingly emphasized that they expect this standard of product reliability without undue premiums in prices they pay to manufacturers. As one knowledgeable purchaser has noted,[1]

"There is a strong tendency in some industries . . . to consider all reliability requirements as something 'extra.' This is like a haberdasher who offers to sell a new fedora for $10 and a few minutes later qualifies his price by saying that a fedora that really fits will cost $12. One simply does not buy a hat that does not fit.

"We all recognize that increased effort in any area necessitates extra expenditure. Just as any other customer . . . [we] must be willing to pay for those specific costs incurred to improve reliability; however, we must separate the traditional and basic elements of good management and engineering from those unusual and justifiable expenditures for higher reliability achievement. We must insist that the term, 'reliability,' not be used as camouflage for additional charges for those functions which are an intrinsic part of an effective industrial operation."

It is to assist in such circumstances by stripping away the camouflage and identifying the areas in which attention is really required that quality costs are broken down into their respective elements. Insofar as the reliability elements of quality cost are concerned, many segments of reliability costs have been considered already in the discussion of over-all quality costs as thoroughly reviewed in Chap. 5:

[1] Funk, Ben I., "Cost of Reliability," *Industrial Quality Control,* Vol. XVII, No. 3, September, 1960.

· Certain reliability-related costs must be incurred in planning the quality system and monitoring it to assure that the desired reliability is attained: these are included as parts of prevention and appraisal costs.

· These costs must be balanced against failure costs to achieve the specified product reliability.

· The total costs of quality within the company quality system must be optimized to meet company quality objectives, including their reliability component.

Definition and Measurement of Reliability

14.3 What Is Product Reliability?

Product reliability is one of the qualities of a product. Quite simply, it is the quality that measures the probability that the product or device "will work."

As a definition:

Product reliability is the probability of a product performing its intended function over its intended life and under the operating conditions encountered.

Four of the significant elements in the concept of reliability are

1. Probability.
2. Performance.
3. Time.
4. Environment.

1. The first element in reliability is the consideration of variation, discussed in Chap. 10, which makes of reliability a *probability*. Each individual unit of product will vary somewhat from other units; some may have a relatively short life and others a relatively long life. Further, a group of units may have a certain average life. Thus it is possible to identify frequency distributions of product failure which permit prediction of the life of units of product.

2. The second consideration contained in the definition is that reliability is a *performance* quality characteristic. For a product to be reliable, it must perform a certain function or do a certain job when called upon. For example, a heating pad must give the intended degree of heat when it is switched onto the low setting and must do the same for the medium and high settings.

Implied in the phrase, "performing its intended function," is that the device is intended for a certain application. In the case of the heating pad, the intended application is that of applying warmth to various areas of the human body. If, instead, it is used out-of-doors to keep a large container of coffee at a certain temperature, the heating pad might be inadequate because of changes in rate of heat transfer and greater volume to be heated, as well as a change in environment.

3. The third element in the definition of reliability is that of *time*. Reliability, stated as a probability of the product's performing a function, must be identified for a stated period of time.

An analogy is life insurance actuary tables. The probability of an individual's living through the next year is a different number than the probability of his living through the next decade. By the same token, a statement about the reliability of a product must be coupled to its intended life, whether 10 minutes or 10 years or whatever the life span is.

4. The fourth consideration in the definition is that of *environmental conditions*. These include the application and operating circumstances under which the product is put to use. These factors establish the stresses that will be imposed on the product. They need to be viewed broadly enough to include storage and transportation conditions, since these also can have significant effects on product reliability.

The environment which a product "sees" will greatly affect its life span and its performance. In the case of the heating pad, for example, the out-of-doors environment of the container of coffee is quite different from the relatively dry environment of a room and would significantly alter reliability of the pad.

The term *inherent reliability* has become popular for describing the potential reliability that the designer is able to create with his design. This is presumed to be the highest reliability that the particular design will afford. When the design is actually produced in the form of "hardware," it has some reliability value always less than the inherent reliability. This is usually considered as the achieved reliability.

The *achieved reliability* of a device is the reliability demonstrated by the physical product. Hence, it includes the manufacturing effects on product reliability, which, in reality, are always present for a physical product.

As a practical matter, the physical product is measured and analyzed to determine what effects are causing the achieved reliability to fall short of the inherent reliability. This calls for a study of the failure mechanism for the product under consideration.

Failure mechanism may be defined as the chronological series of events which logically lead to product failure. An understanding of these events, and the causes for them, permits elimination of those factors responsible for low achieved reliability.

14.4 The Measurement of Reliability

A basic measurement of the probability of the reliability of a product—that is, its probability of survival—is that of *mean time* between failures. This measurement leads, in turn, to the equally basic product parameter of *failure rate* for the same system, product, or component.

Much of reliability analysis has been founded on statistical studies to identify, product by product and component by component, distinct patterns of failure versus time during the life cycle of products and components. An increasing amount of such reliability data is becoming available, as a result of studies by manufacturers, research institutes, and

Bare-bulb temperature, °C	% Survival, 1,000 hours	% Survival, 2,000 hours	% Survival, 3,000 hours
			TYPE 6005/6AQ5W
220	97	97	97
237	78	64	
261	34	19	10
316	8	3	2
347	0		
			TYPE 5654/6AK5W
125	92	89	57
192	72	52	43
263	33	17	50
312	9	1	

General Electric: Tube-temperature study on Sig. Corps Contract DA-36-039-SC-72-42524.

FIG. 14.1. Tube-temperature study.

other agencies for use by companies that are considering use of the product. Figure 14.1 illustrates such data.

One pattern, for example, that seems basic for most electronic product systems is shown in Fig. 14.2. The life cycle consists of three distinct periods:

- The first period is termed the *infant mortality period* and is caused by early failure of weak components due principally to "assignable causes" of a nonrandom nature. This period is typified by a fairly high failure rate which drops off rapidly, perhaps a period of 100 hours or less.

· The second period is typified by a fairly constant rate of failure. Failures occur in the random manner associated with a constant cause system.

· The third period is termed the *wear-out period* in which the failure rate starts to rise rapidly as the number of survivors approaches zero until all units have failed and no more are "left to die."[2]

The reason for establishing these patterns is similar to that discussed in Chap. 10 in connection with rather more simple frequency distribution plots: when these patterns become known, they then permit the application to them of established mathematical probability distributions for measuring and predicting the failure rates of given products and components from sample data.

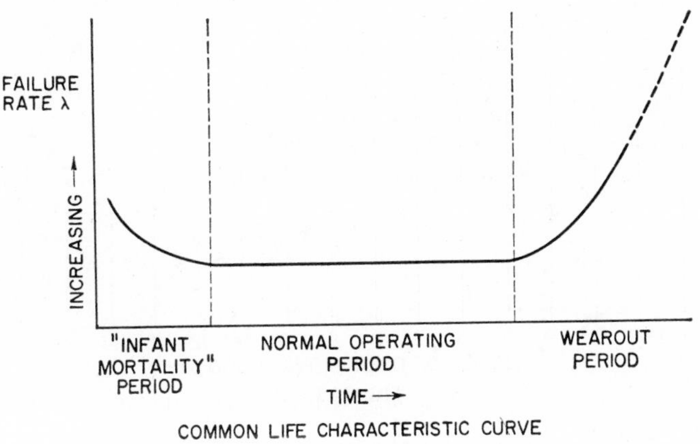

FIG. 14.2.

Frequency Distribution of Life for 200 Switches. As an example, let us start with the frequency distribution in Fig. 14.3 and show how it can be used to measure product reliability. This shows the lifetimes of 200 switches in terms of numbers of operations during the normal operating portion of switch life, i.e., after the infant mortality, or debugging, period and before the wear-out phase. This is the second period shown in Fig. 14.2.

As shown in Fig. 14.3, 20 switches failed during the first 1,000 operations, 18 between 1,000 and 2,000 operations, and so on. By the time the switches had operated 8,000 times, a total of 114 had failed—57 per cent of those that started on the test.

[2] The reader will note the similarity between the terminology of reliability and that of actuarial practice.

Relative Frequency of Failures Based on a Sample. As was shown in Chap. 12, such a sample can give us information that permits us to describe the nature of the larger lot which the sample represents.

Where experience with a new design is limited, as is usually the case, it is necessary to rely on representative samples to provide the logical basis on which to predict the expected failures. Thus, in the observations of a sample of N components taken at random from a large group of similar components, if n_t of them have lifetimes that end during the time period t, the statistical probability that similar results will be obtained from the

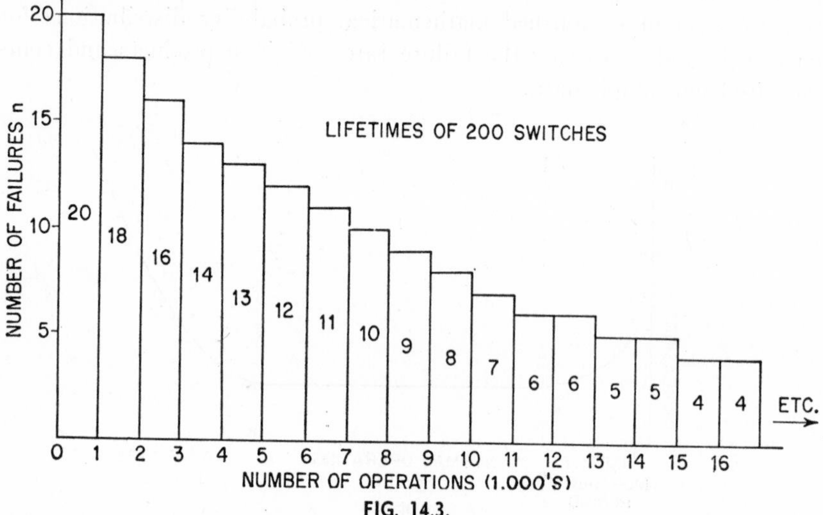

FIG. 14.3.

remainder (untested items) of the group is defined as the *relative frequency:*

$$P_t = \frac{n_t}{N} \tag{39}$$

where P_t = probability of failure during period t
n_t = number of items having lifetimes ending during period t
N = total number of items in sample

Applying equation (39) to the data presented in Fig. 14.3, the probability that a switch will fail after 5,000 and before 6,000 operations is $^{12}/_{200} = 0.06$.

Confidence in this estimate increases, of course, with larger sample sizes. As the sample size approaches the total number of units produced, confidence in the parameters of this lot approaches certainty. Putting it another way, there is a greater chance that the ratio n_t/N, computed for each of two equal sample sizes taken from the same lot, will more closely agree with each other when the sample size is large rather than small. And this ratio, n_t/N, can be regarded as an experimental value of a constant P_t, related to the time period t and referred to as the *probability of occurrence for the period t.*

Reliability Related to Relative Frequency of Failure. In the definition of reliability given in Sec. 14.3, performance over intended life was one criterion. The intended or required life T can be measured in different ways; i.e., total elapsed time, energized time, number of operating cycles, and the like. In order to obtain a measurement for reliability, the actual life t must be compared to the required life T.

The relationship between the reliability of a component and the frequency diagram of lifetimes can be illustrated by using Fig. 14.3. If the area of the combined bars, assuming all 200 switches were run to destruction, is set equal to 1, then the probability, or relative frequency of a particular class of lifetimes—say, 5,000–6,000 operations—equals the area of the bar representing that class of lifetimes; in this case, the bar labeled 12. Note that this is equivalent to plotting relative frequency n_t/N rather than n_t along the ordinate of Fig. 14.3. Also, the relative frequency of failures in the interval $0 \leq t \leq T$ is $(20 + 18 + 16 + 14 + 13 + 12)/200 = 93/200 = 0.465$ when T equals 6,000 operations; so that the probability of a switch failure during the first 6,000 operations is $P_{t=T} = 0.465$. Conversely, the probability that a switch will *survive* the first 6,000 operations (i.e., its *reliability* R_T) is $1.00 - 0.465 = 0.535$, or symbolically,

$$R_T = 1 - P_{t=T} = 1.0 - \frac{1}{N} \Sigma_0^T n_t \tag{40}$$

The symbol Σ (Greek letter capital sigma) denotes arithmetic summation. Thus the term $\Sigma_0^T n_t$ in the above formula is read "the summation of the number of items having lifetimes ending during period t, (n_t), where t ranges from zero to the required life T.

Development of a Continuous (Smooth) Curve and Summing of Areas. If Fig. 14.3 had presented data for 1,000 switches rather than 200 switches, and if the abscissa were to be subdivided into hundreds of operations, 170 slender rectangles would result and their tops would approximate a smooth curve. The limiting form of the frequency diagram, as the fineness of divisions and the number of observations increased indefinitely, is, in general, a smooth curve like that shown in Fig. 14.4. The relative frequency n_t/N is seen to be a function of time $f(t)$ so that

$$R_T = 1.0 - \int_0^T f(t)\, dt \tag{41}$$

As the number of observations increases indefinitely, the summation of a particular area under the curve, in this case from 0 to T, is computed by integration rather than by a straight arithmetic summation. The interested reader is referred to any of the standard textbooks on the calculus for a more detailed explanation of this technique.

It is generally easier to measure the failure rate of a class of units than it is to measure its reliability directly by constructing frequency diagrams like the one appearing as Fig. 14.3. Less time is required, and also fewer samples are destroyed. However, failure-rate data are of little value unless judgment or theoretical considerations can be relied upon to indicate the general form of the frequency diagram that would be generated if sufficient data were available.

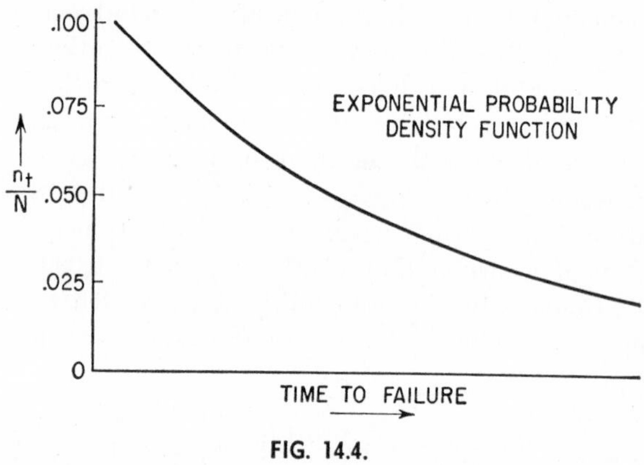

FIG. 14.4.

Constant Failure Rate Results from Exponential Probability Density Function. As was pointed out at the beginning of this section and in Fig. 14.2, a constant failure rate is commonly encountered and should be expected for those parts and components that are so complex as to offer failure mechanisms with different rates. If approximately the same *percentage* of parts remaining at the start of each time interval fail during the interval, the failure rate is constant. For example, Fig. 14.3 depicts a situation for a constant failure rate of approximately 10 per cent. In the first cell $^{20}/_{200} = 10$ per cent; in the second cell $^{18}/_{180} = 10$ per cent; in the third cell $^{16}/_{162} = 9.9$ per cent, etc.

The exponential probability density function, which describes the constant-failure-rate situation, results in a frequency curve as shown in Fig. 14.4 and is represented by the formula

$$f(t) = \frac{1}{\theta} e^{-t/\theta} \tag{42}$$

If this function is substituted in equation (41), the following results:

$$R_T = 1.0 - \int_0^T \frac{1}{\theta} e^{-t/\theta}\, dt = e^{-T/\theta} \tag{43}$$

where T = the required life
θ = the mean life or mean time to failure
e = a constant (2.7183) (see footnote 3)

Reliability Determined Directly from Failure Rate. The failure rate λ by definition is the reciprocal of the mean time to failure and can be substituted in equation (43), giving

$$R_T = e^{-\lambda T} \tag{44}$$

In this example the failure rate λ approximates 10 per cent, or $\lambda \simeq 0.10$. From equation (44), the probability of a switch of the type described by Fig. 14.3 surviving 6.0 (thousand) operations is

$$R_T \cong e^{(-0.10)(6.0)} \cong 0.55$$

which is in close agreement with 0.535, determined from the relative frequencies of the data given in Fig. 14.3.

Note that, in this case, the required life T is expressed in thousands of operations because the data are in terms of failures per thousand operations.

Failure Rates, Other than Constant, Described by Other Density Functions. The example discussed here was one involving a constant failure rate which derives from the exponential probability density function.

Although this is a frequently encountered pattern of failure, there are other density functions which accommodate most of the patterns encountered in practice. These include the following density functions:[4]

1. Normal.
2. Gamma.
3. Weibull.

Figure 14.5 illustrates representations of these functions in practice.

Need for Characterizing Failure Patterns. Although significant technical effort and substantial funds have been devoted to reliability studies, great continuing effort is required to establish progressively more meaningful failure rate patterns since

1. Many more product tests are required than can be justified economically on certain commercial components and products, so that

[3] Naperian base used for natural logarithms.

[4] For a discussion, see Herd, G. Ronald, "Some Statistical Concepts and Techniques for Reliability Analysis and Prediction," *Proceedings, Fifth National Symposium on Reliability and Quality Control,* Philadelphia, Pa., Jan. 12–14, 1959.

these reliability parameters have frequently been analytical projections for which much more actual sampling evidence is still required.

2. Many extremely expensive components, particularly those used in research products, have not been extensively tested for reliability data because of the attendant destruction of the component.

3. In one- or few-of-a-kind products and components, failure-rate patterns have necessarily been somewhat speculative.

4. Interaction of components, one on the other, has resulted in a

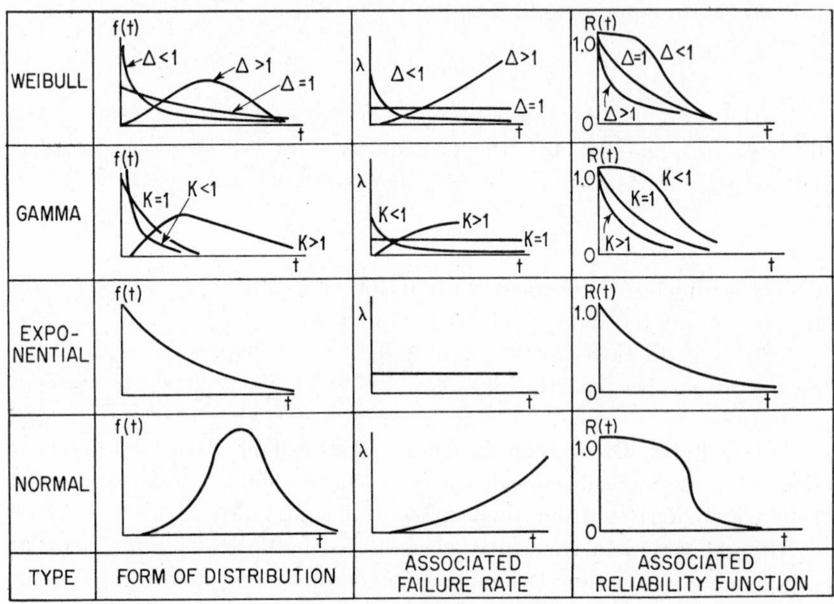

TYPES OF PROBABILITY DISTRIBUTIONS ENCOUNTERED IN RELIABILITY AND THEIR ASSOCIATED FAILURE RATES AND RELIABILITY FUNCTIONS

FIG. 14.5.

reliability value for the system quite different from that which would be estimated on the basis of the components in the system.[5]

Combining Component Reliabilities to Get Product Reliability. *Series Combination.* If a product is an assembly of m components, each with its own reliability R_{T_i}, and if failure of any component will cause failure

[5] Theoretically, the reliability of a system made of a series of components can be obtained by multiplying together all the individual reliability values for the various components discussed later in the section. This assumes no interaction. In practice it is difficult to simulate tests for components that represent the environment of the system under end-use conditions. Actual values in practice may depart from predicted values, in either direction, as much as 200 to 300 per cent.

of the product, then the product reliability will be predicted by the following:

$$R_T = R_{T_1} \times R_{T_2} \times R_{T_3} \times \cdots \times R_{T_m} \qquad (45)$$

Such a system is schematically illustrated by Fig. 14.6.

If the components in Fig. 14.6 fail in accordance with the exponential probability density function, then equation (45) can be written as

$$R_T = (e^{-\lambda_1 T})(e^{-\lambda_2 T})(e^{-\lambda_3 T}) \cdots (e^{-\lambda_m T}) \qquad (46)$$

or

$$R_T = e^{-T(\lambda_1+\lambda_2+\lambda_3+\cdots+\lambda_m)} \qquad (47)$$

in which λ_1, λ_2, λ_3, . . . , λ_m are the failure rates of the M components as determined by component testing, reference to catalogs, or theoretical considerations.

For example, consider the problem of predicting the 10-hour reliability of a product containing the components listed below:

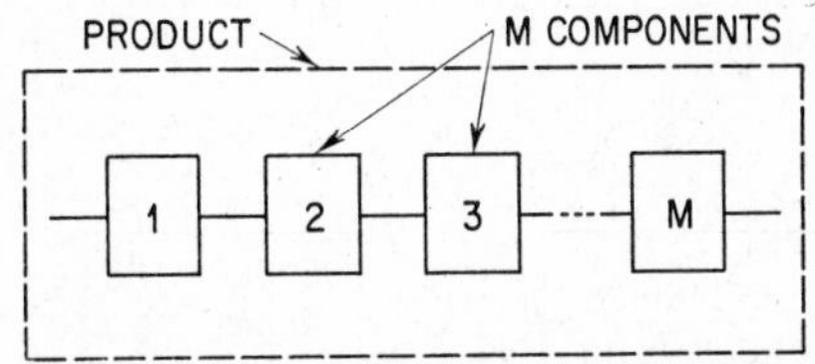

FIG. 14.6. Series arrangement of components.

Component or part	No. in product (m)	Failure rate, λ per hour	Combined failure rate, $(m)(\lambda)$
Diode	52	120×10^{-6}	6.240×10^{-3}
Motor	3	100	.300
Relay	18	145	2.610
Resistor	213	10	2.130
Potentiometer	26	70	1.820
Switch	82	25	2.050
Transformer	21	20	.420
Soldered joint	341	18	6.138
			$\Sigma\lambda = 21.708 \times 10^{-3}$

The summation of the component failure rate is the predicted failure rate of the product in terms of product failures per hour. The product failure rate is 21.708×10^{-3}, and the 10-hour product reliability, using equation (47), is

$$R_{10} = e^{-(10)(0.0217)} = e^{-.217} = .805$$

The Basic Reliability Activities in the Quality System

14.5 Activities of Reliability

The activities in the quality system that are geared to the establishment and control of a product's failure rate, in terms of the elements of probability, of time, of performance, and of environment, represent important elements of work that are carried on in four jobs of total quality control. These reliability activities may be grouped under four headings:

1. Establishing the Product Reliability Requirements, discussed in Sec. 14.6.

2. Developing the Reliability Program to Meet the Requirements Including Product Design, Manufacturing Processes, and Transportation, discussed in Secs. 14.7 through 14.13.

3. Continuing Control of Reliability, discussed in Sec. 14.14.

4. Continuing Reliability Analysis, discussed in Sec. 14.15.

Activities 1, 2, and 4 are among the key activities in the new-design-control job. Activity 3 is a vital portion of the product-control job.

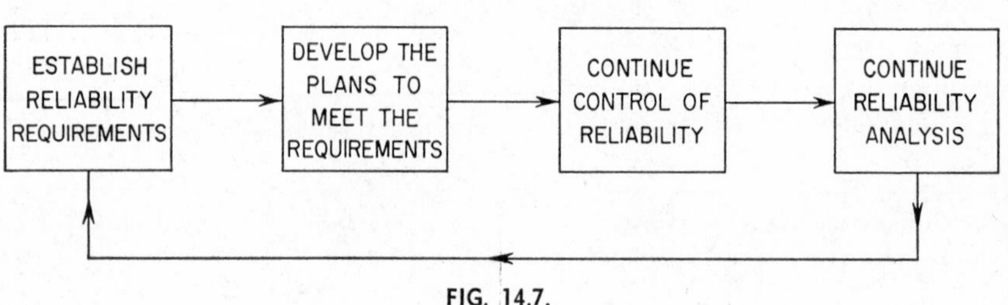

FIG. 14.7.

Fig. 14.7 shows the relationship among these four activities. The data drawn from continuing analysis of product reliability are fed back so that requirements are regularly reviewed with respect to adequacy in terms of product design, process design, and the related control systems.

14.6 Establishing the Product Reliability Requirements

The initial new design control activity involves establishing the standards for mean time to failure and whatever other reliability targets may be indicated to meet the inherent reliability required for the product. As was discussed in Sec. 14.2, the cost of attaining an incremental increase in reliability must be balanced against the costs associated with not attaining it.

Since this over-all balance is of primary interest to the customer, the selected reliability target should be a matter of agreement between the customer (or his representative) and the manufacturer, in such areas as industrial products and military equipment. In the case of consumer products, where the customer will not be present at the reliability review, every effort should be made by the manufacturer to represent him as realistically as possible.

The selection of a reliability standard should be a practical matter rather than a speculative exercise. The standard must be chosen with due attention to the state of the technical art and with understanding of what it will take to extend this art beyond current limits. It must be obtainable within economic bounds.

Too often these elements have not been realistically considered when reliability standards have been created, and unrealistic reliability specifications and costs have been the result.

To be meaningful, the reliability targets must be within reach at a planned date.

This means separation of the reliability analysis into two areas:

- Reliability considerations that can be currently established in relation to current capabilities.
- Considerations that require further analysis, testing, and development before satisfactory data can be considered as established, i.e., new components, new use of old components, etc.

The reliability specified may thus require further technical advances before it can be attained. To accomplish these advances requires that the greatest effort be placed where it is needed. A careful analysis of the proposed system will reveal the components with the highest failure rates. These should be "split out" of the package for further research and development work.

Required reliability values may ultimately be realized only after the product has been placed in production. Some of the increase in reliability is due to increased skill as a result of the learning process. The major portion, however, is afforded by basic refinements to both product design and process design. This is made possible by sufficient numbers of units and accompanying data on which fundamental decisions can be based for reliability improvement.

Throughout it must be remembered that the objective is that of achieving the optimum value for the reliability parameter of product quality—rather than the establishment of any particular special means for this purpose. This means emphasis on simplicity to the extent possible. As an observer has noted, "The present trend toward complexity of missile systems must be reversed before it becomes a limitation. Is it reasonable to expect reliability of an inverted pyramid of four gadgets to cure the bugs in two gadgets which are necessary because the original device was inadequate? How much better to use a simple well-thought-out design in the first place. We fear that many are so confused they think a clever fix is the equal of good design. Reliability unsupported by crutches, no matter how artistically they are carved, should always be the end in view."

14.7 Developing the Reliability Program to Meet the Requirements, Including Product Design, Manufacturing Processes, and Transportation

The plan by which the product reliability requirements are to be attained involves the product-engineering specification which establishes the system, components and configuration; the manufacturing-process specification by which the product is to be made; the packaging and transportation specifications in which the product will be protected; and the selection of the transportation by which it will be moved to the customer. Each of these plans, and some of the considerations that must be taken into account in doing each specific part of the planning, are discussed in the following sections.

Attention is first directed toward determination of product reliability requirements and the design-engineering considerations necessary in specifying a product to meet these requirements. It becomes the problem of the design engineer to specify the design, manufactured by a certain process, that will meet certain reliability requirements within the economic limitations involved.

Where does the design engineer start? Usually, the desired product function, on which a reliability requirement is placed, determines the reliability of the product that is to provide that function. The product, however, is composed of many individual components. Each of these components contributes its share to the reliability of the product, as was shown by the example near the end of Sec. 14.4.

The design engineer starts by considering the arrangement of components he must have to provide the supporting functions essential to the over-all product function. He then evaluates the reliability of the product on the basis of the individual component reliabilities. If certain individual component reliabilities are unknown, it may be necessary to evaluate them by simulation tests. Where analysis shows certain type components to have a critical effect on the reliability of the product, it may be necessary to alter the design so less use of such critical components is made possible. Or it may be necessary to obtain components with a higher reliability or to use components with higher ratings or to provide redundancy in the design. These alternatives are discussed in Secs. 14.8 to 14.10.

When the optimum theoretical product design has been created on paper, it is prudent to build a prototype and test it, measuring its performance and thereby determining its reliability. Such tests show up the weak components, where additional reliability improvement is required. It is then possible to concentrate on these component types, thereby improving product reliability to the required standard of inherent reliability.

The larger the number of components in a product, the more serious the reliability problem becomes. If a product must have a reliability of .90 and is composed of 10 components, then the reliability of each component must be approximately .99; however, if the product employed 1,000 components, the reliability of each component would have to be .9999. When the reliability requirements get this high, as noted above, an almost unbelievable amount of testing is required. The only practical solution appears to be the designing of products with adequate design margins and the manufacturing of products with satisfactory precision and control.

The important considerations involved in the designing process and related to the product are

Design Margin, discussed in Sec. 14.8.

Derating, discussed in Sec. 14.9.

Redundancy, discussed in Sec. 14.10.

Other considerations involved in assuring a reliable product are reserved for later sections. Manufacturing process and transporation considerations are discussed in Secs. 14.11 and 14.12.

Evaluation of the reliability planning resulting from all these considerations is accomplished by means of tests. These are discussed in Sec. 14.13.

14.8 Design Margin

One of the most important concepts in designing a reliable product is that of *design margin*. This is comparable to the so-called factor of safety that civil engineers have been using for centuries. For example, if a bridge is designed with a factor of safety of 4, this simply means that the bridge is four times stronger than necessary to meet the ordinarily expected stresses. This has often been called the "ignorance factor." In other words, this factor of safety covered unknown stresses that might occur, variability in the strength of the materials used, variability due to workmanship, etc. As knowledge increases and variability decreases, it is possible to use lower safety factors.

A better idea of how design margin relates to product strength variability[6] can be gained from Fig. 14.8. As discussed in Chap. 10, product variability is measured in units of standard deviation (sigma). One recommended practice for designing missiles with adequate reliability, for example, is to allow a margin of 5 sigma between the lowest strength product item that will be encountered and the maximum stress

[6] The term *product strength,* as used here, refers to a quality of a product to endure against the stresses of its specific environment and use. It is a comparative term rather than absolute; i.e., the product strength of a footbridge might be greater than that of a railroad bridge, although the former is of lighter construction.

imposed by the environment that the product will encounter. Thus, this 5-sigma margin becomes the *design margin.*

To design intelligently, using any specified margin, it is necessary to know the variability of product strengths and the maximum stresses imposed by the environment. Often neither are known with sufficient accuracy. This necessitates building the product and subjecting it to the environments it will encounter in service. In this way, the product weaknesses (lack of product strengths) are determined in relation to a given environment by a trial-and-error process. In this manner, the "weak

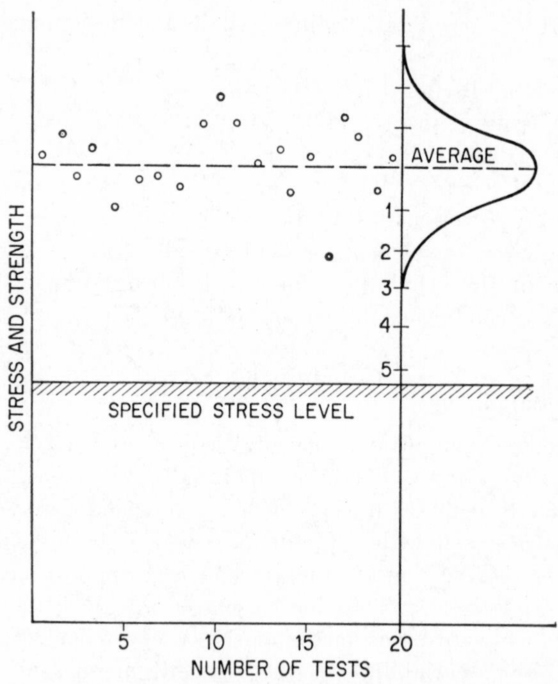

FIG. 14.8. Product strength versus stress.

links" in the chain are identified and strengthened to provide the required design margin.

Both product strength and environmental stress values can be affected, sometimes drastically, by what happens during manufacture. Much of the variability that the design engineer must work with is caused by the variability of manufacturing processes. It is the manufacturing process that causes variability in the strength of materials due to nonhomogeneity, variations in dimensions, and variation in composition.

The same can be said of the electrical characteristics of components. For example, the use of transistors in designs was not practical until manufacturing processes and techniques could be developed to provide the required purity of semiconductor material. A significant contribution to the reliability program comes from studying the effects of process capabilities and process stability so necessary process improvements can be made. A more detailed treatment of manufacturing effect on reliability is reserved for Sec. 14.11.

14.9 Derating

One technique of design in providing a greater margin between design strengths and environmental stresses is to derate components. Derating simply means that the component is being assigned to a task somewhat less arduous than that for which it was originally designed. For example, a 3,000-ohm resistor may have originally been rated at a standard of 70°C ambient temperature and a 1-watt power dissipation. If this resistor were selected for an application where the ambient temperature is 60°C and power dissipation ½ watt, it might be derated for both ambient temperature and wattage dissipation. The effect of such derating would be to put less stress on the part; hence one would expect less deviation of resistance values from the original resistance over a given period of time.

14.10 Redundancy

The reliability of products can be increased by providing a spare component that can be brought into use in case a component fails. The use of a spare tire on an automobile is a homely example of redundancy. Of course, in electronic systems provision is made automatically to switch the spare component into the circuit in the event the original component performing the specific desired function should fail.

Usually redundancy is employed as a last resort and only for those functions that have reliabilities that seriously reduce the total reliability of the system. In airborne equipment, redundancy increases weight; hence it is to be avoided if possible. In any application, redundancy increases initial costs and maintenance costs. Care must also be taken to see that reliability is not adversely affected by introducing redundancy into the design. This may happen as a result of the interaction between redundant components and other components of a system.

14.11 The Manufacturing Process: An Integral Part of the Reliability Program

If there is a "best product design," there has to be a related "best manufacturing process." There is always a manufacturing process present when a device is brought into being, be it a prototype or a production item. In order to determine what maximum reliability is possible, from a given design, it is necessary at some point to build something and make it operate in order to see what it will do.

Inherent reliability thus must always be referred to a given product design and to the process used to produce it. A higher reliability value might be attained by changing the design or the process or both.

When this point of view is identified, it can be seen that the manufacturing function of a company has a major contribution to make in programming product reliability. Manufacturing people can take aggressive, dynamic action in pushing the frontiers of knowledge ahead in their specialty fields to improve product reliability.

One of the important contributions that manufacturing can make is the identification of process conditions as to their effects on product reliability. For example, what dip-solder temperature gives electrical connections on a printed circuit board the highest reliability? What are the effects of solder-flux removal by certain solvents on dielectric strength of printed boards?

These are two simple examples of the kinds of questions to which answers must be found if desired product reliability is to be attained. This involves careful research and development of manufacturing processes and entails the use of scientific experimentation. Maximum information can be gained by making use of designs of experiments as discussed in Chap. 13.

14.12 Packaging and Transportation Planning: An Essential Part of the Reliability Program

The only product reliability that counts is what the customer can actually experience. There is not much point in having a device with a highly reliable design, carefully manufactured, if its reliability is seriously deteriorated because of poor protection and rough handling during shipping.

In many companies, the design of packaging is all too frequently regarded as a secondary matter; yet in other companies, specialists are assigned this responsibility. Even though the size of some companies cannot justify packaging specialists, the responsibility should be assigned to an organizational component with the required competence.

After packages have been designed, they should be evaluated. If simulated shipping tests are conducted by means of impact testers, vibration tables, compression testers, etc., the parameters of the stresses that the packaged product will experience during shipment must be known.

If actual trial shipments are made, care must be used to see that they are representative of what may be encountered shipment upon shipment. A single shipment can hardly be expected to render conclusive results. Routes, method of transportation, and extremes of temperature and humidity should be represented in such tests.

14.13 Evaluation of Reliability Plans by Means of Tests

Whether the reliability planning be for product, process, or packaging designs, it should be tested at appropriate points during the reliability program. Early design proposals will be checked out by means of so-called breadboard tests. Proposed manufacturing processes will be tested by trial runs and further proved out by means of pilot runs. As discussed in Sec. 14.12, packaging may be proved by laboratory tests and trial shipments.

In order to obtain the most information from reliability tests, it is necessary to run the devices to failure. In this manner, the failure mechanism can be determined, as well as the distribution of failures with time. This should be accomplished early in a product-development plan during the prototype stage.

Since such tests are destructive and usually expensive to conduct, the desire is to test as few samples as possible over as short a time as possible. As a consequence, such tests are often run under accelerated conditions obtained by increasing loading and environmental stresses and terminating the tests prior to failure. If accelerated tests are used, they must correlate reasonably well with actual operating experience in the field. An indication of the time involved in testing for moderately high reliability values is suggested in the following example:[7]

If it is desired to evaluate a product to a .990 reliability at a 90 per cent confidence level, it is necessary to test 230 unit-minutes for each operational unit-minute without a failure. This means that if a device is to be operational over a period of one year, a sample of 230 units would have to operate over a year's time without a failure. Or using a trade-off of number of devices with time, 460 units could be tested over a six-month period. This assumes an exponential chance failure curve and must be well ahead of the device's wear-out portion of the life curve.

14.14 Continuing Control of Reliability

At the conclusion of new design control work, the next activity in the reliability program is that of continuing control. The product-control job of total quality control includes work in all areas that will affect product reliability: incoming components, process control, transportation, and so forth.

[7] Fritz, E. L., and J. S. Youtcheff, "Sequential Life Testing in Systems Development," Missile and Space Vehicles Department, General Electric Company.

For example, when a manufacturing process is improved and a new standard of reliability is established, it needs to be "pegged," so there will be no slipping back to old standards.

How can this be accomplished? How can it be determined when the process is slipping? It was shown earlier that variation is inherent in any manufacturing process. How, then, can there be determined the difference between a slippage from the newly pegged standard and a normal variation from that standard. This is one of the areas in which the technique of process-control engineering contributes to product reliability.

It is possible statistically to determine the limiting values of the pattern that typifies the controlled state. This is the basis for the control chart which is discussed in Chap. 11. A controlled process is a predictable process, and an uncontrolled process is not predictable; hence, a controlled process is essential to achieving a product with a specific reliability. As has been noted: "A state of statistical control must be the goal of our entire effort—design, production and testing. This is the only known path to reliability. It is inescapable; it is incontrovertible."[8]

The process-control engineer, in endeavoring to bring about a state of control for a process critical to product reliability, should carefully consider the control function served by modern quality information equipment. Especially those processes that are subject to drift due to tool wear, exhaustion of chemicals, temperature effects, and other environmental influences can be automatically adjusted to compensate for such effects and kept in a state of statistical control. Becoming increasingly available are specialized $\bar{X}$, σ computers that can take measurement information, statistically analyze it, and automatically feed back information to adjust the process the required amount to maintain the subject quality characteristic within specified limits. Such systems were discussed more fully in Chap. 9.

Measurements of quality characteristics and their analyses by means of control charts or computers detect a change in processing that could have a decided influence on the reliability of the product; however, a process-control engineer's responsibility does not end here. What would be the result if some important quality characteristic were completely overlooked and no measurements taken? The only safeguard against such a possibility is actually to measure the end result, specifically the reliability of the product after manufacture. This has to be done on a continuing basis with actual production units to protect against the intrusion of some unknown factor.

[8] Kellogg, Harold R., "Statistical Quality Control and Reliability," *Industrial Quality Control,* Vol. XVI, No. 11, May, 1960.

14.15 Continuing Reliability Analysis

Product reliability is seldom, if ever, a "one-shot" effort. Even in those cases where only a few prototypes are produced as part of a research and development program, intensive study and extensive reliability testing are continuously performed to gain knowledge that can be used for succeeding generations of similar products.

This sustained new-design-control effort is made to increase reliability in the majority of cases because

1. State of the art may not yet have advanced to a point where the required reliability has been realized in the product in question.
2. The costs, because of low reliability, may be excessive because of too many premature product failures.
3. Maintenance and repair costs during the expected life of the product may be excessively high.
4. Consequences of product failure may be serious in terms of lost life, property damage, lost income, or inconvenience.
5. Competitive products may be pushing to higher reliability values.
6. Customers may be dissatisfied and may be demanding higher reliability values.

Research and Development Programs for Reliability Improvement. In a few cases, the value of a highly reliable product is so great as to justify multimillion-dollar research and development programs to gain an increase of a few per cent in the reliability of a critical component or system. For most industrial and consumer products, however, no such expenditures can be justified. Improvement in reliability comes as the result of a sustained effort on the part of the technical and factory personnel normally assigned to the particular product under consideration. The efforts of such personnel are directed to a considerable extent by a continuing, thorough reliability analysis of the product.

Continual Testing to Evaluate Product Reliability. Continual testing is not only necessary for purposes of control, as discussed in Sec. 14.14; it is also necessary for providing exhaustive data on which to base reliability improvement programs. Such data eventually would accumulate as a result of field experience; however, for most products, elapsed time extends far beyond useful limits. The product might become obsolete before its reliability could be improved. Hence, it is necessary to intensify testing, not only by testing large samples of product as discussed in Sec. 14.13, but also by crowding as many operating hours as possible into as short a time as possible. This may require operation under simulated field conditions.

As an example of a product that requires such intensified testing, consider the electric hand iron. It is used only 4 hours per week in the average home. Under such conditions, it would take 10 years to determine its life. Certainly, such a lengthy wait for data is out of the question when an analysis is required for sustained product reliability improvement.

An intensive test established in a hand laundry or shirt factory would log 16 hours per day, or 80 hours per week. This is a twentyfold increase in energized time and gives an answer in 6 months instead of 10 years. Even 6 months is longer than is desirable, and the conditions encountered are not equivalent to those encountered in the home; e.g., the iron is not being turned off and on as frequently per operating hour. Weakness due to differential expansion and contraction of parts might not become as apparent. Conceivably, a simulated test might be established that could be run 24 hours per day with an arbitrary number of heat-up and cool-down cycles. Here the quality information equipment engineer can make an important contribution in simulating time cycles and duration of environmental stresses for equipment to evaluate product reliability.

Accelerated Tests as a Means for Obtaining Results Promptly. Accelerated tests are often used where the nature of the device permits it. This is done by increasing the environmental stress to show product weaknesses in the shortest period of time. In the case of the electric hand iron, this might be accomplished by operating it at 150 volts rather than the rated 120 volts. This would have the effect of making the heating element operate at a higher temperature; hence, it would tend to burn out more readily, thereby showing up defects affecting reliability in the shortest time, e.g., nicks in the resistance wire used in the heating element. The increased voltage would also require the thermostat to break higher current values, thereby increasing arcing and attrition of the contacts.

Accelerated life tests are of value only to the degree to which they correlate with actual-use life tests or intensive life tests. There is a definite limit to severity of conditions. Beyond this limit, other factors, quite different from those encountered in actual use, enter to give misleading and false evaluation of life. There are many devices that do not lend themselves to accelerated testing to any appreciable extent. An electron vacuum tube is one such device.

Importance of Preserving Failure Mechanism. If the device being subjected to accelerated testing is fairly simple and its life depends on a simple failure mechanism that can be speeded up by increasing certain stresses, fairly good correlation can be obtained. Capacitors and resistors lend themselves to accelerated testing. Many other components and assemblies, including electron tubes, cannot be accelerated because the increased stresses create additional failure mechanisms rather than merely speeding up those that are present under normal operation. For example, if increased voltage causes arcing, the electron tube is "killed." Under normal voltages, such arcing probably would not have occurred, and its life might well have been exceptionally long.

Importance of Correlation. Whatever tests are used, they must be standardized as to conditions of environment, and the resultant mean time between failures must be referenced to some standard of reliability. The referencing must be done through use of a regression line that correlates the test-condition results with the actual-use-condition results. This is necessary to obtain meaningful data.

If it is found through experience that there is a poor correlation between tests run under simulated conditions (or accelerated conditions) and actual end-use conditions, it will be necessary to change the standard test conditions until reasonably good correlation is established.

Efficiency of Tests. Reliability testing is expensive. It requires elaborate test setups to simulate environmental conditions; testing extends over relatively long periods of time; the devices tested are usually consumed as a result of the test; power requirements are often high where high loads are necessary. Furthermore, when the testing is done to monitor the process and to discover where it can be improved, it must be done on a continuing basis. It is not a one-shot test, such as used when qualifying a design. It is, in effect, a matter of continually requalifying the design and the current process.

Because of the expense involved, it is important to get the maximum efficiency out of tests, i.e., the most information in the shortest time for the least expenditure of money. Full use should be made of statistical techniques in proving the specified reliability at the required confidence level.

Field-test Data. As has been pointed out earlier in this section, data resulting from use of the product in the field, while slow to accumulate, are essential for correlation with accelerated tests to determine the latter's effectiveness. Field data, when available, are most valuable and certainly should not be ignored. Every effort should be made to see that they are accurately recorded and fed back to the plant for analysis on a continuing basis.

Data Collection and Analysis Sometimes a Contractual Requirement. In many contracts involving the production of weapons systems, the collection and analysis of field data for reliability improvement is made a contractual requirement. A complete log is kept on each system and follows the device throughout its life. Its complete history is recorded: transport, storage, tests, service, maintenance, and use. To keep account of energized time, clocks are often inserted in specific circuits. The clock accumulates the time during which the current is on. All data on all systems of a given type are brought to a data center, where they are processed and analyzed. Periodic reports are issued to the procurement agencies.

Reliability Improvement Is the Objective. Continual reliability testing, as discussed in this section, provides test data, the analysis of which shows where the technical effort must be placed to improve reliability. Certain components will show up as the "weak links" in the system. These must then be studied as to their failure mechanism. When the true failure mechanism has been identified, it is often possible to tell whether the answer to the problem involves a change in product design or manufacturing methods or simply better control of established manufacturing processes. A consistent upgrading of reliability through a series of effective design changes, method changes, and improved quality control generally provides an economic means for attaining required product reliability goals.

Achievement of Product Reliability Through the Quality System

14.16 Total Quality Control and Its Reliability Process

Since product reliability is one of the more important "qualities" of the product, it cannot be operationally or systematically separated from other product-quality considerations. The first six chapters of this book quite thoroughly reviewed this total quality concept. This section will further relate this concept and its reliability component.

As was noted in Chap. 4, responsibilities for product quality thread throughout the entire company organization. This is true for reliability, just as it is for all components of quality, with specific assignments being made to appropriate positions.

Chapter 6 reviewed the constitution of the quality system: the network of administrative and technical procedures for carrying out these related yet separate responsibilities in parts of quality work. The individual actions required to assure product reliability are delineated in this quality system and are an integral part of it.

Three of the subsystems of the quality system will be used as illustrations of how the assurance of reliability results from operation of the system.

1. Preproduction Quality Evaluation, discussed in Sec. 14.17.
2. Purchased-material Quality Planning, Evaluation, and Control, discussed in Sec. 14.18.
3. Postproduction Quality Service, discussed in Sec. 14.19.

14.17 Preproduction Quality Evaluation

This subsystem involves such product-reliability activities as the following:

• Determining the standard of reliability required by the customer for the product.

• Clearly identifying the environment the product will encounter.

• Determining the economic balance between reliability and total costs to obtain it.

• Optimizing the design to obtain the required product reliability.

• Selecting processes and process parameters that contribute to high product reliability.

• Proving by means of prototype and pilot-run tests that required reliability is attainable.

• Eliminating from product design and process design, so far as possible, any threats to product reliability.

14.18 Purchased-material Quality Planning, Evaluation, and Control

This subsystem involves product-reliability activities of which the following are examples:

• Clear delineation of reliability requirements to vendors.

• Evaluation of vendors' capabilities for producing products of the required reliability.

• Evaluation of vendors' product reliability on a continuing basis.

• Servicing of vendors for product-reliability improvement.

14.19 Postproduction Quality Service

This subsystem involves the following product reliability activities:

• Review of guarantees and warranties with respect to product reliability and their equitable adjustment.

• Reliability evaluations of competitive products.

• Information flow from factory to field with reference to anticipated reliability problems and corrective action.

• Information flow from field to factory with reference to reliability problems encountered and corrective action.

• Certification of product reliability to the customer.

• Audit of product reliability after shipment, during and after warehousing, after installation, and in use.

• Reliability maintenance through adequate instructions concerning installation, maintenance, and use; serviceability of product; tools and techniques for repairs; quality cost and timeliness of field service.

• Measuring of product-reliability performance in the field by costs and failure rates.

Summary

14.20 Summary of Part Four

The statistical point of view toward industrial product quality may be briefly summarized: *variation* in product quality must be constantly studied within batches of product, on processing equipments, between different lots of the same article, on critical quality characteristics and standards, in regard to the pilot runs of a newly designed article. This variation may best be studied by the analysis of samples selected from the product lots or from units produced by the processing equipments.

There are five statistical tools which have been found useful in making practical application of this point of view in the four quality-control jobs. These tools are

1. Frequency distribution.
2. Control charts.
3. Sampling tables.
4. Special methods.
5. Reliability prediction.

These five techniques, though highly useful in many cases, represent in the final analysis only one of the technologies that are used in an over-all total-quality-control program for a company. These statistical tools have been discussed in detail in Part Four of this book primarily because they are one of the most used of the quality-control technologies.

A few applications of these statistical tools have been presented in Part Four, but fuller discussion of their use along with the other quality-control technical methods is reserved for Part Five.

14.21 Glossary of Important Symbols and Terms Used in Part Four

X an observed value of a quality characteristic. Specific observed values are designated X_1, X_2, X_3, etc.

$\overline{X}$ the average, or arithmetic mean. The average of a set of n observed values is the sum of the observed values divided by n.

n the number of observed values; the sample size, or number of units (articles, parts, specimens, etc.) in the sample.

σ the standard deviation, the root-mean-square (rms) deviation of the observed values from their average.

R the range, the difference between the largest observed value and the smallest observed value in a sample.

p_1 the fraction defective, the ratio of the number of defective units (articles, parts, specimens, etc.) to the total number of units under consideration, sometimes referred to as the "proportion defective." The use of per cent defective (p) is often preferred. $p = 100p_1$.

p_1n the number of defectives (defective units) in a sample of n units.

c the number of defects, usually the number of defects in a sample of stated size.

$\overline{\overline{X}}, \bar{\sigma}, \overline{R}, \bar{p}_1, \bar{p}_1n, \bar{c}$ the average of a set of values of $\overline{X}, \sigma, R, p_1, p_1n, c$.

N lot size as used with sampling inspection tables.

σ' the "true value" of σ, usually an estimate from samples.

Q a constant that is related to the modified control limit.
d_2 a constant that varies with n, relating the average range $\overline{R}$ for samples of n observed values each to the "true" standard deviation.
$A_1, A_2, B_3, B_4, D_3, D_4$ factors for computing control limits.
M, L factors for computing process limits from control limits.
R_T the reliability of a product having intended life T.
T the intended life of product.
θ the mean life of mean time to failure.
λ the failure rate in terms of items of product failing per unit time.
piece, part, unit one of a number of similar articles, specimens, etc.
sample a portion of material or a group of units taken from a large quantity of material or collection of units which serves to provide information that can be used as a basis for action on the larger quantity or on the production process. Samples are here presumed to be obtained by a method of sampling that is acceptable from a statistical as well as other viewpoints.
lot a specific quantity of similar material or collection of similar units from a common source; in inspection work, the quantity offered for inspection and acceptance at any one time. It may be a collection of raw materials, parts, or subassemblies inspected during production or a consignment of finished product to be sent out for service. It may also represent a stream of production from a common source.
defect a failing or fault, a failure to meet a requirement imposed on a unit with respect to a single quality characteristic, also an irregularity in material, surface finish, etc. In inspection, requirements often include so-called accepted standards of good workmanship as well as specifically stated limitations.
a defective a defective unit (article, part, specimen, etc.), one containing one or more defects with respect to the quality characteristic(s) under consideration.
quality characteristic a property of a unit, part, piece affecting performance or customer satisfaction, such as a dimension or weight or viscosity.
reliability the probability of a product performing its intended function over its intended life and under the operating conditions encountered.
failure mechanism the chronological series of events which logically lead to product failure.

14.22 Important Formulas Used in Part Four

Chapter 10: Frequency Distributions

Average:

$$\overline{X} = \frac{X_1 + X_2 + X_3 + \cdots + X_n}{n} \quad (1)$$

$$= \frac{\Sigma f X}{n} \quad (3)$$

Standard deviation:

$$\sigma = \sqrt{\frac{(X_1 - \overline{X})^2 + (X_2 - \overline{X}^2) + (X_3 - \overline{X}) + \cdots + (X_n - \overline{X})^2}{n}} \tag{4}$$

$$= \sqrt{\frac{\Sigma f X^2}{n} - \overline{X}^2} \tag{5}$$

Range: $R = X_{\text{high}} - X_{\text{low}}$ (6)

Chapter 11: Control Charts

Limits in Relation to Process Averages

Using the Range as the Measure of Spread

Averages: Lower limit $= \overline{\overline{X}} - A_2\overline{R}$ (13)
Center line $= \overline{\overline{X}}$
Upper limit $= \overline{\overline{X}} + A_2\overline{R}$ (14)

Ranges: Lower limit $= D_3\overline{R}$ (15)
Center line $= \overline{R}$
Upper limit $= D_4\overline{R}$ (16)

Using the Standard Deviation as the Measure of Spread

Averages: Lower limit $= \overline{\overline{X}} - A_1\bar{\sigma}$ (17)
Center line $= \overline{\overline{X}}$
Upper limit $= \overline{\overline{X}} + A_1\bar{\sigma}$ (18)

Standard deviations: Lower limit $= B_3\bar{\sigma}$ (19)
Center line $= \bar{\sigma}$
Upper limit $= B_4\bar{\sigma}$ (20)

Limits in Relation to Specifications

Lower limit = lower specification limit + Q (26)
Upper limit = upper specification limit − Q (27)

Go and Not-go Limits

Per cent-defective control limits $= \overline{p} \pm 3\sqrt{\frac{\overline{p}(100 - \overline{p})}{n}}$ (30)

Fraction-defective control limits $= \overline{p}_1 \pm 3\sqrt{\frac{\overline{p}_1(1 - \overline{p}_1)}{n}}$ (31)

Number-defective control limits $= \overline{p}_1 n \pm 3\sqrt{n\overline{p}_1(1 - \overline{p}_1)}$ (34)

Number of defects control limits $= \bar{c} \pm 3\sqrt{\bar{c}}$ (35)

Chapter 13: Special Methods

Tolerance build-up: $T_t = \sqrt{T_1^2 + T_2^2 + T_3^2 + \cdots + T_n^2}$ (38)

Chapter 14: Product Reliability

Reliability: $R_T = e^{-T/\theta}$ (43)

$R_T = e^{-\lambda T}$ (44)

$R_T = R_{T_1} \cdot R_{T_2} \cdot R_T \cdots R_{T_m}$ (45)

14.23 Bibliography on Statistics for Use in Quality Control

For those readers who wish to secure more detailed information on statistics for use in quality control, a brief bibliography is listed below:

Books and Pamphlets

Sampling Plans

Bowker, A. H., and H. P. Goode, "Sampling Inspection by Variables," McGraw-Hill Book Company, Inc., New York, 1952.

Dodge, Harold, and Harry F. Romig, "Sampling Inspection Tables," 2d ed., John Wiley & Sons, Inc., New York, 1959.

Freeman, H. A., Milton Freedman, Frederick Mosteller, and W. Allen Wallis, "Sampling Inspection," McGraw-Hill Book Company, Inc., New York, 1948.

"Sampling Procedures and Tables for Inspection by Attributes," MIL-STD-105A, U.S. Government Printing Office, 1950.

"Sampling Procedures and Tables for Inspection by Variables for Percent Defective," MIL-STD-414, U.S. Government Printing Office, 1957.

Wald, Abraham, "Sequential Analysis," John Wiley & Sons, Inc., New York, 1947.

Statistics and Control

"ASTM Manual on Quality Control of Materials," American Society for Testing Materials, Philadelphia, Pa., 1951.

Bennett, C. A., and N. L. Franklin, "Statistical Analysis in Chemistry and the Chemical Industry," John Wiley & Sons, Inc., New York, 1954.

Bowker, A. H., and Gerald J. Lieberman, "Handbook of Industrial Statistics," Prentice-Hall, Inc., Englewood Cliffs, N.J., 1955.

Cochran, M. G., and G. M. Cox, "Experimental Designs," 2d ed., John Wiley & Sons, Inc., New York, 1957.

Cowden, Dudley J., "Statistical Methods in Quality Control," Prentice-Hall, Inc., Englewood Cliffs, N.J., 1957.

Croxton, F. E., and D. J. Cowden, "Applied General Statistics," 2d ed., Prentice-Hall, Inc., Englewood Cliffs, N.J., 1955.

Dixon, W. J., and F. J. Massey, "Introduction to Statistical Analysis," 2d ed., McGraw-Hill Book Company, Inc., New York, 1957.

Duncan, A. J., "Quality Control and Industrial Statistics," Richard D. Irwin, Inc., Chicago, Ill., 1959.

Elderton, W. P., "Frequency Curves and Correlation," 4th ed., Harren Press, Washington, D.C., 1953.

Enrick, N. L., "Quality Control," 4th ed., The Industrial Press, New York, 1960.

Grant, E. L., "Statistical Quality Control," 2d ed., McGraw-Hill Book Company, Inc., New York, 1952.

Hoel, P. G., "Introduction to Mathematical Statistics," 2d ed., John Wiley & Sons, Inc., New York, 1954.

Juran, J. M., "Quality Control Handbook," McGraw-Hill Book Company, Inc., New York, 1951.

Kendall, M. G., "The Advanced Theory of Statistics," 4th ed., Charles Griffin & Co., Ltd., London, 1948.

Mood, A., "Introduction to the Theory of Statistics," McGraw-Hill Book Company, Inc., New York, 1950.

Moroney, M. J., "Facts from Figures," 2d ed., Penguin Books, Baltimore, Md., 1956.

Peach, Paul, "Introduction to Industrial Statistics and Quality Control," Edwards Broughton, Raleigh, N.C., 1947.

Schrock, E. M., "Quality Control and Statistical Methods," 2d ed., Reinhold Publishing Corporation, New York, 1957.

Snedecor, G. W., "Statistical Methods Applied to Experiments in Agriculture and Biology," 5th ed., Collegiate Press, Inc., of Iowa State College, Ames, Iowa, 1956.

Villars, D. S., "Statistical Design and Analysis of Experiments for Development Research," Wm. C. Brown Co., Dubuque, Iowa, 1951.

Wallis, W. A., and H. V. Roberts, "Statistics: A New Approach," The Free Press, Glencoe, Ill., 1956.

Reliability

Chorafas, Dimitras N., "Statistical Processes and Reliability Engineering," D. Van Nostrand Co., Inc., Princeton, N.J., 1960.

Dummer, G. W. A., and N. B. Griffin, "Electronic Equipment Reliability," John Wiley & Sons, Inc., New York, 1960.

Electronic Industries Association, "Reliable Application of Electron Tubes," Engineering Publishers, Elizabeth, N.J., 1956.

Electronic Industries Association, "Reliability of Electrical Connections," Engineering Publishers, Elizabeth, N.J., 1954.

Henney, Keith, "Reliability of Factors for Ground Electronic Equipment," McGraw-Hill Book Company, Inc., New York, 1956.

Walsh, C., and T. C. Tsao, "Electron Tube Life Factors," Engineering Publishers, Elizabeth, N.J., 1960.

Magazines and Journals

Annals of Mathematical Statistics, published by the Institute of Mathematical Statistics, Stanford University, Stanford, Calif.

Industrial Quality Control, published by the American Society for Quality Control, 161 W. Wisconsin Ave., Milwaukee 3, Wis.

Journal of the American Statistical Association, published by the American Statistical Association, 1757 K St., N.W., Washington 6, D.C.

Quality Control and Applied Statistics Abstract Service, Interscience Publishers, Inc., 250 Fifth Ave., New York 1, N.Y.

Proceedings of Annual National Symposia on Reliability and Quality Control in Electronics, Institute of Radio Engineers, New York, N.Y.

Technometrics, published quarterly by American Society for Quality Control and American Statistical Association, Washington 4, D.C.

PART FIVE

APPLYING TOTAL QUALITY CONTROL IN THE COMPANY

CHAPTER 15

NEW-DESIGN CONTROL

Product quality is affected at all stages of the production process. The engineer who writes specifications and guarantees affects quality fully as much as does the inspector who examines the product for conformance to these specifications. The methods specialist who develops manufacturing facilities is similarly involved, as is the foreman, the shop operator, the purchasing agent, or the reliability analyst.

Historically each of these separate quality activities has come to be carried on quite independently of the others. What organization has existed among them has been haphazard and often ineffective from a technological as well as an administrative point of view.

The increasing precision demanded of products and the corresponding complexity of factory operations have made this hit-or-miss type of organization no longer satisfactory for meeting a company's total quality goal. The core of quality control is the positive organization by management of these separate activities into a company-wide quality-control program.

Part One of this book discussed how these company quality-control activities are integrated into an over-all administrative pattern which operates from the time a product is designed and sold to the time it is packaged, shipped, and received by a satisfied customer.

Part Two broke up this over-all program into four classifications called quality-control jobs. These classifications are

1. *New-design control,* which involves preproduction quality-control activities.

2. *Incoming-material control,* which involves the activities carried on while purchased parts and materials are received and examined.

3. *Product control,* which involves quality-control activities carried on during active production and field service.

4. *Special process studies,* which involve the trouble shooting of quality problems.

Chapter 6, Part Two, described the company quality system within which these four jobs are carried on. Part Three then reviewed the quality-control engineering, process-control engineering, and quality information engineering technologies that provide the technical tools used. Part Four presented the statistical point of view, which provides the analytical basis for work done in the four jobs of total quality control.

With this foundation established, Part Five of this book discusses these quality-control jobs successively in its four chapters. Each of these four quality-control jobs is described in two ways.

Organizational Practices and Routines. It is people who, in the final analysis, build and maintain quality. Effective quality control must, therefore, mean effective human relations—including satisfactory organization planning and sound administrative practices and routines. Chapter 4 reviewed the principles underlying such planning, practices, and routines. It also emphasized that the applications of these principles must be directed to particular company situations. It is to the particular applications of these principles that the discussion in Part Five is directed.

While there are common patterns among these organizational practices as used throughout industry, the accompanying routines are extremely flexible, varying in their details to meet the needs of various companies.

Technological Practices. Many quality problems are extremely complex technically. Proper attitude, organization, and spirit among personnel—although extremely important—cannot alone solve these problems. There must be the support of modern quality-control techniques to aid them in this task.

Several of these tools have been used in industry for many years, often neither termed *quality-control techniques* nor recognized as part of the company activities in controlling quality. Others of the methods are relatively new. Parts Three and Four concentrated their review of the technological and analytical techniques of quality control upon concept and principle. Part Five is oriented to direct applications of the techniques to particular segments of the quality-control jobs. Additional techniques, the application of which is confined to such segments, will also be discussed.

These two factors—organizational routines and technological practices—become merged, of course, in actual plant quality-control programs. For ease of presenting the fundamentals of total quality control, however, the discussion below will discuss these factors independently as well as together. Emphasis will be placed throughout the discussion upon the systematic approach required for a total quality-control program rather than upon the details of individual plans used in quality-control jobs.

15.1 Organizing the Quality-control Jobs

The human effort required in the four quality-control jobs comes chiefly from company personnel to whom these activities are integral parts of broader responsibilities. Thus, development and design engineers or manufacturing engineering people may bear the brunt of work in new-design control, while process-control engineering may carry on the majority of incoming-material control activity.

Obviously, if these individual responsibilities are to be dovetailed into a company-wide program, some over-all quality-control plan must be established. Responsibility for organizing this program is in the hands of company top management, aided in the larger companies by the quality-control component.

Chapter 4 has discussed the responsibilities of management and its quality-control component in organizing and later operating with such a program. The material to follow in Part Five assumes that this organizing job has been done, that the time necessary for development to maturity of the quality-control jobs has elapsed, and that an active quality-control component is in place.

The concentration of Chaps. 15 to 18 is, therefore, upon the actual application of over-all quality-control procedures in the plant. Problems of developing the quality-control program to a point where it is capable of carrying on this broad function of the quality-control job is reserved for Part Six.

Chapters 15 to 18 cover the over-all application of the several techniques used in each of the quality-control jobs. It must be emphasized that some actual company installations of the individual quality-control jobs may incorporate only a portion of these techniques and still operate most effectively. The degree to which these techniques are used in any company situation depends, as pointed out in Chap. 5, upon the economy of that particular situation; these economic decisions must be worked out for each case individually.

15.2 The Needs for New-design Control

Every company has the example of a product the quality standards of which have been continually troublesome to maintain. The quality problems resulting from manufacture of this product are often never solved because "it would be too expensive to do so."

Similarly universal is the conflict between shopmen and design engineers on those parts tolerances which the shopmen insist are far narrower than the use of the part requires. On these parts engineers may privately admit that "we call for ±0.002 inch only because it increases the likelihood of our getting ±0.005 inch."

When a situation of this sort exists, it inevitably results in lack of respect for tolerances established on drawings and on specification sheets. It is also accompanied by excessive expense in securing and using manufacturing facilities of unnecessarily high precision.

A somewhat different situation is the perennial case of the engineer who has carefully designed his product, rigorously tested two or three toolmakers' models which perform satisfactorily, and then complains bitterly about the "factory's incompetence" when large percentages of the product fail to perform properly when produced in mass quantities. Yet this poor performance may have been inevitable owing to overly great tolerance build-ups or to a statistically unsound testing program of the sort discussed in Sec. 10.6.

These situations are some of the more readily apparent illustrations of the need for a properly coordinated, regularly scheduled program, directed toward analyzing newly designed products for possible quality troubles before active production is started. This type of program tends also to improve several less obvious situations that may have long existed in the factory without even being recognized as problems affecting the quality of new designs.

There may, for example, be no organized means for feeding back to the design engineer information from the plant laboratory about new materials or processes. Mechanical inspection or electrical testing groups may be forced to wait for information on what they should inspect or test until production has actively started and many defective units have been scrapped. Parts tolerances may be selected with no knowledge of or reference to the accuracies that may be actually held on the plant's machine tools and processes.

Sales efforts in product planning and merchandising may work in directions opposed to the design actually being developed. Desirable cost standards for parts inspection sampling and bogeys for manufacturing losses may be established only after the design has been in active production for a considerable length of time.

Again, the issue of what really are realistic reliability requirements for a product or component is a continual concern in every company that deals with high-performance articles. Too frequently, meaningful part and product data are not available for the environmental conditions to be encountered; yet a decision must nonetheless be made about proposals to be placed before the prospective customer.

Under such circumstances, the company will be served neither by optimism nor by pessimism based upon speculation. It can incur a long-term product hazard if it is loosely committed by an overly optimistic sales engineer who works on the assumption that his company "can provide any reliability requirement you want." Or it can lose the opportunity to obtain a sizable contract which provides an extremely favorable entry into a high-precision product market by accepting the overly pessimistic view of the development engineer who refuses to identify any range of reliability targets "unless years of exhaustive components tests have been concluded."

Only a systematic quality-control logic, backed by meaningful technical procedures, can serve here. It will provide alternatives as to how far the company may (1) firmly commit itself to reliability levels, reasonably attainable with current know-how about components, and (2) identify the developmental work required before new reliability levels can be firmly committed.

In a somewhat different area, data on field tests and performance of units in the customer's plants may not be effectively reported by the field organization for use by the engineer in the design of products similar to the one under development. Guarantees may be established based upon the performance of a few specially made models rather than upon a sufficient quantity of actual production units. Company efforts toward standardization and product simplification may be thwarted by the fact that the new design calls for many new and special parts. Manufacturing employees may be considerably handicapped by the nonexistence of adequate quality specifications.

These problems are too often faced and solved long after the product design has been frozen and a considerable investment has been made in inventory and in processing equipment. The latitude of decisions affecting process improvements or inspection schedules after the actual design has been completed is obviously much more limited than it is during the development stage of the product.

Thus it is important to view the new-design-control activity as being much more than merely seeing that a design is ready to manufacture. It must have its influence early in the product-planning stage when the wants and needs of the customer are first being considered. It must assure that suitable data about components and parts are made available and that a thorough preproduction and environmental testing program is considered. It must assure the availability of experience with previous similar products, which will be of great value in delineating the likes and dislikes of consumers. Likewise, the new-design activity should assist the design engineer in his efforts to "get around" quality problems that previous designs may have engendered, in either the factory or the field. It must create an awareness of such quality problems.

That considerations of this sort should be faced and solved has been recognized as a "good idea" for some time. Action on the good idea has frequently been lacking, however, because no machinery has been developed to carry out the required program. The quality-control job called *new-design control* has been developed to provide this machinery.

15.3 Defining New-design Control

As a definition:

New-design control involves the establishment and specification of the desirable cost-quality, performance-quality, and reliability-quality standards for the product, including the elimination or location of possible sources of quality troubles before the start of formal production.

This tool is a planned method for balancing the quality costs of a new product design with the service that the new product must render if it is fully to satisfy the customer. New-design-control procedures aim to minimize these costs and to maximize customer satisfaction.

New-design-control activity includes all the quality-control efforts on a new product while its marketable characteristics are being decided; while it is being designed, sold to the customer, planned for manufacture, and initially costed; and while its quality standards are being specified and inspection and test routines are being established to maintain these standards.[1] In the case of quantity production, new-design-control activities end when pilot runs have given proof of satisfactory production performance. With job-shop production, the routine ends as work is being started on manufacture of component parts.

The very nature of new-design control makes its application an art more than a science. The task of eliminating and predicting potential product-quality troubles is subject to at least two sources of error: (1) human beings, with all their susceptibility to faults in judgment, carry on the work; (2) it is excessively costly to make *all* the tests that may be indicated during initial new-design-control planning.

As a result, fine questions of selection and interpretation arise—decisions as to what quality characteristics are particularly critical, as to which tests can be eliminated and which must be made. It requires experience in making these decisions to provide personnel with assurance as to which tests and what specifications will be most useful.

The effectiveness of new-design control tends, therefore, considerably to increase as those carrying on the activity in the company develop the

[1] The term *new design* as used in this chapter does not, of course, refer only to an entirely new product. It refers also to designs which are modifications of existing products.

art of its application. This increase in effectiveness applies generally throughout the technical groups of the company owing to the formal nature of a new-design-control program, as opposed to the increase in effectiveness for only a few individuals as in the case of the uncoordinated, sprawling types of individual design-control activities. The younger men in the technical groups benefit particularly in the plant with a well-organized new-design-control program, since the quality phases of their product development experience may be greatly expedited.

Hence the advantages of considering quality control as a system are further confirmed. The technologies of quality control discussed in Part Three presented the organized body of knowledge that provides the techniques used in doing quality-control work.

All three of the technologies of total quality control have application in new-design control, as does the entire range of the statistical point of view. In particular, quality-control engineering (Chap. 7) and quality information engineering (Chap. 9) are the technologies used most intensively. Frequency distribution (Chap. 10), special methods (Chap. 13), and product reliability (Chap. 14) are the statistical areas that are most often brought to use.

The application of these techniques in a systematized orderly fashion is provided through the planning of the quality system discussed in Chap. 6.

15.4 The Scope of New-design-control Application

New-design control has general application throughout industry. The same basic fundamentals obtain in this activity no matter what type of production conditions are being faced. The detailed new-design-control approaches vary, of course, from company to company, depending upon such factors as products, plant size, and type of personnel available.

One of the major differences is the distinction between the approach used in the mass-production type of manufacture and that used in the job-shop type of production, where only one or a few of a given design are to be manufactured.

In the former case new-design-control activities may make extensive use of such tools as pilot runs and the development of sampling quality levels. Job-shop new-design control, on the other hand, must rely upon such techniques as the establishment of quality standards and analysis of the quality performance of previous designs similar to the one under development.

New-design control is of particularly great importance to a company quality-control program under these job-shop conditions. When only one or a few units are to be produced, "make it right the first time" becomes more than a slogan—it becomes a necessity.

Product-control routines may "catch" a defective turbine shell whose design is such that a satisfactory shell is difficult to cast, but the expense of recasting the shell to new specifications may be excessive. A special process study may discover that the cause of the malfunctioning of an engine at final test is due to faulty specifications, but the loss of customer good will because of the need for additional time to rebuild the engine may be a genuine disaster. An adequate new-design-control program is a quality-control "must" in the plants producing these products.

Another major difference in the application of new-design control is the distinction between the approach used in the research-and-development-oriented company and that for the company which concentrates upon products which essentially use existing engineering and manufacturing know-how.

In the former case, new-design-control activities may make extensive use of such techniques as environmental testing and reliability analyses in their various forms as applied to new components or to new uses of old components. In the latter case, the orientation may be more heavily toward such techniques as process-capability studies to assure compatibility between the existing production facilities and the new product, and to techniques for analysis of quality performance of similar products.

There is thus a considerable difference in the emphasis, in the application, and in the investment that is warranted on new-design-control activity as between a newly designed space vehicle or a newly designed household refrigerator, or as between a new electron tube for early-warning radar and the new control element in an automobile regulator, or as between the design of a home oil-fired furnace and the design of a brazing torch. These differences in degree are determined by the judgments of those in charge of the activity in a company; the objective of assuring a good quality of design is the same in all cases.

Indeed, the quality-control engineer who has become experienced in new-design-control activity ultimately learns that the similarity in concept and technique among all such products is greater than the difference. It is for this reason, among many others, that the quality-control engineer, who is truly skilled in the technologies of total quality control, can make a professional contribution to the new-design-control activity of a very wide range of products.

15.5 Organizing for New-design Control

For the new-design-control activity of a company to be fully effective, a definite routine must be established and maintained for it within the framework of the over-all company plan for its quality system. This routine is developed by the quality-control-engineering unit in cooperation with the concerned functional groups like Engineering.

Before this routine can be initiated, a basic decision must be made as to the classifications of new products which will be subject to the new-design-control routine. Many plants include all their new products in such routines; others include only those products which are new in development concept or sufficiently costly or are produced in sufficiently large quantities.

This decision is made according to the economic circumstances in each company, based upon answers to such questions as "Can we afford not to have a new-design-control routine for this product?" and "How extensive a testing program can we afford in the new-design-control routine for this article?"

In the special case of those products upon which safety of humans and property is dependent, a complete new-design-control program may be required for all products, apart from direct economic considerations.

Once these classifications have been established, each new product that is subject to the new-design-control routine should then be geared into the steps of the routine. The action should be an automatic one. It should not be necessary for members of the quality-control component to ferret out the existence of a new design or to hear of it after considerable time has passed.

A typical report letter from a quality-control engineer, to gain necessary information from design engineers on new products, is shown in Fig. 15.1. Figure 15.2 shows the attached sheet that was returned.

Engineering is the key functional group in new-design-control activities. As "quality planning," the activity is an important complement to the design engineer's main responsibility of developing the most useful and ingenious product possible.

Also important in new-design control are other members of the company technical groups such as laboratory engineers, manufacturing engineering people, and inspection and test personnel. Manufacturing supervision, production-control, marketing, and other groups act chiefly in a consultative capacity.

The quality-control-engineering unit of the company quality-control component has the responsibility to assure the progress and integration of the new-design-control activity for the company. In many areas where quality-control equipment is, or will be, required, the quality information equipment engineering segment has the responsibility to become directly involved.

As discussed in Chap. 4, there are several ways of assigning specific responsibility for new-design control to the quality-control-engineering unit. In the case of some companies with heavy research-and-development content in each new product, it may be most useful to make new-design-control activity for all new products a specialized assignment; it may thus become the responsibility of one or more quality-control engineers. In other companies, the quality-control engineer in charge of the quality system for a product line or product grouping will also be assigned responsibility for the new-design work on the new products to be added to that line; thus there will be as many new-design-control assignments as there are quality-system engineers. For small companies, new-design control may become the part-time responsibility of the single quality-control engineer, or of the Quality Control Manager himself, if he acts as

SUBJECT: QUALITY CONTROL INVESTIGATIONS
ON NEW DESIGNS

3/1/60

To Engineering Section Heads:

Messrs. J. Jones
R. Roe
J. Doe

Will you please fill in the indicated information on the attached sheet A and return it to me

J. J. Smith
Quality Control
Engineer

FIG. 15.1.

his own quality-control engineer. Similar alternatives are available for structuring quality information equipment engineering assignments.

However the activity is assigned within the quality-control component, it is often the case that the responsible quality-control engineer will join with the representatives of other company functional components to form a project team to carry out the new-design activity on a particular product.

Much valuable information is available in development and design engineering, manufacturing engineering, and marketing groups in a plant as a result of accumulated past product experience. Since the project

SUBJECT: QUALITY CONTROL INVESTIGATIONS ON NEW DESIGNS

SHEET A

DATE 3/3/60

TO: Mr. J. J. SMITH

Information concerning equipment now being developed in my section is given below.

BRIEF FUNCTIONAL DESCRIPTION OF EQUIPMENT. IS IT SIMILAR TO EQUIPMENT PREVIOUSLY BUILT?

Aircraft relay, model 4ZP96B3
similar in function to 4ZP83CZ
but rated 600 amps

EXPECTED QUANTITY 40,000 *

DESIGN WILL BE COMPLETED APPROXIMATELY 6 months

PRODUCTION IS EXPECTED TO START APPROXIMATELY 9 months

REMARKS:

*This is of the order of magnitude
but it may be 50%-75% wrong

J. Jones

ENGINEERING SECTION HEAD

FIG. 15.2.

team will be made up of representatives of these various groups, it can use their past experience to the benefit of the quality of the new product design.

15.6 Pattern for the New-design-control Routine within the Quality-system Plan

The cycle for developing a new product that takes place in many companies may be summarized below. Several steps may be consolidated in some companies; the order of steps may be interchanged in others.

1. A new design is contemplated.
2. Technical and marketing analyses are made of the design.
3. General specifications are written. They may be in the form of
   a. Sales propositions in the case of job-lot production.
   b. Rough functional specifications for products that will be manufactured in mass quantity.
   c. Broad outline of the coverage of the quality-system plan for the product.
4. Preliminary design is made.
5. An extensive program of testing the characteristics of this design is carried out, including the components and subassemblies to be used.
6. Intermediate design is made, including production drawings.
7. Tests are made on this intermediate design.
8. Final design is completed along with final specifications, standards, guarantees, quality-system planning, and production drawings. Life and performance tests are culminated before final design completion; release for manufacture of production tools and facilities is given parallel with final design completion.
9. Pilot runs are made using samples composed of production units. The results of the tests of these samples are incorporated into the design specifications if and as required.
10. The unit is released for active production.

Some steps of this sequence are quite general for both job-lot and high-quantity production; a few steps apply chiefly to units produced in mass quantities.

The fundamental elements of new-design-control routines within the total-quality-system plan mesh into this sequence. These elements are summarized below:

1. *Establishment of the quality standards for the product.* This involves analyses which culminate in specifications which incorporate performance and reliability requirements and the cost-quality balance for the product and the components. It includes development of that portion of the quality-system plan which covers the preproduction evaluation and testing of the product.

2. *Design of a product which meets these standards.* This involves the establishment of the detailed drawings for the product, as well as the preparation of the related engineering instructions. It includes following the quality-system plan for the carrying on of environmental and other tests to determine the inherent reliability of components and subassemblies. It also includes field tests and performance studies of assembled prototypes or of handmade samples. Simulation studies of product quality may be made where physical prototypes cannot be made available.

3. *Planning to assure maintenance of the required quality.* This involves the formal development of the details of that portion of the quality-system plan which covers the control of purchased material, the maintenance of quality during processing and production, and the assurance of quality during field installation and product servicing. It also includes the development of the final specifications for the quality information equipments which are required for incoming material, for in-process control, and for field testing and evaluation.

4. *Preproduction final review of the new design and its manufacturing facilities; formal release for active production.* This involves the planned, formal evaluation of the designed product to assure its capability of meeting its warranties and guarantees under conditions of actual use. It also involves analyses of the capabilities of the processes which will be required to produce the product. A series of performance tests will be conducted, in terms required by the quality-system plan, to review the product in all important customer end-use aspects.

Particular emphasis is placed upon components testing under conditions which simulate actual customer use. These reliability tests also couple components into subassemblies to evaluate the effect of different combinations upon quality.

These four elements are quite basic in new-design-control programs of plants which produce such a wide variety of products as fluids, textiles, detail parts, small components like springs and bellows, permanent magnets, many forms of chemicals, and complex assemblies. Because of the wide scope of the accompanying routines, the discussion of new-design control to follow will concentrate upon procedures used in companies which manufacture these complex assemblies; similar features apply, however, to the routines of the other product types.

15.7 A Typical New-design-control Routine

A factory manufacturing small precision electrical regulating and relaying products ties its new-design-control program directly to the cycle of Sec. 15.6, with the following steps:

1. The quality-control engineer circulates a monthly letter to the other design engineers on which they list new designs and the anticipated

quantity of the units that will be produced. Because of the low cost of each individual product, only designs on which there will be a production of over 500 units are made subject to the new-design-control routine.

2. When a new design is reported, the quality-control engineer initiates a project team. He then calls a meeting of the project team.

The design engineer of the new product attends the meeting. Its purposes are to discover critical features of the design, to anticipate troubles the factory may have in producing the product, to initiate any changes in the design that seem immediately required, and to consider the tests of components that seem indicated to evaluate compatibility and reliability.

3. The engineers outline and carry out a test program aimed at finding answers to questions generated in step **2**.

4. The findings from this special test program are incorporated in the design. Preliminary production drawings and specifications are then issued to Manufacturing.

5*a*. Manufacturing makes prototypes from these drawings and submits them to the design engineer for approval tests. If the performance of the models is not satisfactory, tests and design changes are made until difficulties are eliminated. These changes are incorporated in the drawings and specifications.

5*b*. While these tests are in progress, manufacturing engineers complete the planning for all processing equipments and tooling. Those component parts which are critical are so specified, and inspection and test routines are planned for them. Where possible and desirable, AQL or AOQL values are established for parts sampling.

5*c*. The individual pieces of quality information equipment are specified. The various elements of the quality-system plan are brought together by the quality-control engineer and suitably documented for later use by Process Control Engineering (including inspection and test).

6. When the production tools and processing equipments are received, manufacturing begins the output of component parts on production tools. A pilot assembly run is started.

7. Engineering, Manufacturing, and Quality Control analyze the performance of the pilot runs. They also study the quality of parts and assemblies produced for the pilot run by the processes and tools that will be used for the new product. This design review procedure is quite intensive.

8. Results of these analyses are incorporated by the designer into the final design specifications, standards, and guarantees. Studies on processes and tools are used to guide any appropriate action to change tooling, manufacturing, or the quality-system plan.

15.8 Operation of This New-design-control Routine

The actual operation of the routine of this plant may be illustrated by following through the new-design-control program for the new relay, 4ZP96B3, which was reported in the letter shown in Fig. 15.2.

When the development for the new design starts, the designer makes several studies before writing his preliminary specifications of the product characteristics. He analyzes performance reports obtained from field data on products which the 4ZP96B3 is to replace or supplant. He studies data taken from internal factory and inspection reports on these similar products and from information on the best of competitive products. He meets with marketing and sales people, so that their product planning and merchandising activities may properly and adequately be recognized in the development program under way for the new relay design.

The designer examines various standards—Underwriters, NEMA, American Institute of Electrical Engineers, etc.—which contain requirements set down as the result of experience in attaining high-quality products. He goes over data and reports from the plant laboratory on new developments in processes, theories of operation, and materials. He makes extensive use—by discussions, study of reports, and any other means available—of the wide background of experience accumulated in the plant on previous development and new-design-control activities. The five statistical tools discussed in Part Four may be very useful to the designer in these several studies.

The designer then makes the final decision on the economic balance that must be reflected in the characteristics of the relay between cost and service that will be rendered by the device. The 4ZP96B3 is a commercial device so that the limits open to the designer in this cost balance are quite rigidly specified. If the device were developmental, these cost limits might be much more flexible.

Since the new relay replaces units already in production, the designer will strive to develop product characteristics which will give assurance of fully satisfying the requirements necessary completely to replace the devices now in production. He will not wish to fall into a situation where the product will be merely an addition to rather than a replacement for these other devices.

When the design has reached the rough model stage, the quality-control engineer arranges for the initial new-design-control meeting. This session is attended by representatives from Engineering, Manufacturing Engineering, and, depending upon the nature of the device, Marketing. The design engineer for the new relay attends the meeting and exhibits a model of the 4ZP96B3, describes its operation, and points out those component parts which are critical to proper operation. Manufacturing representatives bring up their questions concerning tolerances and possible machining and assembly difficulties. They challenge tolerances that cannot be held with the present manufacturing facilities of the plant, as shown by the results of process-capability studies.

They raise such questions as "Can we make this part from phosphor bronze instead of beryllium copper?" "Can this blind tapped hole be changed to a through hole?" "A tolerance of ±0.001 inch on this hole necessitates a reaming operation. How about calling for ±0.003 inch so we can drill the hole?"

While these questions are being raised, the designer is himself bringing up questions, such as "That spring carries current; will its resistance be too high if I make it from phosphor bronze?" "Will a through hole cut down my magnetic section too much?" "Will the pin fit be satisfactory with a ±0.003-inch tolerance?"

The quality-control engineer and other technical members of the project team may raise an additional series of questions, such as "Will silver-contact tips of this configuration and composition actually have the required life if the relay is installed in an extremely hot climate?" "Can the manufacturers of the small-discharge capacitors that will be used actually maintain their guarantee of ±1 per cent performance over the production lot? No one has been able to do it before." "Since even small quantities of moisture will affect performance and life, is the case for the relay truly moisture- and humidity-proof?"

And the design engineer will be raising reliability questions of his own, as well as those that will affect maintainability and serviceability, such as "This beryllium-copper spring will perform millions of operations during the life of the relay. Are we safe enough, metallurgically, with this particular composition, and do we know enough about the special requirements of heat-treating?" "Are we completely safe in assuming that the relay will be installed where the customer has told us it will be? Is there any possibility of application where it will be much colder or much warmer, or where there will be much more possibility of electrical interference?"

To find answers to the questions raised in this first meeting, a testing program will be outlined. In most companies, the design engineer has the key responsibility for assuring the carrying out of the testing program, since it relates to his basic responsibility for establishing the final product design. He will be assisted by whatever design-reliability specialists there are on the design-engineering staff. He will be closely and actively joined by the quality-control engineer. Other members of the new-design-control project team, as indicated, may be called upon for help.

Many techniques are used in the tests. The engineers use one of them —the frequency distribution—to great advantage. One particular useful frequency-distribution application[2] is the tests of the strength under torsion of one of the relay's subassemblies. This subassembly consists of a knurled part forced into a hole in a phenolic plastic part with the minimum allowable interference (amount the knurled teeth must cut into the plastic molding).

Figure 15.3 shows the frequency-distribution analysis of this knurled part. The analysis illustrates that the minimum force indicated to the design engineer is about 5 inches-pounds ($\overline{X} - 3\sigma$) and that the design engineer should expect an occasional reading lower than that. He uses this information to adjust his design specification.

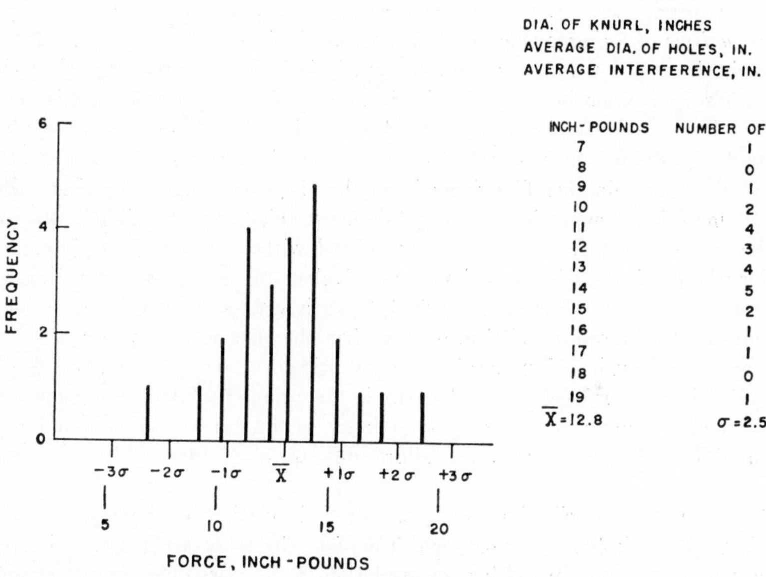

FIG. 15.3.

Extensive testing programs are frequently undertaken for the purpose of gaining technical information that will enable the design engineer to increase the reliability of the device. Some of these tests may be used later by the process-control engineer in evaluating the reliability of current product. Tests of a nondestructive nature that pinpoint the mode of failure are particularly useful in controlling the reliability of continuing production. Information from such tests also provides an important feedback to the design engineer so he can continually improve his designs. Figure 15.4 shows a page covering reliability tests for

[2] Figure 15.3 and this example are adapted from W. H. Bloodworth, "How the Designer Can Tie in with Statistical Quality Control," *Electrical Manufacturing,* May, 1946.

Mechanisms of failure	*Present nondestructive testing*	*Future nondestructive testing*
Contact contamination	Contact resistance test	IR inspection of hot solenoid
Decomposition of organic films	Direct-voltage insulation check	Contact pressure measurement with piezoelectric crystal
Incorrect pull-in and drop-out	Contact pressure measurement with gram gage	
Contact wear and deformation		

Mechanisms of Failure: One manufacturer has indicated that contact contamination is the major reason for relay failure. This is particularly true when the relay finds application in a dry circuit (i.e., one where the current level is low). Even in hermetically sealed relays, the decomposition of organic matter within the unit causes films which cover up to 90 per cent of the contact face. The thickness of the contaminating film depends on the absorption characteristics of the contact material. Penetration of the preliminary thickness of a film is possible by the tunnel effect (i.e., electrons transmitted without energy loss through a barrier whose thickness is approximately equivalent to the electron wavelength). Thicker films can be punctured by field-strength voltage (i.e., coherer action). The latter, also known as *fritting*, occurs when the electric field within the film becomes large enough to form a minute metal bridge through the film. Oil, deeply embedded in the surfaces of metal parts, is the primary source of organic material which decomposes to form contaminating films. It has been found that activated carbon getters prevent failure due to films formed from organic decomposition.

The next major contribution to relay failure is insulation breakdown. Very fine wire is used to wind the solenoids which actuate the relay armature. It is very difficult to apply uniform coatings of insulation to this wire. The uneven coating breaks and causes hot spots and short circuits, which render the relay useless. Relays which do not meet specifications can be considered to have failed. An example of this is incorrect pull-in drop-out current or voltage. Pull-in current or voltage is the maximum current or voltage required to operate the relay. Drop-out current or voltage is the minimum current or voltage required to release the relay. Excessive contact pressure causes abnormal wear of the contact surface, greatly decreasing the reliable life of the relay. Arcs which burn during the recorded time of bouncing are sufficient to cause disturbances by transferring material. This latter effect causes pitting which deforms and weakens the contact surface. Enough pressure must be supplied to prevent excessive bouncing, but care must be taken not to increase the erosion rate.

FIG. 15.4

electrical relays taken from an extensive report covering many electrical component types.[3]

At the completion of the test program, the design engineer issues a report which is presented to a formal design-review meeting of the new-

Page 1

4ZP96B3 – QUALITY CONTROL STUDY

CONTACTOR CALIBRATIONS AND ACTION

Purpose of Study

The purpose of this study is to anticipate difficulties in obtaining the desired calibrations and action of the contactor resulting from variations in dimensions or properties of parts, each of which is within the tolerances of the drawing but which accumulate to produce extreme effects. No such difficulties have been experienced with the handmade samples, twelve of which have been tested; but it is unlikely that all of the possible variations have existed or have been cumulative.

The principal factors to be studied are:

(1) Variation in deflection of the main spring when the relay is picked up.

(2) Variation in stiffness of the main spring and of the wipe spring.

(3) Variation in air gap at the junctions of various parts of the magnetic circuit.

(4) Variation in magnetic properties of the various portions of the magnetic circuit.

(5) Variation in coil resistance.

Only one adjustment is provided to compensate for all of the possible variations; this is the adjustment of the pole piece. The pole piece will be adjusted to provide the desired drop-out voltage, and all of the rest of the calibrations must come as they will.

The desired calibrations and action are as follows:

(1) Pick-up voltage (cold) – 15.0 volts or less.

(2) Seal-in voltage (cold) – less than pickup.

(3) Drop-out voltage (cold) – 4.8 to 3.2 volts.

(4) Air Gap – 0.015 in. or more.

(5) No hesitation during any part of the pick-up or drop-out stroke.

(6) No bouncing on pickup.

The pages of this report summarize tests made:

FIG. 15.5.

design project team. Figures 15.5 and 15.6 show the first two pages of such a report.[4]

On the basis of information obtained from the program of investigatory tests, final production drawings are completed and issued. At this point

[3] Figure 15.4 is after a study by R. Warr and Associates, Ithaca, N.Y.

[4] Figure 15.5 is after a study by C. R. Mason and W. J. Warnock.

1. The manufacturing quality-control project team member takes over and has several prototypes built. "Several" may be 20 to 100 in the new-design-control routine of the plant, depending upon the cost and complexity of the device and the statistical accuracy required in the analysis.

Page 2

4ZP96B3 – QUALITY CONTROL STUDY

CONTACTOR CALIBRATIONS AND ACTION

TEST RESULTS

Results:

The resistance of the coil was found to be 74.1 ohms at 24.0 C.

Table I shows the pick-up, drop-out, and seal-in voltages for various shim thickness and gaps at the end of the plunger in the picked up position. The voltages were calculated from the average values of current using a resistance of 74.1 ohms, and the gap was calculated from the angle through which the pole piece had to be turned to close the gap. As the table shows, the only point where "hang-up" occurred was during pick-up with zero shim thickness and a 21.2 mil gap; for this case, the seal-in value higher than the pick-up value.

TABLE I

Shim Thickness Mils	Gap Mils	Pick-up Volts	Seal-in Volts	Drop-out Volts
0	17.5	13.75	13.15	4.01
5	17.3	14.20	13.95	3.87
11	18.1	15.25	14.00	3.91
16	18.1	15.55	14.22	3.82
0	20.1	15.95	15.13	3.93
5	20.1	18.10	18.05	3.95
11	20.1	17.50	15.35	3.97
16	20.1	17.45	15.40	4.09
20	20.1	17.60	16.10	4.04
26	20.3	18.15	15.30	3.99
31	20.3	18.85	15.50	4.05
40	19.05	19.80	15.39	3.93
45	19.05	21.10	15.50	3.96
52	19.05	20.57	15.98	4.08
56	19.05	21.10	15.95	3.88
61	19.05	22.79	17.97	3.89
0	21.2	15.50	16.85	5.90
31	10.5	16.35	12.95	2.48
61	0	18.20	10.66	2.04

The results of contact-closing bounce tests are shown in Table II. These tests were made using an electronic bounce recorder. For these tests the gap at the poles was set to 0.020 in., and the coil was energized at 28.0 volts. The contact bar was 1/8 in. thick instead of 5/32 in. which it will be in the manufactured device.

TABLE II

Drum Speed	Shim Thickness	Number of Operations			
		No Bounce	1 Bounce	2 Bounces	3 Bounces
Fast	0	34	0	0	0
Fast	0.031 in.	2	33	5	
Slower	0.061 in.	0	30	7	11*

* It was almost impossible to tell whether there were 2 or 3 bounces, but it looked like 3.

FIG. 15.6.

Limitations of sizes lower than 50 are clearly recognized and are used only as applicable. For the 4ZP96B3, 25 models, manufactured in accordance with production drawings, are turned over to the design engineer, who tests them to determine whether or not they meet specifications.

On those features of the models where performance is not satisfactory, Engineering makes changes and carries on tests until acceptable operation is obtained.

2. While the activity of 1 above is going on, the manufacturing engineer completes the planning for all processing and tooling necessary for the job.

3. The quality-control engineer completes the preliminary planning

QUALITY SYSTEMS PLAN
GENERAL PROCEDURE FOR INSPECTION BY
"OPERATOR" OF SEALED RELAY ASSEMBLIES

I. SUBASSEMBLY

Process instructions and/or other supplementary written instructions will exist at work stations describing such things as:

A) Setup
B) Method of test or inspection
C) Number of samples and frequency of operator check
D) Instructions as to action in the event of failure. One failure constitutes rejection unless otherwise specified
E) A log and/or samples indicating time of operator and inspector check for purpose of "evidence of inspection"

II. ASSEMBLY AND ADJUST OVERCHECK

Unless otherwise specified by check lists, the following inspections and/or tests are made on each relay:

A) Tip pressure
B) Tip gap
C) Pick up and drop out
D) Hi-pot (after cover assembly)
E) Contact resistance (after sealing)
F) Leak test

III. AUDIT (ROVING) INSPECTION

Each relay line type will have at least one in-process inspector who will monitor each operation to ascertain "process in control" by:

A) Sampling in accordance with the method described for the particular operation
B) Examining evidence of operator inspection
C) Stamping the log in the appropriate column, accept or reject
D) Taking the necessary action in the event of reject by tagging operation, impounding material, continuing investigation beyond the particular work station to ascertain extent of "process out of control"

Immediately on rejection, notifying the manufacturing foreman and quality control foreman, as required so that immediate corrective action can be instituted.

W. E. John
SUPERVISOR
QUALITY CONTROL

FIG. 15.7. An element of a quality-system plan.

of the quality system, including the inspection and testing requirements as well as the operation guides, to control product quality: when the material will be received, when the product will be manufactured, and when it will be shipped, installed, and serviced. Figure 15.7 shows a section of the quality-system plan covering operator inspection of sealed relays.

4. The quality information equipment engineer either concludes his own preliminary design or arranges with vendors for the procurement of the necessary quality-control equipment. Figure 15.8 shows a part of a specification for such quality information equipment.

When changes indicated by the tests on prototypes have been incorporated in the drawings and planning cards and the necessary processing equipment has been secured, manufacturing begins output of a small number of parts on production tools. As soon as enough parts are available, a pilot assembly run is started.

SPECIAL ASSEMBLY TESTER
APCAT
SPECIFICATIONS

A. Purpose

The purpose of this specification is to outline in general terms the requirements for an item of information equipment that will provide a static and/or dynamic functional test on all circuits of each printed circuit assembly manufactured by this company.

B. General Specifications

I. Power Supplies

a. D. C. Voltage Power Supplies

This company has standardized on input D. C. voltage levels of 6 volt multiples; ie., 6, 12, 24, 48, and 18 VDC. The input voltages should be variable over a ra... Ripple should be ...

readi...

the 250 cycle sine w... 500 ma.

II. Input Power Program Requirements

a. All D. C. input voltages should be capable of being programmed into the tester distributor over a range of ±20% full scale.

b. The A. C. power supply shall be capable of being programmed into the tester distributor at 208 cyc., 250 cyc, and 312 cyc. ±5%

c. The one shot step pulse input shall be capable of being programmed repetitively of from 1 to 10 pulses.

III. Programmed Load Requirements

a. M...

b. The following circuit must be connected to various output terminals to provide a clamp voltage at the gate outputs:

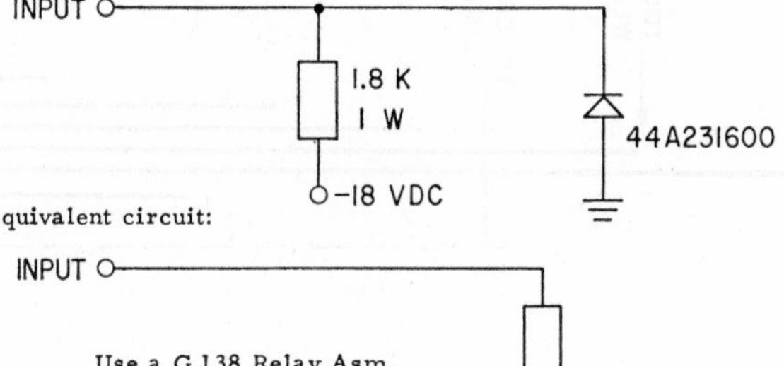

c. Relay equivalent circuit:

INPUT

Use a G 138 Relay Asm.

− 18 VDC

d. Provisions should be made for adding equivalent load circuits at a future date (a minimum of 10).

IV. Output Measurements

a. It shall be necessary to measure the following:

1. Output pulse rise and fall time of from .05 to 5u Sec. ±5%.
2. Steady state D. C. output voltage levels of either zero or +6 volts ±5%.
3. The duration of a pulse of from 1 micro-seconds to 5 milli-seconds ±2%-- pulse width.
4. The delay time between the leading edge of one pulse to the leading edge of a following pulse of from .1 micro seconds to 5 micro seconds.
5. In order to establish and verify the input pulse conditions, it shall be necessary to measure pulse frequencies up to 2 MC and pulse widths to .1 micro seconds. This can be done with an oscilloscope to set up the initial test conditions.

V. Programmed Resistance Comparison

a. In order to test for the forward and reverse resistance of diodes mounted on a diode gate board, it will be required to program standard resistance values

FIG. 15.8. Quality information equipment specification.

In the collection of information from this pilot run on the first production parts and assemblies, the statistical tools of quality control are again used to good advantage. Frequency-distribution studies are made on the important dimensions on the critical parts in the assembly. Such distributions reveal whether the manufacturing processes, in their present condition, will produce parts within the specified tolerances.

Figures 15.9 to 15.11 illustrate such analyses on parts produced by three punch-press tools—drawings 934782, 934784, and 934787. These

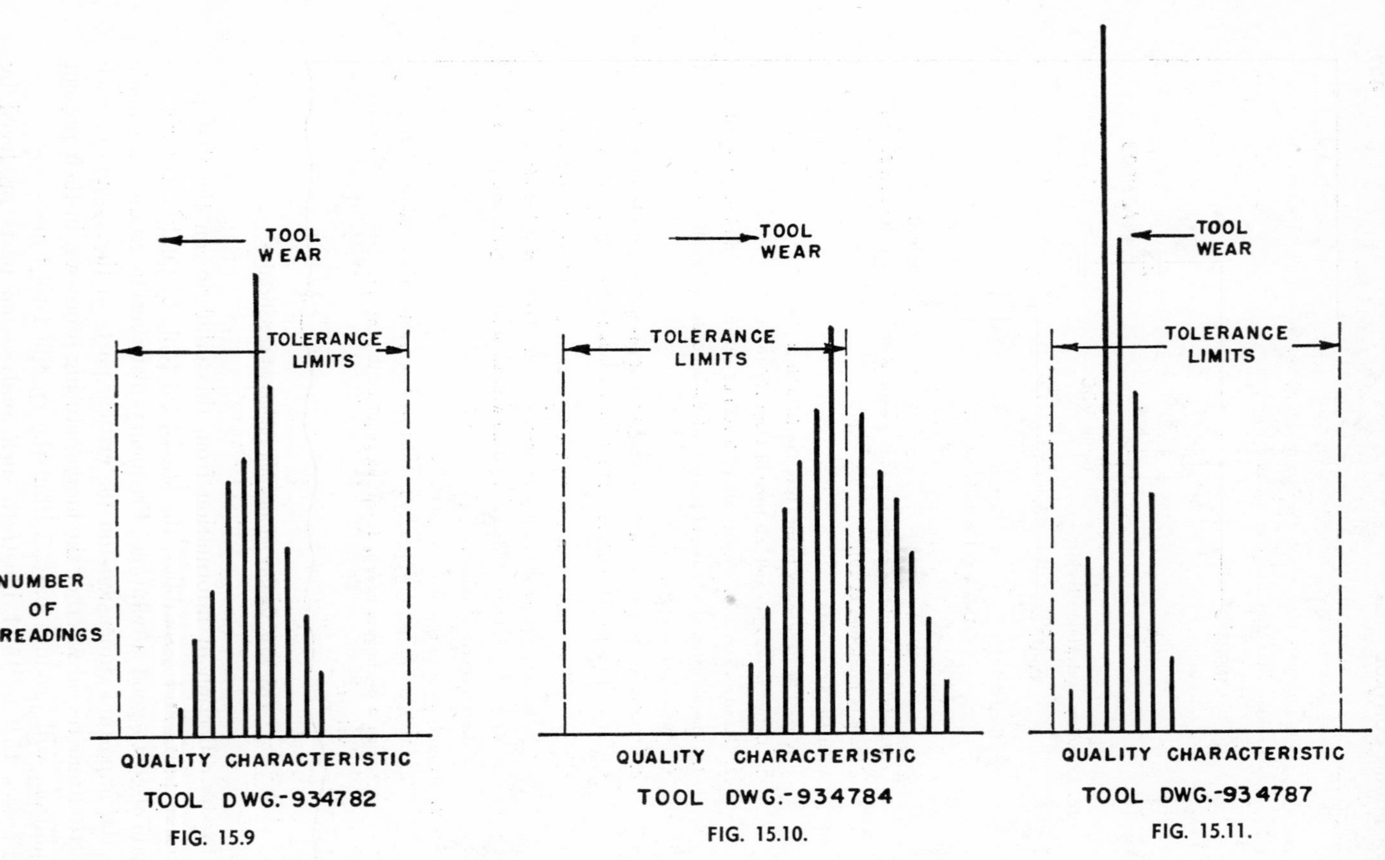

TOOL DWG.-934782

FIG. 15.9

TOOL DWG.-934784

FIG. 15.10.

TOOL DWG.-934787

FIG. 15.11.

tools, developed specially for production of 4ZP96B3 components, are set up on presses in the plant tool room. Fifty parts are manufactured by each tool.

The frequency distribution of Fig. 15.9 illustrates that tool drawing 934782 will produce parts satisfactorily within tolerance. Figure 15.10 shows that parts produced by tool drawing 934784 do not meet specification limits. The frequency-distribution picture indicates that this tool must be repaired or replaced before it is used for regular production.

Tool drawing 934787 also must be repaired or replaced, but for a different reason. Figure 15.11 shows that the tool produces parts within tolerance limits but that the parts thus produced are very close to the tolerance limit in the direction of tool wear. If this tool were used during production in its present condition, it would have a much shorter life before a repair was necessary than would be economical and would soon begin to produce defective parts.

Quality Control is interested in frequency-distribution analyses of parts from several points of view: sampling inspection of outside-vendor die-cast parts, approval of molds, etc. The design engineer's chief interest in these pilot-run analyses, rather than in such studies of individual parts, is in measurements distributions of the over-all functional performance of the device. Such performance characteristics as contact pickup voltage, motor starting current, switch actuator travel, and power-supply voltage output are expressed by him in terms of frequency distributions.

By sketching specification limits on the frequency-distribution pictures, the engineer secures at a glance an indication as to whether the 4ZP96B3, as designed, will perform within specification limits and whether the company can expect a minimum of rejects if specifications are followed throughout. In those cases where poor performance or a substantial number of rejects are forecast by the distribution, the engineer will wish to determine how the unsatisfactory conditions can be eliminated. Special methods may be used by the engineer in those instances where the solution of the problem is particularly complex.

In those cases where the required product improvements are difficult to make or where the expenditures necessary to eliminate the difficulties would be very high, the decision as to whether or not to "live with" the rejects resolves into a problem of economics that must be solved by plant top management.

The conclusion of these new-design-control activities is the formal release, after a final design review by the project team, of the 4ZP96B3 for active production. This step is taken as an indication that, if specifications and drawings are rigidly followed, satisfactory quality performance related to its guarantees can be expected from the new device in

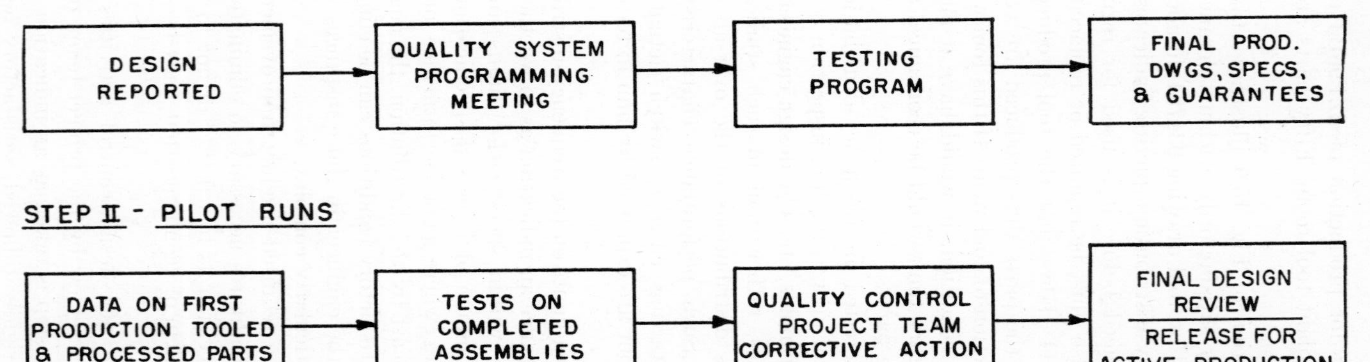
NEW DESIGN CONTROL SEQUENCE
STEP I - PRE-PRODUCTION ANALYSIS
DESIGN REPORTED
QUALITY SYSTEM PROGRAMMING MEETING
TESTING PROGRAM
FINAL PROD. DWGS, SPECS, & GUARANTEES
STEP II - PILOT RUNS
DATA ON FIRST PRODUCTION TOOLED & PROCESSED PARTS
TESTS ON COMPLETED ASSEMBLIES
QUALITY CONTROL PROJECT TEAM CORRECTIVE ACTION
FINAL DESIGN REVIEW
RELEASE FOR ACTIVE PRODUCTION
STEP III - THE QUALITY SYSTEM PLAN FOR MAINTAINING PERMANENT CONTROL DURING PRODUCTION
INCOMING MATERIAL CONTROL (CHAPTER 16)
PRODUCT CONTROL (CHAPTER 17)
SPECIAL PROCESS STUDIES (CHAPTER 18)

FIG. 15.12.

the field and a minimum of rejects may be expected on the production line.

Figure 15.12 shows the general sequence of the new-design-control routine used by this company.

15.9 Techniques Used in New-design Control

A large number of technical methods are used in new-design-control activities of the sort described above.[5]

Many of these were reviewed in Parts Three and Four. It may be worthwhile, however, to summarize some of the more significant of these that apply to new-design-control activity:

Merchandising and Product Planning. The new-design control portion of these activities is carried on from the standpoint of establishing the most economic quality standards for incorporation in a product which will sell well on the market and will satisfy its customers.

Statistical Analysis of New Designs. Frequency distributions, special methods and reliability studies are especially useful in answering such questions as "Have enough test runs been made?" "Is the variation to be expected from this product too great for manufacturing purposes?" "What performance can we guarantee for this product?"

Vendor and Purchasing Department Records. These records are used so as to employ in the new product only parts purchased from those vendors who are most reliable, most quality-minded, and most economical and so that costs for "quality extras" can be eliminated in material purchases.

Process-capability Studies. Records of the accuracies that can be maintained with the factory manufacturing facilities are of great value in decisions as to the type of product design and parts tolerances to be established.

Data on Old and New Materials. Extensive use is made of the results of laboratory and research engineering's analyses of old methods and their experiments with new materials, processes, and theories of product operation.

Accumulated Past Product Experience. Examination is made of plant quality data on the actual production performance of earlier models of similar design.

Special Tests in the Plant on Production Units Similar to the New Design. This is particularly useful in new-design-control activity under job-shop conditions, since it replaces the mass-production type of pilot run.

[5] The term *technical methods* is used throughout to refer to the various individual techniques used in quality-control activities. Thus the term as used here refers not only to such mechanical techniques as tool and die control but also to the several human relations approaches used in quality control.

Field Tests and Reports. This technique is a complement to that of the preceding paragraph. Maximum use is made of data from field performance of similar designs. Special tests may be established for this purpose in the field where possible and practical.

Tolerance Analysis. Activity here is threefold: to establish the widest possible manufacturing tolerances, to be assured that the "build-up" of these tolerances will not be excessive for proper functioning of the device, and to ensure that the various component parts will fit together when assembled.

Shop-practice Tolerance Sheets. These sheets furnish data on the dimensions that can be maintained on standard factory operations which may be called for in the new design.

Standards. Reference is made to plant-wide, industry-wide, possibly national and international standards for the product in question and its components. These standards may be available in several areas—trade associations, professional societies, government agencies—or by statute as in the case of products like many chemicals.

Standardization and Simplification. Techniques for this purpose are used as an aid to the sound design of a new product and for the achievement of the most economical performance-cost balance.

Drawings. With the specifications of the preceding paragraph, drawings constitute the basic core of representing the new product, its tolerances and dimensions, materials, etc.

Quality Guarantees, and Reports for Sales Purposes. These data highlight the important quality standards for the product; for advertising purposes, they may include how these standards will be controlled during production.

Pilot Runs. This procedure involves the production and testing of samples composed of units of the actual product. It is usually carried out with production parts and the use of production facilities. It helps to determine, before the start of active production, those process improvements or design changes which may be required to enable a minimum of quality difficulties during production.

Planned Inspection. Vitally important during new-design control is the selection of the quality characteristics to be inspected, the gages to be used, and the physical location of inspection stations so that suitable guide cards can be prepared for the use and training of the inspection force.

Planned Packaging and Shipping. The choice of the proper container and the proper shipping routine is important for the receipt by the customer of a satisfactory product with a minimum of shifts in adjustment, scratches in finishes, or other quality defects.

Statistical Analyses of Tools and Facilities Specially Purchased for Manufacturing the New Product. The frequency distribution and process-capability studies are most useful here.

Development of Statistical Sampling Quality Levels. AQL and AOQL values may be established for use on production parts in the planned inspection guide cards.

Establishment of a Definite Time Schedule for the New-design-control Routine. This administrative device is most useful under fast-moving, modern industrial conditions to minimize and eliminate the ever-present hazard of bypassing essential phases of the new-design-control activity.

Several of these techniques have been made the subject for intensive study both throughout industry and in the universities. The literature reflects much of this attention in such fields as the making and dimensioning of production drawings and the writing of specifications.

Yet the fundamentals of these technical methods are quite straightforward and are relatively uniform in their applications throughout industry. Specific details of each technique are, of course, adapted to the needs of individual plants.

Several of these new-design-control techniques have been described in detail elsewhere in the book. Those readers interested in considerable detail on others may wish to refer to the literature in the fields in question.

For illustrative purposes, details of three of these new-design-control techniques will be described below, as follows: Tolerance Analysis, in Sec. 15.10; Planned Inspection, in Sec. 15.11; Statistical Analyses of Tools Specially Purchased, in Sec. 15.12.

15.10 Tolerance Analysis

The technique of tolerance analysis takes many forms in various companies. The procedure used in an Atlantic area plant represents, however, the typical fundamentals. This procedure is listed below:[6]

1. A tolerance analysis is required on all new devices before they are placed in production.
2. The analysis must be recorded on a special drawing.
3. The reference number of this analysis drawing must be recorded on the device drawing.
4. The design engineer's signature must appear on the tolerance-analysis drawing before it is completed.
5. The proper time in the new-design-control routine for making the tolerance analysis is determined by the design engineer and the quality-control engineer.

[6] This discussion is adapted from a procedure developed by R. H. Schmitt and associates, Schenectady, N.Y.

6. In those unusual cases where the design engineer waives a tolerance analysis, the analysis drawing must be made out. The facts must be so stated on this drawing, and a number assigned to it and recorded on the device drawing.

7. The analysis will be made by the draftsman for the device, with the assistance of the design engineer.

8. An analysis will be made on old existing designs only when a problem arises in the factory requiring such an analysis.

9. The analysis will cover such points as follows:

a. All important functional dimensions.

b. All specified limits either on assembly drawings or in specifications.

c. All parts which have to be assembled and which must fit together.

d. All spring loads at various compression, tension, or torsional stages, depending on the variations of the spring space available. If necessary, this analysis can be made on graph paper and assigned a number. This number must be cross-referenced on the tolerance-analysis record drawing.

e. Such other auxiliaries as bellows, bimetals, etc., must also be treated as outlined in paragraph *d.*

10. All changes or additions made on detail drawings which will affect the analysis must be properly recorded on the analysis drawings.

11. Whenever possible, a single drawing number should be used for the analysis with the use of additional sheets where needed.

Figure 15.13 illustrates one example of such a tolerance record sheet.

The tolerance analysis made according to this routine may be developed in two ways:

1. Using the time-honored procedure where tolerances of parts are added together arithmetically.

2. Using the procedure of formula (38), as discussed in Sec. 13.8.

Which of the two alternatives that will be chosen will depend upon the circumstances of each individual product. Where it is possible to run the risk of a certain percentage of assemblies which do not fit together and where the other limitations of formula (38) can be observed, use of this formula proves practical and economical.

15.11 Planned Inspection

An important factor during the final development of the details of the quality-system plan for a new design is the establishment of the kind and location of inspection that will be required during active production. Without precautions of this sort, parts may be presented for inspection at the time when the inspector does not have proper gages

Z-9846352

REASON FOR THIS ANALYSIS NEW DEVICE

REFERENCE	NOM.	MAX.	MIN.
A	.312	.322	
B			.109
C	.375		.365
D	.375	.385	
E	.187		.183
F		.102	
G	.625		.619
H			.819
J	.625	.628	
K		.818	
L	.312		.302
M	.375		.372
N			.125
P			.182
R	.312	.316	
S	.375	.380	
T		.112	
U		.176	
V	.164	.164	
W	.190	.190	
X	.213		.208
Y	.205		.200

SKETCHES

REMARKS

QUALITY CONTROL
TOLERANCE ANALYSIS RECORD
DEVICE--4ZP96B3
EST. YEARLY PROD. 50,000 ENGINEER J. G JONES

FIG. 15.13.

either available or accessible to him. Examination of the product may be after the tenth operation when it may be the third operation that is critical and troublesome for quality.

Product and process-quality planning is a new-design-control technique which establishes within the total-quality-system plan the quan-

TITLE SUPPORT		IDEN. 6908866	PT.	GR.	PT. NO.	MATERIAL			
DRAWING CHANGES		RATING				SIZE	NO. OUT	SPECIFICATION	R ST. SN.
						.075 X 1"			
PRICED	DATE / BY	FIRST PLAN QTY.	CARD NO.	NO. OF CARDS	DISTR.	B11-H16-A1			
PLANNED	DATE / BY	PLAN-CHGS	OPER. NO. / DATE / SIGNED						

OPER. NO.	OPERATION	PRICE			PER	RTG. SYM.	S/U	A.E.R.	WORK STATION NO	TOOLS	MACHINE
1	SLIT 1" WIDE								15-1		
2	PRC & BLK								15-1	DIE 6908865 .096" GAGE	
3	ANNEAL								TOOL ROOM	TOOLROOM TO CHECK FOR PROPER ANNEAL	
4	1 ST. FORM								15-1	DIE 6908865 GAGE FOR .218 ± .005 INSP. FOR SQ. BEND	
5	FINAL FORM								15-1	DIE 6908865 GAGE FOR .130 ± .005	
6	TRIM SHORT LEG								15-1	DIE 6908865 GAGE FOR .019 ± .002	
7	FINAL INSPECTION BEFORE SHIP'T										

FIG. 15.14.

tity and location of the required types of inspection before active production is started. It assures the presence of suitable gages and fixtures. Hit-or-miss inspection procedures are thereby minimized.

As used in a metalworking shop, planned inspection is developed under guidance of the quality-control engineer. The details of the planning sequence are as follows:

1. Determine the critical dimensions for each operation.

2. While making out the regular card which describes in sequence the required metalworking operations, list the critical dimensions for each of these operations and specify the measuring equipments, gages, or templates required.

3. Place orders for those gages or measuring equipments which are not available in the plant, so that the equipments will be present for the start of formal production.

4. Make out an inspection guide card, which lists the essential inspection information required for each part.

Figure 15.14 illustrates a planning card, which includes planned inspection for the punch-press work on a support.[7] Figure 15.15 illustrates an inspection guide card used for a yoke plate in the plant.[8]

15.12 Statistical Analysis of Tools Specially Purchased for the New Product

Large quantities of defective component parts for a new design may be produced before the inaccuracy of a new punch-press tool is discovered. Both high scrap losses and production holdups may result. Statistical analysis of new tools and processes is a new-design-control method which aims to eliminate this condition by examining a sample of the parts produced by the tool or process as soon as it has been received from the outside vendor or from the toolroom of the plant.

A typical routine for accomplishing this objective is listed[9] below as it operates in actual practice.

All new tools shall be identified with yellow-colored metal disks and shall be subjected to the following routine before being used in regular production:

1. The tool section shall make 25 consecutive sample units using the new tools.

2. The person making the 25 units shall fill out 2 lavender tags, indicating drawing number of tool, one to be attached to the tool and the other to the 25 samples.

[7] Adapted from a discussion by A. L. Fuller, Schenectady, N.Y.

[8] Adapted from a card developed by H. C. Thompson, Schenectady, N.Y.

[9] Adapted from a routine developed by W. T. Short, W. E. Polozie, and associates, Schenectady, N.Y.

Drg. 8647954-2 Part No. ____ Change No. ____

Yoke Plate INSPECTION INSTRUCTIONS

IMII CHECK	IMII GAGES
1. Ck frac. dims. ∓ 1/8" flat within SR tol.	1. 12" scale
R2A	
2. Square within SR tol. Check burrs	2. Scale & square hd.
IMII	
3. Check 2" dim. of cutout	3. Scale
4. Check 3/8R & 1/2"	4. Radius gage
5. Check 1-9/16 & 154 hls.	5. #23 drill pin & scale
R2B	
6. After finding one conforming to dwg., by layout method, use this as template to ck. reaming plate	6. Layout tools and Instruments
R2A	
7. Check tap holes	7. 6-32 male thd. gage
8. Check dia. of 9/32 drill holes	8. #12 drill pin

INSPECTION SCHEDULE

AVERAGE QUALITY LEVEL - 2% MAXIMUM DEFECTS PER LOT - 5%

LOT SIZE	SIZE FIRST SAMPLE	ALLOWABLE DEFECTS SAMPLE # 1	SIZE SECOND SAMPLE	ALLOWABLE DEFECTS SAMPLE 1 PLUS 2
1-15	ALL PIECES	—	—	—
16-109	10	0	20	1
110-179	15	0	30	1
180-299	25	1	50	2
300-499	35	1	70	3
500-799	50	2	100	4
800-1299	75	3	150	5
1300-3199	100	3	200	8
3200-8000	150	5	300	13

Note: Split Lots of Over 8000 Pieces

NO.	VENDOR	NO.	VENDOR
1		4	
2		5	
3		6	

FIG. 15.15.

3. The 25 pieces shall be given to the inspection unit for checking. The tool shall remain in the tool section and not be used for production until proper approval is received from Inspection on the 25 pieces.

4. The inspection unit shall inspect all 25 pieces for their critical or functional dimensions as indicated on the planning card, using gages furnished. One of the pieces shall be inspected for all dimensions as called for on the drawing. If any dimensions are found to be wrong on

the piece inspected, four additional pieces shall be inspected for the wrong dimension only. All data shall be recorded on a suitable tally card.

5. The tally card, after being filled in by the inspector in duplicate, shall be presented to the process-control engineer, who will make any calculations required.

6. The results of the calculations will be turned over to the tool section foreman and the design engineer, who will accept, reject, or recommend further change in the tools.

7. If further change is necessary, the new-tool-approval routine shall be repeated until the tool is accepted for production.

8. After 25 tool-made parts have received approval, the inspector shall O.K. the lavender tag on the tool, which shall be filed in the tool crib. The lavender tag on the parts shall be filed in the inspector's office by the inspector.

15.13 Some Practical Aspects of New-design Control

Among the major benefits that a plant may gain from the new-design-control programs that have been discussed in this chapter are

1. More effective administration of a coordinated program of quality-system planning.

2. More effective technical methods for use in controlling newly designed products.

The first of these benefits is a matter of administration. It is, therefore, one whose value will take some time to prove. This circumstance is a major problem faced by quality-control proponents who wish to institute new-design control in a plant.

These quality-control people, in describing and trying to "sell" company personnel on the ultimate results from the required new-design-control procedures, may meet considerable passive resistance. This resistance may be typified by the statement: "There's nothing new in that program—we've been doing the work all along. Our interest is in the new technical methods for accomplishing the new-design-control objective."

In introducing new-design control under the quite common conditions of this sort, there is no substitute for practical results. It is only these results which will eliminate the passive resistance and will bring home a basic fact to those who question the value of the program; new-design control *does* bring something new and necessary solely in its role of an administrative device which ties together already existing practices, entirely apart from its statistical methods, pilot runs, or tool and die program.

Quality-control proponents might fail in achieving their new-design-control objective were they merely to allow these individual technical methods to be added to the already large host of uncoordinated design-control activities in the factory. The purpose of new-design control—integrated quality planning for new products—can be accomplished through no other means than by the administrative integration of *all* the design-control activities in the plant. New technical methods can be added to this program as they are required *after* it has been organized.

Several other practical problems are generated because of the administrative objectives of new-design control. There is, for example, the very delicate organizational problem of minimizing friction among the participants in a well-operating program of new-design control. Technical men—designing engineers, manufacturing engineers, laboratory technicians—will be the key individuals in the program. It is they who have the direct responsibility for important elements of the new-design-control program. Yet their activities in this regard are integrated by the quality-control component, which is responsible for integration of quality-control activities but not for the direct responsibilities of these technical men. Sound organization, skillful administration, and wise staff work by the quality-control men are essential to the achievement of the teamwork required for proper performance under the necessary but delicate organizational plan for effective new-design control.

An administrative problem of a somewhat different sort may also be described. It is represented in the ever-present vigilance required of the quality-control people for maintenance of the company new-design-control routine once it has been established.

Many new-product designs are pushed through the factory under pressure; it is desired to place the product on the market as soon as possible. All possible short cuts are taken and all possible obstacles eliminated to permit speedy production of the new articles. Always vulnerable in these drives for short cuts are elements of the new-design-control routine—reliability analysis, field tests, tests of prototype samples, tool- and die-control, and pilot runs.

Periodically, the quality-control organization may be requested to eliminate portions of this routine to help expedite a "really hot" product. The circumstances of the case may make possible the elimination of a few portions in the new-design-control program for some products; circumstances may make such an elimination equally impossible for other products.

When the pressure for elimination still continues on these latter products, it may be necessary in extreme cases for the Quality Control Manager to refer the matter to his superior—company top management—for a decision. Obviously the ultimate strength of the new-design-control program will be directly dependent upon the support given the

Quality Control Manager in these instances by company top management.

Indeed, the quality-control component is making one of its fundamental contributions to the health of the company when it opposes the release of a product whose quality is not well enough established for actual production. Particularly with military and consumer products, where an effort to go to market with new features more quickly than competitors is always present, premature production releases have ruined the customer acceptance of several companies without adequate new-design procedures.

On certain "very rush" new products, some plants provide a special routine which achieves the objective of quality planning but which involves a much more concentrated program of new-design-control activities than that used under normal conditions. This routine is still an effective one, but it may involve relatively high expense. Both the quality-control component and plant top management must approve the use of this routine for a given product, and it is used only in very special cases.

Special new-design-control routines for a somewhat different purpose are also established in many companies. These plants have established satisfactory new-design-control routines for all the new designs coming through the plant, and they wish to gain benefits from these activities in respect to old designs currently in production.

To accomplish this purpose, they use appropriate elements of the new-design-control program for reviewing these old designs. Such new-design-control techniques as reliability analysis often produce some extremely effective results in programs of this sort in helping to improve the quality of the old designs being reviewed.

Practical problems faced by quality-control men in a plant are not all confined to difficulties in establishing the administrative aspects of a new-design-control program. Problems are also encountered in judging how far it is desirable to go in instituting additional design-control technical activities.

The issue is one of long-range economic considerations. New-design-control activities should be established in a plant to the extent that the expense of their operation is justified by the value received in minimizing within factory rejects, in maximizing customer acceptance of the quality of the product, in improving liaison among the plant functional groups. This value must be judged by the long-range influence of quality planning on plant economics and not merely upon its effect on day-to-day quality-cost data.

There are many companies wherein quality-control proponents can and should justify a wide extension of design-control activities. It must be recognized, however, that there are other plants where it may be uneconomic to concentrate much additional effort on new-design control; other quality-control jobs may warrant this attention.

There are plants, for example, in which a well-developed new-design-control program has grown over the years out of sound company planning. This program may not have formally been recognized as a quality-control activity, nor can its routines be described in currently fashionable quality-control language. The individuals involved in the program may be reluctant to accept or show interest in either the administrative or technical method aspects of the proposed new-design-control program.

This situation may be particularly true in those job shops which may have had to develop new-design-control programs for sheer self-preservation in the early days of the plant. A great deal of prudence may be wise for quality-control proponents in situations such as these. Much of the publicity accorded new-design control has been devoted to programs on products produced in mass quantities. This publicity has included "success stories" on highly developed and highly specialized technical methods.

Far less polished methods, on the other hand, may be perfectly satisfactory in accomplishing equally satisfactory quality-planning objectives for the job shop. Here, rapid turnover of types of articles may make it overly expensive to develop sets of techniques as highly specialized as those often publicized in connection with mass production.

In plant situations such as these, quality-control proponents should assure themselves that they propose technical methods on the merits of these methods alone in accomplishing the new-design-control objective, apart from the amount of "window dressing" that may accompany inauguration of these methods. The quality-control proponents should be certain that they are not promoting new technical methods simply because these methods seem to be necessary for a "completely well-seeming program of new-design control." In effect, therefore, quality-control proponents must be certain that the methods and techniques they propose are those which are best adapted to the needs of the particular plant, apart from those which may simply look good on paper.

Because new-design-control programs throughout industry reflect this effort to adapt the type of routines used to the needs of individual plants, these programs take many forms. The activities accompanying them may be described in a wide variety of ways. Discussed below are two examples of new-design-control activities of this sort as used in industry:

1. Section 15.14 discusses the application of an individual technical method—pilot runs—as part of a new-design-control program.

2. Section 15.15 describes the over-all new-design-control program established for planning the quality of a new electromechanical switch.

15.14 Pilot Run to Determine Spring Specification

Part of the program on the pilot run of a new mechanical product was aimed to determine the specification that should be established for the tension of a main spring at the final preshipment test on the product. An upper limit for this spring tension was desired.

The design engineer wished to establish this upper limit during the pilot-run program on the new article. This pilot run was made on units manufactured by actual production facilities.

Data were taken on the spring tension of the first 100 assemblies that were put through the pilot run. All these units performed properly functionally. Figure 15.16 shows the frequency distribution of these data taken on spring tension of these satisfactory units.

TENSION IN GRAMS	TALLY
7	x x x x
8	x x x x x x x x x x x
9	x x x x x x x x x x x x x x x x x
10	x x x x x x x x x x x x x x x x x x x x x x x x x x x x x x x x x x x x x
11	x x x x x x x x x x x x x x x x
12	x x x x x x x x x
13	x x x x x x

FIG. 15.16.

From this information the design engineer made a probability-paper plot, which is shown on Fig. 15.17. From this plot and its accompanying calculations he was able to establish an upper spring tension limit of 15 grams.

Experience during actual production of the new device indicated that this upper limit value aided in the production of products of satisfactory quality.

15.15. Over-all New-design-control Program on a New Electromechanical Switch

In facing the problem of designing a new electromechanical switch better to aid the company to meet competition from other manufacturers and to provide a product of high quality, an Eastern factory drew great benefit from its new-design-control routine.[10] The steps of this routine, as they were applied to the new switch, are listed below.

[10] This discussion follows a study made by A. W. Bedford, Jr., and associates, Schenectady, N.Y.

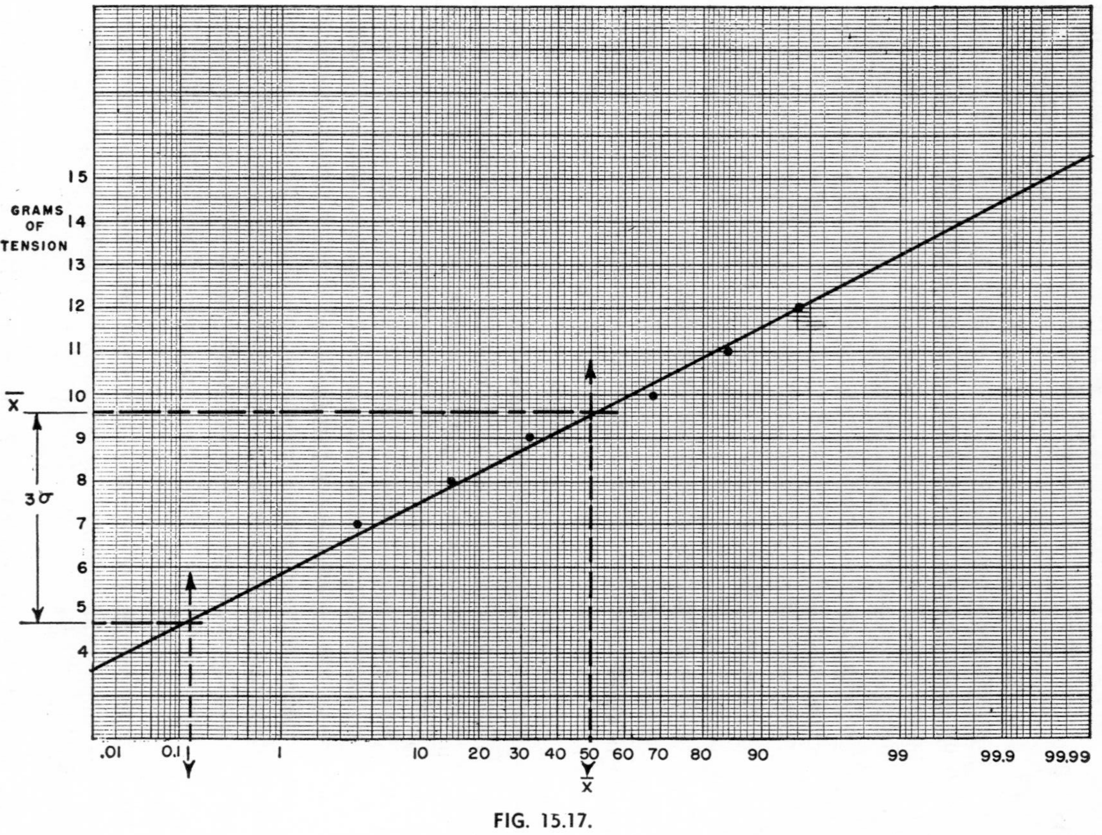

GRAMS OF TENSION
15
14
13
12
11
10
9
8
7
6
5
4
X̄
3σ
.01
0.1
1
10
20
30
40
50
60
70
80
90
99
99.9
99.99
X̄

FIG. 15.17.

Establishing the Quality Standards. The first step in establishing the quality standards for the new switch was a product evaluation. Existing switches were compared in regard to their mechanical and electrical characteristics, accessibility for repair, and ease of inspection and servicing. Mechanical and electrical life tests were run on several samples of each switch type used in the study, and careful analysis of other characteristics was made. The result was factual data on mechanical and electrical reliability and a tabulation of other desirable features for the quality required in the new switch.

The wide background of experience available in the company from previous new-design-control activities was a second source of quality standards. This know-how in the minds of the design engineers draws them away from designs that might later be subject to trouble. It correspondingly draws them toward new standards of quality derived from knowledge gained from past mistakes and troubles or gained from specialized experience in the application of other switch designs. A similar type of experience was available in the form of various standards, such as NEMA, Underwriters, and AIEE. These standards contain many requirements set down as the result of experience in obtaining high-quality component parts such as enclosures and contacts. They are generally expressed in the form of data such as temperature rises, ratings, or test requirements.

A third source of quality standards was new developments in materials, processes, and understanding of the theory of electromechanical switch operation. These developments pointed the way to new quality standards. Many quality improvements incorporated in the new switch were made possible because of these new developments.

The accumulation of these quality standards resulted in the writing of functional specifications for the new product. These specifications outlined the performance standards required.

Completing the New Design. The specifications that were thus written served as the bench mark for preliminary production drawings and prototypes of the new switch. The design engineers looked to these specifications for the required mechanical and electrical reliability, the standards to be followed, demands for corrosion protection, types of enclosures required for special conditions, voltage ranges, and special requirements.

While design of the new product proceeded, consultants and experts from the engineering group of the plant and from its laboratory were frequently called upon for advice in the selection and use of materials and processes. Working through the purchasing agent of the plant, the design engineers and planning people cooperated with outside vendors to determine the highest reliability parts available at acceptable cost.

Evaluating the New Design. After preliminary production drawings were prepared, prototype samples of the new switch were manufactured. These samples were critically analyzed and tested. The test program amounted to an audit of the new design by qualified persons. The original functional specifications were used as the criterion of performance.

The evaluation carried on during this test program consisted of three phases. The first was analysis of over-all switch performance, having to do with such functional features as arc interruption, temperature rise, pick-up voltage, and noise level. The second phase was materials examination by experts to evaluate whether or not proper use was made of materials in the new design. The third phase involved mechanical and load reliability tests on samples containing an ample number of switches. The objective here was to determine the life that could be expected from the new device under actual end-use environmental conditions. The three phases of this test program culminated in a report which was critically analyzed by a project team in a review of the design.

The results of these tests were incorporated into final production drawings. When actual production tools and facilities were available, a pilot run of production units was manufactured and a critical evaluation again made of all phases of switch performance. Any quality problems showing up in this pilot run were immediately analyzed, and the required corrections were made in the design of the new switch and in the plan for the quality system that would control the switch.

Groundwork for Maintaining Quality during Actual Manufacture. One of the most useful means for assuring the maintenance of quality during manufacture was the completion of a program of tolerance analysis of all major parts and assemblies. This analysis was made an integral part of the production drawing structure, so that it could not be bypassed. Figure 15.18 shows an example of such a tolerance analysis.

The tolerance-analysis program was also applied to many factors affecting operation of the device, such as the effect of coil turns and resistance on pickup voltage. The performance of the device throughout the possible mechanical variation of its components was thus established.

Early in the development of the new device, close liaison and a clear channel of communications were established among the design engineers, manufacturing engineers, quality-control engineers, and other concerned parties. As a result, the manufacturing organization understood why certain parts types were required and why it was necessary to set up to provide the required quality for these parts. On the other hand, Engineering was informed about potential difficulties in producing certain parts, about economies that could be effected by certain design changes, etc.

To assist the manufacturing people, specifications were established by

Engineering to cover many often overlooked shop details, such as screw-tightening torques, screw and lock-washer hardness, and hardness of the contact tips.

As part of the pilot-run procedure, samples of parts from the new pro-

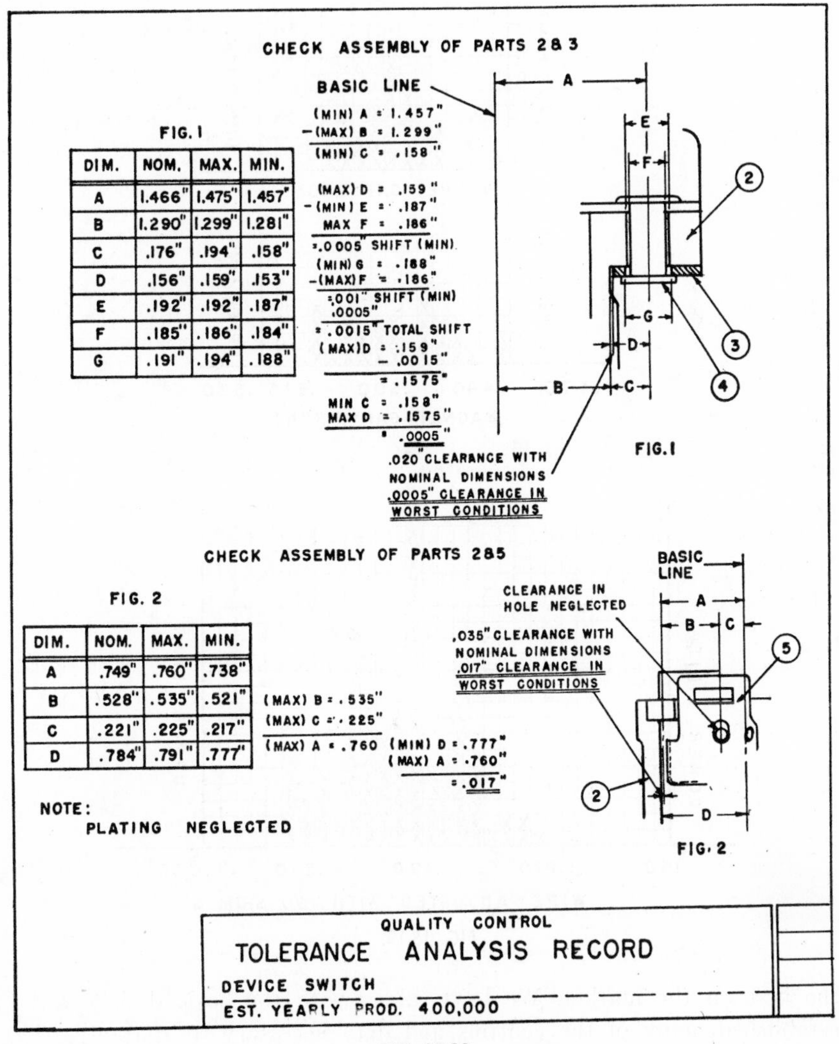

FIG. 1

DIM.	NOM.	MAX.	MIN.
A	1.466"	1.475"	1.457"
B	1.290"	1.299"	1.281"
C	.176"	.194"	.158"
D	.156"	.159"	.153"
E	.192"	.192"	.187"
F	.185"	.186"	.184"
G	.191"	.194"	.188"

FIG. 2

DIM.	NOM.	MAX.	MIN.
A	.749"	.760"	.738"
B	.528"	.535"	.521"
C	.221"	.225"	.217"
D	.784"	.791"	.777"

FIG. 15.18.

duction tools were carefully inspected for variations in their quality characteristics. Frequency-distribution analyses were made as required. Figure 15.19 illustrates some typical distributions made on important switch adjustments.

The plant summarized the benefits it received from this comprehensive new-design-control program on its new electromechanical switch: "As a result of this work, we know that the new line of devices is technically

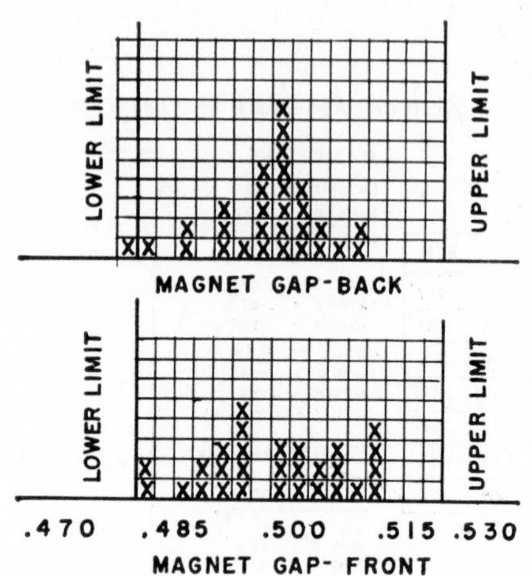

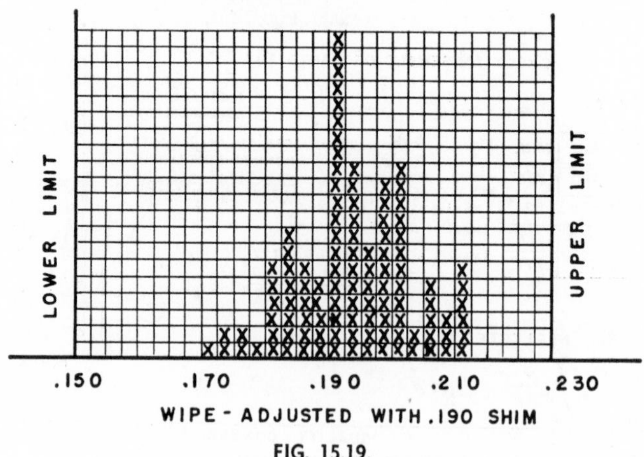

FIG. 15.19.

the best on the market. We have, along with the basic design work, established many of the controls and data necessary to guarantee the maintenance of this high level of quality as production proceeds."

CHAPTER 16

INCOMING-MATERIAL CONTROL

Materials of many types are purchased by companies for use in their manufacturing operations. Steel sheet, iron rod, castings, forgings, punchings, machined parts, fluids, tapes, and hardware are typical examples.

It is essential that the quality of these materials conform with requirements for their use in production. The most effectively designed product cannot properly be produced unless the materials used for its manufacture are satisfactory.

There is a long history of industrial activity to achieve the required control over the quality of incoming materials. This history reflects the fact that a wide variety of approaches have been used for this control purpose.

At the one extreme have been those plants either with no control procedures at all or with very informal ones. These plants have trusted to luck that incoming material will be acceptable when used in production.

At the other extreme have been those plants which inspect their material virtually "to death." These plants have spent more time and money than is necessary to gain adequate control of material quality.

The second of the quality-control jobs, incoming-material control, deals with techniques for achieving the objective of control while avoiding these extremes. After new-design-control activity has resulted in the specification of a well-designed product, incoming-material-control techniques have the task of assuring, at the most economical levels of cost, that material of proper quality will be available for use during actual manufacture of the new product.

It is the purpose of this chapter to discuss various aspects of incoming-material-control procedures.

16.1 The Needs for Incoming-material Control

Visualize the following situation: a battery of turret lathes has started to machine a lot of casting bodies. Tools start to break; castings fail to "clean up." The machine-shop foreman reports to his superintendent that the entire lot is defective because of "hard spots." Since these are the only casting bodies available in the factory, the assembly line on which they are to be used must shut down until new castings can be secured from the foundry. Production stops; employees on the assembly line are sent home.

Visualize an additional situation involving castings: precision machining is performed at high cost on a pump casting. At the twelfth machining operation, blowholes and porosity show up. These defects cause the scrapping of the casting and the loss of the effort spent on the previous 11 operations.

In both these instances, ineffective control over incoming castings was the direct cause of the manufacturing difficulties.

Here is still another case: a small cross-shaped flat spring is carefully inspected for critical dimensions as it is produced by a battery of punch presses. The material specified for this spring is beryllium copper. After they are punched out, the springs are assembled to small electrical devices. The springs serve on these devices as a mechanical counterbalance to the electrical force in the coil.

When the devices have been completely assembled, they are tested. After several weeks of satisfactory production-line performance, the devices suddenly begin to fail to meet specifications at this test.

After considerable time, expense, and a long production holdup, the cause of these failures is discovered. A batch of the cross-shaped springs has been punched from phosphor bronze instead of from beryllium copper; when assembled to the electrical device, the phosphor bronze springs have been unable to provide the proper mechanical counterbalancing force.

The entire production holdup on the device was caused by ineffective material-control activities. An incoming lot was accepted as beryllium copper simply because the material in the lot was "reddish brown and shiny"—a characteristic common to phosphor bronze as well as to beryllium copper.

These are failures detected before shipment. Many similar situations could be cited involving quality troubles in the field. This is one example: bearings on a certain motor type begin to fail prematurely after only 1 year of operation in the plant of the customer which purchased the motors. The failures are finally traced to low-quality materials that were originally manufactured into the bearing linings.

Since no adequate reliability preshipment test had been performed on the motors, it was only on the control of incoming bearing lining materials that quality depended. An unsatisfactory incoming control routine resulted in the considerable customer dissatisfaction developing from these bearing failures.

Control over incoming material may also suffer because of inadequacy of quality information equipment in the plant or because of careless maintenance of this equipment. Incoming inspectors may lack proper training or sufficient understanding of inspection objectives. They may not be provided with satisfactory specifications for judging conformance of materials.

Inadequate utilization may be made of modern statistical acceptance sampling tables. Incoming material may be damaged by poor handling during its receipt and travel through the plant. Certain materials which are placed on the shelf after incoming acceptance—insulating strips, bellows which require "aging"—may be harmed owing to improper storage facilities. Ineffective means for tagging and disposing materials found defective may result in occasional lots of the material finding their way into active production.

These instances illustrate the first of the two aspects in which the incoming-material procedures of many factories have been unsatisfactory in assisting plant management to achieve its quality-product goal: these incoming-material procedures have too often permitted defective materials to be accepted by the plant for use on its production lines.

The second aspect in which these incoming control procedures have been inadequate is more directly related to economics. In some plants, incoming-material routines have been unnecessarily cumbersome and drawn out. Too much time and money have been spent to achieve the amount of control that is required for the materials and parts received.

A case of this sort may be briefly described: one manufacturer discovered that his inspection force had been 100 per cent inspecting all incoming brass rod for its outer-diameter dimensions. The inspection force kept several charts and incoming-material inspection records on this brass rod. These charts showed the quality performance of the vendor in considerable detail.

The inspection force was quite proud of its extensive control routine for this material. Yet for 14 months there had not been a single reject of brass rod at incoming-material inspection. Obviously, the 100 per cent inspection as well as the very considerable charting and recording routine was unnecessarily expensive.

Situations could also be cited illustrating uneconomical material purchase prices that result from an inadequate program of material control. In too many instances, materials—steels, forgings, detail parts, springs—have been bought at prices which reflect excessive costs for unnecessary quality extras or for special tests and inspections. These special requirements may have been required for applications of these materials at one time; they may, however, have been retained in purchase specifications long after the need for them has passed.

The purchasing group may consider that plant quality-control activities are concerned exclusively with internal factory quality problems and so may fail to gain contributions from these activities. Long-range purchasing efforts to establish "approved supplier" lists may suffer because of inadequate plant records on the quality of shipments by various vendors.

Company relations with respected vendors may be strained in several ways: Purchasing, Engineering, even Manufacturing may make independent, inconsistent contacts with one vendor on a single quality problem. Another vendor may complain bitterly about the rejection of thousands of his parts because of defective finish; he may insist that, according to the standards of his own plant, he has met the purchase specification requirement which states only that "fine finish is required." Still another vendor may embarrass a multidivision plant by pointing out that there is a completely nonuniform interpretation of specifications on the same material among the divisions of the plant.

It is the purpose of incoming-material-control procedures to provide the mechanism required to eliminate from company activities these aspects in which earlier control procedures have been unsatisfactory.

16.2 Defining Incoming-material Control

As a definition:

Incoming-material control involves the receiving and stocking, at the most economical levels of quality, of only those parts whose quality conforms to the specification requirements.

All three of the technologies of total quality control have application in incoming-material control, as does the statistical point of view in all its aspects. The planning techniques of quality-control engineering (Chap. 7) and the equipment techniques of quality information engineering (Chap. 9) are extensively used to establish the foundation for incoming-material-control activity in the company. It is, however, the actual day-to-day control techniques of process-control engineering (Chap. 8) which are most intensively used in the second job of total quality control.

Among the analytical tools of statistics, it is the sampling tables (Chap. 12) that are most actively employed.

There are two phases in incoming-material control:

1. Control on materials and parts received from outside sources.
2. Control on parts processed by other plants of the same company or other divisions of the plant.

The scope of incoming-material-control routines covers all quality-control activities carried on while material purchase contracts and prices are being arranged and while these materials are being received, inspected, and stocked by the purchaser plant. Incoming-material control involves techniques in purchasing, process-control engineering, laboratory, and materials handling as well as in other functional fields. It concerns relations with vendors as far as quality is concerned. It applies to all parts and materials received by the factory for use in production; in some plants it also includes control over materials used in such plant-service activities as maintenance and plant protection. Its importance to a soundly operating, company-wide quality-control program is very great under any type of manufacturing condition; under some conditions—chemical batch manufacture, for example—control of incoming material may be the single most important quality-control activity in the plant.

Early material-control routines concentrated most heavily upon incoming inspection procedures. Large areas lined with inspection equipment and peopled with an extensive inspection force were taken to be representative of sound control programs.

Present-day incoming-material-control technique is not so directed. It recognizes that widespread incoming inspection does not, of itself, relate to the preventive approach of total quality control. Modern incoming-material-control activities place strong emphasis on control of material at its source—in effect, upon close product-quality relationships between the vendor and the purchaser.

Receiving inspection, though recognized as very important, is used as an adjunct to this relationship rather than as the whole of incoming-material control. Further to streamline this incoming inspection, statistical acceptance sampling tables are used as widely as possible in place of 100 per cent, spot-check, or no inspection.[1]

The vendor whose material is being controlled may be another plant or division of the same company. In these cases, incoming control procedures are far less extensive than when the vendor is an outside source.

With outside source vendors, the objective of close vendor-purchaser relations imposes a definite set of administrative problems upon the com-

[1] Chapter 12 discussed quite extensively the comparison of acceptance sampling tables with 100 per cent, spot-check, and other forms of inspection.

pany quality-control program. These problems differ in one important respect from those in the other three quality-control jobs: vendor contacts in incoming-material control involve product-quality relationships by plant quality control with individuals and groups who, except as is provided in contractual relationships, are fully independent of the purchaser plant and who represent a sovereign legal unit. Obligations of these individuals to top management of the purchaser plant may be nothing more than those required by the ethics of business practice.

The accepted cyclical alternation between sellers' and buyers' markets may make the plant reluctant formally and officially to suggest overly rigid adjustments—the adoption of acceptance sampling tables, for example—in the practice of these vendors, particularly those who are highly respected and who represent the major source of supply of an item. In their turn, the desires of these vendors to adapt their practice best to aid the quality-control program of the purchaser plant may range from warm cooperation to passive resistance.

A premium may, therefore, be placed upon the gradual development by plant Quality Control of friendly yet firm relations with vendors in respect to product quality and modern means for its control. Wise vendors will soon come to recognize the commercial advantage to them of these relationships.

The contacts may take many forms. At the one extreme, there may be the occasional interchange of correspondence. At the other extreme, there may be almost daily visits by the purchaser plant quality-control component to the vendor's plant to assist in its efforts to develop a total quality control program.

16.3 Organizing for Incoming-material Control

The effectiveness of incoming control activity in a plant is directly dependent upon the caliber of the plan established.

The application of the various techniques of quality control are systematized in that segment of the quality-system plan which relates to incoming material. This plan is generally developed by the company quality-control-engineering unit, in close collaboration with the process-control-engineering unit (also including inspection and testing), which must make the plan work. Collaboration in the development of the plan is also sought from Purchasing, Engineering, and other concerned functional groups. Objective of this planning is to assure that all materials received in the plant will be controlled to the extent required for their satisfactory use in production.

The amount of control required for each type of material received will vary from plant to plant and among the materials received by any given plant. In establishing control procedures for material, consideration must be given to such factors as the size of the inspection force that should most economically be available, the laboratory testing facilities in the plant, and the quality variations allowed by material specifications. The routines must allow flexibility in such matters as inspection sampling schedules, so that economical adjustments can readily be made for different incoming-material situations.

The key groups for incoming-material-control organization are the plant laboratory, Purchasing, and Process Control Engineering.

Laboratory people enter into the incoming-material-control picture by maintaining adequate quality specifications for basic raw materials and by carrying on some of the detailed tests specified by the quality plan for acceptance of complex incoming materials and parts.

Purchasing's responsibility is to work as part of the plant quality-control team so that materials are ordered which are of the proper quality and which reflect the right cost so far as quality is concerned. For the purpose of developing approved supplier lists, Purchasing must assure that a close check is maintained to determine the quality performance of vendors once these orders have been placed and shipments have begun. Purchasing must therefore keep close contact with the incoming inspection records maintained in the plant.

Through this quality-control activity, Purchasing is better enabled to challenge purchase requirements established by plant technical groups, to question prices quoted by vendors in meeting the quality requirements, to keep these prices flexible in line with changing quality needs, and to assure that adequate contacts are being maintained on vendor quality relationships.

The process-control-engineering unit of the company quality-control component has the responsibility to assure the progress and the integration of the incoming-material-control activity for the company. It must work in terms of the plan developed by the quality-control-engineering unit, and must make use of the equipment provided by the quality information equipment engineers.

Chapter 4 discussed the principal responsibilities of the process-control-engineering unit, pointing out that quality liaison between the company and its vendors, to assure that the burden of quality proof rests with the vendor, is a major assignment. For one example, problems the vendor has in meeting company quality requirements may, at the suggestion of the company's purchasing component, be reviewed by a process-control engineer and necessary assistance provided the vendor.

As discussed in Chap. 4, there are several ways of assigning specific responsibilities for incoming-material control to the process-control-engineering unit. In the case of those companies where the receiving and acceptance of incoming materials is a major element in the business, particularly in companies which are predominantly assemblers of purchased components, it may be most useful to make incoming-material control a specialized activity. It may thus become the responsibility of one or more process-control engineers. In other companies, where incoming-material receiving is a less significant factor, it may be added to the in-process and final-product control responsibilities of a process-control engineer who is assigned to a particular group of products and processes; thus there will be as many incoming-material-control assignments as there are process-control engineers with product responsibilities.

Chapter 4 noted that the men and women who perform routine incoming-materials inspection may also be assigned in several ways. They may be assigned to the process-control-engineering unit itself, when this inspection has not yet been satisfactorily routinized and where technical judgments play a significant part in decisions. This is particularly true in rapidly expanding companies with new products for which quality planning has not yet been adequately definitized.

Where incoming inspection has been routinized but where it is still a major factor in incoming-material control because adequate vendor-relations practices have not yet been established, the inspection unit may report through a supervisor directly to the manager of the company quality-control component. Here, process-control engineering audits the adequacy of incoming inspection and is able to concentrate on the technical aspects of vendor-company quality relations.

Where these relations have developed to the point where incoming inspection has been significantly reduced and is highly routinized, the inspectors may be assigned to the appropriate plant manager of Shop Operations. Process Control Engineering carefully audits the adequacy and performance of this inspection.

However these activities may be assigned within the process-control-engineering unit of a particular plant, the appropriate process-control engineers will join with the other functional groups to assure the establishment and maintenance of a sound, thorough, and economical program which will provide the right quality material for the plant.

16.4 Pattern for the Incoming-material-control Procedure within the Quality-system Plan

Summarized below are important elements in the cycle used by many plants for ordering and accepting parts and materials from vendors:

1. Materials and parts are requested—generally by plant production control in establishing production schedules.

2. Specifications and drawings are secured or developed.

3. A purchasing analysis is made to determine the most suitable

vendor or vendors. Commercial purchase specifications may be written, and purchase inquiries may be sent to several vendors.

4. Appraisals are made of vendor's facilities, quality system, and quality capabilities.
5. Orders are placed.
6. Contacts are maintained with the vendor (or vendors) while he is in process of producing or securing the material. This includes the approval of his preproduction samples if required.
7. Material is received by the purchaser plant. It is properly tagged and routed.
8. Material is examined for conformance to specifications.
9. Material is disposed.
10. Appropriate records are kept.
11. Vendor relations are maintained during the course of shipments by the supplier.
12. Information about the material being received is pumped back to the concerned plant technical and purchasing people.
13. The records kept are used regularly to review inspection and purchasing procedures on the material.

Quality-control activity on incoming material correlates directly with this cycle. The activity falls in six fundamental steps within the total quality-system plan, common to the incoming-material-control routines of most plants. Quality-control work is carried on during

1. Material request and material specification.
2. Order placement.
3. Material receipt.
4. Material examination.
5. Material disposal.
6. Record keeping and follow-through.

16.5 A Typical Incoming-material-control Procedure

A plant incoming-material-control routine can be described which illustrates some details of these six steps. The routine applies to all materials purchased from outside sources for use in active production.

These materials range from steels, castings, and fluids to detail parts and subassemblies. They are received in the plant in quantities ranging from one to two forgings of a certain type to hundreds of thousands of items of hardware.

Material Request and Material Specification. Before Purchasing can act on requests by the plant production-control people for placement of orders for a certain material, it must have adequate specifications for the material. Some of these specifications are made available to Purchasing directly from the company new-design-control routine; others are developed as one of the initial steps of the incoming-material-control routine.

Among the classifications of materials and parts required by the plant are (1) those for new products, (2) those called for in reorders on old products currently in production, and (3) those required in orders of basic raw materials—copper, lubricants—which are needed for all products of the plant and which are ordered in large quantities for purposes of economy.

The quality-control program in this plant is relatively new. One of the first steps in its establishment involved the development of effective new-design control. Specifications for material of classification 1—new-product parts—become available to Purchasing as one of the results of this new-design-control routine.

Material of classification 2—old-product parts—are not, however, available with equal adequacy, since new-design-control procedures had not been in operation when these parts were first designed. Adequate specifications for basic raw materials are also lacking, even in the case of those required for new products on which new-design-control procedures have operated.

The new-design-control specifications in this plant are primarily geared to cover parts in terms of individual products. They are not geared to cover raw materials which are required quite generally for all products and which are purchased in bulk to specifications which apply to requirements for a wide variety of these products. The raw-material specifications which were available to Purchasing at the start of the new incoming-control routine were, as a result, merely the overly informal ones developed over a period of years as an incident to other plant activities. They covered only a few portions of the actual quality requirements for the raw materials.

An essential step taken in establishing the incoming-material-control routine of this plant, therefore, was to make one of its elements the development of the specifications required for old-product parts and for basic raw materials. A large quantity of these specifications was involved. As a result, priorities were established for their development.

Parts for old designs were specified based on the reorders for these parts; projects for establishing these specifications were set up when reorders for these parts were in prospect. The parts specifications were developed through the use of a modified form of new-design-control routine, in which the design engineer assigned to the product acted as key man.

In the case of basic raw materials, priorities were similarly assigned. In contrast to specifications for old parts, however, this work was organized as a continuing project; as discussed above, the plant recognized that all new basic raw materials would not fully be specified during new-design-control activity which concentrates upon individual products.

The raw-material specifications are developed by plant laboratory personnel in cooperation with design engineering. Among these laboratory people are experts in such fields as welding, surface finishes, lubricants, chemical testing, and magnetic and radiographic work. The specifications developed by them include such quality requirements for materials as chemical composition, necessary physical properties, surface finishes, and allowable variations in dimensions.

The quality-control component advises the laboratory people in determining some of the elements for these specifications: sampling levels required; physical form in which the product should be shipped to the plant for inspection; preproduction samples that may be required; types of tagging, color coding, or other designations necessary to identify the material and to keep it segregated; the procedures under which vendor's certification of inspection and test will be accepted at the plant without requiring further inspection. When materials or parts require some form of approval by government service agencies, procedures to gain this approval may also be included in the specifications.

While old parts or basic raw materials are being specified as a part of incoming-material-control activity, inspection-planning studies have been conducted just as they are in the normal new-design-control routine of the plant. Regular inspection-planning cards are prepared, which indicate such details as the dimensions and features to be inspected, the gages to be used, the type of stamp to be used to denote inspection approval, and the location of this inspection stamp on the material.

These planning cards identify so-called A materials—those which cannot properly be inspected with standard inspection gages but which must be submitted to the plant laboratory for special tests or for approval of vendors' certificates of inspection and test.

Order Placement. After specifications have been made available to Purchasing, a study is initiated to determine where the material order should be placed to permit most economical purchase prices, proper quality, and other essential requirements. The first question to be decided here is "Make or buy?" that is, to decide whether or not the part or material should be placed with an outside vendor. This fundamental decision influences those portions of the plant incoming-material control which will apply thereafter to the material.

There are two major sources from which the plant draws its parts and materials:

1. From other divisions or plants of the same company.
2. From outside vendors.

Other Divisions or Plants of the Same Company. A minimum of incoming-material-control activity is required for those parts and materials processed by other plants of the same company. Except in unusual situations—an experimental part, a lot of material never before used—the purchaser plant does no incoming inspection on this material; the inspection stamp of the other plant is accepted as evidence of material quality. When, as in unusual times, this procedure results in the acceptance of some material of poor quality, temporary sorting activities may be undertaken by the purchaser plant. At the same time, however, corrective action at the vendor plant is demanded by the Quality Control manager at the company central office. Double inspection—examination both at the vendor plant and at the purchaser plant—is recognized by this company as extremely uneconomical under usual incoming-material situations.

Were the plant discussed in this example one of several divisions of the same factory rather than a separate geographic entity, company policy would insist that the same philosophy of minimizing incoming-material-control activity be followed. It would insist that these other divisions make more effective use of their product-control routines if defective materials were received from them. Costs for sorting the defective materials and for the manufacturing losses caused by these materials would be billed by the purchaser division back to the vendor divisions.

Outside Vendors. When the decision for order placement favors the selection of an outside vendor, a much more extensive incoming-material-control routine than for the preceding example is brought into play. Vendors considered for placement of the order are compared with respect to their price, quality, and ability to deliver on schedule.

Plant incoming-inspection vendor records are examined to gain a view of the past quality performance of the vendors being considered. Approved supplier lists, developed in part from these records, are consulted.

Purchase inquiries are sent to several vendors. On critical materials, these may include essential inspection data listed on standard forms, of which Fig. 16.1 is a typical blank.[2] These forms specify to the vendor the acceptable quality level that must be met by vendor shipments and the quality characteristics to which these AQLs will apply.

In the case of certain materials and parts where the vendor's ability consistently to produce satisfactory quality is in question, his plant may be visited by the best qualified members of the quality-control component. Vendor facilities for welding, for example, may be tested by a process-control engineer. An experienced member of the manufacturing group may join with Quality Control to survey the vendor's manufacturing equipments.

[2] The form shown in Fig. 16.1 has been developed by C. D. Ferris and associates, Bridgeport, Conn.

PART NAME | DWG. NO. | SPEC. NO.

QUALITY CONTROL INSPECTION PLAN | PER STANDING INSTRUCTION | SEC.

DIVISION | WORKS

ISSUED BY: | SUPERSEDES: | EFFECT. DATE:

CHARACTERISTICS AND ACCEPTABLE QUALITY LEVELS (AQL)

ITEM NO.	TEST REQUIREMENTS	CODE	CRITICAL CHARACTERISTICS	AQL	MAJOR CHARACTERISTICS	AQL

CODE LETTERS FOR TEST AND AQL'S ARE FOR PURCHASER'S INTERNAL USE ONLY.

ALL PARTS SHOULD BE TO DRAWING SPECIFICATION IN ALL RESPECTS. THE MOST IMPORTANT CHARACTERISTICS TO BE CHECKED WITH THEIR ACCEPTABLE QUALITY LEVELS ARE LISTED ABOVE. INSPECTION BY THE PURCHASER MAY BE MADE BY RECOGNIZED SAMPLING METHODS. LOTS EXCEEDING THE AQL PER CENT DEFECTIVE AS INDICATED BY THE SAMPLE INSPECTION WILL BE REJECTED AND RETURNED TO THE VENDOR OR, IF NECESSARY TO MAINTAIN PRODUCTION, WILL BE SORTED OR REWORKED AT THE VENDOR'S EXPENSE. THE REQUIREMENTS OF THIS INSPECTION PLAN ARE A PART OF EACH PURCHASE ORDER.

FIG. 16.1.

Such investigations may provide a wealth of information as to the vendor's quality competence. A rating form, similar to that shown on Fig. 16.2, may be made out after these visits.

The quality-control component assists Purchasing in these analyses before final order placement. Until the present well-organized incoming-material-control routine was established, purchase orders, based upon study of only one or two vendor samples, could have been placed for tens of thousands of parts. With the present routine in effect, the quality-control component has the opportunity to recommend that a more ade-

VENDOR ______________________ DATE OF VISIT ______________________

FACILITY CHECKED	SUPERIOR	SATISFACTORY	UNSATISFACTORY	REMARKS
MACHINE TOOLS				
WELDERS				
CASTING EQUIPMENT				
TOOLS, FIXTURES, AND JIGS				
HOUSEKEEPING				
MATERIALS HANDLING EQUIPMENT				
PLATING AND FINISHING EQUIPMENT				
PAINTING AND CLEANING EQUIPMENT				
ASSEMBLY FACILITIES				
INSPECTION PROCEDURES AND FACILITIES				
LABORATORY FACILITIES				
QUALITY CONTROL PROGRAM				
TYPE OF EMPLOYEES				
OTHERS (SPECIFY)				

OVERALL VENDOR RATING: SUPERIOR ( ); SATISFACTORY ( ); UNSATISFACTORY ( )
(CHECK ONE)

REMARKS: ______________________

____

SIGNED ______________________

____

____

FIG. 16.2.

quate sample be required from the vendor; the incoming-material troubles resulting from the older practice of inadequate sample size are thus minimized.

On parts and materials whose specifications have become relatively old, members of the quality-control component assist in investigating possible "water" in the prices bid by vendors due to no longer necessary quality extras in the specification. These investigations may take the form of studies of the tolerances being demanded by the specification.[3] The statistical tools discussed in Part Four may be especially useful in these studies.

For reasons of excellent past relationships or possibly the unavailability of other sources, a vendor may be seriously considered whose ability to produce and control satisfactory material quality is in question owing to inadequate procedures or know-how on his part. Members of the quality-control component may visit the vendor's plant in cases of this sort and assist him in establishing adequate quality-control activities.

For reasons of purchasing practice, the actual material order may require the translation of specifications into standard commercial nomenclature. When the order is finally contracted, however, the specification—including AQLs—that his material will be called upon to meet are generally sent to the vendor, with an attention-gaining sticker such as is shown on Fig. 16.3.

ATTENTION

THIS PART MUST CONFORM TO CERTAIN DETAILED PURCHASER SPECIFICATIONS.

DO NOT PERFORM WORK OR APPLY MATERIALS FOR THIS JOB BEFORE FAMILIARIZING YOURSELF WITH APPLICABLE PORTIONS OF SPECIFICATION (MATERIAL) - NO. 8732.

FIG. 16.3.

This plant uses MIL-STD-105A-type, AQL acceptance sampling table to cover its receiving inspection sampling. Determination will be made with the vendor, as the order is closed, of the AQL to be required of a specific part or material. Agreement will also be made with him on sampling procedure and policy for disposing rejected lots. The vendor may be informed of the conditions under which his certificates of test or inspection will be expected and accepted.

These practices, coupled with giving similar details in as many purchasing inquiries as practical, have helped the plant largely to eliminate unpleasant frictions experienced in earlier years with vendors. These frictions resulted from complaints by vendors who insisted that they were not told of certain details of the technical quality standards of the plant until they were informed of the rejections of their material based on failure to conform with these details.

The policy of sending acceptance procedures and quality specifications to vendors has been particularly valuable for those materials to be used on products sold for government use. These materials may require preshipment inspection at the vendor's plant by government service person-

[3] Section 16.11 discusses an interesting example of such a purchasing investigation.

nel. Specifications act as a powerful agent to minimize misinterpretations of quality requirements at this inspection.

When the purchase order is placed with the vendor or vendors finally chosen, particularly with raw-material suppliers, the character of the vendor's business is often noted on the inspection-planning card. The reason for this step can readily be given. Raw materials may be purchased from primary sources, where the manufacturer himself sells the material and where his quality may be quite directly identified. They may also be purchased from secondary sources, where the actual manufacturing origin of the material may not be quite so clear, since the vendor merely purchases from manufacturers and carries on no production himself. Knowledge of the character of the vendor's business may be useful at incoming inspection of raw material in assisting to develop appropriate acceptance procedures.

Material Receipt. After orders have been placed, vendors may require additional interpretation of the specifications while they are setting up to produce the materials. In the case where orders have been placed with several small vendors, these suppliers may require some technical assistance from plant quality-control people.

Purchase contracts on certain materials call for approval of a sample composed of a specified number of preproduction units. When they have been produced by the vendor, these units—castings or forgings, for example—are shipped to the plant for approval. Radiographs may be required with castings; vendors may be required to make fluorescent penetrant or magnetic particle tests on forgings; die forgings may require cross sectioning and etching for study. On these fabricated parts where resistance welding is involved, an adequate sample of test specimens will be required of the vendor.

The units in these preproduction samples are carefully analyzed, often in frequency-distribution form, by process-control-engineering personnel. Results of these analyses may be examined by the concerned design engineers.

When his preproduction sample is found satisfactory, the vendor receives approval to start active production. When his sample is unsatisfactory, the vendor is informed of details on its defects. Technical assistance may be given the vendor by process-control engineers or other appropriate plant personnel. He must then submit another sample for approval.

With materials like castings and forgings, experience with preproduction samples may cause considerable revision of the quality requirements on inspection-planning cards. The types and amounts of radiographic evidence required for approval of castings may, for example, be adjusted to conform with the assurance of casting quality evidenced by a preproduction sample.

When all preliminary approvals have been given, the next step in incoming-material control takes place when the first shipments are received from the vendor. These lots are identified and then tagged so that they will be routed properly. Lots will usually be routed to the incoming inspection area; some designated A material will require action by the plant laboratory in making chemical or physical tests or in corroborating the vendor's certificate of test and inspection. In all cases, the concerned process-control engineer will carefully audit the validity of the conclusions.

This plant, being fairly new and well laid out for material flow, has only one major incoming-material acceptance area to which the parts are routed. It has been possible to centralize all incoming inspection equipments and records. Older plants of the same company are not so fortunate; owing to scattered material flow, some of these plants must carry on incoming acceptance at several areas.

Handling of the materials is carried on rapidly but carefully as they are transported to the appropriate inspection area. In the case of a tank car of lubricant or a hopper filled with a ceramic base, a sample of specified size may be transported directly to the plant laboratory. The entire carload may be held for release until the results of the laboratory test become known.

Material Examination. Material-examination procedures in the incoming inspection area are generally more rigid on first lots shipped by a vendor on a new order than they are on lots of the material received after this "starting inspection" has been completed. Inspection-planning cards for each type of material will be available and will act as a guide to the policy that should be used by the inspectors assigned to this material.

Some cards will apply to those parts—hardware, for example—where sampling may be started on these first lots received. Other cards will apply to critical parts where 100 per cent inspection is required on first lots to gain a picture of vendor quality; the AQL specified on the inspection-planning card may be used in sampling of subsequent lots. Still other cards will apply to that minimum of parts on which 100 per cent inspection must continually be performed on all shipments received during the life of the order.[4]

Figure 16.4 shows the sequence followed on those parts where 100 per cent inspection of first lots is followed by AQL sampling on subsequent lots. If the 100 per cent inspection shows that the vendor's quality is

[4] Considerations involved in properly carrying out acceptance sampling are extensively discussed in Chap. 12.

poorer than required, this sampling may not, of course, economically be started. The vendor will immediately be informed of the results of the 100 per cent inspection and be requested to improve his quality.

The MIL-STD-105A-type acceptance table used by this plant for all its incoming inspection sampling is similar to that shown in Fig. 12.11. Various AQL levels have been established for materials received by the plant. For detail parts, 1 and 2.5 per cent AQLs are most typical, while 4 to 6.5 per cent AQLs are often used for hardware items.

STEP I-100% INSPECTION ON FIRST LOTS

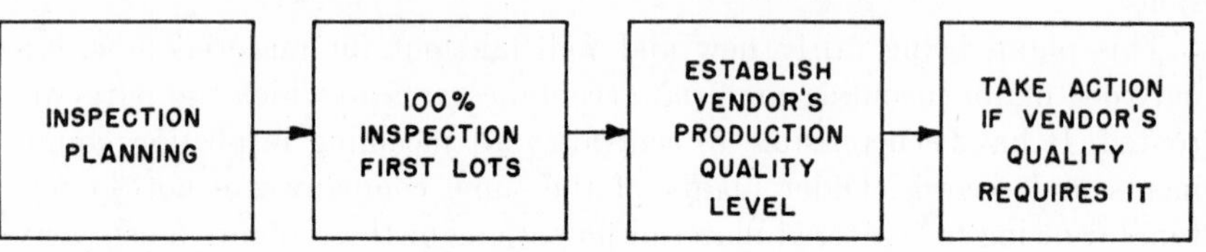

STEP II-SAMPLE INSPECT SUBSEQUENT LOTS

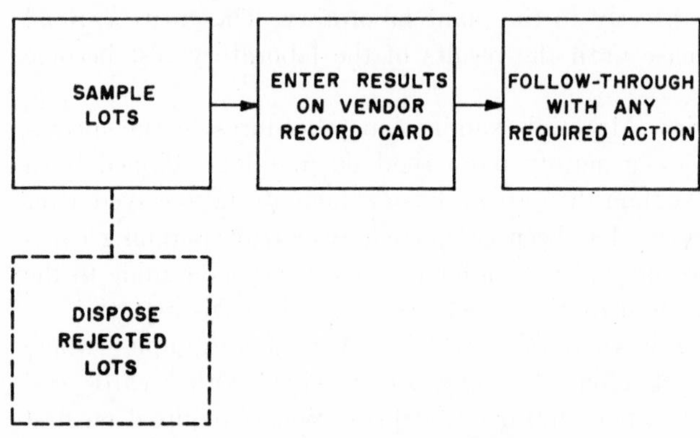

FIG. 16.4.

The incoming sampling procedure provides an automatic routine for going to a reduced sampling table, similar to the table shown in Fig. 12.12, when a sufficient number of successive lots has been approved by normal sampling.

In so far as it can be worked out with the vendor, even these reduced sampling schedules are later replaced by a vendor's certification of test and inspection on his shipments. These certificates take various forms with different materials. They may consist in a certified statement of the chemical and physical composition of a lot of metal; they may consist in a vendor filling in a blank form supplied him by the plant, a typical example being shown in Fig. 16.5; they may merely be frequency-distribution pictures on the results of the vendor's inspection of the shipped lot, of which Fig. 16.6 shows a picture on incoming springs.[5]

Acceptance sampling checks are made only occasionally on lots thus certified unless there is evidence of quality difficulties with the material on production lines.

VENDOR CERTIFICATION OF QUALITY

REPORT NO. ________

ORDER NO. ________

DATE SHIPPED ________

QUANTITY ________

PART NAME: ________ DWG. NO. ________

VENDOR: ________ ADDRESS: ________

SPECIFICATION	NO. CHECKED	RESULTS	REMARKS

SIGNED ________

TITLE ________

FIG. 16.5.

An important element in the procedure of this plant for material acceptance is the training and orientation of the inspection people who carry on this sampling. Every effort is taken by Process Control Engineering to make all required information available to them so that interpretation of material specifications will be uniform and will correspond to the original intent of those writing the specifications.

[5] Figure 16.5 is after a form developed by C. D. Ferris and associates, Bridgeport, Conn.

Strong emphasis is also placed upon the securing and maintenance of adequate quality information equipments for use in acceptance inspection. A complete routine for the regular examination and replacement of such gages as threads and plugs is also carried out through use of a gage color-coding program, each color representing a replacement date.

When material is accepted through these procedures, it is stamped,

PRODUCT COMPRESSION SPRING
CHARACTERISTIC TEST LOAD
METHOD OF TEST TESTER Y
SPECIFIED LIMITS 1.8 # TO 2.4 # @ .281"
RECORDED BY J. G. BROWN
DATE 1-17-59

PART NO. 1816320
VENDOR "C"
ORDER NO. RT-8216
QUANTITY OF LOT 75,000
QUANTITY OF SAMPLE 80
DISPOSITION PASSED

LIMITS

LBS. LOAD	FREQUENCY TALLY	f
1.80		
1.83		
1.86		
1.89		
1.92		
1.95		
1.98		
2.01		
2.04		
2.07	||||| ||	7
2.10	||||| ||||| |||||	15
2.13	||||| ||||| ||||| ||||| ||||	24
2.16	||||| ||||| ||||| ||||	19
2.19	||||| |||	8
2.22	|||||		6
2.25			1
2.28		
2.31		
2.34		
2.37		
2.40		
	TOTAL	80

VENDOR CERTIFICATION
FREQUENCY DISTRIBUTION FORM

FIG. 16.6.

tagged, and made available for transportation out of the inspection area.

Materials like steels, lubricants, and ceramics—the so-called A materials—follow a somewhat different procedure from that required by the standard detail parts. These A materials may require special tests—chemical composition or hardness—which cannot adequately be performed with equipment in the inspection area. The A tests must be made in the plant laboratory.

Many of these tests—those on chemical composition, for example—may be destructive in nature and so make sampling a necessity. This type of sampling is usually carried out on a variables basis.[6] Sample size is sometimes determined statistically; in other instances, where the physical form of the material is a limiting factor, past laboratory experience with the material determines the sampling details.

A case in point is that of a 6-foot 4-inch bar of purchased metal stock, to be machined and processed into a shaft which is about 6 feet long. If a destructive test were required here, the sample must obviously be restricted to one of the ends of the bar; to cut up the bar to produce several pieces for the sample would destroy its value.

A materials of this sort usually remain physically in the inspection area where dimensional checks can be made after the sample is taken and sent to the laboratory.

Vendors' certificates of test, coupons of conformity, or statements of compliance with specification are widely used with A materials. These certificates are sent from the incoming inspection area to the laboratory for its approval.

The laboratory will consult the inspection-planning card for the material, will note any statements on it about the vendor's quality history and whether the vendor is primary or secondary. The material specification will be briefly reviewed to determine the critical nature of the requirements. With many vendors, laboratory personnel may also draw upon their past contacts with him and their experience with his shipments.

Laboratory approval of this material will take into account all these considerations, although with well-known materials from well-known vendors they will be consolidated into a very brief review. Approval may be made directly based upon vendor certification without further tests, or it may involve specific checks of such characteristics as physical properties or surface finishes.

Material approved by the laboratory is inspection stamped and tagged; material found defective is appropriately tagged with that classification.

Material Disposal. Material accepted by incoming inspection or the plant laboratory may not be immediately required for use on production lines. All material accepted, however, is carefully but quickly transported from the incoming inspection area to a storage area, so that the material turnover in the inspection area will be a maximum with a minimum of floor space.

It is, of course, desirable from the point of view of inventory control as well as of quality control that this material be stored for as short a time as possible. During its storage period, material is placed in areas actually

[6] Section 12.18 discusses several aspects of variables sampling.

set aside for this purpose, where temperature and humidity are such that possible damage is minimized and where there will be no deterioration in quality.

Material found defective is also moved rapidly. In this plant, a special caged-in area is used for temporary storage of this material; exceptions are those materials where physical bulk or possibly dangerous inflammables make this practice impossible. A special orange tag, which means to all plant personnel "Do Not Move This Material," is attached to the defective materials in the cage.

Where disposition of defective materials is at issue, a materials review board acts as the quality-control agency to make or to coordinate the making of the required decisions. This board is composed of a concerned process-control engineer, representatives of Design Engineering, Purchasing, and, on material used on products for purchase by government service, the resident government inspector. Available to this board in making a decision about a specific lot of material are five major alternatives:

1. Reject the entire lot, and return it to the vendor.

2. 100 per cent sort the lot, and return the defective units to the vendor. The vendor bears the cost of the sorting inspection.

3. 100 per cent sort the lot at vendor's expense, and repair the defectives right at the purchaser plant. The vendor pays the cost of these repairs.

4. Accept the entire lot, based upon a special disposition which temporarily relaxes specification requirements.

5. Alternatives 2 or 3, except that the purchaser plant bears part or all of the extra inspection and repair costs.

In addition to the major governing factor of effect on product quality, among the considerations governing the material review board's choice among these alternatives are

1. *Cost to the vendor.* Every effort is made to take, if possible, that action which is most economical for the vendor. To small vendors, blanket rejection of an entire lot could mean financial disaster.

2. *Plant production requirements.* Tightness of production schedules on a certain part may make it necessary to accept, by sorting, if possible, some material to keep production lines in operation.

3. *History of the rejected lot.* Account must be taken of possible agreements with the vendor at the time of order placement in respect to how his rejected lots would be disposed. Also out of fairness to the vendor, account must be taken of the rejection cause—for example, was the present specification the result of a revision made *after* the vendor had produced the lot.

Decisions are made rapidly by the materials review board, and the orange-tagged material in the cage is correspondingly disposed at once. This permits the use of a relatively small area for the cage, and it reduces the danger of orange-tagged material "drifting into" the production lines.

Record Keeping and Follow-through. On all materials and parts for which inspection planning is done, vendor records are kept. There is a card for each material type or part number. Among the data shown by these records are dates of the various shipments, vendors' names, lot sizes, inspection results, and the disposition of each lot examined. Lots accepted by vendor's certificate are so noted.

A brief review of vendor performance is made on each card as the results of a new lot are recorded. In addition to this informal check, all cards are periodically reviewed as part of a regular procedure. The quality performance of given vendors is analyzed if and as required.

Results of these analyses are used to inform Purchasing and the plant design-engineering group of the quality performance of specific vendors so that these plant groups may receive counsel for future order placement. Vendor contact does not wait upon these periodic reviews; vendors may be immediately and directly notified as soon as defective shipments are noted. Complaint reports on these shipments will be similar to the gasket rejection recorded in Fig. 16.7. Visits to their plant by the best qualified plant personnel are required for some of these contacts.

The process-control engineer works closely with the other plants of the company so as to assure uniform relations with a single vendor by all plants of the company with respect to such matters as sampling procedures and specification interpretation.

In addition, purchase requirements for material quality are regularly reviewed. As more and more information is gained about production and field performance of a new product, quality specifications for its purchased parts and materials may be radically altered.

The result for the plant of this incoming-material-control routine has been assurance of receiving material of the proper quality at the most economical cost levels. Substantial reductions in material purchase prices and in inspection expense on many materials have been achieved.

Extensive as it is, establishment of this incoming-control routine was accompanied by a decrease for the plant in general expenditures or in overhead. Most of the incoming control activities had been carried on previous to the establishment of the formal routine; they had been carried on in an individual, relatively ineffective, uncoordinated fashion whose duplications and overlaps were eliminated by incoming-material control. As a result, over-all plant quality costs were reduced significantly.

INSPECTOR'S COMPLAINT ON DEFECTIVE MATERIAL

DATE 8/4/60

PAT. NO. ______ DR. NO. 721832

WE HAVE RECEIVED 570 (QUANTITY) GASKETS (NAME OF ARTICLE)
AND
I HAVE INSPECTED 50 (QUANTITY) SAMPLE GASKETS (NAME OF ARTICLE)

FOR BRAKE XR32 (KIND OF MACHINE) (KIND OF MATERIAL)

FROM BROWN CO. (NAME OF MFR.) REQ'N Z-3218P1

AND FIND FOR ALL UNITS IN THE SAMPLE (50)
THE 1/16" DIM. IS O.K.
THE 6-7/8" ID IS +.009" OVER TOLERANCE
THE 4-1/4" OD IS +.010" OVER TOLERANCE

DISPOSITION RETURN LOT TO VENDOR

WHEN DID WE MAKE A SIMILAR COMPLAINT AGAINST THIS VENDOR? 6/24/60

SIGNED J. R. WHITE

FIG. 16.7.

16.6 Techniques Used in Incoming-material Control

Parts Three and Four discussed a wide range of technological and analytical techniques, many of which find application to incoming-material control as reviewed in this chapter. It may be worthwhile, therefore, to summarize some of the more significant of the techniques used in the second job of total quality control.

Several techniques are used in incoming-material-control activities. Major among these, of course, is sound inspection practice, details of which are well known and whose procedures are effectively discussed in the literature. Other technical methods include such tools as statistical acceptance sampling tables, materials specifications, vendor records and contact, statistical analyses of purchased parts, and proper materials handling. Some of the more important of these techniques are summarized below:

Vendor Records. In connection with this important incoming-material-control technique, incoming inspection records are kept on the quality shipped by vendors on materials and parts.

Vendor Relations. Contact is kept with these vendors on matters relating to product quality. The types of relationships range from periodic exchange of correspondence to visits by the process-control engineer to assist the vendor's plant in improving its quality-control procedures.

Quality Information Equipment. The increasing complexity of parts and materials purchased under modern material specifications makes it essential that the inspection of these materials be carried on with modern quality information equipments. The selection and location of these equipments are important incoming control techniques.

Equipment and Gage Maintenance. It is inevitable that delicate measuring equipments will go out of adjustment. It is essential, therefore, that these equipments and gages be properly maintained and that their accuracy be rigidly controlled.

Inspection Training and Education. The quality of materials being released to the shop floor depends to an important degree upon how well incoming inspectors have done their job. To assist them in better performing this task, inspection training is a fundamental requirement. Inspectors may attend training classes, may be given inspection manuals, or may have developed for them inspection guide cards.

Raw-material Specifications. Component parts required by individual product designs will be specified and developed in the plant's new-design-control routine. Basic raw materials which apply quite generally throughout the operations of the plant—steels, insulating materials—may have no such specifications prepared for them in new-design control. These specifications are therefore developed as part of the incoming-material-control routine.

Proper Materials Handling. Inspection activity in assuring conformance will be wasted if the materials received are later damaged, scraped, or battered while being transported through the plant to production lines. It is essential that proper material-handling equipment be available for transporting these materials.

Acceptance Sampling Tables. Chapter 12 discussed in some detail acceptance sampling tables which have wide application in incoming-material inspection. These tables assist both in assuring quality and in enabling its maintenance at low inspection cost.

Proper Storage Facilities. Some materials received by the plant may be shelved for a period after their incoming inspection. If this storage space is inadequate—if it is excessively damp and thus ruins insulating materials or too unprotected from passing battery trucks and thus risks damage to bellows "being aged"—then the incoming-material-control objective will not be achieved. Proper storage facilities are essential to adequate maintenance of incoming-material quality.

Purchase Inquiries and Orders Embodying Quality-control Fundamentals. An important influence upon the effectiveness of incoming-material control is the character of the initial purchase inquiry—the extent to which it informs vendors of the quality requirements, for example—and the effectiveness of the provisions bearing upon quality in the final purchase contract made with the vendor.

Disposal of Defective Materials. Defective materials discovered in incoming inspection must be disposed rapidly. Otherwise, some of this defective material may seep into the production lines, may take up available floor space, or may remain in the purchaser plant for so long a time that the vendor will not or may no longer be obligated to accept it back. Proper tagging, adequate disposal areas, and effective material review routines are essential tools for use here.

Statistical Analysis of Incoming Material. The statistical methods discussed in Part Four may be used to good advantage in analyzing data on materials received by the plant. The frequency distribution is probably most useful for this purpose.

INSPECTION PROCEDURE SHEET -- MI-576 DRAWING NO. (1)

Use In Conjunction With Drg. No. (2)
Part Name (3)
Area (4)
Manufacture (6) A.Q.L. (6) A.Q.L.
1. (5) (6A) (6A)
2.
3.
4.
5.
6.
Prepared By: (7) Date: (8)
Inspected By: (9) Q.C. Approved By: (10)
Gov't. Insp. Coordination: (10A)

CHARACTERISTIC	(13)	.500 + .001 − .0005	(13A)
EQUIP./METHOD	(14)	Air gauge	(14)

DATE	Lot Data NUMBER	SIZE	Disp.	1st Samples			Pcs Rej 100%	A.Q.L.	(12)	100	1%	4%	10%	Insp.
(15)	(22)	(16)	(21)	(17)/(19)	(17)/(19)	(17)/(19)	(20)		(18)				(18A)	(23)
				2/15	3/15					2/15		3/		

FIG. 16.8. (Front)

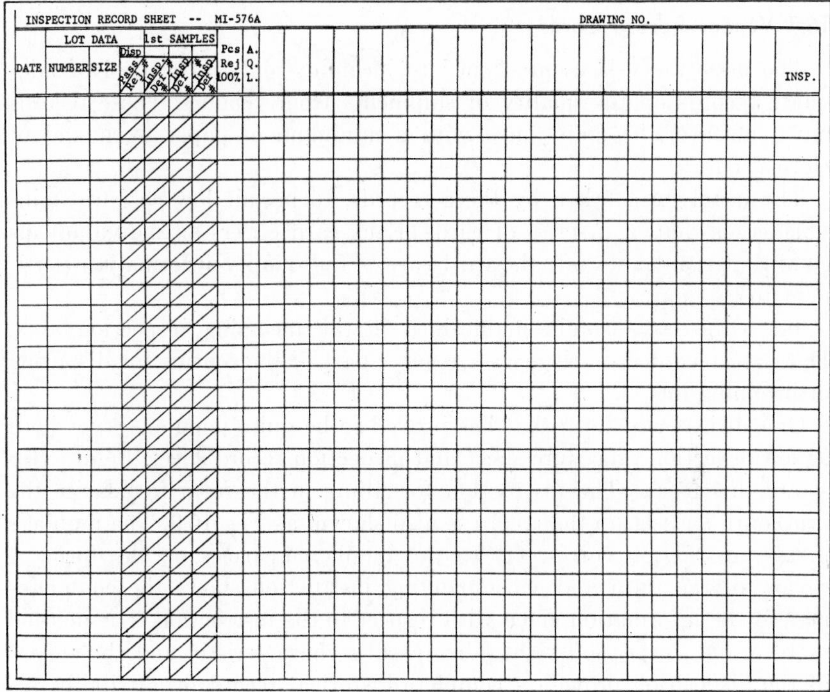

INSPECTION RECORD SHEET -- MI-576A DRAWING NO.

DATE	LOT DATA NUMBER	SIZE	1st SAMPLES Disp Pass Rej	Insp. # Def	Def Insp #	Insp # Def	Pcs Rej 100%	A.Q.L.	INSP.

FIG. 16.8. (Reverse)

Measures of Inspection Performance. Periodic checks on the effectiveness of inspection in maintaining adequate quality of incoming material are essential. The actual details of the techniques used for this purpose will depend upon conditions in individual plants. Work sampling is particularly useful here.

Vendor Certificates. Certification by a vendor of the quality of his material results in both commercial advantage to him and minimum incoming inspection to the purchaser. Techniques for this purpose are important incoming-material-control methods.

Many of these incoming-material technical methods have been discussed in connection with proper quality-control operation at industrial conferences and in trade papers. Others have been effectively presented in the literature of the gage practitioners. The details of these methods naturally vary from company to company, but there is enough uniformity among them to allow concrete discussion of their basic fundamentals.

The discussion below will give examples of three of these technical methods: Vendor Record Cards, in Sec. 16.7; Vendor Relations, in Secs. 16.8 and 16.9; and Gage Control, in Sec. 16.10.

16.7 Vendor Record Cards

The importance is unquestioned to incoming-material control of adequate records on the quality of shipments from vendors. These records must, however, be maintained with a minimum of paper work and of clerical effort.

The usual form taken by these records, to permit low cost of maintenance, is that of a series of cards. Each card covers an individual incoming part or material; the card carries the quality information pertinent to this part.

The cards are usually maintained in the incoming inspection area. Data are recorded on them as a regular part of the routine for disposing of incoming lots.

One such record form that has proved to be quite popular serves both as an inspection procedure sheet and inspection record sheet. Figure 16.8 shows this form.[7] The instruction for filling in the form to initiate the procedure and set up the record is also shown, as Fig. 16.9. The numbers in the instruction correspond to the numbered spaces on the form. A review of the form and accompanying instruction shows the completeness of the information given with respect to the instruction. The method of recording inspection results by quality characteristic and the record of the disposition provide a complete historical record by attributes for a given part from a given vendor.

There are still other types of cards which provide space for plotting a graph of inspection measurements for certain quality characteristics on the part in question.

Vendor record cards supply an invaluable reference library for determination of vendor quality performance and for analysis of difficulties being experienced with given parts and materials. By standardizing the data-recording procedure for incoming parts and materials, they tend to raise the caliber of the hour-by-hour and day-by-day incoming inspection activity.

When all blank spaces on a vendor record card have been filled in, the card is retained on file for a period of time which varies among plants, depending upon such circumstances as the provisions of the purchase contract and the length of the manufacturing cycle. Cards may be retained in a long-manufacturing-cycle plant such as turbines for many months; they may be retained in a short-cycle plant for only a few weeks. Before discarding individual cards on expensive parts and ma-

[7] The form appearing as Fig. 16.8 was developed by Mr. Norman Cheever and associates of Everett, Mass.

Instruction and Procedure for Originating Inspection Procedure Sheet

1. Drawing number, group or part number, and revision letter or number for card identification.
2. Drawing number, group or part number, and revision number or letter.
3. Name of part as designated on drawing.
4. Area where inspection is performed and type of inspection.
5. Outside vendor supplying parts or internal manufacturing area; use one form for each.
6. AQLs in use.

6A. N, T, or R for normal, tightened, or reduced inspection for each supplier.

7. Name of planner or foreman setting up inspection procedure sheet.
8. Date inspection procedure sheet is originated.
9. Signature of inspector.
10. Signature of foreman or general foreman approving inspection procedure sheet for inspection.

10A. Customer's signature as required.

11. Same as 6.
12. AQL for each characteristic or 100 per cent.
13. Characteristics being checked in order of checking. This also includes tests being performed as a separate group.

13A. Setup checks will be listed and the check number of the setup inspector posted in block 18A as required.

14. List inspection equipment or method used.

Instruction and Procedure for Sampling and Recording Results of Inspection on Inspection Procedure Sheet

15. Date.
16. Lot size.
17. Actual sample size inspected.
18. For O.K. characteristics, place inspector's stamp in box. For defects, divide box with diagonal and indicate number over tolerance in upper part and number under tolerance in lower part of box.

18A. Setup inspector's check number opposite setup checks.

19. Total number of defectives for each AQL.
20. Total number of defectives found in 100 per cent inspection.
21. Black in appropriate space for disposition of lot.
22. For internal, laboratory number or serial number; for external, vendor's name and order number.
23. Check number or stamp of inspector completing final check listed.
24. Use sampling tables supplied by Quality Control Engineering.
    a. Select enough pieces for largest sample size required.
    b. Samples to be selected at random from all sections of container or lot.
    c. If several containers constitute lot, divide the sample size by the number of containers and take an equal amount from each container at random.

FIG. 16.9

terials, some plants which require such information summarize their results on master records.

16.8 Vendor Relations

The art of sound vendor relations in incoming-material control consists much more of a philosophy of buyer-seller contacts than it does of any single technique or group of techniques. Basic to this philosophy, of course, is the general ethics of courteous business practice; there are, however, certain features of the relationship which are distinct to quality control.

In the first place, there should be assurance that the vendor is informed about the acceptance procedures of the purchaser plant for the material he ships. Under most desirable conditions, the vendor is a party to the establishment of such of these procedures as quality levels, types of tests made and the importance of these tests, and the character of the inspection on the part.

Much of this information can be interchanged while the purchase contract is being concluded, particularly that which will apply to policies for the return of rejected material. Other practices—assurance that the vendor's inspection and test procedures and equipment are similar to those of the purchaser plant, for example—may have to be reviewed after shipments have started.

Again, the vendor should not be confused by a variety of inconsistent, uncoordinated quality contacts from the purchaser plant. It is essential to sound incoming-material control that these contacts be made as part of the over-all plant quality-control program. All visits to the vendor by the process-control engineer should, for example, be coordinated and/or arranged by plant Purchasing.

The issue of suggesting that a respected vendor improve his quality-control activities may be a particularly ticklish vendor relations problem for the purchaser plant process-control engineer. His efforts in this direction will be successful to the extent that he convinces the vendor that the quality-control organization is a service agency to him as well as to its own employer.

Frequently very effective in this connection is a visit or a series of visits through the vendor's factory, where his complete operation is reviewed. If the vendor can be encouraged to discuss his trouble spots, the process-control engineer may be able to make suggestions regarding technical quality-control methods that may usefully be applied.

Effort toward improved vendor relations in incoming-material control certainly has no effect toward minimizing the obligation of the vendor for the production and shipment of material of specified quality. It does, however, involve realistic recognition by the purchaser-plant quality-control program that its own quality performance and costs may be improved in direct proportion to the improvement in the vendor's quality practices and that aid to the vendor in this direction not only is friendly business courtesy but also involves intelligent self-interest.

16.9 Incoming-material Rating Plan

There have been a considerable number of incoming-material rating plans designed by various companies for the purpose of measuring vendor performance with respect to the quality of the material delivered. Some of these rating plans have had such shortcomings as the following:

1. Vendors have complained about the fairness of plans which compare one vendor against another when the two vendors are receiving ratings on a different "mix" of parts or materials. For example, the vendor that took the tough-to-make parts might receive a poor rating compared to a vendor making a simple, noncritical part.

2. The plan may not take into account the number of shipments or number of items on which the rating is based. Or it may not count a nonconforming item defective unless it is returned to the vendor.

3. Some plans measure the performance of the vendor on only "quality" and neglect two other practical measurements, namely, "price" and "service."

One plan that meets these shortcomings bases its rating on the composite of quality, price, and service. It weighs these factors as follows:

Quality	40 points
Price	35 points
Service	25 points
Total	100 points

This weighting should be flexible from one type of business to another and may be varied to fit a given type of business. The use of this plan is as follows:

1. Its *quality* rating is based on the fraction of total lots received that are acceptable for a given part. For example, if supplier A had 54 lots accepted out of a total of 60 lots delivered, $^{54}\!/_{60}$, or 90 per cent, of the lots were accepted. The quality rating would be $.90 \times 40$ (weighting factor) $= 36$ points.

2. On *price*, the vendor with the lowest net price receives the full 35 points (or whatever weighting factor was chosen for price). If, for example, supplier B had the lowest net price of 93 cents per hundred pieces, his rating on price would be 35 points. If A's price was $1.16, then supplier A's rating would be

$$\frac{.93}{1.16} \times 35 = (.80)(35) = 28 \text{ points}$$

3. The *service* rating can be on the basis of percentage of promises kept. If supplier A kept 90 per cent of his promises, his service rating would be (.90) (25) = 22.5 points.

4. Supplier A's total rating would be, therefore:

Quality	36.0 points
Price	28.0 points
Service	22.5 points
Total	86.5 points

This rating could be compared with comparable vendors on the basis of single-part number or catalog number. These comparisons are then a

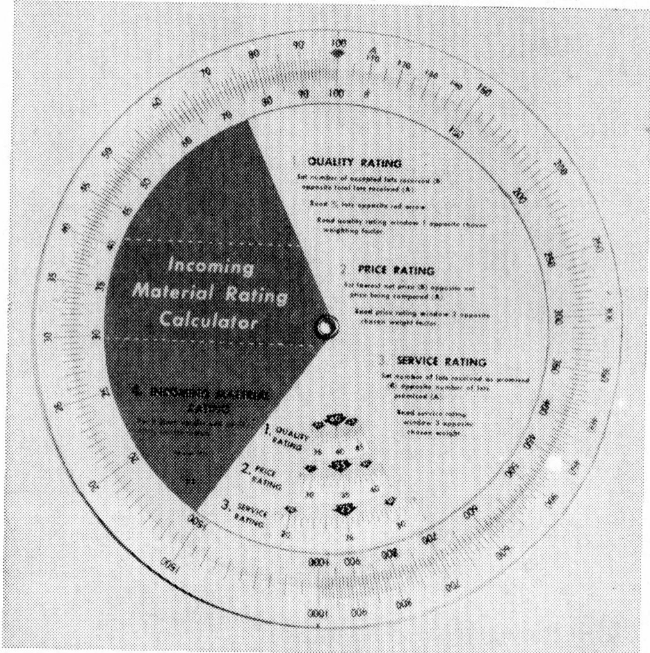

FIG. 16.10. Incoming-material rating calculator.

basis for company-purchasing action in placing future purchase orders.

Figure 16.10 shows a circular slide rule designed with scales and windows that give the rating directly for each of the three factors when using the weightings shown in this example.

16.10 Gage Control

In order to maintain adequate control over incoming materials, it is first of all necessary to be able to measure the quality characteristics of this material. It is frequently necessary to make these measurements through the medium of devices designed specially for this measurements purpose.

These devices range from the relatively simple plug gage to much more complex quality information equipment such as X-ray equipment or supersonic testing devices. They include such inspection and test aids as surface plates, gage blocks, angle plates, plug and snap gages, thread gages, optical gages, air-pressure gages, gear gages, micrometers, pin gages, profilometers, and many others.

A number of simple mechanical gages will be used in the control of incoming material; like other electrical or mechanical equipments subject to wear, it is essential there be assurance that (1) the indication given by the gage is accurate before the gage is used at all, (2) the gage be designed so as to permit its efficient use by personnel, and (3) the gage be maintained so that the indication given is accurate throughout its useful life.

To give this assurance in a plant incoming-material program is the task of gage-control procedures. These may consist in

1. A procedure for approving all new gages before they are used in the factory at all. In large plants, this approval may be obtained by checking the gage with high-precision-measuring equipments which may be located in the plant laboratory or in a special gage-approval area. Small plants may use for this purpose commercial laboratories or government bureaus.

2. A procedure for the periodic recheck of all gages after they have been in use in the factory and for making whatever adjustments or repairs that may be required to enable the gage to be returned to use. This is accomplished through a preventive maintenance program very similar in concept to that used for production machine tools and processes. "Check times" vary, depending upon the type of gage that is being maintained, the amount of usage it receives, etc.

A gage-control procedure for expensive thread gages that check critical tapped holes may be cited as an example: on all new thread gages being checked in the plant laboratory for initial approval, a "pickup card" is made out. Data on this card include type of gage, its serial or drawing number if there is one, its size, the location where the gage is to be used, its particular usage, and any other pertinent information.

When the gage has been given this initial approval, it is then stamped with a special indelible ink whose color dates the gage for its first maintenance check. A definite scheme of colors is used which will show at a glance to incoming inspection personnel the month, week, and even day —in the case of those gages which require such close check—that the gage should be returned to the laboratory for its maintenance checkup.

As a cross check to assure that gages are actually picked up for this check and that the color coding has not been somehow overlooked on the inspection floor, the pickup card for each gage has a color tab clipped to it. The pickup card is then filed in a cabinet along with similar cards, which are regularly reviewed.

During this review, those cards whose tabs call for gage pickup will be pulled from the file and check made to assure that the gage is actually returned to the plant laboratory for proper examination. Where the gage to be picked up has regular production usage, it is necessary with this system to have spare gages which may be placed out on the floor while the regular gage is being checked.[8]

16.11 Study of Rejects on Incoming Plastic Cases

The actual factory operation of both organizational and technical aspects of incoming-material control can best be summarized by a review

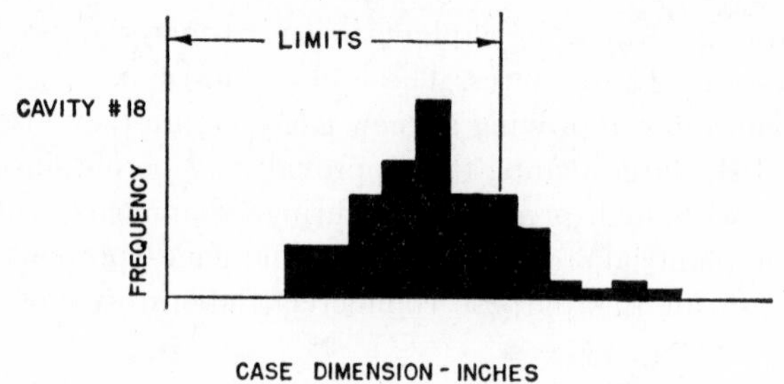

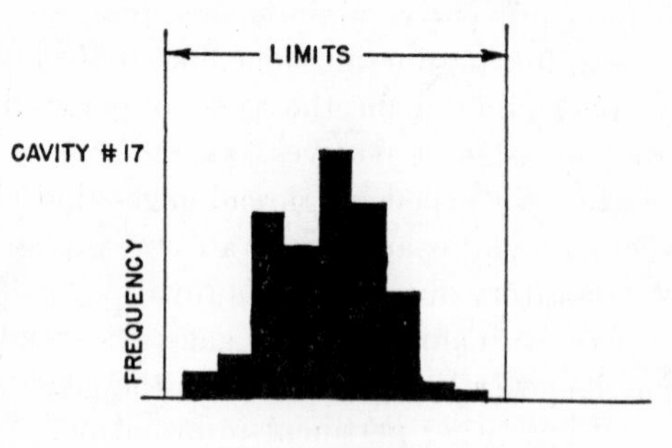

FIG. 16.11.

of three typical case examples. Sections 16.12 and 16.13 will discuss two of these cases, and this section will present the first example, one of a

[8] This color-coding procedure follows a system developed by L. W. Macomber, H. Richards, and associates, Lynn, Mass.

joint vendor-purchaser effort to determine the cause of inferior quality of shipments.

An Eastern factory noted an excessive number of rejected lots at incoming inspection of molded plastic cases. These cases were used on one of the assemblies manufactured by the plant. The molded case was produced by the vendor in a multicavity mold, and cases produced by all the cavities were mingled together in each shipment. There was no means of identifying cases produced by an individual cavity.

It was suggested that there might be an appreciable variation in the quality of cases produced by the different cavities. It was decided, therefore, to undertake a joint investigation with the vendor to determine the influence of the several cavities upon quality.

Figure 16.11 illustrates the results of this analysis as it applied to cavities 17 and 18. As can be seen from Fig. 16.11, cavity 18 was producing out-of-limits cases.

The vendor repaired cavity 18 based upon the results of this analysis. His future shipments reflected a great improvement of quality because of this action.

A further result of this analysis may also be cited. On all multicavity molds thereafter produced for use by this plant, a small number was manufactured into each cavity. Since these numbers were thereafter molded into all plastic cases produced, they enabled ready identification of the cavity from which an individual case had been manufactured.

16.12 Control of Purchased Springs

A plant manufacturing large electrical assemblies purchased a great quantity of springs for use in these assemblies. The plant was dissatisfied with its incoming control procedures on these springs for several reasons:

1. Many lots of springs, rejected at incoming inspection for failure to meet specifications on dimensional accuracy or load limits, were later accepted by the material review procedure for rejected material of the plant.

2. Occasional troubles in assembly and test led to the observation that the plant's go and not-go acceptance sampling routine for springs did not always detect lot variation outside the specification limits.

3. Quality relations between the plant and its spring vendors were not so close as was felt desirable.

4. Purchase prices for some springs were felt to reflect unnecessary, unrealistic, or outmoded spring specification requirements.

Among the steps taken by plant Quality Control to improve these incoming-material situations were three major projects:

1. Establishment of an acceptance sampling procedure by the variables method for springs.

2. Review of spring specifications to assure their mirroring up-to-date quality requirements.

3. Establishment of a procedure for vendor certification of the quality of lots of springs so as to reduce the need for acceptance sampling at the plant.

Each of these three projects is discussed below:[9]

PRODUCT Extension Spring	PART NO. 6172583
CHARACTERISTIC Test Load	VENDOR "B"
METHOD OF TEST Tester 732	ORDER NO. SP-697146-B
SPECIFIED LIMITS .357# to .535# @1.232"	QUANTITY OF LOT 2,250
RECORDED BY T.Green	QUANTITY OF SAMPLE 88
DATE 12-19-60	DISPOSITION Rejected

LIMITS	Lbs. Load	FREQUENCY TALLY	f
→	.355		
↓	.365		
L	.375		
	.385		
I	.395		
	.405		
M	.415		
	.425		
I	.435		
	.445		
T	.455		
	.465		
S	.475		
	.485		
↑	.495		
	.505		
	.515		
	.525	II	2
→	.535	IIIII II	7
	.545	IIIII IIIII I	11
	.555	IIIII IIIII IIIII III	18
	.565	IIIII IIIII IIIII IIIII	20
	.575	IIIII IIIII IIIII	15
	.585	IIIII IIII	9
	.595	IIIII	5
	.605	I	1
	.615	TOTAL	88

FIG. 16.12.

Variables Sampling Procedure. The first project initiated was that of replacing the go and not-go acceptance sampling procedure with one by the variables method. A new spring tester was obtained to make possible the recording of the individual measurements on springs. This tester was used in the following procedure:

A frequency-distribution tally was made by incoming inspection on a sample of springs from each incoming lot. Actual spring readings were plotted on this tally, an example of which is shown on Fig. 16.12. No

[9] From a study by R. S. Inglis and W. J. Masser, Philadelphia, Pa.

definite sample size was specified to the inspector for these tallies; the picture of the build-up of the sample distribution, with respect to the specification limits, indicated to him the number of springs to check from each lot. Those lots were passed the sample distributions of which were properly located in relation to the specification limits. The lot represented by Fig. 16.12 was rejected on this basis.

The tally reports thus made were forwarded to Purchasing for comparison of the performance of various vendors and for whatever action was shown necessary by this comparison. When lot variations were outside specification limits, as in the case of Fig. 16.12, Purchasing would forward a copy of this report to the vendor if and as required.

Purchasing frequently reviewed these tallies with vendors' sales representatives. These salesmen often requested that copies of the tallies be sent to individuals in their own companies; plant quality control many times noted considerable improvement in the quality of subsequent shipments when such improvement was necessary.

Among the advantages obtained from this variables sampling plan are the following:

1. It reflects, at a glance, both the amount of variation in the lot and the relation of the average value to the specification limits. Far more effective data than mere go and not-go information are therefore available for consideration on rejected lots which enter the materials-review procedure of the plant.

2. It provides a ready comparison between vendors, aids individual vendors in making decisions on disposition of rejected lots, and decreases the amount of incoming inspection time as compared with the previous sampling method.

3. It provides vendors with more detailed information on causes for rejection, tends to encourage the use of this tally sheet practice by vendors, and provides plant engineers establishing tolerances for new designs with a useful reference library on the amount of variation to be expected in lots of purchased springs.

Review of Spring Specifications. The distributions made on these incoming lots of springs highlighted several areas in which the spring specifications of the plant were unsatisfactory. Only one of these instances will be cited: those specifications which called for acceptance limits much narrower than could be met by the normal manufacturing variation in the vendors' processes. Springs of this sort had to be 100 per cent sorted by the vendors or 100 per cent tested by the purchaser—either step adding to the spring cost.

It was suspected that some of these specifications were the result of outmoded formulas for calculating spring limits rather than the result of actual assembly-quality requirements. Subsequent analysis proved that this was so in a number of cases, and specifications were consequently adapted. New formulas, reflecting modern spring-manufacturing technique, were made available to the design engineers of the plant. Many cost improvements on springs were a result of these steps.

Vendor Certification. A number of acceptance inspection distribution tallies were made on lots of springs purchased from one vendor. Process Control Engineering and Purchasing discussed the results of the tallies with this vendor, who made such tallies for his own record on every lot of springs shipped to this purchaser.

An arrangement was later made for the vendor to make a photostat of this tally for each lot and to forward this photostat to the plant. The plant was soon able to minimize its own acceptance inspection in favor of this form of vendor certification. Only periodic sampling checks are now made on lots shipped by this vendor.

The purchaser plant has summarized the benefits it has received from this incoming-control procedure:

1. Improved spring test facilities and more effective incoming-inspection methods.
2. Realistic revision of spring specifications, better understanding of spring materials and characteristics, and improvement of spring quality.
3. Better purchaser-vendor relations and closer quality comparison among vendors.
4. Reduction in lost time in assembly due to poor-quality springs and reduction in spring costs by reducing the former 100 per cent testing and by receipt of vendor certificates of test.
5. Reduction in purchased price of many springs as produced by the vendor.

The following excerpt from a letter concerning a single spring type by the vendor to the purchaser plant may be of interest in this connection: ". . . these changes, which were in accordance with your new standards, eliminated the gaging and adjusting operations which had previously been necessary. The savings to your plant on this order amounts to $400. In looking back over previous purchases on this spring, we find that the savings due to the use of your new specifications will amount to over $8,900 per year at the present purchase rate."

16.13 Instituting Improved Control over Incoming Material in a Going Business

A heavy-equipment manufacturer was able for many years to control the quality of his incoming materials through, in part, the medium of very light incoming inspection. Recently, however, some degree of change in the character of his business forced him to buy widely from vendors with whom he had had little previous experience.

The quality produced by these vendors was so spotty that it soon became evident that the manufacturer required a more rigid form of incoming inspection routine. To meet this need, Quality Control developed a formal incoming acceptance procedure through use of a MIL-STD-105A-type acceptance sampling table.

The steps taken to establish this routine were

1. Thorough analysis of the purchased material arriving in the plant.
2. Provision of adequate inspection equipments for this material.
3. Establishment of an appropriate inspection routine.
4. Selection of the most useful acceptance sampling table.

Steps 2 and 4 were carried on jointly, of course. For discussion purposes, however, each of the steps will be discussed independently below:[10]

Analysis of Incoming Material. Several incoming-material analyses were made of the type of materials accepted at the incoming stations, of the lot sizes in which this material was received, and of those incoming lots which were causing the gravest quality difficulties on the production lines. It was found that material was being received and inspected at five different locations in the plant; in some cases, the same type of material was received at two different locations because of nearness of these stations to the various assembly points.

Results of these analyses indicated that a concentration of incoming inspection effort should be placed at one station which could be adequately laid out and provided with proper equipment. The parts which were most critical to quality were to be funneled through this one location. The five incoming inspection stations should be reduced to a total of three—one for critical materials and the other two for general materials which could satisfactorily be accepted close to their point of use.

The analysis also pointed up the relatively small size of the typical incoming lot. It was found that these lots were generally 1,000 pieces or under, calling for a sampling procedure which would be most useful at these lot sizes. Relatively few parts and materials were found to be received in large lot quantities.

Provision of Inspection Equipment. The parts and materials received by this plant are widely varied. They include castings, bar stock, terminal screws, fabricated parts, complicated die-cast gear cases, sand-cast cams, and frames.

Inspection of materials of this character requires for a basic inspection kit such tools as surface plates, gage blocks, sine bars, and plug and snap gages; specialized gages are also required for those high-production parts which are critical.

Where they had not been previously available, the required tools were

[10] This discussion follows a study made by A. J. Showler and associates, Erie, Pa.

secured. Specialized gages were developed to the extent that they would be required by high production parts. Inspection-planning procedures were applied to those parts where they were appropriate.

Inspection Routine. Critical parts, formerly routed among the five original inspection stations, were rerouted to the single acceptance station for parts of this nature. The routine was established so that all incoming parts were accompanied both by a copy of the original material requisition and also be a receiving notice.

A vendor-record card-file system was established, based upon drawing numbers of parts and materials. A file based upon vendor names was also established for those parts received from several vendors.

Incoming-material inspectors record data on these cards in the fashion discussed in Sec. 16.7, and the cards are used in the manner described.

Acceptance Sampling Table. Because of the wide variety of types of lots received by the plant, a very comprehensive MIL-STD-105A-type acceptance sampling table was chosen. This table provided fourteen AQLs, ranging from .015 to 10 per cent.

In the case of some individual materials and parts, various of these AQLs are applied. For the great majority of incoming lots, however, a 2.5 per cent AQL is used. Break-even-point analysis, on an experience basis, showed that this 2.5 per cent AQL is generally appropriate for the type of materials received; the single AQL greatly simplifies the sampling procedure required for incoming material in the factory.

Company Quality Control has summarized the results from this program:

1. Far better quality is being received from vendors.
2. Quality troubles on assembly lines have been reduced.
3. Purchasing has obtained better information about vendor's quality shipments.
4. Vendors have developed a far better sense of their quality responsibility.

CHAPTER 17

PRODUCT CONTROL

The acid test of the adequacy of a quality-control program comes during actual product manufacture. Product control provides the mechanism for this phase of quality control.

Product control has often been publicized for its technical aspects—control charts, quality audits, tool and jig control. The vitally important human relations activity that must be involved in successful product control has frequently been minimized in these discussions. Without high plant morale, without a genuine desire throughout the company to produce products of high quality, without adequate communication of quality objectives throughout the plant, the more technical product-control methods can have few lasting results.

This situation was brought forcibly home to a young quality-control man who had established an elaborate control-charting procedure for a very critical lathe operation on pump fan blades. The frequency-distribution analysis, which had preceded establishment of the control charts, had convinced the quality-control man that the lathe could maintain the ±0.0005-inch tolerance required by the blade job; his regular review of the charts themselves gave him confidence that the job was a stable one and that the blades produced were well "in control."

One Monday morning, however, the control charts told the quality-control man that the blade job was no longer stable or in control. The variation on blades had increased to several thousandths of an inch.

The veteran operator who had operated the lathe for many years had retired at the end of the previous week. Investigation into causes of the out-of-control operation finally disclosed that the lathe had a very definite taper in its ways; the veteran operator had known his machine so well that he had been able to "nurse it along" in the production of satisfactory blades, and the new operator was simply unable to match the performance of the veteran.

The result of this analysis was location of the job on another machine. Several changes were made in its tooling. In establishing a control-chart procedure for the new machine, the young quality-control man was much more humble in making conclusions, based upon purely technical factors, from his analyses.

Modern product-control activities take full cognizance of this overwhelming influence that human beings exert upon the results from technical methods for controlling quality. This influence is reflected in the nature of the techniques and organizational methods of the third of the quality-control jobs. The purpose of this chapter is to discuss these product-control techniques.

17.1 The Needs for Product Control

The percentage of internal failure costs to total planned direct labor cost reflects, for many plants, startling evidence of the effect of inadequate control of product quality during manufacture. These manufacturing losses—composed of such elements as costs for scrapping and/or reworking material of unsatisfactory quality—represent a ratio of as high as 20 to 40 per cent in some plants.

High costs for the inspection of manufactured parts and materials may be another evidence of inadequate control. These high appraisal costs were once justified in some quarters as a reflection of good control of product quality. Modern industrial thinking now recognizes that these costs in some plants may, on the contrary, result because control has been poor. Satisfactory quality may not have been built into the products *before* they were presented for inspection. This modern thinking recognizes that high appraisal costs may merely be a different side of the high-internal-failure coin, with both types of expenditure directly traceable to unsatisfactory control over plant quality.

Yet high appraisal costs and high internal failure costs may indicate that some portion of control has been exercised over quality, namely, that unsatisfactory parts and materials are being "caught" before they are shipped to customers. Even more distressing for many plants are the problems which develop when this unsatisfactory material is actually shipped to customers. Arising from these situations are the numerous customer complaints, the high external failure costs which result either from the need for completely replacing the complainant's material or from the need for repairing or servicing it.

The immediate financial loss due to complaints is only part of this particular problem. While less tangible to a company in the short run, the loss of customer good will from these complaints will ultimately have a direct bearing upon the marketing position of the company. Every reader has heard a purchaser—either industrial or consumer—comment about a manufacturer that "You can't depend upon that company's products." Such statements may presage a serious decline in the company's commercial position.

Another aspect of the complaint situation relates to those products upon whose proper performance human comfort and safety depend. Poor quality of these products may raise much more serious and immediate issues than long-term decline in the company's commercial position. One poor-quality lot received by customers may be all that is required to put a firm out of business.

Poor control over quality during active production may cause financial problems of a more subtle form than that of losses or complaint expense. It may be reflected in the increases in planned cost on a part to allow for second operations like finish tapping or grinding "just to be safe." It may be reflected in unbalanced inventory conditions due to periodic rejections of lots of parts, which force production holdups while additional lots are being manufactured. It may be reflected in machine overruns or in the informal procedure of order clerks to "order a few per cent more just to allow for possible rejections."

These cost situations tend broadly to indicate the needs of a plant for adequate control of products. Other somewhat more specific factors may also be cited:

There may, for example, be inadequate maintenance of the condition of processing equipments and tools or lack of knowledge of the capabilities of these processing equipments. There may be ineffective utilization in the plant of such quality-control technical methods as the control chart or the process sampling table. There may be imperfect use of engineering specifications or of data developed by the company new-design-control routine.

There may be lack of quality-mindedness among plant employees. This failure in attitude may revolve in a vicious circle with such conditions as poor housekeeping and loose inspection performance. There may be failure to keep operators informed of plant quality objectives or to go over with them defective work they have produced. In plants which have extensive report systems covering such elements as car loadings and labor take-home records, there may not even be the crudest attempt at informing management of the quality index of the manufacturing operations of the plant.

Solution of problems of this sort may most effectively be achieved in those plants which operate a total quality control program. Their solution depends upon a foundation of satisfactory new-design and incoming-material-control activities; in particular, it depends upon a broadly conceived and efficiently operating series of product-control routines.

17.2 Defining Product Control

As a definition:

Product control involves the control of products at the source of production and through field service so that departures from the quality specification can be corrected before defective products are manufactured and so proper product service can be maintained in the field.

This tool includes all quality-control activity on a product from the time it is approved for production and its materials are received to the time it is packaged, shipped, and received by a customer who remains satisfied with it.

The emphasis upon prevention and control at the source of production may be readily appreciated. The product whose quality is poor during manufacture faces the strong likelihood of high manufacturing losses, high inspection and test costs, and high complaint expense in the field. For the sake of example, such an article may be termed product A.

Another article—product B—whose quality is high during manufacture will represent a better situation. The likelihood is that this article will experience a good loss, cost, and complaint record.

Figure 17.1 reflects this situation from the statistical point of view. The quality of product B has been controlled at the source, and the frequency distribution shown is that of the product as it is presented for inspection.

Product A is an article without effective control at the source. Its inspection costs have been very high. They have, however, never resulted in sufficiently dependable activities to erase the high complaint expense due to articles which have "slipped through" inspection or those whose characteristics have "drifted" after inspection. Internal failure costs have also remained at correspondingly high levels.

The product-control concept itself, as noted in the definition, is expressed in widely differing details of application among varying types of manufacturing conditions. Chemical processes, as contrasted to those for mechanical products, may be cited as an example.

Product control of quality at the source may, for one of its phases, be very effectively operated in a machine shop or on an assembly conveyor belt by selecting periodic samples during the progress of product manufacture. By showing trends of tool wear or of increasingly less satisfactory operator skill, these samples may "red-flag" potential causes of defects before rejections occur.

In contrast, selection of comparable samples from a batch chemical process may be an ineffective means of control. Selection of samples may be both physically difficult and of questionable practical value.

After the components of the chemical have been measured and the vat

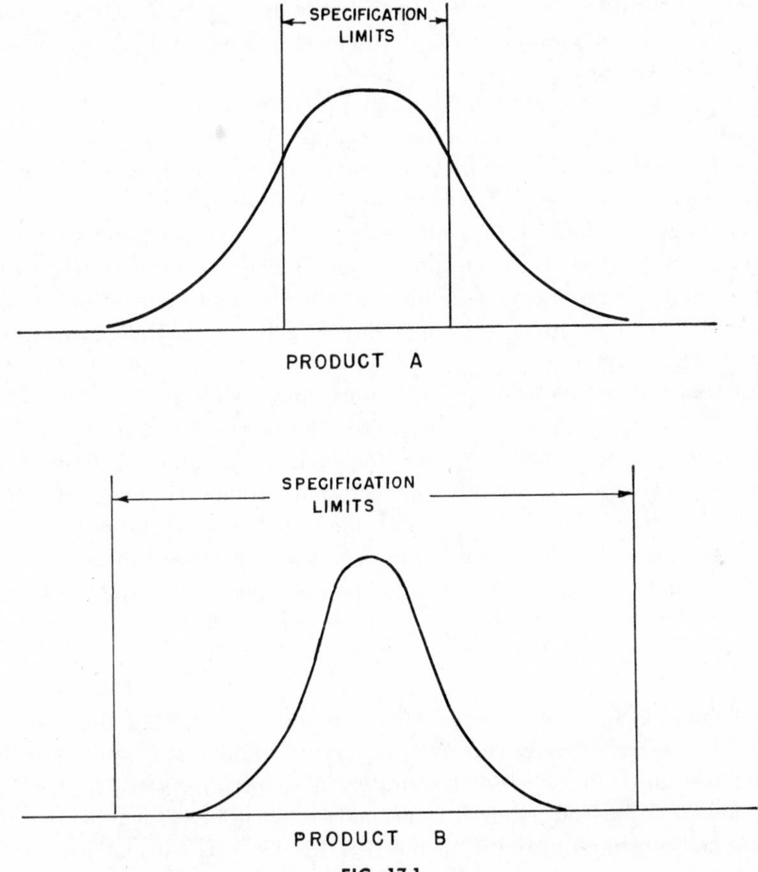

FIG. 17.1.

valves set for the manufacture of a large batch of material, there may be little opportunity for periodic product sampling checks until the material is pumped in final form from the system. And even if it is possible to select these samples, reactions during the processing period may cause results at the final test of the batch which differ from those of the periodic samples.

Some batch operations may, therefore, require product-control activity that is based on corrective action from final product analyses rather than from periodic sampling. The preventive approach here is developed toward the *over-all batch process* rather than toward individual lots passing through this process.

Continuous-flow process operations furnish another illustration of these possible chemical versus mechanical product-control differences.[1] In some of these flow processes, chemists have for some time been selecting samples consisting of a single unit of product—often selected at regularly scheduled intervals.

Before unquestioningly rejecting this procedure in favor of including in the product-control routine the more typical technique of selecting samples composed of several units, the wise quality-control man determines the operational meaning of such a several-unit sample. Does the variation among the units of the sample have the same meaning in a continuous-flow process as it has in a machining process where a several-unit sample is generally a requirement? Are those variations which appear in the flow process sample due largely to the influence of the testing device alone?

The answer to questions of this sort may show that a single-unit sample is desirable in several instances for the most practical and most economical product-control routine for such a continuous process.

These illustrations point up the fact that product-control procedures must be tailored for the particular manufacturing situation at hand rather than be adapted in total from a routine developed for a so-called similar situation. While the basic emphasis upon prevention is fundamental to product control among all these manufacturing situations, the technical details of the application of the principle will vary widely from shop to shop.

It cannot be overemphasized that the purpose of a product-control procedure is that of tangible results in quality maintenance and improvement; the individual techniques employed to produce these results are only means to an end—they are not ends in themselves. Quality-control men must continually guard themselves from concentration upon these individual product-control techniques lest the specialists' perspective be narrowed in regard to the over-all plant quality-control program.

17.3 Organizing for Product Control

Key man in the quality control procedures for product control is the shop foreman. All procedures are built around him and the employees

[1] An interesting discussion of this point is given in Charles A. Bicking, "Quality Control in the Chemical Industry, I," *Industrial Quality Control,* Vol. III, No. 4.

he supervises, since it is of and through them that the great bulk of product-control activities must be carried on. Also involved in a very important degree are mechanical inspection and electrical test activities.

Detailed planning of that segment of the quality-system plan which relates to product and process control is accomplished by the quality-control engineer assigned for the particular product line. In establishing the planned procedures, he may consult Product Engineering, Manufacturing Engineering, Production Control, Cost Accounting, and Shop Operations.

As much quality checking as is practicable is made the responsibility of the shop operators who are generating the quality characteristics. This technique has been called *source control* or, more recently, *station control*. Quality characteristics are measured at those points in the product flow which are the economic and strategic "stations" for control of product and process. At other "stations" an independent quality audit may be conducted by Process Control Engineering personnel.

Implementation of the product and process quality-control plan is the responsibility of the process-control engineer. He may be said to be the key quality-control man in this third job of total quality control. If for any reason the established quality-system plan cannot be applied, he does necessary emergency planning to permit continuation of production at required quality levels. If the situation that necessitated emergency planning is more than transitory, the process-control engineer requests that essential changes be made in the established plan by the quality-control engineer. The process-control engineer also keeps process capability studies up to date and analyzes quality problems as they arise on a day-to-day basis. He may request help of the quality-control engineer or bring other functional specialties to bear on the problem.

It should be noted in this discussion of organization that product-control activities are inevitably bound up with the work of the other management programs used by a plant in its manufacturing operations.

If a plant has ineffective personnel policies and is willing to hire low-caliber employees and then spend little time in training them; if its production-control scheduling and routing procedures impair shop morale by imposing a maximum of red tape and a minimum of orderly material flow through the factory, if materials handling is still in a primitive stage, then the effect and nature of product-control procedures will themselves be strongly influenced.

Whether product control will exert a tug on these other functions sufficiently strong to raise their effectiveness or will be dragged down to their level will depend upon the particular plant situation and the strength of the personalities and policies involved. Certainly it is a basic error to suppose that the mere establishment of a product-control procedure will automatically solve shop quality problems that have been generated by misuse of other management programs.

As a corollary, of course, it must be noted that it is equally erroneous to suppose that a weak product-control procedure will suffice simply because some other management programs are strong. The answer here is a matter of balance; a plant must be assured both that it has adequate product-control procedures and that its other management programs include satisfactory practices that may influence these product-control procedures.

17.4 Procedures for Product Control within the Quality-system Plan

Definite procedures are operated by members of the process-control unit to assure that the product-control activities are an integral part of plant practice. These procedures are established within the total-quality-system plan by the quality-control-engineering unit assisted by the shop foremen and the concerned functional people. Because of the wide variety of manufacturing activities that may exist even within one plant, the procedures must cover a number of different control conditions that can be grouped under two general headings:

1. Control of machining or processing of component parts.
2. Control of assemblies and packaging and on batches.

Procedures required for these control conditions on the factory floor may cover control of work passing through the machine shop, materials being processed through welders or furnaces, assemblies being built up from component subassemblies, chemicals being produced in a batch process, and wire being coated in a continuous-flow process. The procedures may involve control of tools, jigs, and fixtures; preventive maintenance; utilization of process-capability studies; means for improving operator quality-mindedness; application of control-chart and process sampling plans; strategic placement of mechanical inspection and electrical test stations; development of product-quality indices.

These procedures will depend upon proper material flow and sound plant layout for as large a degree as possible of "built-in quality" through the basic manufacturing plan. They will emphasize rigid procedures for disposal of defective parts and for establishing proper reject analyses.

The procedures depend upon good factory supervision as much as upon sound technical methods. They require adequate product-control organization throughout the factory, and genuine acceptance throughout the plant of the point of view of total quality control. They are built around procedures which enable corrective action when such action is required; they involve the taking of data only to the extent that this data may be a basis for action.

Building the Product-control Procedure

17.5 The Pattern

Product-control procedures may cover the entire cycle of actual manufacture where raw materials and purchased parts are, through one process or another, converted into a finished product. They may cover only the component-parts-processing portion of this cycle—as in the case of a processing plant or processing division of a large plant. The procedures may cover only the assembly portion of the cycle.

Whatever coverage is taken by the procedures, they will gear into a flow of manufactured parts and materials which, for many manufacturing floors, often pursues at least six identifiable steps:

1. Receipt of order for the part, material, or assembly in the manufacturing area.
2. Examination of the requirements of the order and taking the steps required to make the order ready for production.
3. Release of order for production.
4. Control of material while in process of manufacture.
5. Final approval of product.
6. Packaging and shipment. If a component part, the product may merely be transported to the area where it will be used in assembly.

Product-control activities which carry through these six steps may be considered in two major divisions:

1. Setting and maintenance of standards (carried on during steps 1 through 3).
2. Control of material during actual manufacture (carried on during steps 4 through 6).

Sections 17.6 and 17.7 will discuss factors that must be taken into account while developing procedures involving each of these two divisions.

17.6 Standards

In building the standards portions of a product-control procedure, the quality-control organization must first take into account such factors as

1. *Product requirements:* the article's specifications, its guarantees, and tolerances.
2. *How it is to be made:* the quality elements of planning for manufacture, determination of processing equipments upon which the article may be produced, and selection of required tools, jigs, and fixtures.
3. *What is important on article:* critical, major, and minor dimensions; inspection and test requirements; point of inspection or test; quality levels for sampling.

If the product has been subject to new-design-control activity, information about these three factors will have been sent to the manufacturing area along with the order in the form of such media as the quality planning for the article. If there has been no new-design-control activity on the product, then the over-all product-control procedure must incorporate an abbreviated form of this activity in order to produce comparable information.

It is not best practice for product-control procedures thus to attempt to backtrack over these required new-design-control steps for an article. Particularly in the development of specifications and guarantees and in the establishment of inspection and test requirements and of quality levels, such a backtrack is both less economical and less satisfactory technically than a straightforward new-design-control program would be. The "design trail" of the article may already have gone cold, and the design engineers concerned may no longer be readily available for consultation. Proper equipment may not be available for making the required tests; tight production requirements may permit no time for adequate analyses.

There are, of course, certain conditions which make it inevitable that such a necessarily sketchy new-design-control program be incorporated in product-control procedures. A plant which has just initiated new-design-control activities will be forced for some time to cover such activities in its product-control procedures which apply to existing articles.

Also, there is the quite typical situation of the plant which does only the machining or assembly of articles designed or specified in another plant. Similar is the case of the so-called contributing divisions (screw machines, punch presses, etc.) of a large plant. These plants or divisions may merely receive a bare drawing or sketch of the part or possibly simply a written order for it, from which they must establish manufacturing, material-ordering, and quality procedures.

There is nothing unique about the techniques used in this so-called new-design phase of product control. The techniques are simply those regular procedures discussed in Chap. 15 adapted to particular situations as needed.

Process-capability studies are particularly widely applied in this work. In the often-encountered plant which has just initiated new-design control, tabulations of the results of these process studies are generally used by the plant engineers during the growth of their formal design-control activities.

17.7 Manufacturing Control

When these standards for the article have been incorporated in the procedure, actual shop control activities may then be developed. Typical of the factors that must be evaluated during this consideration are:

1. *Type of manufacturing process:* is it an assembly being built up on a conveyor? A part being worked at several successive machine tools? Material being processed as individual batches?

2. *Manufacturing quantities:* are there high quantities, same material day after day? Job lots, different parts always? High quantities but short runs of different parts?

3. *Type of shop personnel:* skilled workmen, each a quality-conscious craftsman? Relatively unskilled operators, each performing a repetitive operation? Experienced, competent factory foremen? Newly appointed, inexperienced supervisors?

4. *Type of product:* is it a precision machined part? Intricate assembly? Material with loose quality requirements?

5. *Product-control procedures on other processes in the shop:* can the controls for this process be easily integrated with those in effect on other processes, with corresponding simplicity of administration and minimum of expense? If they cannot be thus integrated, will the control procedure conflict with these other instructions, resulting in confusion?

6. *Acceptance of product control:* is there acceptance among the concerned personnel of the value of total quality control? How can the details of the product-control procedure employ, to the greatest possible extent, the language and practice best understood in the shop? How can the principles of the product-control procedure best be sold to shop personnel?

If the article is to be produced as a relatively small element in the over-all production of a large machine shop or an extensive assembly area, it is likely that its control procedure will merely be absorbed into the standard, over-all product-control procedure for the area, as suggested in factor 5 above. Such over-all procedures, which incorporate the same control principles for all parts, may be both practical and economical when properly established. They are particularly useful in those areas where quality requirements are relatively uniform even though production consists in a wide variety of types of articles.

The article may, however, be produced as a major element of over-all shop production, perhaps in an area devoted largely or exclusively to its manufacture. In cases of this sort, individual control procedures will be developed for sole application to the product.

This discussion of factors involved in developing control activities cannot be concluded without emphasis upon factor 6 above relating to shop acceptance. A product-control procedure which is excellent technically but which either is not or cannot be sold to the personnel who must work with it is of little positive value and may actually be detrimental.

17.8 High Quantities versus Job Lots

It may be emphasized that the two divisions discussed above—standards and manufacturing controls—are quite generally applicable as the basis for product-control procedures. This is true whether production is job lot or high quantity, whether output takes the form of individual parts or intricate assemblies, whether production time required is several days or only a few minutes.

Section 3.8 summarized its general review of this job-lot–high-quantity issue in the following conclusion:

"In mass-production manufacturing, quality-control activities center on the *product,* while in job-lot manufacturing, it is a matter of controlling the *process.*

"For example, in the mass-production manufacture of coils, the emphasis of quality-control activities is on the coil type itself—its dimensions, fiber wrappings, etc. But where varying types and sizes of coils are produced on a job-lot basis, the quality-control activities center on the common manufacturing process for producing the coils."

This conclusion may be paraphrased in the language developed in this chapter: when production is high-quantity and will run for a sufficient length of time, techniques may be used in the product-control procedure both for setting and maintaining standards and for controlling parts during manufacture. When production is job-lot or of short duration, the techniques used may concentrate almost entirely upon setting and maintaining of standards. The process and processing equipment is thus controlled rather than the parts themselves.

If a screw machine is set up for a production run which will involve thousands of parts over a several-day period, it may be useful and effective both to set and maintain standards—through such means as tool and die control or process-capability studies—and to establish manufacturing controls—through such means as patrol inspection or process sampling or control charts. If a punch press is set for a production run which will involve 300 to 400 parts but which will be completed in less than an hour, it may be impractical and uneconomical to concentrate upon any techniques other than proper standards setting. If a large shaft is being slowly turned and faced, control-chart technique may be very inappropriate and the setting of standards may again be the indicated product-control technique.

The details of the various individual standards and manufacturing control techniques used in the accompanying product-control routines will be discussed in Sec. 17.13.

Typical Product-control Procedures

The actual forms taken by product-control procedures vary much more widely throughout industry than the forms taken by procedures of any of the other quality-control jobs. This situation is probably due to the very wide variety of manufacturing situations involved. It is, therefore, most useful to discuss typical product-control procedures in relation to actual industrial cases rather than to more abstract, generalized examples.

Four actual examples will be discussed below, covering major situations encountered in the over-all product-control activity: (1) Job-lot Machine Shop, in Sec. **17.9**; (2) Process Sampling in a Machine Shop, in Sec. 17.10; (3) High-quantity Subassembly, in Sec. 17.11; (4) Assembly, in Sec. 17.12.

17.9 Job-lot Machine Shop[2]

The production machine shop in a Middle Atlantic area factory includes sensitive drill presses, radial drill presses, milling machines, lathes, screw machines, punch presses, grinders, welders, brazing and burning equipment, etc. One hundred to one hundred fifty jobs go through this shop daily, with average lot sizes of less than 100 pieces. A large proportion of these jobs are nonrepetitive; they may not pass through the shop again for a period of from 6 months to 2 years.

Each job lot passing through the shop requires several operations before completion. A typical part may require not only turning but also milling and drilling.

The importance for control purposes of adequate standards setting and maintenance activity under conditions of this sort is recognized in this shop in several ways. One such is its emphasis upon the utilization of the results of process-capability studies. In so far as possible, jobs are planned for and placed upon processing equipments known through these studies to be capable of maintaining the required dimensions.

A preventive maintenance program is actively followed to keep these processing equipments in proper condition. Tools, dies, jigs, and fixtures are closely controlled so that they will be in adequate shape to assist in producing work of the quality called for in new-design-control specifications.

Were this standards activity the only element in the product-control procedure for this plant, the shop would suffer from the occurrence of such defects as

[2] This discussion closely follows an unpublished paper "Quality Control Applied to Job Shop Production," W. J. Masser and R. S. Inglis, Philadelphia, Pa.

1. An undersized or an oversized hole when all that was required was the proper-sized drill.
2. A radius being ground on the wrong side.
3. A hole being drilled out of location.
4. The wrong side being milled.
5. A missed operation.
6. Holes countersunk on the wrong side or not deep enough.
7. Defective burring.
8. Damage during processing.

To eliminate defects of this sort, the shop complements its standards activity with an effective procedure for control during manufacture. This procedure embraces five major elements:

1. First-piece inspection. Operators make their own process checks thereafter, and gages are provided them for this purpose.
2. Acceptance sampling inspection of completed lots.
3. Control through data from final inspection.
4. Quality audit by process-control engineer.
5. Follow-through to gain corrective action from final inspection-control data and quality audits.

It will be noted that these five elements do not include process sampling or patrol inspection, which often characterize the preventive approach in a machine shop. Both analyses and experience have shown this type of sampling to be uneconomical and relatively impractical in this shop. Production quantities are very small, runs are short, jobs may be completed and shipped between inspection checks, and it has been found practical in this shop to place responsibility for periodic checks upon the operators themselves.

Emphasis is, therefore, upon one interpretation of the job-lot product-control approach discussed in Sec. 17.8. *Control is set up for the entire production shop, the "process" in this particular case.* It is not based upon an individual part or job.

With this fundamental established, each of the five steps in the machine-shop control may be briefly reviewed:

First-piece Inspection. All jobs receive a first-piece inspection. If the inspector approves the first piece, the job is allowed to run and the operator will thereafter periodically check this work.

All jobs receive a first-piece inspection at each operation. It is therefore possible for one lot to receive three, four, or five such inspections.

Acceptance Sampling of Completed Lots. Completed lots are routed to a final inspection area, well stocked with measuring equipments. Here the lots are sampled through use of a MIL-STD-105A-type acceptance sampling table.

It has been found practical and economical to use a single AQL for the great majority of lots entering the final inspection area. The quality level used was determined through use of the type of analysis discussed in Chap. 12 of this book.

Figure 17.2 illustrates graphically the inspection sequence followed in this acceptance procedure.

Control through Data from Final Inspection. Data are taken on each lot passing through final inspection. For purposes of corrective action and so as to reduce record keeping to the required minimum, detailed data are kept only on the jobs found defective.

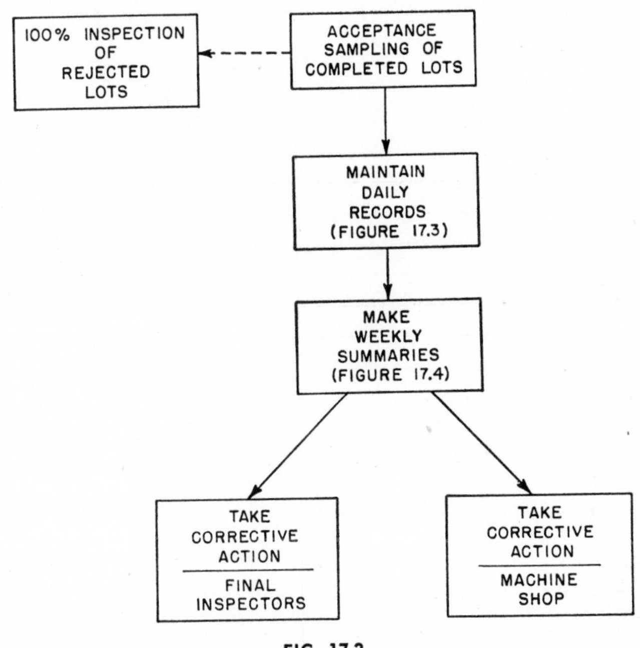

FIG. 17.2.

Figure 17.3 presents the form on which this record is kept. It is made out daily by the final inspectors. These inspectors record the total number of jobs accepted and rejected, as well as the total number of first-piece inspections and rejections. For all defective lots, they record the drawing number, lot size, quantity inspected, quantity rejected, the operation responsible for the defect, the type of defect, and the disposition of the lot.

The operation responsible for the defect and the type of defect are, of course, the most important items on the form. The various types of operations are listed by numbers, and the various types of defects are listed by letters. For example, reference to Fig. 17.3 shows that, for a lot rejected owing to an undersize dimension on a milling operation, the inspector would record 11 (milling operation) and T (undersize).

The record kept on the form of lot size, quantity inspected, and quan-

Date__________

Jobs Passed__________ Jobs Rejected__________

OPERATIONS

1 - Brazing/Burning
2 - Broaching
3 - Engineering Errors
4 - Drilling "Sen."
5 - Drilling "Rad."
6 - File Bench
7 - Forming (brake)
8 - Grinding
9 - Lathe
10 - Layout & Brush Gr.
11 - Milling
12 - Other Divisions
13 - Production Errors
14 - Punch Press
15 - Sawing
16 - Steel Fabrication
17 - Welding
18 - Screw Mach.
19 -
20 -

DEFECTS

A - Compound Group
B - Countersinking
C - Def. Burring
D - Def. Material
E - Def. Threads
F - Def. Radius
G - Finish too rough
H - Missed Operations
J - Mixed Parts
K - No Job Tag
L - No Print
M - Other Faults
N - Out of Location
O - Oversize
P - Plating
Q - Reaming
R - Rough Handling
S - Shortage
T - Undersize
U -
V -
X -

DRAWING NO.	JOB QUAN.	QUAN. INSP.	QUAN. DEF.	OPERATION & DEFECT	DISPOSITION REJ.	DISPOSITION PASSED

No. of 1st piece Inspections______
No. of 1st piece Rejections______

Inspector__________

FIG. 17.3.

tity rejected provides primarily the opportunity for a check by the process-control engineer to determine if the acceptance sampling table is strictly adhered to. The data also furnish the basis for gaining some degree of indication of the per cent defective in the lot.

The record kept of drawing numbers is of value in a frequency-of-occurrence analysis. Corrective action—whether change in engineering design or in manufacturing method—may then be requested by the process-control engineer.

The daily record form of Fig. 17.3 is summarized weekly. Figure 17.4 shows the form used, one particularly useful for weekly process-control-engineering reviews to determine the basis for corrective action.

Quality Audit. The process-control engineer, as part of his job of implementing the quality system, monitors the quality-control procedures being used throughout the shop.

In addition to this activity, he periodically conducts an audit to evaluate the quality that is being shipped from the machine shop. This is a customer-centered audit, the process-control engineer playing the role of the assembly supervisors who must use the machined parts. These periodic evaluations provide a continuous monitoring of the machine shop's quality-system plan. Any weakness discovered in the parts calls for a review of the system and for necessary changes in the planning by the quality-control engineer to assure the desired parts quality.

Follow-through to Gain Corrective Action. Whether discrepancies in parts quality are noted on the daily inspection records or as a result of the quality audits, it is essential that prompt investigation be made and proper corrective action taken. Data from the record sheets usually show in this shop that two or three operations and two or three types of defects are responsible for 75 to 85 per cent of all rejections. These data are reviewed weekly by the process-control engineer. Decisions upon corrective action represent the essence of the work, since the futility of record keeping without corresponding action is recognized. This action may take such forms as the following:

1. The foremen will notify their instructors or leaders to concentrate upon the operations found to be defective.

2. Manufacturing Engineering may start to design foolproof jigs or fixtures on these operations.

3. In the rare case of epidemics, patrol inspection may be temporarily established for the troublesome processing operation.

4. Defective work is returned for the instruction of the operators who produced it. These operators are correspondingly provided with further guidance and training.

A number of steps are taken in this plant to improve the quality-consciousness and quality-mindedness of all employees. In addition to such factors as operator training, good supervision, and quality campaigns, the quality-control personnel make several specific moves which are integrated with the data-recording activity at final inspection. The results of the weekly analyses of Fig. 17.4 are posted prominently in the plant in the form of two charts. One chart shows the percentage of effective jobs for each operation. The second chart shows the per cent-defective trend of all jobs passing through final inspection.

Week Ending ____________

SUMMARY SHEET

	Jobs Passed	Jobs Rej.	Jobs. Insp.	% Defect.
Monday				
Tuesday				
Wednes.				
Thursday				
Friday				
Saturday				
TOTAL				

	TOTAL	W-	V-	U-	T- Undersize	S- Shortage	R- Rough Handling	Q- Reaming	P- Plating	O- Oversize	N- Out of Location	M- Other Faults	L- No Print	K- No Job Tag	J- Mixed Parts	H- Missed Operation	G- Finish Too Rough	F- Def. Radius	E- Def. Threads	D- Def. Material	C- Def. Burring	B- Countersinking	A- Compound Group
1- Brazing/Burning																							
2- Broaching																							
3- Engineering Errors																							
4- Drilling "Sen."																							
5- Drilling "Rad."																							
6- File Bench																							
7- Forming (Brake)																							
8- Grinding																							
9- Lathe																							
10- Layout & Brush Group																							
11- Milling																							
12- Other Divisions																							
13- Production Errors																							
14- Punch Press																							
15- Sawing																							
16- Steel Fabrication																							
17- Welding																							
18- Screw Machine																							
19-																							
20-																							
21-																							
TOTAL																							

FIG. 17.4.

In addition, particularly troublesome parts scrapped at final inspection are displayed each week. Cards attached to these parts explain the defects, show the amount of money lost owing to the defects, and may indicate any information as to business lost owing to the scrappage.

The plant using this product-control procedure recognizes that it does not employ some of the more highly publicized techniques whose value has been analyzed and found uneconomical for this particular situation. Plant personnel feel that they have gained considerable advantage from the procedures tailor-made to their job-lot machine shop. Among these advantages the plant lists

1. Ease and economy of the operation of the procedure.
2. Its complete analysis of shop quality.
3. Its provision for continually monitoring the output of the quality system by the process-control engineer.
4. Its red-flagging of needs for corrective action.
5. Its indication of the effects of corrective action.
6. The fashion in which the procedures point out those individuals—operators, inspectors, or others—who require further instruction.
7. The reductions in losses and increases in output that have accompanied operation of the procedures.
8. The reductions in inspection time that have resulted from quality improvements developing from operation of the procedures.

17.10 Process Sampling in a Machine Shop

A product-control procedure which utilizes several different techniques from those discussed in the preceding section operates very successfully for the machine shop of a New York State factory. This machine shop includes milling machines, drill presses, lathes, and other similar tools. Work passing through the shop requires only a fair degree of precision, ranging from tolerances of plus or minus two- or three-thousandths of an inch to tolerances expressed in fractional terms:

Production quantities range from job lots to high-quantity runs. Many lots are nonrepetitive; others are processed regularly. Work passing through the shop consists chiefly of relatively small parts, each of comparatively low cost. As many as a dozen individual operations may be performed on these parts.

Shop employees are well trained in the operation of the machine tool to which they are assigned. Most of these machine operators are not, however, skilled mechanics; some are women.

This shop carries on some standards-setting and -maintenance activity. This consists largely of the same techniques as those noted in Sec. 17.9—preventive maintenance, process-capability studies, tool and die control, etc.

Because of the character of this machine shop, its primary quality emphasis is placed upon the control of parts during processing. After a dozen operations have been performed and the parts have been degreased and cleaned, it is virtually impossible at a final inspection to do more than sort the bad parts from the good. There is, for example, no room on the small parts for operators' identification stamps.

Both experience and analytical studies have shown the management of this shop that it is most practical and economical to carry out its control of parts through process sampling. This process-sampling activity covers all parts manufactured in the machine shop. A process-sampling table is used similar to that discussed in Sec. 12.22 and shown in Fig. 12.19. A single AQL has been determined to apply to all parts, and a single shop-wide patrol inspection schedule is operated.

The process-sampling procedure used in this shop has four major steps, as follows:

1. The setup for a job is made by the operator or setup man. When he is satisfied that it is correct, first-piece inspection is made by the process inspector. When the piece is approved, the inspector punches a record card which is hung at each machine and the operator starts the production run.

2. The operator checks his work at regular intervals. If he discovers a defect, the process is corrected. The new setup must thereupon be approved by the process inspector.

3. At the intervals specified by the process-sampling table, the patrol inspector checks the required number of parts. These parts may be chosen consecutively or at random, depending upon the job circumstances.[3] If no rejects are found, the inspector segregates work that has been processed since the last check, punches the record card "O.K.," and production continues.

4. If defects are found by the process inspector, he notifies the proper authority to get the process corrected immediately. The parts that have accumulated since the last inspection are set aside for sorting. The inspector punches the reason for rejection on the record card. When the process is corrected, approval by the process inspector must be obtained before production is allowed to continue.

Except for an occasional final acceptance sampling check on lots periodically to audit the continued effectiveness of the process-sampling procedure, no final inspection is required in this shop. Process sampling has been proved so satisfactory that lots are merely transported to the assembly area after their completion.

In addition to the immediate follow-through gained through this process-sampling procedure, the process-control engineer regularly reviews the record cards taken from the machines. Corrective action is decided upon, and responsibilities are assigned to appropriate positions. Special process studies (see Chap. 18) may be initiated in particularly trouble-

[3] For a discussion of this matter, see particularly Sec. 12.22.

some problem situations. Figure 17.5 shows the sequence followed in this procedure.

The value the factory has gained from this procedure is due not only to these sampling techniques but also to the extensive program of quality education carried on in the plant. Employee participation in "better quality" drives, periodic slogan and poster campaigns in the plant newspaper, and both preliminary and refresher training of operators are examples of this educational activity.

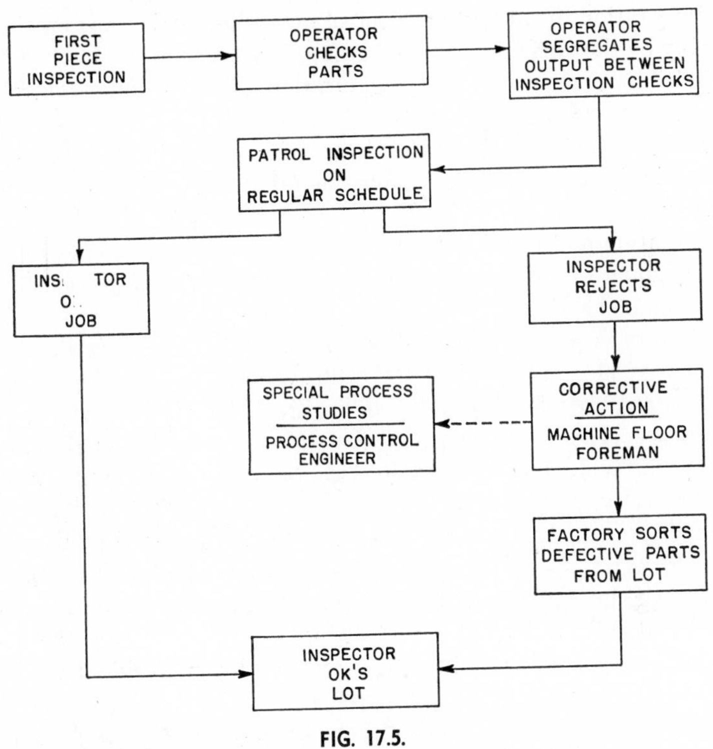

FIG. 17.5.

17.11 High-quantity, High Reliability Subassembly

A New England factory manufactures, as one of its major products, a small electrical component which consists essentially of a series of windings enclosed in a leakproof, canlike case.[4] This electrical component—termed here a *subassembly*—is both shipped directly to customers and used as a subassembly for other products manufactured by the plant.

[4] This discussion directly follows an unpublished paper by D. A. Gensheimer, Pittsfield, Mass.

Applications of the subassembly require that its quality be high. While total production quantities of the article are large, a number of different types are manufactured each week. All articles, however, pass through essentially the same manufacturing cycle involving the same operations and processes. The article's reliability must be high.

Product control on this article was initiated by a quality-control engineer. His responsibilities include

1. Integration of all product-control activities carried out on the subassembly by the various functional groups concerned.
2. Initiation, approval, and organization of all product-control procedures.
3. Issuance of quality-control instructions covering product-control routines in inspection, test, quality-maintenance, and quality-auditing procedures.
4. Initiation and revision of the quality reports required.
5. Assigning of projects, as required, to appropriate positions for investigation and action.

An approach to the manufacturing-control aspects of the over-all product-control procedure for the subassembly, as developed by the quality-control engineer, is shown in Fig. 17.6. This figure shows a product-flow chart indicating both the several processing operations and the eight individual control stations that are the keys in the product-control activity.

A quality-control instruction has been written for each of these eight stations, clearly specifying the product-control techniques to be used. Shown in these instructions is such information as the sampling tables to be used and the quality levels to be applied. Also shown are the inspection- and test-planning data that were developed during new-design-control activity on the subassembly.

Figure 17.7 illustrates one of these quality-control instructions. It covers the product-control procedures for control station 4 and is self-explanatory.

Of particular interest in product control for this subassembly is control station 7. It involves a final quality audit of the outgoing product and consists of checks over and above the normal factory inspection and tests. Acceptance of the day's production depends upon the outcome of this audit.

The quality-audit procedure includes selection of a random sample of the day's production and subjection of these units to three groups of acceptance tests, which are comparable to regular production tests previously made. These tests include the following:

1. Mechanical inspection.
2. Electrical test.

3. Oven leak test and other reliability tests.

Each of these three tests is conducted and judged to a 0.65 per cent AQL. Records of the tests are made on conventional per cent-defective control charts. These charts are used to determine the amount of sampling required on future lots.

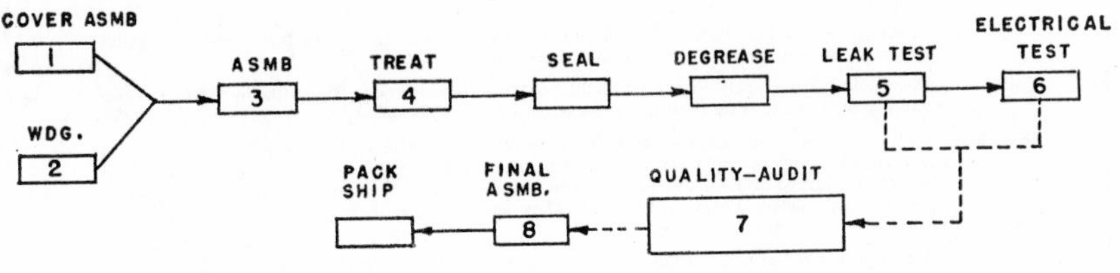

NOTE: EACH NUMBER (1, 2, ETC.) REFERS TO AN INDIVIDUAL CONTROL STATION

DESCRIPTION OF CONTROL STATIONS:

1. PATROL INSPECTION.
   ELECTRICAL TEST (100%),
   FINAL LOT SAMPLING CHECK (1% A.Q.L.).
2. DRY TEST (100%) OPEN CIRCUITS.
3. LOT SAMPLING CHECK (1% A.Q.L.)
   SPLIT LIGHT TEST FOR SHORTS AND GROUNDS (100%)
4. POWER FACTOR AND OTHER ELECTRICAL SAMPLE CHECKS ON THE QUALITY OF THE TREATING OPERATION.
5. LEAK TEST (100%)
6. ELECTRICAL TEST (100%)----- ANALYSIS OF ELECTRICAL FAILURE EXCEEDING EXPECTED %.
7. QUALITY- AUDIT---- FINAL PRODUCTION SAMPLE TEST PERFORMED IN A SEPARATE ROOM DESIGNED ESPECIALLY FOR THIS PURPOSE
8. FINAL SAMPLING INSPECTION (0.65% A.Q.L.)

PRODUCT CONTROL

HIGH QUANTITY SUB-ASSEMBLY

FIG. 17.6.

The charts are analyzed in the following fashion to determine the amount of sampling: If the quality level shown by previous audits is running less than ¼ per cent, a reduced sampling plan is employed. If the quality level is between ¼ per cent and the upper limit on the control chart, a normal sampling plan is used. If the quality level exceeds the upper control limit, then a more rigid sampling plan is used.[5]

[5] Reduced, normal, and more rigid sampling plans were reviewed in Sec. 12.12.

Q. C. INSTRUCTION NO. 5.04

Subject: Product Control Tests – Class 7321-7322 Sub-assembly Treating.

Purpose:

1. To detect unsatisfactory sub-assembly characteristics caused by faulty operation of the sub-assembly treating system.

2. To detect such characteristics as soon after treat as possible, before the doubtful sub-assemblies become mixed with previously treated sub-assemblies.

General: These instructions apply to all Class 7321-7322 sub-assemblies treated with any of the treating materials and in any of the treating processes covered by Laboratory and Engineering Instructions.

Procedure: Each day, three sub-assemblies, all of the same catalog number, shall be taken from each treating tank unloaded between 8:00 AM and 5:00 PM. These sub-assemblies shall be selected after the baskets are turned over for unloading, where baskets are loaded on their sides, but shall be taken before actual unloading begins. Sub-assemblies shall be taken from the center of one of the top baskets.

Over a period of days, all catalog numbers of Class 7321 and 7322 sub-assemblies being built in quantity shall be sampled.

The samples selected shall be immediately sealed, degreased, and placed in a forced circulation oven operating at 70° C, with a minimum of elapsed time between selection of samples and placing them in the oven. Sub-assemblies shall remain in the oven long enough to bring their dielectric temperatures within the range of 65° - 75° C after which they shall be measured for power factor and capacity at either rated 60-cycle volts, or at a 60-cycle voltage in accordance with the following table if sub-assemblies are rated for DC voltage.

DC Rated Volts	60-cycle Test Volts	DC Rated Volts	60-cycle Test Volts
400	220	1500	660
600	330	2000	880
1000	440	Over 2000	35% of DC rating

In the event the desired test voltage exceeds the maximum rated voltage of the bridge, measurements may be taken at the maximum voltage available.

If the power factors obtained exceed those given in the tabulation given below for the applicable case style, voltage rating and treating material, the tank load of sub-assemblies represented by the sample shall be removed from the production flow and an additional sample shall be taken and measured. Results of tests on both samples shall be referred to the Engineering Department for decision as to disposition of the tank load in question.

If elevated temperature power factors are satisfactory, the samples shall be cooled to a dielectric temperature of 20°-30° C and the power factor and capacity measurements repeated at the same voltage as was used for the previous measurements.

65° - 75° C POWER-FACTOR LIMITS

Case Style and Size	*Rated AC Volts	Max % P.F. 1476	1436	Oil
All round cans	660 and below	.50	.50	.30
All round cans	Above 660	.40	.40	.25
2 in. x 2-1/2 in. oval	660 and below	.50	.50	.30
1-3/4 in. x 2-1/2 in. oval	Above 660	.40	.40	.25
All other oval	All	.40	.40	.25
All rectangular	660 and below	.50	.50	.30
All rectangular	Above 660	.40	.40	.25
Bathtubs	All	.60	.60	.30
AVDG	All	.60	.60	.30

* For DC sub-assemblies - consider 1500 V DC equivalent to 660 V AC.

Records: A permanent record of all measurements shall be kept in the office of the Quality Control Manager. Each week the over-all Quality Performance report for Class 7321-7322 sub-assemblies shall include a record of the number of tanks sampled and the number of tanks whose samples had high power factors.

A. R. JONES
Eng. Department

APPROVED:

B. F. SMITH Mfg. Superintendent

T. D. GREEN Mgr. - Q. C.

R. M. BROWN Eng. Department

FIG. 17.7.

When a sample is rejected as a result of this audit, the manufacturing group is required to sort out all of that type of subassembly for the specified defect before the lot can be released.

The quality-audit procedure has been particularly useful for this subassembly, which is a relatively precise electrical component whose characteristics make it impossible by regular production 100 per cent testing to

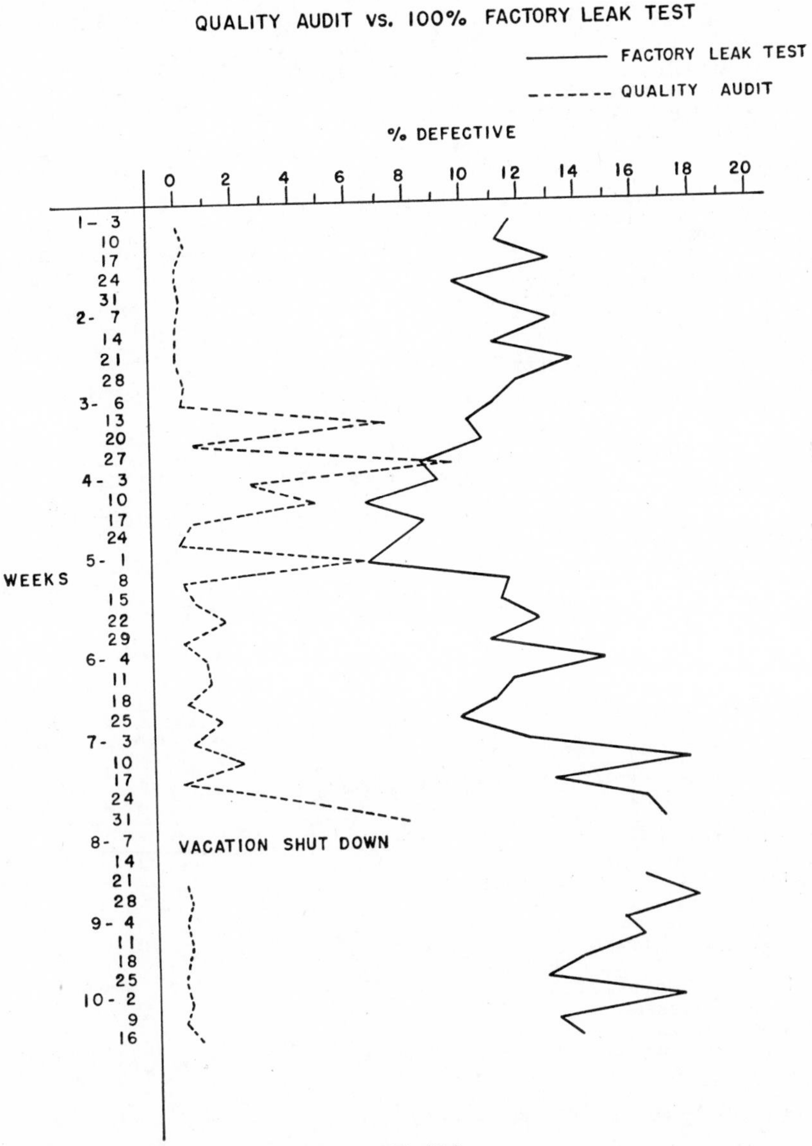

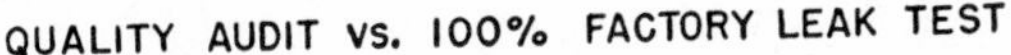

FIG. 17.8.

weed out all articles which may become defective early in actual operation. This is particularly true of possible borderline cases, where a second test is all that is required to show up the defect.

The value of the audit is further illustrated in Fig. 17.8, which compares the results of the regular production 100 per cent leak test with the

QUALITY PERFORMANCE—CLASS 6241 SUB-ASSEMBLIES

W/E 1-16

	QTY.	%	
COVERS			
ASSEMBLED	74,306		
MECHANICAL REJECTS	309	.42	B
COVERS 100% ELEC. TESTED	1,806		
NO. FAILURES	13	.72	B
WINDING			
ROLL PRODUCTION	113,226		
PARTIAL ROLL LOSS	5,672	5.	B
TEST LOSS	1,523	1.3	B
TREATING 70° P.F. CHECK			
LOTS CHECKED	10		
LOTS REJECTED	0	0	
BASE DEFLECTION LEAK TEST			
TESTED			
REJECTED	NONE		
OVEN LEAK TEST			
TESTED	8,526 *		
REJECTED	538	6.3	A
FINAL ELECTRICAL TEST			
TESTED	64,625		
REJECTED	2,556	4.	AB
% ACT. SCRAP — YR. TO DATE		4.7	B
B. D. ELIMINATION			
LOTS TESTED	9		
LOTS REJECTED	0		
PROCESS AVERAGE	1/1085	.09	A
FINAL PRODUCTION SAMPLING TEST			
MECHANICAL — INSPECTION (0.65% AQL)			
LOTS CHECKED	35		
LOTS REJECTED	0		
PROCESS AVERAGE	20/3960	.51	A
ELECTRICAL TEST (0.65% AQL)			
LOTS CHECKED	35		
LOTS REJECTED	2		
PROCESS AVERAGE	29/4395	.66	A
LEAK TEST (0.65% AQL)			
LOTS CHECKED	27		
LOTS REJECTED	0		
PROCESS AVERAGE	5/3055	.16	

A---REPAIRED B---SCRAPPED

* THIS SIZE PROD. SAMPLE TAKEN TO OBTAIN %

FIG. 17.9.

quality-audit samples. During the latter part of February, a sharp decline is shown in the percentage of leaks found by operators at the regular production test. Simultaneously, an increase in leaks is shown in the quality-audit sample results.

Investigation of this situation was initiated because of these dissimilar results. It revealed faulty operations of process ovens such that many of the subassemblies were not receiving the heat-treatment required to reveal a leaky unit. Had not the quality audit both rejected the defective lots before shipment and highlighted the need for corrective action, no steps might have been taken until floods of complaints began pouring in from customers.

Figure 17.9 shows a typical quality performance report, which presents a regular picture of subassembly-quality result. This report shows a quality index for each of the eight control stations. It is reviewed periodically by the process-control engineer as a basis for corrective action.

17.12 Assembly

An electromechanical assembly, composed of a number of intricate parts and built for extremely rigid customer quality requirements, is produced in the highest quantities of any product manufactured in a 1,000-employee plant. The assembly, subject to very high rejections at final electrical test and mechanical inspection, had been designed and in production before the plant instituted its total-quality-control program.

One of the first steps in developing an over-all quality-control plan for the assembly was carrying through a necessarily extremely abbreviated version of new-design-control activity. Most of the parts used in the assembly were purchased from outside vendors. Using requirements and quality levels developed during the new-design studies, an incoming-material-control routine was established through which these vendor parts would pass.

Those component parts processed by the plant itself were manufactured in a small-parts machine shop, where a process-sampling program had been instituted. The few subassemblies which were not purchased from outside sources were also made subject to process sampling.

When product-control activity was started for the assembly, its initial phase was utilization for standards-setting purposes of the new-design-control information. Several assembly fixtures were altered, regular maintenance checks were established for certain of these fixtures, and similar standards steps were taken.

Certain basic changes affecting the design, which the brief new-design studies showed would reduce rejections although not affect quality performance in the field, had to be bypassed, however. Excessive expense

QUALITY CONTROL CHART NUMBER X-1

PRODUCT Electro-mechanical Assembly MONTH January

STATION Final Inspection & Test CHARACTERISTIC All Defects

PER CENT DEFECTIVE

0 1 2 3 4 5 10 15

DATE	INSP.	DEF.	$
1/1	205	20	9.8
1/2	355	48	13.5
1/3	210	21	10
1/4	254	26	10.2
1/5	291	30	10.3
1/6	180	5	2.8
	1495	150	10
1/8	405	59	14.6
1/9	224	38	17
1/10	203	32	15.8
1/11	300	35	10.2
1/12	391	32	11
1/13	293	40	13.7
	1716	236	13,8
1/15	469	89	19
1/16	403	50	12.4
1/17	271	22	8.1
1/18	456	72	15.8
1/19	374	65	17.4
1/20	290	32	11
	2263	330	14.6
1/22	459	57	12.4
1/23	315	49	15.6
1/24	443	60	13.5
1/25	349	58	16.6
1/26	432	61	14.
1/27	592	85	14.4
	2590	370	14.3
1/29	473	110	23,3
1/30	446	67	15
1/31	312	34	10.8
2/1	514	73	14.2
2/2	184	25	13.6
2/3	428	51	11.9
	2 357	360	11.

1WK	1495	150	10
2WK	1716	236	13.8
3WK	2263	330	14.6
4WK	2590	370	14.3
5WK	2 357	360	13.9

MO	10421	1446	13,9

FIG. 17.10.

would otherwise have been incurred on an assembly where a large investment had been sunk in processing facilities and inventory.

The assembly itself was manufactured rapidly on a long bench, at which several employees were seated whose successive operations in applying parts and subassemblies quickly built up the product to its final form. Because of the critical quality specification, the assemblies were 100 per cent tested for performance and 100 per cent inspected for mechanical defects at the end of the bench.

The nature and speed of the assembly process made patrol inspection impractical and uneconomical as a phase in the control aspects of the product-control routine. The major control point, therefore, was at the final inspection and the final test stations.

Go and not-go control charts were plotted here, both charts for major individual quality characteristics and a single chart for all inspection and test defects combined. These control charts were directly tied in with daily reject breakdowns which, with the charts, were reviewed each morning as the basis for corrective action by the process-control engineer. Even more rapid hour-by-hour corrective action was initiated by the shop foreman based upon reject analyses provided him.

Frequency distributions on major performance characteristics were plotted semiweekly by the test organization, using random samples each composed of 50 assemblies. Each week, a quality audit sample of several units was selected from assemblies being packed for shipment; this sample was sent to the plant laboratory for rigorous test and examination. Data from these laboratory investigations were used for review by the Manager–Quality Control.

Figures 17.10 to 17.12 illustrate one aspect of the results produced by this over-all program. These figures show the "all defects combined" control chart plotted after final inspection and test and directly posted on the manufacturing floor. Figure 17.10 pictures the reject situation for the month of January, a situation that had existed on the assembly for the several-month period since it had reached its full weekly production rate.

Figure 17.11 pictures the February reject report, showing the gradual effect of the newly initiated quality-control program—fast corrective action initiated by process-control engineering on individual reject problems, the psychological effect on operators of control-chart posting, etc.

Figure 17.12 illustrates the situation for the month of March, the first month for which a control limit was plotted for shop view.[6] Shop management had decided that the 7 per cent all-reject level could be lived with and maintained economically, upon recognition that the highly expensive

[6] Figure 17.12 is similar to the control chart whose technical background was amplified in Sec. 11.27.

QUALITY CONTROL CHART NUMBER X-2

PRODUCT Electro-mechanical Assembly MONTH February

STATION Final Inspection & Test CHARACTERISTIC All Defects

DATE	INSP.	DEF.	$
2-5	472	63	13.3
2-6	359	57	15.9
2-7	303	38	12,5
2-8	381	41	10.8
2-9	429	54	12.8
2-10	443	54	12.9
	2387	307	12.9
2-12	445	46	10.1
2-13	328	48	14.6
2-14	190	32	16.8
2-15	469	51	10.9
2-16	527	40	7.6
2-17	504	58	11.5
	2373	278	11.5
2-19	379	40	10.6
2-20	380	56	14.7
2-21	371	38	10.2
2-22	329	47	14.3
2-23	465	65	14.
2-24	436	32	7.3
	2360	278	11.8
2-26	393	40	10.2
2-27	472	39	8.3
2-28	356	24	6.7
3-1	291	14	6.8
3-2	393	42	10.7
3-3	362	26	7.2
	2267	185	8.2

PER CENT DEFECTIVE

0 1 2 3 4 5 10 15 20 25

1 WK	2387	307	12.9
2 WK	2373	278	11.5
3 WK	2360	278	11.8
4 WK	2267	185	8.2
5 WK			

MO	9387	1043	11.1

FIG. 17.11.

QUALITY CONTROL CHART NUMBER X-3

PRODUCT Electro-mechanical Assembly MONTH March

STATION Final Inspection & Test CHARACTERISTIC All Defects

DATE	INSP.	DEF.	$
3/5	300	19	6.3
3/6	210	19	9
3/7	356	21	5.8
3/8	490	30	6.1
3/9	416	31	9.5
3/10	309	16	5.2
	2081	136	6.5
3/12	403	21	5.3
3/13	408	29	7.1
3/14	331	18	5.4
3/15	344	18	5.2
3/16	324	22	6.7
3/17	313	28	8.9
	2123	136	6.5
3/19	336	26	7.7
3/20	420	28	6.7
3/21	332	20	6
3/22	375	25	6.7
3/23	343	30	8.7
3/24	290	24	8
	2105	153	8
3/26	442	27	6.1
3/27	443	27	6.1
3/28	392	36	9.2
3/29	425	34	8
3/30	452	23	5.1
3/31	60	2	3.3
	2214	149	6.7

PER CENT DEFECTIVE

0 1 2 3 4 5 10 15

UPPER CONTROL LIMIT

1WK	2081	136	6.5
2WK	2123	136	6.5
3WK	2105	153	8.
4WK	2214	149	6.7
5WK			

MO	8523	607	7.1

FIG. 17.12.

design and processing changes suggested by the new-design studies would have to be made before this reject level could be substantially lowered.

This control situation was thereafter maintained for the assembly until its order commitments had been satisfied and production was ended in favor of a new model upon which extensive new-design-control activity had been conducted and whose design features permitted sharp reduction in the 7 per cent reject level.

17.13 Techniques Used in Product Control

As demonstrated by the procedures discussed above, there are a great many individual techniques that can be used in product control. These technical methods include a host of elements ranging from such readily identifiable quality-control techniques as process sampling and effective inspection procedures to such more general factors as adequate floor area, good factory housekeeping, and air conditioning.

Many of these were reviewed in Parts Three and Four. It may be worthwhile, however, to summarize some of the more significant of these that apply to product-control activity.

Setting and Maintenance of Standards. *Process-capability Studies.* With given combinations of materials, speeds, feeds, temperatures, coolants, etc., almost all processing operations have an inherent variation. This process "capability" is largely independent of specification tolerances for parts to be manufactured on the process. It is necessarily important to determine these capabilities as fundamental to product-control standards setting. Process-capability studies provide a basis for this determination and its related assignment of parts to those facilities which can economically maintain the required tolerances.

Tool, Die, Jig, and Fixture Control. Proper tooling is essential for control of product quality under all circumstances; with low-quantity, short-duration production, tooling is a basic product-control technique. New-design-control activities may specify the proper tools and dies; it is a fundamental product-control necessity to be thereafter assured of the continued effectiveness of these tools by regular examination before and/or after production runs to determine the desirability of sharpening, replacement, etc.

Preventive Maintenance. Machine tools and other major manufacturing equipment inevitably will wear under constant use. The resulting loose bearings and worn pins may cause poor-quality products. A program of preventive maintenance is an important quality-control technique, since it enables a regularly scheduled examination of processing facilities *before* they break down.

Accounting Standards on Quality. Quality-control data concerning inspection and test requirements, quality levels, and other quality cost factors are the most effective information available to accountants for the determination of the quality cost elements to be included in standard costs. Quality-cost goals can similarly be determined from these data. Such accounting determinations are a quality-control essential, since they furnish the economic basis for much of a plant quality-control program.

Control during Manufacture. *Shop Personnel Quality-mindedness.* Selection of employees with the proper aptitudes, training of these individuals in machine operating skills and in sound attitudes toward both the importance of product quality and their jobs in general, continued stimulation of the quality interests of these operators through their direct participation in plant quality activity and in refresher training if required, the return to and review with operators of the defective parts they have produced, regular physical examinations of employees to determine the need for such physical aids as glasses, competent supervision to provide the leadership needed on the shop floor for quality-mindedness —all are basic to product control.

Proper Material Flow. Quality can be economically and consistently built in material only if the factory floor layout permits proper routing of material accompanied by efficient materials handling which, at the very minimum, eliminates damage to parts in transit. Similarly important are satisfactory balances of inventory so that a lot of one type of part need not be subject to damage and deterioration on a stock-room shelf while its release to the assembly floor awaits a matching lot of another type of part.

System Planning for Mechanical Inspection and Electrical Test Procedures. Well-trained inspection and test personnel, supplied with the right gages and measuring equipments and placed at strategic locations in the production process, provide one of the most important elements of the manufacturing-control aspects of product control. The types of inspection or test that can be used vary all the way from first-piece checks to rigid 100 per cent examination—the choice being dependent upon the particular quality situation.

Control Charts. The control chart, by red-flagging potential causes of defects before they result in rejections, is the most useful of the statistical methods used in product control. With machine-shop parts, this complement to inspection effectiveness usually appears in the form of a measurements control chart, and its usual adaptation for assemblies is as a go and not-go chart.

Process-sampling Tables. Statistical process-sampling methods provide an efficient foundation for process-control activities. Process sampling is especially useful in component part processing, frequently in instances where the control chart is not readily applicable. Process sampling also is found valuable in control of subassembly manufacturing operations. This sampling may take the form of the regular selection of the same number of units every period. Or it may be a continuous "random-order" plan of the sort discussed in Sec. 12.25.

Tool-wear Studies. Reliable knowledge on the wear of tools is valuable information for many production decisions, as well as for product-control considerations involving matters like process-sampling frequencies. Measurements-control charts provide an excellent medium for studying wear, as illustrated by the wear pattern shown in Fig. 17.13. This figure illustrates one of the several tool-wear patterns; the tool literally seems to "cave in."

Acceptance Sampling Tables. Lots of parts may require a final sampling check before shipment. Acceptance sampling tables are generally used during this type of inspection.

Quality Audit. Experience has shown the usefulness of selecting a small

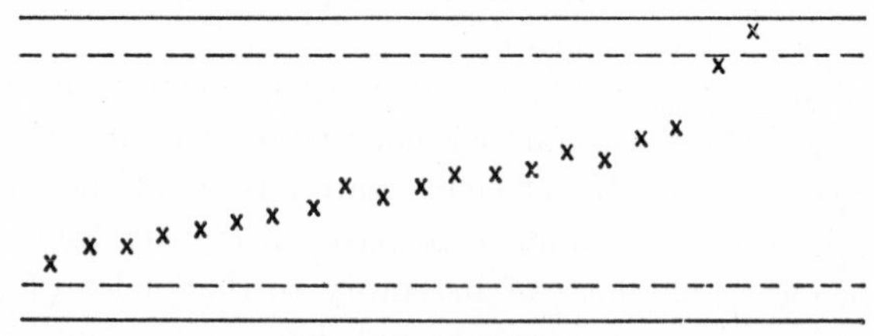

MEASUREMENTS CONTROL CHART SHOWING TOOL WEAR

FIG. 17.13.

sample from the production output after all other regular inspections and tests have been performed. This quality "audit" takes various forms under various circumstances: it may or may not be the basis for the release for shipment of the lot sampled; it may or may not be conducted on a more rigorous basis than the regular inspections or tests; it may or may not provide the data for a quality index for the product. Most quality audits point toward corrective action relating to equipment performance, inspection efficiency, operator skill, etc.

Quality Index. Of prime importance as a mirror of the effectiveness of a quality-control program on a product is maintenance of a regular index of the quality of that product. Such an index may be compiled from results of sampling, from 100 per cent inspection data, from quality-audit information. It may be developed by giving equal weight to all defects or by varying these weights.[7] The quality index is reported to manage-

[7] Section 11.23 discusses such indices.

ment on the same basis as the information received by management on production output, average labor take-home earnings, and other elements of the business.

Automatic Control Devices. There are small, specialized computers commercially available for calculating $\overline{X}$ (X-bar) and σ (sigma) for a given set of data. Chapter 9 discusses some of the techniques used for designing such quality information equipment. Some equipments are included in closed-loop arrangements whereby the manufacturing process is directly controlled by the feedback of quality information.

Disposing Defective Parts. Because of the danger that rejected parts may, without approval, find their way back into the production process, it is important that procedures be available for rapid disposition of such parts. These procedures will involve a rigid system of tagging, "holding for disposition," and routing. They will include a quality-control-component-sponsored review for disposition of those parts which have been rejected but which may be approved for repair. They will include a similar review of those rejects which may be approved for use "as is" in such special cases as when the cause for rejection is not critical to quality.

Major-part Record Forms. Particularly with expensive parts that are produced individually or in job lots for ultimate manufacture in an assembly, data forms may be maintained for control and record purposes. Figure 17.14 shows a portion of a typical form developed in connection with a shaft type.

Complaint Analyses. Records and analyses of customer complaint reports from the field furnish useful product-control information. While usually a considerable time lag exists between these reports and current production, they nonetheless both reflect the effectiveness of control programs and highlight those defects on which more aggressive corrective action must be initiated. Complaint reports on individual articles may also be the basis for intensification of product-control activity on similar articles.

Regular Quality Performance or Reject Breakdown Reports. A much more immediate indication than complaint reports of the adequacy of control measures is a quality performance record. Such a record, often in the form of a reject breakdown report, is frequently posted every hour, day, or week in conspicuous view of the manufacturing area. Figure 17.15 shows such a form for an armature assembly, in the form of a breakdown by individual charts on each of the major quality characteristics on which inspections and tests are made.

Control of Quality in Packaging and Shipping. A common quality danger for all products is damage during shipment. With intricate, finely adjusted assemblies that are improperly packaged, a severe jar during transportation may cause a shift in quality characteristics; with certain

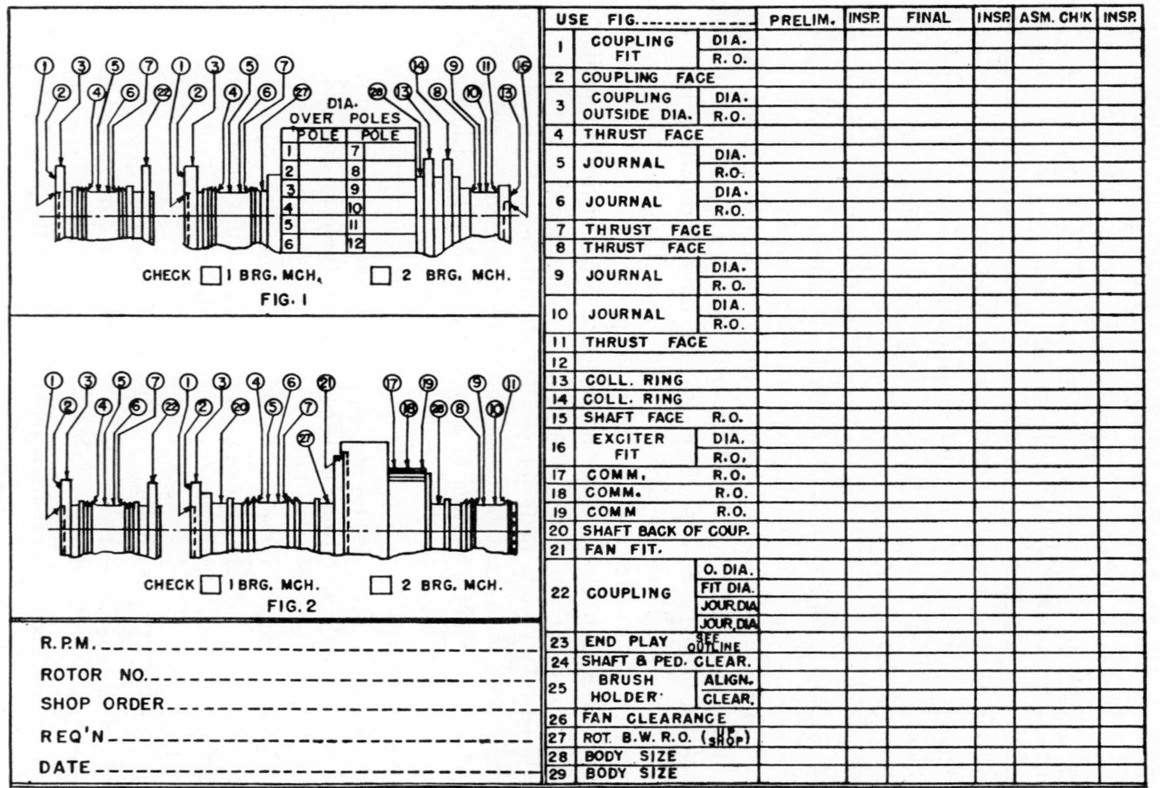

DIA. OVER POLES

POLE		POLE	
1		7	
2		8	
3		9	
4		10	
5		11	
6		12	

CHECK ☐ 1 BRG. MCH. ☐ 2 BRG. MCH.

FIG. 1

CHECK ☐ 1 BRG. MCH. ☐ 2 BRG. MCH.

FIG. 2

R.P.M. ______________________

ROTOR NO. ______________________

SHOP ORDER ______________________

REQ'N ______________________

DATE ______________________

USE FIG. ________			PRELIM.	INSP.	FINAL	INSP.	ASM. CH'K	INSP.
1	COUPLING FIT	DIA.						
		R.O.						
2	COUPLING FACE							
3	COUPLING OUTSIDE DIA.	DIA.						
		R.O.						
4	THRUST FACE							
5	JOURNAL	DIA.						
		R.O.						
6	JOURNAL	DIA.						
		R.O.						
7	THRUST FACE							
8	THRUST FACE							
9	JOURNAL	DIA.						
		R.O.						
10	JOURNAL	DIA.						
		R.O.						
11	THRUST FACE							
12								
13	COLL. RING							
14	COLL. RING							
15	SHAFT FACE	R.O.						
16	EXCITER FIT	DIA.						
		R.O.						
17	COMM.	R.O.						
18	COMM.	R.O.						
19	COMM	R.O.						
20	SHAFT BACK OF COUP.							
21	FAN FIT.							
22	COUPLING	O. DIA.						
		FIT DIA.						
		JOUR. DIA.						
		JOUR. DIA.						
23	END PLAY	SEE OUTLINE						
24	SHAFT & PED. CLEAR.							
25	BRUSH HOLDER	ALIGN.						
		CLEAR.						
26	FAN CLEARANCE							
27	ROT. B.W. R.O. (HP / SHOP)							
28	BODY SIZE							
29	BODY SIZE							

FIG. 17.14.

chemicals, a change in temperature during transit may cause product ruin. Great importance rests, therefore, upon adequate quality activity both during the design of the product container and during actual placement by shipping employees of the article in its container. The mode of transportation, the climate and temperature conditions, etc., all must be considered during this important phase of product control.

Control of Field Service. Although control of quality during manufacture of a product may have been excellent, there remain subsequent points for control. The importance of packing and shipping has been discussed. The next important point occurs at time of installation. For certain products this may be a very critical stage requiring the services of expert craftsmen. The installation of an air-conditioning system falls in this category. Any dirt entering the piping for the refrigerant can ruin the compressor, completely negating the precision machining done at the factory. If moisture is allowed to enter the system, its effectiveness is greatly diminished.

The quality-system plan for a device should include complete installation instructions prepared with great care so that they will be understood and followed by the craftsman of average ability.

Also important is the quality of workmanship used in later servicing and repairing of a device. This is especially true where the product requires service due to some deficiency on the part of the manufacturer. Such deficiency might be forgiven by the customer if he can get prompt, courteous service at little or no cost to him. If, however, the service is slow, or expensive, or requires repeated service calls, the customer becomes not only dissatisfied but irate. He may not only refuse to purchase the offending company's products, but he may also actively condemn the company and its products to his associates. The value of an efficient, well-trained field-service organization as a builder of good will can scarcely be over-emphasized.

Details of two representative examples of these technical methods will be discussed below, as follows: Process-capability Studies, in Secs. 17.14 through 17.18; Quality Audit, in Secs. 17.19 and 17.20.

Process-capability Studies

17.14 Background

The facilities selected for manufacture of a part are an important determinant of the cost and quality of the resulting production. If the processing equipment selected is sufficiently accurate to meet the quality target as established by drawing tolerances, then reasonable costs and acceptable quality can be expected. If the processing equipment cannot

ARMATURE CHARTS

WEEK ENDING ....

WINDING

BOGEY: 0.00 0.05 0.10 0.15 0.20 0.25 0.30

	NAME →	PREVIOUS WEEK →	DAY'S SUMMARY
M	NUMBER REJECTS		
	NUMBER STARTED		
	% DEFECTIVE		
T	NUMBER REJECTS		
	NUMBER STARTED		
	% DEFECTIVE		
W	NUMBER REJECTS		
	NUMBER STARTED		
	% DEFECTIVE		
T	NUMBER REJECTS		
	NUMBER STARTED		
	% DEFECTIVE		
F	NUMBER REJECTS		
	NUMBER STARTED		
	% DEFECTIVE		
S	NUMBER REJECTS		
	NUMBER STARTED		
	% DEFECTIVE		

PRE-BALANCE

BOGEY: 0 .02 .04 .06 .08 .10 .12

	NAME →	PREVIOUS WEEK →	DAY'S SUMMARY
M	NUMBER REJECTS		
	NUMBER STARTED		
	% DEFECTIVE		
T	NUMBER REJECTS		
	NUMBER STARTED		
	% DEFECTIVE		
W	NUMBER REJECTS		
	NUMBER STARTED		
	% DEFECTIVE		
T	NUMBER REJECTS		
	NUMBER STARTED		
	% DEFECTIVE		
F	NUMBER REJECTS		
	NUMBER STARTED		
	% DEFECTIVE		
S	NUMBER REJECTS		
	NUMBER STARTED		
	% DEFECTIVE		

ELECTRICAL TEST AFTER LEAD CLEANING

	NAME →	PREVIOUS WEEK →	DAY'S SUMMARY
M	NUMBER REJECTS		
	NUMBER STARTED		
	% DEFECTIVE		
T	NUMBER REJECTS		
	NUMBER STARTED		
	% DEFECTIVE		
W	NUMBER REJECTS		
	NUMBER STARTED		
	% DEFECTIVE		
T	NUMBER REJECTS		
	NUMBER STARTED		
	% DEFECTIVE		
F	NUMBER REJECTS		
	NUMBER STARTED		
	% DEFECTIVE		
S	NUMBER REJECTS		
	NUMBER STARTED		
	% DEFECTIVE		

FINAL ELECTRICAL TEST

BOGEY: 2.00 2.50 3.00 3.50 4.00 4.50 5.00

	NAME →	PREVIOUS WEEK →	DAY'S SUMMARY
M	NUMBER REJECTS		
	NUMBER STARTED		
	% DEFECTIVE		
T	NUMBER REJECTS		
	NUMBER STARTED		
	% DEFECTIVE		
W	NUMBER REJECTS		
	NUMBER STARTED		
	% DEFECTIVE		
T	NUMBER REJECTS		
	NUMBER STARTED		
	% DEFECTIVE		
F	NUMBER REJECTS		
	NUMBER STARTED		
	% DEFECTIVE		
S	NUMBER REJECTS		
	NUMBER STARTED		
	% DEFECTIVE		

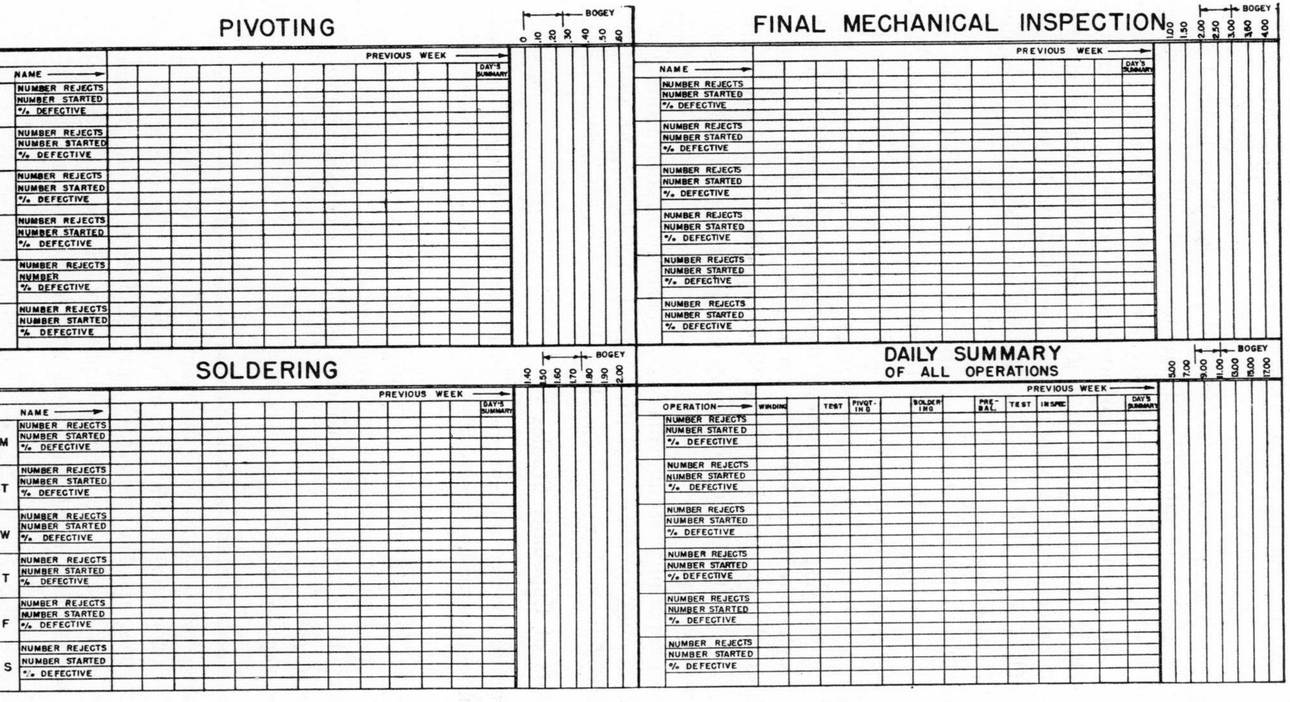
PIVOTING
BOGEY
0 .10 .20 .30 .40 .50 .60
PREVIOUS WEEK
NAME
DAY'S SUMMARY
NUMBER REJECTS
NUMBER STARTED
% DEFECTIVE
FINAL MECHANICAL INSPECTION
1.00 1.50 2.00 2.50 3.00 3.50 4.00
SOLDERING
1.40 1.50 1.60 1.70 1.80 1.90 2.00
M
T
W
T
F
S
DAILY SUMMARY
OF ALL OPERATIONS
5.00 7.00 9.00 11.00 13.00 15.00 17.00
OPERATION
WINDING
TEST
PIVOTING
SOLDERING
PRE-BAL.
TEST
INSPEC

FIG. 17.15.

consistently meet the quality target, then high costs, scrap, and reworked materials are inevitable outcomes.

In some shops, experienced operators and foremen have learned from long experience that "Machine 27 can handle the close turning work up to ±0.002 inch and machine 33 is better for the work from ±0.003 to ±0.006 inch." Not all shops are so fortunate as to possess this experience however. Even in the shops where a great deal is known about the capabilities of processing equipments, it is very rare to have this information in such a form that it can be shared with designing engineers, planners, and manufacturing engineers.

Since such knowledge about the performance capability of processing equipment is essential to the proper functioning of a quality-control program, many plants have made scientific investigation of these capabilities a keystone of their entire product- and process-control program. In so doing, they were forced to develop techniques for this investigation which were more effective for quality-control purposes than the old rule-of-thumb techniques that had prevailed for many years. One of the most useful of the techniques developed for this work is the process-capability study.

The process-capability study consists essentially of determining the capability of a single process operation, always in relation to the individual quality characteristic of a part. It is discussed in some detail below.

17.15 Concepts of Capability Studies

Process capability is a measurement with respect to the inherent precision of a manufacturing process.

As a definition:

Process capability is quality-performance capability of the process with given factors and under normal, in-control conditions.

Two significant elements in this concept of process capability are

1. Process *factors*
2. Process *conditions*

1. The first consideration necessary to the concept of process capability is that a process is made up of a number of distinct factors. These factors include raw material, machine or equipment, the operator's skill, measuring devices, and the inspector's skill. A change in one or more of these factors may change the process capability. Hence, a process capability to be meaningful must be stated with respect to a given set of specifically listed process factors.

2. The second element contained in the definition is that involving process conditions. For a process capability study to be meaningful, the process being analyzed should be one that has measurements *normally distributed and in a state of statistical control.* As was shown in Chap. 10,

normality is essential to the identification of a process pattern and determination of how that pattern relates to the specification requirement. Chap. 11 discussed statistical control and showed that only a controlled process is a predictable process. A process capability value to be useful must have an established pattern that is consistent over a period of time.

Mathematically the process capability is defined as six standard deviation units (6σ). As was developed in Chapter 10, 99.73 per cent of all the readings for a normal distribution fall within the area bounded by plus and minus 3 standard deviation units from the mean. So, a process capability study, mathematically, is merely a well-organized, carefully disciplined frequency distribution analysis of the appropriate process data. The formula for the process capability is, therefore, formula (4) for sigma in Chap. 10 multiplied by 6. It is

$$\text{Process capability} = 6\sigma = 6\sqrt{\frac{\Sigma(X - \overline{X})^2}{n}}$$

where σ = standard deviation of the sample
$X_1, X_2, \cdots, X_n$ = individual measurements
$\overline{X}$ = arithmetic mean of the individual measurements
n = number of individual measurements

Conducting the Study. A process capability study should be conducted under normal operating conditions with a single set of factors making up the manufacturing process. For example, a study should use a single batch of raw material, a single operator, and a single inspector throughout the period during which data are being collected. The operator should avoid feeding "corrections" into the process or making adjustments during the study.

Recalibration of the measuring equipment during this period should be avoided unless it is "normally" calibrated at frequent intervals. All of these separate factors are subject to variation over long periods of time, so it is advisable to make several separate studies at widely separated intervals to determine the effects of normally varying factors on the process capability.

The capability study should contain a sufficient number of measurement readings so that a representative sample is obtained. For most operations, a minimum of 50 readings should be adequate.

The order of the readings should be preserved. It is advisable to tag items with a numbered tag as they come off the process. Their identity is then retained. If some question arises later with regard to the accuracy of measurement, a recheck can be made. Caution should be exercised in making rechecks to take into account possible changes that might occur with time, i.e., change in dimension due to a part dropping in temperature, decrease in moisture content, etc.

If the recorded readings are plotted in order of production on an ordinary graph, it is often possible to gain further information about the process than if the readings were merely accumulated into a frequency distribution. This simple technique often reveals short, erratic periods in the process. Since such erratic periods are not predictable, they need to be eliminated and controlled before a meaningful process-capability study can be made.

17.16 Calculation of the Process Capability

There are several ways of calculating the capability of a process. One is to go through the rather cumbersome procedure of using formula (4).

A rather rapid method for calculating a process capability will be discussed here. This method involves the use of a process capability worksheet used in conjunction with a nomograph. It uses a variation of formula (4)—shown below as formula (39). A worksheet, shown in Fig. 17.17, assists in computing the two factors Σfd and Σfd^2 in this formula:

$$\sigma = i\sqrt{\frac{\Sigma fd^2}{n} - \left(\frac{\Sigma fd}{n}\right)^2} \tag{39}$$

The white-on-black numbers (hereafter called white numbers) are the fd values, and the black-on-white numbers (hereafter called black numbers) are the fd^2 values. The sheet (Fig. 17.17) is arranged so that the vertical scale is the quality characteristic under investigation and the horizontal scale is the frequency with which the various sizes of the characteristic are encountered in the sample taken.

To illustrate its use, a process capability will be calculated for a process used for milling stainless steel bars to a thickness of 0.12 ± .003 inch. A capability study was run on milling machine #3 during the first shift with stainless steel on operation #35. Measurements in inches were:

1	.1220	11	.1200	21	.1205	31	.1210	41	.1205
2	.1205	12	.1215	22	.1200	32	.1220	42	.1200
3	.1210	13	.1210	23	.1220	33	.1200	43	.1210
4	.1210	14	.1220	24	.1205	34	.1215	44	.1210
5	.1210	15	.1210	25	.1210	35	.1210	45	.1215
6	.1215	16	.1215	26	.1215	36	.1200	46	.1210
7	.1210	17	.1215	27	.1205	37	.1225	47	.1205
8	.1215	18	.1220	28	.1205	38	.1210	48	.1205
9	.1205	19	.1210	29	.1215	39	.1210	49	.1210
10	.1210	20	.1195	30	.1210	40	.1215	50	.1215

In Fig. 17.16, these readings are plotted in the order which they were produced over time and also are cumulated into a frequency distribution.

The steps in calculating the process capability on the basis of these readings are as follows:

1. Average the first 5 measurements. This average (.1211) shows that the distribution is tending to center around .1210.

2. Establish this (.1210) as the nominal point (zero) in the "variation from nominal column" (Fig. 17.17).

If some other value, such as .1215 or .1205, were chosen, this would not affect the result. The objective is to center the distribution so there will be an adequate number of cells on both sides of the mean to accommodate all the data.

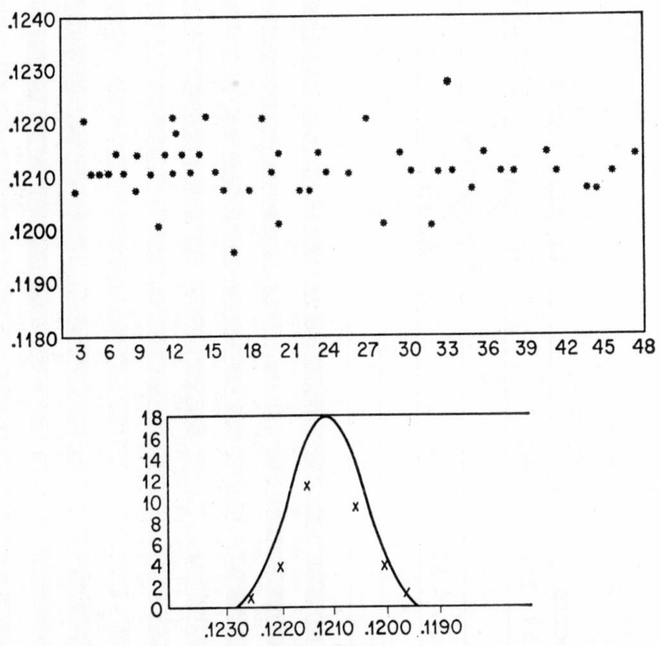

FIG. 17.16. Measurements in sequence and frequency distribution.

3. Assign appropriate "coded" values to each cell and write these in the column headed "actual size" opposite respective cells. In this example, the measurements are in increments of .0005 inch. If .1210 is chosen as the 0 cell, then .1215 is written opposite the +1 cell, .1205 opposite the −1 cell, etc.

4. Circle the single set of white and black numbers in the frequency (f) column that corresponds to the frequency of occurrence in each respective cell.

5. Transcribe white and black numbers to their respective columns

PROCESS CAPABILITY STUDY

MACHINE OR PROCESS MILLING #3

DATE 11/20/59 FIRST SHIFT

TOOLS

CYCLE TIME 2. 4 MINUTES

PROCESS CAPABILITY VALUE .0037"

MATERIAL STAINLESS STEEL

OPERATION #35

SIGNED

THICKNESS

Frequency - f

ACTUAL SIZE	Variation from Nominal	1	2	3	4	5	6	7	8	9	10	11	12	13	14	15	16	17	18	19	20	21	22	23	24	25	White	Black
	+ 10	10	20	30	40	50	60	70	80	90	100	110	120	130	140	150	160	170	180	190	200	210	220	230	240	250	+	
		100	200	300	400	500	600	700	800	900	1000	1100	1200	1300	1400	1500	1600	1700	1800	1900	2000	2100	2200	2300	2400	2500		
	+ 9	9	18	27	36	45	54	63	72	81	90	99	108	117	126	135	144	153	162	171	180	189	198	207	216	225	+	
		81	162	243	324	405	486	567	648	729	810	891	972	1053	1134	1215	1296	1377	1458	1539	1620	1701	1782	1863	1944	2025		
	+ 8	8	16	24	32	40	48	56	64	72	80	88	96	104	112	120	128	136	144	152	160	168	176	184	192	200	+	
		64	128	192	256	320	384	448	512	576	640	704	768	832	896	960	1024	1088	1152	1216	1280	1344	1408	1472	1536	1600		
	+ 7	7	14	21	28	35	42	49	56	63	70	77	84	91	98	105	112	119	126	133	140	147	154	161	168	175	+	
		49	98	147	196	245	294	343	392	441	490	539	588	637	686	735	784	833	882	931	980	1029	1078	1127	1196	1225		
	+ 6	6	12	18	24	30	36	42	48	54	60	66	72	78	84	90	96	102	108	114	120	126	132	138	144	150	+	
		36	72	108	144	180	216	252	288	324	360	396	432	468	504	540	576	612	648	684	720	756	792	828	864	900		
	+ 5	5	10	15	20	25	30	35	40	45	50	55	60	65	70	75	80	85	90	95	100	105	110	115	120	125	+	
		25	50	75	100	125	150	175	200	225	250	275	300	325	350	375	400	425	450	475	500	525	550	575	600	625		
	+ 4	4	8	12	16	20	24	28	32	36	40	44	48	52	56	60	64	68	72	76	80	84	88	92	96	100	+	
		16	32	48	64	80	96	112	128	144	160	176	192	208	224	240	256	272	288	304	320	336	352	368	384	400		
.1225"	+ 3	3	6	9	12	15	18	21	24	27	30	33	36	39	42	45	48	51	54	57	60	63	66	69	72	75	+ 3	9
		9	18	27	36	45	54	63	72	81	90	99	108	117	126	135	144	153	162	171	180	189	198	207	216	225		
.1220	+ 2	2	4	6	8	10	12	14	16	18	20	22	24	26	28	30	32	34	36	38	40	42	44	46	48	50	+ 10	20
		4	8	12	16	20	24	28	32	36	40	44	48	52	56	60	64	68	72	76	80	84	88	92	96	100		
.1215	+ 1	1	2	3	4	5	6	7	8	9	10	11	12	13	14	15	16	17	18	19	20	21	22	23	24	25	+ 11	11
		1	2	3	4	5	6	7	8	9	10	11	12	13	14	15	16	17	18	19	20	21	22	23	24	25		

	Variation																										White	Black
.1210	0	0	0	0	0	0	0	0	0	0	0	0	0	0	0	0	0	0	0	0	0	0	0	0	0	0		
.1205	- 1	1	2	3	4	5	6	7	8	9	10	11	12	13	14	15	16	17	18	19	20	21	22	23	24	25	- 9	9
		1	2	3	4	5	6	7	8	9	10	11	12	13	14	15	16	17	18	19	20	21	22	23	24	25		
.1200	- 2	2	4	6	8	10	12	14	16	18	20	22	24	26	28	30	32	34	36	38	40	42	44	46	48	50	- 10	20
		4	8	12	16	20	24	28	32	36	40	44	48	52	56	60	64	68	72	76	80	84	88	92	96	100		
.1195	- 3	3	6	9	12	15	18	21	24	27	30	33	36	39	42	45	48	51	54	57	60	63	66	69	72	75	- 3	9
		9	18	27	36	45	54	63	72	81	90	99	108	117	126	135	144	153	162	171	180	189	198	207	216	225		
	- 4	4	8	12	16	20	24	28	32	36	40	44	48	52	56	60	64	68	72	76	80	84	88	92	96	100	-	
		16	32	48	64	80	96	112	128	144	160	176	192	208	224	240	256	272	288	304	320	336	352	368	384	400		
	- 5	5	10	15	20	25	30	35	40	45	50	55	60	65	70	75	80	85	90	95	100	105	110	115	120	125	-	
		25	50	75	100	125	150	175	200	225	250	275	300	325	350	375	400	425	450	475	500	525	550	575	600	625		
	- 6	6	12	18	24	30	36	42	48	54	60	66	72	78	84	90	96	102	108	114	120	126	132	138	144	150	-	
		36	72	108	144	180	216	252	288	324	360	396	432	468	504	540	576	612	648	684	720	756	792	828	864	900		
	- 7	7	14	21	28	35	42	49	56	63	70	77	84	91	98	105	112	119	126	133	140	147	154	161	168	175	-	
		49	98	147	196	245	294	343	392	441	490	539	588	637	686	735	784	833	882	931	980	1029	1078	1127	1196	1225		
	- 8	8	16	24	32	40	48	56	64	72	80	88	96	104	112	120	128	136	144	152	160	168	176	184	192	200	-	
		64	128	192	256	320	384	448	512	576	640	704	768	832	896	960	1024	1088	1152	1216	1280	1344	1408	1472	1536	1600		
	- 9	9	18	27	36	45	54	63	72	81	90	99	108	117	126	135	144	153	162	171	180	189	198	207	216	225	-	
		81	162	243	324	405	486	567	648	729	810	891	972	1053	1134	1215	1296	1377	1458	1539	1620	1701	1782	1863	1944	2025		
	- 10	10	20	30	40	50	60	70	80	90	100	110	120	130	140	150	160	170	180	190	200	210	220	230	240	250	-	
		100	200	300	400	500	600	700	800	900	1000	1100	1200	1300	1400	1500	1600	1700	1800	1900	2000	2100	2200	2300	2400	2500		
																										Totals White & Black	+2	78

INSTRUCTIONS

1. Sample size must be 25 or 50 pieces. These should be the first 25 or 50 pieces produced after the machine or process has been set up and properly adjusted.

2. Measurement should be done with accurate gages, i.e., micrometers, electro-limit gages, etc.

3. The tally of the pieces checked can be accomplished by circling the red and black number combination which corresponds to the proper frequency (f) and the proper variation from nominal.

4. After the tally has been completed, the largest value circled for each individual variation should be carried to the proper column at the right of the table.

   a. The White numbers should be placed in the White column and the black numbers in the Black column.
   b. The White column must be added algebraically and the total placed in the box marked Total White.
   c. The Black column must be added arithmetically and the total placed in the box marked Total Black.

5. These totals White and Black can now be transferred to the process-capability nomograph to obtain process capability value.

6. The unit probability value will depend on the unit assigned to the sample, i.e., .0001", .001", etc.

FIG. 17.17. Process-capability sheet.

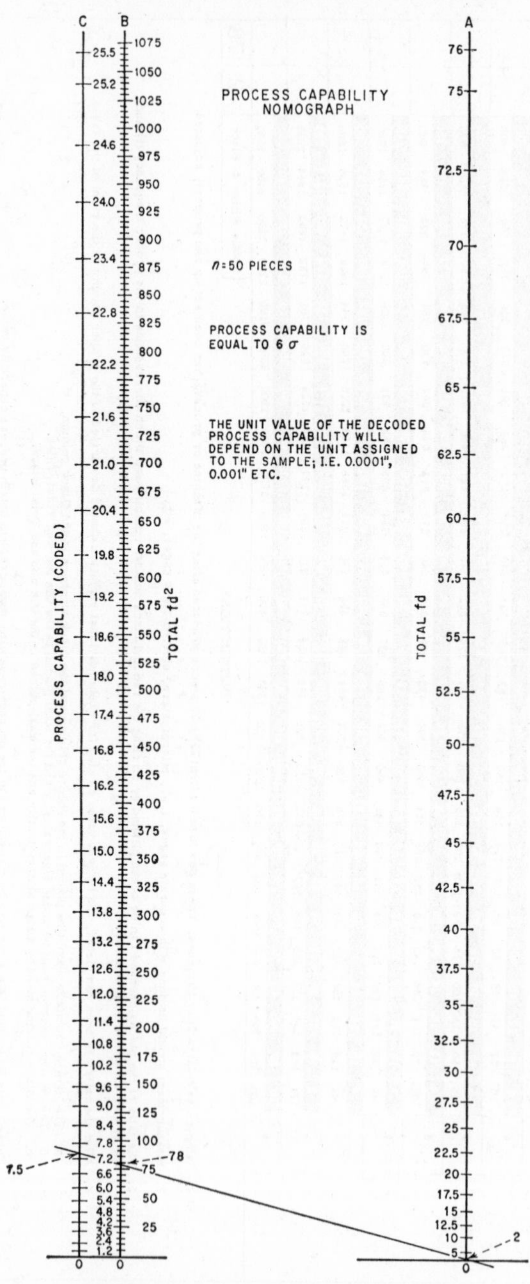

FIG. 17.18. Process-capability nomograph.

on the extreme right-hand edge of the worksheet. These columns are added. Note that the "white" column contains both positive and negative numbers and must be added algebraically. The "white" sum corresponds to Σfd and the "black" sum to Σfd^2 values computed by the longhand method of calculation shown in Sec. 10.15.

6. The white numbers' and black numbers' totals, 2 and 78, are then entered in columns A and B, respectively, on the process-capability nomograph shown in Fig. 17.18. A straight line is passed through these points on columns A and B to intersect column C. At this point, the coded process capability is read in column C, which in this case is 7.5.

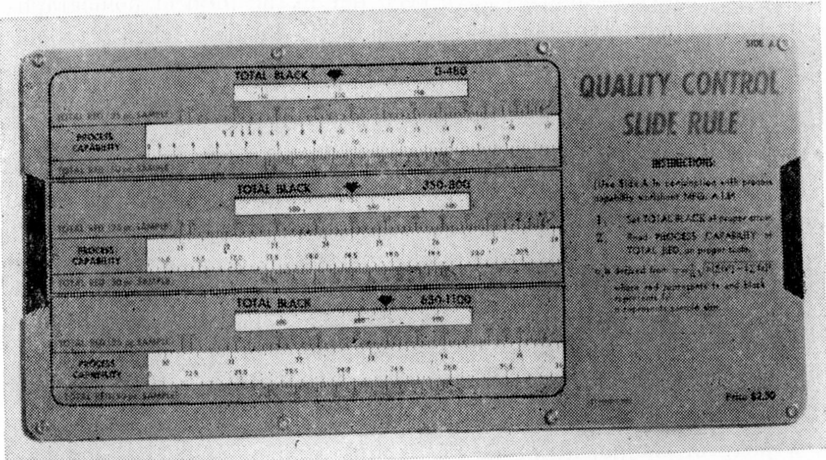

FIG. 17.19. Process-capability slide rule.

7. "Decode" the process capability value read in column C by multiplying it by the incremental value represented by one cell width, in this case, .0005 inch. The result is the process capability of .0037 inch.

Slide rules have been developed that accomplish the same purpose as the nomograph. Figure 17.19 shows such a slide rule. The worksheet could have been used independently of the nomograph by substituting the white numbers' and black numbers' totals into the equation.

$$\text{Process capability} = 6\sigma = 6i\sqrt{\frac{\Sigma fd^2}{n} + \left(\frac{\Sigma fd}{n}\right)^2}$$

$$= 6(.0005 \text{ inch})\sqrt{\frac{78}{50} + \left(\frac{2}{50}\right)^2}$$

$$= .0037 \text{ inch}$$

17.17 Use of Process-capability Studies

Now that methods for computing process capability have been demonstrated, the application of the results next will be considered.

The applications considered here include

1. Information to facilitate the design of the product.
2. Acceptance of a new or reconditioned piece of equipment.
3. Scheduling work to machines.
4. Selection of operators.
5. Setting up the machine for a production run.
6. Establishing control limits for equipment that has a narrow process capability in comparison with the allowable tolerance band.
7. Determining the economic nominal around which to operate when the process capability exceeds the tolerance.

The last three techniques have been put in the form of nomographs.

1. Information to Facilitate the Design of the Product. When a product is being designed, an important area to be considered is the machines available to manufacture such a product. Process-capability values for the available machines and the corresponding quality characteristics provide the designer with a realistic approach to his work. New equipment needs will be highlighted when the present machines are not capable of producing the tolerances required by the design. Designing products both to fit existing equipment capabilities and to highlight new equipment needs will help in quality planning. Furthermore, reduced losses, smoother conversion to the new design, and faster scheduling will result.

2. Acceptance of a New or Reconditioned Piece of Equipment. The new equipment needs that were mentioned above must be fulfilled and must be capable of producing the dimension required. Before accepting the new piece of equipment, process-capability studies should be conducted for assurance that the machine is adequate for the job to be performed. Process-capability studies can also be used by a manufacturer before shipping a piece of equipment to assure that it meets its guaranteed performance.

3. Scheduling Work to Machines. Different machines that create the same type of characteristics may have different process capabilities because of such factors as make, size, age, model, and the like. Various product designs, scheduled through the manufacturing, may have different tolerances for the same type of characteristics to be generated. By knowing the capabilities of the machines, these products can be so scheduled to minimize or eliminate rework and scrap costs. To illustrate this, consider a machine shop with three lathes of different makes. The characteristic that they are creating is the turned diameter of the parts produced. After a series of process-capability studies, the results are tabulated below. It not only is found that the lathes are different in capability but also that they will vary according to the material used.

Lathe	Process-capability value	
	Soft brass	Stainless steel
A	.001 inch	.003 inch
B	.002 inch	.004 inch
C	.005 inch	.007 inch

With this information in hand, it is possible to assign work such that the tolerance specified on a given job determines the machine to which that job is assigned. For example, if a turned diameter of soft brass were specified as $0.969 \pm .002$ inch, the total tolerance band is .004 inch. This job would necessarily have to be assigned to either lathe B or lathe A, since these are the only lathes in the shop capable of producing that class of work. If there is a possibility that parts with a tighter tolerance than this might be scheduled during this time, in all probability, lathe B would be used for this particular job.

It is advisable, whenever possible, that the process-capability value should not exceed 75 per cent of the total tolerance.

4. Selection of Operators. It should be pointed out that process-capability studies can be run where no machine is involved. Take one case that was studied, namely, the adjustment of thermostats. These were adjusted by means of an adjusting screw which was turned until an indicator light came on. The only tool involved was a knob which had no influence on the process. Twelve operators were involved, and the thermostats were all of the same design and went to the operators in a random manner from the fabrication process. The effectiveness of the adjusting process was measured by the temperature at which the thermostat closed under operating conditions.

Some very interesting results were obtained. As might be expected, the process-capability value was large when an operator first started on the job and generally narrowed appreciably with experience. However, there were two operators who showed no improvement. They were finally placed in other jobs since they were incapable of adjusting thermostats. On the other hand, there was one operator who exhibited outstanding skill, having a process-capability value (6σ) of approximately half the average operators. Figure 17.20 shows schematically how the process-capability value changed with time for each operator. Here is a good example of how a process-capability study enabled a foreman to select operators best fitted for a certain exacting operation.

5. Setting Up a Machine for a Production Run. When readying a piece of equipment for a production run, it is necessary to assure that the machine will be set up to produce parts that are within the engineering tolerance. This is done by measuring some of the first parts produced, and on the basis of what is found, the machine is either accepted for that production run or is readjusted and other parts subsequently checked. The questions raised are (1) "How many measurements need to be made?" (2) "Between what limits should these measurements fall to assure that the machine is properly set?" (3) "The measurements falling outside of what limits indicate that the machine needs to be readjusted?" In order to answer these questions, one must first know the

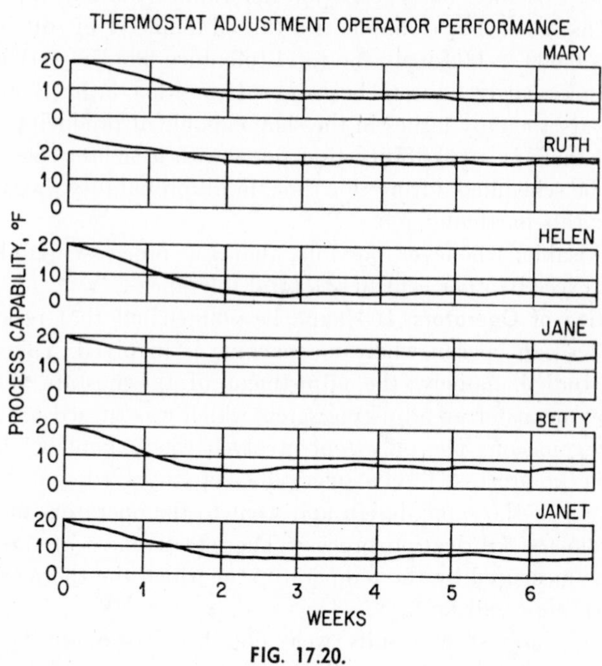

FIG. 17.20.

process capability of the machine and the acceptable quality level of the characteristic created.

With this information, the above questions can then be answered. A nomograph has been developed for easy calculation of this information. To illustrate the use of the nomograph shown in Fig. 17.21, consider the example just used and presented in the preceding section. In this example, a turned diameter of soft brass was specified as 0.969 ± .002 inch, for a total tolerance band of .004 inch. This job was assigned to lathe B, which had a process capability of .002 inch for soft brass. So the process capability of the lathe expressed as a per cent of the tolerance is .002 inch/.004 inch = 50 per cent. This point is so marked on Fig. 17.21 and labeled point D. The quality level (AQL) for this dimension is 2.5

per cent and is marked point E on Fig. 17.21. A straight line (1) is drawn connecting points D and E and extended until it intersects pivot line 2 at point F. The sample size now is chosen and marked on the scale labeled

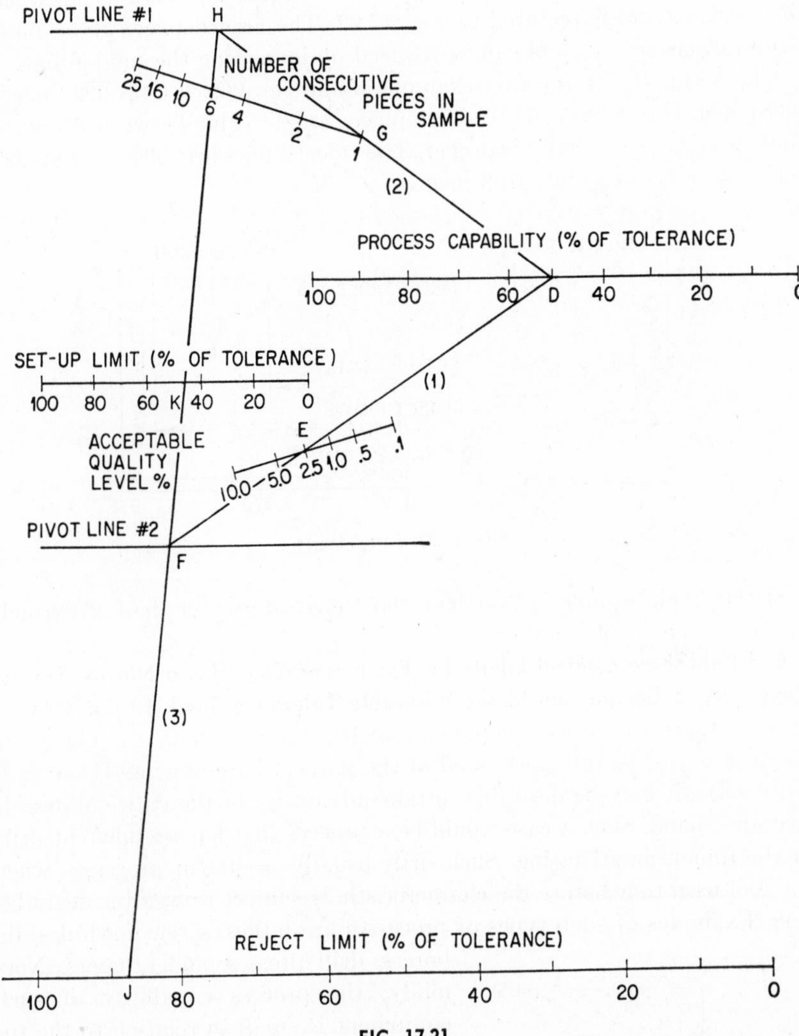

FIG. 17.21.

"Number of Consecutive Pieces in Sample." Assume that only a single piece is desired in the sample. This is marked as point G. A straight line (2) is drawn connecting points D and G and extended until it intersects pivot line 1 at point H. A straight line (3) is now drawn connecting points

F and H and extended to intersect the reject limit, marked point J. The point at which this line bisects the setup limit (point K) yields the limit within which the setup is acceptable. This limit is expressed as a per cent of tolerance and is pictured in Fig. 17.22. The point at which this line intersects the reject limit (point J) yields the limit outside of which the setup needs to be adjusted. Once again, this limit is expressed as a per cent of tolerance and is pictured in Fig. 17.22. The area between these limits is an indecision area and can be reduced by increasing the sample size.

The setup limits for this example would be .969 ± (.45).002 inch = .9681 inch and .9699 inch. A single piece sample value between these two limits indicates the setup is proper. The reject limits are .969 ± (.88) (.002 inch) = .9672 inch and .9708 inch.

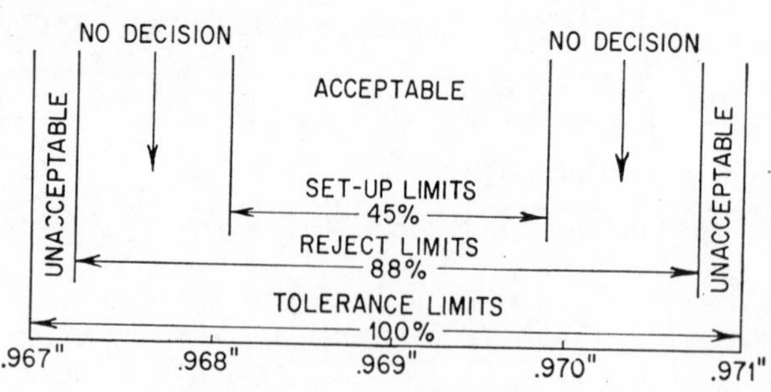

FIG. 17.22. Setup limits.

If the single sample is less than .9672 inch or greater than .9709 inch, the setup should be readjusted.

6. Establishing Control Limits for Equipment That Has a Narrow Process Capability in Comparison to the Allowable Tolerance Band. In many types of operations, the process capability of the equipment used is narrow in comparison to the tolerance band of the parts it is producing. When such is the case, it may be desirable to take advantage of the entire allowable tolerance band. Such a case would be a process that has an inherent drift in the dimensional setting. Such drift usually occurs in processes when the tool used to generate the characteristic is subject to wear or degradation. Examples of such types of processes are lathes, screw machines, jig borers, drill presses, and grinders. Normally, the process capability of such equipment is small in relation to the total allowable tolerance, and the setting can drift within tolerances. Such a condition is shown in Fig. 17.23.

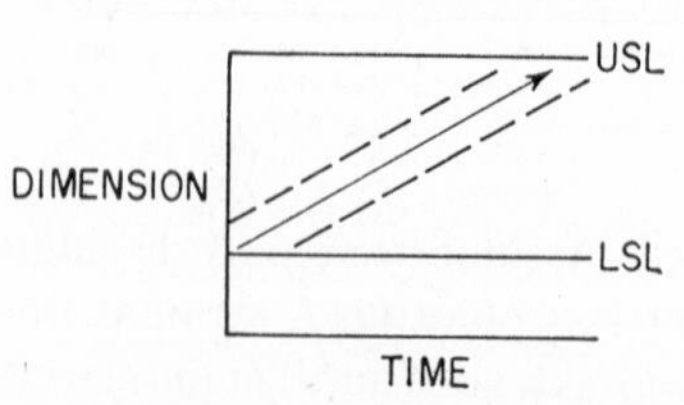

FIG. 17.23. Tool-wear rate.

The problem that arises in such cases is to set control limits that will allow one to take full advantage of the tolerance band and yet have assurance that an excessive number of parts out of tolerance are not being produced.

A nomograph has been derived to assist in determining the proper control limits. This is shown in Fig. 17.24 and consists of four variables. Once two of these variables are chosen, the other two are fixed. These variables are

1. The sample size used (n). This is column A.
2. p_1 per cent (column B). This is the minimum per cent of parts out of tolerance that one could expect if the average of the sample fell directly on the control limit.
3. p_2 per cent (column C). This is the maximum per cent of parts out of tolerance one could expect if the average of the sample fell directly on the control limit.
4. The distance the control limit is inside the specification limit and expressed as a per cent of the process capability (column D).

For instance, consider the example used previously where a turned diameter of soft brass was specified as 0.969 ± .002 inch for a tolerance band of .004 inch.

Previously, this job was assigned to lathe B with a process capability of .002 inch, but for this example, it is assigned to lathe A with a process capability of .001 inch. Here the process capability is small in comparison to the total allowable tolerance (25 per cent). A sample size of 4 is taken periodically. This is marked as point R on Fig. 17.24. Further, a maximum of 2 per cent parts out of limits at any time is established. This is marked as point S on Fig. 17.24. A straight line (1) is drawn between points R and S. This establishes the distance between the control limit and the specification limit to be 45 per cent of the capability (point T), and the minimum per cent out of tolerance, for a sample falling on this control limit, to be .05 per cent (point U).

7. Determining the Economic Nominal Around Which to Operate When the Process Capability Exceeds the Tolerance. Many dimensions are so set that an undersize part will result in scrap and an oversize part can be reworked. The cost of scrap may be greater than that for rework, or it may be that the rework cost is greater than the scrap cost. If the process capability of such a process for some reason exceeds the tolerance band, it may be necessary to continue the operation until such time as the process capability can be improved. However, during that time defective parts have been made, resulting in scrap and rework dollars. Rather than minimize the per cent defective produced, a shift of the nominal toward the lesser cost side of the tolerance may be desirable to reduce the total defective-quality dollars to a minimum.

A nomograph has been derived to assist in computing the amount to shift the average from nominal to realize the lowest cost situation. This consists in four variables and is shown in Fig. 17.25. These variables are

1. Tolerance band. This is the width of the tolerance band beyond which the parts produced will result in either scrap or rework (column 1).
2. Process capability *at the time being studied* (column 2).

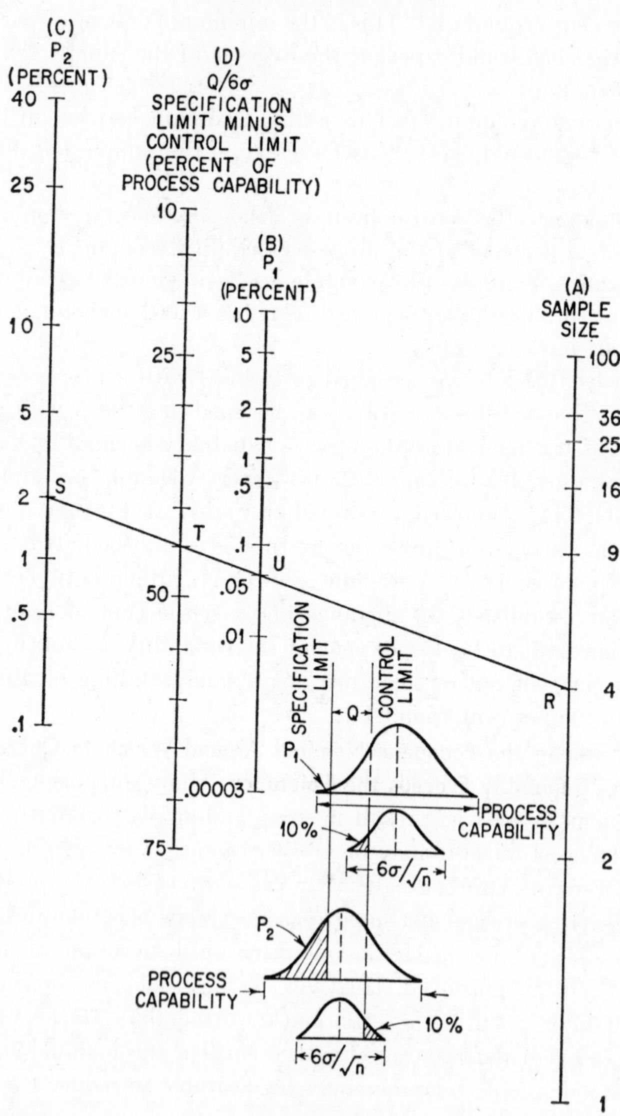

FIG. 17.24.

3. The cost ratio. This is the ratio of the greater cost divided by the lesser cost (column 3).

4. The amount to shift the average from nominal. This shift is always toward the tolerance limit with the lesser associated cost (column 4).

To illustrate the use of this nomograph, consider once again the example given near the beginning of this section. If the turned diameter of .969 ±

NOMOGRAPH FOR DETERMINING MINIMUM SCRAP AND REWORK COST

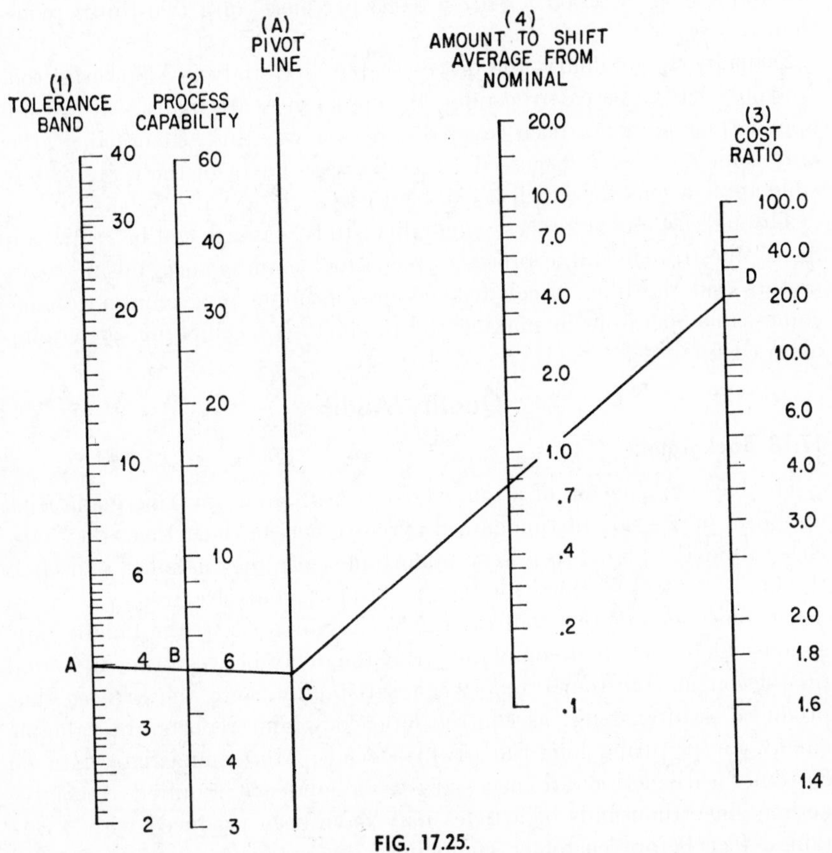

FIG. 17.25.

.002 inch is too small, the shaft is scrapped at a cost of $10. However, if the turned diameter is oversize, it can be reworked at a cost of $.50 per shaft. Lathe B's capability normally is .002 inch but suddenly changes to .006 inch, and replacement parts for the lathe are temporarily unavailable. The shaft order is necessary to maintain production, so it is decided to keep producing despite the scrap and rework cost. If the present nominal is maintained, the defective-quality cost will be ($10) (.023) +

\$.50 (.023) = \$.246 per piece.[8] Using the nomograph with a tolerance band of 4 mils (point A) and a process capability of 6 mils (point B) will yield point C on the pivot line when connected with a straight line. The cost ratio is \$10/\$.50 = 20 and is marked point D. Connecting points C and D with a straight line shows that a shift of approximately .75 mils will minimize the total defective-quality dollars. The nominal is shifted to .9697 inch, with a resultant 10.6 per cent of the parts reworked and .3 per cent of the parts scrapped. So the total defective-quality cost now is (.106 × \$.50) + (.003 × \$10) = \$.083 per piece, or a two-thirds reduction.

Summary. In summary, the process-capability study is a powerful tool. Not only can it be easily computed, but its uses are many. All possible applications have not been covered here, nor was this attempted. Rather only some have been discussed, so as to give a flavor of the types of possible applications for which it can be used.

Through use of the process-capability study, savings can be realized in losses due to inadequate processes, poor tool maintenance, unskilled operators and the like. It can help assure optimum programming of machines and operators in making the product to specification at a minimum cost.

Quality Audit

17.18 Background

The basic evaluation of a quality-control program must be made from appraisal of the satisfaction gained by customers in the articles they purchase from the plant. In a very important sense the customer himself is the final "control station" for factory product-control activity.

Customer satisfaction will eventually be mirrored by the number and seriousness of customer complaints. But the delay between time of actual production and customer reports on satisfaction with the articles thus produced is often long; as control data, complaint reports are valuable chiefly for picturing long-run quality trends. More immediate data on customer satisfaction are necessary as a guide to required corrective action, since thousands of articles may have been produced with a certain defect before customer complaints are received on the first such defective article shipped.

Since it provides customer-viewpoint data of the sort thus required, the quality audit has assumed increasing importance as a quality-control technique. In principle, it usually represents

1. Selection of a sample of product from a lot upon which all opera-

[8] .023 is the area on one side under the normal curve beyond 2σ. In this example, after the change in the process capability, the tolerance band only includes $\pm 2\sigma$ of the process distribution.

tions, tests, and inspections have been performed and which awaits shipment. Size of this sample is usually relatively small and may include as few as 10 or 15 units, although a 50-unit sample is desirable when such a sample size is economical.

2. The units in the sample are examined by the process-control engineer from the viewpoint of a critical customer. This examination in some cases uses the same standards as those for the regular production inspection and tests. In many instances, it uses much more rigorous standards than those used for regular production, including accelerated life tests and product tear-downs.

3. Results from this examination are used as the basis for action of various sorts:

a. In some instances, the quality audit must result in approval of the sample before the lot from which it was drawn may be released for shipment.

b. In most instances, release does not await the quality-audit results. These results are, however, used by the process-control engineer to show trends and to guide corrective action that may be required.

4. The frequency of quality audits varies widely from plant to plant, depending upon economic and quality requirements. Some plants require a quality audit of each lot shipped, others require an audit periodically —each day, each week, each month.

5. Some plants publish quality-audit results as the quality index for the product studied for the period covered by the audit.

Audit samples are most easily selected where the product is small and where units can be easily handled. The same approach has been applied to larger apparatus, however, often through the medium of selecting important subassemblies or critical component parts.

In substance, therefore, this technique is just what its title states—an audit of quality—and is directly comparable in need and in principle to the more widely known accounting audit. The quality audit is not a control measure in the full preventive sense, since the articles examined by the process-control engineer have already been manufactured along with the lot from which they have been drawn. It may, however, be an extremely useful and economically productive overcheck on the effectiveness of the regular day-by-day plant routines for controlling quality—involving inspection skill, test performance, operator care, etc. It may also provide a ready customer-viewpoint quality barometer.

17.19 An Example

The approach taken by a Massachusetts plant represents an interesting example of one approach to quality auditing. This plant manufactures a variety of measurements devices which are intricate, highly precise assemblies, many of which can be held readily by a man in one of his hands.

The audit operates as follows:

The process-control engineer selects samples of finished apparatus after final inspection in the factory. The units in each sample are brought to the plant laboratory and are carefully tested and inspected by experienced personnel who take the viewpoint of an exacting customer. It has not been found practical to sample on a basis of much greater than 1 per cent for a high-production line; low-production lines, where value of each article is high, may have samples of from 5 to 15 per cent of output.

Defects found in the audit are divided into two major classes: (1) calibration and (2) mechanical.

Calibration defects are noted when the device being examined is found to be outside the performance limits required by engineering specifications.

Mechanical defects are divided into major and minor classifications as follows:

1. *Major defect* is any defect of such nature that the customer may reasonably complain about its occurrence. This may be appearance, operative failure, improper operation, hazard of operation failure, and even improper design.

2. *Minor defect* is any defect representing a substandard practice that may not be cause for customer complaint but should nonetheless be brought to attention of the process-control engineer. Slight appearance defects are an example here.

Major defects found at the audit are charted and reported weekly to appropriate positions who are held responsible for corrective action as required. When defects are found which, in the process-control engineer's opinion, should receive immediate consideration, they do not await the weekly summary but are at once brought to the attention of the concerned parties.

This plant has found that it derives several benefits from this audit procedure, three of which are listed below:

1. It provides an indication of quality trend, thereby showing the desirability for concentrating corrective efforts where they may be most required.

2. It provides an index of customer acceptance in advance of actual complaint reports, thereby allowing corrective action to be taken earlier.

3. It highlights faulty operations of the quality-control procedures as soon after their occurrence as possible while their operations may be corrected before serious consequences have resulted.

CHAPTER 18

SPECIAL PROCESS STUDIES

In factories which do not possess well-operating total-quality-control programs, an epidemic of production-line quality failures or a sudden avalanche of customer complaints may sound the starting gun for a host of independent, uncoordinated approaches to what is hoped to be rapid elimination of the causes of the trouble.

These approaches are often conflicting and overlapping; sometimes they are actually directed to contradictory interpretations of the problem to be faced. Too frequently they cause a slow rather than a fast solution; the answer finally decided upon may be one that does not really solve but merely transfers the problem elsewhere.

In plants which enjoy total-quality-control activity, these critical quality problems generally arise in parallel with product-control operations. To provide a channel for carrying through the major project effort required to deal with them, special process studies have been established as the fourth of the quality-control jobs.

These process studies provide the total-quality-control medium through which basic product-quality problems can be effectively faced and rapidly solved. It is the purpose of this chapter briefly to review special process studies.

18.1 Defining Special Process Studies

As a definition:

Special process studies involve investigations and tests to locate the causes of defective products and to determine the possibility of improving quality characteristics.

These studies are directed to major, usually nonrepetitive quality problems requiring activity from more than one group in the company organization. There may, for example, be the sudden appearance at final assembly of high rejects which cannot be eliminated by readily available methods or a controversy between Design Engineering and Manufacturing Supervision as to whether or not a new and tightened tolerance is required for a high-quantity expensive part or the need for making a long-range study of the cause of a field complaint.

As noted in the definition, by no means all the problems passing through the special studies activity are those generated by factory quality troubles. These studies are also used for many of the major investigations initiated by Product Engineering, Manufacturing Engineering, and other groups to determine the feasibility of improving quality standards on existing products or facilities.

Experience has taught plant management that basic problems demanding major project effort should be faced by a quality-control activity organized of and by itself. Before the institution of the special process studies job, consolidation of these nonrepetitive projects with the product-control routines designed to deal with regular, repetitive quality issues too often resulted in disservice both to the regular procedures and to the nonrepetitive projects.

18.2 The Elements of Special Process Studies

Fundamental to all special process studies are two elements:

1. *Coordination of company effort* so as to utilize all resources in an integrated approach to the problem.

2. *Employment of the best technical methods* in order both to enable a sound technological attack on the problem and to encourage a solution whose reliability or lack of it is quite definitely understood.

For many special studies, coordination of effort and the taking of rapid and simple action are all that are required when the problem under consideration has been analyzed. Indicated steps may be a drawing change by Engineering, a process adaptation by Manufacturing Engineering, an increase in care by Shop Operations; all may readily be dovetailed together to eliminate the causes of the trouble.

In contrast, determination of the causes and solutions of other quality problems may be technologically very complex. Every plant has experienced the case of product failures which seemed to have been caused by factors which are "mysterious" and "unidentifiable."

A situation in point is that of the assembly plant whose mechanical-device quality was so poor that, on occasional days, more units were rejected than were shipped. There were so many variables which "could" cause the rejections that factory personnel found it difficult to make even a satisfactory start on the problem of isolating the possible causes.

Operators might have been at fault, test stands might have been defective, materials might have been unsatisfactory, design specifications might have been unsound. And when some process change was made which temporarily seemed to improve quality, factory personnel were faced with the question of how much confidence could be placed in the long-term value of the apparent problem solution.

In knotty cases of this sort, extensive utilization of quality-control technical methods must supplement special process studies coordination activity. Sound understanding of the philosophy of scientific industrial experimentation is essential as the foundation upon which effective applications of these technical methods may be built.

The statistical point of view is especially useful here. Special methods in particular find their widest value with special process studies in analyzing problems, examining causes, and suggesting solutions of given statistical reliability.

The technical methods used in process studies are merely adaptations of the quality-control methods already listed in Chaps. 7 to 14. The statistical point of view has itself been reviewed in Part Four. Especially to be emphasized for consideration in relation to special process studies are the sections in Chap. 13 which review the fundamental philosophy of the design of experiments as well as those which cover such techniques as correlation, tests of significance, and analysis of variance.

18.3 Organizing for Special Process Studies

Involved in special process studies organization are the regular members of the company quality-control component. When a major quality problem arises which demands a special study, the problem is immediately discussed and analyzed as far as possible by process-control engineers and quality-control engineers.

Responsibilities are assigned for carrying out the various individual steps required for the investigation. As soon as the results of these individual analyses become known, they are tied together into a problem solution.

Corrective steps that must be taken to bring this solution to reality are assigned to appropriate personnel. In the cases of shop-quality problems, these corrective steps also include assurance that a control is built into the solution such that the quality problem will not recur.

Key man in the organization for special process studies is the process-control engineer. He acts in a role comparable to that of a "T formation" football quarterback in assuring that the problem is handed to the proper

SPECIAL PROCESS STUDIES CASE # 112

PROBLEM 72E4 Relays, which had been adjusted and tested in Preliminary Test, were out of limits in Final Test on the Pick-up Volts Quality Characteristic.

LOCATION –72E4 Line

PRESENTED BY Test DATE July, 1960

*****

PAST DATA ON PROBLEM See Condition I on FIGURE 18.2

*****

CONTROL DATA TO BE TAKEN (1) Distribution data on pickup voltage and dropout current for 50 relays at Final Test.

(2) Trend data for 14 consecutive days on 10 relays.

ACTION TAKEN (1) Test limits were widened from .4–.5 to .35–.65 for pickup volts.

(2) Constant current hereafter to be held in main contactor coil during test of differential element.

(3) Phosphor bronze springs, which had gotten on the line by mistake, were scrapped.

RESULTS See present condition on FIGURE 18.2

R. J. Johnson
PROCESS CONTROL ENGINEER

DATE 8/15/60

FIG. 18.1.

individuals and groups. Since he is usually fully grounded in the application of quality-control technical methods and particularly in statistics, the process-control engineer is well qualified to integrate special study projects.

Procedures established by plants for this activity are usually very simple in nature. These procedures merely assure identification of such factors as

1. *Types of problems to be entered in the special process studies channel.* The major distinction between problems which may and those which may not be entered is one of cost; problems are carried through the channel only when they are sufficiently important economically to balance the cost of the required investigation.
2. *Specification of the procedure for rapidly bringing these problems to the attention of the process-control engineer.* Most of the special process studies involving factory quality troubles are initiated by report of the factory foreman—as key man in the product-control routine through which most of these issues arise—on problems which he and his people cannot alone solve.
3. *Outline of the general steps that must be taken for final problem solutions by the quality-control component.* Such procedures frequently require that case reports be placed upon file after completion of a special study. A file of these reports thus provides a store of know-how for approaching similar problems which may arise.

Figures 18.1 and 18.2 illustrate essential portions of a case report filed after solution of a problem involving electrical devices which would not meet a specification at final test.

Special Process Studies Examples

18.4 Thermometal

Section 18.2 emphasized that the approach to process studies is characterized by two elements fundamental to all such investigations: (1) coordination of effort and (2) employment of the best technical methods. After this basic approach has been established, the detailed development of an analysis may demand—particularly on complex processes—comprehensive knowledge of the related process technology.

Active participation in special studies may, therefore, be required from plant process specialists and technologists—in electroplating when unsatisfactorily uneven finish thicknesses are being experienced, in drilling and reaming when there is excessive variation in distances between hole centers, in casting when quality is spotty on steel motor casings, in porcelain glazing when cracks appear after heat-treatment of bushings. The following examples are concerned with two distinctive types of proc-

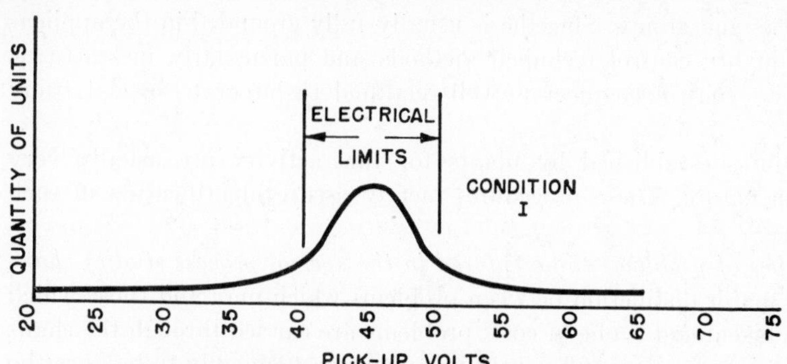

CONCLUSION: REPORT MADE THAT LIMITS COULD NOT BE MET WITHOUT HIGH REJECTS; LIMITS THAT COULD BE MET WERE CALCULATED, AND NEED FOR IMPROVEMENT IN METHODS AND OPERATION REPORTED.

STEPS TAKEN: METHODS IMPROVED. LIMITS WIDENED AS MUCH AS POSSIBLE OUT OF SPECIFICATION SPRING MATERIAL FOUND.

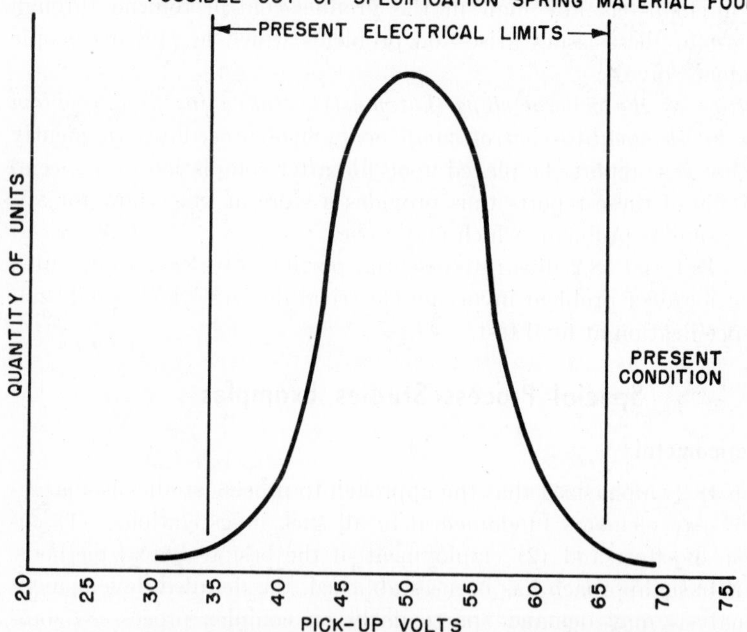

CONCLUSION: NEW LIMITS MADE POSSIBLE A REASONABLE QUANTITY OF REJECTS; NECESSITY FOR IMPROVING OPERATING CHARACTERISTICS REPORTED, WHICH WORK IS NOW UNDER WAY.

FIG. 18.2.

ess technology where specialists' assistance was required for successful completion of the study: adjustment of thermometal strip subassemblies in this Sec. 18.4; castings of sintered metal blocks in Sec. 18.5.

Because the purpose of this chapter is application of quality-control techniques, discussion of these examples will be concentrated primarily upon the various quality-control techniques employed; in spite of its importance to the solution, the appropriate process know-how will be reviewed only to a necessary minimum.[1]

Thermometal subassemblies act as the tripping mechanism for relays which are used as protective devices on motor starters. Electrical load conditions, which may endanger the motor starter, generate heat that activates the bimetallic thermo strip. The relay is then tripped, thus preventing the load hazard from damaging the starter.[2]

The thermometals are manufactured in a sequence with essentially the following steps:

1. Receipt on the production line of the metallic elements.
2. Assembly of the thermometal strip subassembly.
3. Mechanical adjustment of the strip for proper operation in accordance with engineering specifications. Adjustment tolerance is ± 0.005 inch, but strips are set at the specification nominal value.
4. Oven annealing heat-treatment of the subassembly.
5. Transport of the completed subassembly to the relay production line, where it is assembled to a completed relay. This relay is later tested electrically, and the tripping operation of the thermometal is the major quality characteristic checked by this test.

During actual manufacture, steps 3 and 4 are combined into a single job held by one operator. In production of the thermometal assembled as the activating mechanism in the 403A protective relay, there are two of these combination stations in operation, each with an adjusting fixture and an operator and each using a common heat-treat oven.

On this 403A relay, rejections at the final test in step 5 above, amounted, before a special study on the process, to 75 per cent. The distribution shown in Fig. 18.3 pictures the adjustment setting values on thermometals in a defective lot of 403A relays from which the thermometal had been disassembled and its adjusted setting checked.

This figure illustrates the very large proportion of strips that were found to be out of limits. Yet the two operators at the adjust stations were known to be conscientious, quality-conscious employees who insisted

[1] For a discussion on analyses of technically highly complex problems in whose solution special methods played a major part see Secs. 13.15 and 13.16.

[2] This discussion follows a study made by W. T. Short and associates, Schenectady, N.Y.

that the adjustments had been at the specification nominal when the subassemblies had left the adjust fixtures.

After considerable effort toward solving this problem of high rejects at final electrical test caused by out-of-limits thermometal subassemblies, the concerned shop foreman called for assistance from the process-control engineer. The engineer initiated a special process studies project, which had the final result of reducing the rejection rate on the thermometal subassembly from 75 per cent to an acceptable figure of 1 per cent.

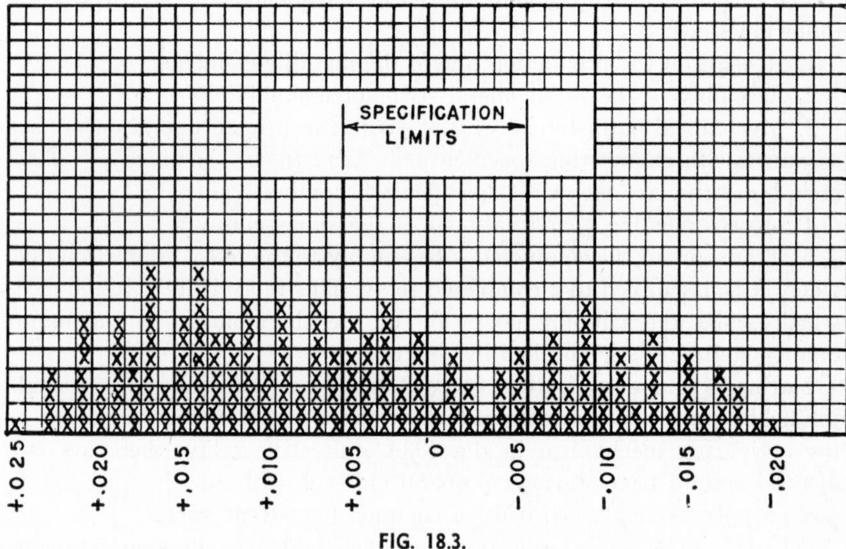

FIG. 18.3.

In bringing this special study to a successful conclusion, the following activities were carried through:

Preliminary Analysis and Action. A preliminary analysis by the process-control engineer concerned initiated a series of investigations which disclosed four faulty process features, corrected as follows:

Faulty feature	*Corrective action*
Each of the two adjusting fixtures permitted inaccurate and discrepant settings, due to worn mechanical parts in the fixtures.	Fixtures were repaired, and their settings were correlated one against the other. Fixtures were made subject to regular review through the plant preventive maintenance program.

Faulty feature	*Corrective action*
Excessive variation in temperatures was experienced within the heat-treat oven.	Temperature variation was reduced to an acceptable amount by installation of a blower.
Errors in establishment and maintenance of the average temperature value held on the oven were experienced.	A master control switch was installed which eliminated the problem.
The metallic elements received for use on the production line were coming from different sources. Materials from each source differed from the other sources in trip characteristics after heat-treat, even though the same adjustment had been made throughout. Figure 18.4 shows the two-peaked distribution curve of one of these mixed thermometal lots. This distribution picture gave the first indication of the presence and importance of two sources of metal.	Material received from each source was identified before use on the production line. Procedures were established for differences in the adjustment of metal from each source so as to compensate for the effect of the heat-treatment.

After this activity, the process-control engineer ran a sample lot of thermometal subassemblies through the production sequence. The final

BI-METAL ASSEMBLY
AFTER I HOUR ANNEAL
TOLERANCE ±.005

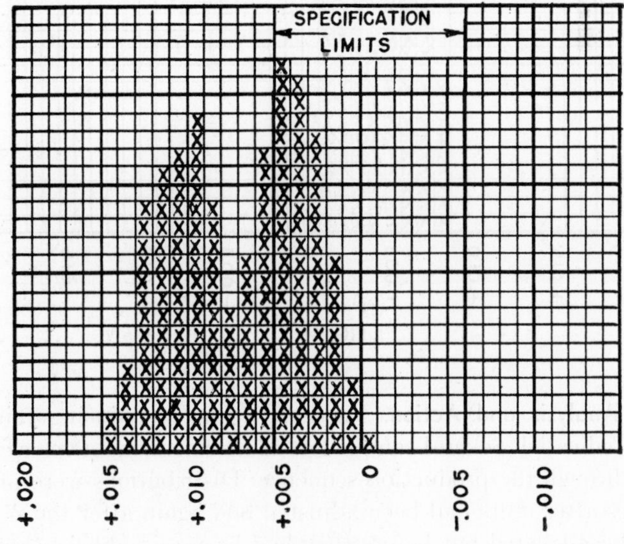

FIG. 18.4.

electrical test results on this sample showed that 30 per cent rejects were still being experienced. Frequency-distribution analysis of the adjustment setting of the thermometal strips in the sample assemblies showed that the average strip setting was still several thousandths of an inch on the "high side" of the specification nominal value.

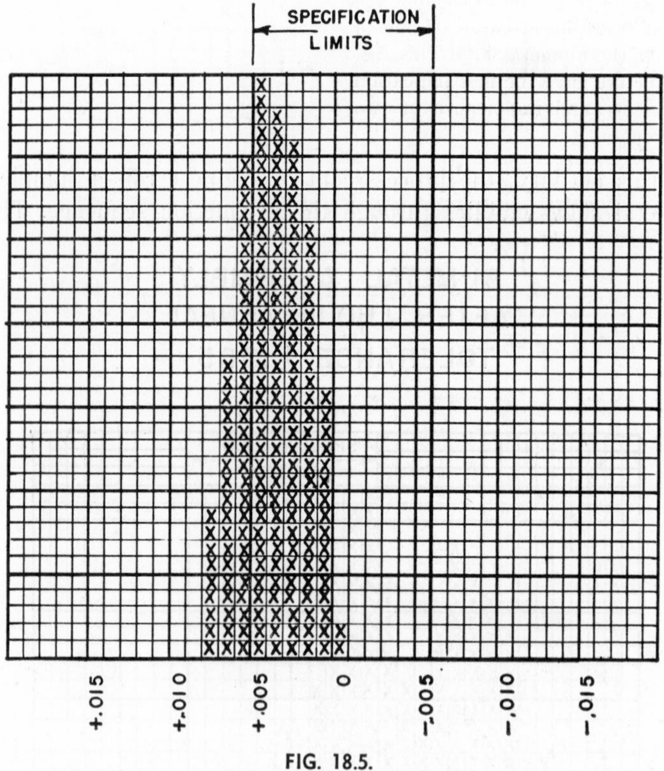

FIG. 18.5.

Further Analysis and Action. Further action in reducing rejects was obviously indicated. Several sample lots of thermometal strips were therefore sent through the production sequence. Distributions were plotted on the samples after units had been adjusted and again after the same units had been heat-treated but before they had been assembled to relays.

These same plots showed that the trip settings of thermometal strips drawn from the same source had a very definite and discernible tendency to "drift" after heat-treat.

A sample lot was then sent through the process adjusted and heat-treated as usual. Its distribution plot is shown in Fig. 18.5. This distribu-

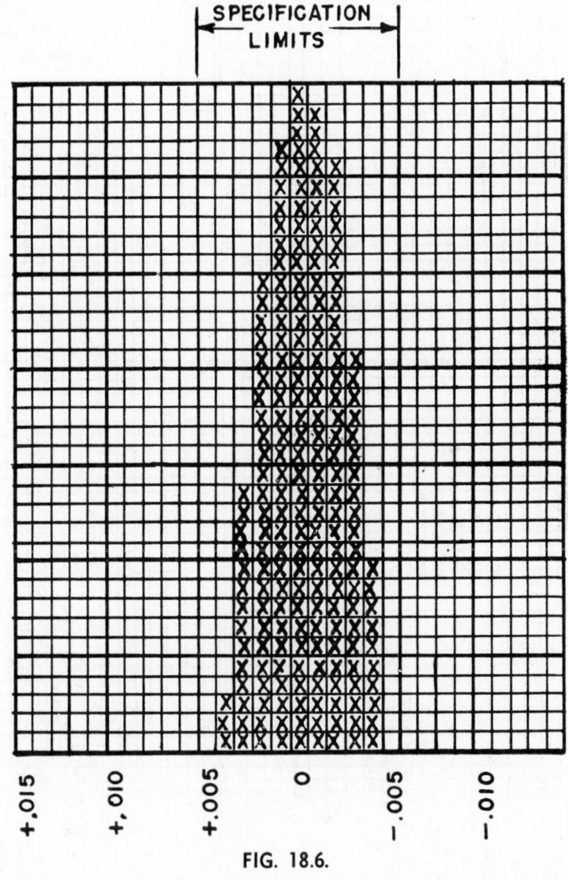

FIG. 18.6.

tion was analyzed for its average value, which was shown to be 0.004 inch above the specification nominal value.

A second lot, with thermometal drawn from the same source, was then sent through the process, with the initial adjustment 0.004 inch *below* the specification nominal value. Figure 18.6 pictures the resulting distribu-

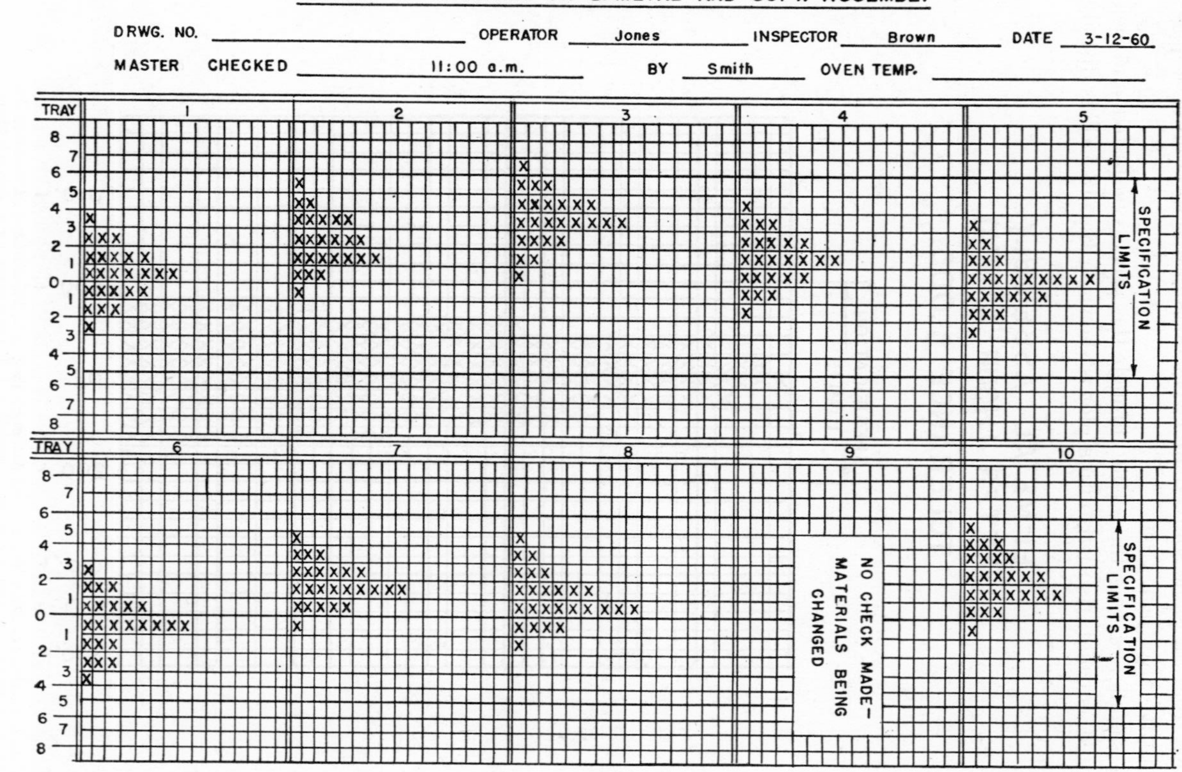
SETTING OF BI-METALS ON BI-METAL AND SUPT. ASSEMBLY
DRWG. NO.
OPERATOR Jones
INSPECTOR Brown
DATE 3-12-60
MASTER CHECKED 11:00 a.m.
BY Smith
OVEN TEMP.
TRAY
1
2
3
4
5
SPECIFICATION LIMITS
TRAY
6
7
8
9
10
NO CHECK MADE— MATERIALS BEING CHANGED
SPECIFICATION LIMITS

FIG. 18.7.

tion, showing the first lot of thermometals whose quality was satisfactory after heat-treatment.

Final Action and Control. Satisfied that the thermometal setting had an inherent tendency to drift as a result of heat-treat, the process-control engineer established a procedure whereby this quality hazard would be eliminated. Operators at the adjust and heat-treat stations were first furnished masters for the thermometal settings. They were then asked to follow a very simple procedure:

1. When a new batch of metallic elements was received, operators were to assemble and adjust a sample of the thermometal subassembly, heat-treat the sample, then check the adjustment settings, and plot them in tally form.

2. Operators were then to compensate for the drift tendency as shown by the average value for this sample, by adjusting strips from that lot the required amount above or below the specification nominal.

3. Operators finally had the responsibility for periodically sampling the resulting subassemblies after heat-treat. Whatever adjustment compensations seemed indicated could be made by operators on the subsequent lots.

Figure 18.7 shows the tally form used by operators for the purpose outlined in step 3.

Soon after this procedure was instituted, the following results could be seen:

Rejects at final electrical test of the 403A relay stabilized at about 1 per cent.

The adjust operators were highly satisfied with a simple procedure which removed from them the onus of poor workmanship.

The shop foreman was able to get out relay production without being forced to pass back and forth lot after lot of relays for readjustment of the thermometal.

In his file report on the completion of this study, the process-control engineer included the following summary comments:

"If the investigation had ended after fixtures, furnace, and source of supply were corrected, the factory would still have had 30 per cent rejections. From the results obtained in reducing this figure to 1 per cent, it is obvious that the use of quality-control techniques aids greatly in solving factory quality problems on a permanent basis."

18.5 Casting of Sintered Blocks

Sintered metal blocks are produced in a process the basic steps of which are shown in Fig. 18.8. One type of these blocks possesses magnetic properties.

Output of this block was subject to 25 per cent rejections at the test of

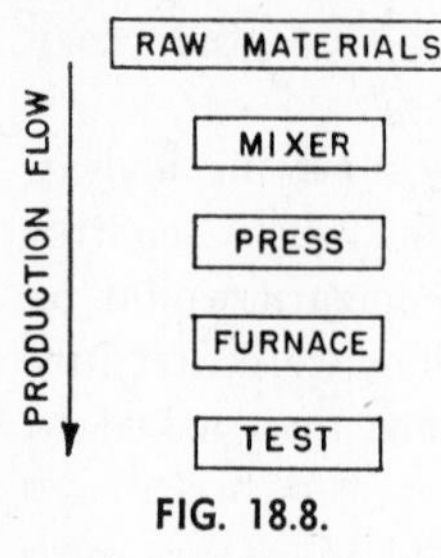

FIG. 18.8.

its magnetic properties. To reduce these rejections and the attendant manufacturing losses, a special process studies investigation was begun on the entire process of casting sintered magnetic blocks.[3]

The casting process is rather intricate, with many possible variables. There would consequently be a great deal of difficulty in making a step-by-step analysis of the process unless some indication was available of the type of variable for which to watch.

It was decided, therefore, that the process study would be begun by analysis of the quality of blocks received at final test; potential reject causes would then be traced back from that point. As first step in the investigation, a sample of 150 blocks was sent through the regular production process.

Each block in the sample remained untouched until the final test, at which point the magnetic properties of each was recorded in the distribution shown on Fig. 18.9.

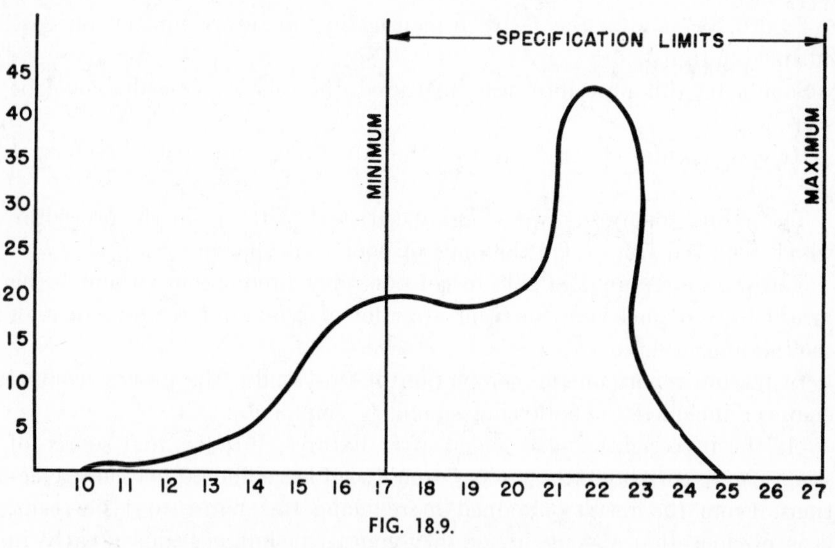

FIG. 18.9.

The two-peaked distribution in this figure pointed to the possibility of two influential source factors affecting magnetic quality. Hypothesizing that two such factors operating at the same point in the process were at work, the production sequence was analyzed for their possible location.

[3] This discussion follows a study by G. S. Berge and associates, New York, N.Y.

After a step-by-step study, evidence began to point to possible major discrepancies between blocks produced by two sintering furnaces, called here furnace 1 and furnace 2. To explore the effect of these furnaces, a sample lot was sent through the regular process, with a portion of the blocks passing through sintering furnace 1 and the remaining blocks passing through sintering furnace 2.

The blocks passing through each furnace were so identified. After the rest of the processing period had been completed, test results on each block were recorded as shown on Fig. 18.10.

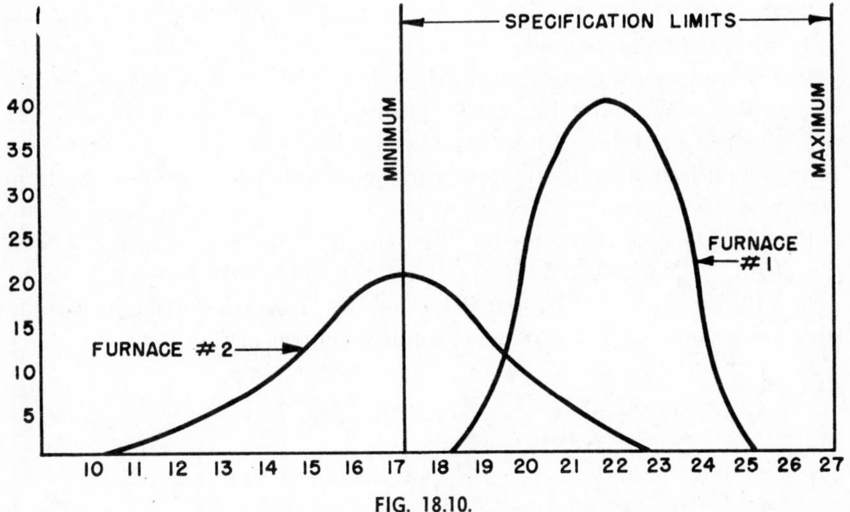

FIG. 18.10.

This figure showed that furnace 1 was producing blocks of acceptable quality. Both the average and spread were satisfactory for the distribution plotted for blocks which had passed through this furnace.

On the other hand, furnace 2 was producing blocks which were approximately 50 per cent defective. Both the average and spread were unsatisfactory for its distribution.

Owing to this analysis, furnace 2 was made subject to a searching methods study. It was found that there was an uneven heat distribution internally which set up hot and cold zones within the furnace. Changes were at once made in furnace structure, which resulted in a much more even internal heat distribution.

With furnace 2 repaired, rejects at final test dropped sharply from the 25 per cent level. To assist in maintaining the much improved quality level, a procedure for periodic sampling of sintering furnace output was made a part of the plant product-control procedure.

18.6 Summary of Part Five

Quality is affected at all major stages of the production process. Effective control of quality must, therefore, involve quality-control activities which start while a product is being sold and designed and end only when the product is received by a fully satisfied customer.

These activities fall into four natural classifications termed the jobs of quality control, which are

1. New-design control.
2. Incoming-material control.
3. Product control.
4. Special process studies.

Part Five has discussed each of these jobs with emphasis upon the two major phases involved in each: (1) organizational practices and (2) technological routines. While organization practices are relatively uniform for all four jobs, there are a variety of technical routines unique to each.

Part Five has assumed for its discussion that quality control has been thoroughly "sold to" and accepted by the concerned personnel in the plant. Part Six of this book will review the issues involved in gaining such acceptance while introducing quality control in the plant.

PART SIX

QUALITY-CONTROL EDUCATION AND TRAINING

CHAPTER 19

COMMUNICATING TOTAL QUALITY CONTROL

Discussion in this book has been largely concentrated upon organizational techniques and technical methods. But even sound organization and adequate methods cannot alone assure success for a quality-control program. These techniques must be supported by a foundation of positive attitudes among company personnel toward quality and the modern means for its control.

Positive quality attitudes in a company are primarily represented by the very intangible but extremely important spirit of "quality-mindedness" extending from top management right through to the men and women at the bench. Such attitudes will not automatically develop through the total installation of a quality-control program. They must be earned through action by members of the quality-control organization and through the results gained from activities in the quality-control jobs.

These attitudes can be earned through what may be described as essentially a process of responsible "selling" by the proponents of quality control. Whatever is new about the total-quality-control program is gradually and successfully introduced step by step to the entire company organization so as to obtain its willing acceptance, cooperation, and participation. New and strange quality-control procedures are not introduced in the shop without considerable forewarning and smoothing of the way; descriptions of quality-control technical methods are not couched in the mysterious language of the mathematician or technologist but are presented in shop terminology.

Selling the total-quality-control program is basically a matter of sound human relations activity. It requires clear, concise, and sustained communications with all persons and groups that play a role in total quality control.

It is the purpose of this chapter to discuss the communications and education job. There are two points of focus: first, *internal,* within the company for development of its personnel; second, *external,* outside the company for development of suppliers, customers, and "the public." Sections 19.1 to 19.5 will discuss internal communications. Sections 19.6 to 19.15 will discuss internal education. Sections 19.16 to 19.18 will discuss external communications.

Internal Communications

19.1 Where Does the Initiative for Proposing a Modern Quality-control Program Come from?

The suggestion that a plant undertake a total-quality-control program may come from any of several quarters in the company. It may be initiated by top management, which may have been impressed with the necessity for improved quality-control activity in the company or have seen success of such a program in other plants. It may be proposed by functional heads such as the Chief Inspector, the Managing Engineer, or the Manufacturing Superintendent. Quite frequently, it is suggested by relatively young members of the company organization who are technical specialists.

The proposal to initiate total quality control may be made as a sheer defense mechanism in the face of severe pressure on the company, in the form of many field complaints, extremely high manufacturing losses, or bitter internal feelings among plant personnel caused by unresolved quality problems. The initiatory proposal may be made as a suggestion to improve an already operating series of activities devoted toward the control of quality.

Wherever the total-quality-control proposal is born and under whatever circumstances, the first major task for its proponents is a uniform one: a concrete, practical, salable plan must be developed for approaching the initiation and for outlining the ultimate objectives of a quality-control program for the plant.[1]

It is very possible that the quality-control proponent will not be a top-echelon member of the company organization. He must then gear his plan for a review by top management so that management will be "sold" on deciding that total-quality-control prospects are so attractive that the company should "give it a try."

[1] Chapter 6 has discussed in some detail the quality system analysis of a plant in terms of its strong and weak quality elements, so that a program can be developed which is directly integrated with the needs of the plant.

At least four general considerations must be taken into account during development of this plan:

Individual Tailoring. An essential requirement is that the company's quality needs should first be carefully analyzed. The quality-control plan being introduced should be one with procedures and terminology tailored to the individual plant requirements determined from this analysis. It should not be a "prepackaged" program lifted bodily from another company or from the literature in the field.

Economic Balance. The scope of the quality-control activities recommended by the plan should be based upon sound economic analysis rather than developed without reference to the economics of company quality needs. The scope should be determined by striking a balance between the range of the quality problems in the company and the cost of the minimum amount of control required to face and solve them.[2]

The field of quality costs, as reviewed in Chap. 5, offers many of the tools needed for this analysis. Problems that quality-control components encounter when introducing their proposals in terms of their technical details alone disappear quickly when they show the potentialities in the business language of quality costs.

Participation. The quality-control plan will undoubtedly recommend action and cooperation from many functional groups and persons in the plant. The support, involvement, and motivation of these persons and groups are far more likely to be secured if they have participated in formulation of the plan and of the quality-control program it recommends.

Emphasis upon Benefits. The plan should emphasize the tangible benefits that may be derived from quality control and should indicate the measuring sticks that will be regularly used in the program to evaluate the results produced. To the extent that actual applications can be cited of individual quality-control projects that have been successfully carried on in the plant, the salability of the entire plan will be much enhanced.

It must be noted, in connection with the development of such a plan, that attention should be paid to the circumstances under which the total-quality-control proposal is being initiated. Appreciation of these circumstances should strongly influence the approach planned for introduction of the program.

The program, sponsored by top management, for example, will have to point toward the encouragement of spontaneous and genuine approval and participation by the lower-echelon members of the company organization. The program promoted by functional heads will have to overcome the immediate reaction by members of other functions that total

[2] Chapter 5 has discussed this economic balance.

quality control represents simply an "empire-building" device on the part of the Chief Inspector or the Managing Engineer.

The program which is developed primarily because of high manufacturing losses must guard against restricting its coverage solely to the product-control aspects of total quality control. The program generated by numerous field complaints must exercise caution against concentrating primarily upon special process studies trouble shooting.

19.2 Sequence for Selling Quality Control

Acceptance of the proposed quality-control plan by top management, with whatever adaptations and improvements it wishes to make, is an essential without which no further genuinely effective selling can be done in the factory. Quality-control proponents in many plants may properly be called upon to render considerable tangible evidence of the value of the activity before this approval is obtained for their plan. The approval may well be tentative, with complete acceptance contingent upon the results from initial quality-control applications.

When the plan has been accepted by management, tentatively or otherwise, a sequence of several steps will be followed to bring its proposals into actual operating reality in the plant. This sequence will develop the plan through the stage where widespread tangible evidence will be available to all members of the company organization on the actual value of quality-control activities. It will carry on the plan to the ultimate point where an over-all, company-wide program of quality is in operation of the sort discussed in this book.

This "sales sequence" includes at least four general steps which are quite fundamental in introducing total quality control under a wide variety of industrial circumstances. These steps are

1. Introduction by top management to concerned key personnel of the quality-control plan and the initial steps for placing it in operation. In the larger companies which may require such an individual, a report is made of selection of the head of the quality-control component if his assignment has not heretofore been made known.

2. A systematic project-by-project quality-control beginning in the company, with full management support for these projects. In this connection, the "check-list" appraisal of the elements of the company's quality system—as discussed in Chapter 6—becomes a very effective tool both for programming the necessary projects and for emphasizing factually the need for the program. Analysis and presentation of the company's quality costs, and an evaluation of the opportunities for substantial improvement in them, is also extremely effective in encouraging top-level support for the program.

3. Regular appraisal of tangible results from the projects; growth of

the number of projects and their gradual evolution and integration toward the form of the planned company-wide total-quality-control system.

4. Communication of quality objectives and of information on quality-control activities to all company personnel; encouragement of as wide a degree of participation as possible in the program from personnel; establishment of quality-control education and training work.

Each of these four steps is discussed in Sec. 19.3.

19.3 Steps in Selling Quality Control

Introduction of Program by Top Management. Some degree of resistance among company personnel to a program like total quality control is inevitable. This resistance is generally caused by lack of information as to the procedures and objectives of the program.

Before any action is taken for establishing the activities proposed by the basic quality-control plan, therefore, it is highly desirable that top management should present the essentials of this plan to all key people. A presentation of this sort accomplishes several purposes: it provides a means for communicating to key personnel the basis for total quality control; it tangibly demonstrates that the proposed program has genuine top-management support; it furnishes a channel wherein those individuals who have not yet had such an opportunity may participate in an over-all review of the proposed activities.

This introduction by management may be carried on quietly and informally if a private meeting is deemed best for company conditions. Or management may wish to encourage widespread enthusiasm in the launching of total quality control by holding a "full-dress" promotional meeting.

The promotional meeting may begin with formal presentation of the program by top management, possibly followed by some device such as a slide film with commentary to review the details of the quality-control activity.

This introductory meeting furnishes an excellent opportunity for announcing the selection of the individual who will be assigned the quality-control management responsibility. The individual who will "spark-plug" the program may be immediately assigned on a full-time basis. He may, on the other hand, initially devote only part of his time to quality control, with full time to be given to the activity as it develops. Wherever possible and practical, it may be most beneficial that the individual thus selected be a man who is already a member of the company organization, familiar with its quality problems and personally familiar with many of the individuals in the plant.

A Project-by-project Beginning. When the introductory meeting gives way to actual initiation of company quality-control activity, only a few projects will be selected as the first steps. They may be carried on in the new-design-control field, in the incoming-material-control phase of quality control, or in either of the other two major jobs.

This project-by-project approach aids in selling the program to company personnel through the medium of tangible quality-control results. It also provides a practical means for tailoring the general quality-control routines to the particular needs of the company.

By selecting two or three of the most troublesome quality problems of the plant, obtaining success in attacking and solving them, and then selecting more projects, the over-all program of the four quality-control jobs will gradually evolve in a form best adapted to the requirements of the plant.

Tangible Results. Since growth of the quality-control program will be directly dependent upon the results it produces, it is extremely important that adequate means for reporting these results be established. These reports are made by the Quality Control Manager to top management and other key personnel on a periodic basis, perhaps monthly. The initial reports are made on the first individual projects, and the coverage of the report is expanded as the quality-control activities expand. Great care is exercised in the reports to point out that the quality-control results are due to the cooperative efforts of several functional groups and individuals rather than to the personal successes of the quality-control people.

The measuring sticks used may be drawn from a wide variety of elements, depending upon the situation. Of great importance is the use of quality costs as a key measuring stick. Others are improvements in design and in manufacturing process, improvements in customer acceptance, enhancement of personnel quality-mindedness, and reductions in overruns.

Many of the important results thus reported will be intangibles. But the most effective of all these results is that which can be measured against the very tangible measuring stick of dollars-and-cents savings. Quality-control reports used during this phase of the selling process may tend, therefore, to give quality-cost savings the most prominent place among all the measuring sticks used.

Communication and Participation. The greatest quality resource of a plant is conscientious workmanship. Essential, therefore, to the genuine selling of quality control is the development of a real feeling of quality responsibility among all members of the company organization.

Growth of this attitude is fostered by communication of quality objectives to all personnel in the plant. Media that can be used are the plant newspaper, special quality-control publicity releases, meetings with employees to review the quality features of products of the plant, quality cartoons posted on bulletin boards, and presentations before employee-information meetings of skits, discussions, and sound or slide films on quality. Most effective of all means for communicating quality objectives and quality-control activities is the face-to-face relationship between supervisor and employees, whereby the required information is passed along. This chain of communication starts, of course, with top management.

Growth of quality-mindedness is also fostered by encouragement of employee participation in actual quality activities. Plant-wide quality drives with definite objectives, shop quality committees which meet periodically to make and review recommendations for quality improvements—each may be extremely effective. Encouragement at employee-information meetings of two-way discussions between supervisor and employee on the identification and solution of quality problems is also of great importance.

Success of this phase of quality-control selling is judged by the extent to which all employees in the company come to recognize the importance of their individual efforts to the design, manufacture, sale, and shipment of a product of acceptable quality.

19.4 The Sales Attitude for Quality-control Proponents

Important to the success of the proponents of the quality-control program in carrying through the selling process discussed above is the basic attitude they bring to the task of introducing total quality control into the plant. It is interesting to note, in this connection, that there is much in common between the attitude of the effective quality-control proponent and that of the successful sales engineer for industrial products.

When the successful, well-trained sales engineer makes a call to sell his product to a new and prospective customer, he proceeds according to a carefully planned course of action. He may use selling materials—samples, charts, etc.—whose value has been carefully tested. He will recognize that the burden of proof is upon him and that the prospects will be interested only if they can be shown that sufficient benefit will be gained from the product to justify its purchase.

The sales engineer is able to adapt his sales arguments to meet the interests of his prospects. With the design engineer, he must be able to discuss technical details; with top management, he must be able to talk of the dollars-and-cents benefits to be derived from his product; with manufacturing people, he must be able to talk about the effects upon plant personnel of the installation of the product.

As with the industrial sales engineer, two basic sales precepts that the quality-control proponent must follow are that

1. He must always concentrate in sales discussions upon the benefits of his product, which is quality control.

2. He must always be able to discuss these quality-control benefits

from the individual viewpoint of the "prospect"; in his case, the design engineer, the shop supervisor, the purchasing agent, the inspector, or top management.

While the quality-control proponent may himself be personally impressed, for example, with the logic and clarity of the statistical aspects of the activity, he must not simply assume that everyone else in the plant is similarly impressed. If the organizational aspects of quality control are of interest, this phase must be emphasized in sales discussions and not statistics; if human relations aspects are of interest, this matter must be emphasized.

Again as with the sales engineer, the successful quality-control proponent does not blame his failure upon the prospect when he does not make a sale. Instead, he tries to analyze that part of his approach which failed to make a satisfactory impression. Perhaps the costs quoted for the program were unduly or unrealistically high; perhaps there was excessive emphasis upon the organizational and administrative aspects of quality control; perhaps there was too little emphasis upon the benefits to be gained from application of quality-control technology. If the fault was in the approach used, the quality-control proponent tries to improve his approach; if the fault was in the form of the quality-control program proposed, he will rework the program, if deemed necessary, so that its undesirable features will be eliminated.

Throughout, the quality-control proponent leans upon his deep conviction of the benefits to be gained by his company from quality-control applications; he recognizes, however, that these benefits will probably never be realized unless he can so present them that he will be joined in his acceptance of and enthusiasm for quality control by the great majority of the plant organization and particularly by top management.

19.5 Introducing Quality Control in the Multiplant Company

Much of the discussion in this chapter has implicitly assumed that the organization to which total quality control is being introduced is a company with a single plant. Quality-control programs must, of course, also be sold under other conditions: in the company which operates many plants at different geographic locations and in the plant at a single geographic location which includes several semi-independent operating divisions.

The approach used in this multiplant or multidivision situation is, however, similar in principle to that reviewed above with reference to the company with the single plant. A quality-control plan must be prepared, approval must be obtained from top management, and a project-by-project beginning is highly desirable.

Selling quality control in the large, multiplant company will naturally call for a great deal of flexibility in the basic quality-control plan presented to company top management. This plan must be adaptable to meet the different needs of the various plants of the company, and it must be in such a form that it can also be sold to the managements of these plants.

As compared with the single plant, quality-control selling in the multiplant company may require a wider degree of initial participation in plan development and also much more extensive way-paving before applications may be initiated. Since there will, however, be a larger organization to support the associated expense, the multiplant situation may have the advantage that more attention can be devoted to preparation of extensive quality-control materials for use in the early phases of the introduction of the program.

As the quality-control program is being sold on a project-by-project basis or on an operating, section-by-section basis, it is necessary to develop concurrently a hard core of plant personnel who have developed the proper quality attitudes, quality knowledge, and quality skills successfully to support the quality control program. Section 19.6 discusses the means by which such personnel education and development can be extended throughout the company to support the expanded quality control program.

Internal Education

19.6 Three Key Characteristics Required by Company Personnel

The design, manufacture, and sale by a company of products of consistently good quality requires a high degree of effectiveness in at least three key characteristics of company personnel:

First: Their quality *attitudes.* Essential here is the genuine belief by company employees in the importance of good quality, excellent workmanship, well-conceived designs, and service-centered selling.

Second: Their quality *knowledge.* Vital in this connection is employee understanding of the kinds of quality problems that bear both upon their individual jobs and upon the plant in general; appreciation by the employees of the existence of up-to-date methods for solving their specific quality problems; positive acceptance by them of the principles, facts, and practices of modern means for building, maintaining, and controlling quality.

Third: Their quality *skills.* Important here are the abilities, both physical and mental, through which plant personnel actually perform the operations essential to quality as they are called for.

In effect, the company whose work force has sound quality attitudes, keen quality knowledge, and adequate quality skills is the company whose work force has the greatest likelihood of designing, manufacturing, and selling high-quality products.

19.7 Objective for Quality Education

The basic management objective for company quality education may, therefore, be readily formulated. This objective may be stated as *the development for company personnel—in all functions and at all levels—of those attitudes, that knowledge, and those skills in quality which may contribute to production of company products at minimum cost consistent with full customer satisfaction.*

Such an objective is not a new one. Long before total-quality-control programs had attracted widespread attention, plant managements were attempting to emphasize quality in the training of new operators, in the courses designed for foremen and supervisors, and in the types of assignments used in the planned rotation of engineers and salesmen.

The objective is one whose achievement can be based only in part upon the use of formalized classroom types of training such as those just cited. Much of the quality learning process—especially in attitudes, but to an appreciable extent also in knowledge and skills—takes place very informally and almost imperceptibly during the course of a man's regular working day. Part of it is forced upon him during the finger-burning of on-the-job experience; a great deal of it comes about as a result of the daily contacts between the man and his boss; part of it results from the exposure of the man to his fellow workers.

The management quality-education objective is one for which the means of achievement vary widely over periods of time. Quality problems have only one certainty: their content will be subject to continual change. Hence the solutions to quality problems will be a book to which chapters are constantly being added but for which the final chapter is never written. Quality education never ends for the healthy, aggressive company whose products compete effectively in the fast-moving American economy.

19.8 Quality Education as a Process

So education in the quality problem is a process that, with varying degrees of effectiveness, has been taking place in industry for many years, in many forms, and in many ways. In their desire to modernize this process so as better to achieve the management objective for company quality education, realistic company managers and quality-control engineers recognize that they begin with an existing fund of quality attitudes, knowledge, and skills—good or bad, current or hopelessly antiquated—on the part of company personnel. They recognize that they begin with a regularly functioning, informal learning process which is continually adding to this fund of education. They recognize that they begin with, to the extent that such activities have been in operation, a formal process of on-the-job, vestibule, orientation, and classroom training activities in job skills as related to quality.

It is interesting to observe that many of the modern quality-education efforts that have proved unsuccessful for American companies during the past 10 years are those which have paid little or no attention to this principle that, to determine where a man or a program or a quality-education activity is going, it is first necessary to learn where that man or program or educational activity has come from, and then to act accordingly. Although much attention was lavished on their content and teaching methodology, the unsuccessful company quality-education activities never really fitted deeply into the company for which they were presumably designed. Some were offered prematurely or were not sufficiently down to earth; others were couched in quality terminology that completely threw overboard the traditional plant designations for rejects, losses, and quality faults; still others took no advantage at all of the quality-education process that had been going on in the plant for many years; collectively, they never really came to grips with the company and its quality problems as they really existed at the time the educational programs were begun.

Experience seems strongly to indicate, therefore, that the first step for a quality-control engineer in appraising his plant's needs for modern quality education is carefully to analyze the *existing* company quality-education process, determine its characteristics and its strengths and weaknesses, and then build his educational planning from there.

19.9 Analysis of the Existing Quality-education Process

There are three basic questions that the quality-control engineer will ask about the existing quality-education process during this analysis:

QUESTION ONE: *What are the scope, magnitude, and effectiveness of the company's formalized training for plant personnel in the specific job knowledge and skills that are required for the designing, building, and maintenance of good quality?*

Even if a company has an officially designated training staff which carries on all formal training activity and which may have ready well-organized answers for him on this question, it is important for the quality-control engineer to go much deeper than the analysis that would be provided through this type of evaluation by these training men and women whose horizon is almost necessarily highly specialized. The quality-control engineer should go to the grass roots of this training effort to see and analyze for himself the emphasis placed by the apprentice school on relative types of quality knowledge and skills; the amount of time that is actually spent in the vestibule room in teaching new operators job skills relating to quality; the reaction of foremen to the caliber of the knowledge and skills gained by employees in such training; the reality, as compared with the company's current quality problems, of the inspection-training manual used in the plant; the degree to which development and design engineers come to be acquainted with the realities of modern requirements for product reliability and the analytical techniques for dealing with these requirements.

If the company has no formal training staff, the quality-control engineer may have to dig deeply even to establish just what formal training efforts in quality are being carried on by various sections and supervisors. It is vital that he establish such facts, for a major purpose of his analysis of the current quality education process is to gain a picture of the total hours—hence total dollars—being expended on formal training for quality.

QUESTION TWO: *What is the net effect on the quality thinking of company personnel due to the informal, on-the-job, day-by-day influences of experience, contacts, and exposure that is so basic to the process of quality education in a company?*

The single most useful criterion that the quality-control engineer has with which to answer this question is the degree of quality-mindedness that exists, section by section, throughout the company. While no techniques for the quantitative measurement of quality-mindedness seem yet to have been developed, quality-mindedness can be sharply and readily appraised qualitatively by an experienced quality-control man.

QUESTION THREE: *What are the scope, magnitude, and effectiveness of the company's formalized efforts to train plant personnel in the modern concepts of quality and in the programs and methods of total quality control?*

Typically in the early days of installation of a total-quality-control program for a company, the answer to this question was "Almost nothing is being done." It remains, however, a very useful practical question to ask. It is surprising how often material that relates directly to modern quality and its control techniques may turn up in some dark corner of the company's educational process. Years ago someone may have inserted such material in a foreman's training course in which it has effectively though obscurely since been used. Possibly some supervisor or workman, to whom the terms $\overline{X}$, R, or *p charts* would be a new language, has instinctively found how useful it seems to be to chart reject percentages or to tally readings on parts from certain machine tools, and this supervisor or workman has educated or is trying to educate those around him in the value of these methods. Such home-grown material, as well as the people who have used and developed it, can be tremendous assets in any formalized quality-control training courses being planned. To use such material, however, requires that the quality-control engineer know that it exists.

19.10 Use of Answers to the Questions

Answers to these three questions provide the quality-control engineer, who recognizes that the totality of the company's quality-education process is one of the most important influences that must be utilized on behalf of the company's quality-control program, with much of the basic material he needs for planning the types and kinds of modernization that must take place to bring this educational process up to date.

Specific action to be taken in the area of question One—*formalized training in specific job knowledge and skills as related to quality production*—represents a major problem of industrial education in itself. It relates to the quality aspects of training apprentices, cadet or student engineers, and new employees. As such, it is more suitable for review in books which concentrate upon industrial education, and it is to such volumes that quality-control engineers should turn for direction in this area.

In the area of question Two—*the informal process of quality education*—what is involved in solution to the various problems of developing and maintaining quality-mindedness, again a major field for quality-control attention in itself. This subject will be reviewed in Sec. 19.11 below.

Question Three—*the formal training of personnel in modern quality problems and in control techniques*—is the issue usually of prime interest to quality-control engineers who are endeavoring to modernize their company's quality-education process. It will be considered in Sec. 19.12 below.

19.11 Quality-mindedness

One of the three objectives for company education in total quality control, noted above in Sec. 19.7, is in the matter of attitudes.

Quality attitudes of plant personnel historically have been shaped by a broad process of quality education which involves not only formal quality-control courses but also, to a much larger extent, many informal quality influences. These influences are the actions and deeds that occur daily in connection with the job and which probably are the most significant factors in molding the attitudes of the individual.

The individual operator in the plant is the key man required for the production of products of satisfactory quality. In most instances, he wants to do a good job; it is important, however, that the correct "climate" must be provided for this accomplishment. He looks to his supervisors and managers to provide the necessary quality system, the tools with the required capability, suitable training for the development of necessary skills, and quality information equipment to measure his performance and guide the operation of the process for which he is responsible. In the final analysis, it is this man—the individual operator—around whom the quality system plan of the company is designed.

But this plan is normally a technological one; it must be supplemented by a human climate which motivates the individual operators to *want* to use the plan to produce good quality. This motivation is largely supplied by the actions and deeds of the supervisor. For example, unless *top* management shows continued interest in product quality by deed as well as word, not much will happen in the balance of the organization. Intermediate managers tend to concern themselves with those problems that appear important to top management.

Quality-mindedness for top management must be more than a matter of lip service. The most earth-shaking pronouncement in support of product quality fades into nothingness for shop operators when an order comes down to the factory to ship products of substandard quality in order to meet a delivery commitment.

Interest in quality has to be genuine and be borne out by action, by periodic meetings to discuss quality problems, by adherence to the quality policy for the company, and by balanced interest in behalf of product quality. Unless such interest is in evidence, lack of support is felt by those who daily seek to attain quality standards. If this support is withheld for long periods, morale begins to suffer and ineffectiveness inevitably results. Resistance to compromising product quality may be lacking when such resistance is most needed.

The functional managers of the business are expected to carry out the policies of top management and at the same time get functional work done according to plan. Unfortunately, things don't always work according to plan, and conflicts arise. For example, a new design may have hit a snag, creating a quality problem. There may be an introductory date that has to be met. Will half measures be used, and a temporary fix be used—and not proved—to meet the introductory date? It is at times like these that quality-mindedness is really put to the test and the integrity of the individual put on trial. Certain loyalties develop, both to the organization and to the product. At times like these, functional managers can do much to set the tone of quality-mindedness in the plant by their actions in behalf of sound product quality.

One of the key figures in any quality-mindedness campaign is the shop foreman. He represents first-line management, in fact as well as name, to the people who report to him. If a good employee relations program is in place and working, the foreman's position as part of management is well established, as are also the lines of communication. The employees look to the foreman to keep them informed on the company's problems and successes. Thus in a quality-mindedness campaign, the foreman is the spokesman for the company. Furthermore, the foreman's actions in behalf of product quality must be backed by intermediate and top managers all the way up the line. If this is done, the foreman is sure of his ground and will champion the cause of product quality.

This is the positive situation the worker likes to see. He takes pride in belonging to an organization where the day-to-day actions of his supervisors are consistent with the aims of the enterprise. To him, it typifies a strong organization that knows where it is headed. He is challenged as an individual to put his best effort and skill into producing quality products when he knows that the best of research work and the best of engineering, manufacturing, and marketing work have been used to provide the customer a product of satisfactory quality.

In promoting quality-mindedness throughout the organization it is important to obtain the participation of all personnel. This provides a group appeal. If the individual has not fully appreciated the value to himself in producing product quality, he may consider its importance to the group. Thus the individual may feel that the welfare of the group is important to his own welfare. This builds an *esprit de corps* throughout the organization.

There are a number of media that can be used to appeal to the individual and the group in promoting quality-mindedness. These media should be used over a predetermined period—say, 2 to 3 months. Even a modest promotion can effectively use the following devices:

1. Short write-ups in plant paper.
2. Cartoons in plant paper.
3. Poster displays in work area. (These can be of a general nature of showing "Why do it better" or "How to do it better.")
4. Quality slogans.
5. Increased suggestion awards for quality-improvement suggestions.

19.12 Formalized Training in Quality Control

Members of the teaching profession who have studied the learning process of groups and individuals at all levels of the modern company have repeatedly told us of their unanimous conclusion: adult men and women in industry will learn and retain only those things which they think they need to know, which they genuinely believe will help them in their work, which they think will most likely help them to solve the problems which daily plague them, and which, in effect, they really want to learn.

It follows from this, and experience in quality education certainly confirms it, that the most effective quality-control training courses are those which are quality-problem-centered rather than quality-theory-centered; those whose course content is built around specific assistance in helping men and women do their quality job better; those whose objective is the dissemination of principles and practices for solving basic, down-to-earth quality issues rather than the dissemination of broad, general theories for quality discussion only.

The *first* and most universal principle in building a quality-control training program, therefore, is the following:

Principle 1. Keep it down to earth and centered upon real company quality problems. Concentrate upon practical, meaningful quality material and case studies.

Several other principles have simmered out of the past decade of industrial experience and may be readily cited:

Principle 2. In developing quality-control training programs, the quality-control engineer and training staff should work and consult with the line organization to the fullest extent possible, especially in regard to the scope and kinds of material to be used in the programs. After all, the line organization must do the bulk of quality problem solving for the company and, from a marketing point of view, represents with its employees the customer for quality-control training. Line people should, therefore, be encouraged to feel that course work is being carried on by Quality Control Engineering as an assistance to the line rather than as a substitute for it.

Principle 3. The quality-control training programs should be based upon recognition that the solutions to industrial problems—therefore, the solutions to quality problems—are always changing; consequently, education in quality-control methods and techniques can never be considered as completed, including education for the educators themselves. It follows that participants in the quality-control courses should be strongly encouraged to continue their education on a self-training basis after completion of the formal course, through whatever means are most appropriate for this purpose. It also follows that formal quality-control training courses should have definite, organized provisions for periodic, brief refresher courses for plant personnel who have completed the basic training courses.

Principle 4. The training programs should, in the long run, include and involve as participants all levels of personnel from general management through to the skilled machinists. Since interests and objectives differ widely among organization levels, individual courses in the quality-control training program should be tailored to fit these several needs;

no attempt should be made to force a single quality-control training course to fit such widely different needs as those of the general manager, the quality-control trainee, and the inspection foreman.

19.13 The Range Covered by Quality-control Training Programs

In large companies a long-range program of quality-control training may include any or all of such training activities as the following:

1. A brief and general course for first-line supervision in modern methods of planning and controlling quality, concentrating essentially upon the physical elements affecting product quality.

2. A general orientation discussion for middle- and upper-management levels, portraying total quality control as a management planning and control technique and concentrating upon the financial aspects of quality as well as on the general outline of the technologies of quality control itself.

3. Orientation training in quality for new company employees. This work may be carried on as a part of regular new-employee plant-orientation activity.

4. A brief, simple, visual presentation of some of the machine and assembly aspects of quality control for skilled workmen and assembly operators.

5. A course in the practice of quality-control techniques for inspectors, testers, laboratory men, selected foremen, and others whose daily work requires new and better quality training. Such a course emphasizes engineering, manufacturing, sales, testing, and inspection phases of quality control. It will cover a general and brief review of the technological and statistical methods that may be involved.

6. A course in the technologies and statistical methodology of total quality control for company technical men—development or design engineers, manufacturing engineers, etc.—whose work in the total-quality-control system makes such training essential.

7. Detailed training courses for persons who are, or may become, full-time members of the quality-control organization or whose work and background make such training desirable. Such courses involve not only detailed discussion of practical quality techniques and methods but also provide a basic knowledge of the statistical methods that may be useful in a total-quality-control program.

These detailed courses will involve depth training in the three technologies of total quality control:

- Quality-control engineering.
- Process-control engineering.
- Quality information equipment engineering.

19.14 Alternate Resources for Quality-control Training Programs

Whether a company is large or small will not influence the content of the training courses to any appreciable extent. For the smaller company not wishing to develop special training material, a number of textbooks on quality control are available. If the number of persons to be trained is limited, some of the groups listed in Sec. 19.13 may be combined into a single course. For example, executives and engineers could make up one group, with executives attending only the initial sessions on indoctrination and the engineers continuing to study the technical and statistical aspects of quality control in the latter sessions. Another group could be made up of shop personnel, including operators and inspectors.

For the company that does not wish to undertake its own in-plant training in quality control, a number of universities and colleges offer suitable quality-control courses. Although these institutions may offer quality-control courses as part of the regular curriculum, they present special courses to cater to those regularly engaged in industry. These courses are of two types: the first is an intensive course of 1 to 2 weeks' duration; the second is an evening course given 1 or 2 nights a week over a period of 12 to 15 weeks. Although many of these courses have a statistical quality-control orientation, some have become broader in scope to include consideration of other aspects of total quality control.

There is another source of instruction in quality control available from seminars and conferences sponsored by different professional associations. The American Society for Quality Control, 161 W. Wisconsin Ave., Milwaukee 3, Wisconsin, offers several workshop seminars each year. These are given in different locations as a matter of convenience and economy for the attendees. *Industrial Quality Control,* the journal of the American Society for Quality Control, announces these seminars and publishes a directory covering short courses in quality control.

The American Management Association, 1515 Broadway, New York 36, New York, also offers several sessions during the course of a year as part of their workshop and orientation seminar program. These are held at various locations, convenient to different parts of the United States and Canada.

19.15 Responsibility for Quality-control Training

Over-all authority for, and cognizance of, this quality-control training program in a company are the responsibilities of the quality-control component, although the actual operating details of some of the training courses may be delegated by it to the company training staff. Members of the plant organization are used to the widest extent possible as instructors and guest speakers in these courses, further to emphasize their quality-problem-centered nature. Outside consultants may sometimes be profitably employed both in the early days of quality-control training, when the quality-control component has not yet developed sufficient competency to direct the programs, and during the operating phases of the training programs so as to provide a broad point of view and an outside-the-plant perspective.

Of fundamental importance to the success of these quality-control training courses is that they be consistent among themselves within the company in the point of view they take toward total quality control and that this point of view also be consistent with the actual operating company quality-control policies and practices. The course should not teach one thing while the company practices another.

External Communications

19.16 Communicating the Total-quality-control Program to Vendors

The previous sections of this chapter have considered the quality-control communications job to educate and motivate the people within the company organization. To complete the communication of total quality control requires reaching certain individuals and groups outside the company that are really also a part of the company's quality system. Prominent among these are the vendors on whom the company depends for meeting the quality required in purchased materials. Also, of greatest importance is "king customer" for whom products of good quality have been provided. The remaining sections of this chapter discuss ways in which these groups can be reached and the professional relationships the quality-control engineer must develop, both with the industrial managers and with the public.

The importance of communicating the quality plan to all persons who play a role in producing product quality can readily be appreciated. One of the most important of these persons is the vendor who provides basic materials, parts, and components to the company and thus greatly influences final product quality.

Communicating the total-quality-control program to vendors involves the same basic principles that are used to communicate the program internally; i.e., the vendor must be led to appreciate the benefits that he will gain by using total quality control.

A number of companies have published attractive brochures encouraging their suppliers to join with them in specific quality-improvement and quality-control programs. One such company[3] agrees to do certain things

[3] See Personal Products Corporation, Milltown, N.J., "Principles of Good Source Relations."

for the benefit of the vendor; the vendor, in turn, agrees to do certain things for the supplier.

In general, the purchaser company may agree to do the following:

1. To let the vendor know all the facts in connection with an order, including all the quality requirements.

2. To encourage exchange visits to promote understanding and solution of mutual problems.

3. To place, whenever possible, facilities of research, development, and technical service at the disposal of suppliers in helping to solve quality problems and improve quality.

4. To plan procurement schedule sufficiently in advance of requirement dates.

5. To supply the vendor with a written understanding concerning the quality system to be followed by supplier and purchaser.

6. To arrive at an understanding with respect to handling of unsatisfactory material.

7. To maintain a consistent cost policy.

8. When mistakes are made, to acknowledge them quickly and take corrective action quickly.

9. To develop with the supplier the knowledge and conviction that the most important requirement is the quality of the end product.

10. To preserve the dignity of the relationship with the supplier.

In turn, the supplier's responsibilities may include

1. To supply materials to specification on schedule.

2. To maintain quality-control procedures which assure consistent meeting of specifications.

3. To be willing to negotiate concerning disposition of unacceptable product.

4. To inform the purchaser as far in advance as possible of circumstances affecting cost.

5. To maintain efficiency of operation that assures competitive costs.

6. To maintain a progressive viewpoint aimed at constant quality improvement.

7. To grow with the purchaser's business.

8. To service the customer and thereby protect the best interests of the consuming public.

9. To bring attention of purchaser promptly to any factors which may impair the relationship.

10. To look upon association as a long-term partnership.

Along these same lines a large aircraft manufacturer[4] has sought to promote product quality with its suppliers by means of a very attractive

[4] After a brochure by Boeing Airplane Company, Seattle 24, Wash.

brochure. In summary, it outlines eight specific mutual benefits from purchaser-vendor relationships:

1. Improved definition of product design.
2. Better initial design.
3. Reduction of costly mistakes.
4. Less retesting.
5. Better schedule control.
6. Pertinent information on product performance.
7. Timely corrective action.
8. Earliest possible delivery . . . and payment.

A number of companies have conducted "vendor clinics." These consist in an organized program whereby vendors are brought into the host plant in groups to hear presentations by various managers and quality-control personnel with respect to quality policy, quality levels, quality-control procedures, handling of engineering changes, and similar subjects. Opportunity is taken to show the vendor where the part he furnishes fits into the final product and why certain requirements are important. Brochures or programs are printed, including a résumé of subjects discussed.

The representative from the vendor establishment should be a man of responsibility. He should be in a position high enough in the vendor organization to bring about changes in policy and procedures. The host plant usually provides the guests with luncheon and assists with hotel accommodations; however, the vendor usually takes care of his own traveling and living expenses.

The size of the groups attending a "vendor's clinic" may vary from 10 to several thousand persons. This will depend on what is to be accomplished. If announcement of a new policy is being made, it can be done in a large group. However, if two-way communication is necessary, the smaller group will encourage more response from the vendor or his representatives.

19.17 Product Quality as a Sales Mover

It is an established fact that customers will buy where they receive the greatest value. Some of the values customers look for in products are durability, convenience, reliability, attractiveness, adequate performance —all these are *qualities* of the product. The manufacturer who can provide these desired qualities without exceeding the price for competitive offerings gains product leadership.

If a manufacturer has provided the customer good values and met his quality expectation, he has established his reputation with the customer and can expect the customer's continued patronage. Even beyond that, the customer may become an active booster for the company's products and recommend them to his associates. Any salesman knows the advantages of being able to sell quality as compared with selling price.

When a manufacturer has established his reputation as a producer of quality products, there is a great deal of advantage in his advertising the fact. This is a case where acts must back up words. If they do not, the words can prove to be very embarrassing and very damaging to the manufacturer. Examples can be identified where firms are no longer in business because they could not back their claims for quality products. On the other hand, those companies which have been able truthfully to advertise themselves as producers of quality products have established themselves in a very sound position.

The best product-quality assurance a manufacturer can provide his customers is the operation of a total-quality-control program.

The company with a well-established, effective total-quality-control program in place can emphasize it as an added value for the customer. Well-documented quality-control procedures build confidence and serve to assure the customer that great care is used in delivering a quality product to him.

Government procurement agencies, for example, are placing increasing reliance on suppliers having a well-organized quality system in place. Experience has shown that less inspection and fewer rejections have to be made on the part of the procuring agency where the supplier has a sound quality-control system.

This viewpoint with respect to the quality system is of equal importance to industrial customers. Plant visitations can be effectively used to demonstrate to customers just how the company's total quality system operates: how materials are controlled, reliability tests conducted, quality check points operated, and product quality certified.

For example, a Midwestern electrical manufacturer had tried unsuccessfully to secure the account of a large appliance manufacturer for his motor requirements. It was not until he arranged a thorough visit for the appliance company's purchasing agent and its quality-control manager that he was able to establish the favorable climate needed for obtaining the order. A review of the plant convinced the potential customers that the motor concern had an added value to offer its customers in the form of its well-planned quality system.

In effect, the use of product quality as a sales mover is an example of "the art of being good, qualitywise, and getting credit for it."

19.18 The Growing Professional Nature of Quality-control Work

Quality-engineering work is increasingly acquiring the characteristics that are the hallmark of professional activity:

1. An organized body of knowledge is required for its purposeful application.

2. Ethical requirements are great. Integrity of product quality must be maintained by the manufacturer in the face of pressures for short-range monetary gain.

3. An area of public service exists in conserving materials and manpower through the elimination of waste due to scrap, rework, and broken-down products.

There are some unique requirements in the quality field in the United States which place quality-engineering work today in the position where efforts to make it professional are both currently indicated and technically meaningful. One of the facts increasingly in the area of product quality is the requirement for the same kind of unquestioned dedication to good practices that was developed in the field of finance many years past with respect to accountancy practices and over many years in several of the more traditional areas of engineering.

Certain elements of quality-engineering work, which is basic to the new, total quality control, had been previously performed on a sporadic basis. But the quality engineer[5] himself is something new under the industrial sun. Quality engineering is not merely a new label for the inspection-planning package, nor a fresh designation for the test-equipment engineer, nor a technologically flavored title for the industrial statistician.

It is, instead, a specialized technical activity characterized by a unique combination of skills in the appropriate phases of product and process technology, as well as in quality-control technique itself. Quality-engineering work is the product of the cross-fertilization of modern developments in several fields: statistical methodology; fast-response, high-precision quality information equipment; and management-engineering progress in understanding the nature of the control function in modern business. In quality-engineering work, the economy is witnessing the evolution of a genuinely new sector of the engineering profession.

In experience, education, aptitude, and attitude, the man entering quality-engineering work today is, in fact, not very different from the man entering other longer-established major technical fields; for example, product engineering or manufacturing engineering. He possesses, or has the capacity to acquire, the necessary product and process background, the personal characteristics to work effectively in a dynamic atmosphere with people of diverse interests, a technical background which enables him to acquire, if he does not already have it, the growing

[5] This term is used to encompass the three technologies of the field: quality-control engineering, process-control engineering, and quality information equipment engineering.

body of quality-engineering knowledge, and the analytical ability to use this knowledge in solving new and different quality problems.

With product quality becoming so important as a motivation for customer purchases, and with quality costs looming as one of the most significant elements of product cost that must be minimized to permit the setting of the right price to the customer, total quality control has become one of the most potent new professional work areas in modern business today for improving sales, productivity, and profitability.

The culmination of these developments will be that total quality control—the basis for quality-engineering professionalism—will take its place as the newest of the major technological and managerial areas that make fundamental contributions to those businesses that grow, prosper, and contribute to general economic well-being. Total quality control in technical action is the future for the quality-control man and his function. It is a future that, with proper application of effort, will be a happy and productive one for him and his professional career, for the prosperity of his company and its customers, and for the optimum utilization of resources in the economy as a whole.

INDEX

Abbott, W. H., 377*n*.
Accelerated tests, 426
Acceptable quality level (AQL), 315, 320, 356–357
Acceptance number, 316–317
Acceptance sampling, 139, 308–354
(*See also* Sampling)
Action, corrective, 528, 537
courses of, planned, 107
Activities (work elements), 54–60, 64
American Management Association, 614
American Society for Quality Control, 614
Analysis of variance, 392
Appraisal costs, 84
Appraisal of quality, 67
Area of normal curve, 220–221
Armstrong, G. R., 396
Assignable cause, 249*n*.
Attributes, 253
control charts for (*see* Control charts)
Audit, example, 577–578
procedures, 164
quality, 554, 576–578
quality effectiveness, 164
technique, 576–577
Authority, 14, 51–54
delegation of, 48
Automatic relay tester, 187–188
Automation, 22
Average, 215, 228
in measurements control charts, 257–259, 261–264, 269, 278
true, 227
Average outgoing quality limit (AOQL), 315, 321

Batch process, 526
Bell Telephone Laboratories, 248, 314
Bicking, Charles A., 526*n*.
Bimodal curve, 231–232
Bogey, 252
Break-even point (BEP), 342–346
Brinell hardness, 386
Brochure for quality promotion, 149
Business system, relationship to quality system, 120

Calculators, mechanical and electronic, 218, 512, 567
Cells, 208, 215
Central tendency, measure of, 214–216, 257, 271–272
Certificates, vendor, 307, 495, 497, 507
Certification, materials, 144
Chance factors, 213–214
Characteristics, classification, 138
multiple, sampling, 346–348
Clarke, P. C., 396
Classification, of characteristics, 138
of defects, 294–295, 346–347
Cochran, W. G., 392*n*.
Coding of data, 218
Color code for gage control, 513–514
Combined process control, 185
Communication, 146, 595–620
external, 615–620
internal, 81, 598–605
Comparison bases, quality costs, 89
Complaints, comparisons, 96
Computers, 146
Consumer requirements, 24
Consumer's risk, 318, 321
Continuous production, sampling, 361–363
Contributed value, 95
Control, 14, 48
meaning of, 12
process of, 48–49
Control charts, 40, 159, 248–306
for attributes, 253, 279–297
analysis, 285–290
application, 298–300
computation, 285–290, 297
demerits, 294–296
form, 281–285, 291

Control charts, for attributes, gaging, 291–293
major and minor defects, 294–296
number defective, 290
number of defects, 290–291
per cent defective, 279, 298–300
precontrol, 293–294
quality, 294–296
sample size, 280–281
bogey, 252
concept of, 248–250
costs related to, 252
definition of, 250
measurements, 254–279, 300–306
application, 272–278, 300–306
average, 257–259, 261–264, 269, 278
central tendency, 257, 272
computation, 261–267, 270–275
costs, 266–270
economics, 266–270
form, 254–257
limits, 257–278
process averages related to, 261
range, 256–262, 264, 267–269, 278
sample size, 255–257, 271–272
specification limits related to, 275–278
spread, 257–259
standard deviation, 258–259, 265, 267–269, 271
tolerances related to, 248–249, 252
types, 253
uses, 251–252
variation in, 250–251, 254
Control gaging, 291
Controlled process, 253
Correlation, graphical, 385–386
mathematical, 394–395
Costs, 11, 15, 21
Costs of quality, 26, 83–102
analysis, 89, 157
applications, 97
appraisal, 84
budgeting tool, 98
comparison bases, 92, 94
definitions, 83–89
distribution, 84
example, 99
failure, 84, 97
external, 97
internal, 97
goals, 97
indirect, 99
measurement bases, 92
measurement tool, 97
operating, 83–99
optimization, 133
prevention, 83
process-quality analysis tool, 98
product line, 90
programming tool, 98
ratio of elements, 84
reduction, 83–85
reports, 91
sources, 89
Cowden, Dudley J., 236*n.*, 281*n.*, 395*n.*
Cox, G. M., 392*n.*
Crawford, James R., 331
Croxton, F. E., 395*n.*

Data, classification, 188
processing, 146
Decision identification in policy formulation, 126
Decision making, managerial, 104
measurements for, 102
Defective, definition, 279*n.*
Defects, classification, 294–296, 346–347
definition, 279*n.*
major and minor, 294–296, 578
Demerits, 294–296
Density functions, 412–414
Derating, 421
Design control (*see* New-design control)
Design margin, 419–421
Design review, 132
Design specifications, 461
Designed experiments, 131, 391–394
Discovery sampling, 331
Discrepant material, disposition of, 163
Dispersion (spread), 208, 214, 257
Division of labor, 108
Dodge, Harold F., 296*n.*, 314, 325*n.*, 361, 363
Dodge-Romig sampling tables, 318, 325–328, 331, 346
Double sampling plans, 324–325
Drawings, interpretation of, 162
Drift, 251, 266–267
limits for, 572
Dudding, B. P., 293*n.*

Education, internal, 605–615
analysis for, 607–609
objective, 606
process, learning, 606–607
training, formalized, 611–613
training programs, range, 613
Effectiveness measurements, 103
End-use effects, analysis, 132
Engineer, process-control, 50, 487–488
quality-control, 17, 50
quality information equipment, 50, 115–116
systems, 26
Environmental effects, analysis, 132
Epstein, B., 390
Equipment development, advanced, 171
Equipment quality costs, 99
Experiments, design of, 131, 391, 394
Exponential density function, 412–413

"*F*" test, 391
Failure, frequency of, 411
mean time between, 407–408
Failure costs, 84
Failure mechanism, 407, 426–427
Failure rate, 408
Feedback, quality information, 114, 145, 147, 186

Feedback cycle, 67
Feedback loop, 66
Field complaint analysis, 158
Field performance, 295–296
First-piece inspection, 534
Fisher, R. A., 392*n*.
Formulas, summary, 431–433
Freeman, H. A., 34*n*.
Frequency distribution, 203–247
  analysis, 209, 221–224
  average, 215–216, 219
  bimodal, 231–232
  calculation, 222, 224–225
  central value, 208
  concept of variation, 205, 210–212
  costs, 229
  data presented as, 376–378
  definition, 207
  example, 207–208, 226–228, 240–247
  grand average, 215
  J shape, 231
  median, 215–216
  nonnormal, 234–236
  normality, 233–234
  100 per cent inspection curves, 232–233
  with reference to tolerance, 208, 212
  sample size, 226–230
  shape, 212–213, 230–236
  skewed, 230
  spread of values, 208, 214
  true average, 227
  true standard deviation, 227
  uses, 236–240
Functions, organizational, 46, 49, 108
    communication with, 146

Gage control, 512–514
Glossary, symbols and terms, 430–431
Go and not-go data, control charts, 279–297
Graeco-Latin square, 393–394
  example, 398–402
Grand average, 215
Grant, E. L., 388*n*.
Grouping readings in series, 217–218

Herd, G. Ronald, 413*n*.
High-quantity production, 41
Hoel, Paul G., 391*n*.
Homogeneous lot, 334
Human factors, 27
Human relations, 81–82, 521–522

Incoming-material control, 38, 155, 481–520
  definition, 36, 484–486
  disposal, 501–503
  examples, 514–520
  gage control, 512–514
  inspection, 497–501
  inspection forms, 506–507
  jobs, of, 35
  needs for, 482–484
  organizing for, 486–488
Incoming-material control, pattern for system, 488–489
  records, 503–504, 508–512
  sampling plans, 498–501
  technical methods, 504–507
  typical procedure, 489–514
Incoming-material rating plan, 511–514
Indirect quality costs, 99
Industrial cycle, 16
Infant mortality period, 408
Information analysis, 186
Information recording, 186
Information system, quality (*see under* Quality information)
In-process control, 158, 181
Inspection, assignment in organization, 64
  first-piece, 163
  planned, 466
  responsibility for, 17
Inspection guide card, 470
Inspection planning card, 468
Inspectors, patrol or roving, 307–308
  reducing force of, 368–369
Instrumentation, quality information system, 115
Internal control procedures, 294–295

J-shaped curves, 231
Jennett, W. J., 293*n*.
Job lot, 41, 533–539
Jobs, quality control, 33, 41–42
Juran, J. M., 281*n*.

Kellog, Harold R., 424*n*.
Kendall, Maurice G., 393*n*.

Laboratory, 487, 491, 501
Large company organization, 75
Latin square, 392–393
Layers, organizational, 70
Lieberman, G. J., 364
Life characteristic curve, 409
Lifetimes, frequency distribution, 409–411
Lot, 226–228
Lot characteristic, 236
Lot-quality protection, 321–323
Lot size, 334–335
Lot tolerance per cent defective (LTPD), 315, 320–323

Machine capability (*see* Process-capability studies)
Machine setup, 569–572
  for cost, minimum, 573–576
  limits, 572
  nominal, selection, 573–576
Machines and methods, 27
Magnets, permanent, 28
Maintainability, 13
Maintenance, preventive, 552–553
Management, 26, 43, 48–49
  of quality-control function, 118
Manager, attitude of, 43–44, 609–611
  business, 18–19
Manager–Quality Control, 51–53

Manuals, 161
Manuele, Joseph, 364
Manufacturing control, 530–531. 553–557
Marketing, 46
Markets, 25
Material, incoming (*see* Incoming-material control)
Material disposal, 501–503
Material examination, 497–501
Material handling, 505
Material receipt, 496–497
Material specification, 489–491
Materials, 26
  certification of, 144
  new, evaluation of, 132
Mean time between failures, 407–408
Measurement operation, evaluation and analysis, 189
Measurements, combined, 105
  for decision making, 102
  for effectiveness, 103
  of productivity, 102
  product quality, planning, 140–141
  timeliness of action, 103
Measurements control charts (*see* Control charts)
Measuring equipment, 115
  capability, 154
  maintenance, 113
  requirements, 141
Measuring techniques, 115–116
Mechanization, degree of, for control of processes, 178
Median, 215–216
Methods, new, evaluation of, 132
Models, mathematical, 134
Multiplant company, 71
  selling quality control in, 604–605
Multiple characteristics, sampling of, 346–348
Multiple sampling plans, 324–325
Multiproduct plant, organization for, 75
Multispindle machines, 272

New-design control, 38, 437–480
  application and scope, 443–444
  definitions, 442–443
  examples, 475–480
  jobs of, 33
  need for, 439–442
  operation of routine, 451–465
  organizing for, 444–448
  pattern for routine, 448–449
  planned inspection, 466–469
  practical aspects. 471–474
  sequence chart, 462
  techniques, 463–471
  tolerance analysis, 465–466
  tools, statistical analysis, 469–471
  typical routine, 449–450
Normal curve, 219–221
  area of, 220–221

Odds, 213
Operating characteristic curve, 319–321
Operating quality costs, 83–99
  definitions of items, 86–89
  example, 99
Operator, responsibility for quality, 12, 22
  selection of, 569
  service to, 113
Order placement, 491–496
Organization, 43–82
  authority, 48
  automated factory, 75
  centralized, 63, 78
  common errors, 44–45
  decentralized, 63
  division of labor, 108–109
  economic balance, 82
  examples, 66–80
  human relations, 81–82
  inspection and test, 64
  location of function, 78
  multiplant, 71
  in past, 44–46
  problems, 80
  product line, 72
  for reliability, 79
  responsibility of, 46–48, 51–62
  setup, 23
  size, 74, 75, 82
  technological basis, 73
Organizational criteria, 62, 70–78
Organizational structuring, 63, 70
Organizing principles, 49–50

p charts, 253
Parts, renewal, 147–148
Patrol inspectors, 308
Per cent defective control charts, 279–290, 298–300
Personnel, characteristics, 605–606
  quality control, 50
  requirements, 141
Pilot run, 154, 244, 464
Planning, approaches to, 134–135
  quality (*see* Quality control; Quality planning)
  temporary, 114, 162
Policy documentation, 127
Position guide, Manager–Quality Control, 51–53
Postprocess control, 183
Post-production quality service, 117
Precision in manufacturing, 152, 166–167
Precontrol, 293–294
Preprocess measurement and control, 180
Preproduction quality evaluation, 111
Prevention costs, 83
Preventive action, 33–35
Principles, quality control, 1–6
Probability, 213–214
Probability-paper graphing, 378–385
  example, 382–385
Problem identification in policy formulation, 127
Problems, quality, 27–30
Process analysis, techniques, 152
Process average, 261

Process-capability studies, 153, 557–576
  calculation, 562–567
  concepts, 560–561
  conduct, 561–562
  example, 562–567
  use, 567–576
Process control, 150, 354–364
  sampling tables, 354–357
Process-control engineering, 50, 487–488
  technology, 150–165
    definition, 151
  work elements, 57
Process limits, 210, 220, 254–257, 269–270, 278
Process sampling, 354–357
Process variation analysis, 156
Processes, new, evaluation, 132
Producer's risk, 318–323
Producibility, 19
Product control, 38, 521–578
  definition, 524–526
  examples, 533–552
  human relations in, 521–522
  jobs of, 35
  in manufacturing, 530–531, 553–557
  needs for, 522–524
  organizing for, 526–528
  pattern for system, 529
  procedures, 528–552
  process capability studies, 557–576
  quality audit, 576–577
    example, 577–578
  standards, 529–530
  techniques, 552–557
Product design, process-capability studies, 568
  review, 132
Product and process, adjustment for compatibility, 133
Product- and process-quality evaluation and control, 113
Product- and process-quality planning, 112
Product quality, 11, 13
  analysis, 67, 125, 129
  challenge, 14–16
  level of, 13
  promotion to customer, 149
  sales mover, 617–618
Product reliability (*see* Reliability)
Production testing, 156
Productivity, 19
Professional work, 618–620
Profit, contributions to, 84–85
Profitability, 19
Program, quality control, proposal, 598–600
  written, 29–30, 100–101
Promotion of quality to the customer, 149
Protection against sampling risk, 315
Prototype tests, analysis, 131
Purchased-material quality planning, evaluation, and control, 112
Purchasing responsibility, 487

Quality, appraisal, 67
  factors affecting, 25
Quality, fundamentals, 25
  product (*see* Product quality)
Quality assurance inspection, 155
Quality audit, 554, 576–578
  example, 577–578
Quality characteristics, 14, 254–257
Quality control, application, 21
  benefits, 18, 599–600
  definition, 1, 12
  evolution, 17
  factors in, 24–30
  introducing, 598–605
  jobs of, 107, 109–110
  as management tool, 12
  objectives, 21–22
  organization for, 43–82
  planning, 107
  principles, 1–6
  professional nature, 618–620
  program, proposal, 598–600
    written, 29–30, 100–101
  selling, 597–605
  total, 1–6, 12, 16
Quality-control engineering, 17, 50
  analytical techniques, 130
  work elements, 54–60, 64
Quality-control engineering technology, 123–149
  definition, 124
Quality-control function, centralization and decentralization, 63
  location, 78
  organization of, 62
Quality costs (*see* Costs of quality)
Quality index, 294–296, 554
Quality information analysis, 114–115, 186
Quality information equipment, 115, 167, 505
  cost factors, check list, 173
  design, procurement, and construction, 196–197
  development schedule, 174
  examples, 170
  installation, check-out and follow-up, 197–199
  points of process for application, 180
  specification, 174, 193–196
Quality information equipment engineering, 50, 115–116
  definition, 168
  technology, 166–199
  work elements, 57
Quality information feedback, 114, 145, 186
  from field, 147
Quality information system, concept, 177
Quality-measuring equipment (*see* Measuring equipment)
Quality-mindedness, 597–598, 609–611
Quality objectives, 126
Quality planning, 28–29, 66, 134
  documentation, 141
  implementation, 161
  interpretation, 162

Quality planning, temporary, 162
(*See also* Planning)
Quality policy, 126–129
decision identification, 126
documentation, 127
formulation, techniques, 126
problem identification, 127
quality objectives, 126
Quality problems, 27–30
Quality reputation, 24–25
Quality requirements, 14
delineation, 130
Quality responsibility, 14, 43–48
Quality system, 107–120
business system related to, 120
definition, 108
elements, 111
necessity for, 108
plan, 109
documentation, 109–110
responsibility for, 109
for self-evaluation, 118
subsystems, 111–118
Quality training, orientation, and manpower development, 116

Random sample, 334
Range, 215, 218–219
in measurements control charts, 256–270
Rating, of components, 164
of personnel, 164
Reduced inspection, 330–333
Reduced sampling plan, 338–342
Redundancy, 421
Reject quality level (RQL), 321
Rejection number, 316–317
Relationships charts, 61
Relay tester, automatic, 187–188
Reliability, product, 13, 403–429
achieved, 407
activities for, 415–428
analysis, continuing, 425
and automation, 403–405
of components, 414–415
definition, 406–407
evaluation, 423, 425–426
improvement, 425, 428
inherent, 407
manufacturing effects, 421–422
measurement, 407–415
organizing for, 79
packaging for, 422–423
and product complexity, 403–405
programs for, 418–419
and quality system, 428–429
requirements, 416–417
of system, 415
tests, 425–428
transportation planning, 422–423
Reliability test equipment, 185
Renewal parts quality control, 147
Repeatability, 154
Reputation, quality, 24

Responsibility, 43, 46–49
delegation of, 14, 43
distribution of, 47, 50
functional, 46
integration of, 44
Rework analysis, 157
Risk, sampling, 315, 318
Romig, Harry F., 314, 325*n.*
Root-mean-square, 216–217
Ross, K. E., 311*n.*

Safety factor, 419
Salability, 18
Sample, representative, 210–212, 236–237
selection of, 334
size of, 226–230, 255–257, 272, 280, 315
when taken, 342–345
Sampling, acceptance, 139, 308–354
applications, 349–354
early forms, 310–311
features, 311–314
versus 100 per cent inspection, 309–310
reasons for, 308–310
specifications, 315
spot check, 310–314
statistical sampling tables (*see* Sampling tables)
variables, 348–354
of continuous production, 361–363
for process control, 364–365
single, double, multiple, 324–325
by variables, 348–349
Sampling plans (*see* Sampling tables)
Sampling risk, 315, 318
Sampling tables, 307–373
attribute, sections, 334–338
uses, 342–348
average outgoing quality protection, 323–324
Columbia, 330
cost considerations, 318
definition, 318–319
Dodge-Romig, 318, 325–328, 331, 346
double sampling, 324–325
lot-quality protection, 321–323
Military Standard 105 (MIL-STD-105A), 325, 328–330, 334, 342–343, 495
Military Standard 414 (MIL-STD-414), 349
multiple sampling, 324–325
normal inspection, 330
OC curves, 319–321
process-control, 354–364
types, 354–357
use, 358–361
reduced inspection, 330–331, 338–339, 342
sequential plans, 325, 328–330, 332–333
single sampling, 324–325
tightened inspection, 330
types, 319–321
uses, 364–369
examples, 369–373
variables, 348–354
example, 350–35

Schrock, E. M., 291–292
Scrap analysis, 157
Seder, Leonard A., 392
Selling quality control, 597–605
  attitude, 603–604
  initiative, 598–599
  multiplant company, 604–605
  promotion, 601–603, 611
  sequence, 600–605
Sequential analysis, 395
Sequential sampling plans, 325, 328–330, 332–333
Serviceability, 13
Setup acceptance, nomograph for, 571
Shewhart, Walter A., 248, 395*n.*
Shop operations, quality responsibility, 64
Shop practice, 248–250
Sigma, 216, 219–221
Significance, test of, 390–391
    example, 397–398
Simon, Leslie E., 229*n.*, 395*n.*
Simulation techniques, 134
Single sampling plans, 324–325
Sintered metal casting, 591–594
Skewed curves, 230–232
Slide rule, process capability, 567
Small company organization, 74
Snap gages, 291–293
Solomon, H., 364
Sorting inspection, 156
Spans, organizational, 70
Special methods, 40, 374–402
  examples, 395–402
Special process studies, 579–594
  definition, 37, 579–580
  elements, 580–581
  examples, 583–594
  jobs, 35, 39
  organizing for, 581–583
Special quality studies, 118
Specification, interpretation of, 162
Specification limit, 209–210
  measurements control charts related to, 275–277
Spot check, 307, 311
Spread, 208, 214, 257
Standard deviation, 216–225, 234–235, 244
  in measurements control charts, 258–261, 267–269
  true, 227
Standard quality, establishment of, 114
Standing instructions, 161
Statistical methods, 203–204, 391–395
Statistical sampling tables (*see* Sampling tables)
Statistical tolerance analysis, 387–390
Statistics, bibliography, 433–434
  as point of view, 204
  tools of, 204
  training in, 203
Storage facilities, 505
Strength, product, 419–421
Structure table, 159
Structuring, organizational, 63, 70
Subsystems of quality system, 111–118
Suppliers, approved, 484
Systems engineering, 26, 107–108

"*t*" test, 391
Tables (*see* Sampling tables)
TAG chart (test automation growth chart), 190–193
Tally card, 206
Taylor, Ervin F., 331*n.*
Technological triangle, 123–124
Technologies, of quality control, 123–199
  specialized, organization for, 73
Test-data analysis, 157
Tests, accelerated, 426
  prototype, analysis of, 131
  of significance, 390–391
Thermometal subassemblies, 585–591
Tightened inspection, 330–331
Timeliness measurements, 103–104
Tolerance, drawing, 209
  shop, 245–247
Tolerance analysis, 387–390, 465–466
Tolerance sheets, 248–250
Tolerances, economic partitioning, 131
Tool control, 552
Tools, statistical analysis, 465, 471
Torrey, M. N., 363
Total quality control, 1–6, 16
  definition, 12
Training, quality-control, 116, 597–620
    principles, 612–613
  programs, 116, 613
  range, 613
  resources, 614
  responsibility for, 614–615
Triangle, technological, 123–124
True average, 227
True standard deviation, 227

Unassignable cause, 249*n.*
Underwriters, 451
Unprofitable cycle, 84

Variance, analysis of, 392
Variation, concept of, 205, 210–212
  recording, 205–207
  usual and unusual, 249–250, 254
Vendor, certification, 307, 495, 497, 507
  communications, 615–617
    quality requirements, 143, 492
  facilities evaluation, 133, 492–495
  purchaser relationships, 112–113, 485–488, 495, 505, 510–511
  rating, 158
  record cards, 508–510
  servicing, 144, 495–496
Villars, D. C., 388*n.*

Wald, A., 363, 395*n.*
Wear-out period, 409
Work elements, fixed elements, 64
  quality control, 54–60
  variable elements, 64
Work sampling, 160